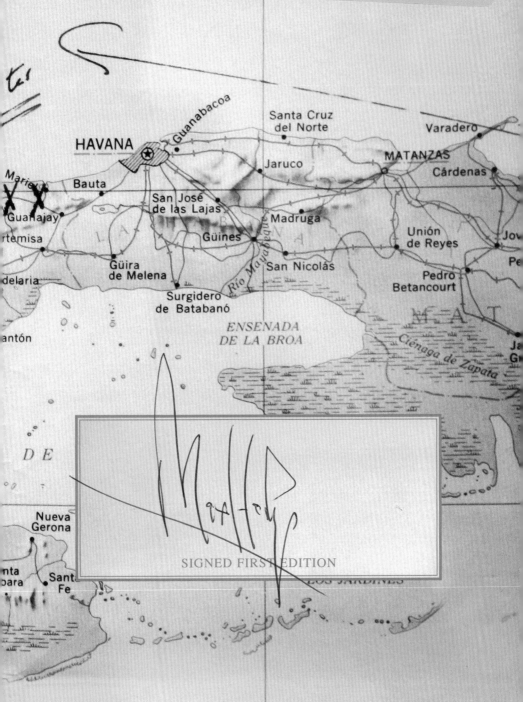

HAVANA

Guanabacoa

Santa Cruz
del Norte

Varadero

MATANZAS

Cárdenas

Mariel

Bauta

Jaruco

San José
de las Lajas

Madruga

Unión
de Reyes

Jov

Guanajay

Güines

Pe

rtemisa

Güira
de Melena

San Nicolás

Pedro
Betancourt

delaria

Surgidero
de Batabanó

M A T

antón

ENSENADA
DE LA BROA

Ciénaga de Zapata

Ja
G

D E

Nueva
Gerona

SIGNED FIRST EDITION

LOS JARDINES

nta
bara

Sant
Fe

The annotations on this map were made in October 1962, by President John F. Kennedy

ABYSS

Also by Max Hastings

REPORTAGE

America 1968: The Fire this Time
Ulster 1969: The Struggle for Civil Rights in Northern Ireland
The Battle for the Falklands (with Simon Jenkins)

BIOGRAPHY

Montrose: The King's Champion
Yoni: Hero of Entebbe

AUTOBIOGRAPHY

Did You Really Shoot the Television?
Going to the Wars
Editor

HISTORY

Bomber Command
The Battle of Britain (with Len Deighton)
Das Reich
Overlord: D-Day and the Battle for Normandy
Victory in Europe
The Korean War
Warriors: Extraordinary Tales from the Battlefield
Armageddon: The Battle for Germany 1944–45
Nemesis: The Battle for Japan 1944–45
Finest Years: Churchill as Warlord 1940–45
All Hell Let Loose: The World at War 1939–45
Catastrophe: Europe Goes to War 1914
The Secret War: Spies, Codes and Guerrillas 1939–1945
Vietnam: An Epic Tragedy 1945–1975
Chastise: The Dambusters Story 1943
Operation Pedestal: The Fleet That Battled to Malta 1942

COUNTRYSIDE WRITING

Outside Days
Scattered Shots
Country Fair

ANTHOLOGY (EDITED)

The Oxford Book of Military Anecdotes
Soldiers: Great Stories of War and Peace

MAX HASTINGS

ABYSS

THE CUBAN MISSILE CRISIS 1962

WILLIAM
COLLINS

William Collins
An imprint of HarperCollins*Publishers*
1 London Bridge Street
London SE1 9GF

WilliamCollinsBooks.com

HarperCollins*Publishers*
1st Floor, Watermarque Building, Ringsend Road
Dublin 4, Ireland

First published in Great Britain in 2022 by William Collins

1

A catalogue record for this book is
available from the British Library

HB ISBN 978-0-00-836499-1
TPB ISBN 978-0-00-836500-4

Maps and silhouettes by Martin Brown

Typeset in Minion Pro
Printed and bound in the UK using 100%
renewable electricity at CPI Group (UK) Ltd

MIX
Paper | Supporting
responsible forestry
FSC
www.fsc.org   FSC™ C007454

This book is produced from independently certified FSC™ paper
to ensure responsible forest management.

For more information visit: www.harpercollins.co.uk/green

For HARRY HASTINGS
who loves Latin America and its peoples so much

'And we will all go together when we go/ What a comforting fact that is to know/ Universal bereavement/ An inspiring achievement/ Yes, we will all go together when we go'

Tom Lehrer song, 1959

'We were truly on the verge of war'

Nikita Khrushchev, 30 October 1962

'Nobody wants to go through what we went through in Cuba very often'

John F. Kennedy, December 1962

Contents

List of Illustrations   xiii

Introduction   xvii

A Timeline of Significant Global Events
    during the Cold War Era   xxvii

Principal Participants in the Missile Crisis   xxxv

Time Zones and Spellings   xxxviii

PROLOGUE: Operation Zapata
    17–19 April 1961   1

1   *Cuba Libre*   23
    1 THE AMERICAN COLONY   23
    2 GRANMA   35
    3 THE LIBERATOR   45

2   Mother Russia   58
    1 TRIUMPH IN SPACE, HUNGER ON EARTH   58
    2 'THE SHARK'   71
    3 KHRUSHCHEV ABROAD   84

3   *Yanquis, Amerikantsy*   99
    1 AMERICAN PIE   99
    2 JACK   107
    3 NUKES   119

4   The Red Gambit: Operation Anadyr   135

5   The Shock   174

6	Drumbeat	209
	1 THE PRESIDENT IS TOLD	209
	2 THE WARMAKERS	222

7	'They Think We're Slightly Demented on This Subject'	234
	1 BEHIND CLOSED DOORS	234
	2 'IRON ASS'	247
	3 THE DECISION	253

8	The President Speaks	266
	1 KENNEDY CONFRONTS HIS PEOPLE	266
	2 KHRUSHCHEV CONFRONTS DISASTER	285

9	Blockade	290
	1 HIGH, CONFUSED SEA	290
	2 'SHOOT THE RUDDERS OFF!'	309

10	'The Other Fellow Just Blinked'	326
	1 HAIR TRIGGERS	326
	2 'SHOULD I TAKE OUT CUBA?'	330

11	Khrushchev Looks for an Out	343
	1 'EVERYTHING TO PREVENT WAR'	343
	2 THE KREMLIN DECISION	352
	3 'A TRIAL OF WILL'	364

12	Black Saturday	371
	1 CASTRO FRIGHTENS KHRUSHCHEV	371
	2 THE SOVIETS SHOOT	383

13	The Brink	390
	1 IMPASSE	390
	2 THE HOUNDING OF B-59	407
	3 THE OFFER	413

14	Endgame	424
	1 TIME RUNS OUT	424
	2 THE CUBANS CUT UP ROUGH	440

15   'This Strange and Still Scarcely
        Explicable Affair'   450

     Acknowledgements   481
     Notes and References   485
     Bibliography   507
     Index   515

Illustrations

p. 134 – Unclassified 1962 memo *(National Security Archive)*

p. 312 – *New York Times* front page, 23 October 1962 *(John Frost Newspapers/Alamy Stock Photo)*

p. 313 – *Chicago Sun-Times* front page, 23 October 1962 *(John Frost Newspapers/Alamy Stock Photo)*

Cartoons

p. 299 – British couple reflecting on the missile crisis cartoons by Osbert Lancaster, published in the *Daily Express (Courtesy of Clare Hastings)*

p. 319 – 'Gone Far Enough' cartoon by Eddie Germano, published in the *Brockton Enterprise Times*

p. 392 – 'Intolerable Having Your Rockets on My Doorstep' cartoon by Victor Weisz, published in the *Evening Standard*

p. 421 – Khrushchev and Kennedy arm wrestle cartoon by Leslie Gilbert Illingworth, published in the *Daily Mail*

Picture inserts

Collier's magazine front page, 3 August 1950 *(Courtesy of the Advertising Archives)*

Cuban freedom fighters *(Hulton Deutsch/Getty)*

The 'Rough Riders' charging up San Juan Hill, illustrated by Frederic Remington *(North Wind Picture Archives/Alamy)*

Earl Smith and Fulgencio Batista *(Bettmann/Getty)*

Castro and his men disembarking from *Granma*

Che Guevara *(Dom Slike/Alamy)*

Camilo Cienfuegos *(Courtesy of Centro de Información Científico Técnica)*

Juan Almeida *(Courtesy of Oficina de Asuntos Históricos, Havana)*

Castro on his progress to Havana *(Bettmann/Getty)*

Marita Lorenz

Mirta Francisca de la Caridad

Naty Revuelta *(Polaris/Eyevine)*

Celia Sánchez and Vilma Espín *(Narique Meneses/Shutterstock)*

Castro interviewed by Ed Sullivan *(CBS Photo Archive/Getty)*

Castro embracing Khrushchev *(Underwood Archives/Getty)*

Fighting during the Bay of Pigs invasion

Manuel Artime *(Hank Walker/The LIFE Picture Collection/ Shutterstock)*

Cuban soldiers interrogating 'Pepe' San Romain

Kennedy with wife Jackie Kennedy and poet Robert Frost *(Bettmann/Getty)*

Khrushchev with defence minister, Malinovsky *(Bettmann/ Getty)*

Robert Frost at Idlewild *(Jacob Harris/AP/REX/Shutterstock)*

Russian missiles in Cuba *(National Security Archive)*

America's trainee astronauts *(CBW/Alamy)*

Protests at the University of Mississippi *(Bettmann/Getty)*

James Meredith escorted across the University of Mississippi campus *(Glasshouse Images/Alamy)*

May Day parade, Moscow, 1962 *(Sovfoto/Universal Images Group/ Shutterstock)*

The June 1962 protest in Novocherkassk

Sherman Kent

Richard Bissell *(AP/Shutterstock)*

Edward Lansdale *(AP/Shutterstock)*

John McCone *(Ted Russell/The LIFE Picture Collection/ Shutterstock)*

Juanita Moody *(National Security Archive)*

Georgy Bolshakov

Oleg Penkovsky *(Bettmann/Getty)*

Aleksandr Alekseev *(AP/Shutterstock)*

Oleg Troyanovsky *(Keystone Press/Alamy)*

Anatoly Dobrynin *(Pictorial Parade/Staff/Getty)*

Aleksandr Feklisov

Aerial photo of a Soviet missile base in Cuba *(PA Images/Alamy)*

Kennedy with Soviet ministers in the White House *(Keystone/ Getty)*

Walter Lippmann *(Everett Collection Inc/Alamy)*

Richard Russell

The Joint Chiefs of Staff *(Bettmann/Getty)*

Russian men parading in civilian clothes *(Courtesy of Michael Dobbs)*

Georgi Voronkov with the officers who shot down Rudy Anderson's U-2 *(Courtesy of Michael Dobbs)*

Kennedy makes his White House address *(Pictorial Press Ltd/ Alamy)*

American people listening to the broadcast *(Ralph Crane/The LIFE Picture Collection/Shutterstock)*

Members of EXCOM at a White House meeting *(Ken Hawkins/ Alamy)*

A Soviet Foxtrot submarine trailed by the US Navy *(NARA)*

SAC chief Gen. Thomas Power with staff *(Courtesy of Michael Dobbs)*

McGeorge Bundy *(Francis Miller/The LIFE Picture Collection/ Shutterstock)*

Dean Rusk *(Gibson Ross/Alamy)*

George Ball *(Evening Standard/Getty)*

David Ormsby Gore *(Keystone France/Getty)*

Ted Sorensen

Curtis LeMay *(Bettmann/Getty)*

Robert F. Kennedy

Llewellyn Thompson *(Bettmann/Getty)*

Robert McNamara *(World of Triss/Alamy Stock Photo)*

Adlai Stevenson presents at the UN *(Balfore Archive Images/ Alamy)*

Adlai Stevenson

Harold Macmillan with Khrushchev in Moscow *(Keystone Press/ Alamy)*

The Kennedy brothers at the White House *(Cecil Stoughton, JFK Library)*

British protesters on the streets of London *(GL Archive/Alamy)*

Jerome Hines performing as Boris Godunov *(Ralph Morse/The LIFE Picture Collection/Shutterstock)*

Cuban street propaganda *(imageBROKER/Alamy)*

Cruiser being stopped by blockade *(Underwood Archives/Getty)*

Anti-aircraft guns in Cuba *(HO/AFP/Getty)*

Raúl Castro with Pliev *(Courtesy of Michael Dobbs)*

Khrushchev with advisers *(Keystone Press/Alamy)*

Life magazine cover, 15 September 1961 *(Ralph Morse/The LIFE Picture Collection/Shutterstock)*

Chuck Maultsby *(National Security Archive)*

Rudolf Anderson

U-2 pilot *(US Air Force Photo/Alamy)*

US Navy pilots after a sortie over Cuba *(Courtesy of Michael Dobbs)*

US Navy aerial photo of Soviet military headquarters *(Courtesy of Michael Dobbs)*

U-2 in flight *(US Air Force)*

Castro with Pliev *(Courtesy of Michael Dobbs)*

Mikoyan with Alekseev *(Courtesy of Michael Dobbs)*

An abandoned missile in Cuba *(Vadim Nefedov/Alamy)*

Kennedy at SAC headquarters *(National Security Archive)*

Introduction

Four years ago my friend Robert Harris wrote a novel entitled *The Second Sleep*, set in a primitive medieval community in south-west England. Only well into the book does a critical moment come, when the priest who is the principal character chances upon an ancient artefact that the reader, but not the man of God, can identify as a cellphone. Thus it becomes apparent that the action is taking place not in the remote past, but centuries into the future, when the planet has reverted to a depopulated wilderness through successive catastrophes initially precipitated by an internet collapse. Here is a glimpse of what might be residual humankind's future following a superpower conflict, which must almost inevitably prove to be a nuclear one. Robert's fantasy, set amid the likely irreversible consequences of doomsday, lingered in my mind as I researched and wrote this book, about events sixty years ago. More recently my narrative, which seemed of solely historical interest when I embarked upon it, has gained a shocking new immediacy and relevance, thanks to the Russian invasion and rape of Ukraine.

In the course of more than four decades of the Cold War, each side was responsible for its share of perilous lunges and blunders. In the Soviet camp, there was the failed strangulation of West Berlin in 1948–49, and the June 1950 North Korean invasion of the South. Five months on, the hubristic Gen. Douglas MacArthur led UN forces racing to North Korea's border with China, and later advocated the use of nuclear weapons, by way of retribution for the battlefield humiliation which 'volunteers' from Mao

Zedong's People's Liberation Army had inflicted upon him. Later came the 1956 Soviet suppression of the Hungarian Uprising, and the Anglo-French invasion of Egypt to regain possession of the Suez Canal. The April 1961 US-sponsored assault on Cuba rocked the freshman Kennedy administration. In 1968 Soviet troops bloodily suppressed the 'Prague Spring'. Two years later the Gdansk shipyard strikes were likewise terminated by gunfire. The 1979–89 intervention in Afghanistan proved a disaster for the Soviet Union, vying with that generated by America's long Vietnam agony, which became a much more profound tragedy for the peoples of Indochina.

Yet none of these events, nor others involving the two sides' clients, matched the peril created by the 1962 Cuban Missile Crisis. Today some historians seek to diminish its gravity. They assert: neither side wanted nuclear war. This is true, but it seems wholly mistaken thus to suppose that the worst was unlikely to happen. At a 1992 Havana conference on the Crisis, former US defense secretary Robert McNamara expressed astonishment on hearing revelations about the arsenal at the disposal of the Soviet defenders of Cuba thirty years earlier, including tactical nuclear weapons. He told a reporter: 'That was horrifying. It meant that had a U.S. invasion been carried out, if the missiles had not been pulled out, there was a 99 per cent probability that nuclear war would have been initiated.' McNamara said this, of course, during his *mea culpa* years, following the destruction of his reputation in Vietnam. His '99 per cent' guesstimate was way over the top. Nonetheless, his sense of shock was well-merited.

During October 1962, John F. Kennedy frequently cited Barbara Tuchman's celebrated bestseller *August 1914*, published a few months earlier – in Britain, by the family firm of prime minister Harold Macmillan. Tuchman's account is disputed by some modern scholars. On one point, however, her view seems incontrovertible. None of the belligerent powers wanted the big war they got. But Austria-Hungary and Germany willed a small one, to crush and dismember Serbia, and some German generals were eager to seize an opportunity to humble Russia before her rising military might became overwhelming. The players lost control of events, with consequences for Europe that proved calamitous.*

In the first days of the 1962 crisis, America's armed forces' chiefs of staff delivered to the White House a unanimous recommendation for bombing of Cuba, followed by invasion and occupation of the island. It is chilling today to read in the USAF archives subsequent testimony by its senior officers asserting their impenitence for having urged war; their enduring conviction that America might have secured a 'decisive victory'; their contempt for the president and the civilians around him, who 'chickened out'.

There were several moments during the Thirteen Days – 16–28 October – at which John F. Kennedy came under immense pressure from some of his own White House team, including national security adviser McGeorge Bundy, to yield to the hawks. 'Ken, you will never know how much bad advice I received,' the president later told Kenneth Galbraith. It seems rash to assume that, whatever the contrary views of the Kremlin, Russian officers on the ground in Cuba would have accepted thousands of casualties among their 43,000 troops, together with local defeat, without unleashing some of the tactical nuclear weapons under their control. There were no technological safeguards to prevent crews from firing at commanders' discretion. Once the invaders had suffered their own heavy losses from even a small nuclear explosion, it is unlikely that the American people would have permitted Kennedy to refuse to escalate.

Details are disputed, of such episodes as that involving a Russian Foxtrot submarine six hundred miles out in the Atlantic: its captain, uncertain whether on the surface war had broken out, allegedly threatened to fire his nuclear torpedo when harassed by US warships. The fundamentals are that both sides groped through the Crisis under huge misapprehensions, and that some subordinate officers enjoyed a control over the use of weapons of mass destruction which could have unleashed a catastrophe unintended by

---

* For the author's 2013 study of that colossal tragedy, see *Catastrophe: Europe Goes to War 1914*.

either the Kremlin or the White House. The longer I write historical narratives, the more chilled I become by the fog of ignorance in
which governments make big decisions. In the twenty-first century,
the US, Russia and China understand each other little better than
they did six decades ago. It is no easier for the White House to
divine the intentions of the angry and half-deranged autocrat who
tenants the Kremlin in 2022 than it was those of his predecessor in
1962. All three superpower governments, not to mention lesser
nuclear nations, take risks that could one day prove disastrous for
humanity, because somebody miscalculates, overreaches or
concedes to subordinates opportunities to do so.

An important point about the Crisis is often missed: it was overwhelmingly a political issue, not a strategic one. John Lewis Gaddis
has written: 'Nuclear weapons ... had a remarkably *theatrical* effect
on the course of the high Cold War. They created the mood of dark
foreboding that transfixed the world as the late 1950s became the
early 1960s. They required statesmen to become actors: success or
failure depended, or so it seemed, not upon what one was really
doing, but on what one *appeared* to be doing.' Rationally, and
viewed over any but the shortest time-frame, the installation of
Soviet nuclear weapons in Cuba did not make Americans significantly more vulnerable than they were before: both sides'
submarine-launched ballistic missiles were becoming ubiquitous
realities in the oceans of the world. The issue was instead a percep-
tional one: the United States felt obliged to respond to the
indisputably aggressive *intent* of the Soviets' Cuban gesture.

If the 1950–53 Korean conflict was the bloodiest battlefield clash
of the Cold War, the Missile Crisis was its most perilous episode,
embracing an extraordinary cast of characters on all sides – we
must obviously include the Cubans alongside the Americans and
Russians. It seems to me a weakness of many accounts that they
confine themselves to what took place in the pivotal Thirteen Days.
I have attempted instead to frame the events of October in the
context of what America then was, and the USSR, and Cuba. How
else to make sense of the behaviour of the players, standard-bearers
for their respective societies and products of their very different

historical experiences? It was only nine years since Nikita Khrushchev had played a prominent role in the black comedy of the death of the satanic Josef Stalin; less than four months since he had beforehand authorized and afterwards endorsed the shooting of unarmed industrial protesters in Novocherkassk.

Weeks before Cuba erupted, Kennedy faced the bitterly divisive University of Mississippi riot, staged by white supremacists resisting the admission of a black student. Fidel Castro, meanwhile, had achieved his lifelong ambition to become the most famous revolutionary in the world, despite heading one of its smaller states. Some historians claim that personalities play only a minor part in determining the course of history, which is instead dominated by tides of events and ideas. After studying the Missile Crisis, it is hard to sustain this thesis as a universal truth. Three extraordinary men – Castro, Khrushchev and Kennedy – made its decisions and decided its outcome.

The US president remains a divisive figure among historians. His heroically glamorous persona hid large character flaws. Yet during his thousand days at the White House, his was a towering and inspirational role in the Cold War, contributing some of its most memorable rhetoric. A host of people who know little American history recall the line in his January 1961 inaugural speech 'Ask not what your country can do for you – ask what you can do for your country.' Europeans will never forget his June 1963 appearance in beleaguered West Berlin, where he won hysterical applause from a million people for asserting '*Ich bin ein Berliner.*' His part in the Cuban Missile Crisis represents his best claim upon greatness, as this book will argue, even if it will also acknowledge the American policy blunders and failures that preceded and, indeed, followed it.

The mood of those days in the Western world is not easy to recapture. There was an instinctive disbelief in the threat of annihilation, amid soothing commonplaces that were all around us – I myself was a teenage schoolboy, preoccupied with evading the football field. Yet we saw acknowledgements of peril reflected in newspaper headlines; the ubiquity within the United States of nuclear shelters and air-raid drills; in Britain, of pathetic civil defence preparations to succour survivors of catastrophe. The historian Peter Hennessy has written wittily of his horror on discovering that the Soviet Union had earmarked five nuclear megatons for the British port of Liverpool. Had these been unleashed in 1962, he remarks, before the imminent dawning of the age of the Beatles and 'Liverpool sound', whatever posterity was left after the city's vaporization might have supposed that Cliff Richard represented the creative summit of British popular music.

Graham Perry was a seventeen-year-old grammar school sixth-former in Kent. He and his fellow pupils, while waiting for their maths teacher to arrive for a lesson during the Thirteen Days, discussed the nuclear stand-off. A very pretty girl named Gillian – and remember that these were still relatively virginal teenage times – explained how, if doom beckoned, she and her friends proposed to spend their last moments on earth, with some fortunate boys. Then she added: 'You know, if there's one of these four-minute warnings, then it turns out to have been a false alarm, some of us girls are going to look pretty stupid.' Wing-Commander Perry, who sent me that recollection, commented wryly that, in the course of a long subsequent career in the RAF, some of it on secondment to the USAF, 'I never heard a more succinct or profound analysis of the implications of Mutually Assured Destruction.'

As for my own credentials to write this story, I doubt that I would have presumed to attempt it had I not lived and reported in the US for almost two years in 1967–68, and thus vividly recall the country of that decade. It may be worth something that I met many contemporary giants, including Robert Kennedy, Robert McNamara, Dean Rusk, Lyndon Johnson; I later came to know Arthur Schlesinger pretty well. Less than six years after the Missile Crisis, I sat in the White House Cabinet Room where were held most of the meetings of Excom – the Executive Committee of the National Security Council – hearing John F. Kennedy's presidential successor expound passionately about another national trauma, Vietnam.

I also visited the War Room at USAF Strategic Air Command headquarters outside Omaha, Nebraska, surmounted by the proud sign, immortalized in Stanley Kubrick's film *Dr. Strangelove*,

PEACE IS OUR PROFESSION. Earlier, in 1966, within the hull of a submerged Royal Navy submarine, I heard the echoing hammer blows generated by exploding practice charges dropped by harassing warships, as had the crew of the Soviet B-59 that was hunted through the Missile Crisis by the US Navy.

Thousands of books have been written about the events of October 1962. I do not aspire to rival, for instance, Sheldon Stern's or James Hershberg's meticulous analyses of the Excom meetings, nor other specialists' explorations of the nuclear balance and much else. This is a narrative for the general reader, which seeks to set the extraordinary story in the context of its times, personalities and the wider world, for a new generation outside the defence and academic communities, and indeed beyond the United States, which has always claimed proprietorship of the Crisis. I should like to hope that anybody who reads this book will understand a little more not merely about the Cuban saga, but about the Cold War as a whole.

Since countless millions of us, although not ourselves Russian, Cuban or American, would have become victims had the outcome of the Thirteen Days been different, it seems not unreasonable that we, also, should assert claims as stakeholders in its memory. I have devoted somewhat more space to the British perspective, and especially to that of Harold Macmillan, than our spectators' role justifies. In the former prime minister's old age, I occasionally heard him expound about the Crisis. Americans, and explicitly American historians, sometimes fail to acknowledge that while allies publicly applauded President Kennedy's performance, during the unfolding of events they were as fearful of a possible US misjudgement as of a Soviet one.

Winston Churchill observed with wry complacency during the Second World War that its history would treat him kindly, because he himself would write it, as indeed he did. Something of the same is true of John F. Kennedy and the Cuban Missile Crisis. During daily and sometimes almost hourly White House meetings, tapes were made, of which the transcripts comprise the foremost source for historians analysing American conduct. Only two participants knew that the machines were turning – the president and his younger brother. There is no reason to believe that this significantly influenced their words and deeds, but there must have been moments when the president, especially, recalled that he was preserving for future generations a chronicle of his conduct in crisis.

In the summer of 1940, Churchill often murmured aloud in the presence of his staff Andrew Marvell's line on King Charles I's 1649 execution: 'He nothing common did, or mean, upon that memorable scene.' Churchill was, of course, consciously determined that posterity should say the same about him. It may be that John F. Kennedy, a keen student of Churchill, thought something of the same in October 1962. Meanwhile others, when the taping was revealed in 1973, felt betrayed. Dean Rusk telephoned the Kennedy Library to protest in vehement terms, about such a record having been kept without the knowledge of Cabinet members such as himself.

Some contemporary witnesses have asserted that there were disparities between what Kennedy and others said during Excom meetings, and opinions that they voiced at other times and places during those thirteen days, which went uncaptured on tape. No such asides invalidate the transcripts, which are much more credible than the written minutes of great international conferences. *Pace* Rusk and others, it seems fabulous that we have such a record, of a kind unprecedented in history.

All the significant American archives are today accessible, including those of the intelligence services. One among many reasons for admiring the culture of the United States is its willingness to expose past national follies and blunders, as well as triumphs, to the scrutiny of historians. The Russian sources, by contrast, are much less comprehensive; records were only very selectively available to scholars during the precious 1990s window of *glasnost*. The tenant of today's Kremlin is no more willing than were his twentieth-century predecessors to come clean about bygone events, far less contemporary ones.

I must pay special tribute, as do most writers about these events, to the 1997 account by Aleksandr Fursenko and Timothy Naftali,

'One Hell of a Gamble', a ground-breaker because they were the first authors to enjoy opportunities to access some Moscow archives. I also admire the primary research carried out by Michael Dobbs for his 2008 *One Minute to Midnight*. Among more recent narratives, Serhii Plokhy's 2021 *Nuclear Folly* made good use of Ukrainian sources. Ada Ferrer's 2021 *Cuba: An American History* seems by far the best recent treatment of the island's experience, probably because of the author's background as a Cuban-American.

On Russian issues addressed in this book, as in all my recent works, I have profited from the wonderful efforts of my own researcher and translator Dr Lyuba Vinogradova, who has provided me with hundreds of pages of translated material, especially including contemporary diaries and subsequent recollections of life in the USSR of that era. She also arranged interviews in Ukraine with veterans who served in Khrushchev's 1962 Cuban army. No Soviet diplomat's recollections can be swallowed whole, but those of the remarkable Anatoly Dobrynin, who served for twenty-four years as the USSR's Washington ambassador, seem to possess uncommon value – not in detailing the Crisis, but instead by telling us much about who on Moscow's side knew what and when. Anastas Mikoyan's memoirs likewise represent one of the least incredible accounts by a Soviet Presidium participant. The recollections of Oleg Troyanovsky, Khrushchev's foreign policy adviser, are also invaluable.

For more than forty years, I have prided myself upon conducting primary research for my books in the countries about which I write, including France, Germany, China, Russia, Vietnam, Korea, Japan, as well as passing many long and happy sojourns in the US. In addressing this story, however, like every other working historian around the world, I have been handicapped by the closure of archives in consequence of Covid-19, and by the protracted impossibility of long-haul travel. Yet it is almost miraculous how much primary source material is these days available online, especially from the US National Security Archive and the Wilson Center in Washington. The Miller Center in Virginia is another treasure trove, not least in making it possible to listen to audio extracts from the tapes of the White House Excom meetings, matched by simultaneous screen transcripts showing which participants were saying what. My dear friend Professor Margaret MacMillan has contributed immeasurably, by flagging US resources which she knows intimately.

When I was obliged to cancel planned trips to Cuba, Alexander Correa Iglesias conducted interviews on my behalf with people on the island who recalled their experiences, not only of October 1962, but of mid-twentieth-century Cuban life and politics, which deserve to be collected and published in their own right. I suspect that those old men and women spoke more freely and vividly in Spanish to Alex than they might have done to me, through an interpreter. Cuba survives as an almost uncompromising communist society, a showcase for the ideology's failure, longer than has done any other nation on the planet save North Korea. Today, as the last of the *barbudos*' generation of revolutionaries fade from power, mass protests in the streets of Havana have shown the craving for change. The fact that the revolutionaries have sustained their grip for so long is at least partially due to the dogged hostility of the United States, still frustrated and even embittered by the Castro brothers' sixty-year defiance.

The abiding cause for gratitude about the Missile Crisis is, of course, that we are here to read and write about it. Today, in the wake of Russia's monstrous new acts of aggression, the story possesses a shocking immediacy. It shows the perils of great powers venturing to the edge of an abyss from which in 1962 they mercifully drew back. The world cannot be assured that we shall always be so fortunate as to see national leaders display comparable wisdom.

MAX HASTINGS
Chilton Foliat, West Berkshire
June 2022

A Timeline of Significant Global Events during the Cold War Era

1945

4–11 February Stalin's hegemony over Eastern Europe is conceded by the Western allies at the Yalta Conference

8 May World War II in Europe is declared at an end by the Western allies, while the USSR set its own VE Day twenty-four hours later

17 July–2 August The post-war partition of Germany is agreed at the Potsdam Conference, during which Western leaders hear news of the 16 July successful atomic bomb test at Alamogordo. Stalin commits to declaring war on Japan

6 August USAAF drops an atomic bomb on Hiroshima

8 August USSR declares war on Japan

9 August USAAF drops an atomic bomb on Nagasaki

14 August Japan surrenders

24 October United Nations formally established in San Francisco

1946

9 February Stalin makes speech declaring the irreconcilability of communism and capitalism, appearing to reject peaceful co-existence

5 March Churchill delivers his 'Iron Curtain' speech at Fulton, Missouri

1 July US conducts first of twenty-three peacetime atomic bomb tests on Bikini Atoll

1947

12 March US president asserts the 'Truman Doctrine' in speech to Congress, declaring America's will to resist communist expansion, immediately so in Greece

5 June Marshall Plan announced in a speech at Harvard by secretary of state George Marshall, offering massive US financial aid – $13 billion – to devastated Europe. USSR rejects Eastern Europe's proposed share of the money, announces alternative Molotov Plan

15 August India achieves independence, and is partitioned through the creation of Muslim East & West Pakistan

2 September US convenes conference which proclaims the 'Rio Pact', a hemispheric security zone

1948

25 February Communists seize control of the Czech government. Foreign minister Jan Masaryk is found dead two weeks later

17 March Brussels Pact declares the intent of European governments to resist communism

14 May State of Israel proclaimed

24 June Stalin imposes Berlin Blockade, which persists for eleven months, during which the city is fuelled and fed by massive round-the-clock Western allied airlift

Yugoslavia withdraws from Soviet bloc, following which Tito conducts wholesale purges of Stalinists & accepts US economic aid

1949

4 April Creation of NATO ratified

12 April Berlin Blockade lifted by Moscow

23 May German Federal Republic established by Western allies, with Bonn as its capital

29 August USSR tests its first atomic bomb

1 October Mao Zedong emerges as victor of Chinese Civil War, and proclaims People's Republic of China. Defeated Nationalist leader Chiang Kai-shek retires to Formosa – modern Taiwan – where he announces his own rival government, protected by the US Navy

7 October Moscow creates German Democratic Republic in its Eastern occupation zone

1950

30 January Truman approves development of US H-Bomb

February Wisconsin senator Joseph McCarthy launches witch-hunt against 'communists in high places' inside the US, forcing the introduction of loyalty tests for government servants

24 June Soviet-armed North Korea invades the South with Stalin's blessing. American and small British forces intervene to preserve the South, and during a Soviet boycott of the United Nations Security Council the Americans successfully carry a vote mandating the US to become prime movers in a UN effort to reverse North Korean aggression

November/December Chinese 'volunteers' – eventually 2.3 million served – enter North Korea to save its polity from Gen. Douglas MacArthur's advancing army. They inflict battlefield humiliation on US/UN forces before their offensive is checked in the midst of the peninsula

1951

18 February Greece and Turkey accepted as members of NATO

11 April Truman sacks MacArthur as US/UN supreme commander in Korea, for appearing to urge the use of nuclear weapons against China

1952

3 October Britain tests its first atomic bomb

1 November US tests first thermonuclear weapon

4 November Eisenhower elected US president

1953

5 March Stalin dies

17–24 June Strikes and protests across East Germany involving some 230,000 workers, some of them former Nazis, are suppressed by Soviet troops and tanks, with scores of fatalities, at least forty executions and thousands imprisoned

27 July Armistice signed at Panmunjom, ending the war in Korea, close to original North/South partition line. Acute tensions between the two states persist into the twenty-first century, with forces confronting each other across the Armistice line

12 August Soviets test their first thermonuclear bomb

1954

1 March US tests first H-Bomb on Bikini Atoll

7 May French forces suffer crushing defeat by Ho Chi Minh's communist forces at Dienbienphu, ensuring France's loss of its war against Indochinese nationalists

July Vietnam, largest element of the former French Indochina, is partitioned at the 17th Parallel, under terms of Geneva Agreement

September–December China's PLA bombards offshore islands of Quemoy & Matsu, held by Chiang Kai-shek's Nationalists

1955

14 May The Warsaw Pact, a military alliance of the armed forces of the Soviet empire, is formed. Red Army withdraws from Austria, as do Western occupation forces. Austria becomes neutral

September Khrushchev prevails following two-year Kremlin power struggle, becoming Soviet leader, First Secretary of the Communist Party

22 November USSR tests its first H-Bomb

1956

14–25 February USSR's XXth Communist Party Congress marks start of deStalinization

29 June USSR commits tanks to Poznań, Poland, to suppress workers' demonstrations

October–November Hungarian Uprising against Soviet rule suppressed by Soviet forces

29 October Suez Crisis, which began on 26 July with President Nasser's nationalization of the Suez Canal, dramatically escalates with an Israeli invasion of Egypt, secretly arranged by the British and French governments to justify their own 5 November amphibious assault on Egypt, abruptly aborted at the insistence of US President Dwight Eisenhower. Anglo-French forces withdraw in December

1957

25 March Treaty of Rome establishes European Economic Community and European Atomic Energy Community

26 August Vostok rocket launches the Soviet Union's first ICBM

4 October Sputnik satellite launched into orbit

3 November Sputnik II launched, carrying the first living creature to enter space from earth – the dog Laika, which dies during the flight
8 November British test their own first thermonuclear weapon

1958
1 June Gen. Charles de Gaulle reassumes power in France
21 July NASA initiates Mercury space project, using an Atlas rocket
August Quemoy & Matsu blockaded by Chinese
November Khrushchev demands the withdrawal of Western troops from their sectors of Berlin

1959
January Fidel Castro assumes power in Cuba, following the flight of Fulgencio Batista
June USSR revokes Sino-Soviet nuclear cooperation agreement
15–27 September Khrushchev visits United States

1960
13 February In the Sahara France detonates its first atomic device, in pursuit of creating an independent national nuclear '*force de frappe*'
1 May Soviet SAM missiles shoot down a US U-2 spyplane in Soviet airspace
5 May Khrushchev announces the capture of U-2 pilot Gary Powers
15/16 May Abortive Paris summit meeting of Khrushchev, Eisenhower, Macmillan, de Gaulle
US Navy launches the first of forty-one Polaris nuclear-missile submarines
8 November John F. Kennedy defeats Richard Nixon to become US president-elect
19 December Castro declares commitment to alignment with the USSR and communism

1961
12 April Yuri Gagarin becomes world's first spaceman
17 April CIA launches the Bay of Pigs invasion by Cuban exiles
21–26 April Failed French generals' putsch against de Gaulle in Algiers
5 May First US manned space flight
4 June Vienna summit meeting between Kennedy and Khrushchev
12–13 August The East German border is sealed, and on the 17th construction of Berlin Wall begins

1962
US involvement in Vietnam deepens
18 March At Evian, France signs Algerian ceasefire, as a preliminary to conceding independence
April Khrushchev conceives Operation Anadyr, the USSR's nuclear missile deployment in Cuba
June USSR's Presidium formally endorses Operation Anadyr. In Novocherkassk troops kill twenty-six unarmed protesters
July First shipments of Anadyr personnel and weapons sail for Cuba
14 October U-2 sortie over Cuba secures the first photographs of the missile sites on the island

16 October US president informed about the missiles

22 October Kennedy addresses American people on TV, revealing discovery of the missiles

23 October US naval blockade of Cuba implemented

28 October Khrushchev writes to Kennedy, his letter broadcast by Radio Moscow, undertaking to remove the missiles

20 November USSR also agrees to remove nuclear-capable IL-28 bombers from Cuba, and in response US naval blockade is lifted

21 December Bilateral US/UK summit in Nassau concludes agreement to provide Polaris missiles for British nuclear deterrent

1963

25 July After only twelve days of negotiations, US, USSR and UK agree a partial atmospheric nuclear test ban treaty

2 November In Saigon President Ngo Dinh Diem is murdered by South Vietnamese generals during a US-sponsored coup

22 November John F. Kennedy assassinated in Dallas

1964

August Gulf of Tonkin incident and subsequent congressional resolution signals escalation of the US commitment in Vietnam

13/14 October Khrushchev removed from power in the Kremlin, replaced by a collective leadership dominated by Leonid Brezhnev

16 October China explodes its first nuclear device

1965

30 April US Marines and Airborne forces land in Dominican Republic to prevent threatened communist takeover, perceived in Washington as a replay of the Cuban Revolution

July Announcement of deployment of 200,000 US troops in Vietnam, followed by start of B-52 bombing of the North

August India and Pakistan fight a short war over Kashmir, which ends in September

1 October An alleged pro-communist coup takes place in Indonesia, reversed by the army

1967

Massive anti-Vietnam war protests worldwide, especially in the US

5–10 June Israel secures a devastating victory over Egypt, Syria and Jordan in the Six-Day War

9 October Che Guevara, aged thirty-nine, executed by the Bolivian Army

1968

January Britain announces decision to withdraw by 1971 all its armed forces deployed east of Suez

23 January North Koreans seize spy ship USS *Pueblo*. It remains disputed whether the vessel was in international waters, as the US claimed. Its eighty-two surviving crew members – one had been killed – are held prisoner for eleven months

31 January Vietnamese communists launch devastating Tet offensive, which stuns America, despite eventual US military victory

31 March President Lyndon Johnson announces on nationwide TV that he will
    not seek re-election
6 June Senator Robert Kennedy assassinated in Los Angeles
20/21 August Soviet forces crush the 'Prague Spring' revolt against Soviet rule in
    Czechoslovakia
5 November Richard Nixon elected US president

1969
28 April De Gaulle resigns French presidency
20 July Apollo 11 lands on the moon, a decisive American triumph in the 'space
    race' with the USSR

1970
28 April Nixon launches US-South Vietnamese offensive in Cambodia
December Normalization of diplomatic relations between Poland and West
    Germany

1971
3–16 December Indo-Pakistan war: West Pakistan becomes state of Bangla Desh

1972
21–28 February President Nixon visits China
26 May SALT I arms limitation treaty between US and USSR signed in Moscow
    during summit between Nixon and Brezhnev
21 December East and West Germany recognize each other's sovereignty and
    statehood, as part of Chancellor Willy Brandt's *Ostpolitik* – moves towards
    détente

1973
1 January Britain, Ireland and Denmark join the EEC
27 January US-communist ceasefire in Vietnam, following signing of Paris Peace
    Agreement by Kissinger and Le Duc Tho
11 September US-sponsored army coup overthrows communist government of
    Chile, whose leader Salvador Allende is killed during assault on presidential
    palace
6–25 October Egypt and Syria attack Israel. A ceasefire is brokered by the US after
    Israel belatedly achieves overwhelming victory. The US supplants USSR as the
    dominant foreign influence upon Egypt's governance

1974
18 May India explodes a nuclear device
20 July Following a Greek coup in Cyprus on the 15th, Turkey invades the island,
    which is thereafter partitioned
8 August Richard Nixon resigns as US president following Watergate. Replaced by
    Gerald Ford

1975
30 April Saigon falls to communist forces, completing defeat of US-backed forces
    in South Vietnam; country reunified under Hanoi rule

1976
Soviet and Cuban forces help to install a communist government in Angola
9 September Death of Mao Zedong
2 November Jimmy Carter elected US president

1979
1 January China and US establish formal diplomatic relations
17 January The Shah of Iran, a prominent American client, flees Tehran after overthrow of his regime by Islamists led by the Ayatollah Khomeini
17 February China invades Vietnam, in retaliation for Vietnam's overthrow of the Chinese-backed Khmer Rouge regime in Cambodia. Clashes continue until 16 March
4 May Margaret Thatcher becomes British prime minister
18 June SALT II arms limitation agreement signed
4 November Fifty-two US embassy staff in Tehran seized to initiate the 'Hostage Crisis', which continued for 444 days
12 December NATO decision to deploy 572 US cruise and Pershing missiles in Europe, in response to Soviet SS-20 deployment
25 December Soviet forces enter Afghanistan to support Kremlin puppet regime in Kabul installed by coup, initiating ten-year civil war

1980
1 January China and the US establish formal diplomatic relations
3 January US Senate suspends SALT II agreement, in response to invasion of Afghanistan
24 April Eagle Claw, a military operation to rescue the Iranian embassy hostages, fails disastrously, inflicting crippling damage upon the credibility of both the Carter presidency and the US military
4 May President Josip Broz Tito of Yugoslavia dies
14 August Polish shipyard workers strike and the Solidarity trade union is created, with Lech Wałęsa as its leader, immediately a popular hero
4 November Ronald Reagan elected US president

1982
2 April Argentina invades and occupies Falkland Islands
6 June Israel invades Lebanon
14 June Argentine forces in the Falklands surrender
10 November USSR's leader Leonid Brezhnev dies, replaced by Yuri Andropov

1983
23 March President Reagan announces 'Star Wars' Strategic Defense Initiative, a technological fantasy which nonetheless terrifies the Soviets, who believe that it threatens to destroy the 'Balance of Terror' and render the USSR newly vulnerable to an American nuclear First Strike
25 October US forces invade the former British island colony of Grenada to evict its left-wing government, without consulting British prime minister Margaret Thatcher

1985

March Mikhail Gorbachev becomes leader of the Soviet Union, succeeding Konstantin Chernenko. He initiates a programme of openness – *glasnost* – and reorganization – *perestroika*

19/20 November Reagan and First Secretary Gorbachev hold their first bilateral summit in Geneva, which ends inconclusively

1986

26 April Chernobyl nuclear plant explodes, the worst nuclear accident in history

11/12 October Reagan and Gorbachev conduct historic summit meeting in Reykjavik, at which they agree to remove intermediate nuclear missiles from Europe. This proves a critical landmark in the ebbing of the Cold War

1987

October Reagan and Gorbachev agree to remove medium- and short-range missiles from Europe

8/10 December The US and Soviet leaders stage a third bilateral summit meeting in Washington DC. Disarmament talks collapse at the last minute, but pave the way for the so-called INF Treaty on arms reduction

1988

8 November Vice-President George H.W. Bush elected US president

1989

January Soviet forces withdraw from Afghanistan

4 June Poland becomes independent, following Solidarity's overwhelming election victory

23 October Hungary declares itself an independent republic

9 November Berlin Wall is demolished and East Germans gain unrestricted access to the West

December Communist governments are removed in Czechoslovakia, Bulgaria and Romania

1990

March Lithuania secures independence from Russia

29 May Boris Yeltsin elected president of Russia

2 August Iraq invades Kuwait

3 October Germany reunified

22 November Margaret Thatcher resigns as Britain's prime minister

1991

16 January US-led coalition launches air campaign against Iraq

15 February Coalition ground forces begin assault on Kuwait

28 February President George Bush announces conclusion of major combat operations, liberation of Kuwait

25 June Yugoslavia begins to break up

26 December Dissolution of the Soviet Union marks the conclusion of the Cold War

Principal Participants in the Missile Crisis

IN THE US
John F. Kennedy (1917–63) President of the United States
Lyndon Johnson (1908–73) Vice-President of the US
Dean Rusk (1909–94) Secretary of State
Robert McNamara (1916–2009) Secretary of Defense
Gen. Maxwell Taylor (1901–87) Chairman of the Joint Chiefs of Staff
Gen. Curtis LeMay (1906–90) Chief of Staff of the USAF
Adm. George Anderson (1906–92) Chief of Naval Operations
John McCone (1902–91) Director of the CIA
Theodore Sorensen (1928–2010) President's political adviser,
    speechwriter and Special Counsel
Llewellyn Thompson (1904–72) Ambassador at Large for Soviet
    Affairs, former ambassador in Moscow
George Ball (1909–94) Under-Secretary of State

US Intelligence Agencies in 1962
The Central Intelligence Agency or CIA, established in 1947, was the principal civilian covert foreign information-gathering arm of the US government, also responsible for intelligence analysis and paramilitary activities abroad, its director appointed by and reporting to the president, in his capacity as chairman of the National Security Council, established in 1947. The CIA's 1962 budget was double that of the State Department. Its ONE cell – the Office of National Estimates – was responsible for making the Agency's strategic judgements; this should not be confused with the Office of Net Assessment, the ONA, created in 1973 as a branch of the Defense Department because the latter so often disagreed with ONE's judgements.

The National Security Agency or NSA, established in 1952 on foundations laid in World War II by the US Army's Arlington Hall codebreakers, reported to the Secretary of Defense, and addressed SIGINT – electronic eavesdropping, cipher-making and breaking. The Defense Intelligence Agency or DIA, created in 1961 and centred on the Pentagon, gathered information directly relevant to the activities of US armed forces, each of which had its own intelligence centre, reporting to its respective service chief of staff. The National Intelligence Board was founded in 1957 as an advisory group with a membership across the intelligence community, including representatives of the FBI, the US's domestic intelligence-gathering as well as federal law enforcement body. The National Photographic Interpretation Center or NPIC was started in 1961, to provide services both to the CIA and the defence intelligence services.

There was considerable tension, confusion and rivalry between these organizations, and especially between the CIA and Department of Defense, but working relationships were somehow sustained.

IN THE SOVIET UNION
Members of the ruling Presidium of the Communist Party (sometimes known as the *politburo*) who attended some or all of the key meetings during the Crisis:
Nikita Khrushchev (1894–1971) Premier, First Secretary of the Communist Party and Chairman of the Council of Ministers
Frol Kozlov (1908–65) Second Secretary of the Communist Party
Anastas Mikoyan (1895–1978) First Deputy Chairman of the Council of Ministers
Leonid Brezhnev (1906–82) an NK protégé who was Party General Secretary
Aleksei Kosygin (1904–80) First Deputy Premier
Dmitry Polyansky (1917–2001) head of the Communist Party of the Russian Republic and later Chairman of the Council of Ministers
Mikhail Suslov (1902–82) ideologist and strong opponent of Khrushchev
Nikolai Shvernik (1888–1970) former Presidium chairman and trades union chief
Candidate member Viktor Grishin (1914–92) later Moscow CP chief

Secretaries P.N. Demichev, L.F. Ilichev, B.N. Ponomarev, A.N. Shelepin, V.V. Kuznetsov

In attendance: Andrei Gromyko (1909–89) Soviet Minister of Foreign Affairs

Gen. Rodion Malinovsky (1898–1967) Minister of Defence

Gen. Issa Pliev (1903–79) Soviet C-in-C in Cuba

Aleksandr Alekseev (1913–2001) KGB officer, 1962–68 Soviet ambassador in Cuba

Soviet Governance in 1962

The Union of Soviet Socialist Republics, created in 1922, is described in the ensuing narrative variously as the USSR, Soviet Union or Russia, merely to avoid relentless repetition. It was ruled by the Communist Party, which held congresses every five years to elect a Central Committee of the three hundred most influential Party officials. This body in turn chose an executive body or cabinet of around a dozen members known as the Presidium or *politburo* – Russians used both words interchangeably – which exercised the real power. The Central Committee also chose 'secretaries' or *apparatchiks* as Party administrators, of whom Khrushchev was foremost. The national parliament or Supreme Soviet exercised largely ceremonial functions, and elected a Council of Ministers, of which in 1958 Khrushchev also assumed the chairmanship. Meanwhile Leonid Brezhnev, as chairman of the Supreme Soviet, was nominal head of state. Little of the above detail matters to the account that follows. Khrushchev exercised dictatorial authority for as long as he could claim to command the confidence, or at least the acquiescence, of the Party Presidium.

IN CUBA

Osvaldo Dorticós Torrado (1919–83) President

Fidel Castro (1926–2016) Prime Minister & First Secretary of the United Party for the Socialist Revolution of Cuba

Raúl Castro (1931–) Minister of Defence

Ernesto 'Che' Guevara (1928–67) Minister of Industries

Raúl Roa García (1909–82) Foreign Minister

Emilio Aragones (1928–2007) close associate of Guevara and later Organizing Secretary of the Cuban Communist Party

José Abrantes Fernandez (1935–91) Chief of State Security, later Interior Minister

Time Zones and Spellings

Timings are inescapably confusing, but can only be ascribed to events in the locations in which they took place. Much of the action happened in the eastern United States, here recorded by EDT or Eastern Daylight (saving) Time. Cuba then set its clocks one hour ahead of this to CST or year-round Cuban Standard Time; London was five hours ahead of Washington; Moscow seven hours ahead. This changed at 2 a.m. on 28 October, when the US set back its clocks by one hour, increasing the time difference between Moscow and America's East Coast to eight hours.

In quoting both American documents and spoken words, I retain American spellings: thus, for instance, 'defense' and 'center'.

Prologue
Operation Zapata 17–19 April 1961

Just before midnight on 16 April 1961, five rustbucket transport vessels dropped anchor two thousand yards off the coast of Cuba, to launch one of the most disastrous military operations in history. Would-be liberators aboard the ships, clad in camouflage-pattern fatigues and now donning web equipment and taking up weapons, were surprised to find the shoreline showing lights: American briefers had told them they would land at a deserted resort area. They went ahead anyway. Frogmen scrambled clumsily down into rubber boats, then set forth to place guidance beacons for the assault force to follow. Against orders, their American instructors accompanied the teams as they laid the markers. They opened fire upon a jeep moving up the beach, causing the shore lights to vanish. Wild shooting followed, from both attackers afloat and local militia among the palms and mangroves. Back on a transport José Pérez 'Pepe' San Romain, one of the operation's Cuban commanders, urged on by Central Intelligence Agency touchline coaches, set about landing his men. He was a twenty-nine-year-old former army officer imprisoned by the old Havana regime, liberated in January 1959 by the victorious revolutionaries. He had later broken with Fidel Castro; was again briefly imprisoned; then fled to the United States. His claims on command at Playa Giron, designated 'Blue Beach', were that he was one of only a small minority of the invaders who knew something about soldiering, albeit nothing about war.

San Romain was sufficiently realistic about the prospects to hand to an American for safe-keeping $10,000 in US currency and

$25,000 in forged Cuban pesos that he had been given as a cash float to pay local people once a beachhead was established. When his own boat touched the shore, he made a suitably theatrical gesture by kissing the sand. San Romain's arrival was smoother than that of most of the invaders. CIA planners had failed to notice offshore coral reefs, on which several craft stranded. As exile officer Erneido Oliva and his staff jumped down from their transport into a light aluminium boat, one landed on top of its helmsman, knocking him into the sea. The boat drifted away bearing seven men, none of whom knew how to start the outboard motor. They bobbed in limbo for forty-five minutes, watching spectacular pyrotechnics on the beach and listening to explosions and bursts of fire, until rescued and towed in by a launch. Most of the outboard motors proved unserviceable, so that by 5.30 a.m. on 17 April the landing schedule was wildly awry, with one infantry battalion still stuck on a transport, together with the ammunition for the entire force.

The invaders had been assured by their American mentors that they could expect to land unopposed; that it would take Fidel Castro seventy-two hours to deploy regular troops to meet them. As it was, thoroughly alerted militia were firing furiously, and heavy metal was on its way to support them. The liberators had also been told that the Cuban air force would be neutralized by their own attacking planes, disguised as Havana's. In reality, the renegade fliers failed to inflict decisive damage, though killing and wounding sufficient people to present Castro with a propaganda coup. One aircraft, damaged apparently by Cuban flak, caused a sensation by forced-landing at Miami International Airport, where the authorities asserted that it was flown by Castro defectors.

When the Havana regime's planes started to attack the invasion flotilla soon after 7 a.m., consequences were catastrophic. The *Houston* was hit by a rocket that passed through the hull without exploding, but made a hole big enough to cause the captain to feel obliged to beach his vessel two hours later. A Hawker Sea Fury, originally sold to the Batista regime by the British, hit the *Rio Escondido*, which promptly blew up. This one ship carried the expedition's entire stores of fuel, medical supplies, communications equipment, rations and ammunition. Meanwhile inland, a force of exile paratroops descended into a chaos matching that on the beaches. Many landed amid swamps, and almost all found themselves lost.

Within a few hours it became apparent that the exiles were doomed, their deaths or surrender delayed only by the sluggishness of the defenders. The shooting, confined to a few thousand yards of sand, mangrove and palms within sight of the sea, continued for three days. It was intended by its American planners to precipitate a mass uprising by the oppressed Cuban people, eager to throw off the shackles of Castro. Instead, exile prisoners found themselves taunted by furious cries from crowds of local people, who spat in their faces: *'Paredon! Paredon! Paredon!'* – 'The Wall! The Wall! The Wall!' Cubans were baying for blood, and not that of Fidel: this was local shorthand for a demand for the 'liberators" execution.

The surviving transport ships offshore sailed away to save themselves, leaving the rump of the invaders to their fate. The world learned to know the invasion place as the Bay of Pigs, *Bahia de Cochinos*. The Cuban people, however, sought to endow the event with a title more resonant and grandiose, and chose instead another local place-name *Playa Giron*, which is how to this day the attack is known and celebrated on the island. President John F. Kennedy, commander-in-chief of the planet's most powerful nation, had granted to Fidel Castro, commander-in-chief of one of the weakest, a priceless victory, which strengthened the Cuban's bizarrely inflated status, his superstar celebrity.

To understand the Missile Crisis that came almost eighteen months later, it is essential to set the events of October 1962 in the context of those of April 1961. The Bay of Pigs invasion, codenamed by the CIA Operation Zapata, had been conceived more than a year earlier. President Dwight Eisenhower, exasperated by Castro's relentless taunting of himself and the United States, authorized the Central Intelligence Agency to raise and train an expeditionary force to overthrow him, recruited from among Cuban exiles in Florida. One of the first of these to come forward was twenty-eight-year-old Manuel Artime, a devout Catholic reared by Jesuits; short and stocky, with a rasping voice that impressed by its harshness. After he was interviewed by CIA agents, one of them told him: 'OK, Artime, you are our friend and we are going to be very close friends of yours.' He was flown to Mexico City and thereafter to a succession of training camps, first in the Panama Canal Zone, later in Guatemala. Another CIA man, German-born Gerard Droller, who masqueraded as a steel tycoon under the pseudonym 'Frank Bender', told an exile political representative in New York: 'Remember Manolo, I am not a member of the US government, I have nothing to do with the US government, I am only working for a powerful company that wants to fight communism.' 'Bender's' credibility was not enhanced by the fact that he spoke no Spanish.

At first the Americans planned to create a guerrilla force. Soon, however, they acknowledged that only a conventional invasion could aspire to topple the two-year-old Havana regime. Five thousand men should be enough, the Agency's chiefs figured: they recalled how few insurgents had accompanied Castro, when he broke forth from the mountains after Christmas 1958, to overthrow President Fulgencio Batista.

Another early recruit to Zapata was Erneido Oliva, a twenty-nine-year-old Cuban army officer. In the summer of 1960, he was contacted in Havana by friends: 'They said there was going to be an invasion. They were organizing troops in a camp in Latin America, with a recruiting office in the US, and they wanted me to join.' He was also black, which was then a thing not much more comfortable to be in Cuba than in the US. He flew to Miami, leaving behind a wife and baby daughter; signed up with the counter-revolution. The Americans contracted to pay each recruit $175 a month, plus $50 for a wife and $25 for each further dependant.

The Cuban exile community in America was riven by faction, especially between former Castro and ex-Batista soldiers. Some urged Oliva not to join the invasion force, because Fidel had become too strong to overthrow. The freshly-minted dictator never ceased to bait his vast neighbour: in September 1960, he recognized Red China and denounced the United States as 'a vulture ... feeding on humanity'. CIA recruits continued to be shipped south from Miami in batches of forty or fifty. By 4 November that year, the training camp in Guatemala held 430 men. It was designated a brigade, 2506 – the serial number of a man who died in training – with Pepe San Romain as its commander. Two weeks later, John F. Kennedy was briefed about the exile invasion plan by CIA chief Allen Dulles. The president-elect, following his narrow victory over Richard Nixon, was conscious that he needed some conservative friends to burnish his anti-communist credentials. He wanted action, and decided that the CIA's paramilitaries were the people to deliver it to him. The Agency's prestige had been much enhanced, in the eyes of Washington policy-makers, by its 1954 success in organizing the overthrow of Guatemala's radical President Jacobo Arbenz, at the behest of the United Fruit Company. That coup had been made relatively easy by Arbenz's lack of popular support. Subsequent regime changes proved tougher to manage, and frequently went awry.

Kennedy took over the Cuban project as a going concern. He said publicly: 'We must attempt to strengthen the non-Batista democratic forces in exile, and in Cuba itself, who offer eventual hope of overthrowing Castro. Thus far these fighters for freedom have had virtually no support from our government.' The CIA operation was among the worst-kept secrets in the hemisphere. As early as October 1960, a Guatemalan newspaper revealed both the American training camp in its jungle and the intention to invade Cuba. The New York Times, The Nation and other publications followed up on the story. On New Year's Day 1961, Castro spoke publicly in Havana about the prospect that his people would soon face US attack. Two days later, Eisenhower, in one of the last significant acts of his presidency, broke off diplomatic relations with Cuba, which had been growing progressively more rancorous and confrontational.

Publicity about the invasion project triggered a late rush of recruits in Miami. In Guatemala and Cuba, however, chaos descended upon the counter-revolutionaries' activities. A succession of infiltration groups, bound for the island, found themselves stranded: one party had to swim ashore naked, after their boat capsized. Following internecine disputes at the camp in Guatemala, Pepe San Romain resigned as brigade commander, appointing Oliva to succeed him. This upheaval caused half the trainees to demand to quit. With difficulty, order was restored. San Romain was reinstated. The principal mutineers were taken into custody and isolated.

In Washington, Dulles and his deputy Richard Bissell, who was directly responsible for the exile operation, urged the new president to move fast to authorize invasion. Bissell, regarded as one of the Agency's most brilliant senior officers and midwife of the U-2 spyplane project, said in old age: 'My philosophy ... was that the ends justified the means and I wasn't going to be held back.' Evan Thomas, a historian of the CIA, writes that Bissell 'personified American hubris in the post-war era'. Success was assured, he and Dulles told the president, if they went soon. Delay, however, would be fatal, because of a flood of Warsaw Pact weaponry reaching Castro, following his embrace of Soviet leader Nikita Khrushchev: May would be too late. If Kennedy swung the other way – pulled the rug from under the whole undertaking – he was warned that he would face ferocious hostile publicity. Conservatives on Capitol Hill and in the country would punish him for his debility. The wrath of more than a hundred thousand Cuban exiles in Miami would be reinforced by that of their American supporters.

The clincher was that the joint chiefs of staff – the US armed forces' top brass – came out in favour of the operation. Just as America's military leaders viewed with professional contempt the communist insurgents of South-East Asia, they likewise despised Castro's army. Following an inspection of San Romain's men by Pentagon officers, on 10 March 1961 the military reported enthusiastically upon the exiles' state of readiness. An officer told Washington that Brigade 2506 was 'raring to go, absolutely fit for battle'.

A generation earlier, Winston Churchill had rejected the targeted killing of national leaders, even of Adolf Hitler, as a tool of democratic governments' war-making. Yet in the years before President John F. Kennedy was himself assassinated, he endorsed or at least acquiesced in American efforts to contrive the removal and/or liquidation of several national leaders, those of Cuba, South Vietnam and the Congolese Republic foremost among them. Arthur Schlesinger, historian standard-bearer for the memory of the Kennedy brothers, sternly rejected the charge that they were complicit in plans for Castro's killing. It is impossible, however, to accept his protestations of their innocence.

The earliest known CIA plot against the Havana regime involved an offer, during Eisenhower's presidency, of $10,000 to the pilot of a plane scheduled to carry Fidel's brother Raúl from Prague to Havana, to arrange a fatal 'accident' during the flight. The money was to be paid on successful completion of the mission, and the pilot was also promised a college education for his two sons, if he himself failed to survive. Nothing came of the plan, or others even more far-fetched.

As for the Bay of Pigs, McGeorge Bundy, Kennedy's national security adviser, said long afterwards: 'We all felt that the Castro regime had hardened into a very tight dictatorship, that there really had been an extinction of free choice, that it was not wrong to let a group of Cubans have a test, and that the national thinking in Cuba as a whole was genuinely unenthusiastic about Castro. We reached that decision on less than perfect evidence. There was a fairly general view, which may sound funny now, not only in the administration but in the country as a whole, that any time you had a Communist takeover in a country, most people in that country really wouldn't like it and would be in favor of liberation.' The Cuba Study Group dominated by Robert Kennedy and Gen. Max Taylor agreed: 'There can be no long-term living with Castro as a neighbour.' Senator Mike Mansfield was one of the few influential voices on the Hill who urged caution in both US rhetoric and conduct towards the Havana regime.

The Kennedy administration might have saved itself grief by heeding the wise counsel of a Latin American leader who liked Cuba's leadership no more than did the White House. In January

1961 President Arturo Frondizi of Argentina told a visiting US delegation: 'The elimination of Castro will not solve the fundamental question. What is required is an attack on the conditions that produced him. If he is eliminated and these conditions are left unchanged, new Castros will arise all over the continent.'

The CIA initially intended a landing in March 1961 at a site near the town of Trinidad, on the south-east coast. Under scrutiny, however, the planners decided that this location was too prominent and exposed; somewhere 'more discreet' was urged, not least by the president, so that the invaders would have time to get established, before the defenders awoke to their arrival. A night H-Hour was substituted for a dawn one. During a series of Washington meetings at the State Department and the CIA's headquarters, it was agreed that Brigade 2506 would seize and hold a bridgehead until the Cuban exiles' 'Revolutionary Council' declared itself a 'government in arms' and could utilize the airstrip abutting the landing zone. Pepe San Romain afterwards asserted that he was told that if the invasion got into trouble, American ground and air forces would intervene.

The president chaired an 11 March 1961 White House meeting to formalize authorization. This was attended by many of the luminaries of America's governing establishment: Mac Bundy, Dean Rusk, Robert McNamara, Paul Nitze, Richard Goodwin, Arthur Schlesinger, Senator William Fulbright. In Schlesinger's words, 'we all listened transfixed' to Richard Bissell's exposition of the Bay of Pigs plan. Schlesinger was instructed to prepare a draft presidential statement, to be used once the invasion had taken place, to explain to the world that 'our objection isn't to the Cuban Revolution; it is to the fact that Castro has turned it over to the communists'. Schlesinger wrote, for Kennedy's delivery: 'The people of Cuba remain our brothers. We acknowledge past omissions and errors in our relationship to them. The United States ... expresses a profound determination to assure future democratic governments in Cuba full and positive support in their efforts to help the Cuban people achieve freedom, democracy and social justice.' The historian discussed with the president a series of recent *New York Herald*

Tribune articles by Joseph Newman, newly returned from a visit to the island, testifying to the continuing strength of pro-Castro popular sentiment.

He later admitted that Kennedy's final decision to go ahead was driven by hubris, 'an enormous confidence in his own luck. Everything had broken right for him since 1956 ... Everyone around him thought he had the Midas touch and could not lose.' They were told of an intelligence report which stated that 'the Cuban air force is entirely disorganized and lacks experienced pilots and specialists trained in maintenance and communications ... The planes are for the most part obsolete and inoperative ... The combat efficiency of the Air Force is almost non-existent.' The president went around the table asking: did anybody oppose the scheme? On that occasion Fulbright was the only man to express vociferous opposition to the plan, though Arthur Schlesinger afterwards penned two memoranda for Bundy, expressing deep misgivings, which were also read by Kennedy. These went unheeded ... until afterwards.

By way of preparing the ground for what was to follow, on 3 April the State Department issued a statement, asserting its considered judgement that 'the Castro regime in Cuba offers a clear and present danger ... to the whole hope of spreading political liberty, economic development and social progress through all the republics of the hemisphere ... The present situation in Cuba confronts the Western hemisphere and the inter-American system with a grave and urgent challenge ... What began as a movement to enlarge Cuban democracy has been perverted ... into a mechanism for the destruction of free institutions in Cuba, for the seizure by international communism of a base and bridgehead to the Americas.'

Exile leader José Miró Cardona, who had been Castro's first prime minister, issued a gaudily-worded call to arms: 'Cubans! We must conquer or we shall die choked by slavery. In the name of God we assure you all that after the victory we shall have peace, human solidarity, general wellbeing and absolute respect for the dignity of Cubans without exception. Duty calls us to the war against the executioners of our brethren. Cubans! To Victory! For Democracy! For the Constitution! For Liberty!'

At a presidential press conference held in the State Department auditorium on 12 April, the first question concerned Cuba. JFK ruled out any role for US armed forces in an assault on Castro's regime, saying: 'The basic issue is not one between the United States and Cuba. It is between the Cubans themselves.' The *Jornal do Brasil* in Rio applauded such a public assurance of non-intervention: 'All this is very good because it shows the US is beginning to understand Latin American psychology.' Robert Kennedy never afterwards owned up to a bullying intervention of his own: at a Washington meeting, the attorney-general asserted that the president had made his decision to support the exile invasion; thus he, RFK,* wished to hear no further voice raised against it.

It is astonishing that the CIA, the US military and some senior diplomats persuaded themselves that a Cuban exile force which numbered not even the five thousand originally planned, but instead a mere fifteen hundred men, could overthrow the Castro regime. Former secretary of state Dean Acheson made a withering comment later: 'You don't have to call in Price Waterhouse to discover that fifteen hundred Cubans aren't as good as twenty-five thousand Cubans [at Castro's immediate disposal].' Yet the cultural conceit that contributed so much to America's later catastrophe in Indochina also influenced thinking in April 1961. The government and people of the US despised alike Castro and his armed forces.

Moreover, even after the president explicitly ordered that no Americans were to participate in the landing, few of its CIA sponsors took him at his word. They believed – as the exiles certainly did – that once they established a fighting presence ashore, however precarious, the mighty United States would never allow the enterprise to fail. Throughout Zapata, a US naval force lingered offshore just outside Cuban waters, anticipating an order that never came, to intervene with air and firepower. Once the shooting started,

---

* I dislike using initials for the Kennedy brothers, yet it seems indispensable in such a narrative as this, to avoid confusion between the two.

believed those in the conspiracy, Washington would throw to the winds its previous caution and commit whatever American forces seemed necessary. Pepe San Romain said: 'Most of the Cubans were there because they knew the whole operation was going to be conducted by the Americans ... They did not trust me or anyone else. They just trusted the Americans.'

San Romain addressed his exultant troops before they left their bases on 10 April. Many sang songs, including Cuba's traditional national anthem. Oliva said: 'It was a great spectacle, very touching. Playing music, the *charanga*, singing, people saying *vivas*.' On 13 April, the *Miami Herald* carried a banner headline, reporting that the exile force was on the move towards action. At Puerto Cabezas in Nicaragua, the men boarded aged cargo vessels chartered by the CIA. The loading of weapons and stores was delayed by rickety, protesting winches and derricks. Although the Americans provided purpose-built landing craft to carry a handful of M-41 tanks and some vehicles, the infantrymen would go ashore from open boats. Meanwhile at the air base, exiles who were to attack Castro's airfields and his headquarters at Columbia, outside Havana, saw that their twin-engined B-26 Invaders had been adorned with Castro's Cuban wing markings. In the early hours of 15 April, the pilots were briefed on their targets.

Luis Somoza, Nicaragua's dictator, as usual face-powdered to indulge his peculiar vanity, came down to the dock to bid farewell to the amphibious Cubans. He shouted: 'Bring me a couple of hairs from Castro's beard.' The men of the four battalions – as the invasion units were designated, though in truth they had the numerical strength of mere companies – were given identification scarves: black, red, blue, yellow, according to which of four colour-code-named beaches they were tasked to assault. Once at sea, ammunition was issued and there was more hasty arms training. On one ship, *Atlantico*, a clumsy gunner sprayed the deck with .50-calibre machine-gun fire, killing one man and wounding two. The fatal casualty was ceremoniously buried over the side.

Who were those Cubans? The largest single category, 240 men, were ex-students; there were also 135 former soldiers, together with teachers, mechanics, journalists, geologists, cattlemen and three Catholic priests. Fifty were black. There were several Jews, but no women. Many *brigadistas*, as they styled themselves, had never held a weapon before that weekend. Some had a much closer cultural affinity to the US than to their supposed homeland. San Romain was damned by other exile factions as a Batista stooge. Manuel Ray Rivero, a former Castro minister who later testified to the Taylor inquiry, established by the White House principally to whitewash its own role in the sorry story, said: 'The operation didn't go deep with the people of Cuba. Many of the people that were in the force did not know what they were fighting for ... There was too much US control ... Many of the elements in the force represented the old army.'

In darkness on that Saturday, 15 April, the reconnaissance party for a 164-strong diversionary force which was to land thirty miles east of the American base at Guantánamo Bay, at the opposite end of the island to Playa Giron, closed in on the shore. This group was hampered by the fact that four days earlier, its intended leader was demonstrating the use of a hand grenade to his team when it exploded and, in the words of the subsequent Taylor report, 'blew up the detail'. The replacement group, after inspecting the coast, motored back over the flat sea to the transport, to report themselves unable to land, because militia ashore were alert. Their American instructors administered furious rebukes, but could not move the fainthearts. They stayed aboard the 'mother ship' *La Playa* until CIA chiefs abandoned this subsidiary operation, much to its protagonists' relief.

At 6 a.m. on that same Saturday, almost forty-eight hours ahead of the amphibious landing, eight B-26 prop-driven Invader light bombers, purchased by the CIA and now crewed by exiles, attacked three Cuban airfields. They destroyed a handful of military and civilian planes without significantly diminishing Castro's air force, but CIA officers aboard the invasion transports told Pepe San Romain and his comrades that the attacks had been successful. Several crippled B-26s were obliged to forced-land or ditch in the sea. The bomber that landed at Miami airport, however, was not damaged by ground fire, but instead had been ornamented with some decorative bullet-holes before take-off, to participate in a CIA deception. Its pilot Mario Zuniga, who flew under the false name of Juan Garcia, claimed to be a defector from Castro's air force, newly arrived from Cuba. 'Garcia' was solemnly granted asylum by US immigration officials.

At the United Nations in New York the Cuban foreign minister denounced the attacks, prompting a vehement denial of responsibility by America's UN ambassador Adlai Stevenson. No US personnel had participated in the bombing, he assured the General Assembly; the US government would do everything in its powers to prevent Cuban exiles from doing such things in the future. In making these claims Stevenson was himself the victim of CIA deceits in which, of course, the White House was complicit. Few American reporters were fooled by the clumsy stunt. A CIA contract pilot later said bitterly that these early attacks 'only served to make Castro angry and gave him time to rally his forces'.

President Kennedy now prevaricated – frankly, suffered a loss of nerve. He issued an order which remained in force for the rest of the weekend, to cancel further air attacks. This prohibition was lifted only on the morning of the 17th, as the seaborne invaders went ashore. The bombings triggered a wave of repressive measures by the Castro government throughout Cuba. Thousands of men and women suspected of disloyalty were arrested and confined at such facilities as Havana's Karl Marx Theatre, the Principe Castle and the baseball park at Matanzas. Several anti-Castro groups, mobilized by the CIA, launched local attacks and acts of sabotage, most conspicuously by setting fire to Havana's El Encanto department store, killing one of its staff. The Cuban Revolutionary Council, in almost permanent session at New York City's Hotel Lexington, issued a stream of bellicose statements through a Manhattan public relations agency.

Meanwhile on the island, in an extraordinary fashion Operation Zapata united the Cuban people. José Ramón Linares Ferrara was a young architecture student in Havana. He had become a sceptic about aspects of the Revolution, but was electrified in its support by the bombings and what followed: 'We were in the middle of a class with the architect Ricardo Porro when we felt explosions. He panicked and told us all to lie flat. Then we spent a week in the basement of one of the university buildings, up to our elbows in grease as we unpacked and learned how to handle Czech PPSh sub-machine guns. Giron moved the whole country tremendously, redrew the boundaries of political argument. It was a defining moment.' They queued to donate blood at the university hospital and shared guard duties with a host of other highly-charged young men and women. At the funeral of seven victims of the bombings Castro said, accurately: 'The US sponsored this attack because it cannot forgive us for achieving a Socialist revolution under their noses!' He denounced the raids as 'twice as criminal, twice as cowardly' as those by the Japanese on Pearl Harbor in 1941. A crowd roared in response: 'Fidel, Khrushchev, we are with you! War! War!'

On the night of Sunday 16 April, Brigade 2506's paratroop contingent, 176 strong, was given a steak dinner, together with apples to carry for their breakfasts, before they boarded five C-46 transports, which flew them through darkness towards landing zones inshore from the assault beaches. Their American instructors voiced anger about being denied authorization to jump with their pupils, though one did so anyway. The drops were reasonably accurate, but many weapons and much heavy equipment fell into swamps. The paratroopers failed in their designated task – to block Cuban reinforcements making for the beachhead. A few of the airborne contingent were killed, and most quickly became prisoners.

At sea, thirty miles south of Cienfuegos the transports rendez-voused with a flotilla of landing craft from Puerto Rico that carried the expedition's tanks and heavy equipment. On all the ships, hundreds of impassioned voices joined in choruses of patriotic songs.

On the morning of the amphibious landings and parachute drops, Monday 17 April, rebel planes were permitted to renew their bombing and strafing attacks, inflicting casualties on a column of militia marching towards the beaches. The B-26s were progressively shot down by the defenders, or obliged to land on British Grand Cayman, in the Nicaraguan jungle or the sea. At 1.20 p.m., a bulletin was issued in New York by the Cuban Revolutionary Council: 'Peasants, workers and militia are joining the freedom front and aiding the rapidly expanding area already liberated.'

Both sides' heroic narratives of the fighting around the beachhead must be treated with scepticism, because they were designed to promote rival legends. Neither appears to have shown much tactical genius. The Taylor report deplored the way the Cuban exiles 'wasted their ammunition in excessive firing, displaying the poor discipline which is common to troops in their first combat'. It also criticized the 'apparent lethargy' of those entrusted with offloading munitions and supplies. A CIA officer who gave evidence to Taylor said that on Red Beach, in his opinion, 'there was not much fighting done'. It was never plausible that a small, ill-trained and poorly-equipped invasion force should do more than hold a perimeter for a time, even had its ammunition and stores escaped destruction. The leaders ashore conducted fierce arguments over voice radio with the ships. San Romain said: 'We were raising hell, sending everybody to hell and asking for things.' Command was impeded by the fact that many radio sets proved unserviceable after contact with the sea. Following the destruction of *Houston* and *Rio Escondido*, the surviving vessels fled into international waters, ensuring that the invaders' fate was sealed.

Cuba's defenders were far more numerous and better-armed. Gen. Max Taylor admitted: 'The effectiveness of the Castro military forces, as well as that of his police measures, was not entirely anticipated.' On the afternoon of the 17th, Fidel arrived to take personal command of the battle. Reinforcements of infantry, 122mm howitzers, T-34 and later Stalin tanks carried on flatbed trucks came in a steady procession. On 19 April, a final wave of air attacks was launched in support of the invaders. Contrary to the US president's orders, American CIA contract personnel manned four of the five aircraft that bombed Cuban targets. One of the pilots later told the Taylor inquiry: 'When the going got tough, we had trouble even getting [the Cubans] into the aircraft. On D + 2 it took us several hours to get some of their crews [airborne] and then they aborted the mission.'

In the course of 18/19 April, some US warships moved close inshore, and aircraft from the fleet conducted repeated reconnaissance missions. American naval officers expected every hour to receive orders to intervene in support of the beleaguered invaders. Late on the evening of Wednesday 19th, two US destroyers sought to approach the shore and evacuate survivors, but withdrew after coming under fire from Castro's forces. Pepe San Romain and most of his comrades surrendered when they ran out of ammunition, or Castro's troops closed in upon their pockets of resistance. Some fugitives took to the swamps – Manuel Artime remained at liberty for thirteen days. Although a few of those captured were summarily killed, Castro ordered the militia not to execute prisoners, probably because he anticipated their utility as bargaining chips and for propaganda purposes; perhaps also because he feared American retribution if the exiles were shot. There is evidence that Kennedy warned Havana through a Brazilian back-channel of a severe US reaction if the prisoners were harshly treated. By late afternoon on the 19th, all firing had died out in western Cuba.

The world's front pages became dominated by photos shot by Castro's victorious forces, of beaches where blackened and wrecked vehicles still smoked, while corpses, abandoned weapons and equipment were strewn across the sand. Operation Zapata was at an end. Sixty-seven members of Brigade 2506 were killed in the fighting, and a further forty-odd perished in captivity or while attempting to escape after the battle ended. The Havana government declared 176 of its own troops to have been killed in action, though the exiles claimed that larger numbers perished in the air attacks. Four American airmen and one US paratrooper also died. Two American CIA contract personnel, detained inland, were among hundreds executed by the regime after fighting ended. The overwhelming proportion of the invasion force which wound up in Cuban captivity confirms that it attempted no heroic sacrificial stand, though lack of ammunition probably rendered such an anti-climax inevitable.

The reasoning of the CIA chiefs who promoted and orchestrated this farce was later explained, privately at least, by some of the Agency's most senior executives. They expected to be able to blackmail their own president into salvaging the invasion with American might, once an armed stand on the island became an accomplished reality, however shambolic. Beyond the moral baseness and political rashness of such behaviour, the hawks were probably also wrong about practicalities. Had US warships and aircraft intervened, they could have inflicted heavy casualties on Castro's forces, and created a murderous mess. It is unlikely, however, that in the absence of a pre-arranged plan for a follow-up invasion and occupation by US troops, they could have changed the outcome of Operation Zapata. Kennedy showed belated sense, in cutting America's losses.

In Moscow, Soviet leader Nikita Khrushchev was as baffled by White House vacillation as were the CIA chiefs. On the afternoon of the 18th, Khrushchev blustered to Washington that Russia would not stand idly by while the Americans assaulted its client nation. In reality, however, the Soviet premier expected the US administration to finish what it had started. He afterwards mused to his son: 'I don't understand Kennedy. What's wrong with him? Can he really be that indecisive?' Khrushchev anticipated that the Americans, rather than accept the verdict of Playa Giron, would swiftly launch their own military operation, such as he himself had unleashed against Budapest. Washington could fabricate claims that the US base at Guantánamo Bay had come under Cuban attack; start an offensive in 'self-defence' which, predicted Khrushchev's generals, would require only a few days to mop up Castro's rabble. As it was, the Bay of Pigs fiasco and Kennedy's limp acceptance of defeat confirmed Khrushchev's belief that the young president was green, weak, ripe for bullying. A Kremlin mindset was established for what would follow a year later.

A small number of survivors from the beaches were rescued offshore by the US Navy. Twenty-two set out for Florida in a sailboat, of whom just twelve survived thirteen days at sea, to reach safety. Common to all the surviving *brigadistas* was a rage towards the US, which had incited them to this great patriotic adventure, then betrayed them. Meanwhile the Cubans gleefully catalogued their prisoners, whom they alleged to include a hundred plantation owners, sixty-seven landlords of apartment houses, thirty-five factory owners, 112 businessmen, 179 men who lived off unearned income and 194 ex-Batista soldiers. Some exile prisoners, together with an unknown number of local suspects, certainly running into hundreds, were executed in the wake of the landings.

A further 1,113 captives were eventually ransomed by the US, after twenty months' imprisonment, for nicely-judged prices that ranged from half a million dollars apiece for the leaders, down through $100,000 for senior officers and $50,000 for junior ones, to $25,000 a head for 'other ranks'. In total, the US paid $53 million in food and medical supplies, allegedly raised from private sources rather than by the government, to redeem the captives. Around a thousand of the prisoners' dependants on the island were permitted to accompany them into exile. Castro drove to the prison, personally to inform the *brigadistas* that they would be flown to Miami. Pepe San Romain asked if it might not be dangerous to the regime to release them. Castro responded contemptuously: 'None of you will come back. But if you do, I don't care if a thousand more come with you. It wouldn't make any difference.' The Cuban leader was proved right. Whereas before Operation Zapata the Havana regime faced serious domestic opposition, thereafter this almost ceased to exist. Many Cubans who hated Castro fled the island, while those who remained acquiesced in his rule.

As for reactions back in the US, the Harvard student Todd Gitlin, who later became a prominent radical, wrote: 'Harvard's dissidents took the Kennedy administration personally. To the social-democratic and left-liberal instructors, the Bay of Pigs was not just a crime, it was a violation of the implied contract binding John F. Kennedy '40 to Harvard.' The *New York Times* editorialized: 'We looked like fools to our friends, rascals to our enemies, and incompetents to the rest.' Mac Bundy said of Zapata: 'I underestimated the cost of failure by a very great deal.' A journalist at an off-the-record briefing on 25 April asked Kennedy how, after his first three months, he was enjoying the presidency. The question, as well as the rueful response, prompted laughter: 'Well, I liked it better up to about nine days ago.' This was a skilful exercise in exploiting a show of frankness to shrug off a huge failure of presidential judgement.

The *New York Herald Tribune*'s front-page story on 26 April, based on an off-the-record briefing by Allen Dulles, reported: 'The CIA insists its information was accurate and was correctly analyzed. The fault, in this view, was not an intelligence miscalculation, but a military failure – the inability of the anti-Castro forces to hold a beachhead.' Dulles also sought to blame the administration's refusal to authorize serious air support, and the Pentagon's endorsement of the invasion plans. He concluded that 'there had been no real test of whether there could be a popular uprising against Castro, as there had to be an occupied area in being and available before the defections could start'. The CIA chief meant that it was realistic to expect local support for Castro to start to crumble only when the opposition – the exiles – controlled some portion of the island.

The secret report on Operation Zapata, commissioned by the White House for the administration's internal consumption and orchestrated by Kennedy's personal military adviser Gen. Maxwell Taylor, unsurprisingly exonerated the president by attributing failure to a mistaken belief that so large an operation 'could be plausibly disclaimed'. Secretary of state Dean Rusk, by contrast, blamed the disaster squarely on the CIA for launching a 'shoe-string operation run by amateurs'. Which was about right. Dulles's public prestige as an intelligence chief, dating back to World War II, always much exceeded his abilities, achievements and judgement.

Kennedy, chastened that he himself was obliged to take the rap without avowal of the follies of his professional advisers, said resignedly to press secretary Pierre Salinger: 'What could I have said that would have helped the situation at all? That we took the beating of our lives? That the CIA and the Pentagon are stupid?' The *New York Times* had deliberately withheld from publication in the interests of national security its knowledge of the invasion plan ahead of the event. Kennedy told the paper's publisher 'that he wished the newspaper had printed stories that revealed in great detail what the U.S. government was about to do'. Such exposure, he said, 'might have induced him to cancel the whole operation'.

Before April 1961 the Kennedys appear to have cherished no private passion about Cuba, one way or the other. The abortive invasion, however, transformed them into Castro-haters. This tinpot dictator had inflicted on the administration an extraordinary humiliation, for which neither the president nor his brother ever forgave him. An administration official was described as saying plaintively soon after the invasion that 'probably some countries can't be saved from communism anyway, and we'll just have to get used to it'. The writer observed that his source 'seemed to be suffering from shock in the aftermath of Cuba'. Yet no such spirit of resignation or acquiescence prevailed at the White House, hereafter pervaded, in the words of a historian of the CIA, by anti-Castro sentiment that became 'an obsession of the Kennedy brothers and some CIA officials. The Kennedys' responses stemmed, in part, from a desire to get even.'

Arthur Schlesinger observed that RFK had 'seized the lead in Cuban policy'. In the immediate aftermath of the Bay of Pigs, the attorney-general urged his brother to double up on his bet against Castro: 'The time has come for a showdown, for in a year or two years the situation will be vastly worse. If we don't want Russia to set up missile bases in Cuba, we had better decide now what we are willing to do to stop it.' At the end of November 1961, JFK signed a top-secret order, authorizing the CIA 'to use our available assets ... to help Cuba overthrow the communist regime'. The Agency set up 'Task Force W' to implement the president's wishes. Robert Kennedy was given responsibility to oversee Operation Mongoose, as it was dubbed, though it is hard to see how eliminating Castro had anything to do with his nominal responsibility for the Justice Department. The appointment merely emphasized how personal had become the confrontation with Castro. Incoming CIA chief John McCone appointed Richard Helms to be his 'man for Cuba'.

The administration rejected an August 1961 olive branch from Havana. Che Guevara met in Uruguay with presidential adviser

Richard Goodwin, and proposed a deal: the Cubans would back off the relationship with Moscow, and offer compensation for sequestrated US property in Cuba, if only the Americans would accept a modus vivendi with the Socialist Revolution. When Goodwin reported back on this conversation to the White House, explicitly to Kennedy and Bundy, they did not deign even to respond to Guevara's astonishing proposal.

In January 1962 Robert Kennedy told a meeting in his office of those charged with implementing Mongoose that regime change in Cuba was the foremost foreign policy objective of the Kennedy administration, a foolish assertion, all the more so if true. Richard Helms described RFK as exerting relentless pressure for Cuban action. Yet the CIA man admitted much later: 'However ambitious, our sabotage efforts never amounted to more than pinpricks. The notion that an underground resistance might be created on the island remained a remote, romantic myth.' The president sometimes expressed regret that he had not appointed his brother to head the CIA. If he had done so, however, RFK would have been saddled with explicit responsibility for some disastrous Agency follies, in South-East Asia as well as Cuba.

The morning after the Bay of Pigs failure, the president mused to Walt Rostow that Britain had been traumatized for years by the failure of its 1956 Egyptian invasion, likewise France by its long bloodletting in Algeria, 'but Britain and France were six or seven per cent of the free world. The United States was seventy per cent of the free world, and we could not afford a Suez sickness, an Algeria sickness.' A few days later Arthur Schlesinger was among guests at the White House Mansion breakfast table. Mac Bundy reminded the president that the historian had opposed Zapata. This prompted a characteristic flash of presidential wit. Kennedy observed that Schlesinger's two papers, setting out his objections, would look good when he wrote his inevitable book about the administration. Then Kennedy jibed, maybe only half in jest, about the spectre of a one-term presidency: 'He better not publish that memorandum while I'm still alive ... And I have a title for his book – *Kennedy: The Only Years.*'

Perversely, however, the American people seemed to applaud any attempt to topple Castro, even such a fiasco as this one: in Zapata's wake, Kennedy's poll ratings soared. Moreover, the 35th president was not done with that hairy-bearded tropical island, not by a long shot. England's Queen Mary said after she presided over the 1558 loss of her country's last foothold in France that when she died, 'Calais will be found inscribed on my heart.' John F. Kennedy might have said the same about Cuba, a small neighbouring country with which, for some good and at least as much ill, his presidency would forever be coupled.

1

Cuba Libre

1 THE AMERICAN COLONY

It was hot. Often wet. Fabulously lush, green. Cubans, an intensely proud people, like to remind foreigners, and especially Americans, that when Christopher Columbus 'discovered the New World' in 1492, he did not set foot in the continental United States, but instead explored the Bahamas – and Cuba. For more than three hundred years thereafter, the island's geographical location between the Caribbean and the Gulf Stream made it the most important way station for almost every ship voyaging to or from Europe and Spain's empire in the Americas. In the late eighteenth century Fyodor Karzhavin, a Russian who became an impassioned supporter of American independence, toured the island, then under Spanish suzerainty, and wrote of its people: 'Their demeanour reflects dreaminess and melancholy. Their extreme laziness makes it almost impossible to persuade them to render any service to a European. It is extraordinarily dangerous to insult them in any way, because they have an unlimited capacity for extracting revenge.' Slave trading was abolished only in 1886. As young Lt. Winston Churchill approached Havana for a few weeks' war tourism in 1895, during the country's struggle for independence, he wrote later: 'I felt as if I had sailed with Captain Silver and gazed on Treasure Island … Cuba is … lovely … Well have the Spanish named it "the pearl of the Antilles". Here was a place where anything might happen.' Its twentieth-century national poet Nicolás Guillén described his homeland as 'the big green lizard with eyes of moist stone'.

The American people cherish a myth that, unlike the old European powers, they have never been imperialists. In truth, of course, their empire began in their own continent, where they almost extinguished the native inhabitants with a ruthlessness that would have impressed Spain's *conquistadores*. They ruled the Philippines for more than half a century, and dominated Latin America for much longer. 'These islands are natural appendages of the North American continent,' John Quincy Adams wrote in 1823, 'and one of them, almost within sight of our shores, has become an object of transcendent importance to the commercial and political interests of our Union.' That island, slightly smaller than Pennsylvania, provided the stage for Theodore Roosevelt to secure one of the fastest-earned military reputations in history, leading his volunteer 'Rough Riders' up San Juan Hill on 1 July 1898 against Spanish colonialists, who in 1902 were compelled to cede Cuba's independence from themselves, though not from the United States. Robert Kagan has written in his magisterial history of US foreign policy that the Spanish war was a decisive event in the creation of modern America's self-image, 'as the advance guard of civilization, leading the way against backward and barbaric nations and empires'.

Twentieth-century *yanquis* loved Cuba above all the southern continent, while deploring the tendency of its people, when not performing samba or tango, to defy Washington's interpretation of their best interests. Havana was where Sky Masterson took Sister Sarah to seduce her in *Guys and Dolls*. The nation's fifties dictator, Fulgencio Batista, sold its gambling licences to the Mob in return for a monthly suitcase of cash such as would cost overweight on any airline, delivered to the president's office. NBC's *Steve Allen Plymouth Show* once broadcast live from the Riviera Hotel, with Allen showcasing its link with a notorious mobster: 'Here we are in Havana, home of the pineapple and Meyer Lansky.' Somerset Maugham found it 'just like Atlantic City'. Cuba was also favourite residence of the big bullshitter with the mustache, Nobel Prize and a procession of wives, the Ernest Hemingway who wrote books about bullfighting, doomed warriors and doomed fishermen, and was prodigiously admired even by Russian communists. Graham Greene, another writer who hung out in fifties Cuba, titled one of the best satirical novels ever written about espionage *Our Man in Havana*, published in 1958.

If you lived in Sioux Falls, South Dakota, or even Tarrytown, New York, the island represented an exoticism that was hard to find on your own patch, and a great place to do stuff you would not want to be caught doing at home. The Americans linked their gift of Cuban independence to a twitch of congressional legislation known as the Platt Amendment, which granted Washington licence to wield authority in the country whenever its own interests seemed to demand this: 'That the government of Cuba consents that the United States may exercise the right to intervene ... that all acts of the United States in Cuba during its military occupancy thereof are ratified and validated.' In 1934, Platt was replaced by a new bilateral Treaty of Relations, but the deal was the same: the US held land-lord's rights. The Cuban government was merely leaseholder, empowered to make a good thing out of casinos and electricity franchises, while peasants went barefoot. Even back in 1898, no local freedom-fighters were invited to the Americans' victory cele-brations in Havana. Teddy Roosevelt might have heard of José Martí, Cubans' proudest 1895 martyr of the independence struggle, but precious few of his countrymen had done so.

Among the spiritual descendants of those Cubans was the island's most famous, or notorious, revolutionary. New Year 1959 witnessed the triumph of a guerrilla superstar, whose bearded followers – *los barbudos* – stormed into Havana, following the abrupt flight of President Batista. Thirty-two-year-old Fidel Castro was introduced to the American people by TV's greatest talent impresario. On 11 January, fifty million viewers tuned in for their weekly fix of variety from *The Ed Sullivan Show*. The host who had sold Elvis to middle America and would soon do the same for the Beatles, now showed them their new Caribbean neighbour.

Sullivan started in by telling the audience they were about to meet 'a wonderful group of revolutionary youngsters'. Castro spoke in English, emphasizing his Catholicism and enthusiasm for baseball. Then Sullivan embraced the precocious Cuban onscreen, saying: 'You know this is a very fine young man and a very smart young man, and with the help of God and our prayers, and with the help of the American government, he will come up with the sort of democracy down there that America should have.' The host was far from alone in rhapsodizing about the new leader. Scores of other journalists and stars, from Ed Murrow to Errol Flynn, sang the same song. American tourists poured into Cuba, to explore its revolution for themselves.

Then, abruptly, it all went sour. Within a matter of months, the Eisenhower administration and most of the American people decided that the cigar-chomping revolutionary was a public enemy. The United States clung to its addictive habit of insisting upon the right to decide who should run Cuba and how. Prompted by a wave of nationalizations of US-owned enterprises, Washington concluded that this should not be Fidel Castro. Thereafter, and in considerable degree into the twenty-first century, the removal or killing of the leader of one of the least powerful countries on earth became a major US policy objective. And almost nobody in Washington saw anything unreasonable or presumptuous about reaching such a determination, and seeking to act upon it.

The root cause of the 1960 falling-out between Castro and the American people was that Batista's monstrous excesses under US sponsorship licensed Castro to undertake a revolution that systematically erased everything associated with the old regime, including its rising middle class. In the previous decade Cuba had recorded the third highest per capita income in Latin America. In 1958 it had ranked fifth in manufacturing, top in per capita distribution of cars and radios. It was not far behind in education, literacy, social services. Yet yawning disparities existed in wealth distribution between white and black, city and country. Some 30 to 40 per cent of the island's children suffered malnutrition, according to a World Bank report, rising to 60 per cent in rural areas. María de la Concepcion Pietro y Alfonso was born in 1930, daughter of Spanish immigrants who worked for the famous Havana department store

El Encanto. Most of its staff lived in dormitories on its upper floors, and her father was obliged to ask the Spanish owner's consent to marry her mother.

The overwhelming bulk of the country's earnings were either exported to American investors or concentrated among Cuba's rich or middle class. Sugar, fruit and cigar exports yielded handsome profits, the lion's share of which were remitted to US companies which controlled the country's telephone and utility enterprises, oil and sugar refining, together with much else. Foreigners owned 70 per cent of arable land. Many Cubans blamed their predicament on the *yanquis*, who decided almost everything that happened in Havana. 'We are responsible for keeping order in the hemisphere,' 1938–44 assistant secretary of state Adolf Berle, one of Washington's veteran Latin America specialists, said without apology.

Juan Melo, born the son of peasants in 1941, grew up in a house with the usual palm-leaf roof, but his family was fortunate enough also to boast the refinements of a concrete floor and ownership of a radio set: neighbours visited each evening to listen in. Morality was a big deal to those ragged people. As a child in Calimete, little Maximo Gomez had trouble persuading his parents to let him go to see the Mexican movies featuring their idols – stars like Ana Luisa Peluffo, Mapita Cortés, Christiane Martel – because the cinema stood next door to the local brothel. The vast majority of Cubans cooked on wood or charcoal. Melo, having been fortunate enough to secure an education, embraced Marxist literature and doctrine in his teens; he came to dismiss such children's comic heroes as Superman as anti-communist propaganda, and to spurn *Reader's Digest* for the same reason. He hated Cuba's ruler.

Fulgencio Batista was a soldier who had first gained significant influence in the so-called Sergeants' Coup of 1933. He became president in 1940; was deposed four years later when, after losing an election, he retired to a comfortably cushioned exile in Florida. He returned eight years on through an unopposed new coup, to make his second presidency one of the most lucrative franchises in Latin America, yielding him US$1.25 million a month from Meyer Lansky alone. His death squads roamed the country, murdering in the hundreds every year real or supposed enemies of the regime. Corruption was institutionalized. Privileged people boasted of possessing a *botella* – a bottle – local slang for holding a government post for which they were paid, but did no work. The United States provided almost unqualified support for the regime, including military aid. At the eastern extremity of the island lay Guantánamo Bay naval base, forty-five square miles of Cuba that had been annexed as US territory. This was no less imperialist than Britain's 'sovereign base areas' on Cyprus, Spain's Moroccan enclave and the Russians' Kaliningrad on the Baltic, seized by Stalin in 1945. At the wired perimeter of Guantánamo there was an American gate, guarded by US Marines, and beyond it a Cuban gate, manned by the regime's soldiers.

The smartest and richest white Cubans sent their children to a local American school, Ruston Academy. Among its pupils was Manuel Yepe, born in 1936, whose parents ran a successful tourist business, overwhelmingly American: 'When you finished at Ruston, you knew more about the US than about Cuba.' Parents paid seventy-five pesos a month for every child, as against two pesos to attend a local village school. But the fees were worth it for the connections kids made, not least with the Batista family, who had sons there. Another ex-pupil, Marta Nuñez, observed somewhat cattily that 'it was where all the rancid bourgeoisie – the *bitonguita* – sent their children'.

When Yepe went on to Havana University, like many of his generation he joined the Revolutionary Movement and steeped himself in idealistic literature, heedless of his privileged background. Sixty years later he still quoted proudly from memory a passage from the leftist philosopher José Ingenieros, which he learned in his student days: 'When you draw your fantasy bow towards a star and set your imagined wings towards elusive heights, striving for perfection and impatient of mediocrity, you carry within you the mystic flame of an ideal. Do not let it die, because if it does you are relegated to cold, motionless human slop.' Yepe said: 'For us, that was a catechism in those days. We were united by our conviction that Batista must go.'

Most of Cuba's seven million people hated the president and his foreign sponsors. Yet the man who overthrew him, becoming a world figure despite representing an unimportant state, himself grew up as a child of privilege. Fidel was the son of a rags-to-riches sugar plantation owner, Angel Castro, and a servant girl who bore him seven children before he married her. The boy, born in 1926, became the only pupil attending his elementary school who could boast shoes. He grew up big, strong, bright, wayward, stubborn and prone to tantrums. When he was sent away to a smart Jesuit boarding school in Santiago, he was nicknamed *El Loco* for his stunts. Notable among these was to ride his bike full-tilt into a wall for a bet, which he won at the cost of concussion.

He loved the countryside and especially mountains; sat well on a horse. He was good with guns. A young American friend, Jack Skelly, was swimming inshore one day at a beach club near Guantánamo when he heard the repeated cracks of a rifle and saw wavelets flurry around himself. Hastily turning in the water, he saw Fidel sitting on the beach house porch with a .22, cigar in his mouth, laughing and yelling, '*Te la voy a pelar, Americano!*' – 'I'm going to scalp you, American!' Only in a wild place, among wild young men, would such a joke have played so well. Stubborn and determined, like many very tall men – he stood six foot three – Fidel was physically ill-coordinated. He was a lazy student, but had a photographic memory. Gregarious and naturally dominating, he was curious about everything, but preferred action to reflection; was determined to lead.

From an early age, he showed a conviction of his own future greatness, practising oratory for hours before a mirror, embracing the legends of Alexander the Great and Julius Caesar. Aged thirteen, he attempted to organize a wages strike among his father's workers. Yet a few years later the forgiving Angel presented him with a Chevrolet – representing untold wealth in Cuban society – and agreed that this obsessively fluent teenager, who never stopped talking, should study law at Havana University. Once enrolled, Fidel ignored classes in favour of radical politics. As a student leader, he travelled widely in South America, proselytizing against

US imperialism. It was among his virtues that he treated everybody the same, prince or pauper. But like many revolutionaries, he developed an exaggerated reverence for a peasant ideal, matched by a disdain for the bourgeoisie from which he himself came.

In 1949, aged twenty-three, he completed his law degree and married a fellow-student from a smart family named Mirta Francisca de la Caridad. Fidel boasted that he carried a pistol to the church ceremony, lest the security police come for him. Whether or not this was true, the remark reflected his passion for self-dramatization. His indulgent father gave him a wedding gift of ten thousand pesos, US$100,000 in modern money. He spent most of it on a protracted American honeymoon, including a three-month idyll in New York, some of it riding in a glitzy Lincoln convertible. The city delighted him, without abating his anger towards Southern racial segregation and *yanqui* treatment of his own country.

If Cubans such as Castro were extravagant in holding the US responsible for all its woes – few Caribbean islands were in better shape – it was indisputable that American corporations controlled the island's principal industries. If brutes and incompetents ruled in Havana, they were licensed by Washington. If mafiosi ran the casinos, this was possible only with US government acquiescence. 'The people and I are the dictators,' announced Batista triumphantly, on his return to power in March 1952. Washington immediately recognized his regime; offered weapons and counter-insurgency instructors.

In those days when Wisconsin senator Joseph McCarthy was a big man on Capitol Hill, leading his obsessive anti-communist crusade, the US government's overarching anxiety was to combat the perceived plague virus of revolution, not least in Latin America. The incoming Eisenhower administration pledged support to every regime that would promote this objective. Opponents of the continent's anti-communist dictators also became enemies of the United States. Batista's name was a byword for corruption and cruelty, yet he settled himself to enjoy a life of unembarrassed luxury while his hit squads roamed the streets in pursuit of his opponents. He relaxed by playing canasta and watching horror movies in the home cinema of a heavily-guarded estate outside Havana, basking in the protection of the only godfather who mattered, the US ambassador, who often shared his card table.

Fidel's lifestyle, meanwhile, was shamelessly feckless. He sought to provide legal assistance to the poor, but took no heed of his responsibility to Mirta and their baby son, who relied on family handouts to escape destitution. Castro and his friends became a tightly-knit group whose members existed in an atmosphere not unlike that of the US West Coast radicals of the late 1960s. Most were children of privilege, nursing fantasies of violence and revolution – and in thrall to the personality of Fidel, undisputed leader of 'the Movement'. There is agreement among Castro's contemporaries that he had no interest in ideology, Marxist or otherwise: his preoccupation was the dispossession of Batista; the attainment of power for himself.

On 26 July 1953 Fidel, together with his younger brother Raúl and 160 of their friends and fellow-members of the Movement attempted to seize control of the great Moncada barracks in Santiago, home to a thousand troops. It was the last night of the annual carnival: the rebels anticipated that the soldiers would be sleeping off the party. They were wrong. The moment shooting started around the gates, alarm bells rang throughout the Moncada. Most of the attackers fled in confusion, some taking refuge in a nearby hospital where they were soon identified, seized and shot by vengeful soldiers. Though only eight rebels were killed in the initial shoot-out, twenty-five of those who surrendered were executed – just five of that group survived. Elsewhere Castro was captured asleep in a peasant hut with thirteen companions, including his brother Raúl, born in 1931 and as impassioned and committed a revolutionary as himself, despite lacking seven inches of his height. They had the good fortune to fall into the hands of a humane officer, who prevented his men from shooting them out of hand. Fidel, handcuffed in an army truck, asked the lieutenant wonderingly why he had not killed them. Pedro Manuel Sarria, a fifty-three-year-old Afro-Cuban, said: 'I am not that sort of man, *muchacho.*' Castro's father Angel, a famously reserved figure, broke down in tears when he heard that two of his sons had headed the Moncada assault.

Fidel spent more than two months in solitary confinement before facing a show trial, held in a hospital near the barracks. His two-hour oration in his own defence became a revolutionary sacred text – Castro considerably refined his words between their court-room delivery and later publication. He quoted Thomas Paine, Jean-Jacques Rousseau and Balzac in support of the argument that Cubans had a duty to resist the Batista tyranny. He concluded with the ringing words: 'Condemn me. It does not matter. History will absolve me.' He was sentenced to fifteen years' imprisonment, while supporters gathered to cheer him in the street outside.

The Moncada attack had been a farce, but put Fidel on the map. Cuban-American historian Ada Ferrer has written: 'It was not that a majority of Cubans supported the attack on the barracks, nor that they even knew anything about the attackers and their specific goals. It was rather, that the response of an already unpopular government was so intemperate and brutal that public sympathy immediately gravitated to the young rebels.' Castro became identi-fied around the world as a prominent face of opposition to Batista, who did not dare to execute him. Here was a familiar manifestation of dictatorships supported by the US: they were sufficiently harsh and predatory to incur the revulsion of the world and hatred of their own people. They were insufficiently effective, however, to suppress dissent. Cuba's rapidly improving economic fortunes might have enabled the dictatorship to survive, the Revolution to be averted, but for the cruelty, corruption and incompetence of Batista's governance.

As it was, Fidel Castro and his closest associates – brother Raúl, Juan Almeida, Pedro Miret – used their time in prison to transform themselves from the shadowy Movement into a coherent revolu-tionary organization. Fidel wrote to Naty Revuelta, a socialite who became a devoted supporter, on 29 December 1953: 'Naty, what a formidable school this prison is! It is here that I am forging my vision of the world and can complete the task of giving my life purpose.'

He read hugely, everything from Somerset Maugham's *Cakes and Ale* and Victor Hugo's *Les Misérables* to Axel Munthe's *Story of San Michele*. Though Castro for years insisted that he was not a communist, in prison he taught a course on political economy that featured Marx's *Das Kapital*; he read Lenin's *State and Revolution*. Batista responded to Fidel's growing international fame by ordering the prisoner's isolation, but his fan mail grew exponentially, much of it from women. His wife Mirta wearied of marriage to a celebrity revolutionary. She decamped to New York with their young son, and filed for divorce.

Fidel rejected Batista's offers of a conditional freedom in exchange for an undertaking to renounce armed rebellion, and this gamble paid off. On 6 May 1955, the dictator succumbed to popular pressure and signed an unconditional amnesty for the rebels. Castro and the other '*Moncadistas*' had spent just nineteen months behind bars. They emerged to meet a throng of admirers and reporters, for whom Fidel raised high his arm in token of victory. He announced that henceforward the dissidents would be known as 'the 26th July Revolutionary Movement' or M-26-7 for short. In Cuba the number 26 has ever since remained shorthand for Castroism.

Six weeks later, Fidel was granted a Mexican tourist visa that enabled him to leave his homeland. He feared, probably rightly, that if he lingered in Havana Batista's death squads would get to him. The most conspicuous legacy of his brief freedom in the capital was conception of a daughter, Alina, by Naty Revuelta, who swiftly abandoned the fiction that the baby was her husband's. Batista had the worst of all worlds. Fidel Castro was free, and committed to renewing his campaign, even as Cuba's president became ever more bitterly hated by his people. If Castro was a clumsy revolutionary, he was a propagandist of genius. He displayed a strength of purpose which Batista was quite unable to match.

During the ensuing months of exile in Mexico City, Castro had one of the most influential encounters of his life, with a twenty-seven-year-old Argentine, a doctor by training and Marxist by vocation, Ernesto Guevara, the man who, as 'Che' – 'Buddy' – which the Cubans dubbed him, would attain immortality alongside Fidel. Following their first meeting at a dinner party, the two adjourned to a café where they sustained a conversation for ten hours. The Argentine threw in his lot with the indigent young men of M-26-7. Che wanted to attach himself to a revolution, and Fidel's offered the most accessible one on offer. There was a profound empathy between the two young men which endured for years, until poisoned by Fidel's megalomania and Che's inalienable commitment to the romance of jungle revolution. Castro continued to receive a small allowance from his father until Angel's death a few months later, but the group's most immediately useful source of funds was a rich Cuban named María Antonia González, married to a Mexican wrestler. Her big apartment became their safe house and rendezvous. The exhibitionist Fidel embraced the soulful Che. Other members of the group decided that these two had one thing in common beyond politics – they were almost the only men in Latin America who could not dance.

Che asked Hilda Gadea, his Peruvian fiancée, her views on Fidel's evolving plan for an invasion of Cuba. It was madness, said this forceful ideologue, 'but we must be with it'. He hugged her and said that he had already decided to sail with the rebels, as their medic. When Washington somewhat surprisingly granted Fidel a US visa, he staged a highly successful fund-raising trip. He made headlines in Cuba as well as in the *New York Times* by asserting, 'In 1956 we shall be free men or we shall be martyrs.' Cuba's previous president, Carlos Prío Socarrás, in exile in Miami, gave $50,000 to Castro which was readily accepted – by 1959, Prío's contribution had swelled to $250,000, for which he later received from the beneficiary … nothing. The group felt rich enough to start providing its members with a living allowance – eighty cents a day. By the spring of 1956, Fidel could claim a following of sixty, who hiked in pursuit of fitness, and began military training at a ranch outside Mexico City. Che, chronically asthmatic, struggled with the long marches, but doggedly persisted. He knew that they would soon be doing such things for real.

2 GRANMA

That summer Castro's band swelled in number to 120. At the river port of Tuxpan, one day they chanced upon an almost derelict sixty-three-foot cruiser, named the *Granma*. The owner, a retired American dentist, sold it to the Cubans for $20,000, and given the boat's condition he was probably thrilled with his deal. They set about arranging its repair, increasingly anxious and impatient because the Mexicans had tired of their subversive activities – police seized several Movement arms caches. The world, in those weeks before the rebels set forth, was preoccupied with simultaneous headline crises in Budapest, where early in November Soviet forces suppressed a Hungarian popular uprising with exemplary brutality, and Egypt where the Anglo-French-Israeli invasion ended in a humiliating withdrawal, at American insistence.

On 24 November Fidel, sitting in a car by the port, scrawled a will. He and his volunteers then approached the dockside in darkness and a rainstorm. Those seeing the *Granma* for the first time were unimpressed by its size and condition. One man, Universo Sánchez, assumed that the launch was merely conveying them to an offshore transport. He demanded: 'When do we get to the real ship?' Nonetheless he clambered aboard with the others, lugging weapons and stores, supervised by Che in a long black rain cape. Chaos followed. When just eighty-two men had been packed into the hull, Fidel reluctantly accepted that there was no room for more. At 2 a.m., *Granma* slid away from the dock, leaving on the shore fifty other frustrated revolutionaries. The boat, completely darkened, headed towards the estuary at low speed, to avoid attracting official attention. When it reached open water, many of the passengers swiftly wished that it had not. A storm was brewing, and 1,235 miles of sea lay ahead.

The ensuing week was hellish. Che wrote: 'The entire ship soon assumed a ridiculously tragic aspect. Men … held their stomachs while their faces reflected their anguish. Some buried their heads in buckets while others were lying about, motionless, their clothes covered with vomit.' Most had never before been afloat. In heavy seas, the twenty-three-year-old former US Navy boat, designed to carry twelve crew, began to take in water. Soon passengers including Fidel were wielding buckets to bail. When the storm abated after two days, they discovered that during the early panic, much of their food had been thrown overboard. As they neared Cuba, the prospective guerrillas scuttled below decks whenever a plane or boat appeared: the Mexicans had indeed alerted Batista's police that *Granma* was at sea. The invaders had no wireless transmitter, and thus could not warn expectant M-26-7 reception parties ashore that they were running late.

On Saturday 1 December, with their water tanks empty and the volunteers desperately hungry, Fidel announced that they would land next morning. Men were issued with military fatigues and brand-new boots – the latter a blistering mistake. In a symbolic gesture, the aspiring guerrillas flung their old civilian clothes over the side. As darkness faded, early next morning they rammed a sandbank sixty yards offshore. In the first light of day, amid clouds of mosquitoes the ragtag band scrambled down from *Granma* into the shallows; began to lug arms and equipment ashore. Exhausted and forlorn after their experiences at sea, they waded through the swamps on the remote coastline of south-eastern Cuba, clutching their weapons and wearing red-and-black armbands adorned with the symbols 'M-26-7'. Che Guevara frankly avowed later, 'It was less an invasion than a shipwreck.' Their leader nonetheless addressed the first peasant they met with grandiloquent words: 'Have no fear. My name is Fidel Castro and we have come to liberate the Cuban people!'

The days that followed were a nightmare for young men most of whom were city-reared. They had no experience of the wilderness with its strange noises, predatory insects, cloying heat and almost impenetrable vegetation. Thirty years earlier, a witty young British adventurer in the Brazilian jungle wrote that his first impression of South America was of 'a continent with imperfect self-control'. This extended to Cuba, with its exuberant lushness yet merciless absence of creature comforts. Such food as the invaders obtained from peasants or tiny shops – cassava, rice and beans, tinned condensed milk – inflicted dysentery, the guerrillas' curse.

On the morning of 5 December, Batista's troops, who had been tracking them since the landing, attacked their camp. In a storm of fire Che was hit in the neck. He exclaimed laconically, '*Estoy jodido!*' – 'I'm fucked!' – and expected death. Then he realized that he had suffered only a flesh wound, and bolted for the forest. Fidel ran into high sugar cane, clutching a cherished telescopic-sighted Swiss hunting rifle. Of the eighty-two aspiring guerrillas, three were killed outright, seventeen were wounded and captured. The survivors scattered into clusters, seeking escape. Most were betrayed, captured and executed during the days that followed. Batista announced publicly that the invading group had been wiped out, prompting an article in the *New York Times* headed 'The Violent Cubans' and deploring their absurdity: 'Could anything be madder?' Headlines in Cuba proclaimed 'FIDEL CASTRO MUERTO'.

Yet Castro was not merely not dead but remained irrepressible, deranged. When he and two companions met Raúl and four others, the rebel leader asked his brother how many guns had been saved. Five, said Raúl. Fidel exulted: 'Well, we have two! That makes seven. Now we've won the war.' Three days later, eight more ragged figures joined them, among them Che Guevara, who had marched allegedly east, guided by what the Argentine confidently declared to be the North Star, until after two days they found themselves on Cuba's south coast.

The shrunken band plunged into the mountains of the Sierra Maestra, where they remained through the ensuing two years. Their sufferings were very great, from weather, sickness and privation. Some local recruits who joined them faded away home after experiencing a few days in the wilderness. They mounted sporadic attacks on army outposts, which seldom offered much resistance, and provided a trickle of arms, ammunition, food, rum. Batista's aircraft bombed them, with little effect. Castro recognized that his foremost challenge was not one of tactics, but instead of public relations. He needed to show the world that he was alive; and still in the revolution business.

His agent in achieving this was yet another of the adoring, well-connected women who played notable roles in his ascent. Celia Sánchez contacted Herbert Matthews, an adventurous fifty-seven-year-old *New York Times* journalist. She offered him the scoop of an interview with Cuba's most wanted fugitive. Matthews arrived on the island masquerading as a rich tourist. He was driven much of the way to the guerrilla camp by women friends of Sánchez, then hiked into the mountains. He first encountered Raúl Castro, to whom he talked in Spanish that he had acquired while reporting Spain's civil war, two decades earlier. At dawn on 17 February 1957 Fidel joined them, to meet for the first time Celia, who would become his lover and much more. She lost one argument – to persuade him to return to Mexico and restart his revolution from the outset. Otherwise, however, she proved an administrative wizard, imposing a coherence on Castro's ramshackle campaign that it had hitherto lacked.

As for Matthews, he was entranced by the guerrillas, who had been at pains to clean themselves up for the encounter. They staged a little charade to convince the journalist of their strength, parading the same men past him in a continuous loop. His front-page dispatch appeared in 24 February's *New York Times*. Castro was 'quite a man ... the rebel leader of Cuba's youth', according to the star-struck reporter. Fidel was not merely alive, but fighting fiercely in the almost impenetrable mountains. Matthews praised his 'extraordinary eloquence ... the personality of the man is overpowering'.

The Batista regime denounced as fictions both the interview and Matthews' account of the guerrilla force in the mountains, but nobody believed Havana's version. The story appeared at a time when several other revolutionary groups were active in Cuba, competing with Castro for legitimacy as the nation's principal opposition movement: on 13 March 1957, student insurgents shot their way into Batista's palace before being overwhelmed. There was nothing inevitable about Castro's assumption of the role of natural successor to the Havana regime, but he proved himself a brilliant self-publicist long before he became a successful guerrilla.

Once the outside world discovered that he was accessible, it could not hear enough about him. Castro told a Spanish journalist: 'I hate Soviet imperialism as much as Yankee imperialism. I'm not breaking my neck fighting one dictatorship to fall into the hands of another.' He said that he was targeting aristocracy, exploitation, privilege, and was committed to agrarian reform.

The guerrillas' strength rose to two hundred, many of them known to each other by nicknames – Lalo, Yayo, Pepe, Paco, Chichi, Chucho, Chino. Fidel himself was dubbed *El Caballo* – 'The Horse'. They all stank; affected the extravagant beards that made them famous as *los barbudos*. Accidents with weapons proved a persistent feature of their mountain lives, but as fighters they became progressively bolder, more skilful and successful. On 28 May 1957, they attacked Batista soldiers garrisoning a barracks at El Uvero, a remote fishing village. The defenders surrendered after six rebels, fourteen soldiers and five pet parrots had been killed. In this battle, as in others, Che Guevara displayed suicidal courage, while afterwards he used his medical skills to hold clinics for local peasants. The army recognized that isolated posts could not be held, and began a progressive withdrawal from the Sierra. Elsewhere urban rebel groups pledged to Castro conducted shoot-outs with police, which raised their profile even if they secured no great victories.

It is extraordinary that the Havana regime, with its army of secret policemen and killers, proved to lack the will or skill to locate and destroy Fidel, but so it was. The world heard ever more about the man and his indisputably romantic, apparently indestructible band. There was Camilo Cienfuegos, always quoting from *Don Quixote*; Juan Almeida, a poetry-loving ex-bricklayer; the supremely handsome Che Guevara, a sea-green incorruptible whom women went crazy for, and who now embarked on a relationship with eighteen-year-old blacksmith's daughter Zoila Rodríguez. Raúl Castro once met Che riding through moonlit jungle on a white horse, ahead of a captured army jeep and supply truck. Yet the doctor, almost certainly psychopathic, also enjoyed personally executing alleged stool-pigeons.

In February 1958 the rebels achieved a propaganda coup. Juan Fangio, the Argentine racing driver who was five times world champion, arrived in Havana for the Cuban Grand Prix ... and was promptly kidnapped by 'Fidelistas'. He missed the race, but was released at midnight to hold a press conference, at which he spoke of 'my friends the kidnappers. If what the rebels did was in a good cause then I accept it.' Yet Batista still had a paper strength of forty thousand soldiers and policemen, against three hundred in Fidel's jungle camp. On 9 April 1958 a nationwide general strike against the regime failed miserably.

In its wake the president's SIM secret police killed two hundred supporters of the 26 July Movement. That summer, Havana launched Operation *Fin de Fidel*, to hunt down its leader. After seventy-four days of pursuit and skirmishes the rebels, aided by excellent intelligence provided by local peasants, were still armed and free. Celia Sanchez organized a permanent base for the leadership more comfortable and settled than anything the *barbudos* had hitherto known, where they occupied log cabins erected on the side of Pico Turquino mountain, lit by a generator. Castro greeted Karl Meyer of the *Washington Post*, one among a procession of visiting journalists, with the words 'Welcome to Free Cuba'. Celia remained devoted to 'the Horse', but was exasperated by his tantrums and lack of self-discipline. His temper was not improved by painful troubles with his teeth.

In Cuba's cities, insurgent bomb attacks and firefights with police became everyday occurrences. Meanwhile the outside world grew ever more disgusted by Batista's atrocities. While the US government remained formally supportive of the regime, many of the most influential members of the State Department and CIA had become covertly hostile. Washington halted shipments of heavy weapons and aircraft to Batista, although the shameless British stepped in to provide him with Hawker Sea Furies.

Castro was nonetheless conscious that his prospects of succeeding the dictator remained uncertain. Washington people were talking to exiled Cubans in Miami, among whom they aspired to identify leaders for a new puppet regime: they feared that if Castro secured power, he would rule as brutally as Batista. Contrarily US ambassador Earl Smith, a prominent Florida Republican, regarded the guerrilla leader as the sole cause of Cuba's instability, and implored the State Department to lift its partial arms embargo. Some deliveries to Batista indeed continued, but Foggy Bottom urged Smith to be discreet about them.

The rebels staged ever more spectacular publicity stunts: in June 1958, in Oriente province Raúl Castro kidnapped ten Americans and two Canadians from a US mining facility, then next day added to his haul twenty-four US servicemen, on leave from Guantánamo Bay. The hostages provided a human shield, which forced the regime temporarily to stop bombing the guerrillas. Fidel was initially furious about the hostile American publicity which these actions prompted. He changed his mind, however, as the detainees were released in small groups to tell the world of their generous treatment, and even to express support for the Revolution. A twenty-two-year-old US Navy flier, Thomas Mosnes from Iowa, said that he 'had had a ball', especially when his captors threw a Fourth of July barbecue for the prisoners, before taking them on a tour of bombed villages.

The guerrillas' ranks by now included some American *renegados*, all of them disreputable. The most notorious was twenty-nine-year-old petty crook, army deserter and all-around loser William Morgan. Under Che, he was promoted to the rank of *comandante*, but by the time Morgan was executed as an alleged double agent, he was unlamented. During negotiations for the hostage releases, a US consul was rash enough to claim that his country was giving no assistance to Batista. Raúl Castro responded by showing him photographs of Cuban air force planes refuelling at Guantánamo Bay. Nonetheless, Fidel sent Raúl, who was then accompanied by Che, a message warning against avowing their communist convictions to the foreign reporters who interviewed them.

The rebels steadily extended their hold on the Sierra Maestra, and established a surprisingly efficient system of governance. Meanwhile in the course of Operation Fin de Fidel, a thousand government troops were landed from the sea to stage a new assault on the guerrillas' stronghold, led by a former college-mate of Fidel named Major José Quevedo. With irresistible cheek Fidel sent the officer an affectionate note 'just to greet you and to wish you, very sincerely, good luck'. After seventy-four days of desultory operations in which the guerrillas lost thirty-one men killed, Quevedo quit. He joined the rebel ranks following a mass troop surrender and prisoner exchange brokered by a seventeen-year-old girl named Tete. A Sherman tank that had bogged down was commandeered by the victors. Batista's forces conducted a wholesale withdrawal from the region, enabling Castro's men to declare it a 'Free Zone'. Che and Camilo led 148 men on a 350-mile trek half the length of Cuba, to open a new front in the east. Their privations were appalling, and they lost twenty-nine of their number in a government ambush. But they kept fighting.

The atmosphere of the guerrilla struggle thereafter became increasingly picaresque, even carnival: 13 August 1958 was Fidel's thirty-second birthday, for which Celia organized a surprise party. During a truce with the regime for a prisoner exchange, an army helicopter took Castro, his lover and Che on an air tour of the Sierra Maestra. He armed a new women's platoon. The teenage Tete later recounted how, after the meeting that voted to endorse its formation, Fidel addressed the girls: '*Muchachitas*, you have seen how much I had to argue for you so that you can fight. Don't make me look bad.'

That summer of 1958, it had become apparent to all save Ambassador Smith that Batista's days were numbered. Uncertainty persisted, however, about what would follow. US business, the big investors in Cuba, wanted neither the incumbent president nor Castro. Fidel himself was nervous that a military coup might pre-empt a grab for power by his own followers. The State Department dispatched former ambassador William Pawley to Havana to urge Batista that he should leave quietly. The dictator sent Pawley packing, saying that he rejected any approach from Washington that was not open and official. On 3 November, he staged a clumsily-rigged election to nominate his successor, and announced as victor his lackey Andrés Agüero, with 70 per cent of the vote. Not even the Eisenhower administration, however, professed to view the poll as legitimate.

Thereafter, events in Cuba moved swiftly. Fidel, his band by now swollen to eight hundred, albeit mostly green recruits, descended from the hills. Guerrillas laden with captured ammunition blazed it at everything in their path. Money poured into the Movement's coffers. In December Washington informed Earl Smith, most loyal of Batista's remaining supporters, that it could no longer recognize the regime. At a secret meeting on the night of the 17th, the ambassador reluctantly told the dictator that he must leave, and not towards any American destination.

On 27 December Che Guevara led a force of 340 men to the city of Santa Clara, in the centre of the island. After two days of street fighting, the rebels triumphed over Batista loyalists. In the early hours of New Year's Day 1959, the dictator flew away from Cuba towards eventual exile in Portugal, without a public word to a soul. The mobster Meyer Lansky also fled, leaving his casinos to be looted and trashed by an exultant local crowd. The last Batista fighters in Santa Clara surrendered on hearing the news, and were executed that afternoon. Fidel, stunned by the suddenness of events, drove into the city of Santiago, to be greeted by adoring crowds, which he addressed for two hours: 'The Revolution is now beginning ... For the first time, the people will have what they deserve ... This war was won by the people.'

Camilo Cienfuegos led a column of grimy guerrillas to accept the surrender of five thousand troops at Camp Columbia, outside Havana. Their commanders graciously conceded to the Fidelistas bar privileges at the officers' club. In the middle of the night Che arrived in the capital, which he had never before seen, and took over the old fortress of La Cabana. There was brief uncertainty about whether others would challenge Castro for the governance of Cuba. For a few hours, the Americans deluded themselves that Colonel Ramón Barquín might form a new military dictatorship. Havana University was occupied by armed students who cherished short-lived notions of supplanting the *barbudos*. It was their misfortune, however, that Batista's men, during the previous two years, had murdered their most effective leaders.

Fidel now swept away the political pretensions of the survivors, with yet another supremely theatrical gesture. He could have taken a plane from Santiago to Havana. Instead, he chose to lead a motorcade the length of the island, on a week-long parade that became a Roman triumph. Some of his men rode on tanks decorated as if they were carnival floats. Almost every mile of the route, rejoicing crowds strewed their path with flowers as they cheered the victors hysterically. Castro temporarily discarded the spectacles he had worn all his life, saying: 'A leader does not wear glasses.' His nine-year-old son Fidelito, brought home from exile in Miami to share his father's victory and now clad in cut-down military fatigues, joined him as he rode a tank borne on a flatbed truck.

By the time the Castros reached Havana, the last vestige of doubt had vanished about who would rule Cuba. Fidel told a *Chicago Tribune* reporter who scooped the first interview with the conqueror: 'You can be sure we shall be friendly towards the US if the US is friendly to us.' He established his headquarters and temporary home in the Havana Hilton, of which the ballroom became a guerrilla mess hall. Everybody loves a winner: Che Guevara's parents flew in from Buenos Aires, to applaud their son in his hour of glory. Che and Camilo's men busied themselves disarming fourteen thousand Batista soldiers. On 12 January some seventy officers of the SIM secret police were shot in front of an open trench in Santiago. Vengeance was popular: a banner at a Castroist rally demanded 'Let the firing squads continue!' A sadistic American ex-convict from Milwaukee named Herman Marks enjoyed supervising a succession of executions. US diplomatic protests about these actions prompted Cuban indignation: many people saw much to be avenged. Fidel ruled, with the impassioned backing of millions.

3 THE LIBERATOR

Castro's attainment of heroic status was his own achievement, but his retention of it reflected American clumsiness. The power of his personality was indisputable, but it would have been a long stretch to characterize him as either an admirable human being or a successful father to his people. He had in common with many revolutionaries energy, charisma and fluency, allied to an impracticality which killed most of his followers during the guerrilla struggle, and would eventually bring millions of Cubans to the brink of starvation. In this, he matched the contemporaneous achievements of Ho Chi Minh in North Vietnam, Kim Il-Sung in North Korea and the Great Leader himself, Mao Zedong in China. Fidel and Che were ultimately heartless: they cared vastly for the cause; little or nothing for the individual save – especially in the case of the former – themselves.

Guevara would call for the creation of 'two, three, many Vietnams' to ensnare the US in Africa and Latin America; he eventually denounced Soviet imperialism as indistinguishable in its iniquity from the American brand. Meanwhile Castro's obsession with the cult of personality was nicely illustrated by an episode in February 1959, within weeks of his assuming power. On a whim, he boarded the visiting cruise ship MS *Berlin* in Havana harbour, and introduced himself to her captain's pretty nineteen-year-old daughter, Marita Lorenz, by saying: 'Do you know who I am? I am Cuba!' Despite his claims of personal asceticism, after deciding to add Marita to his harem, he dispatched a plane to New York to fetch her to Havana.

In the years following his triumph, one by one he removed every leading personality who appeared to represent a challenge to his absolute power. At an 8 January 1959 rally, Castro broke off a speech to ask an old guerrilla *compadre*, beside him on the platform: 'Am I doing alright, Camilo?', to which his comrade responded 'You're doing fine, Fidel', which was promptly echoed by the crowd and became a slogan of the Revolution. The handsome, dashing Camilo Cienfuegos was too popular for Castro's liking. At such rallies the leader appeared unwilling to allow his comrade a turn at the microphone, despite repeated shouts of 'Let Camilo speak!' Cienfuegos, a *Granma* veteran who held the title of *comandante* of Cuba's armed forces, disappeared forever in a mysterious offshore plane crash on 28 October 1959, aged twenty-seven.

In the same period Huber Matos, military chief of Camagüey province, fell from grace: he had attacked Castro for promoting communists to key positions. At a trial in December, Raúl Castro and Che Guevara – the Revolution's most enthusiastic avowed Marxists – demanded Matos' execution; instead, he served twenty years' imprisonment without remission, being released only in 1979. Others, notably including Che himself, fell from favour later. Only Raúl Castro was deemed unimpeachably loyal, safe: intelligent and ruthless, he was nonetheless devoid of his brother's charisma and popularity. As armed forces minister he wielded extensive influence, but his authority was dependent upon his giant sibling.

Nobody knows, or probably will ever know, how many 'enemies of the Revolution' were executed by the Castro regime in the first year after he assumed power, but three thousand is considered a reasonable guesstimate. One supporter said, 'We began to be afraid of what to do, and what not to do.' Architecture student José Ferrara admired Fidel boundlessly, and saw him as striving to reconcile revolutionaries, communists and counter-revolutionaries, but Ferrara acknowledged later that 'the revolution became heavy-handed. The expulsions of students from universities [for political deviation] became very harsh and did a lot of damage to our cultural life.' The list of banned books became interminable, so that Ferrara could read – for instance – Thomas Mann's *The Magic Mountain* and *Death in Venice* only when a friend secretly lent them to him.

The new rulers were morbidly sensitive about the United States, and especially about the alleged arrogance of its representatives in Havana. Manuel Yepe, the foreign ministry's twenty-three-year-old head of protocol, said: 'Americans of every kind just marched into my office without warning. When I asked them who had given them authority, they always responded that they were from the Embassy. They still thought they owned our country. I told them to go to hell, saying "We are now a sovereign state!"' Castro's puppet president Osvaldo Dorticós Torrado congratulated a Cuban audience on now having secured 'the privilege of living in a country where the United States ambassador means little'.

It is often the case that inspirational figures who win wars of liberation prove unfit to govern thereafter. Cuba, a small country corruptly ruled for generations, was bereft of an effective bureaucracy. The tools for successful administration are order, process, planning. Castro, Che and their henchmen not merely lacked experience of these disciplines, but denied a requirement for them. Revolutionary zeal – whatever that might mean – and loyalty to Fidel were the only talents deemed necessary to build the new Cuba. 'Most of us did not know what socialism was', as a comrade said ruefully, long afterwards.

It is hard to overstate the damage done to US interests by Washington's support for Batista long after it had become plain to the world that the dictator was, politically, a dead man walking. John F. Kennedy admitted in an October 1960 speech that the Eisenhower administration had failed 'to help Cuba meet its desperate need for economic progress' ... had employed 'the influence of our Government to advance the interests and increase the profits of the private American companies which dominated the island's economy, [and had given] stature and support to one of the most bloody and repressive dictatorships in the long history of Latin America'. An entire generation of Cubans, embracing all save the fattest of the nation's fat cats, grew up identifying America not with freedom and justice, but with oppression and deprivation. Even as Fidel Castro set about creating his own tyranny, this was legitimized – just as was the brutal Hanoi communist regime – by the fact that these were respectively a Cuban tyranny and a Vietnamese one, not the puppets of foreign imperialists.

In the spring of 1959, Cuba's economy was in free fall. Herbert Matthews, the *New York Times* reporter who had boosted Castro towards fame with his interview in the Sierra Maestra, suggested that the new leader should make a visit to the US, to win friends. The eleven-day trip, which took place in April, fulfilled one of its objectives by propelling the Cuban leader into a stratosphere of fame. More than a few of Eisenhower's people briefly enthused about Castro. A legion of American women, if disappointed in fantasies of sleeping with Elvis Presley or TV's Cuban heartthrob Desi Arnaz, would have been equally content to embrace the bearded guerrilla. A New Yorker said ecstatically: 'I don't know if I'm interested in the Revolution, but Fidel Castro is the biggest thing to happen to North American women since Rudolph Valentino.' In the Big Apple he met Mayor Robert Wagner; addressed a crowd of twenty thousand people; stuck his hand in the tiger's cage at the Bronx Zoo. Arthur Schlesinger wrote later of Castro's visit to Harvard, where several thousand students applauded the Cuban hero: 'They saw in him, I think, the hipster who in the era of the Organization Man had joyfully defied the system, summoned a dozen friends and overturned a government of wicked men.'

As a path to building bridges with the US government, however, the trip was a resounding failure. A sulky President Eisenhower, having considered denying Castro a visa because he had not awaited an invitation from the White House, disappeared to play golf at Augusta. Officials whom the visitor met found him childishly ignorant about matters of state, and especially economics. On 19 April Vice-President Richard Nixon spent three hours with Castro, then wrote a memorandum that proved shrewd, asserting that he was 'either incredibly naïve about Communism, or under Communist discipline'. He also described the Cuban as having 'those indefinable qualities which make him a leader of men'. Whatever Americans might think, 'he is going to be a great factor in the development of Cuba and very possibly in Latin American affairs generally'. It may not be too fanciful to suggest that Castro's extrovert passion evoked in the morbidly repressed Nixon a microcosm of envy as well as respect – not for the dictator, but for the man.

In May 1959 Castro announced agrarian reforms which included wholesale confiscations of US-owned assets. New regulations limited the size of private agricultural holdings to a thousand acres, with all excess holdings being confiscated by the government, without compensation to the former owners. A year later, all American businesses on the island were declared forfeit. Fidel's closest associates, notably brother Raúl and Che Guevara, were now pursuing an agenda that included suppression of 'state enemies' and, indeed, of all dissent. While the first revolutionary government included some conspicuous moderates, these were cast aside during the months that followed victory, as Castro's grip on power became more confident.

Cuba's 'haves', who had enjoyed privileged lives under the old regime, found themselves stripped of property and in many cases forced into exile: some 250,000 people quit the island in Castro's first years, and more would follow. Maximo Gomez had a special class schoolfriend in Calimete, a chunky boy named Tomasito who was the local apothecary's son. When Tomasito stopped coming, the twelve-year-old asked insistently about his absence, until he was told sternly, 'Don't talk about Tomasito any more, or his sister Rosinda. They moved.' It was only long afterwards that Maximo learned that they, like many others, had gone to Florida with 'Operation Peter Pan', which evacuated thousands of bourgeois schoolchildren.

Castro's government established a reputation for extravagant rhetoric, administrative incompetence, irresponsibility and cruelty. Marta Nuñez was the daughter of a successful and prosperous journalist with close American connections. In her big home as a child, only the maids listened to Cuban radio; she and her parents tuned to American stations. Although her father embraced the Revolution, at the age of fifteen and afterwards, she found it hard to come to terms with what it meant for her own life – no more smart schooling; an end to clothes from the US; a confrontation with poverty, to which she had never been exposed; a breach with the Catholic faith of her childhood, which ended with her throwing away the image of the Virgin she had always carried in her pocket: 'My father was a gourmet. One day he took a photograph of the pork ration that we were allowed, because it was so small. I had to work hard not to be anti-communist.'

Although her father kept on Fermin, his long-time driver, when Marta rode in the family car she now sat democratically beside him, instead of in the back. The last book she read at Ruston Academy before the school shut down was *Gone with the Wind*, which she found disturbingly close to home. Many, many parents disapproved of the Revolution, and especially of their daughters adopting trousers as part of their new militia women's uniforms. María Regueiro's impeccably middle-class father, who owned a Havana store, admired Fidel personally, but recoiled from his embrace of communism. Caring passionately for his daughter's gentility, he resisted her decision, aged seventeen, to participate in the government's mass literacy campaign by taking a job as a teacher out in the countryside. She went anyway.

Yet millions of Cubans – the have-nots who made up most of the population – continued to love and revere Castro and those around him, partly because memories of Batista, of *yanqui* imperialism and social deprivation, were so vivid. '"*Después del triunfo*" – "after the triumph" – is Cuban shorthand for everything that has happened since Fidel and Raúl Castro grabbed power in 1959', in the words of Anthony DePalma, an American reporter who knows the country intimately. Cubans had experienced centuries of oppression, poverty and privation. From 1959, they could console themselves that now, instead, they were enduring home-grown varieties of such things, not those imposed by avaricious foreigners. Marcolfa Valido, born the daughter of peasants in 1939, has always remembered Castro with gratitude and admiration: 'He gave Cuba a sense of worth. Of course he was not perfect, but he did many good things, even if some people are today ungrateful.' Maximo Gomez was likewise thankful, because under Fidel's rule he, born into poverty, was able to study art history and eventually to make a career in museums and galleries: 'Without the Revolution that would have been impossible.'

Teenage revolutionary Juan Melo recalled a popular saying of those days: 'I don't know what communism is, but if Fidel is a

communist, I'm a communist too!' The intimacy of Castro's relationship with his people was manifest whenever he addressed a
mass meeting. Women would shout from the crowd, 'Don't be too
long, Fidel! We have babies to feed!' Castro would shout back reassurance – then hold forth for four hours. One night he spoke at
Havana University. Pablo, a uniformed janitor whom students
traditionally bribed to supply them with copies of lecture notes,
cried out from the crowd: 'Fidel, give me a cigar!' The old man, who
was black, had worked there when the leader was studying, so they
knew each other well. Castro shouted back: 'Pablito, you are always
begging! Do some work and buy your own cigars!' The janitor
riposted: 'Damn you, Fidel, you're a real tight-wad! When I gave
you your notes all those years ago you never tipped me. And now
you don't want to give me a smoke!' The students loved it, of course.

José Ferrara, who was eighteen in 1960, described Castro as 'a
great politician, a great statesman, a man with a great vision of the
future. He was not a good ruler – leading and administering are
two different things.' Ferrara nonetheless continues to respect
Fidel, as do many of his fellow-countrymen, as a towering figure in
his country's history. Marcolfa Valido was haunted by wretched
childhood memories: she was once refused access to a bus, to take
her and another little girl to confession, because they were so
raggedly dressed: 'Things like that happened, and I could not
understand them.' She remembered the railway line near her family's tiny apartment, because there were often corpses beside it, left
there by Batista's killing squads. 'I have a lot to thank the Revolution
for, because I compare it with what went before. There was progress,
education.' Such a woman as Marcolfa, who in the 1960s became a
teacher, was insufficiently ideological to be bothered by the regime's
persecution of dissenters. She and her family, hereditary 'have-
nots', had no cause to care about what the Revolution took from
Cuba's 'haves'. They themselves were merely grateful for access to
schooling, some medical care, and the end of institutionalized
racial discrimination.

José Bell Lara was twenty-two, an enthusiastic revolutionary who
was prominent in the Havana airport workers' union. Like a host of

Cubans, he ever afterwards remembered the successive crises of the early Castro years as good times, because they brought people together: 'We relied for the country's defence not much on organization, but instead on the spontaneous enthusiasm of the people. Many who were not revolutionaries joined the Revolution, shared in its defence. Attack [from abroad] does a lot to bring people together.'

At Castro's first meeting in Havana with KGB officer Aleksandr Alekseev in October 1959, the Cuban said he would not be seeking arms from Russia, for fear of provoking US retaliation. Moreover, a few months later he asserted that the real danger to his country was not military but instead 'Cuba's economic weakness and its economic dependence on the US ... [the] US could destroy the Cuban economy'. He was persuaded to change his mind, however, and to accept Soviet weapons, following a massive explosion in Havana harbour on 4 March 1960, which destroyed a ship bringing Belgian weapons for the Cuban army. Castro, not unreasonably, was convinced that this was the CIA's work, though no evidence has ever emerged to support this allegation. 'The Americans are deciding on extreme measures,' he told Alekseev two days later. After Vice-President Nixon met Castro, he urged Eisenhower: 'Because he has the power to lead, we have no choice but at least to try to orient him in the right direction.' The president disagreed, determining instead to dispose of this noisy, tiresome Latino gadfly. In December 1959 Col. J.C. King, chief of the CIA's Western Hemisphere Division, recorded his recommendation that 'thorough consideration' be given to the elimination of Fidel Castro to 'accelerate the fall of his government', a view endorsed by Allen Dulles and Richard Bissell.

By the time Castro next visited New York, to address the United Nations in September 1960, relations between Washington and Havana had turned glacial. A Gallup poll showed 84 per cent of Americans holding a negative view of the Cuban against 4 per cent positive, 12 per cent having no opinion. The only people who welcomed him were fellow-revolutionaries, such as the Black Power leader Malcolm X. One editorial denounced him as 'a spoilt brat with a gun'. Staten Island residents burned him in effigy.

Eisenhower hosted a lunch for Latin American leaders to which Castro was pointedly not invited. A final insult came when the Cuban was about to fly home, and discovered that the Americans had impounded his plane. Soviet leader Nikita Khrushchev promptly lent him a Russian one. Huge posters began to adorn Havana: 'NIKITA FIDEL AMIGOS'.

It was not the case that American policy towards Castro drove him into the arms of Moscow. Expropriation of US assets and wholesale executions of *Batistianos* preceded, and did not follow, Washington's explicit declaration of hostility. Nonetheless confiscation of the Esso, Shell and Texaco refineries on the island was provoked by those companies' refusal to process Soviet oil, first fruits of the new trade agreement with Moscow. Washington broke off diplomatic relations with Havana in January 1961, following a Cuban demand for an arbitrary reduction of US embassy staff to eleven people, inside forty-eight hours. In March that year John F. Kennedy announced the creation of the Alliance for Progress, a proclaimed successor to the Marshall Plan, designed to boost the fortunes of Latin America: its purpose was to offer an alternative to Cuban advances, which came with a Marxist top-dressing. There was never a realistic prospect that the US would reach an accord with Castro. This was a period when Washington still supported some of the ugliest dictatorships in the world merely because they were anti-communist.

Stripped to essentials, Americans wanted the new Cuban leader to shave, figuratively speaking; restore forfeited economic assets; accept its direction. Why should he have done so? The US had created the conditions for the new impasse, by almost everything it had done to the island since 1898. Cubans were then, as they remain today, exasperated by America's claim upon their historic gratitude for having allegedly 'given' independence to their country. In truth, their own people had waged a long, bitter and ultimately successful war to expel the Spanish, which Teddy Roosevelt and his friends joined only at the last hurrah.

The US and Cuba shared mirror grievances, rooted in mutual charges of ingratitude and unreason. The former colonial master –

the US, not Spain – now found itself suffering the sort of treatment that Ireland accorded to Britain for decades after securing state-hood in 1921. This caused Eire, as the Irish dominion was then known, to stay out of World War II; its prime minister to visit the German embassy in Dublin in May 1945, to offer formal condolences on the death of Hitler. The wise and witty writer Sydney Smith did not much exaggerate when he wrote two centuries ago about John Bull's other island: 'The moment the very name of Ireland is mentioned, the English seem to bid adieu to common feeling, common prudence and common sense.' The same words might be applied to the conduct of the United States towards its own small, unbiddable neighbour. The Cubans, like the Irish, drove a wagon train of just grievances. Arthur Schlesinger wrote: 'It was true that revolutionary Cuba had a reckless and anarchic verve unknown in any other communist state, that it had abolished corruption, that it was educating and inspiring its people, that it had triumphantly reclaimed a national identity, that it was traduced and slandered in the foreign press.' He added, equally correctly, that 'these truths blotted out harsher truths and subtler corruptions' about Castro's misgovernment.

The CIA established a propaganda broadcast unit in the Swan Islands, and began to dispatch aid to little knots of anti-Castro rebels in the mountains – *Contras*, as Havana branded them – and to plan bigger things, which eventually became Operation Zapata, approved by Eisenhower in March 1960. By way of retaliation, in 1961 Castro's station began to broadcast programmes under the banner of 'Radio Free Dixie', fronted by self-exiled US civil rights spokesman Robert Williams, aimed at alienated African-Americans, which ran until 1965. There has been interminable debate among historians and biographers about whether Fidel was always a communist or merely became one. Without immediately addressing that question, it is hard to imagine any means whereby Castro could have sustained mass enthusiasm for his Revolution without the expropriation of American-owned assets and land. He needed to quarrel with the powerful interests that had backed Batista – not merely the mafia bosses who ran the casinos, but some of America's largest corporations. He had to sustain a sense of excitement among his people. It seems significant that unlike, for instance, the rulers of China and North Vietnam, Cuba's ruling group chose to represent themselves as warriors even after they had won their war. Though they had been less than brilliant guerrillas – there was no General Giap among them – in public appearances they continued to affect military fatigues, combat boots and personal weapons. Castro was a sensationalist: he excelled at creating sensations. His 269-minute rant to the United Nations on 26 September 1960 was grotesque in its excess, but supremely newsworthy, because it stood among the longest speeches the General Assembly has ever been obliged to endure.

Hundreds of thousands of bitter, clamorous Cuban exiles were now domiciled in Florida, where they commanded support from American conservatives: their numbers would progressively swell to the twenty-first century's 1.53 million, with a further half million elsewhere in the US, as Cubans at home suffered ever-mounting hardships. Margarita Alducín, born in 1943, was the daughter of a kitchenware salesman and a housewife who 'sewed for the street'. Her mother had been disinherited by her rich family 'because she fell in love with a black man, a mulatto' – her father. When the Revolution came, she devoted herself to stitching flags for M-26-7, and her modest home became a hiding place for revolutionaries, some of them later well-known – Eduardo García Lavandero, Juan Niuri, Chomón.

By 1961, however, Margarita and her mother had soured on the regime. They recoiled from 'the mess of whether the revolution was going to be communist ... Almost everybody in our neighbourhood had left [Cuba] – the owner of the local pharmacy, the wineries – everybody. People told my mother that we should go, but she said no.' Margarita's sister did leave, however. Senora Rivas forbade her son Filiberto, a militiaman, to read the government newspaper *Granma* in their home. 'First the shortages began. They gave you a ration card, and permission to buy things, though you had to queue for hours. Everything was regulated.' As a schoolboy, Maximo Gomez was aching to start what would become a lifetime of service in Cuba's cultural institutions, when he was summarily removed to cut sugar cane, along with thousands of other high school pupils: 'It was hard. When we returned we had to make good all that lost class time.'

A climate of chronic suspicion overtook what was once middle-class Cuba, as neighbours and workmates looked askance at each other, each wondering where now lay the private loyalties of others. Conchita Alfonso, mother of three children and wife of a paid-up revolutionary, said later: 'There was mistrust if you were a revolutionary, if you pretended to be a revolutionary or if you wanted to leave the country. If you wanted to go, you were already an enemy.' Her brother was asleep one night when his wife woke him by throwing some revolutionary literature at his head. She said: 'Either we all leave Cuba, or I go with my family.' Conchita told her husband she wished to go too, because the rest of her family was leaving. He responded: 'I will help you go, if you wish, but my daughters stay here.' Thus, of course, she stayed.

Once Castro became an avowed foe of capitalism, as well as a persecutor of Cuba's 'haves', it was almost inevitable that the US would attempt to undo by force the island's Revolution. British prime minister Harold Macmillan expressed sympathy to the White House: 'Castro really is the very devil ... I feel sure Castro has to be got rid of, but it is a tricky operation for you to contrive, and I only hope you succeed.' These words reflected the usual British eagerness to appease American sentiment. In truth, the prime minister regarded the US's Cuba fixation as overdone, and dangerous to European interests. He urged that if Washington pushed too hard, 'many Cubans who might otherwise have gradually drifted into opposition to Castro will instead be inclined to regard him – and themselves – as martyrs'.

Given the respective mindsets in Washington and Havana, Cuba now had little choice save to seek the assistance of the Soviet Union. Castro dispatched Che Guevara to Moscow, to demand arms – and, indeed, missiles. The Soviets, in the mood of the times and of the Cold War, were almost bound to respond sympathetically, as they did. The island under Fidel Castro remained one of the worst-governed countries on earth, albeit in a different fashion from Batista's polity. Margarita Ríos Alducín observed wearily in old age that their high hopes of the early Revolution went unfulfilled: 'The troubles of the poor are always the same.' Nobody ever did anything specially bad to the Alducíns, but nor did successive regimes in power ever give them anything good.

Castro was transforming Cuba into a theatre for his own self-aggrandizement, and his thespian skills secured a global audience for the performance. As the Soviet Union and Nikita Khrushchev drew the island into an ever-closer embrace, thoughtful observers perceived Cuba's potential for a Great Power showdown. A British *Spectator* editorial, written in mid-October 1962, was headed 'Avoiding Adventures'. It observed: 'As in Berlin so in Cuba a good deal of care has been taken by the Russian leader not to go too far.' The writer added, however, 'a new situation would, of course, arise were the Russian government to try to turn Cuba into a missile base. But some care has presumably been taken to make this clear to Mr. Khrushchev, and provocation of this kind would go far beyond the cautious pattern which has so far prevailed in Soviet diplomacy. Both Berlin and Cuba have the makings of first-class international crises. But they will only become so if the Russian government imagines it can safely go beyond the bounds of prudence.'

All unknown in London, America's principal Cold War adversary was already advancing far 'beyond the bounds of prudence'. The Soviet Union had harnessed Fidel Castro to an adventure that would shortly terrify the world.

2

Mother Russia

1 TRIUMPH IN SPACE, HUNGER ON EARTH

In 1957 the bleeping Sputnik satellite delivered to its Russian owners, bursting with pride, their biggest propaganda triumph since victory in the Great Patriotic War, twelve years earlier. Sputnik supposedly implied a capability to dominate US skies with nuclear weapons. In April 1961, there followed another space achievement which put the fear of God, or rather of the godless communists, into millions of patriotic Americans: the USSR won the race to become the first to propel a man into earth orbit. Yuri Gagarin's space flight made a superstar of the handsome young lieutenant, promptly elevated to major. In homes across Russia news of his flight, broadcast by the famous Radio Moscow announcer Yuri Levitan, prompted an orgy of national rejoicing. 'People ran out into the street, laughed, congratulated each other,' wrote young Muscovite Galina Artemieva. 'It was such a happy, unforgettable day!' The world nervously hailed a superpower seen to be outpacing America. Many people, some of them in Washington, saw the Soviet spaceman as symbolic of a communist society apparently advancing by giant steps. They even began to delude themselves that some of the blizzard of statistics emerging from the Soviet Union, asserting its own military, economic and social achievements, might be authentic.

Extraordinary though it seems today, such influential gurus as Paul Samuelson and J.K. Galbraith predicted that the Soviet economy was likely within a generation to overtake that of the United

States. Henry Kissinger, then teaching at Harvard, wrote that 'the United States cannot afford another decline like that which has characterized the past decade and half', which threatened to 'find us reduced to Fortress America in a world in which we had become largely irrelevant'.

The full Gagarin story did not emerge for decades. It lays bare the rickety, rackety, mortally dangerous technology that was deployed to make possible the Soviet Union's achievement. As the pilot accelerated through the atmosphere, for several terrifying seconds his rocket's third-stage engine signalled a malfunction. Later, as the Vostok 1 spacecraft decelerated from 18,000 mph for re-entry, it failed to slow sufficiently quickly for its braking engine to fall away. The capsule spun wildly; Gagarin could feel its protective shell cracking, burning. He was reprieved only when the braking engine cable snapped. Having ejected above Russia after 106 minutes, the spaceman's survival pack fell off and the breathing valve on his helmet stuck. His reserve parachute blew open accidentally, which could have killed him. When he finally landed in a potato field near the Volga, the world's first cosmonaut was obliged to borrow a horse to get to a phone to summon rescuers.

Here was, indeed, a symbolic vision of post-Stalin Russia: a society endowed with remarkable scientific and technical skills, unmatched by production capability. The country could not build a car, washing machine or electric toaster that anyone outside its own borders would choose to buy. Mice once invaded an arsenal in central Russia and ate the insulation on missiles stored there: hundreds of cats had to be recruited to address the plague. When Sergei Korolev, the Soviet rocket designer who played a prominent part in Gagarin's flight, heard of this, he was reduced to hysterical laughter. The general in charge of the arsenal was sacked; fortunate not to be shot. In October 1960 a new R-16 rocket exploded on its launch pad, incinerating almost a hundred people including the officer in command of Soviet missile forces, whose remains were identified only by a marshal's shoulder pad and half-melted office key found in the ashes.

The Party, chained to centralized bureaucracy and Marxist ideology, laid its dead hand upon everything from factory work norms to agricultural practice. All human affairs were viewed through an ideological prism. A contemporary Moscow street joke has a listener phone in to a fictional Radio Armenia, asking for a cure for baldness. He is told stonily: 'We do not answer political questions.' The secretary of the Ukraine Communist Party, Petr Shelest, wrote in his 1962 diary: 'Khrushchev is right to say that we must be open about our difficulties, if we are to overcome them. Unfortunately, however, we often create these difficulties for ourselves, then battle against them, and at last regard success in overcoming them as an achievement.'

A mass migration was taking place from the Russian countryside to cities: thirteen million people made such a move between 1956 and 1959, sustaining a chronic urban housing shortage. Conditions for most of Khrushchev's people were appalling – average living-room available to each person, excluding communal space, was just fifty-four square feet, half that decreed as a norm four decades earlier, in the first flush of the Revolution. Aziz Chirakhov, who ran a string of market stalls, lived in an old block in which seventeen families each occupied a single room on either side of a long corridor 'along which small kids rode their tricycles', with a single shared toilet and common kitchen for all. He said: 'My neighbours fought so much that I found another place, with a less good room but just three families.' Khrushchev enjoyed a notable success, in moving many such urban dwellers out of wooden *barak* – huts – into apartment buildings, but these were basic. Space was everywhere at a premium, so that only the Party could book hotels. 'At that time they were building the Rossiya Hotel. As soon as the first wall went up, somebody chalked on it "No Rooms Available".'

As a Leningrad child Svetlana Mikhlova attended a specialist English-language school where she enjoyed the rare privilege of reading foreign authors – Dickens, Galsworthy, Jack London, *An American Tragedy* and *The Catcher in the Rye*. She was fascinated to learn from their pages that Westerners were free to live wherever they chose, in contrast to her own homeland, where every citizen was obliged to register their domicile; to travel internally only with official authorization.

It was a contradiction that there were many good things in the shops and markets, at least in Moscow and other big cities. Housewives could gaze upon tubs of red and black caviar, while tins of crab rusted on the shelves, because almost no one had money enough to buy them. Among prized domestic items, telephone lines were accessible only to those with influential friends. In the decade that began with Stalin's death, Soviet industry produced just a hundred thousand private cars a year, barely a week's output from US auto plants. An unskilled worker might earn sixty roubles a month, the price of two pairs of shoes. The standard of consumer goods was lamentable. At least 40 per cent of the average family income had to be spent on food, barely adequate in quantity, and no treat for the taste buds. Some families had primitive KVN TVs, with tiny screens that viewers watched with the aid of a water-filled glass magnifying lens. More affluent households aspired to a Start-3 model, which did not require magnification. Alcoholism was a chronic blight, partly because vodka offered the holiday from reality most accessible and affordable by the Soviet Union's 214 million people.

The entire national narrative since the 1917 Revolution depicted sacrifice: of lives, in millions; of freedom of choice and speech. Until at least 1942, Josef Stalin was responsible for far more deaths than Adolf Hitler. Then there were the privations, often trending to starvation, imposed by invasion and civil war; followed by institutionalized mismanagement; then again by invasion; then by further fabulous mismanagement. Any person within the borders of the USSR who pointed out that, before 1914, Russia under the tsars had been set on a spectacular upward economic trajectory, would have been fortunate to escape the Gulag, but spoke the truth.

The nation's leaders imposed hardships and madnesses industrial, agricultural, military and social, backed by draconian sanctions for expressions of dissent. No one who had lived through the Great Patriotic War would forget that in 1942 some citizens of Leningrad resorted to cannibalism amid starvation, cold and

disease that killed three-quarters of a million of the city's inhabitants – far more people than the USA, Britain or France forfeited in
the course of the entire war. Almost every Russian had suffered
personal loss between 1941 and 1945 – parents or close relations
dead or maimed; communities devastated. More than 1,700 towns
had been obliterated; such cities as Minsk and Kiev became largely
uninhabitable.

Following such experiences it seemed intolerable to many
Russians, and especially to their leaders, that America should wax
fat, rich, complacent, arrogant, while their own great socialist
nation – which had borne the lion's share of the burden of allied
loss and devastation for defeating the Nazis – struggled to provide
its people with a minimal acceptable standard of living. In
Aleksandr Solzhenitsyn's novella *Matryona's Home*, his epony-
mous heroine laboured, despite age and infirmity, 'not for money,
but for ... the marks recording labour-days in her well-thumbed
work-books'. A teacher named Saveliev, in the countryside outside
Leningrad, recorded in a July 1962 diary entry that he saw old
women dragging two goats to be sold for meat, because of an
absurd new tax on 'excess' private livestock. If they had kept the
animals, they would have been obliged to pay an impost of fifteen
roubles apiece: 'A goat now equals a cow! One is allowed to keep
other livestock together with a goat, but not two goats ... This is so
stupid and shameful. Who managed to come up with such an idea?!
And so the old women went, cursing their fate, their bosses and the
new rules!'

A month later, the same man recorded: 'Potatoes have been
harvested. This year they are bigger than last, and the harvest is
better. We immediately handed over to the state 60 kg at 8 kopecks
per kg, as in the south the harvest is extremely poor due to a
drought. Therefore, there is a decree ordering us "voluntarily" to
hand over 10 kg from each 100 square meters. They have started
limiting sales of bread, and no flour is available.' A month on, he
added: 'While there is more or less enough black bread, there are
no rolls. Livestock numbers are also being cut, which means it's
going to be tough. They have started making bread with 20 per cent

additives. People are saying that in the Tselina' – the wildernesses of the steppes – 'bread ration cards are being issued.'

Ivan Seleznev wrote in his diary expressing dismay about the poor harvests, and deploring the priority given to maize on the orders of the first secretary of the Communist Party: 'Illiterate *muzhiks* ploughing fields during the time of the Romanovs got much better yields. Why was that? This year [1962] they have put up prices for meat, butter and related products, on average by 20–30 per cent. Life has become hard for the working class.' Productivity in Soviet industry was less than half that of the US, worse in some sectors: an American miner produced fourteen tons of coal a day, his Soviet counterpart 2.1 tons [1963 figure]. Capital projects were never costed; prices both of consumer goods and industrial products were arbitrarily fixed. Most people were dependent upon buses to travel within their country – the railways prioritized freight.

While a shrinking minority of leftists clung to a fantasy of the Soviet Union as a socialist paradise, the West's predominant image was of a grey, monolithic society, suffused with hardship. This was real enough, but only part of the story: a surprising number of Russians nonetheless contrived to enjoy their lives. They took pride in heroic resilience in the face of hardship, and in the slow, painful, dogged recovery from wartime devastation. A sensitivity to perceived Western slights and condescension, so often displayed by Nikita Khrushchev, was shared by his people. It is striking to notice how few of the Russians who served in the West as diplomats or spies sought to defect. They lived among Western plenty, sometimes for years. Yet they chose thereafter to return to relative poverty – albeit privileged poverty, given their status – at home, rather than embrace a foreign culture which most found irredeemably unsympathetic. Aleksandr Solzhenitsyn would become Russia's most prominent dissident. Yet when he was eventually deported to Germany and later took up residence in the US, admirers thronging to embrace him were affronted by the harshness with which he attacked the West's perceived decadence and materialism. This great writer, who fought the Soviet system for so long and suffered so much at its hands, remained an impassioned Russian.

Long-serving ambassador Anatoly Dobrynin, born in 1919, was working as an aircraft engineer when, in 1944, he was plucked forth to attend the Higher Diplomatic School, an invitation that bewildered and alarmed him because, in the Soviet universe, he was nobody. A plumber's son, with a mother who worked as an usher at a Moscow theatre. Many years later, he learned from Molotov that it had been Stalin's personal decision to recruit some young men from technical backgrounds to represent Russia abroad. Before being posted, as well as attending language classes they were instructed in bourgeois etiquette, one lesson being conducted at a table set with an array of glasses and cutlery. Imaginary waiters brought in imaginary dishes.

Dobrynin was first posted to Washington as a counsellor in 1952, and like most foreign visitors was awed by its wealth. He wrote in his memoirs that it took him years to come to terms with America, then – he added, a little grudgingly – 'eventually to like it'. The Korean War was raging, as was McCarthyism. He found the US to be 'going through a period of anti-communist and anti-Soviet hysteria'. He himself was a committed Marxist-Leninist, and was convinced that sooner or later the US would attack his country.

In order to understand the events of October 1962, it is important to acknowledge such sentiments and indeed passions, even among intelligent and informed Russians. Throughout Khrushchev's decade of power old people suffered more than young ones, especially in 1961, when bread ran short and so-called currency reform devalued people's savings overnight. Tamara Kosykh, born in 1947, was one of four children reared by their mother, a factory worker, in a two-roomed apartment in the Urals. They lived harsh lives by Western standards, yet she afterwards remembered gratefully that the state offered them more benefits than successor generations receive in the twenty-first century: a crèche, free milk, free young pioneer camps, free hospitals and kindergartens.

'The 'Fifties were a time of hope,' wrote Galina Artemieva. 'The [Gulag] prisoners were being released, the war wounds were healing, our faith was growing in a different, better future.' Galina, born in 1950, described herself as one of the first Soviet generation not to have experienced war, or fear. 'We were children of the victors! We believed that we lived in the best country on the planet. We knew that things would get better, sunnier, more just. [We thought]: "Hey, it's great to be living in a Soviet country!"' Yet in many areas, children attended school in two shifts, a necessity prompted by the 1950s baby boom, which created a shortage of classrooms. Thus, Galina found herself doing homework in the morning, attending classes in the afternoons. Because she was young, she was oblivious of the USSR's oppressive culture.

Valery Galenkov, born in 1944, grew up in rural poverty, but likewise cherished memories of a happy childhood, alone with his grandmother in a wooden shack with a big birch tree in its garden, which he loved to jump from, especially in winter when there was heaped snow beneath. They had an outside toilet; a washbasin behind the stove; a sleeping bench above it. When his grandmother was out, Valery catered for himself: a piece of bread, a ladle of water. Once a week in winter, less often in summer, they bathed at a huge local public bathhouse. 'Life seemed good,' he said. 'It was only much later that I realized how mean and poor it was.' At the village club, there were film shows that always started with a propaganda movie about happy Russian life, with a title such as *The Soviet Urals*. Then came some heroic epic: 'We saw *Kuban Cossacks*, *Girls*, *Quiet Flows the Don*. Those were real masterpieces, and the Don's vast fields became dear to us.'

When the lights came up after each screening, their village boss – the head of the local Party – harangued them: 'He was a good, simple, merry fellow. Only later, when we grew older, did we realize that he was a pretty rough peasant type, and that a lot of what he told us was lies.' Their pleasures included much music, singing and dancing accompanied by accordionists or guitar-players. When Galenkov was a young man, people participated enthusiastically in Party demonstrations and rallies; cynicism did not take over until later, when compulsion became necessary to enforce attendance.

Such rural areas had access only to 'wired' radio sets, facto-
ry-configured to deny access to Western stations. But seventy
foreign Russian-language outlets beamed transmissions to the
Soviet Union, and now that Khrushchev's people owned seventy
million shortwave sets, it was impossible for Moscow to jam them
all. Pop music became the West's most effective propaganda tool.
Conversely, while sophisticated Russians and especially Muscovites
trusted the BBC more than Radio Moscow, American propaganda
was too crude to make much impact. During the Missile Crisis, the
CIA-funded station Radio Liberty broadcast such messages as 'for
every Soviet missile in Cuba, enough money, material and labour
have been expended to provide shoes for 25,000 people'. Yet as late
as the 1968 Prague Spring, evidence suggests that many Russians
preferred to accept Moscow's version of events to that of any
foreigner, and this was even more so six years earlier.

Galenkov said of those days: 'We could not compare our country
with any other, because we lived behind the Iron Curtain. We felt
that if we stuck things out, they would get better – and they did.'
Tamara Kosykh, who was then fifteen, said: 'We knew absolutely
nothing about America except that it was very far away. We did not
feel jealous of what Americans had, because we lived in isolation
and knew only our own situation. It seemed to us that we had
everything we needed. We weren't miserable, you know. There was
much devastation, in the aftermath of the war, but people were
working hard to restore the country, and they were doing it enthusiastically.'

The Soviet Union's highs and lows of 1962 were characteristic of
the entire communist era. On 17 June, its submarine K-3 voyaged
beneath the ice to reach the North Pole, a pioneering achievement.
Two weeks later, however, on the 30th, Aeroflot Flight 902, a
Tu-104 on an internal scheduled flight, crashed near Krasnoyarsk,
killing all eighty-four passengers. Although the cause of the tragedy
has never been acknowledged, it was almost certainly precipitated
by a rogue missile that ran amok during an air defence exercise.

There were serious public protests against government policies.
During Khrushchev's ten-year dominance, an estimated half a

million Soviet citizens dared at some time to participate in demonstrations, disorders or strikes. Some paid with their lives, and many more were dispatched to labour camps. If the Khrushchev era was incomparably less brutal than that of Stalin, it can scarcely be characterized as liberal. Sixty-four-year-old Boris Vronsky, writing a diary in 1961, mocked Khrushchev's personality cult and claims for Soviet achievement: '"Life is better now, life is more fun", as our giant of science and genius of humankind declares. His portrait offends one's eyes absolutely everywhere. He pontificates: "Things are going great with us." However, we can see for ourselves how great they are going. There is a strike in Odessa where freight workers discovered that butter was being shipped off to Cuba and refused to load it; there is unrest over food supplies in Krasnodar; a strike at the Voroshilov plant in Krasnoyarsk and other stoppages in other places.'

On 17 May 1962 the Presidium approved a decree raising retail prices by one-third for meat and poultry products, up to 25 per cent for milk and butter. Factory output norms were also increased, without any rise in wages, and in some cases with a reduction.

In Riga that summer, even as the Cuban crisis loomed, crowds gathered around a Lenin statue, shouting anti-government slogans. In Moscow, Leningrad, Donetsk and Kiev leaflets called for protests against price rises. Galina Artemieva's aunt Anya was so fearful of famine that she made her own bread with a mixture of flour and semolina, to go further, before drying and storing it in cotton pillowcases. Flyposters appeared on the walls of the city of Chita: 'Comrades! How much longer shall we live half-starving and destitute?' A few months earlier Nina Barbachuk, a forty-three-year-old Minsk doctor, was jailed for writing a series of anonymous letters to President Kennedy care of the US embassy in Moscow, warning him not to accept the Soviet leadership's professions of enthusiasm for peace, and describing the mean living standards of Soviet people.

Two Ukrainians released from labour camps found themselves rearrested and imprisoned for allegedly making threats against communists in Smolensk and 'approving of life in the U.S.'. When a young schoolteacher started a new job at a school near Yaroslavl, she was obliged to bring with her a mattress cover which she stuffed with dried sedge grass, to lay upon the metal bedframe that was the sole furniture of her room. Bread was brought to the village in locked containers because it was a precious commodity, liable to be stolen. Another Central Committee decree tightened the screws on dietary concessions, abolishing city canteens where it had been possible to buy a cup of tea for one kopeck and receive a free issue of bread – this had been especially important to hungry young students.

The most serious display of discontent took place in the industrial city of Novocherkassk, an event that – like the accidental airliner shootdown – was rigorously concealed from the Russian people for three decades afterwards. Trouble began with a strike by several thousand workers at NEBF, the Budyenni locomotive construction works, a major local employer, to protest the increased production norms and higher food prices. An official who sought to calm the crowd was showered with sticks and bottles. Some of the first troops summoned to the scene fraternized with the strikers, while others were injured by flying missiles. On 2 June, the unrest escalated into a mass protest in the city centre, where demonstrators broke into the public administration building. Soldiers opened fire, killing twenty-six unarmed people, who were secretly buried in unmarked graves, and wounding a further eighty-seven. Although reporting of the massacre was suppressed, rumours spread across the Soviet Union, including claims – probably false – of much larger numbers of deaths. Among those arrested, 114 were subjected to show trials. Fourteen supposed ringleaders of the demonstrations were convicted of 'banditry', 'vandalism' and other crimes. Seven death sentences were commuted, but all those in the dock received terms of imprisonment.

Foremost among important facts about the Novocherkassk tragedy, which became the subject of *Dear Comrades*, an international award-winning 2020 feature film, was that Anastas Mikoyan and Frol Kozlov, Khrushchev's deputies, arrived in the city to investigate on behalf of the Presidium before the army started shooting:

thus, the Kremlin was directly complicit in the bloodshed. Mikoyan wrote in his self-serving memoirs: 'I realized that the workers' demands were justified, and that their unrest was caused by major grievances.' He claimed that, even as he sought to negotiate with the strikers, his fellow-emissary Kozlov telephoned the Kremlin to demand approval to open fire – 'which he received from Khrushchev'. Kozlov also ordered trains to be prepared, for mass deportations of the dissidents to Siberia – 'a shameful act!', in Mikoyan's words. One senior officer on the spot, Gen. Matvey Kuzmich Shaposhnikov, commanding a tank unit, refused to order his men to fire on the demonstrators: for this display of scruples, he was later demoted. His superior, Gen. Issa Pliev, unhesitatingly exercised the authority granted by Moscow to order his men to shoot to kill.

The protesters did not demonstrate against communism – on the contrary, they carried images and slogans of its heroes: it was the now-masters of the Kremlin whom they denounced. In Novocherkassk, in the words of a Western historian, 'they did not tear down portraits of Lenin; it was Khrushchev they reviled'.

The Revolution – the Soviet Union's march towards a socialist utopia – still commanded the support of an overwhelming majority of Russians. It was those now implementing it, members of the ruling Presidium of the Central Committee of the Communist Party, who incurred their wrath. Even the KGB admitted that the Novocherkassk workers had been much provoked. A slogan was chalked on the side of a locomotive halted by protesters on the tracks outside the city: 'Cut up Khrushchev for meat!' Portraits and posters depicting the Presidium's chairman were torn down and burned. Nikolai Barsukov has written about the mood that provoked the protests: 'The disillusionment and dissatisfaction of the masses were exacerbated by the sharp contrast between the recent promise of imminent paradise and the reality of existence.'

Sergei Khrushchev later asserted that his father, until the end of his days, was racked by guilt about the shootings. He described him coming home during the disturbances and saying crossly:

'The workers kicked up a row and the local idiots started shooting.'
This benign view is hard to credit. The leader makes no mention of
Novocherkassk in his memoirs, while admitting other mistakes.
Khrushchev is elsewhere recorded as telling Kozlov: 'Since millions
have already perished for the Soviet cause, we were correct to use
force.' That remark seems both credible and important.
Novocherkassk was not unique: in 1962, anti-government protesters were killed in other cities including Murom and Aleksandrovsk,
albeit in smaller numbers. The first secretary's generation of
Bolsheviks had already borne witness to, and often initiated, so
much bloodshed in the cause of the Revolution, that it seemed
necessary to double down, to sustain a stone face in the presence
of death, rather than to risk imperilling the triumph of socialism.
Such a mindset would persist within the Kremlin, in considerable
measure, until the last years before the collapse of the Soviet
Union.

The *shestidesyatniki* – 'Sixties generation', which would make an
impact on Russia almost as powerful as that of their contemporaries in the West upon their own societies – had yet to take wing,
though New Wave Russian cinema promoted some remarkably
original ideas, especially about the nature of war. Many young
Muscovites adopted a trendy cropped hairstyle which was so close
to a soldier's cut that the teenagers who embraced it were said to be
'ready for war tomorrow'. Red Army veteran Grigory Chukhrai
made such famous films as *The Forty-First*, *Ballad of a Soldier* and
Clear Skies; Mikhail Kalatozov directed *Cranes Are Flying*. One of
the greatest American Westerns ever made, *The Magnificent Seven*,
was granted Russian screenings. The overarching cultural mood,
however, remained sternly conformist. Official repression of
dissent increased in 1962. In the Gulag, camps holding political
prisoners were ordered to adopt an 'intensified' and then a 'strict'
regime, rendering even harsher the conditions in which prisoners
were held.

Perversely, the freest communities in Russia were its scientific
secret cities, the principal inhabitants of which were permitted to
exchange ideas and voice opinions with a freedom unthinkable

outside. Even the Presidium understood that there was no prospect that Russia could win its race for space, nuclear parity, medicine or any scientific or technological achievement, unless its cleverest practitioners were permitted to think for themselves and exchange ideas, as other Soviet citizens could not. By 1962 the scientific-military-industrial complex embraced 966 plants, research institutes, research laboratories and manufacturing installations, employing 3.7 million people. Soviet scientists came to form the spearhead of their country's nascent intellectual culture. Physicist Andrei Sakharov enraged Khrushchev by warning against resuming nuclear testing. The latter said contemptuously: 'I'd be a jellyfish and not chairman of the Council of Ministers if I listened to people like Sakharov.' Khrushchev remained implacably committed to showing his Presidium comrades, and the world, that if he was not a mass murderer of remotely the same appetites as his predecessor, he, too, was a man of steel.

2 'THE SHARK'

In the eyes of the world Stalin was a monster, of whom his own people were the principal victims. Almost a decade after his death, however, many Russians mourned him as architect of their restored might, the nation's saviour in the Great Patriotic War. Veteran Viktor Nekrasov wrote: 'The victors are above judgement! We had forgiven Stalin all his misdeeds.' Amid a Marxist universe in which the cruellest famine was that of truth, rumour held sway. One of the most popular held that a Jewish conspiracy, embracing Stalin's doctors, had murdered him. When Khrushchev's sensational 1956 XXth Congress speech was circulated, denouncing Stalin's mass murders, a major, talking with fellow-officers of his tank unit in the Moscow Military District, demanded angrily: 'Why was all this published? They should put all this away in the archives so that people's souls would not be disturbed or devastated!'

Another officer said wonderingly: 'After this speech you don't know whom to believe ...' A colonel added: 'And where was Khrushchev himself? Why did he keep quiet back then, but begin to spout all this muck on Stalin now that he's dead? I somehow do not trust all the facts that are laid out ... Stalin raised me on his ideas from my childhood, and I will not reject those ideas now.' The same officer referred to the great novelist Boris Pasternak, author of *Dr Zhivago* which of course he had not been permitted to read, as 'Judas, a renegade, a weed, a frog in the swamp'. He said of Khrushchev: 'The country was ruled for so long by a madman, a murderer, and now – by a fool and a pig.' To this day, to acknowledge the towering iniquity of Stalin seems to many patriotic Russians to demand a renunciation of their people's sufferings and sacrifices in the cause of socialism since 1917.

Galina Artemieva, as a communist Young Pioneer in the 1950s, was granted the special privilege of being allowed to visit the Leaders' mausoleum in Red Square without queuing: 'We were hushed by the solemnity of the moment. I had never seen a corpse. The leaders represented a strange pair. One [Lenin], the great example of wisdom and humanity, small and yellow-faced, lay there in a neat suit and tie and did not look impressive next to the Generalissimo. Stalin looked quite alive, just asleep, ready at any moment to open his eyes as soon as he tired of lying there in front of the audience. I felt sorry for both of them, thinking it somehow offensive that they should be exposed to everyone's gaze.' In October 1961 Khrushchev erased the cause for her pity, decreeing the overnight removal of Stalin's corpse from public display; it was buried nearby, symbolically beneath several feet of concrete.

In February 1962, a person never identified mailed in Moscow a mass of letters addressed by name to prominent communists, including members of the Presidium, denouncing Russia's leader: 'There is no limit to Khrushchev's adventurism, and because of the inevitability of the collapse of these adventures, he will always need scapegoats.' The leaflets raised the possibility that the Russian people, who had thus far engaged only in local sabotage of his economic and social measures, 'will suddenly rise up and undertake something that eclipses all Budapests' – a reference to the 1956 Hungarian Uprising.

Nikita Khrushchev was certainly not a humane Soviet leader, but he was a much less inhumane one than Stalin. In many respects a brute, devoid of grace or manners, uncomfortable with culture and dismissive of dissidents 'on the wrong side of history', he indulged spasms of liberalism, realism and generosity that incurred the enmity of Kremlin hardliners. He possessed energy, enthusiasm, wit and a taste for clowning, qualities not customarily associated with Soviet leaders. He released from the Gulag at least a million political prisoners – some historians put the number much higher. His dispossessed rivals in the 1953–55 Kremlin power struggle, from which Khrushchev emerged supreme, were merely exiled to the provinces, rather than being shot. During the preceding decades, however, the Party first secretary and chairman of the Central Committee had ascended a mountain of corpses to win the trust of Stalin, to become his protégé and eventual successor.

Khrushchev was described by British Labour Party leader Hugh Gaitskell in 1960 as resembling 'a rather agreeable pig', though that was after meeting him in benign mood. He was born in 1894 into an impoverished peasant family in Kursk province, Ukraine. He began working in factories and mines at the age of twelve. Nelson Rockefeller once taunted him about the half million Russians who migrated to the US in the early twentieth century in search of free-dom. The Soviet premier responded dismissively: 'Don't give me that stuff. They only came to get higher wages. I was almost one of them.' Fiercely ambitious and materialistic, but for the 1917 Revolution Khrushchev would probably have become a successful industrial manager. Himself a proficient metalworker, he cherished a lifelong respect for those possessed of technical skills, and a prickly ambivalence towards those who had the academic educa-tion of which he himself was bereft. He had scarcely ever, indeed, read a book.

As a teenager he became a precocious anti-tsarist activist, boast-ing a police file for collecting money for victims of a massacre of striking miners in the Lena goldfields. Joining the Bolsheviks in 1918, he spent the Civil War as a political commissar. When it ended, he became a factory manager in the Donbas, Ukraine.

Thereafter, as a protégé of Stalin's murderous acolyte Lazar Kaganovich, his rise through the Communist Party was meteoric. In the mid-1930s, he became city manager of Moscow and overseer of its huge Metro construction project. He was also complicit in the Terror – Stalin's ideological purges. His biographer William Taubman writes: 'Khrushchev assisted in the arrest and liquidation of his own colleagues and friends. Of 38 top officials of Moscow city and province party organizations, only 3 survived. Of 146 party secretaries of other cities and districts in the Moscow region, 136 were, to use the post-Stalin euphemism, "repressed".' Mikoyan speculated cynically in his memoirs about Khrushchev's startling ascent. It happened, he said, 'because they had put everybody else behind bars'.

Or shot them. William Hayter, 1953–57 British ambassador in Moscow, wrote in 1970 of the Presidium of Stalin's era: 'Those who survived … did so because of their willingness to join in betraying their colleagues and persecuting the rest of the population. Passivity under Stalin was not enough: active participation in terror was required, and the survivors must have terrible burdens on their conscience. This hideous background must never be forgotten in estimating the present Soviet leaders.' Modern historian Vladimir Naumov has written of Khrushchev: 'He was transported and bewitched by Stalin's genius and wisdom; his very proximity to the leader had a huge impact on such an emotional nature as Khrushchev's. I think even his feeling of personal gratitude for the attention Stalin showed him was overshadowed by his profound euphoria at being involved in the great events happening in the country under Stalin's leadership.'

In 1938, Khrushchev became the Kremlin's viceroy in Ukraine, a post he held until 1949, with only a brief interruption. He developed a reputation for indiscretion and vulgarity, sometimes directed against his mighty mentor, yet retained his post and his life by displaying administrative effectiveness and animal cunning. He spent the war as a senior commissar, emerging with the military rank of lieutenant-general, having attended some of Russia's greatest battles: he never forgot the stink of incinerated corpses in the wrecked tanks at Kursk, under the summer sun of 1943. He witnessed the sufferings of the rural population in the 1946–47 famine which may have killed as many as two million people, victims of drought and post-war agricultural destitution. In 1947 Khrushchev was temporarily removed from his post as Ukraine Party secretary, and for a time feared for his own life. Yet later that year he was rehabilitated and restored to office.

His ascent was assisted by the fact that most of those who met him, both Russians and foreigners, underrated him. It does not seem frivolous to suggest that Stalin, morbidly sensitive about his own lack of inches, relished the fact that his protégé was even shorter – five foot five. He waddled, rather than walked. Beyond a fierce strength of will, Khrushchev displayed talents for duplicity and equivocation, bluff and persiflage. No man attained the summit of the Soviet Union by asserting unwelcome realities; indeed, an affinity to truth was an insuperable obstacle to high office. This should be remembered, in the context of the Missile Crisis.

Khrushchev's 1953–57 rival Georgy Malenkov seemed to a Westerner 'easily the most intelligent and quickest to grasp what was being said'. By comparison Khrushchev appeared bovine, frighteningly ignorant of the world. He was 'quick but not intelligent', according to William Hayter, 'like a little bull who if aimed the right way would charge along and be certain to arrive with a crash at his objective, knocking down anything that was in his way'. The 1953–57 US ambassador in Moscow, Charles 'Chip' Bohlen, viewed Khrushchev among those animalistic top Soviet functionaries with whom 'there was no meeting point, no common language'.

Following Stalin's black farcical expiry in March 1953, Malenkov for a time replaced him. Khrushchev engineered the arrest, then execution of the blood-steeped Lavrenti Beria. Thereafter, he progressively elbowed aside his enemies in the Presidium, until by late 1955 he himself had secured dominance. He became an enthusiastic foreign traveller, covering more distance than any Russian leader since Tsar Nicholas II. In November–December, he made a long tour of Asia with Nikolai Bulganin, a trip which included considerable clowning for cameramen, and a ride on an elephant.

In February of the following year, he performed the decisive political act of his life – delivering a four-hour 'secret' speech to the XXth Congress of the Soviet Communist Party – later leaked by a Polish communist to an Israeli intelligence officer, thence to the CIA who passed it to the *New York Times* – denouncing Stalinism; calling Stalin's crimes 'deformations of socialism'. In 1957 Molotov, Malenkov and Kaganovich were all branded Stalinists, and expelled from the Presidium. Kaganovich pleaded for his life. Khrushchev declined to relieve him from mortal dread, saying laconically, 'We'll think about it.' Eventually, his old chief was dispatched to manage the Urals potash works and lived until 1991. None of the vanquished was shot, which caused other members of the Kremlin inner circle to sleep more easily in their beds than they had done under Stalin.

Yet few people, inside or outside Russia, supposed for a moment that the USSR's leader had banished fear as an instrument of governance. A story is told which may be apocryphal, but captures a truth, of an assembly at which a Stalinist shouted forth from the crowd after one of Khrushchev's rhetorical assaults on his predecessor: 'And where were you, when all these crimes were committed?' Khrushchev barked back: 'Who said that?' A terrified silence fell upon the gathering – in which, Khrushchev later claimed, he himself shared. Under his leadership, the Party reassumed collective control of what passed for the justice system, and mass terror ended. But there was no pretence of an evidence-based rule of law, and he possessed a long streak of vindictiveness. Secrecy – the concealment of political discussions, decisions and above all embarrassments and failures – remained institutionalized. Lest anyone doubt the horror of the system over which Khrushchev presided, recall the account by the philosopher Isaiah Berlin, of a 1958 visit to Oxford by the great composer Dmitri Shostakovich. At any mention of political matters, recorded Berlin, the visitor fell into 'terrified silence ... I have never seen anyone so frightened and crushed in all my life.'

In the previous year, Khrushchev's grasp on power became secure. He was recognized as *Vozhd*, or Leader, and remained so until October 1964. His first three years proved the most successful, both in presiding over economic achievements at home – record harvests – and raising Soviet prestige abroad. Yet few of his people loved him. 'The paradox or, conversely, the logic of the times', in the words of Nikolai Barsukov, 'is that Khrushchev attained supreme power precisely when that power lost its support both from below (as daily life became worse and worse, people lost their Communist illusions and, with them, faith in Khrushchev) and from above (when Khrushchev started taking everything upon himself).' Nikolai Kozakov, an aspiring Gorky poet in his late twenties, kept a diary during those years in which he referred contemptuously to his nation's leader as 'the shark'.

Ivan Seleznev, another private diarist, wrote in November 1961 deploring Khrushchev's leadership: 'Stalin is nowadays branded almost a criminal, beyond the pale in this most democratic of all nations that he led for almost 30 years. They try to present this new man at the helm, this waste of space, as a fount of wisdom and brilliance. Since he can show nothing to justify that claim, instead the sacrifice and vilification of Stalin are used to fuel the new personality cult ... the vanity of one person, whom fate has placed in charge ... Stalingrad has been renamed Volgograd.' Seleznev added sardonically: 'It turns out that there was a Battle of Volgograd, not a Battle of Stalingrad.' Two state-sponsored composers wrote a song in the new leader's praise, of which the refrain ran:

He went through battles together with our people.
He is leading our land to happiness,
May our friend Comrade Khrushchev be praised,
Sing, o people, of him!

Yet more than a few Russians were unwilling to do anything of the sort. A family friend of Galina Artemieva, a woman from a once-noble family, referred to the leader as 'Krushch', a word for a tree-eating beetle: 'It's not a face he's got, it's an arse ... Didn't he drown the Ukraine in blood? Wasn't he Stalin's absolute toady?' Khrushchev possessed a ferocious energy and appetite for work, together with a moodiness that sometimes caused him to exult and laugh even with foreigners, sometimes also plunged him into gloom. Khrushchev's wife, Nina Petrovna, said: 'He's either all the way up or all the way down.'

His domestic affairs were no less tangled than those of most top Bolsheviks. One of his sons, Leonid, killed a sailor while drunkenly attempting to shoot a bottle off the man's head; the reprobate afterwards perished as a wartime pilot. Leonid's widow Lyubov Illarionovna Sizykh, Khrushchev's daughter-in-law, in the 1940s served a long term of imprisonment for alleged espionage. Nina, Khrushchev's weighty third wife, was better educated than he was; she taught Party history and Marxist-Leninist theory. Nina was his partner through the years of power, but he cherished a lingering guilt about her two predecessors, whom he had abandoned. He had a fondness for animals, so that his dachas often featured menageries which included at different times squirrels, a fox cub, a deer, rabbits, ducks and dogs.

He was a compulsive talker, prone to caustic mockery, sometimes during discussions on the most serious issues. At a meeting about building a new strategic bomber with range to reach the US, one designer promised that his version could attack the Americans, then reach sanctuary in Mexico. Khrushchev said contemptuously: 'What do you think Mexico is? Our mother-in-law? You think we can simply go calling any time we want?' He could be authentically amusing, but in a boorish fashion. During a visit to London, he enquired about the figure commemorated by the Albert Memorial. Told that this was Queen Victoria's consort, who performed no state duties, the Soviet leader demanded of his British hosts: 'And what did he do in the daytime?'

Khrushchev once invited Dag Hammarskjöld for a boat ride on the Black Sea. The UN secretary-general expected to luxuriate on a motor cruiser, but instead found himself a passenger, or rather prisoner, in a small rowing boat propelled by his host. Neither man had any common language, and Khrushchev viewed the excursion as a just punishment of the Swede, for boring him with monologues about the UN. Mikoyan wrote of his boss: 'He was a real rough diamond. Despite having very little education, he grasped things quickly and learned fast. He was a natural leader, persistent and stubborn in achieving his goals, courageous and willing to swim against the tide. He was nonetheless prone to extremes, and ... became obstinate in his follies and caprices. He tended to force these on the Central Committee, especially once he had brought in his own people. In consequence, his bad decisions started to seem like "collective" ones. Once he became carried away by a new idea, he would heed no one; kept driving on with the force of a tank.' He often marched alone, adopting policies without much pretence of seeking the views of others in the nominally collective leadership. To the fury of Presidium colleagues, Khrushchev did not consult them before issuing his notorious 'Berlin ultimatum' at a 27 November 1958 Kremlin press conference, demanding the withdrawal of Western troop contingents from their sectors of the city, occupied since 1945.

Perhaps the foremost characteristic of the Soviet leader, the foundation of his ascent to power and the dominant force in all that he did thereafter at home and abroad, was an absolute faith in communism, and centralized planning. He was honest enough to acknowledge, as many Party *apparatchiks* would not, that the Soviet Union was still far from being the Socialist paradise the Bolsheviks had promised. But he continued until his death to believe that it would become so if his people persevered; if they kept faith with the ideals of Marx and Lenin.

In October 1961, Khrushchev presented a grand economic programme to the XXIInd Party Congress. Within a decade, he promised, the whole population would be 'materially provided for'; well before 1971, everyone would 'enjoy a good diet of high quality'. Within ten years, the national housing shortage would also be ended. It is doubtful that a single member of his audience supposed that his vision would be fulfilled. One listener, who shared the Russian people's love of folk jokes, recalled the folk-tale rascal Khodzha, who promised the Emir that in twenty years, he would have taught his favourite donkey to talk. Why twenty years? 'Because he was smart,' said the cynic. 'By that time, either the Emir or the donkey would have dropped dead!' Yet it is possible that

Khrushchev, alone in the hall, swallowed his own rhetoric. His son Sergei wrote that his father's contradictory character 'blended pragmatism and the communist idealism of the twentieth century ... He fervently believed in the worldwide victory of communism, believed as a good Christian believes in heaven. And for him communism was the same as heaven, only it was on earth, where all people would be happy and live in plenitude and satisfaction.'

Khrushchev brought to domestic policy a passion and energy which delivered some benign results and rather more failures, especially in the field of agriculture – his collected speeches on the subject fill eight volumes. An obsession with output numbers, characteristic of the Soviet system, prompted him to emphasize maize production. During his 1959 visit to the US he paid a brief visit to Iowa, where a big farmer named Roswell Garst showed off his maize, machinery and animals. Khrushchev wrote warmly of Garst in his memoirs: 'As a capitalist, he was one of my class enemies. As a man whom I knew and whose guest I was, I treated him with great respect and valued him for his knowledge and unselfish willingness to share his experience with us.'

The Russian returned home with redoubled enthusiasm for corn-growing, in emulation of the Iowan. By 1962 thirty-six million hectares hosted this crop, for which large areas of the USSR were unsuited. Khrushchev empowered an almost deranged Stalinist agronomist named Trofim Lysenko, whose prescriptions underpinned the excesses of this policy. Entertainers were recruited to promote peasant enthusiasm for maize, dancing dressed up as corn cobs for bemused villagers. Maize-mania reflected Khrushchev's instinct to take everything too far. Enemies derided him as a *kukuruznik*, or corn man. Khrushchev's agricultural reforms were not a total failure: on his watch, people no longer starved to death. Substantial numbers, however, went hungry.

Leonid Pliusch, who was to become a prominent critic of the Soviet system, recalled in his memoirs that when, in 1959, he took up a post as a village teacher, he was appalled to find a third of its inhabitants suffering from tuberculosis. Though they had cows, all milk was taken away for sale by the collective. To check the flight to the cities, rural-dwellers were denied internal passports. The default mood of the peasantry, said Pliusch, was apathetic and distressed, because collectivization removed incentives to repair a falling barn, or indeed to do a proper day's work. The saying 'you pretend to pay us and we pretend to work' was a quintessential Soviet-era joke. The irony of all this was that Khrushchev cared more about the fate of the peasants than had any previous Russian ruler in history. It was his misfortune, and that of his people, however, that an iron-clad commitment to centralist, collectivist policies caused him to address the USSR's rural ills with quack remedies.

His policy towards the intellectual world was quixotic, rooted in sensitivity about his own literary ignorance. Boris Pasternak was obliged to renounce his Nobel Prize, on the personal order of Khrushchev. Only in the latter's old age did he confess that he had never read *Dr Zhivago* when he ordered its author's persecution, hastening Pasternak's death in 1960, aged only seventy. Khrushchev claimed to regret this. Contradictorily, in 1962 Aleksandr Solzhenitsyn's famous short novel *One Day in the Life of Ivan Denisovich* received approval for publication. In this the great dissident argued – as Vernon Scannell later put it – that the whole of Soviet society, whether incarcerated in camps or notionally free, 'was bound together in an indissoluble symbiosis … that those in the labour camps were freer than those allegedly and formally "at liberty". Paradoxically, the land of the Gulag was the only place where a Soviet citizen had nothing further to fear.'

Khrushchev's role in the story's publication was black comic. He was informed of a masterpiece by a hitherto unknown writer, and had his personal assistant read extracts aloud to him. These convinced him that the story celebrated the honest labours of Gulag prisoners who remained loyal to the Soviet system. The first secretary thus authorized publication in the literary magazine *Novyi mir*, at almost exactly the period of the Missile Crisis. He subsequently regretted this misbegotten spasm of enlightenment.

Khrushchev also authorized publication of the great nuclear physicist Andrei Sakharov's article acknowledging the consequences of exposure to radioactivity. Sakharov's damascene moment came when he realized that at least ninety people had died as a result of proximity to atmospheric tests of a new nuclear weapon. Soviet observers who attended these affairs found themselves, as did their American counterparts, recoiling in special horror from the many birds which fell victim. Sakharov wrote of the experience of encountering an eagle flapping on the ground with badly singed wings after the first Soviet hydrogen bomb explosion on 12 August 1953: 'It was trying to fly, but couldn't get off the ground. One of the officers killed the eagle with a well-aimed kick, putting it out of its misery. I have been told that thousands of birds are destroyed in every test; they take wing at the flash, then fall to earth, burned and blinded.' It is droll that scientists who had taught themselves to shrug off the deaths of countless human beings in the wake of a nuclear exchange found their imaginations disturbed by the impact upon wild creatures.

Sakharov retained his high status – for the time being. His disgrace came later. Meanwhile Khrushchev inherited an army of more than five million men, and set about reducing it by 20 per cent. He dismissed the generals' fury, observing unoriginally that they always prepared for the last war. He abolished military cadet training in Soviet schools, and slashed procurement programmes. When, with the support of Marshal Zhukov, celebrated commander of the 1944–45 drive to Berlin, he also announced swingeing cuts in the navy and shipbuilding programme, the demoted navy chief Vice-Admiral Nikolai Kuznetsov left an October 1955 meeting after firing a Parthian shot: 'History will not forgive you!'

Khrushchev argued that national defence must rely overwhelmingly upon nuclear missiles, but the human consequences of his economies were severe. A quarter of a million redundant officers were almost literally turned onto the streets to become his implacable foes, as were most Soviet generals and admirals. Even civilians were uneasy about the cuts. 'In spite of all the talk about disarmament,' Ivan Seleznev wrote in his diary, 'there is an arms race and the West German fascists are especially active, with American support. It is important we don't get the sort of sudden kicking we received at the start of World War II.'

While ignoring the simmering rage of his commanders, the leader also seemed oblivious of tensions among the Soviet Union's minorities, excluded from Moscow's decision-making about their own fate. Cultural nationalism was repressed. Between 1958 and 1962, security police broke up many clandestine groups in the Baltic states and Ukraine: several activists were shot. A Ukrainian lawyer was sentenced to death, though reprieved, for promoting a separatist movement. In Kiev, when Komsomol groups started holding Ukrainian cultural events, these were banned as 'nationalist deviations'. Religious sects were likewise ruthlessly persecuted, so that during the early sixties numbers of Orthodox priests and churches halved. In 1962 legislation was passed to make it a criminal offence to give children religious instruction at home. The abuse of psychiatric institutions for the confinement of dissidents and 'anti-social elements' continued into the 1970s.

Yet alongside all this, Russian pride and a yearning for self-assertion remained powerful engines, playing a critical role in the Soviet conduct of foreign policy. However significant might be popular resentment towards their own rulers, Khrushchev's people cherished a much stronger animosity towards the West, rooted in their narrative of World War II. Even in the twenty-first century, most educated Russians brush aside the infamous 1939 Nazi-Soviet Pact, which for almost two years made Stalin Hitler's ally and fellow-predator in Finland, Poland, Romania. Instead, there is an all-consuming awareness of the sacrifice that followed, of twenty-seven million Russian lives; of the devastation of the homeland; of the massively disproportionate share of the burden of allied losses borne by the Red Army, to encompass the defeat of Hitler.

When Yuri Gagarin, the world's first spaceman, was just seven years old, invading Germans seized his family's home, burned his school, strung up his younger brother from a tree – an experience the boy somehow survived – and enslaved his other siblings. His compatriots shared a consciousness that while American and British war veterans went home to education and prosperity, their Red Army counterparts returned to devastation, squalor, disease, hunger and renewed privation. It seemed to them intolerable that

Westerners, who had suffered so little by comparison with themselves, should aspire to rule the world; should condescend to their own nation, with its history and culture far older and deeper than those of the United States. A craving for respect – secured through fear if no other engine proved serviceable – has lain for centuries at the heart of Russian conduct towards other nations. And was seldom more so than in 1962.

3 KHRUSHCHEV ABROAD

Nikita Khrushchev claimed to cherish a private desire to thaw the Cold War, to reduce the tensions between East and West. Oleg Troyanovsky became his assistant for foreign affairs in 1958, and thus by 1962 was experienced in the ways of his master. He had served extensively abroad, first as a junior diplomat at his country's London embassy, later as an interpreter for the Soviet judges at the Nuremberg Trials, before returning to the foreign ministry. Troyanovsky asserted: 'Nikita Khrushchev was the driving force behind the effort to move the world from the edge of the abyss, where it stood at the beginning of 1953', when Moscow was ringed with anti-aircraft guns, ammunition stockpiled beside them. Sergei Khrushchev wrote in his study of his father, 'No one could envisage friendship with the United States or Great Britain. But the era of peaceful coexistence had arrived.'

Yet precious little of this alleged spirit of accommodation was apparent to those who lived through the Khrushchev era, or who governed Western nations during his tenure of the Kremlin. The British historian and defence intellectual Michael Howard observed: 'In the 21st century, it is easy to forget how unspeakably bloody the Russians were, sixty years ago.' Howard, a lifelong liberal and one of the founders of the International Institute for Strategic Studies, was neither a rattler of sabres nor in the least impatient for Armageddon. And of course he spoke before the ghastly reversion represented by the 2022 invasion of Ukraine.

The principal impediment to Khrushchev's wish for détente was his own rage towards the West for its superior wealth, military might, culture, and economic and social achievements, which mocked the languishing of the socialist system to which he had devoted his own life. Moreover, it was indispensable to his hold upon power in the Kremlin that he should be seen to be pursuing the ideological struggle against Western capitalism and its bastions in Europe and elsewhere. To this end, he could never help himself from springing surprises, delivering threats, wilfully upending conference tables. His behaviour was driven partly by a natural impulsiveness; partly by a perceived need to appease bellicose forces within the Kremlin; partly by a belief that the Soviet Union must stand tall in the world to mask its real weakness.

After British leader Harold Macmillan visited Moscow in 1959, Khrushchev boasted to colleagues that he had 'fucked [the prime minister] with a telegraph pole'. Early in 1960, the first secretary said with satisfaction that since the development of intercontinental missiles 'main street Americans have begun to shake from fear for the first time in their lives'. In January 1961, Khrushchev proclaimed general support for worldwide wars of national liberation. His nuclear tests, notably that of a fifty-eight-megaton superbomb at Novaya Zemlya on 30 October 1961, were explicitly designed to frighten Western electorates.

Space programme chief Gen. Nikolai Kamanin wrote in his diary on 9 February 1962: 'There are insistent rumours that there was an assassination attempt on Khrushchev in Minsk. It isn't the rumours that are surprising, but the fact that people believe them. People do not like Khrushchev, with his ceaseless talk and promises. People hope that peace will be maintained and that their material circumstances will improve, but they cannot have both. It is not only Kennedy and [West German chancellor Konrad] Adenauer who are to blame for that, but also our noisy politics, attempts to "poke our noses" into every corner of the globe.'

At the heart of Kremlin foreign policy was a determination to assert the Soviet Union's greatness, founded upon its military strength and achievements, together with its claimed status as ideological leader of the communist world and ruler of an empire that had expanded even as those of the old European powers shrank. It aspired to punish American triumphalism, rooted in economic and nuclear dominance. Khrushchev's son Sergei said: 'We lived all the time here with enemies on the gates. Americans were surrounded by two oceans, they were protected. They were like the strongest predator in the world, like a tiger, but a tiger which grew up in a zoo, and when sent into the jungle they were afraid of everything. Stalin had accepted the [1944–45] American and Churchill deal: "You must be kept in your borders. We agree that you will domi- nate Eastern Europe; the rest is the Western world, it's our world. Don't even put your nose in the Middle East." But my father said: "No. I want to be a world power. I want to be respected as an equal." And Americans don't respect anybody as equal.' Moreover Khrushchev sincerely believed that Cubans, Congolese, Vietnamese and suchlike peoples could enjoy better lives under communism than under exploitative capitalism.

He professed to mock Stalin's fear of war with the nuclear-armed West. William Taubman has written that he 'determined not only to seem fearless but to strike fear into his Western opponents'. The Russian said privately that when first he was briefed about nuclear weapons he could not sleep for several days, but then he realized that it was impossible ever to use them, and thus began to sleep again. Contradictorily, however, he also convinced himself that this reality empowered him to brandish the spectre of nuclear war with- out risking its occurrence. He began to threaten the West with the USSR's R-7 intercontinental ballistic missile before the weapon had even been flight-tested. Following the Anglo-French withdrawal from Egypt after their 1956 invasion, Khrushchev persuaded himself that this was the fruit of Soviet nuclear threats rather than – in reality – of American financial ones. Sergei Khrushchev wrote: 'Father was extraordinarily proud of his victory.' The Soviet leader concluded that nuclear weapons were all-conquering; that the mere fact of possession, together with an apparent willingness to use them, could be wielded as decisive weapons on the world stage.

When Senator Hubert Humphrey visited Moscow in the spring of 1961, Khrushchev accorded him an eight-hour interview. Before they parted, the host enquired where his visitor came from. On being told that his city was Minneapolis, Khrushchev went to a big wall map, drew a circle around the Minnesotan metropolis and said by way of farewell: 'That's so I don't forget to order them to spare it when the rockets fly.' Humphrey reported in Washington on his host as 'a man who is insecure, who thinks [we] are rich and big ... and keep picking on [him] ... [He is] defensive in an offensive way ... demonstrates his insecurity in overstatement'. Humphrey was thinking, no doubt, of the first secretary's assertion that a great stream of missiles was rolling forth from Soviet production lines 'like sausages'.

Herein lay the contradiction at the heart of Khrushchev's strategy, eventually laid bare in the Missile Crisis: he privately acknowledged that he must not go to war with the West, because US nuclear superiority condemned the Soviet Union to annihilation. But he determined to exploit Western popular terror of such a conflict, to bluff his way to tactical successes abroad. Nuclear threats became his default weapons of choice. After drinking heavily at a party following the 1956 Tushino Air Show, Khrushchev 'insulted literally every country in the world', according to William Hayter, brushing aside the desperate efforts of fellow-Politburo members to silence him. His tenure of power was a perpetual high-wire act, which was successful chiefly in persuading moderate opinion in the West that he was a man to fear, impossible to achieve accommodation with. British Labour politician Richard Crossman observed that he would never forget Khrushchev's 'couldn't-careless suggestion that we should join with the Russians because, if not, they would swat us off the face of the earth like a dirty old black beetle'. Aneurin Bevan, another British man of the left, said despairingly, 'He's impossible. It's time he grew up.'

Yet in Khrushchev's worldview, sustained by Russian leaders from earliest times into the twenty-first century, the Soviet empire was besieged by the Western Powers: 'We were surrounded by American air bases,' he complained. 'Our country was literally a great big target range for American bombers operating from airfields in Norway, Germany, South Korea and Japan.' Khrushchev brooded especially on the American Jupiter nuclear missiles, since

1961 deployed in NATO Turkey and Italy. When holidaying on the Black Sea, he would sometimes offer guests binoculars and demand: 'What do you see?' They would respond with bromides about the blue waters, but Khrushchev would then snatch the glasses and exclaim with his accustomed theatricality: '*I* see US missiles in Turkey, aimed at *my* dacha.' In the early post-World War II years, US aircraft constantly overflew Soviet territory, knowing that while those on the ground seethed, they were incapable of engaging the high-altitude intruders. Khrushchev's objection to the 1948 Berlin Blockade was not that Stalin attempted it, but that he failed to think it through. He applauded Kim Il-Sung's June 1950 invasion of South Korea, even in long retrospect, and claimed to lament only that Stalin had provided the North Koreans with insufficient support.

Many Russians, especially those around Stalin, viewed the 1945 atomic bomb-droppings as directed not against Hiroshima and Nagasaki, but instead against themselves. Leading nuclear physicist Yuli Khariton described the Kremlin's view of those explosions as 'atomic blackmail against the USSR, as a threat to unleash a new, even more terrible and devastating war'. This perception powerfully influenced Soviet policy and strategy through the decades that followed, souring the triumph of its victory over Germany, and causing it to fear for the security of its new East European empire.

It is hard to argue that Moscow's fevered impatience to build a Soviet Bomb, to create a balance of terror, was misplaced. Some prominent Americans, notably including members of the armed forces top brass, would continue into the 1960s to urge that the US should exploit its superiority to make explicit its dominance. General Douglas MacArthur was the only prominent officer dismissed for promoting, among other manifestations of hubris, the use of nuclear weapons to advance America's military interests, in Korea in 1951, but he was certainly not alone in holding such views. Admiral Arthur Radford, 1953–57 chairman of the joint chiefs of staff, was a strong supporter of MacArthur, committed to using America's nuclear superiority to impose its will, especially against China. The USAF's Gen. Curtis LeMay, who would become a strident voice in the Missile Crisis, served out a full 1961–65 term as supremo of his service, despite insistently proclaiming his enthusiasm for a showdown with the Soviet Union in which he was confident that the US would prevail.

In the decade that followed Stalin's death in March 1953, the Cold War remained very cold. The Soviet premier rejoiced in springing surprises, most of them ugly, and in fomenting confrontations when and where the West least expected them. He fuelled American paranoia, contriving to inspire a fear of the Soviet Union beyond anything that a rational assessment of its strength could justify. It is arguable that the Russian had no choice save to bang his drum and beat his chest, in order to contain the huge internal stresses within the Soviet empire. Khrushchev told Averell Harriman: 'I am very jealous of my prerogatives, and while I live I will run the Party. If you are trying to bury me, you are engaged in wishful thinking.' Harriman urged John F. Kennedy to brush aside the Soviet leader's bullfrog impersonations rather than rise to them. Joke with him, urged the veteran diplomat; don't debate with him. But it proved easier for many Europeans and a few Americans to give such counsel than to persuade US presidents to take it.

One of the least admirable aspects of Kennedy's 1960 presidential election campaign was that he promoted a myth about a supposed 'missile gap' between the nuclear capabilities of the US and USSR, to Russia's advantage. The Republican administration, he claimed, bore responsibility for this shameful situation, which threatened the safety of the United States. These assertions represented a travesty of the reality, but became credible to millions of Western people, because they mirrored the rhetoric of Khrushchev and appeared confirmed by Soviet space 'firsts'. The Soviet leader inflicted grievous strategic damage on his own nation by goading the West to spend ever more billions on armaments, which it was far better able to afford than was the USSR to match.

Such conduct, like that of today's President Vladimir Putin, reflected consciousness of his nation's real weakness and failures, rather than of its pretended strength and success. Whatever Khrushchev's motives, however, it is hard for civilized posterity to forgive his repeated threats of nuclear annihilation. In August 1961, for instance, at the ballet in Moscow, Khrushchev launched a diatribe against British ambassador Frank Roberts, about the consequences of a nuclear exchange. The US's and USSR's respective sizes, he asserted, would enable both nations to survive. But Britain, West Germany and France would be obliterated on the first day. He asked Roberts how many bombs would be needed to dispose of Britain. Six, hazarded the ambassador. Khrushchev pronounced him a pessimist: 'The Soviet General Staff ... had earmarked several score of bombs for use against the UK', which suggested 'that the Soviet Union had a higher opinion of the UK's resistance capacity tha[n] the UK itself'. Even during the Cold War, these were repulsive remarks for a national leader to utter.

The West extended regular olive branches to Khrushchev, which provoked further insults. At a dinner at Chequers during a 1956 visit to Britain, the guest of honour cheerfully informed his hosts that his missiles 'could easily reach your island, and quite a bit further'. In September 1959, he became the first Soviet leader to make an official visit to the United States, an invitation for which he had angled for years. Here, he told Kremlin colleagues complacently, was evidence that at last the capitalists acknowledged the legitimacy of Russia's socialist state: 'It is our strength that has led to this – they have to recognize our existence and our power.' The allies – Britain, France and West Germany – were alike appalled by Eisenhower's gesture which, they feared, presaged some kind of American sell-out, perhaps on Berlin.

Khrushchev insisted upon flying to Washington in the new Soviet Tu-114 airliner, and was delighted to be informed that it stood so high off the ground that no American airport ramp was tall enough to reach its door. Nobody in Moscow dared to tell him that its stork-legged undercarriage was necessary to prevent its engines ingesting crippling debris from Russia's ill-swept runways. So fearful were Soviet aviation chiefs of the risks of the trip by the unproven new aircraft that they stationed ships in a picket line along its entire ocean flightline to the US, a pitiful precaution against disaster in the clouds.

Collier's

15¢

August 5, 1950

HIROSHIMA, U.S.

Can Anything Be Done About It?

The nightmare of America – and the world – throughout the Cold War, here visualized on a *Collier's* magazine cover.

(Above) Some of the Cuban freedom fighters who fought for decades to secure the nation's 1902 independence from Spain. (Below) The American supporters who secured all the publicity for achieving this. Here, a romantic depiction of the 'Rough Riders' charge up San Juan Hill on 1 July 1898.

(Above) Best friends: The US ambassador in Havana Earl Smith and his frequent canasta partner, 1952–59 dictator Fulgencio Batista. (Below) The only – possibly faked – photo of Castro and his would-be guerrillas disembarking from *Granma* on 2 December 1956.

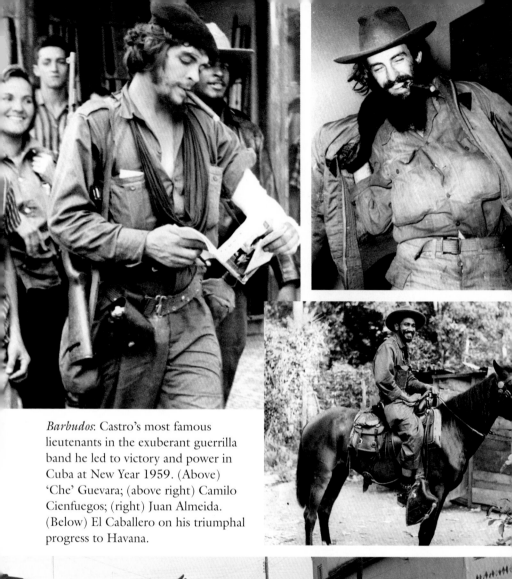

Barbudos: Castro's most famous lieutenants in the exuberant guerrilla band he led to victory and power in Cuba at New Year 1959. (Above) 'Che' Guevara; (above right) Camilo Cienfuegos; (right) Juan Almeida. (Below) El Caballero on his triumphal progress to Havana.

Some members of Castro's adoring harem: (top left) Marita Lorenz; (top right) his first wife, hapless Mirta Francisca de la Caridad; (left) Naty Revuelta; (below) Celia Sánchez (head bent) with Vilma Espín who became Raúl Castro's wife.

The most famous guerrilla in the world. (Above) Castro being interviewed by legendary US TV host Ed Sullivan within days of his victory. (Below) In New York City, in September 1960, Castro meets and embraces his new sponsor, the USSR's Nikita Khrushchev.

An American humiliation: in April 1961, Castro's troops and Soviet-supplied tanks advance to crush the farcical invasion by CIA-backed exiles at the Bay of Pigs. (Right) Exile officer Manuel Artime after his ransomed liberation from captivity. (Below) Cuban soldiers interrogate dejected exile leader 'Pepe' San Romain following his surrender.

知乎 @竹中贤

(Above) The king of Camelot: John F. Kennedy at a White House celebration of Nobel Prize winners with wife Jackie and America's most famous poet, Robert Frost in April 1962. (Below) Kennedy's would-be nemesis, Soviet leader Nikita Khrushchev with his defence minister, Marshal Rodion Malinovsky.

The Soviet premier was told that the US president had invited him to Camp David, which he had never heard of. Instead of being flattered he demanded: 'What sort of camp is it? ... a place they put people they don't trust?' When, during his visit, occasional anti-Soviet protesters appeared, Khrushchev angrily suggested that they represented deliberate insults by the United States. Told that the American government had no power to prevent such personal gestures, he betrayed himself and his society by asserting that in the Soviet Union such things would never be allowed. KGB officer Mikhail Lyubimov said: 'One sometimes felt embarrassed that he was such a hick', adding ruefully, 'at that time we also had some other ministers with just three years of schooling'.

A Soviet diarist named Romen Nazirov, aged twenty-eight, recorded on 20 September: 'Newspapers are full of Khrushchev. The content of his press conference at the [Washington] National Press Club was routine enough, but the style was pretty sharp. A provocative question about the personality cult [of himself] greatly annoyed him. Nikita Sergeevich replied to the question about "Russian intervention" in Hungary: "You see, the so-called Hungarian issue is stuck in some people's gullet like a dead rat: they find it nasty, but can't spit it out. (Laughter in the audience). If you want to talk about that sort of thing, I can provide you with quite a few dead cats. They will still be fresher than the well-known question about the events in Hungary."'

Khrushchev announced after his first meeting with Eisenhower that he would trust him, 'as one war veteran trusts another', but of course did nothing of the sort. The two established no rapport. The Russian's familiar boast that he was unafraid of nuclear war caused the American to respond that he himself certainly was. Khrushchev returned home to report to his Presidium comrades that the US visit had been a triumph. He believed that it emphasized his skills as a negotiator and games-player at the highest international level. Yet all that had been agreed in Washington, after a fashion, was that the Soviet leader withdrew his latest ultimatum for allied withdrawal from Berlin, while the US acknowledged that the city's divided status was 'abnormal', and should not be prolonged indefinitely.

Khrushchev's adviser Oleg Troyanovsky later described 1960 as the worst year of the Cold War for exchanges of invective between the superpowers. Today we know that the confrontation did not explode into nuclear catastrophe. Thus it is easy to forget that seventy years ago, well before the Missile Crisis, many people around the world, especially including officers of the armed forces, expected that sooner or later there would be a war; that the United States and its allies would have to engage the Soviet Union in arms. Michael Howard described his own first visit to the United States in the spring of 1960, as an emissary of Britain's Institute for Strategic Studies. He found Washington 'a *military* capital', with 'almost more uniforms on the street than I remembered in wartime London ... This was a nation that believed itself to be at war ... There was an electric excitement in the air that I found terrifying. This, I thought, was what Europe must have been like before 1914 ... This seemed a people who, in spite of the Second World War and Korea, had not really experienced war, and who found the prospect an invigorating challenge. It was in just such an atmosphere, I thought, that wars began.'

At a New Year's Eve party in the Kremlin on 31 December 1959, Khrushchev summoned together the American, French and British ambassadors, together with a prominent Italian communist, and subjected them to a harangue. He boasted – yet again – that he had thirty atomic bombs earmarked for France and fifty for Britain in the event of war, though the number trained on the US was a state secret. If the forthcoming Paris summit conference failed to produce an agreement on Germany's future, he threatened, he would cut off Western access to Berlin and sign a bilateral treaty with East Germany.

On 1 May, most sacred day in the communist calendar, on his personal orders Soviet air defences shot down an American U-2 reconnaissance plane in Russian airspace. There had already been twenty-four such flights since 1956, authorized by the US president. Khrushchev regarded them as an arrogant intrusion upon Soviet sovereignty: how would the Americans react, he demanded in a fair question, to similar flights by the Soviet air force? The fact that this latest sortie had taken place days before a scheduled four-power summit meeting in Paris caused the Kremlin to consider it a studied insult.

The Russians, hitherto incapable of intercepting the high-flying U-2, had now acquired S-75 missiles with the reach to do so. One such destroyed the American aircraft. By a characteristic lethal Russian miscue, a second SAM missile shot down one of the MiG-19 fighters that were also scrambled to engage the American plane. The U-2's pilot, former USAF officer and now CIA civilian employee Gary Powers, parachuted safely to earth, though for six days he was unknown to be in Moscow's hands. Khrushchev was ecstatic about the U-2 shootdown, and congratulated his air defence chiefs. In old age, however, he mused regretfully that, from that day onwards, nothing ever went quite right for him: 'I was no longer in full control.' Anastas Mikoyan wrote long afterwards about Khrushchev and the U-2 what he would never have dared to say at the time: 'It was his [Khrushchev's] fault that the lowering of [East-West] tensions, which had cost us so much effort, was set back at least fifteen years.'

Khrushchev announced the shootdown on 5 May. He waited a further two days, during which the Americans plunged into a swamp of falsehoods, claiming that their missing plane was a NASA meteorological survey aircraft that had been airborne over Turkey, before disclosing the capture of Powers. The Soviet leader described photographs found in the plane's wreckage, then taunted: 'Our cameras take better pictures.' Thereafter, he kept changing his mind about whether he wanted the Paris summit to go ahead. His pride was sincerely wounded by the U-2 flight, which he branded 'a flagrant violation of international law [and] a gross insult to the Soviet Union'. He also cherished a belief that the more thoroughly he humiliated the Americans in a presidential election year, the greater damage he could inflict upon the prospects of Republican candidate Vice-President Richard Nixon, whom he detested.

Khrushchev anticipated that Eisenhower would save the summit by shifting blame for the U-2 overflight onto his generals or the CIA. Instead the president – against the advice of Llewellyn

Thompson, America's shrewd Moscow ambassador – forced the Russian leader's hand by insisting upon accepting personal responsibility. The U-2 flights, the president told the American people, were vital to national security. There is a good case that he was right, though the timing of the 1 May sortie was foolish.

Only when Khrushchev was aboard his plane en route to Paris did he inform the Soviet delegation that he had decided to wreck the summit, unless Eisenhower apologized for the overflights. After landing in France on 14 May 1960, he held a preliminary meeting with British prime minister Harold Macmillan. Eisenhower, fulminated the first secretary, had claimed to be his 'friend' – he used the English word ironically, and repeatedly. Next morning, at the first heads of state meeting at the Élysée Palace, he lashed himself into a theatrical frenzy, putting an end to any hope of serious negotiations. France's president Charles de Gaulle rebuked him for coming to Paris, and allowing others to do so, when all the causes for his anger were already known. The French president was resigned to abandoning the summit, while Eisenhower was furious. Macmillan was distressed: of them all, he believed most passionately in the value of face-to-face exchanges between Great Power leaders, especially since such meetings enabled Britain to assert its residual claim upon such status.

Khrushchev next held a 150-minute press conference before three thousand journalists assembled in the Palais de Chaillot, at which he announced his refusal to attend a second session unless the Americans accepted his terms in full, which of course they would not. This statement provoked some hisses and hoots which Khrushchev believed to come from Germans. He responded by shaking his fist and shouting, supposedly at 'some of those fascist bastards we didn't finish off at Stalingrad'. He persisted: 'We hit them so hard that we put them ten feet underground right away. If you boo us and attack us again, *look out!* We will hit you so hard there won't be a squeak out of you.'

Khrushchev's behaviour was driven partly by sensitivity about his vulnerability to Kremlin hardliners: he was forever apprehensive that if he talked softly to the West, his authority at home would be jeopardized. Two years later the Missile Crisis would cause him to be branded by posterity as the man who took the world to the edge of the nuclear abyss. In the eyes of some Kremlin associates and of his generals, however, he was a soft touch; an appeaser of 'the fascists'. The East German government was appalled by ill-founded rumours that Washington was considering arming the West German Bundeswehr with nuclear weapons, and constantly urged the Kremlin to act more toughly. The hawks denounced every move Khrushchev had made towards de-escalation: promotion of an armistice in Korea, release of the last German World War II prisoners, withdrawal from Austria and Finland, admission of Stalin's crimes. The USSR, they argued, had gained nothing from such gestures. Khrushchev escaped overthrow only because of fears that a successor might launch a new Terror.

Yet some of the Russians who had flown with their leader to the summit were aghast at the prospect of returning to the iciest days of East-West confrontation. When great issues of war and peace were at stake, his boorishness had long since ceased to seem clever or amusing, even to Presidium colleagues. They were unwilling to share his indignation about the U-2 flights, shrugging that there had always been spies, many of them their own. Deputy foreign minister Valerian Zorin, a habitually unemotional man, wandered the Soviet embassy in Paris shaking his head and exclaiming despairingly, 'What a situation! What a situation!' Defence minister Marshal Rodion Malinovsky appeared to be the only Russian visitor who relished the drama, apart from the man precipitating it. Yet those around the Soviet leader remained too craven to challenge his conduct.

Oddly enough, Khrushchev seldom raised his voice to immediate subordinates. He reserved his bullying tactics for big people, domestic and foreign enemies. When Macmillan deplored Khrushchev's sabotage of the Paris summit, Khrushchev shouted at him: 'You sent your planes over our territory! You are guilty of aggression!' Within weeks of that debacle, the Soviet premier chose also to escalate tensions with China. At the June 1960 Congress of the Romanian Communist Party, he wantonly insulted the Beijing delegation. By thereafter withdrawing all Soviet advisers from China, he denied Moscow access to vital intelligence, as well as confirming the increasingly strident hostility of Mao Zedong.

Later that year, at the United Nations in New York, Khrushchev renewed his verbal assault on the West and its allies. After the representative of the Philippines denounced Soviet imperialism, Khrushchev removed his own shoe and banged it on the table before him, while delivering a storm of invective. Diplomats around the world expended hours attempting to divine how far the Soviet leader's excesses were spontaneous, and how far rehearsed. The answer was probably: a mixture. That day in New York, once he was back in the Soviet delegation's offices, a gleeful Khrushchev told his aide Troyanovsky, who had not been present in the UN Assembly chamber: 'Oh, you missed so much! It was such fun!'

Today it is hard to recall the special Western terrors aroused by the issue of Berlin, hostage city of the Cold War. Germany in 1945 had been partitioned into Soviet, American, British and French zones each, except that of the last, roughly reflecting the areas over-run by the respective armies. In May 1949, the combined American, British and French occupation zones were translated into a new German Federal Republic, with a population of fifty million. The Russians responded in October by declaring their sector, with its eighteen million people, the German Democratic Republic.

West Germany flourished, while Moscow's puppet Eastern state languished. A stream of its most educated citizens fled to the prospering West, enraging its own government and humiliating the Kremlin. Both sides rearmed their respective German clients. In the midst of East Germany lay Berlin, also in 1945 divided into neighbouring occupation zones. American, British and French troops sustained garrisons in western districts linked to the body of West Germany by a ninety-mile-long autobahn and rail line, which the Russians and East Germans intermittently harassed. In 1948–49 Stalin for eleven months severed all land links to the city, precipitating a siege and the legendary airlift to feed its people.

The autobahn and West Berlin, often characterized as the exposed neck and head of Western defences in Europe, remained a source of exasperation to Moscow, because it became the channel through which 'Ostis' – Easterners – fled to embrace capitalism. For the NATO allies, by contrast, the garrisons in West Berlin symbolized their commitment to uphold the victory settlement of 1945, and to defend the liberty of the city's 2.5 million citizens. London *Times* journalist Louis Heren wrote wryly that West Berliners 'probably had the world's lowest expectations and the highest score for survival ... They knew their future would be decided by Washington and Moscow, and for reasons that had little to do with their well-being ... No wonder West Berliners were cockneys, aware that they would not get an even break, but quick-witted and shrewd.'

In Russian eyes, exasperation about the flight of refugees through Berlin was increased by bitterness that the West had any presence in the city at all, given that the Red Army had paid the vast blood price to capture it in 1945, after the British and Americans showed a conspicuous lack of haste to do so. In European capitals, however, whatever other differences simmered between the Western allies, there was an impassioned determination to resist Soviet encroachments, and to nurture America's will to lead the defence of both Berlin and West Germany. Eisenhower acknowledged the contradictions imposed by the Europeans' fixation: 'an instance in which our political posture requires us to assume military positions that are wholly illogical'. Berlin, he said, was 'a can of worms'. Whenever the Russians sought to raise tensions with the West, they threatened to seize the enclave, where Soviet and American tank crews glowered at each other from their respective sectors. Militarily, the Russians could sweep the city in an hour. Yet the inescapable consequent clashes with NATO tripwire forces, before a communist host overwhelmed them, meant that an attack on West Berlin was likely to provoke general war.

We know today that Khrushchev never considered occupying the allied sectors by force. He wanted a deal whereby the Western Powers withdrew from the city, and sought to secure this by blackmail and threats. Nobody in the West, however, was privy at the time to the secret that the Soviets had no intention of starting shooting, a prudence which was at odds with everything they were telling the world. Diplomat Anatoly Dobrynin described as a major strategic blunder Khrushchev's delusion that he might gain advantage by feeding a mood of crisis over Berlin, when everywhere else in Europe the US was willing to acquiesce in the status quo – in Russia's Eastern empire, won in 1945. The ambassador also deplored Khrushchev's role in escalating rhetoric which the US and, in particular, secretary of state Dean Rusk, wished to calm.

National leaders in London, Paris, Bonn and Washington were haunted by the vision of West Berlin and its people as hostages, at the mercy of the surrounding Russians, who were liable at any moment to seize them as prey, victims of the terrifying Cold War chess game. Arthur Schlesinger later wrote: 'Berlin threatened a war which might destroy civilization ... It is hard now to recall the forebodings ... to evoke again the pessimism that shrouded the [US] government.' The stalemate persisted. Khrushchev issued repeated ultimatums, threatening to sign a unilateral Russian treaty with East Germany, and to block Western access to West Berlin. Such a latter step would almost certainly oblige the NATO allies to resist by force. Thus the recurring newspaper headlines 'NEW BERLIN CRISIS' prompted real alarm each time they appeared on the streets of Western capitals. And not just Western capitals. A bleak contemporary joke on the streets of Moscow had a man demand: 'The situation is tense. Will there be a war?', to which the reply came: 'No war, but such a fight for peace there won't be a stone left standing.'

Thus it was, that in the first years of the new decade of the 1960s, the West's leaders thought much about Berlin and remarkably little about Cuba, which the NATO allies of the United States considered a tiresome, exclusively American obsession. The ascent to the presidency of John F. Kennedy was greeted by many Europeans with a sigh of relief. It seemed to offer the possibility of a revised international order, a new and less perilous spirit of the age. While nobody supposed that the Cold War was going away, it seemed reasonable to hope that the bright star now assuming the leadership of the Western world would guide it at least a little further from Armageddon. Nikita Khrushchev might have said: 'Fat chance.'

3

Yanquis, Amerikantsy

1 AMERICAN PIE

The United States was by far the richest and most powerful nation on earth. Between 1947 and 1960 average real incomes had increased by as much as in the previous half-century. *Fortune* magazine claimed smugly that only a million families 'still look really poor'. For the first time a majority of Americans owned the homes in which they lived, as distinct from renting. The building of a car required only half the 310 labour hours needed in 1945. 'Capitalism works,' wrote economist J.K. Galbraith in his 1958 classic study *The Affluent Society*, 'and in the years since World War II, quite brilliantly ... More die in the United States of too much food than of too little.' The book title became shorthand for how the world saw America. Moneybags publisher Malcolm Forbes said complacently: 'The success of capitalism has created such a degree of prosperity, to where now young people don't have to think "How am I going to earn a living?" They can think "How am I going to live?" The economic pressure is off them.'

Many Americans saw themselves as blessed people, uniquely favoured by the Almighty, who was still viewed as an important force in their affairs. So was patriotism. An Englishman making a first visit to Washington was astonished to find his hotel lobby serenaded by a male voice choir performing such numbers as the 'Battle Hymn of the Republic' and 'Over There'. Alcohol consumption was impressive, but away from the East and West Coasts wine was still perceived as an alien, slightly sinister beverage, as against beer, martini and rye. In hot places, circulating fans remained more common than air conditioning. The interstate highway network was growing apace, linking a host of square-cut towns and cities, passing by vast square-cut fields. An Eastern high school poll showed that sick *Mad* magazine was second only to *Life* as favoured student reading. Chubby Checker made it big with the record and film *Twist Around the Clock*, selling a dance that even the most dysfunctional adult or child could perform. Movie audiences were electrified by *West Side Story*, epitome of cool matched by musical and choreographic genius.

A poll asked Americans: 'Taking all things together, how would you say things are these days – would you say you're very happy, pretty happy, or not too happy?' A resounding 80 per cent responded either 'very' or 'pretty' happy. Americans owned more than fifty million TVs, which did not need to be viewed through water-filled magnifiers. Peter Joseph writes of 'that great race for membership in the middle class, and more than ever a person's accumulation of material goods measured his standing'. Walter Lippmann opined: 'We talk about ourselves these days as if we were a completed society, one which has no further great business to transact.'

Yet the country was also troubled by demons, foremost among which was fear of communism, linked to a belief that the Soviet Union was a serious competitor. In four 1959–61 Gallup polls, a majority of Americans identified 'keeping the peace' or 'dealing with the Russians' as the gravest problem facing the United States, way ahead of any domestic issue. A bipolar world, such as existed for forty years after 1945, was an exception to the patterns of history, in which multipolarity and occasionally unipolarity have been the norms. The Second World War had transformed the rivals into super-energetic empires, each with its own sense of mission abroad. The ideological clash between communism and capitalism roused extraordinary passions: in California, the folk singer Woody Guthrie lost his first job because he dared to refuse to condemn Stalin.

H. Rowan Gaither's November 1957 report *Deterrence and Survival In the Nuclear Age*, in the drafting of which an important role was played by Paul Nitze, who became a defense under-secretary in the Kennedy administration, called for Strategic Air Command to be placed on continuous alert and painted a bleak picture of an ever-widening Soviet lead in military and nuclear capability. It proposed a massive civil defence programme to prepare the American people to weather a nuclear strike.

President Eisenhower rejected these proposals, and most of the numbers broadcast by Gaither, a founding member of the RAND think-tank, were later found to be fantasies. However, Kennedy's defense secretary Robert McNamara told the Senate Armed Services Committee that the Russians 'sought not merely conquest but the total obliteration of the enemy'. Teenager Frances Glasspoole, then living with her family inside America's Cuban enclave at Guantánamo Bay, said: 'I believed that Castro and Khrushchev were both maniacs, crazy people.' NASA's Wernher von Braun said ruefully of the early space race: 'Whatever first there was, the Russians had always chalked it up for themselves. We either didn't come in at all, or a poor second.' The 1949 'loss of China' to Mao Zedong's communists still rankled with conservatives. The memory caused them to demand that their presidents should never again display such perceived weakness towards the Reds. The McCarthy witch-hunts in pursuit of communists in high places, which had driven into the wilderness some of the country's greatest creative artists as well as its China specialists, were only a few years in the past.

Gen. Nathan Twining, 1957–60 chairman of the joint chiefs of staff, argued from retirement that the Free World faced a monolithic communist conspiracy 'which for over forty years has been dedicated to an unswerving objective to destroy free institutions, the free way of life and free republican governments'. He believed the US should devote itself to creating 'an unchallengeably superior military technology', which would enable it to eliminate or neutralize the system that threatened it. He dismissed with contempt those who declined to accept his views as 'anti-nuclear intellectuals ... scientists with a bad conscience ... armchair strategists, do-gooders, appeasers'. In September 1961 the patrician conservative

William F. Buckley wrote with lofty disdain: 'Kennedy has chosen to identify himself with that segment of American society which is either unwilling or unable to regard Communism as more than a childish bugaboo.' When Soviet ambassador Anatoly Dobrynin visited Drew Pearson's farm, the muck-raking columnist showed him a row of peas grown from seed given to him by Khrushchev, alongside a row of domestic peas. Pearson said wryly: 'I am the first American who is practising peaceful co-existence and peaceful competition.'

Meanwhile in both the office and the home, women were still perceived as an inferior species. The proportion attending college, by comparison with their male contemporaries, fell from 47 per cent in 1920 to 35 per cent in 1958. On the cusp of the sixties the average marriage age of American girls was twenty. Fourteen million were engaged by age seventeen, a reflection of the fact that only thus would many, or even most, agree to go to bed with a guy – and a guy was what a gal's partner was almost certain to be. A British teacher at Tulane University was nonplussed one day to be requested by one of his female students to sign her certificate of virginity. Stokely Carmichael, who claimed to be not merely a radical but a revolutionary, leader of the Student Nonviolent Coordinating Committee, said: 'The only position for women in SNCC is prone.' The first Playboy Club, a metropolis of male condescension and indeed abuse, had opened two years earlier and was booming so conspicuously that many clones were under construction across America. On 5 August Norma Jeane Mortenson, first *Playboy* magazine centerfold and perhaps the most vulnerable woman in the world, was found dead, aged thirty-six, less than three months after she sang '*Happy Birthday Mr President*' at a Madison Square Garden Democratic fundraiser … as Marilyn Monroe.

There were glimmerings of revolt. CBS TV screened a documentary on 'the trapped housewife' and the *New York Times* ran a piece about educated women 'who feel stifled in their homes … Like shut ins, they feel left out.' Gloria Steinem published her career breakthrough article in *Esquire* magazine, about the pressure on women to choose between a career and marriage. In 1960 the contraceptive pill became widely available, to the horror of many Christians and conservatives. Yet the sixties social revolution had not yet got started. Judith Rodin, then an undergraduate at Penn State University, described those Kennedy years as the '1950s extended: students were very concerned about their own lives, social events and classroom performance, but they were neither politically nor socially active'. It would take JFK's assassination, black civil rights and Vietnam to change that.

In 1961 Congress approved a 50 per cent increase in NASA's budget, as it began training the first astronauts to fulfil Kennedy's pledge to put a man on the moon before 1970. Two Americans followed Gagarin into space: in February 1962 Col. John Glenn completed America's first orbital flight. At Rice University on 12 September, Kennedy told students: 'We choose to go to the moon in this decade, and do ... other things not because they are easy but because they are hard, because that goal will serve to organize and measure the best of our energies and skills, because that challenge is one we are eager to accept, one we are unwilling to postpone, and one which we intend to win.'

The new president promised that you – yes, you there, especially if you were young – could make a difference. Many adolescent Americans were movingly ready to believe in his proclaimed 'New Frontier', to join his Peace Corps and work reasonably unselfishly abroad. William Chafe wrote: 'The whole image of the Administration was of strenuous, exciting, exalted service to a higher cause.' Green shoots of anti-establishment activism were beginning to poke through. Rachel Carson's *Silent Spring*, which became the Old Testament of the environmental movement, was published in 1962. Several hundred New York students joined a demonstration against a routine civil defence drill, by refusing to descend to their designated nuclear shelters. Fifteen thousand people attended a rally at Madison Square Garden to denounce the nuclear arms race and call for a test ban treaty.

Todd Gitlin was a teenage East Coast liberal who would become a conspicuous sixties activist. He looked back on the nation's fifties leadership with contempt: 'I thought President Dwight Eisenhower was a genial deadhead, a semi-literate fuddy-duddy who deserved to be chastised almost as much for excessive golfing and tangled sentences as for embracing Generalissimo Franco [the murderous fascist dictator of Spain].' By contrast, Gitlin watched the newsreels of Castro's *barbudos*, and in their images, surrounded by adoring crowds, 'we read redemption – a revolt of young people, under-dogs, who might just cleanse one scrap of earth of the bloodletting and misery we had heard about all our lives. From a living-room in the Bronx, we saluted our unruly champions.' Joseph Heller's great anti-war novel *Catch-22* was published within months of the Kennedy administration taking office.

But towering over all other social issues was that of race, which through the decade would play a huge part in the travails of the United States. It would be mistaken to memorialize the Kennedy presidency solely in terms of Cuba, or of the early commitment to make war in Vietnam. While both loomed large in their seasons, racial intolerance was a poison seeping through the veins of American society, making headlines month upon month and year after year. In 1960 the Department of Labor reported that the aver-age black worker earned 60 per cent less than his white counterpart. In the eyes of much of the world, American pretensions as stand-ard-bearers for freedom and justice were mocked by institutionalized segregation in the Southern states. Although Adlai Stevenson was a card-carrying liberal, when he stood against Eisenhower as Democratic candidate for the presidency in 1952, he picked as his running-mate Alabama white supremacist John Sparkman, as if a shot of racism was an acceptable dose for even a good Democrat to swallow, in exchange for a chance of getting to the White House.

A decade on, black civil rights had advanced little. During the 1960 Cotton Bowl football game, fighting broke out after a player on the all-white Texas team called one of his Syracuse opponents 'a big black dirty nigger'. When comedian Dick Gregory made his first appearance onstage at the Chicago Playboy Club, a white Southerner in the audience stood up and shouted contemptuously: 'Nigger!' Gregory defined a Southern liberal as 'a guy who will hang you from a low tree'. That year, 1962, he travelled south to march with Martin Luther King, and was routinely beaten up and jailed for his pains. He became a master of one-liners that mocked the tormentors of his race. When told in restaurants 'We don't serve negroes', he responded: 'No problem, I don't eat negroes.'

The 'Whites Only' drinking fountains, separate sections for the races in restaurants, on park benches and buses, seemed to set at naught the grandiose liberal rhetoric spouted on the East and West coasts. The Southern racists fought their corner without doubt or shame. Lester Maddox, owner of an Atlanta fried chicken restaurant and later governor of Georgia, said: 'Every time you pass civil rights legislation for any group of people, you create civil wrongs.' In Louisiana a local white political boss named Leander Perez said desegregation was a conspiracy by 'zionist Jews'. The white commitment to sustain the 'colour bar' was supported by such figures as Sen. William Fulbright of Arkansas and Sen. Richard Russell of Georgia.

Fannie Lou Hamer, a black woman who sought to register to vote in Mississippi, was sacked from her job, jailed, then presented with a $9,000 water bill, though her home had no running water. The Freedom Riders' mixed-race bus demonstrations were met with white violence, especially in Alabama. Southern police forces behaved appallingly. Yale chaplain William Sloane Coffin said later that after seeing one Freedom Rider lying bloody and half-dead after a white assault in Montgomery, 'I doubt that I'd ever been angrier and certainly never more ashamed of the United States.' Coffin himself became a Freedom Rider soon after. Martin Luther King said: 'We will wear you down by our capacity to suffer, and in the process we will win your hearts.' NBC reporter Loyal Gould described his experience covering Ku Klux Klan meetings as well as civil rights marches in the South: 'It was all so frightening, frightening as hell, to see this going on in your own country. To also see this vast amount of white poverty, along with this black poverty, and to realize that those poor souls, these white Klan types, couldn't get it through their bloody heads that they're in the same boat with the black fieldhands down South. It's crazy.'

Even as racial tensions and the tempo of white violence rose across the South, the new administration responded sympathetically but cautiously. Jack Kennedy met King, leader of so many sit-in protests across the South, and later told a group of African diplomats with slightly tasteless flippancy: 'It is in the American tradition to stand up for one's rights – even if the new way to stand up ... is to sit down.' Yet his Justice Department resisted calls to send in federal marshals and troops to protect black protesters from white violence: the president was desperate not to forfeit Southern Democratic votes in Congress.

Then, however, the University of Mississippi defied federal court rulings on racial integration; and persistently blocked the admission of black student James Meredith. The state legislature trumped up a criminal charge against him, to justify the university's veto. Kennedy saw no choice save to mobilize the National Guard and send in his own law-enforcers. On Sunday 30 September 1962, 127 federal marshals and 316 agents of the US Border Patrol were deployed to secure Meredith's admission to the university. This prompted a riot by white students and local citizens who burned cars, and pelted soldiers and federal agents with bricks and rocks. Two people died. Meredith was duly enrolled, and thereafter endured harassment and social isolation before finally graduating with a degree in political science.

All this was making front-page headlines around the world, only weeks before the Missile Crisis broke. Liberals cheered the president's intervention, but Southerners and conservatives closed ranks, expressing rage and disgust at what they characterized as 'an attack on our traditions and states' rights'. Todd Gitlin wrote: 'In mobilizing a mass opposition to race inequality, the movement for the rights of African (and other dark-skinned) Americans had to aggrieve many whites. It also intensified the counter-resentments of the many white have-a-littles who felt hard-pressed by the dark-skinned have-nots', just as the fifties economic boom was running out of steam. America in 1962 was indeed a uniquely fortunate nation, discovered by a host of visiting foreigners to be the most thrilling destination on earth. But it was also a troubled, violent, divided one. And would become more so.

2 JACK

On assuming office in January 1961, John F. Kennedy enjoyed the huge advantage that he was something fresh on the block, the first US president born in the twentieth century. Greek immigrant James Sackellson, who had often waited table for the new chief executive in Washington's Occidental restaurant, said fervently: 'He made Nixon look like two cents.' Eisenhower, in 1952 an infinitely reassuring, fatherly presence, had become a tired one eight years later, forever associated with golf courses. Comedian Bob Newhart sallied during a fictional nuclear crisis: 'Somebody take the putter off Ike.' James 'Scotty' Reston wrote a famous column in the *New York Times*, quizzing his fictitious friend Uniquack about past American leaders. When he left out the last incumbent, Reston demanded: 'What about Eisenhower? Wasn't he president?' Uniquack responded: 'We must await the judgement of history on that.' JFK's image-makers were at pains to conceal the fact that he played a far smarter game of golf than did his predecessor.

The Kennedy White House exuded an aura of power unrivalled by any other centre of government in the world, and indeed unmatched by the twenty-first-century US presidency. Russia's conduct, so little understood even by informed Americans, was characterized by public Kremlin assertions of might, displayed in the May Day military parades through Moscow; coupled with morbid secret sensitivity about weakness. The leaders of the United States, by contrast, enjoyed a justified confidence that their country had scaled peaks unsurpassed by the fallen empires of Rome, Spain, Britain. To understand those who wielded the nation's authority, it is necessary to view them as different people not BC and AD, but instead BV and AV – Before Vietnam and After Vietnam. The year of the missiles was still BV. Those remarkable men – and then, of course, they all were men – were untainted, unscarred, unhumbled by what was to come in South-East Asia. Under-secretary of state George Ball once observed that the Europeans had embarked on colonialism not so much for its economic advantages as for 'the satisfactions of power'. Godfrey Hodgson, a British chronicler of post-war America, commented about Ball: 'It is strange that he did not recognize the echo of his own contemporaries' feelings. Power – the unprecedented economic, military and political power of the United States after 1945 – was their birthright, and they found it satisfying in the highest degree ... The Bay of Pigs, as well as the Marshall Plan, illustrated the range of what they meant by internationalism.'

The administration was densely peopled by the brilliant, the cast of characters who would advise the president through the Missile Crisis. Mac Bundy, the national security adviser of whom much more later, was deemed smartest of the smart. At Defense there was Bob McNamara, of whom jokes were made that early on Sunday mornings, people arriving for extra duty would test the heat of the hood of his vehicle in the Pentagon car park to calculate how long the secretary had already been at his desk. Arthur Schlesinger, meeting McNamara for the first time, saw 'a quiet, agreeable man with rimless glasses, looking like a college professor'.

McNamara was the supreme loyalist, meticulously discreet, the wizard of odds who had made a career out of numbers. After World War II he wanted to return to Harvard, but was instead wooed to run Ford Motors. There, he acquired a reputation for heaping rewards on those who served him well, ruthlessly dispatching those who fell short of his stratospheric standards: he became one of the most admired corporate managers of the 1950s. Margaret Thatcher much later said of one of her British ministers: 'Other people bring me problems. He brings me solutions.' That was what McNamara did, first as a number-cruncher for the wartime USAAF, then for Ford, now for the Kennedy administration. He was profoundly serious, monkishly committed to his responsibilities. With his slicked-down hair and that cruelly disciplined parting, he might have prospered as a Soviet *apparatchik*. He was a rationalist, a master of control, especially at meetings. He was not quite as successful at Ford as his fan club claimed, because his brilliance lay in giving auto buyers what he thought they should want, rather than what they actually did. But he was pretty damn good – as he also was, for a season, at Defense.

He was a decent man, devoted to his wife Marg and family; not much fun, but impossible to sell short. He was wisely fearful of nuclear weapons, as some of his colleagues were not, and determined to limit them. Cynics said that the reason McNamara hung close to the president was that he lacked other friends, especially on the Hill. The secretary worked a fourteen-hour day, and refused to waste any of it on drinking with congressmen. As for the Pentagon chiefs, in 1962 there were few democratic nations in the world where generals and admirals could exercise real clout against political leaders, but the United States was one of them. Many Americans, especially those away from the East Coast, took pride in their armed forces; knew the names of some commanders; respected their opinions. It is hard to overrate the influence wielded by the chiefs of staff – respectively heads of the army, navy, air force and Marine Corps – on Congress and its powerful committee chairmen. The brass wanted more of everything, however futile, and formed alliances with legislators panting for pork – defence contracts for their states. The cost-conscious McNamara fought them up hill and down dale.

The chiefs of staff, like most commanders in most nations throughout history, recoiled from their government's desire to micro-manage armed forces operations. Major Bill Smith, Max Taylor's military aide, said: 'They [the administration] certainly were not great believers in the use of military force ... They didn't think the results that the military were getting or the way they did things were nearly as effective as they ought to be with the equipment they had.' McNamara, instead, liked to speak of 'usable power' – the difference between paper strength and effective military force – a phrase he often deployed to justify denying the chiefs the weapons for which they had an insatiable appetite.

When McNamara spoke at the White House Cabinet table, he did so not as standard-bearer for America's armed forces, but instead as their sceptical, resented political overlord. After the Kennedy men first arrived, notices appeared on walls in the Pentagon: 'The new Administration wants new ideas, diverse opinions, divergent views ... that will enable us to do our job better.' But USAF intelligence chief Robert Breitweiser, one of many uniformed McNamara-haters, said sardonically, 'It soon became evident that any dissenting view was going to be cut off at the knees ... I believe McNamara had an ego that wouldn't quit ... He could fly into a veritable rage at the suggestion that someone else's ideas could be closer to the mark.' There was nothing pacifist about the secretary, but he believed to the roots of his soul that making war was too important to be left to the judgement of military men. He was not, however, a flexible thinker. Once he made up his mind; decided upon the rational response to the evidence as he saw it, he was hard to shift. He was not good at acknowledging that 'facts' were not always facts.

At State – Foggy Bottom – was veteran Dean Rusk, whose most useful function was that he could be relied upon to do what the president told him, albeit a good deal more sluggishly than Kennedy wished. Rusk, though clever and articulate, was also cautious, instinctively unwilling to stick his neck out. He came from the Georgia back country, and surprised the New Frontiersmen by his liberalism on racial matters. A former Oxford Rhodes scholar, he had served in wartime Asia before becoming a Pentagon staff officer, then transferring to the State Department. He was a veteran Cold Warrior, who had played a prominent role in the 1945 parti-tion of Korea. He viewed communist China as not merely mistaken but wicked, home of the 'Yellow Peril'. The Kennedy administra-tion never considered normalizing relations with Mao's country, and showed no interest in rehabilitating John Paton Davies, most brilliant of the State Department's 'old China hands', who had been driven into outer darkness by McCarthy. Rusk was a technician rather than a designer, the only Cabinet member whom Kennedy did not address by his first name. The president discussed with Philip Graham, owner of the *Washington Post*, the case for displac-ing him in favour of McNamara, but Rusk was kept on, deemed a safe pair of hands – which indeed he was.

Closer to the Oval Office were the president's immediate intimates, personal assistant and appointments secretary Kenny
O'Donnell and general counsel Ted Sorensen, that slender, studious
brainbox who had a finger in every pie and most presidential
speeches. It would be mistaken to depict the administration as one
big, happy family: there was relentless jockeying for influence, such
as is inseparable from any centre of power. For starters O'Donnell, a
prominent member of the 'Irish mafia' around JFK, loathed Sorensen.
Kennedy valued the general counsel greatly, however, because his
sole political conviction was personal loyalty to the president.

Attorney-general Bobby Kennedy, he of the mean mouth and
ice-blue eyes, only thirty-six, committed to his brother through
flame and fire, had been a critical force in the campaigns that
propelled JFK to the presidency. He was now the administration's
enforcer, which made him widely disliked, not least by other
Cabinet members, some of whom could never forget that he had
served on the staff of the egregious Senator McCarthy. RFK nonetheless had some common sense, terrific energy, together with a
confidence rooted in intimacy with the president, and another
virtue uncommon in politics: he was willing to change his mind.

In 1962, however, the attorney-general was habitually viewed as
his brother's hitman, licensed thug, who used four-letter language
as if he meant every obscenity: all those teeth were not just for
show. More than a few people around Washington regarded Bobby
as a punk, but nobody around the White House dared to say so.
Thomas Parrott, the official White House note-taker, said: 'He was
a little bastard, but he was the president's brother, the anointed guy,
and you had to listen to him.' Bobby, physically a slighter figure
than Jack, esteemed toughness more than any other quality. He was
in awe of Max Taylor, the ex-paratrooper and authentic World
War II hero recently elevated to chairman of the joint chiefs,
because the soldier also had a brain. David Halberstam wrote ironically – or, if not, it should have been: 'If Harvard produced
generals it would have produced Max Taylor.'

On the fringes were courtiers also brilliant, if less important,
such as the historian and Roosevelt biographer Arthur Schlesinger,

author of the 1949 generational liberal manifesto *The Vital Center: The Politics of Freedom,* now reinvented as speechwriter and favoured Mansion dinner guest. There was Walt Rostow, who wrote one of the most successful of Kennedy's campaign lines: 'Let's get the country moving again'. Ken Galbraith, six feet nine inches tall and mocked on skis by Bill Buckley as 'resembling a drunken pretzel', retained some access to the president even while serving as 1961–63 US ambassador to India.

This was the most conspicuously elitist group ever to have governed America, men of the highest gifts, scarcely any of whom had ever had to get their hands dirty, except maybe a little during the war. The president was the only man around the Cabinet table save Max Taylor who had experienced front-line service, albeit the worst of it because 'they sank my boat', PT-109, a designation that had become a tie-clip presented by the Kennedys to select friends and supporters. McNamara had been a War Department statistician; CIA chief John McCone did ship-building. Mac Bundy witnessed D-Day, but from the comfort of the cruiser *Augusta,* where he was serving as aide to Admiral Alan Kirk, a family friend. Schlesinger had been in the OSS. None of them had been stupid enough to get stuck in the boring old infantry.

Twenty months into the Kennedy presidency, even after the Bay of Pigs they believed that for them, almost anything was possible, especially abroad. Domestic policy – above all, civil rights – remained problematic. On 6 October 1962 the *Economist* voiced disdain for the administration's performance, in terms echoed in other serious organs around the world: 'Manifestly Mr. Kennedy has failed to educate many Democrats about the necessity of his plans to get America moving again. Some candid friends say that he has also failed thus to educate the electorate ... Mr. Kennedy is now being criticised for getting too little and asking too much.' The president frequently held forth to his advisers and friendly journalists about why this, or that, spiky national issue would have to 'wait for the second term'. America was then, as it almost always has been, a conservative country in which supreme industrial and technological energy, imagination and innovation co-existed alongside retro politics. Liberals dominated the judiciary, but nothing else. Sixty or seventy Southern Democrats in Congress were as likely to vote with Republicans as with their own nominal party. Kennedy was the last Democratic candidate for president to win both a majority of the Southern white vote and a majority of the national black one. After 1960, it would prove impossible to secure both constituencies.

Abroad, however, looked a world of opportunities, where American wealth, influence and military might seemed capable of moving mountains. A dominant force in the thinking of presidents, as well as of their people, was the memory of victory in World War II. The United States saw itself as having been prime mover in achieving a decisive termination of the greatest conflict in human history. Many Americans, both in and out of uniform, aspired to gain equally conclusive outcomes to the lesser conflicts that now beset the world. MacArthur had to be sacked after saying in Korea 'there is no substitute for victory', with all his phrase made plain that the aged, vain megalomaniac had in mind. The quest for 'victory' would meet bitter disappointment in South-East Asia and indeed many other places, but in 1962 still loomed large in many minds.

John F. Kennedy had a much better personal understanding of abroad than did most of his people but he, too, cherished a hunger for greatness as a statesman and as standard-bearer for the United States. He wanted not merely to keep the West safe, but somehow also to win the Cold War, though he had no coherent vision of how. He elevated a willingness to make decisions, to choose, into the supreme macho virtue, and disdained those who flinched from them. He was thrilled when the influential columnist Joseph Alsop dubbed him '[Adlai] Stevenson with balls'. Dean Rusk, not a poetic man, used a poetic phrase of the new US chief executive: 'He was on fire, and he tended to set people around him on fire.' Walter Lippmann once wrote: 'In all men who lead multitudes of human beings there is a bit of magic.' In 1960, when he passionately embraced Kennedy – 'a natural leader, organizer and ruler of men' – rival columnist Arthur Krock was prompted to write in disgust: 'I may be getting old and I may be getting senile but at least I don't fall in love with young boys like Walter Lippmann.'

Since the inauguration Kennedy 'had changed somewhat physically', wrote Arthur Schlesinger. 'The face was more lined and furrowed; the features were heavier, less handsome but more powerful.' Theodore H. White, star-struck author of the *Making of the President* books of which the first, describing the 1960 campaign, conferred a sort of sanctity on JFK, wrote of meeting him again after a year in the presidency: 'He seemed very little changed in movement or in gracefulness from the candidate; only his eyes had changed – very dark, very grave, markedly more sunken and lined at the corners than those of the candidate. The candidate had yearned for this office; now all the problems were his; now he must resolve them ... He had always acted as if men were masters of forces, as if all things were possible for men determined in purpose and thought ... This was what he would have to cherish alone in the White House, on which an impatient world waited for miracles.'

Kennedy's usual day began at 7.45 when he was wakened in his second-floor bedroom in the Mansion by his African-American valet, George Thomas, with a breakfast tray and the papers. The children Caroline and John would rush in, watch cartoons on TV while their father read overnight government cables. Around 9 a.m., he would walk over to the Oval Office in the West Wing, often leading a child by the hand. He swam before lunch with his aide Dave Powers, then ate in the Mansion with liberal America's newly-anointed goddess of beauty and culture, his wife Jackie, before a nap in bed, a practice consciously copied from Churchill. Back in the office, he would work until 8 p.m. or so. The First Couple seldom left the White House for private dinners, though Joe Alsop's was one of the houses they enjoyed. Kennedy said: 'The presidency is not a very good place to make new friends' – nor indeed to keep old social relationships green.

He was richly endowed with intelligence and charm. It is only necessary to view one of the countless contemporary TV interviews with the president to perceive how much smarter and more sophisticated he was than have been some of his successors in the office.

He was always curious, which most of us esteem a badge of honour, and possessed extraordinary powers of concentration. Not many 1962 Americans did nuance or irony, but he did. In that respect, as in some others, he was much more a European figure than a man of his own country. He once quoted Madame de Staël on TV's *Meet the Press*, which not only reflected his own extensive reading, but also ran a significant risk of alienating an American audience. He was never as keen on James Bond thrillers as both his own image-makers and Ian Fleming's found it convenient to pretend.

A child of privilege, he introduced into the White House energy, wit and foreign culture. André Malraux, whom not many Americans had heard of, was honoured for his writing. Pablo Casals played his cello in the East Room. Arthur Schlesinger wrote euphorically, 'Never had girls seemed so pretty, tunes so melodious, and evenings so blithe and unconstrained.' Informality was cherished. The worst crime, for Kennedy and those around him, was either to bore or to be bored. Though he knew nothing of the bullets approaching him from the Dallas Book Depository, he was always in a hurry. On a 1951 world trip, this then-congressman with a passion for poetry scribbled lines from Andrew Marvell: '*But at my back I always hear/Time's winged chariot hurrying near*'. He was the best-read, most widely travelled president in US history. From far out in America's boondocks, University of Nebraska student Don Ferguson was one of millions of young Americans who loved the transition from old, old Dwight Eisenhower: 'All at once you had something exciting. You had a young guy who had kids, and who liked to play football on his front lawn. He was a real human being.'

Once during the 1960 campaign Kennedy was asked if he was tired, and responded: no, but he was sure Nixon was. Why so? 'Because I know who I am and I don't have to worry about adapting and changing. All I have to do at each stop is be myself. But Nixon doesn't know who he is, and so each time he makes a speech he has to decide which Nixon he is, and that will be very exhausting.' This proposition may or may not have been true of Nixon, but was debatable about Kennedy himself: he had in common with Franklin

Roosevelt that both were highly disciplined dissemblers. All politicians must in some degree possess thespian skills, but Kennedy was a finer actor than most. Though he was a brilliant listener, which goes far to explain his capacity to please both sexes, David Halberstam characterized him as 'almost British in his style' because of his dislike of showing genuine, spontaneous emotion, while valuing grace under pressure.

There was a chronic tension between his outward appearance, of vigour and openness, and an inner reality of frailty and pain, which his priapic extravagance did not contradict. Kennedy once quoted Somerset Maugham: 'It is not true that suffering ennobles the character; happiness does that sometimes, but suffering, for the most part, makes men petty and vindictive.' Yet if this struck a chord with him, he hid his own physical infirmities well, responding with irritation to anyone who asked him how he felt. He inherited from his disreputable, near-gangster father a profound ruthlessness and lack of sentiment. How extraordinary it was that so unlovely a parent, whose most conspicuous virtue lay in his bank balance, should have produced children so prodigiously good-looking! 'Don't play unless you are captain,' old Joe advised them. 'Second place is failure.' This attitude helps to explain JFK's indifferent record in Congress: he was not important enough on the Hill for the work to command his best shot. Walter Lippmann was among liberal critics who deplored his failure to speak out against the McCarthy witch-hunts.

While some of the president's finest rhetoric addressed the plight of less fortunate humanity, his policies in office showed little practical concern for it. There was an inner coldness, manifested in his obsessive, passionless sexual couplings – Mimi Beardsley plausibly recorded that he never kissed her on the lips. In the words of one intimate, 'he was nice to people, but heedless of people'. When a wartime comrade once lent him $20, important money to 'Red' Ray, the former sailor had to write twice to get it back. Although it seems just to judge Kennedy's promiscuity by a standard of male conduct deemed tolerable in his time – anyway by men – rather than those of our own, it is hard to avoid a measure of disdain towards a president with aspirations to statesmanship, who grappled girls in discreet corners of the White House, even at some moments of crisis.

His capacity for love – real, deep-heat passion – was small. Norman Mailer wrote for *Esquire* during the 1960 campaign that Kennedy was 'mysterious': he had 'the wisdom of a man who senses death within him and gambles that he can ensure it by risking his life'. Kennedy's impersonation of a man like other men was assisted by the fact that he did jokes. That much, and that only, he had in common with Nikita Khrushchev. At many critical moments, including those of October 1962, JFK enchanted those around him by his displays of wit.

He wrote in his book *Profiles in Courage*: 'Great crises produce great men.' Few historians would endorse this view. The world has witnessed many huge events which have been addressed, perforce, by lacklustre national leaders. In September 1962, before the Cuban missile storm broke, many observers of his administration believed that its period of office was thus far distinguished by style, not substance. Despite all the liberal media hype about Camelot, the knights of Jack Kennedy's court seemed to have a clearer view of what kind of armour they wished to wear, which crests should adorn their helmets, than of the foes they would vanquish. Frederic Fox, a Princeton classmate of Kennedy, had worked in the Eisenhower White House. He applauded the mood music of the JFK administration: 'There was a spontaneity to it', then added equivocally, 'but I don't know really whether that's a virtue when you're talking about a nation of two hundred million people'.

Kennedy was more interested in the global competition with the Soviet Union, and with communism, than in anything going on at home. Only in the last months of his life – impelled, somewhat unexpectedly, by RFK's conviction that this had become a vital moral issue – would he commit decisively to black civil rights, after being long pressed by Lyndon Johnson to act, to lead. It is hard to reconcile his professed principles with his earlier request to Sammy Davis Jr. to stay away from his star-studded Washington inaugural ball, because of the perceived public unacceptability of Davis's

interracial marriage to Swedish actress May Britt. Meanwhile
Kennedy declined to confront recalcitrant opponents in Congress,
which had already rejected his proposals for tax reform, public
works, support for public transport and a measure to assist migrant
workers. His only notable domestic success was to have faced down
the nation's steel barons over proposed price increases. '*Thanks,
Mr. President/ For all the things you've done,*' sang Monroe at
Madison Square Garden. '*The battles that you've won/ The way you
deal with U.S. Steel/ And our problems by the ton.*'

In reality, however, his conduct of office, as distinct from his
rhetoric, was not that of a radical. Ken Galbraith would later
describe the role of the administration's liberals such as himself as
resembling that of 'Indians firing occasional arrows into the camp-
site from outside'. Many people could not forget that, in Kennedy's
earlier incarnation in Congress, he had been shamelessly cynical in
support of a hardline US posture abroad, attacking President
Truman for the supposed 'loss of China' and questioning the sack-
ing of Gen. Douglas MacArthur during the Korean War. The great
diplomat Chester Bowles wrote in his diary in May 1961, following
the Bay of Pigs: 'The question which concerns me most about this
new Administration is that it lacks a genuine sense of conviction
about what is right and what is wrong ... The Cuban fiasco demonstrates how far astray a man as brilliant and well-intentioned as
Kennedy can go, who lacks a basic moral reference point.' When
the president was later assassinated, Omaha TV station reporter
Tom Brokaw recorded a colleague saying, 'It's about time somebody got the son-of-a-bitch.' This was, of course, not a widely-shared
view in a traumatized America, but it emphasizes the fact that
the nation's Kennedy-haters, like its earlier Lincoln-haters and
Roosevelt-haters, meant business.

In the fall of 1962, however, there was still absolutely everything
to play for.

3 NUKES

Gen. Omar Bradley said on Armistice Day 1948: 'We live in an age of nuclear giants and ethical infants, in a world that has achieved brilliance without wisdom, power without conscience.' The terminology of Cold War hawks and doves is familiar. But Harvard analysts later identified a third group, which they characterized as 'owls', who believed that 'a nuclear war would not arise from careful calculations but from organizational routines, malfunctions of machines or of minds, misperceptions, misunderstandings and mistakes'. Owls now dominate the historiographical study of the Missile Crisis, and indeed of the Cold War. At the time, Harold Macmillan was prominent among them – and so also was John F. Kennedy.

The president professed a fascination for Barbara Tuchman's *The Guns of August*,* which he read in July 1962, eighteen months after assuming the presidency. He focused especially upon a July 1914 conversation between Germany's Kaiser Wilhelm II and his army chief of staff, Gen. 'Gloomy Gus' Helmuth von Moltke. Kennedy's interest is significant at several levels, first because it is worth asking how many other modern US presidents might have read such a work – surely Barack Obama and possibly George W. Bush, but certainly not Ronald Reagan nor Donald Trump. Nor, for that matter, Nikita Khrushchev, even if a Soviet historian had been permitted to address the theme with frankness.

Then there is the substance of Tuchman's narrative. A moment came in 1914 when the Kaiser panicked at the prospect of a two-front war; he proposed to Moltke that it was unnecessary to invade France before fighting the Russians. The general dismissed such a foolish speculation: the plans were made, and had been set in motion. A thousand trains were rattling west: the die was cast. Kennedy was determined that no such fatalism should prevail on his watch. He cited two other prominent Germans afterwards looking back upon the outbreak of World War I, one of whom asked

---

* US title of *August 1914.*

the other: 'How did it all happen?' The other replied, 'Ah, if only one knew.' Kennedy told his advisers: 'If this planet is ever ravaged by nuclear war ... I do not want one of [the] survivors to ask another "How did it all happen?" and to receive the incredible reply "Ah, if only one knew."' This remark must go far to explain why in July 1962 he secretly installed tape-recorders in the White House, and thus three months later was able to preserve the evidence of much that was said by the principal players, as the world clung to the brink of the abyss.

Like most international rivalries, the competition between the capitalist West and communist East started out as a turf conflict, in the aftermath of World War II. It evolved into the most frightening confrontation in history because first the Americans, and four years later also the Russians, acquired the means not to achieve a 'victory' over each other, but instead to destroy humankind. At a post-Cold War conference (held in 1994) Admiral Stansfield Turner, a former director of the CIA, concluded hours of talk about strategies by saying that in hindsight, all the theological discussion about nuclear warfighting had been meaningless. The core realities were that neither side ever had a realistic prospect of devastating the other's nuclear arsenal beyond risk of unacceptable retaliation. And neither had ever understood the other's fears, perceptions and motivations.

Washington viewed with deadly seriousness Khrushchev's renewed threats to cut off Western access to Berlin. Such hardliners as former secretary of state Dean Acheson in April 1961 urged Kennedy, in the presence of a horrified British prime minister Harold Macmillan, that if they did any such thing the US should dispatch an armoured division to reopen the autobahn. Acheson saw Berlin not as a Soviet grievance, but instead as a pretext, cynically exploited to test Western will to resist, which it was vital should not be found wanting. NATO armies in Europe trained and exercised ceaselessly to repel a feared invasion by Warsaw Pact legions, though privately commanders knew that to succeed in such an endeavour, it would be necessary to employ tactical nuclear weapons.

Rodric Braithwaite has written: 'There is no evidence that the Russians ever hoped to incorporate Western Europe by military means. But Stalin and Khrushchev had some hope that political pressure and blackmail might at least enable them to neutralize West Germany.' Historians who adopt a more malign view, citing Warsaw Pact blueprints for surprise attacks spearheaded by nuclear weapons, seem to confuse intentions with contingency responses to scenarios, such as all armed forces maintain. Churchill in May 1945 caused his chiefs of staff to formulate plans for Operation Unthinkable, an assault by forty-two American and British divisions, supported by the rump of Hitler's Wehrmacht, to liberate Poland from the Red Army. While the Unthinkable file today makes gripping reading in Britain's National Archives, nobody believes that the Western allies ever seriously proposed to execute it. Nor should the Warsaw Pact archives, or such of them as are open to scrutiny, cause us to deduce a Soviet intent to invade Western Europe. The wise and commonsensical American analyst Ray Garthoff wrote in 1991: 'The principal fault of the process of assessing the adversary ... was the inability to empathize with the other side and visualize its interests in other than adversarial terms.'

Fake news is not a twenty-first-century invention. Starting on 23 January 1960, Joseph Alsop published a series of six widely syndicated columns, alleging that the Soviet Union possessed a dominant lead over the US in nuclear missiles. His thesis was partly based on charges laid by Gen. Thomas Power, chief of the USAF's Strategic Air Command, in statements that contradicted the Eisenhower administration's accurate assertions of American superiority. The columnist claimed that the White House was playing Russian roulette with US security, and an astonishing number of Americans believed him, rather than the president. For this their own generals bore as much blame as did the ill-judged boasts of Khrushchev. The consequence of the Soviet leader's missile-rattling, alongside that of American airmen, was to goad the US to a nuclear weapon-building programme that vastly outpaced the resources of the USSR, as well as any sane assessment of its own security needs.

Michael Howard visited America's key military and strategic egghead institutions in 1960. He wrote later: 'By all but a tiny number of experts, the Soviet Union was seen as a force of cosmic evil whose policy and intentions could be divined simply by multiplying Marxist dogma by Soviet military capacity.' Howard found little support for his own view that the Soviets must be viewed as *Russians*, 'with fears and problems of their own, derived from past history and present weakness'. He was shocked to find a discussion taking place at the USAF's RAND think-tank, about how long it would take Los Angeles to reconstitute itself after a nuclear war – 'not long, they reckoned'. He was dismayed by the degree to which the RANDsmen seemed to reduce the strategic debate 'to bean counts of nuclear weapons'.

He wrote of the celebrity strategist Albert Wohlstetter: 'His basic assumption, common to so many of his countrymen, was the insatiable hostility and total ruthlessness of a Soviet Union bent on world conquest, that would run any risk to achieve its ends ... He used this to convince himself and everyone else of the vulnerability of the USA to nuclear attack, which could be overcome only through huge increases in military expenditure.' Howard was heartened, contrarily, by visits to Harvard and MIT, where he met academics headed by Henry Kissinger and Arthur Schlesinger, 'whom I found to be deeply humane men, with a well-founded dread of nuclear war ... but also an understanding of the problem of power, and a mistrust as strong as my own of the terrible simplifications perpetrated by their Californian colleagues.'

In the winter of 1960, president-elect Kennedy authorized some of his scientific advisers to attend a Pugwash disarmament conference in Moscow. This proved to represent wasted motion: the Soviets exploited it as a mere propaganda opportunity; declined seriously to discuss anything save the fantasy of General and Complete Disarmament. In the following fall of 1961, there was a return match in the US. Some prominent Soviet scientists and academics attended another Pugwash meeting, where they clustered in bewildered groups around the translators – no simultaneous translation of speeches in English was available. A Russian sighed to an American delegate after a coach tour of New England: 'How fortunate you are, to live in a country that has never been invaded!' Michael Howard's foremost impression of the occasion was that it emphasized that the Russians were 'just as frightened of the West as we were of them'. The Europeans were also obliged to recognize that the Russians and Americans were interested only in each other. Britain sent some of its top scientists and academics to the conference, but these hapless men struggled to secure a hearing. 'The Americans were politely uninterested in anything we might have to say,' wrote Howard. 'Whether we liked it or not, we were living in a bipolar world.'

A senior British MI6 intelligence officer of the period avowed that 'there were madmen on both sides'. Eight years ahead of the Missile Crisis South Korean president Syngman Rhee, a figure as ruthless and reckless as Castro, though in the Western camp, urged President Eisenhower to deploy the full military power of the United States in support of a worldwide crusade against communism. After a 1955 Soviet thermonuclear test, the physicist Andrei Sakharov suggested to missile supremo Marshal Mitrofan Nedelin that it would be a catastrophe for mankind if such a weapon was ever deployed in conflict. Nedelin responded with a crude joke that signified: mind your own business, make your bombs and leave us to decide how to use them. Sakharov was appalled, but Nedelin's mindset reflected that of other military men on both sides. As early as 1957, Britain's Joint Intelligence Committee anticipated a possible Soviet initiative to send 'volunteers' to a sympathetic country outside the Warsaw Pact, as the Chinese had done to war-torn North Korea in November 1950. The Russians 'might well feel their policies and prestige would suffer a serious blow if they failed to respond to a request to help ... by making nuclear weapons available to [a] non-communist power'.

When Kennedy embarked upon his quest for détente – a less confrontational relationship with the Soviet Union – he sought a reset of the arid US presidential relationship with Khrushchev. The White House sent several designedly positive signals to Moscow, such as abolishing US Post Office censorship of Russian publications. On 6 February 1961, McNamara acknowledged that the supposed 'missile gap' with the Soviet Union, of which he himself had been a promoter, was a myth. Above all, Kennedy proposed a new summit conference, this time to be held in Vienna in June 1961, and attended only by himself and the Soviet leader.

Khrushchev assented. Ahead of the meeting Averell Harriman, the veteran diplomat with immense experience of the Kremlin, warned Kennedy not to take too seriously the Russian's inevitable histrionics. When the president stopped off in Paris on his way to the meeting, de Gaulle told him that if Khrushchev had wanted a war about Berlin, 'he would have acted already'. He also warned that the Soviet leader would test the American: 'Your job, Mr. President, is to make sure Khrushchev believes you are a man who will fight. Stand fast ... Hold on, be firm, be strong.' But Kennedy was still depressed by the Bay of Pigs fiasco a few weeks earlier. He was also suffering pain that obliged him to use strong medication for both his Addison's disease and severe back spasms.

Anastas Mikoyan, Russia's effective deputy premier with the title of first deputy chairman of the Council of Ministers, implored Khrushchev not to bully Kennedy; instead to attempt constructive dialogue. He wasted his breath. Once inside the conference room on 4 June, instead of engaging the US president in the serious negotiations Kennedy sought, about such issues as Berlin and nuclear testing, Khrushchev subjected him to tirades of a coarse violence such as the cultured, lifelong-privileged American had not imagined possible in political intercourse. The Russian leader, who never admitted his own country's mistakes to foreigners, seized upon Kennedy's frank confessions of US policy errors in Korea and Cuba as evidence of weakness. He hurled new threats about Berlin.

Anatoly Dobrynin, then head of the foreign ministry's American Department, wrote in his memoirs: 'When all these questions were discussed at the meetings of the Politburo, no one even thought of the possibility of a military confrontation with the US.' The objective, in Vienna, of making so much of Berlin was merely to exert maximum pressure on the president. The result was that 'an unnecessary fear of war over Berlin affected US diplomacy for many years, starting with Kennedy himself. The question continued to resemble a smouldering fuse.' Khrushchev 'was committed to the peace process but could not often translate that commitment into concrete agreements. His improvisation, his inclination to bluff, and his bad temper were all overlaid by a strong ideology, and this helped turn his discussions with American presidents into heated disputes without helpful results.'

The Vienna meetings which began at the city's US embassy were treated by Khrushchev as raucous saloon bar shouting matches, from which Kennedy emerged stunned. 'Is it always like this?' he asked Llewellyn Thompson, America's formidable Moscow ambassador, veteran of years of experience of attempting to do business with the Russians. Yes, said Thompson. The president told *Time* correspondent Hugh Sidey: 'I never met a man like this. [I] talked about how a nuclear war would kill seventy million people in ten minutes and he just looked at me as if to say, "So what?"' Kennedy said to the columnist 'Scotty' Reston: 'Roughest thing in my life. I think he did it because of the Bay of Pigs. I think he thought that anyone who was so young and inexperienced as to get into that mess could be taken ... So he just beat the hell out of me ... I've got a terrible problem. If he thinks I'm inexperienced and have no guts, until we remove those ideas we won't get anywhere with him. So we have to act.' Dean Rusk wondered if Khrushchev was entirely sane, an uncertainty increasingly shared by several of the first secretary's fellow-Presidium members. JFK said he believed there was a one-in-five chance of a nuclear Armageddon over Berlin, which represented short odds.

The disconsolate president broke his flight back to Washington in London, to discuss his experience privately with Harold Macmillan. Afterwards the prime minister wrung his hands about both the difficulty of managing Khrushchev and American attitudes, confiding to his diary: 'The President seemed rather stunned – baffled, w[oul]d perhaps be fairer.' Macmillan was grateful for the opportunity to talk off the record with Kennedy about the realities of the Berlin situation, as he saw them. The British leader feared that if his own apprehension was publicly avowed, 'Americans w[oul]d think we were "yellow" and [the] French and Germans (who talk "tough" but have no intention of *doing* anything about Berlin) could ride out on us ... But certainly – so far as regards Russia – the prospects are pretty grim.'

Khrushchev returned from Vienna to parade before Kremlin colleagues his contempt for the new US president: 'Compared to him, Eisenhower was a man of intelligence and vision.' He announced to the world a new six-month ultimatum, for Western military withdrawal from the West German hostage city. In response, John F. Kennedy adopted a succession of measures designed to show American willingness to go head to head militarily with the Soviets. He said, 'If we don't meet our commitments in Berlin, it will mean the destruction of NATO and a dangerous situation for the whole world. All Europe is at stake in West Berlin.'

On 25 July 1961 the president made an important post-Vienna speech to the American people. He emphasized that the world did not face a crude choice between humiliation and nuclear war. To promote a widening of options, reflected in Robert McNamara's announcement of a new doctrine of 'flexible response' to replace that of 'massive [nuclear] retaliation', he would invite Congress to boost the defence budget by $3.25 billion, mostly for conventional forces. He announced the call-up of 150,000 reservists and National Guardsmen, together with a dramatic expansion of the military: he tripled draft calls, extended enlistments, enlarged the armed forces by 300,000 and reinforced by forty thousand American troop strength in Europe. He asserted that America would sustain its commitment to the two million free people of Berlin – the city remained 'a great testing place of western courage and will'.

The moderation of the president's speech was nonetheless as striking as its expression of resolve: he recognized that the Kremlin was under immense East German pressure to stem the refugee flood westward. Since 1949 an estimated 2.5 million people, 20 per cent of East Germany's population, had moved to the West. In the first half of 1961, more than 100,000 East Germans fled, with almost twenty thousand crossing into West Berlin in June, 26,000 in July. Khrushchev invited John J. McCloy, Kennedy's disarmament adviser, to visit him at his dacha at Sochi on 26/27 July. The

American took care to lose a tennis match with his host, and listened to a tirade on Berlin. A month later, according to his own account, Khrushchev paid a secret visit to the city, peering out of his car, from which he did not disembark. While he was wholly unwilling to fight for the place, he was stricken to the heart by the humiliation which its role as a bastion of freedom, an escape route from the Soviet empire, was inflicting not only upon East Germany but on the global image of socialism.

Khrushchev faced trouble on two fronts: Mao Zedong's increasingly explicit bid for leadership of the Socialist world, and East German leader Walter Ulbricht's clamorous demands for cash and action to halt the flight of skilled workers from his own statelet. For many months, Western intelligence had anticipated that the communists would establish a physical barrier in Berlin, not to keep capitalists out, but to enforce their own people's captivity. This now became reality. Just after midnight on Sunday 13 August, with Khrushchev's authority, the East Germans began laying a wire barrier; behind it, building the Berlin Wall which became the most grotesque physical manifestation of the Iron Curtain and indeed of the Cold War.

The world was stunned. The president could vow to defend the freedom of West Berliners, but not to go to war to prevent the escape of Easterners. The US made the gesture of dispatching fifteen hundred additional American troops down the autobahn to reinforce the garrison of West Berlin, but went no further. Kennedy himself remained privately calm and sensible: 'This is a way out of [Khrushchev's] predicament. It's not a very nice solution, but a wall is a hell of a lot better than a war.' Harold Macmillan, however, remained unsure of the president's judgement. He wrote in his diary on 12 August: 'The Americans have got very excited, the situation is tense and may become dangerous ... I still feel from Khrushchev's point of view, the East German internal situation was beginning to crumble and something had to be done. But I also believe that he does not want to produce a situation wh[ich] may lead to war. The danger is, of course, that with both sides bluffing, disaster may come by mistake.' Macmillan regarded as ridiculous the subsequent theatrical confrontations between Soviet and US troops with every gun loaded, especially around Berlin's 'Checkpoint Charlie', and he told Kennedy as much. But US voters, as well as Khrushchev's *amour-propre*, demanded no less.

The Wall was a public relations disaster for the Soviet Union, but some Westerners perceived it as an escalation which they feared might presage a full-blooded assault, such as Khrushchev frequently threatened. 'We are the masters of Berlin,' Soviet Gen. Gennady Obaturov wrote smugly in his diary. 'Berlin is hurting America more than it is hurting us. We have got Kennedy by the short and curlies, and we can pull any time. We shall do just that, and not tear it off as long as we need it.' Oleg Troyanovsky was asked in 1999 why, if the Berlin crisis had really been solved by the Wall, Khrushchev continued to hammer at it. Troyanovsky shrugged: 'He had to hammer away at something. After all, there was a Cold War going on.' Such an argument possessed a logic against the background of the relentless pressure on Khrushchev to defend his personal position from Kremlin hawks, the East German regime and Mao Zedong. It did little, however, to support the claims later made by Troyanovsky and others, about Khrushchev's aspirations to promote East-West détente, to draw the world back from the brink of catastrophe.

Through it all, America's vast nuclear arsenal stood at readiness for war. Its strategic superiority over the Soviet Union in deliverable weapons was of the order of seventeen to one. The USAF's Single Integrated Operational Plan, SIOP-62, drafted under the Eisenhower administration, provided for 3,200 nuclear warheads to be launched against targets in the USSR, China and their allied countries within minutes of the president issuing the signal. The joint chiefs of staff calculated that such a strike would kill between 360 and 450 million people. Eisenhower had called for the war plans to be refined, to promise less of an absolute termination of everything Russian if not also American. They remained USAF doctrine when JFK assumed the presidency, however, and became operational policy in April 1961. Kennedy asked his defence chiefs for an update on prospective deaths in a nuclear exchange. The USAF's Gen. Curtis LeMay said that a Russian First Strike could kill sixty million. Harold Brown, director of defence research, said that even if the US launched first, twenty or thirty million Americans would die in the inescapable Soviet counter-strike.

A new plan, SIOP-63, prepared in 1961–62 under Robert McNamara's direction, introduced a range of options and negotiating pauses in the event of a thermonuclear war. This menu included a possible pre-emptive strike in response to unequivocal warning of an impending Soviet attack. The new US strategic concept became public knowledge, and the Russians decided that McNamara was thus seeking to create conditions for military victory, by firing first. As the defense secretary much later came to understand, the Russians 'could not read our intentions with any greater accuracy than we could read theirs'. The USSR's General Staff Academy taught its students that 'in a nuclear war there will be no winner or loser. However Soviet strategic policy is that the victory will belong to socialist countries because their aim in the war is just, the morale of their population is higher, their national economic system is better, and at the head of socialist governments are hard-working people who are members of the Marxist-Leninist Party.' Amid the institutional incoherence of the Soviet system, the military caste concealed much of its thinking even from the Kremlin.

No more than anyone else could Robert McNamara devise a coherent, rational nuclear strategy, because such a thing could not exist. Rodric Braithwaite, an uncommonly wise and informed later British ambassador in Moscow (1988–92), has written: 'American grand strategy proceeded from the premise that the Soviet Union was essentially evil, that it was unremittingly aggressive and expansionist, and that it aimed to impose its philosophy on the rest of the world by peaceful means if possible, but by force if necessary. These propositions were unsupported by real evidence.'

The Russians were dismissive of American talk of 'controlled escalation', 'massive retaliation' – they believed that subtle nuances of nuclear strategy were unrealistic, and they were almost certainly right. They talked of prospective 'victory' only because they believed that it was essential to use such language, to convince the Americans that they themselves would not flinch from a nuclear showdown. Suffusing all Soviet strategic thinking was the haunting memory of June 1941, when Hitler's Operation Barbarossa inflicted a devastating, nigh-fatal surprise on Russia. Her political and military leaders in 1962 had witnessed at close quarters this epochal trauma, and were determined that never again would their country be caught unawares.

Back in April 1954, in the power struggle that followed Stalin's death, Khrushchev attacked Malenkov at a Central Committee meeting for alleged defeatism, after he asserted that there was no practical defence against a nuclear attack, and that a war could end all life on earth. Yet once Khrushchev had elbowed his rival aside, he embraced Malenkov's thesis. After meeting Eisenhower at Geneva in July 1955, he concluded that 'our enemies were afraid of us in the same way as we were of them'. In 1960, the Moscow Party journal *Kommunist* dismissed the notion that nuclear war could further the triumph of socialism.

Yet whatever sensible private convictions both Western and communist leaders harboured – that nuclear war must not be allowed to happen – amid relentless sensational publicity about nuclear scenarios, both factual and fictional and some of it supposedly scientifically based, it is scarcely surprising that hundreds of millions of ordinary people lived in fear. In 1957 Nevil Shute published *On the Beach*, a futuristic horror story set in 1963, about the extinction of humankind following a nuclear conflict. The movie version, starring Gregory Peck and Ava Gardner, was released in 1959 and seen by vast audiences. In 1961–62 the US and USSR tested more than two hundred nuclear weapons. The 15 September 1961 cover of *Life* magazine featured a figure garbed in protective anti-radiation gear. Under the headline 'How You Can SURVIVE FALL-OUT', the sub-heading read: '97 out of 100 people can be saved ... Detail plans for building shelters ...' The great physicist Edward Teller lobbied Kennedy for a $50 billion US civil defence programme.

In October 1961 McNamara's deputy and intimate Roswell Gilpatric, handpicked for his role by JFK, made a carefully crafted public speech to emphasize American knowledge of Soviet weakness. Even after absorbing a full-scale nuclear First Strike, Gilpatric said, so vast was the US nuclear arsenal that 'we have a second-strike capability which is at least as extensive as what the Russians can deliver by striking first. Therefore, we are confident that the Soviets will not provoke a major nuclear conflict.' This made it official: there was indeed a missile gap, but one that drastically favoured the US.

However, while the men at the top believed Khrushchev would not launch an attack that was almost certain to destroy his country, both the US and its allies felt obliged to keep preparing for the worst, because their peoples demanded it, and because the Soviet leader's stability and even sanity seemed in doubt. After a top-secret meeting that autumn, Britain's prime minister Harold Macmillan approved retaliation procedures against the Soviet Union, to be carried out by the RAF's own nuclear bomber force, following authorization by other senior ministers, in the event that he himself should be incinerated by a surprise Russian First Strike. Never short of mordant wit, he minuted the Cabinet Office in October, nominating senior colleagues to exercise authority after his vaporization: 'I agree the following – First Gravedigger ... Mr [Rab] Butler. Second Gravedigger ... Mr [Selwyn] Lloyd.' In that pre-cellphone era, a bizarre communications machinery was created, which remained in existence until 1970, whereby in the event of warning being received of an incoming strike while the prime minister was in his car, the Automobile Association's radio rescue system for motorists would be co-opted to alert the PM's driver, who would then stop at the nearest public telephone box, for Britain's leader to telephone Downing Street. In a final touch of satire, it was suggested that every Downing Street driver should be issued with the four pennies then necessary to operate a public call-box in this eventuality.

Such planning reflected the mismatch between the looming spectre of the end of the world and the pitiful measures available to mitigate its consequences. The British prided themselves upon bleak realism. In contradiction to some informed opinion in the United States, scarcely anyone at Westminster or in Whitehall, from the prime minister downwards, privately believed that anything worth saving would survive a nuclear exchange, least of all themselves. Responsible governance demanded that contingency measures should be taken, including the construction of BURLINGTON, a vast underground emergency leadership bunker near Corsham in Wiltshire. But nobody in high places troubled themselves to ensure that its bedsheets were kept aired to receive them.

Back in Washington, the foremost New Frontiersmen deemed pragmatism the supreme virtue, about nukes along with everything else. That was why McNamara had promoted the non-existent missile gap with the Soviet Union – because it played well on the Hill. Almost every senior member of the Kennedy administration recognized that some negotiated mutual reduction in nuclear weapons was in everybody's interests. But no one did much about progressing this, because the politics went the other way. In August 1962, Kennedy asked if the Jupiter nuclear-armed missiles that had been sited in Turkey since 1959 could be withdrawn – he had been told that they were obsolescent and contributed nothing to Western security. Nonetheless a decision was taken to leave the fifteen launchers in place, because of the impact their removal might make upon the confidence of allies, especially the Turks.

Thus, three leaders and their nations marched towards a fateful rendezvous in the Caribbean, with hapless allies such as the British trailing behind. Fidel Castro was driven by a craving to secure for his small country a celebrity and importance to which it could lay claim only by promoting sensation and even outrage. Nikita Khrushchev cherished no desire for war, but was happy to use the threat of it as a means of asserting the Soviet Union's right to be viewed on the world stage as the equal of the United States. His conduct represented the negation of statesmanship but was, instead, the bitter fruit of the Russian experience since 1917, and arguably even before. Khrushchev probably recognized that he had little prospect of securing the love of his people, never mind that of his Presidium colleagues. However, he needed at least their respect, which he sought by presenting himself as standard-bearer for Russian greatness and socialist revolution. Unfortunately for the cause of peace, however, such a display mightily alarmed the peoples of the West, and especially Americans.

John F. Kennedy was one of the most enlightened men ever to occupy the presidency of the United States. But his instinct towards moderation and compromise, fostered by sophistication and international experience, stood at odds with the conservative worldview of a substantial proportion of his fellow-countrymen, who demanded that America should be seen to be strong. Whereas Khrushchev, in making foreign policy decisions, was seldom obliged to consider a domestic public, as distinct from political, opinion, Kennedy could never neglect his own. His presidency, and above all his conduct of the approaching Crisis, would be characterized by a tension between personal rationality and a determination to be seen by his people to conduct himself in a fashion that did not injure his 1964 re-election prospects. The most frightening aspect of this was that more than a few Americans, especially those who wore uniforms with stars on their shoulders, were less fearful of war than was the rest of the planet.

UNCLASSIFIED ~~SITIVE~~

OFFICE OF THE SECRETARY OF DEFENSE
WASHINGTON 25, D.C.

20 February 1962

EYES ONLY.

EYES ONLY OF ADDRESSEES

FROM: Brig. Gen. Lansdale ~~~~

SUBJECT: The Cuba Project

Transmitted herewith is the projection of actions to help Cubans recapture their freedom. This total plan is EYES ONLY. The lives of many brave people depend on the security of this paper entrusted to you. Any inference that this plan exists could place the President of the United States in a most damaging position.

This is a specific plan, with time phases. It responds to the request of the Special Group (5412) for such a paper. I urge that this paper **not** be made known, in this complete form, beyond yourself and those named as addressees.

The Attorney General
Special Group: General Taylor
State: Secretary Rusk, Alexis Johnson, Richard Goodwin
Defense: Secretary McNamara, Deputy Secretary Gilpatric, Brig. Gen. Craig   Gen. Lemnitzer
CIA: John McCone, Richard Helms, William Harvey
USIA: Ed Murrow, Don Wilson

UNCLASSIFIED ~~SENSITIVE~~

Ten months after the failed Bay of Pigs, the Kennedy administration was still committed to 'liberating' Cuba, a secret mission in which the list of addressees on this memorandum shows that the 'best and brightest' were complicit.

4

The Red Gambit: Operation Anadyr

Nikita Khrushchev was an opportunist. He justified some of his most dangerous gambles by quoting Lenin, who had in turn borrowed from Napoleon: *'On s'engage et puis on voit'* – 'You start something, then see what happens'. In 1961, during one of the several Berlin crises precipitated by Soviet ultimatums, Sergei Khrushchev asked his father nervously what would happen if the Americans failed to yield. The Soviet leader laughed off the young man's fears, saying that no one would start a war over Berlin. But what if the West rejected Moscow's six-month deadline? Wait and see, responded Khrushchev: 'He hoped to give them a good scare, and thereby extract their agreement to negotiate.' Sergei demanded insistently: but what if negotiations fail? 'Then we'll try something else. Something will turn up.' In foreign policy, starting something without considering how to get out of it frequently proves disastrous. Yet this was precisely what the Soviet leader did, when in the late spring of 1962 he informed his Presidium comrades that he proposed to deploy nuclear weapons in Cuba.

After Castro had assumed power more than three years earlier, the Kremlin vacillated about how far to support him. Its initial attitude was wary: it feared that to play war games in America's backyard could provoke an extravagant reaction in Washington. Moreover, Castro himself started out favouring an arm's length relationship: when KGB officer Aleksandr Alekseev applied for a visa as TASS news agency correspondent in February 1959, this was not granted until August. Moscow decided against sending military aid, too. Following Khrushchev's September 1959 US visit, however, with characteristic impulsiveness he reversed course: he began to send weapons to Castro, about whom the Russians still knew little.

In February 1960, he dispatched deputy premier Anastas Mikoyan – 'that shrewd fox from the East', as the leader called him – on an exploratory visit to Havana. The sixty-six-year-old Mikoyan, an Armenian, could scarcely be characterized as a humanitarian since, among many other bloodstains on his record, he was a signatory of Stalin's 1941 order for the secret massacre of more than twenty thousand Polish officers and intellectuals at Katyn. He had also played a key role, as Kremlin representative in Hungary, during the suppression of the 1956 uprising. He was nonetheless a more sensitive, sophisticated figure than most of his fellow-Presidium members. Almost satirically, he lent his name and authority to a bestselling cooking primer – *The Book of Healthy and Tasty Food* – as part of a campaign to raise socialist domestic standards. His political survival skills were legendary – an official described him, with mingled respect and disdain, as the only man capable of walking across Red Square in the rain without getting wet.

When the Soviet delegation arrived in Havana, even Castro's *barbudos* were embarrassed by the logistical shambles which greeted its sombre-suited members. 'Mikoyan's trip was a disaster, because we were completely unprepared to handle a visitor of that eminence,' admitted Manuel Yepe, who at twenty-three had become the Havana foreign ministry's director of protocol, thanks to his earlier fidelity as a student supporter of the Revolution. Yepe had got off to a poor start as a master of ceremonies a few weeks earlier, when the new Czech ambassador flew into the capital. A local band had been trained to play his national anthem. The musicians became confused, however, and instead played the anthem of Yugoslavia, with which Warsaw Pact relations were glacial.

As for Mikoyan, despite the chaos that attended the public engagements of his visit, in private he became as fascinated by Fidel as were many others who met the man. The embryo dictator confided that he had been a closet Marxist since his student days. In truth, it is almost certain that Castro claimed this fragment of autobiography merely because it seemed indispensable to winning friends in Moscow. Having fallen out with the US in a fashion from which there could be no return save by renouncing the Revolution, Castro needed another superpower. Mao's China did not yet qualify, and thus the Soviet Union was the only one in sight.

Mikoyan was delighted. The Cuban leader's exuberant radicalism roused happy memories of 1917. Stalin had cherished a naïve post-World War II hope that the communist ideal would capture the imagination of the German people – explicitly, that Westerners would flock to live in the socialist East. In reality, the reverse happened, so that the Soviet dream of freely uniting Germany under the red flag collapsed. This goes far to explain the enthusiasm of the Russians for their new friends in Cuba. The visitor returned to Moscow to report that Fidel was an authentic revolutionary: 'Completely like us'. Mikoyan later told Dean Rusk: 'You Americans must realize what Cuba means to us old Bolsheviks. We have been waiting all our lives for a country to go Communist without the Red Army. It … makes us feel like boys again!' It is certainly true that there was a juvenility about the behaviour of the revolutionaries, and especially that of Fidel: impulsive, intemperate, cruel, egomaniacal; impervious to moderation or unwelcome advice. Even Khrushchev privately considered premature the Cuban's avowal of a commitment to communism. Nonetheless the Soviet Union signed a trade agreement with Cuba, which granted the bankrupt nation a $100 million loan.

Some of the island's revolutionaries were appalled by this perceived betrayal of their country's non-aligned status, among them Max Lesnik, who subsequently fled to Miami in a small boat. Yet years later he said: 'Fidel was entirely correct … and I was wrong. If we had done what I wanted, that is to say to keep Cuba from forming an alliance with the USSR, the Revolution would have been wiped out by Washington.' Fidel could not have retained power in Cuba for more than half a century without both the support of Russia – at least until the end of the Cold War – and the hostility of the United States. In the 1960s, he found the right friends and the best enemies to suit the mood of the times. Tens of millions of people in Central and South America, groaning beneath the rule of dictatorships dependent upon US sponsorship, embraced the legend of Castro as their culture's supreme freedom fighter, and in due course celebrated his comrade Che Guevara as its principal martyr.

The Russians committed themselves to arm Castro's forces. In June 1960, Khrushchev told a gathering of Russian schoolteachers, 'If need be, Soviet artillerymen can support the Cuban people with their rocket fire, should the aggressive forces in the Pentagon dare to start intervention against Cuba.' In September that year when the Soviet leader visited New York to deliver his most notorious United Nations speech, Castro arrived to do likewise. In a fit of pique the Cuban abandoned the Shelburne Hotel on Lexington Avenue, in favour of taking up residence at the dilapidated Hotel Theresa in black Harlem. The move represented inspired proletarian public relations, promptly matched by a spontaneous gesture of Khrushchev's. The Soviet premier dismayed both the New York police and his own security men by hastening to meet the Cuban.

'Castro was waiting for us at the entrance,' the Russian wrote in his memoirs. 'His eyes sparkled with kindness towards his friends. We greeted each other by embracing ... He bent down and enveloped me with his whole body. While I'm fairly broad abeam, he wasn't so thin either.' Even Khrushchev was taken aback by the squalor and indeed stench of the hotel, but their meeting became a love-in, reprised next day with a public embrace at the UN. Mikoyan thought his leader's impulsive visit 'brilliant ... he was very good at that sort of thing'. The body language between Castro and Khrushchev was extraordinary. The Cuban stood six foot three, the chunky Russian a mere five foot five, but they clutched each other – in those early, illusion-packed days of the relationship – with a warmth that was almost familial.

Khrushchev thereafter succumbed to one of the fits of romantic excitement to which he was vulnerable. He convinced himself that the Cubans, their leader and their revolution possessed an authenticity, a nobility and a courageous defiance of American might, which he must back to the hilt. A torrent of Kremlin propaganda flowed across the USSR, extolling the virtue and romance of the Russian people's new best friends. Khrushchev's son Sergei said: '[The Cubans] became heroes to most of the Soviets, of the youth, who never knew about Cuba before but now they saw these young people fighting against American imperialism.' Teenager Galina Artemieva described herself as 'fascinated by Cuba and its revolution. Here they were, the handsome young *barbudos* ... Our rich and great country was helping all the new countries.'

'For a Soviet person,' two Russian historians have written of those heady days, 'space travel was a symbol of gaining freedom. Stalin's crimes had been exposed, Solzhenitsyn was being published, transistor radios made, and there was talk of personal initiative and criticism. The sensations of [Soviet] power and absolute faith in that power was everywhere – in the poetry, in Siberian construction projects, the first ice hockey triumph ... The example of the young Cuba was reviving beautiful memories of the [1917] Revolution.' Russians hung portraits of Che and Fidel in their homes, and learned the stirring song of the *barbudos*: '*Cuba, my love/ Island of crimson dawns!/ Your music resonates around the earth/ Cuba, my love!*'

Back in 1957 Egyptian journalist Mohammed Heikal, a confidant of President Gamal Abdel Nasser, had visited Moscow and interviewed Khrushchev. The latter, whose social treatment of friends was often little better than that of enemies, became irritated by the cigar Heikal was smoking, which he snatched out of the journalist's mouth, denouncing it as 'a capitalist object'. A few years later Heikal called again at the Kremlin, and was astonished when Khrushchev presented him with an entire box of Havanas. The Egyptian remonstrated, recalling their previous meeting and the chairman's attitude to symbols of capitalism. Khrushchev chuckled: 'I haven't changed. It's these cigars that have changed. Since the revolution in Cuba, these have become Marxist-Leninist cigars!'

The April 1961 exile assault on Playa Giron was repulsed with Soviet weapons. Moreover, in the eyes of much of the world, the Bay of Pigs legitimized Moscow's commitment to assist the Cubans to defend themselves. While nothing was then publicly known about Operation Mongoose, it was plain that the Americans remained determined to overthrow Castro. Why should not his new Russian friends assist him to defend himself? Even such staunch US allies and NATO members as the British were, privately at least, much of this mind.

Sergei Khrushchev asked his father: 'Why not invite Cuba to join the Warsaw Pact?' Khrushchev responded, '"They're too far, we don't know them too well, and if America attacks them we shall have to start nuclear war." It was too dangerous, and he didn't know what Castro would do.' After the Bay of Pigs, the Cuban leader formally declared that he had joined the Soviet bloc. With his accustomed giant arrogance, he then told Khrushchev that the Soviet Union had an obligation to defend all its allies, good or bad: 'Thus it was that Cuba became to the Soviet Union the same as West Berlin to the United States: a useless piece of real estate, deep inside hostile territory, but if you will not defend it, even risking nuclear war, you will lose face as a superpower. So, my father decided what he could do. He cannot defend Cuba diplomatically. He cannot use conventional forces because Americans control all communications. So – send there these weapons, to show the Americans we're serious.'

On 30 January 1962, *Izvestia*'s editor Aleksei Adzhubei, doyen of Soviet journalists because he was married to Khrushchev's daughter Rada, interviewed Kennedy, a year in the White House. The president took the opportunity to warn Moscow against its military empowerment of Castro's Cuba. The American people, said Kennedy, were psychologically unprepared to have a hostile neighbour so close at hand. He suggested that the 'USSR would have the same reaction if a hostile group arose' in its own neighbourhood – he cited the violent Soviet response to the 1956 Hungarian Uprising.

Khrushchev chose to dismiss the president's words. In the following month, he approved an expansion of military aid to Cuba, which was signed off by the Presidium in April. Some of the weapons dispatched were diverted from shipments already promised to Egypt's President Nasser, a reflection of the priority that Castro's island suddenly assumed in Soviet strategy. Some 650

Russian advisers and trainers were sent, to assist the Cuban armed forces. Khrushchev sought no payment for this largesse, which represented a significant call on the USSR's overburdened treasury.

At the same time he was bombarded by his generals with bleak assessments of the disparity between US and Soviet nuclear forces. When, on 30 October 1961, the Soviet Union tested a fifty-megaton bomb, possessing ten times the destructive power of all the explosives detonated in World War II, the ignorant world supposed that such might was unchallengeable. Yet the Soviet leader's military men, most of whom loathed the Kremlin boss, warned that the nation's nuclear forces remained hopelessly outmatched by those in the hands of the Americans. Khrushchev later confessed that his reluctance to admit US weapons inspectors to the Soviet Union, as part of an arms control deal, stemmed partly from unwillingness to let them see how weak was its nuclear firepower.

He was informed by his experts that since Russia's R-16 liquid-fuelled long-range rockets took several hours to prepare for firing, while American Minuteman missiles could be triggered far more swiftly, 'before we get it ready to launch, there won't even be a wet spot left of any of us', in the bleak words of Marshal Kirill Moskalenko. They were acutely aware that their own ICBMs could be utilised only for a First Strike: if the Americans launched first, there was no prospect of Khrushchev's long-range arsenal being brought to readiness sufficiently swiftly to retaliate. Moscow did, however, possess a large inventory of medium- and intermediate-range missiles. If some of these were moved to Cuba, reflected the Soviet leader, 'our missiles would have equalized what the West likes to call "the balance of power". The Americans … would learn just what it feels like to have enemy missiles pointing at you; we'd be doing nothing more than giving them a little of their own medicine … We Russians have suffered three wars over the last half century … America has never had to fight a war on her own soil … and made a fortune as a result. America has [made] billions by bleeding the rest of the world.'

In March 1962, when Anatoly Dobrynin was appointed Soviet Washington ambassador, Khrushchev's parting private advice to him was at odds with his public posture: 'Don't ask for trouble.' The chairman also, however, emphasized his commitment to sign separate peace treaties with East and West Germany, and to make Berlin a 'free city'. In truth, of course, he intended the opposite: to cause the West Berliners to join the captivity of their Eastern brethren. He expressed his sense of grievance about American nuclear missile-launchers poised in Turkey, 'under the very nose of the Soviet Union'. He did not hint at a possible missile deployment in Cuba, but vented his spleen at the arrogance instilled in the US government by its nuclear superiority: 'It's high time their long arms were cut shorter.'

In Khrushchev's memoirs, he asserted that the notion of the Cuban deployment first came to him during a May visit to Bulgaria: 'Something had to be done to make Cuba safe. But what? The idea gradually took on shape in my mind. I didn't tell anyone what I was thinking. This was my personal opinion, my inner torment.' Yet it is generally accepted that he had already mooted the plan while staying at his Black Sea dacha, the very place where he so often peered across the limpid waters through binoculars and inveighed against the American Jupiter missiles sited in neighbouring Turkey. A month earlier when defence minister Marshal Rodion Malinovsky arrived to brief his leader on the latest state of the nuclear balance, as a preliminary to demanding more resources, the chairman had suddenly demanded: 'Rodion Yakovlevich, what if we throw a hedgehog down Uncle Sam's pants?' He had conceived a grandstand play: to make a covert deployment in Cuba, then stun the world with an announcement of it, at his planned UN General Assembly appearance in November, after the US mid-term congressional elections.

The Kremlin appeared to own a factory for producing generals rough-hewn out of granite, serried ranks of whom appeared on the reviewing stand at Moscow May Day parades, adorned with absurd quantities of medals. Physically Malinovsky, who would play a central role in the Missile Crisis, fitted this template. He owed his position to Khrushchev's personal support, rooted in a relationship forged during the war. The defence minister was nonetheless a hawk, who nursed deep-rooted grievances against his boss. Soviet strategy during Malinovsky's long reign over the armed forces represented a sullen compromise between Khrushchev's belief that nuclear weapons had become the dominant force in military affairs, and the marshal's continuing commitment to Soviet armies powerful enough to win conventional campaigns in Europe.

He boasted a brilliant fighting record. Born in 1898, he grew up on the estate of a nobleman where his mother worked as a cook; malicious gossip held that, far from being the honest proletarian claimed in Party literature, Rodion was the count's illegitimate son, genteelly reared alongside his other children. In 1914, aged just fifteen, he stowed away to join a regiment headed for the front, and won his first decoration as a machine-gunner. He then served in France with the Russian Expeditionary Corps, and emerged not merely alive, but speaking some French. After the Revolution he enjoyed a stellar rise to high command, then in the Great Patriotic War fought all the way from the 1941 Black Sea campaign to the 1945 occupation of Czechoslovakia.

Like many Soviet officers, he found time between battles for chess and women. The famous aviation chief Nikolai Kamanin described how he was persuaded by Malinovsky to sit down at a board just before the December 1944 battle for Budapest – and beat him twice: 'I later learned from [the general's] orderly that he likes chess very much, and also dislikes losing. I must lack diplomatic skills.' Russian historian Sergei Borzunov recorded once coming upon a marker in a book of chess problems, 'written on it in Malinovsky's beautiful handwriting *Omnia vincit amor* and *Sic transit gloria mundi*'.

As for the first of those two mottoes – 'Love conquers all' – in 1944 the marshal became the object of some mockery for not only embracing a 'campaign wife' – twenty-eight-year-old Raisa Galperina, of the army's Bath and Laundry Corps – but daring to decorate her with the Order of the Red Banner for fictitious intelligence work in the front line. He then appointed her to his headquarters as head of the Military Council's canteen. 'Malinovsky was a man who loved women,' said Khrushchev, 'especially beautiful women.' After the war, the marshal divorced his wife Larisa and married Raisa, which is more than most Soviet officers did for their campaign mistresses. In 1946, Stalin made him a member of the Supreme Soviet.

While Malinovsky, like most Soviet generals, was an iron man, he was not without a brain. Yet now, he told Khrushchev that his Cuban plan could work. This was an astonishingly naïve judgement, which can only have been rooted in the visceral Russian yearning to strike fear into American breasts, rather than in a rational analysis. Malinovsky knew less about the United States than did Khrushchev. Neither man consulted Anatoly Dobrynin, the Soviet ambassador, nor any other Russian with first-hand knowledge of American personalities and politics. Khrushchev invited his missile chief to explore the prospects of deploying the weapons covertly. He crowed confidently to Yuri Andropov, who was responsible for relations with the USSR's fellow-socialist nations including Cuba: 'When that is done, we shall be able to target them at the soft underbelly of the United States.' On 21 May at the Kremlin, however, when he described his plan to the USSR's Defence Council he emphasized the value of the missiles for defending Cuba, not for shifting the global balance of power.

He himself explained his argument later, telling colleagues that the next American-sponsored assault would be much better prepared than was the Bay of Pigs, and would threaten Fidel's survival: 'I said that we were the only ones who could prevent such a disaster from occurring.' He had become increasingly obsessed with the risks, and the strategic unacceptability, of losing Cuba, the Soviet Union's *avanpost* or bridgehead in the Western hemisphere. At a subsequent Presidium meeting three days later, he again declared his conviction, allegedly backed by intelligence sources, that the US would soon move militarily against the island: 'They must be given to understand that ... they will be dealing not merely with one stubborn country, but also with the nuclear might of the Soviet Union.'

A Soviet diplomat soon to be engaged in the Cuban debate later described the first secretary as 'a revolutionary romantic ...

Khrushchev kept saying that an American invasion could be prevented by such a gesture of deterrence, which would place Cuba at the centre of the world political stage … He expressed his confidence that the pragmatic Americans would not take a mad risk [to remove the missiles], just as we could not do anything about American missiles in Turkey, Italy and West Germany.' Kremlin foreign policy adviser Oleg Troyanovsky has said: 'Khrushchev possessed a rich imagination, and when some idea took hold of him, he was inclined to see in its implementation an easy solution to a particular problem, in this case defending Castro's regime and partially rectifying the nuclear imbalance.'

Troyanovsky was among the doubters, partly because he himself knew the Americans, and anticipated the extreme reaction which the Soviet initiative must provoke. But when he expressed his unease to Khrushchev, the leader merely shrugged that the USSR was doing no more than the US had been doing for years – threatening its perimeter with nuclear weapons, most conspicuously the Jupiters in Turkey. By 1962, wrote Anastas Mikoyan, Khrushchev 'had become extremely conceited, following Gagarin's space flight and the [USSR's] growing influence in Africa and Asia. Instead of exploiting these as an opportunity to lower tensions, he decided to put pressure on the young president.' The missile deployment was 'pure adventurism'.

The proposal appears to have been driven by a mingling of ideological, political and strategic considerations. First, a public fissure had developed inside Cuba, between Castro and traditional pro-Soviet PSP communists led by Anibal Escalante. At a moment when the competition between the Soviet Union and China for leadership of the Socialist world was intensifying, there were fears that Castro might embrace Beijing, or himself be overthrown. The Soviet leader was mortified by Chinese taunts that he himself had 'capitulated to imperialism'. He now supported Castro against Escalante. Meanwhile the Bay of Pigs remained a vivid memory: the American threat to Castro was no figment of Soviet paranoia.

Khrushchev later wrote: 'My thinking went like this. If we installed the missiles secretly, and then the US discovered them after they were poised and ready to strike, the Americans would think twice before trying to liquidate our installations by military means. I knew the US could knock out some, but not all. If a quarter or even a tenth of our missiles survived – even if only one or two big ones were left – we could still hit New York, and there wouldn't be much of New York left ... The main thing was that the deployment of our missiles in Cuba would, I thought, restrain the United States from precipitous military action against Cuba's government.'

This was wildly tendentious, but Khrushchev seems sincerely to have believed it. Throughout the Presidium discussions, Mikoyan argued in support of reinforcing Cuba, but urged that going nuclear might trigger an American invasion, which could 'lose everything'. He was unconvinced by the claims of Marshal Sergei Biryuzov, C-in-C of Soviet strategic missile forces – 'not a very clever man' – that it would be possible to hide the missiles in Cuba. Mikoyan deplored the absence of Biryuzov's predecessor, Mitrofan Nedelin, a much brighter officer who had died in the October 1960 R-16 launch pad disaster. Nedelin, the deputy premier thought, would never have gone along with this scheme. The entire thinking part of the Soviet military knew – and even intermittently acknowledged in its house journal *Voennaya Mysl* – 'Military Thought' – that there could be no winners in a general nuclear war, and certainly not the Soviet Union; thus, that it was grotesque to brandish nuclear weapons in the very faces of the Americans. Khrushchev speechwriter Fyodor Burlatsky later speculated that Stalin would never have risked it, being 'more cruel but more rational. Stalin remembered Yalta, and I don't think it was likely he would have taken such an adventurous step.'

Nobody, however, dared to contradict Khrushchev, as his son Sergei explained: 'During that period the Presidium generally relied on Father. His word was final. It wasn't even a matter of personality. Everything was determined by the structure of centralized power ... Everything depended on the top person. Even Presidium members tried not to push themselves forward unless their own vital interests were gravely affected ... Cuba didn't affect anyone's.' If critics no longer faced a bullet, as was the case in Stalin's time, the habit of submission was so deeply ingrained in these brutalized men that frank debate remained unthinkable. Mikoyan recalled a black comic moment when Khrushchev read aloud a list of Presidium members, omitting one name, that of Andrei Kirilenko. Mikoyan said to his chief: 'What's up? I didn't realise you were going to remove him.' Khrushchev responded: 'I wasn't.' He just forgot, he explained casually. 'Thanks for reminding me.' Yet if the list had gone to press as Khrushchev drafted it, Kirilenko might by default have become the past, because the Leader hated to admit mistakes.

Mikoyan and his sceptical colleagues left the May 1962 Kremlin meeting less alarmed than they should have been, because they considered it unlikely that Castro would accept Soviet nuclear missiles on Cuban soil. Such a deployment must dramatically increase the risk of US military action against the island, while alienating most of anti-nuclear Latin America. Moreover, it would validate American claims – hitherto widely discounted across the region – that Castro planned to make Cuba a Soviet military base. But in Moscow believers and doubters alike now stumbled onwards, to the next stage of this supremely high-stakes decision process.

The Russian in Cuba who was closest to Castro and to Che was forty-eight-year-old Aleksandr Alekseev, born Shitov. Officially, he was a press correspondent. In reality, he was the KGB station chief, a veteran of service in the Spanish Civil War, France, Iran and Argentina. Alekseev enjoyed a far warmer relationship with the Cuban leaders than did the USSR's ambassador. An unexpectedly human figure, the tall, bespectacled spy was a bachelor who wrote verse that Yevgeny Yevtushenko thought quite well of. One day in May, Alekseev was abruptly summoned home. Such a call and such a journey were never comfortable experiences for a Soviet functionary, because history showed that they might as readily augur nemesis as advancement. At the Kremlin, he was informed by Khrushchev personally that he was to assume the role of ambassador, because he possessed the confidence of Castro, as the incumbent did not. This was the good news. The chairman then stunned his visitor by saying: 'Your appointment is linked with our decision to site nuclear-armed missiles there. This is the only way to safeguard Cuba against an outright American invasion. Do you think Fidel Castro will agree to such a move on our part?'

No, responded the KGB officer promptly. The Cuban leader was committed to revolutionary solidarity with other Latin American states, which would be appalled. The ambassador-designate said the whole conversation 'nearly turned me to ice'. Foreign minister Andrei Gromyko confided to Alekseev his own belief that it would prove impossible to deploy the missiles without the Americans finding out. Like his Presidium colleagues, however, Gromyko failed to express overt dissent.

Next day, a Sunday, Khrushchev summoned members of the Presidium and military leaders to an informal meeting at his dacha in the Moscow suburbs. He told them of Alekseev's appointment, and that his immediate task would be to seek Castro's support for the missile deployment. The Cubans would not be told that the commitment had already been decided upon: instead, the envoy would seek to persuade them that only thus could their precious revolution be properly defended against the machinations of the United States. Secrecy would be vital, until the missiles were in place and the US elections had taken place in November. Then, said Khrushchev, 'the Americans will have no choice but to swallow this bitter pill: aren't we compelled to put up with American missiles in Turkey?'

Gen. Anatoly Gribkov of the General Staff was tasked to prepare a plan, which on 24 May was presented to the Soviet Defence Council. Its members ratified a resolution 'to deploy a Group on the island of Cuba composed of all branches of the Soviet Armed Forces'. Khrushchev experienced some difficulty in getting all the council's members to affix their signatures and assent 'za' – 'for'. While it remains unclear whether this was an issue of politics or logistics, some had to be visited at home after the meeting, so that unanimous approval might be recorded. On Sunday 27 May, the Soviet representatives set forth for Havana, after some parting words from the nation's leader. They were to convince Castro, said Khrushchev, that 'if missiles are deployed near the US they [the

Americans] will be even more afraid'. The delegation, nominally led by Sharaf Rashidov, first secretary of the Communist Party of Uzbekistan, included missile chief Marshal Biryuzov. All its members bore false passports, and posed as an agricultural mission. They carried no paperwork about the planned operation, in case their plane was lost en route or some mishap befell its members. They were committed to forgo any radio contact with Moscow about the weapon deployment, even in cipher. Two days later, they arrived in Cuba, to be astonished by Castro's calm, almost serene response to the missile proposal.

The Cuban said: 'That's a very bold move. Before we make it, I must consult my closest associates. But if making such a decision is indispensable for the Socialist camp, I think we shall agree to the deployment of Soviet missiles on our island. May we be the first [guinea-pigs] of a showdown with US imperialism!' Soviet general Gennady Obaturov later wrote contemptuously in his diary about Cuban posturing: '"*Patria o Muerte!*" They know how to die, they are revolutionaries and heroes. But they have no idea how to build an economy. Last year we asked their delegation: "Do cows eat sugar cane?" They didn't know.'

It was a notable feature of the sixties that many young Westerners became passionately enthused by Fidel, Ho Chi Minh, Che Guevara and above all Mao Zedong. It is unsurprising that they should be impressed by revolutionary crusaders for change. But the willingness to kill wholesale and without scruple translated their idols into a different order of humanity. Ho Chi Minh presided over much death, while masking his role in a soft-voiced sanctity which deluded – as it continues in the twenty-first century to delude – his Western admirers. Fidel and Che were different. They enthused about their status as warriors. In 1962, it was less than six years since they had sailed for Cuba in *Granma*. They had ruled the country for barely three. They were veteran disrupters, but novices at government who had already displayed in a hundred ways their immaturity and irresponsibility.

Castro's recklessness should command the awe of posterity. It is understandable, given the history of Cuba, that he hated the United

States sufficiently to wish fire and destruction upon it. It is astounding, however, and was clearly seen as such by most of the Russians who parleyed with him, that he was willing to risk so much in order that 'his' side should be seen to prevail in the confrontation with Cuba's giant neighbour; and, of course, that Khrushchev should seek to shackle the fortunes of the USSR to so wild an ally, so woolly a country.

The Cuban leader chose to visualize his own role in the nuclear deployment as that of a facilitator, who would earn credit from Moscow for supporting the grand design of the world Socialist cause. Aleksandr Alekseev, by contrast, emphasized – largely disingenuously – that its objective was to serve Cuban interests, and defend Castro's revolution. This was one of many glaring follies as well as deceits about the deployment: it was obvious to any thoughtful person that the presence of long-range ballistic missiles on the island made it much less safe from US aggression, not more so – as Alekseev had already pointed out to the Kremlin. Khrushchev could have made a tenuous case for deploying tactical nuclear missiles or even medium-range MRBMs in Cuba for defensive purposes. Moreover these lesser weapons might have been concealed for longer from American eyes. The much larger and longer-range IRBMs, however, would have no possible defensive role, and could not conceivably be hidden.

In further conversations, the Cuban leader expressed doubts that nuclear missiles were necessary, and avowed his unease about reaction elsewhere in Latin America. Finally, however, he said: 'If the far more experienced Soviets wanted to "buttress the defensive power of the entire Socialist camp"', Cuba had 'no right to base our decision on narrow self-interest'. A few weeks later Raúl Castro travelled to Moscow, where he and defence minister Malinovsky signed a secret treaty, ratifying the nuclear deployment. Che Guevara afterwards visited the Kremlin to propose some amendments to this document, before it was ratified in Havana. Khrushchev endorsed these on the nod.

Castro's acceptance of the missiles, which amazed most of the Russians privy to the negotiations, partly reflected the conduct of a lifelong risk-taker. Anthony DePalma has written of 'única ... what Cuban poet Elena Rivero has called "the national insanity" of Cubanness, the exceptionalism of a people of intense passions, the pretensions of a big country on a small island, a nation always playing a much bigger role than it had any right to play.' Facing the desperate condition of his economy and the continuing American threat, the Cuban leader almost certainly felt obliged to accept the Soviet alliance on Moscow's terms, as the price of indispensable military and cash aid.

On one point, however, he and later the Kennedy administration found themselves in unacknowledged agreement: both assumed that the missile deployment must reflect a considered, coherent Soviet strategy, which took account of the inevitability of a drastic US response. Castro was among those who accepted at face value Khrushchev's extravagant rocket rhetoric, his assertions of nuclear parity with the Americans. The Cuban said much later: 'You've got to go back to those times ... don't you remember the great Soviet might, when they first put a man in space with colossal rockets? Don't you remember when Nikita said that the Soviet Union had missiles that could hit a fly in the air? I'll never forget that statement.' Castro assumed that the USSR possessed hundreds of ICBMs; had he instead known the truth of Soviet weakness, 'I would have counselled prudence.' Marshal Biryuzov, who negotiated the deployment agreements, returned to Moscow 'with the impression that Cuba's leaders saw themselves much more as benefactors of the Soviet Union and its Socialist cause than as our dependants'.

For years afterwards, Castro quizzed top Russians about the rationale underlying their actions in the summer and fall of 1962. He never received a rational response, because there could be none. Moreover Castro at the outset displayed greater wisdom than Khrushchev, by urging Moscow to deploy the missiles openly through an announced agreement, such as the Americans had long since signed with the Turks, Italians, British. Had the Kremlin followed such a course, although American rage would have remained unavoidable, the moral and diplomatic positions of both

Cuba and the Soviet Union would have been incomparably stronger.

Within the USSR, the circle privy to the secrets of the deployment remained tight. All planning documents were handwritten, so that typists could be excluded from the 'need-to-knows'. Anatoly Dobrynin, ambassador in Washington, and Valerian Zorin, Russia's permanent representative at the UN Security Council, were told nothing because, in Dobrynin's later words, 'without knowing the facts, we could better defend the government's false version of its strategy. This … remained a moral shock to me for years to come.' The Soviet envoy found himself in exactly the same position as had been Adlai Stevenson a year earlier, when at the UN he professed his country's non-involvement in the Bay of Pigs. The Russian side of the secret of the missiles was sustained: it seems even more remarkable that there was no leak from within Cuba, where the Revolution's principals were no more celebrated for their discretion than for their judgement.

Khrushchev was delighted by his unfolding campaign, displaying an almost childlike enthusiasm for the *konspiratsiya*. He initially suggested dispatching the warheads to Cuba in submarines, until the impracticability of such a course was explained to him. At a pivotal meeting on 10 June, formal Presidium approval was given for the missile deployment. It was named Operation Anadyr, a codeword derived from a Siberian river, to create an impression that it related to military activity within the Soviet Union. Anadyr had grown exponentially since Khrushchev first mooted it, as the military sought to create a coherent expeditionary force, capable both of fulfilling its designed strategic purpose and of defending itself tactically against American air or ground assault. It now embraced thirty-six MRBMs – medium-range (1,200 miles) ballistic missiles – and twenty-four launchers, together with sixteen IRBMs – intermediate-range (2,200 miles) missiles, to be moved from their existing locations in Ukraine and European Russia. Once sited in Cuba, at a stroke they would double the number of Soviet nuclear missiles capable of reaching the US mainland. Their warheads ranged in size from two to eight hundred kilotons.

To protect the installations, Moscow initially mandated the commitment of four motorized rifle regiments; two armoured battalions with thirty-four tanks; twelve SA-2 units and some conventional anti-aircraft gun batteries. There would also be a field hospital, bakeries, workshops, and three months' supply of rations and fuel. The ultimate planned Soviet troop strength on Cuba, including the personnel of five missile regiments with appropriate support, was set at 50,874. The protective fighting elements could constitute only a tripwire force, in the event that the US launched an amphibious assault on Cuba, but Moscow's planners believed they could fulfil the same function as the Western garrisons of Berlin – deny an invader any prospect of a walk-over. Meanwhile the Soviet Navy planned to dispatch two cruisers, four destroyers and twelve missile-armed Komar patrol boats, together with eleven submarines. Khrushchev, it later emerged, supposed that these last were nuclear-powered, whereas in truth all those which deployed to the western Atlantic were diesel-electric, as well as technically unsuited and unequipped for service in tropical waters.

The eventual scale of the deployment represented a compromise, and a bad one: the Russians were sending a force so large that it could scarcely fail to get noticed, but too small to resist an assault such as the Americans could conduct from ports and air bases only a few hours across the sea. The expeditionary force might aspire only to make a sacrificial gesture – unless the Soviets unleashed their tactical nuclear weapons.

Fifty-nine-year-old Gen. Issa Pliev, son of a North Ossetian mountain peasant family, was a bizarre Kremlin choice to command its forces on this most sensitive of missions. Though his courage was undisputed and he possessed a reputation for ruthlessness and indeed brutality, he lacked experience beyond European battlefields. An unswerving Bolshevik, he led pre-war repression operations in Mongolia, and in 1939 wrought terror in Soviet-occupied Poland. Marshal Zhukov and Khrushchev valued him as an inspirational cavalry leader, yet even Stalin and Beria had been dismayed by Pliev's indifference to the 'butcher's bills' – casualty lists – racked up by his wartime operations. Most recently, only weeks before Pliev flew to Cuba, it was he, as commander of the North Caucasian Military District, who in June 1962 directed the murderous suppression of the Novocherkassk strikers. There could be no clearer sign of the approval of Khrushchev and Malinovsky for Pliev's 'firm' handling of the unrest than their appointment of him to Cuba, about which he knew nothing. Sergei Khrushchev recorded his father's assertion that it was Malinovsky who picked Pliev for the appointment. In any event, it was a rash one.

In addition to his cavalier attitude to risk, the general was stubborn and irascible, a condition exacerbated by kidney troubles. A personal doctor followed him to Cuba, where he suffered persistent and sometimes disabling ill-health. Soon after arrival on the island, the general's relations with Castro became fractious, because he declined to accept demands that he should acknowledge the Cuban leader as his superior, empowered to issue orders to him. Pliev's subordinates regarded him as a worn-out old warhorse, wholly unfit for his role. Some of his officers would soon show themselves willing, when the general was indisposed, to take critical decisions on their own initiative.

On 7 July Khrushchev bade an exuberant farewell to the army command party about to leave for Cuba. He repeated his 'hedgehog in Uncle Sam's pants' metaphor, to characterize the thrust which the USSR's missile men were to deliver against the United States. He made plain that he had no intention of starting a war, but was instead merely committed to preventing the Americans from undoing Castro's Revolution. Some officers are alleged to have displayed the courage to warn Khrushchev that the deployment could not possibly be completed in secret, but if they did so there is no record of their dissent.

Only once before had missiles of the Soviet Strategic Rocket Forces left home: during a 1959 Berlin crisis when, unknown to the West until after the Cold War, twelve such nuclear weapons were briefly deployed at secret sites at Vogelsang and Fuerstenberg, north of the city, before being withdrawn when tensions eased. Scarcely a man of the 1962 crews had travelled abroad – or, indeed, been permitted to, save a few who had seen war service. Operation

Anadyr's deception plan included issuing personnel with Arctic clothing. A missile regiment's weapons and equipment weighed eleven thousand tons, requiring five cargo ships to carry each one with its crews to Cuba. The vessel bearing the first consignment, *Maria Ulyanova*, named for Lenin's sister, departed in mid-July, to be followed by eighty-five more such ships, which in the course of the ensuing three months made 150 round trips. They sailed in conditions of darkest secrecy out of six Soviet ports from Sevastopol to Severomorsk, near Murmansk. At the quayside, all personnel were obliged to surrender their uniforms in exchange for civilian clothes, officers being given felt hats, other ranks plastic models, together with identical shirts and trousers. Operation Anadyr was renamed by some of its participants 'Operation Check Shirt'. The troops were to masquerade as 'agricultural advisers'. They were nonetheless bewildered to be greeted on their later arrival by Cubans shouting, *'Bienvenidos, Companheiros!'* – which the Russians assumed meant 'Welcome to the combine harvester operators!' (the word was similar to the Russian *kombainer*) to conform to their cover story.

The lead elements of the expeditionary force were SAM units – surface-to-air missiles and their crews – to provide protection for the nuclear launchers that followed. The missile personnel had thus far spent their entire military service manning launchers on static sites inside the USSR. Their first knowledge that this was about to change had come when instructors arrived to supervise training for field deployments. They were then told that they were to participate in exercises abroad ordered by the Defence Ministry. At the gangplanks as soldiers boarded the transports in Russian ports, frontier guards confiscated each man's identity papers, which left the voyagers feeling disorientated, somehow depersonalized 'as if we were nobodies', in the words of Valentin Alyoshin.

Lt. Vasil Voloshchenko commanded a T-54A tank platoon of the 224th Regiment, which spent a month creeping by rail across the Soviet Union before reaching the closed port of Liepaya on the Baltic. The loading operation was a shambles, with crane cables snapping under the weight of the tanks, 'one of which nearly sank the ship'. Triple-storeyed bunks were erected in the hold, for the tank crews. Several of the unit's officers were abruptly disembarked and sent home, having at the last minute been branded unreliable by the KGB. Voloshchenko said: 'Morale wasn't high – we were all wondering if we were going to come back.' Serhii Plokhy asserts that five hundred officers and a thousand other ranks were removed from the units designated for Cuba, mostly for reasons of possible political unreliability. Be that as it may, overseas duty was especially unwelcome to men close to completion of their term of compulsory military service. If they fulfilled specialist functions, however, they were obliged to embark.

Gennady Chudik ran a missile unit's maintenance workshop. He and his mates, informed that they were headed for somewhere hot and tropical, for some reason decided that this meant Indonesia. They were told that any wives who had KGB clearance and were already serving in the army could accompany their husbands, which delighted Chudik and his wife Olya, who proved eligible: she secured a divisional headquarters administrative posting. From 10 July when they were first alerted, unprecedented security was imposed, with a ban on external phone calls and quitting the base. Thereafter the Chudiks were exceptionally fortunate, travelling to Cuba in a twin-berth cabin aboard the cruise ship *Admiral Nakhimov*. They ate better than at home, though denied alcohol.

The passage was a nightmare for those aboard cargo vessels, with troops battened below decks throughout the hours of daylight, consoled by back-to-back movie screenings. Only when darkness fell were they permitted on deck to exercise and to take saltwater showers. The Turks were bribed to allow the vessels that had loaded at Black Sea ports to sail through the Dardanelles without local pilots beside the helmsmen. Not until they passed the Straits of Gibraltar and entered the Atlantic did captains belatedly inform the passengers of their destination, though by then many had guessed.

Elvira Dubinskaya was a twenty-year-old nurse from Kiev, an ardent communist and Komsomol leader, who was among the first volunteers for an unspecified mission abroad, which her father

Ilyushin IL-28

MiG-21

IRBM R-14 (NATO designation SS-5)

MRBM R-12 (NATO designation SS-4)

FKR-1 Cruise missile

Luna missile (ground to ground)

S-75 ground-to-air missile (NATO designation SA-2)

0   10   20   30 feet

0   5   10 metres

The principal Soviet weapons systems shipped to Cuba.

immediately guessed meant Cuba. She and the rest of her military hospital staff travelled in August aboard the freighter *Stavropol*. The women, like the men, travelled in the hold, often horribly seasick. At intervals barrels of water and pickled cucumbers were lowered to them. The nurses took turns to carry the vomit buckets topside and throw their contents overboard – the only acceptable excuse for appearances on deck in daylight.

The cargo mix of the missile-carrying ships was potentially lethal: if trucks in the hold broke loose in rough weather and smashed into cylinders of the hydrogen peroxide used to power the pumps of the rockets' combustion chambers, devastating explosions could follow. Once the cargo vessels entered the Atlantic, an announcement was made over the broadcast system that they were heading for Cuba to assist its people and 'to defend the Revolution from American imperialism'. In mid-ocean, US aircraft began making low passes over the ships, which Russian passengers travelling in less well-appointed vessels than did the Chudiks found unnerving.

'The sun was merciless,' said Rafael Zakirov, aboard the freighter *Izhevsk*. 'All day we suffocated in the steel box of the hold, tormented by the heat, the swell, the stench and thirst.' The twenty-five-year-old engineer, born in Kazan, had additional cause for unhappiness, because he had just been selected to join the elite cosmonaut training group. When orders arrived for Cuba, his CO refused him permission to take up this thrilling new posting, because of his specialist skills. Nuclear warheads and equipment travelled with them, packed as deck cargo in crates labelled, in English, 'agricultural machinery'. On one troopship, men cultivated sideburns, beards, moustaches, so that they soon looked as if they were auditioning to join Castro's *barbudos*.

The Soviet Navy's Independent Missile Regiment arrived in Cuba on 2 August. Some of its young personnel were thrilled by their first experience abroad. They were bemused, driving through Havana, to see bar signs written in Russian – *Karavai, Balalaika* – which reflected the decades-long presence of a small community of White Russian refugees. They fell in love with mangoes, which none had ever tasted. They thrilled to the exoticism of the palms, flowering shrubs, fruit, though 'we felt at times that the heat was unbearable', in Rafael Zakirov's words, especially when they were given for lunch Russian borsch, made from concentrates and served in army-issue metal bowls that were too hot to hold. Food rotted quickly. Worms, no supplement to morale, often appeared on the dinner plates of disgusted men.

The new arrivals worked throughout the hours of darkness, sweating prodigiously, to offload vehicles and weapons. The ships' derricks could not handle the heavy equipment, and a huge floating crane had to be summoned. The Russians were assisted by some Cuban soldiers, with whom they communicated in broken English, their only common language. The locals told the new arrivals that the Americans had always treated them 'as if their country was US private property'. Thirty-seven Soviet cargo ships docked during August, twenty of them carrying weapons, including SAMs, patrol boats and cruise missiles.

As Vasil Voloshchenko's vessel approached Cuba after a voyage of fifteen days, a platoon was mustered on deck at armed readiness, to resist any American attempt to board. His unit's tanks were offloaded onto covered trailers, which transported them to a Cuban army barracks. Once tents had been erected for men for whom there was no space in the existing wooden hutments, they started intensive combat training. Fidel Castro personally visited the unit and rode in Lt. Voloshchenko's T-54. The young officer was flattered, but he was also surprised to notice that the dictator was wearing darned fatigue trousers: 'He was national leader, for heaven's sake! Surely he could have decent trousers? But they all lived very poorly.' Curiously enough, the Cubans felt the same way about the visitors: they were unimpressed by the Russians' cheap, style-starved clothing. Voloshchenko's tanks were for a time posted twenty yards from a tactical nuclear warhead dump: 'Every day you looked at them and thought "God help us, let's pray that they don't start anything!"'

For the eighty-foot-long ballistic missiles, transiting the island proved a marathon. Peasant shacks had to be demolished to make way for the eighty-six-ton cylinders, which could not manoeuvre around corners in towns and villages. Several of the locations previously pinpointed for missile sites proved unsuitable, so that new ones had to be identified and surveyed. Once arrived, some crews were obliged to sleep in tents, while others were quartered at Cuban army barracks in which at night they covered themselves in water-soaked sheets to assuage the oppressive heat. Meanwhile some infantrymen travelled far and slowly across the island by rail, to a military college in a town near Holguín, which they found beautiful. There, they were stationed alongside a regiment of eight FKR tactical missile-launchers, hidden in bamboo groves, which targeted the US base at Guantánamo.

Rafael Zakirov was responsible for the security of his unit's tactical nuclear warheads, which posed a severe problem because of the heat. The least unsuitable storage site they could find was an old concrete casemate in the Sierra del Cristal mountains, yet the heat and humidity threatened the weapons' electrics. On Castro's orders, the only available air-conditioners, located in Santiago's brothels, were dismantled and moved to the mountains, where newcomers and locals worked together to resolve further problems created by incompatible electricity supplies. Oddly, in a country that was one of the world's major sugar producers, the visitors found that the best treats they could offer local people, who knew only raw cane, were refined white sugar and Russian cigarettes from their rations.

Sergeant Pavel Velichko was a twenty-four-year-old signaller from Mariupol in Ukraine, serving with the 79th Missile Regiment. On arrival in Havana, they travelled all day by truck, soaked to the skin by a rainstorm, before disembarking in a vast field of cane. They were installed in tents, which they shared with plagues of mosquitoes, beetles and other unfriendly insects: 'We were particularly afraid of Black Widow spiders.' The lack of common languages caused occasional tensions with locals: a Cuban who pestered the guards outside a missile site received short shrift until it was discovered that he was searching for a lost cow. The abrupt change of diet caused many men to succumb to dysentery. Vitaly Semenozhenkov and a mate slipped off into a nearby town where they bought cane spirit, became royally drunk, and found themselves arrested. But the Cuban policemen only wanted to be friends, and led them back to the guard hut outside their camp.

Nikolai Probachai was twenty-two, from a small village in Ukraine. His childhood had been punctuated by famines, in which they were reduced to making bread from ground corn cobs: 'There were no potatoes, nothing – we ate weeds. People's stomachs swelled from their hunger.' Until Nikolai was eight, he was deemed too malnourished to attend school. When he joined the army in 1959, he trained as a geodesics specialist, surveying missile-launcher sites. At their home base back in Russia, they had learned by heart the twelve-digit code that determined the settings for their R-12 MRBMs – his own were aimed at a target in Scotland, probably the Faslane nuclear submarine base.

His unit, the 79th Missile Regiment, had sailed for Cuba from Sevastopol on 25 August aboard the 10,825-ton *Omsk*. The passage took sixteen days, spent playing cards in the hold, wearing only underpants. Approaching Cuba there had been a moment of tension as the ship passed Guantánamo, and was caught in the beam of the US base's powerful roving searchlight. No consequences ensued, however. After docking on 9 September, they travelled without incident to their designated site, at Sagua La Grande, in modern Villa Clara province. Probachai felt unhappy. 'It was depressing,' he said, 'to feel that we were not sure we would be alive next day, but we thought the worst that was likely to happen to us was that the Americans would attack us with iron bombs', rather than nuclear weapons. Living conditions on the missile launch sites were harsh. No water was laid on, so that they found themselves washing clothes in holes in which rainwater accumulated after storms. They supplemented meagre rations with soup made from dried vegetables which they purchased. They were fascinated by lemons, coconuts … and Coca-Cola.

Some Russians later testified to strict moral relations with local people, but Probachai and his comrades were disarmed by the appearance in their quarters of a tractor-driver who spoke good Russian, having studied in Rostov. He brought with him a conspicuously pregnant girl, and said: 'Guys, would you like to do it with my sister? You can, she doesn't mind.' The soldiers minded, however, and fortunately there were other women whom they found more appealing. KGB officer Mikhail Lyubimov said: 'Cuba was a wonderfully romantic place and the Cubans were very romantic people. Their women had a very special attitude to love – there was none of that American stodginess that related it to marriage. Everybody there seemed to play the guitar, to do samba. Just walking on the harbour quays, people all around you seemed to be having fun. They were very poor, but very happy.'

This was a romanticized view, but many Russians were eager to share it. Pharmacies sold them medicinal alcohol, which they drank enthusiastically. Local people traded them big sea shells in exchange for pieces of soap or bottles of eau de cologne. Through long hours of sweltering boredom that interspersed almost manic exertions at the missile sites, the visitors chewed sugar cane; chatted to Havana University students who guarded their positions and also manned some ancient anti-aircraft weapons. The heat, punishing enough on normal duty, became brutal for those occasionally confined in the unit's punishment cell – a huge barrel in which defaulters were sent to bake, to atone for crimes. Discipline for the Russians was generally taut: two fellow-nurses in Elvira Dubinskaya's field hospital were abruptly sent home, either for voicing 'incorrect thoughts' or misbehaving with local people. Sgt. Pavel Velichko was obsessed with natural beauty, and loved to paint. At every off-duty moment he took his brushes and addressed the exotic scenery, Cuban peasants, a woman riding a horse. He explained himself to every Cuban by saying 'pintor, pintor' – 'artist, artist' – his only Spanish word. Once he insisted on riding a local horse to show off his skill, despite being warned that it was unruly. The animal duly bolted, but somehow the sergeant stayed in the saddle.

It took time for the Russians to adjust to such novelties as the Cuban habit of sleeping much of the day, then waking in the cool of the night. Valentin Alyoshin of the 428th Missile Regiment said: 'The country amazed us with its cities that never slept and the horrifying poverty – huts that lacked windows, children running after us, pulling our trousers and saying "Cigarettes! Pesos!" We gave them some cigarettes, but we had only 25 pesos each.' Nurse Elvira Dubinskaya gave all the clothes she could spare to a Cuban: 'It wasn't much, but he was so happy.' She thought the island 'like a holiday resort, but the people weren't very well adjusted to real life'.

At her field hospital the 75-strong staff slept on mattresses on the floor of a military school. For many weeks, beneath the cloak of official secrecy they were forbidden either to write or receive letters. When at last the communications ban was lifted, they were given the postal code 'Moscow 400', which caused one bewildered mother living near the capital to write demanding why, when her son was stationed so close to home, he never came to see her. They were repeatedly warned about the ubiquity of 'Contras' – Cuban coun-ter-revolutionaries. Whenever anything bad happened – a cane fire, or a Russian patient admitted to the hospital dying, having been injected with the wrong drug – this was attributed to Contras, rather than to chance or incompetence.

An enduring feature of the Soviet deployment was an obsession with this fear of treacherous attacks on Soviet personnel and facili-ties. Some pinprick assaults indeed took place. A CIA-sponsored sabotage attack on a copper mine was clumsily executed by two Cuban exiles who later spent more than twenty years in Castro's prisons, after being captured. But reports of invasion fleets of exiles offshore being engaged by Soviet and Cuban troops were fantasies, like modern claims by some Russians that they helped to repel the Bay of Pigs invasion. These legends persist into the twenty-first century, however, with a big Russian website dedicated to veterans' accounts of murders, firefights, poisonings, sunken US submarines and downed aircraft, almost all the products of fevered imagina-tions. In reality, the worst perils the Russians faced on the island derived from biting insects, their sorry rations and living conditions.

In the absence of battle casualties, Elvira Dubinskaya and her fellow-nurses found themselves treating mishaps. A Russian soldier began dating one of their comrades, and was caught by his previous girlfriend. In a jealous rage, she almost blinded the man by throwing acid in his face. A Cuban threw his lover from a sixth-floor balcony, an experience which she miraculously survived. The hospital also treated Fidel Castro's mother after she suffered a stroke.

The sexual practices of the World War II Red Army persisted, so that senior officers recruited 'campaign wives' from the women staff. Dubinskaya was bitterly resentful when she was nominated for a Party award, which was instead presented to Raya, the unit cook, lover of Dr Tvardovsky, the senior doctor. The Russians had access to few amusements – only the occasional film show or concert. Once, all the Havana military hospital's Russian nurses were recruited for a dance at the Soviet embassy. Dubinskaya found herself partnering Aleksandr Alekseev himself, but since he was two metres tall and she herself only a metre and a half, they performed *krakoviak*, the supremely energetic Polish folk dance, cavorting opposite each other but apart – 'we did it properly, with all the moves' – while the other guests stood around and clapped in rhythm. After that event, the ambassador several times invited Elvira to the embassy, obviously with more intimate ideas, 'but then he saw that I didn't care at all'.

As for Castro's nation, 'people go to war as if they were off to a party', says a Cuban leading character in the immensely powerful and influential 1968 film about the revolutionary era, *Memorias del Subdesarrollo – 'Memories of Underdevelopment'* – directed by Tomás Gutiérrez Alea. In real life architecture student José Ferrara described the posturing of some of his compatriots, especially the ardent revolutionaries, as they watched the missiles and their crews arriving: 'There was some *machismo*, typical Cuban *machismo*, with people saying things like "We could finish off the United States!" Yet those were very dark days, with posters in the basements of buildings that told us "In case of air attack, shelter here".' Manuel Yepe liked the new Soviet ambassador, but was irked by the portfolio of lies Alekseev presented about himself: first, of course, avowing nothing of his role as a KGB officer: 'saying that he belonged to the International Relations department of the Supreme Soviet, then that he was head of this and that, and I don't know what. But for a

Russian, he was very unusual, and won people over.' José Bell Lara was an enthusiastic young revolutionary, who found the Russians 'very strange people ... but a necessary evil. Their support was fundamental. Without them, we could not have survived three years.'

Thus, through those late summer and autumn weeks of 1962, the Russians on the ground in Cuba laboured much, suffered somewhat, laughed a little, and explored an exotic alien land in a curious spirit of innocence, given the colossal implications of the mission to which their leaders had so insouciantly committed them. So near to them, and yet so far away, 160 million Americans remained in ignorance of what was being done on Castro's island. Back in Moscow Khrushchev himself appeared to take an almost childlike delight in the giant nuclear *bombe surprise* that he was seeking to serve up to the United States. Others in the Kremlin who were privy to the secret, however, nursed fears. They slept poorly in expectation that at any moment, the Americans must discover what was taking place, and respond with potentially ungovernable anger. Yet because Russia was what it was, and the Kremlin likewise, they said little or nothing to the leader, the *Vozhd*.

Khrushchev's biggest mistake was to confuse two objectives – defence of Cuba and the projection of Soviet power to threaten the United States. The first purpose was justifiable, and probably attainable. Several prominent Americans at the time, and some historians since, have asserted that the administration never had any intention of invading Cuba, following the Bay of Pigs fiasco. It was certainly true that there was no immediate commitment to attack. But extensive detailed plans existed, and later denials of aggressive designs by – for instance – Robert McNamara lack credibility. When the Castro regime's defiance of American will remained a running sore in Washington, there was and remains every reason to believe that US forces might have assaulted Cuba, had a pretext presented itself.

The Cubans were in much the same condition as the Chinese, in November 1950. At the height of American triumphalism in the Korean War, US forces stood on China's Yalu river frontier. There was still deep anger in the United States about the 'loss of China' – the triumph of Mao Zedong's communists – little more than a year earlier. Chiang Kai-shek and his Nationalists stood poised on Formosa – modern Taiwan – eager to resume the struggle on the mainland. Douglas MacArthur, a man of limitless hubris, was UN commander-in-chief in Korea. Heedless of whether the Truman administration had the slightest immediate ambition or intention to permit US forces to cross the Yalu and revisit the outcome of the Chinese civil war, it was perfectly rational for Mao in Beijing to view this as an unacceptable risk, and thus to have committed Chinese forces to Korea.

In the same way, it was reasonable for the Castro regime in Havana, and indeed for most of the world, to regard an American invasion of Cuba as plausible, even likely. Given the deployments of US forces around Soviet borders, or within easy range of targets in Russia, the Kennedy administration would have struggled to secure international support to oppose Soviet reinforcement of the defences of Cuba. If Khrushchev had chosen to commit say, a hundred thousand troops to Cuba at Castro's invitation, there was little that Washington could have done about such an initiative, with any hope of allied backing.

The siting of strategic missiles was, however, an entirely different proposition. Khrushchev privately acknowledged as one of his motives, the desire to extend the reach of Soviet nuclear power into America's backyard. The moment that he committed himself to doing this, he compromised the rationale for defending the Cuban Revolution. Khrushchev's second folly was to accept the ludicrous claims of Marshal Biryuzov, endorsed by defence minister Malinovsky, that the missile deployment could be hidden from the Americans, the giant cylinders concealed beneath palm trees. Troyanovsky said later, 'It is … totally beyond my comprehension how, taking into account the tremendous scale of this operation, anyone could seriously hope to keep it secret, whereas its success hinged entirely on springing a surprise.'

Though space satellite photography was still in its infancy, it was already a reality. Nearer the ground, for more than six years, U-2 high-altitude reconnaissance aircraft had been providing astonishingly detailed surface images. In the course of the Cold War the Americans, British and other allies launched many ill-judged initiatives. In the summer of 1962, however, the Russians surpassed them in folly. Only a politician of the most erratic judgement could have expected to get away with shipping manpower and equipment for a small army halfway across the world, through ports within a few minutes' flight time of the United States, without anybody noticing.

Yet that is what Nikita Khrushchev did. Stranger still, there is no evidence that he or his staff prepared any response to the eventuality of exposure. 'Unfortunately,' wrote ambassador Aleksandr Alekseev, long afterwards, 'we did not plan any alternative solutions in case the Americans discovered the missiles before they were operational.' Khrushchev merely started something, then – recalling his favourite maxim – waited to 'see what would happen'. Hitherto, most of the Soviets' initiatives – whether in Germany, the Middle East or elsewhere – had been launched in plain sight, announced to the world by the Kremlin with defiant pride. This time, however, Moscow's move aspired to secrecy, which made it an inherent cause for guilt. When revelation later came, nothing did more to damage Khrushchev's case in the eyes of the world than the fact that he had sought to act in darkness. 'From the start, the undertaking held the seeds of its own failure,' said Gen. Gribkov.

In the Crimea during August, while Khrushchev holidayed he also received a procession of visitors, including Che Guevara and a delegation. Once again, he rejected the Cubans' urgings that he should sign a public defence treaty, such as the Americans made with many of their allies. Instead, he assured the visitors in the presence of Marshal Malinovsky that the Americans would be obliged to acquiesce in the new nuclear-armed reality: 'You don't have to worry – there will be no big reaction from the U.S. and if there is a problem, we will send the Baltic Fleet.' This was absurd, but the Soviet defence minister appeared as willing as Khrushchev to believe it.

On 7 September 1962, Khrushchev authorized further shipments of tactical weapons to Cuba – three detachments of *Luna* missiles, codenamed FROGs by NATO, with a range of twenty miles, twenty-four of them armed with conventional explosives, the other twelve fitted with nuclear warheads, and all mounted on light tank chassis. There were also eighteen FKR-1 nuclear-tipped cruise missile-launchers. These became by far the most dangerous weapons of the deployment, from the viewpoint of threatening to precipitate a global catastrophe. Why send them, unless there was a willingness to use them? Without unleashing such force, there was no possibility of holding Cuba against a conventional American assault. On 8 September Malinovsky's staff at the Defence Ministry drafted an order authorizing Gen. Pliev to fire these weapons on his own initiative, should contact with Moscow be lost during an American invasion. In the event, this message was not sent in writing to the Soviet commander, but its absence changed nothing, since back in July such authority had been granted orally to Pliev, by Khrushchev. Only later, at the height of the subsequent Crisis, was discretion belatedly rescinded.

Also in the first week of September, construction work began on SS-5 missile sites in Guanajay in western Cuba. Conventional forces continued to arrive and deploy. Astoundingly, and to this day incomprehensibly, after all the elaborate security measures attending the shipment of the missiles and troops to Cuba, once on the island no attempt was made to conceal them, even to lay camouflage nets. Sergei Mikoyan, who would shortly accompany his father Anastas to the island, later said: 'The mistake with the camouflage was typically Russian: we had to [make the deployment] speedily, so too many ships were used and the Americans noticed. We worked as we were used to, and we never asked Fidel about camouflage. Fidel said [later] "if you had asked us, we could have disguised the missile bases as agricultural projects". It was very Russian not to ask for additional expertise.' Khrushchev's speechwriter Fyodor Burlatsky joked: 'We are a planned society, but not a real planning society.'

Sergei Khrushchev afterwards claimed that his father was shocked by this failure, which he questioned: 'Father got no sensible answer from Pliev. I didn't hear any more enthusiastic remarks from him about the general, or references to awarding Pliev the rank of marshal.' No convincing orders were given to the missile regiments to try to hide their weapons, and back at home they had no experience or training in attempting to do so. The confusion of Soviet thinking was further emphasized by the provision of additional missiles for the IRBM launchers. There was never a possibility that, if a first salvo was unleashed against the US, the sites would survive long enough to reload and fire again, especially since engineers made no attempt to harden and protect the weapons against conventional air attack, never mind nuclear retaliation. All these failures can be explained only by a confusion that seemed institutionalized in the Soviet armed forces, and was conspicuous in the planning and execution of Operation Anadyr.

Khrushchev was at his new villa, set among pine forests at Pitsunda on the Black Sea east of Crimea and surrounded by a high concrete wall, when on the morning of 5 September he was informed that the Americans appeared to have spotted the arrival of SAM missiles in Cuba. This was perhaps his last, best opportunity to back off the nuclear deployment, because the strategic missiles had not yet then been offloaded. He declined to take it; sustained his commitment. Instead of retreating, he raised his bluff. US interior secretary Stewart Udall, on a tour of Soviet power stations, was suddenly invited to visit the Soviet leader. From the conspicuous luxury of the villa with its indoor swimming pool, oriental rugs and Japanese roof garden, on 6 September Khrushchev subjected the American to a tirade ... about Berlin. Reasserting his familiar threats, he told Kennedy's man: 'We will give him a choice – to go to war or sign a peace treaty ... It's been a long time since you could spank us like a little boy – now we can swat your ass.'

The dispatch to Cuba of most of the designated Soviet warships had been cancelled, partly because their abrupt appearance in the Caribbean would have been incompatible with the intended secrecy of the missile movements. Once the large naval deployment was called off, its principal remaining elements were the four two-thousand-ton Foxtrot-class submarines of the 69th Brigade, built to the poor standard of construction prevailing in Soviet shipyards: all suffered chronic defects. They were notoriously noisy, their turbines being audible to Western eavesdroppers at a distance of twenty miles. One of the boats, B-59, was commanded by Captain Valentin Savitsky, who assumed command only hours before the boat sailed. It also carried on board the flotilla chief of staff, Vasily Arkhipov. A year earlier, he had been aboard a Hotel-class boat which developed a huge leak in its nuclear reactor cooling system. The ensuing crisis prompted a mutiny, and although this was suppressed and the sub reached port, eight members of the crew died soon afterwards, and others later.

The submarine flotilla left Saida Bay near Murmansk at the beginning of October, under orders as confused as all the others attending the Cuban deployment. Admiral Vitaly Fokin, first deputy head of the Soviet Navy, offered characteristically bombastic parting words to the captains: 'If they slap you on the left cheek, do not let them slap you on the right one.' The officers testified later that they had no notion how to interpret the admiral's admonition, though he appeared to be suggesting that they should tolerate no insults from the US Navy. Arkhipov and the brigade's commander Vitaly Agafonov alone knew that the flotilla was destined for Mariel Bay in Cuba. Their subordinates, the boats' captains, were not informed of their destination until they opened sealed orders on entering the Atlantic. Each boat carried twenty-two torpedoes, one of them nuclear-tipped and bearing a ten-kiloton charge almost as destructive as the 1945 Hiroshima bomb. Arkhipov quizzed a senior officer: 'It's not clear to us why we are taking atomic weapons along.' In response, he was told simply: 'That's the directive. You should familiarize yourself with [the nuclear torpedo].' The flotilla commander received no reply at all when he added a further question: 'When and how should we use it?'

Another of the flotilla's captains, Ryurik Ketov, said that the Northern Fleet's chief of staff, Admiral Anatoly Rassokho, ordered

use of 'the special weapon in the following cases. First, if you are
bombed and there is a breach in the pressure hull. Second if you
surface and come under fire and again, if there is a breach. And
third, on orders from Moscow!'

The muddle attending the entire deployment to Cuba was
reflected by the mere dispatch of the boats, with no clear notion
what their presence was to achieve. In the original plan, it had been
intended to send a November-class submarine, to sail directly
beneath the transport ship *Aleksandrovsk*, in an attempt both to
escort the missile-carrying vessel and to conceal its own presence.
This idea was only belatedly abandoned. The Foxtrot boats
proceeded towards Cuba using their electric motors to achieve a
submerged speed of six to nine knots by day, surfacing at night to
make up to fifteen knots on the surface. Captain Dubivko of B-36
said later: 'The higher political leadership determined the timetable
of our arrival in Cuba, and we understood that.' It was as absurd for
Soviet commanders to suppose that they could reach Cuban waters
undetected, as to believe that the missiles ashore could remain
unseen for two months. American and British warships were plot-
ting the Russian boats' approximate movements for days before the
Crisis broke. An Atlantic storm slowed their progress, though also
making it more difficult for surveillance aircraft to pinpoint them.

On 13 October a US Navy tanker spotted a surfaced submarine
130 miles north of Caracas, but was at that time oblivious of its
significance. Two days later, the boats received orders from
Moscow to abandon their passage to Mariel, and instead to take up
positions in the Sargasso Sea, three days' sailing from Cuba – this
change of plan appears to have been prompted by the profoundly
cautious Anastas Mikoyan, and against the wishes of Marshal
Malinovsky. Mikoyan's view prevailed with the Presidium only
when the Soviet Navy's C-in-C Admiral Sergei Gorshkov joined its
meeting and confirmed that the submarines had no hope of
remaining undetected once inshore, in the Caribbean. As it was, in
the Sargasso Sea the exact locations of the Soviet boats remained
unknown to the US Navy through some days that followed, though
in tropical conditions they needed to surface for thirty-six hours

fully to charge their batteries, against a normal ten to twelve, because their electrolytes became so hot. Moreover the diesel engines of B-130 suffered failure, and a hatch leakage on B-36 made it unable to dive below two hundred feet, instead of its designed thousand feet. Here were four more dangerous pieces in the jigsaw Khrushchev was assembling so close to American shores. Much more would be heard about them.

Accompanying Stewart Udall on his Russian tour was America's iconic poet Robert Frost, eighty-eight years old. He, too, had been invited to meet the Leader, but on arrival in the Crimea was overtaken by a fever. He took to his bed and sent word that he was too unwell to visit Khrushchev, who promptly dispatched his personal physician to treat Frost. Soon afterwards, the first secretary himself arrived at the poet's bedside, and stayed for ninety minutes. He enquired if the poet had anything special to say, and Frost responded by delivering a vigorous, obviously carefully-prepared presentation. He called on the US and Soviet Union to engage in a 'noble rivalry', eschewing blunders, 'petty squabbles and blackguarding propaganda' that might precipitate catastrophe. Great nations, he said somewhat fancifully, 'admire and don't take pleasure in belittling each other'.

Khrushchev responded courteously and sensibly. The poet was appropriately flattered. When his visitor left, Frost fell back on his bed, exhausted, and said to his American companion, 'Well we did it, didn't we? He's a great man all right.' All this had taken place even as the Soviet leader was orchestrating for the US its most brutal shock of the Cold War, a knowledge that surely lent spice to his visit to Frost, and made a fool of the poet. The American party landed back at Idlewild on 9 September, where the vain, exhausted old man was met by a throng of reporters, demanding his impressions of Khrushchev. Frost caused a sensation by asserting: 'Khrushchev said ... he thought that we're too liberal to fight – he thinks we will sit on one hand and then the other.' Udall was appalled, mostly because he knew Khrushchev had said no such thing. The phrase 'too liberal to fight' was one that Frost himself often used to tease his dovish friends at Harvard. It nonetheless made a headline in the next day's *Washington Post*: 'Frost Says Khrushchev Sees U.S. as "Too Liberal" to Defend Itself'. The person most stung by the remark was JFK, who had invited the old sage to read a poem at his inauguration. Now, he demanded angrily of Udall, 'Why did he have to say that?'

At the end of September Khrushchev, having received the latest progress report from the military, said to Troyanovsky his adviser, not without the relish he often exhibited amid unfolding melodrama: 'Soon all hell will break loose.' His aide claims to have responded: 'Let's hope the boat will not capsize.' Khrushchev reflected for a few moments before saying, 'Now it's too late to change anything.' Troyanovsky afterwards stated his belief that this was the first moment at which the first secretary seriously contemplated the extreme peril threatened by the gambit to which the Soviet Union's *Vozhd* had committed his great country.

5

The Shock

It is an enduring puzzle of the Missile Crisis that despite the huge intelligence resources of the US, and the extreme sensitivity attached to Soviet activity in the Caribbean, the White House of President John F. Kennedy was slow to learn, or at least to acknowledge, that the Soviet Union was deploying nuclear weapons ninety miles from the mainland of the United States. The subsequent President's Intelligence Board report concluded that 'the near-total intelligence surprise ... resulted in large part from a malfunction of the analytic process'. In short, the US machine gathered evidence that the Soviets must be doing something big in Cuba, but failed to deduce what this might be. This PIB judgement was accurate as far as it went, but failed to acknowledge how far political constraints impinged upon intelligence activities, above all aerial surveillance of Cuba.

Between July and September, Western electronic and aerial surveillance observed the surge of shipping leaving the Barents and Black Seas. Not all US watcher operations were technologically sophisticated: Soviet ships passing through the English Channel were monitored and photographed by a light aircraft piloted by twenty-two-year-old Gordon Janney, flying from the Kent airfield of Lympne and chartered by the US embassy from a little local company named Skyfotos.

The Americans saw that an unusual volume of shipping was bound for Cuba. Moscow was successful, however, in concealing the fact that these vessels carried tens of thousands of military personnel, in place of the mere four thousand estimated by the CIA to have been dispatched to the island. The intelligence community missed a significant trick on 20 July, when a Soviet transport plane made an emergency landing at Nassau, in the British-owned Bahamas. American tourists at the airport enthusiastically photographed check-shirted Russians clustered on the tarmac, but nobody realized that these were the advance parties of the Soviet missile regiments, en route to Havana, together with Gen. Pliev's doctor. Most US analysts believed that the maritime cargoes were composed merely of defensive conventional armaments for the forces of Fidel Castro. They felt obliged to acknowledge that such reinforcements were not unreasonable, given the Soviets' declared commitment to protect Cuba and the administration's known determination to oust Castro. Staff at Washington's NPIC – the National Photographic Interpretation Center – came up with a new word to describe their work on images of Soviet merchant vessels headed for Cuba: 'cratology'. They found themselves seeking to divine the contents of huge wooden containers lashed to the decks of these ships. For weeks, however, they achieved little success.

Thirty-eight-year-old Juanita Moody was one of very few senior women employed by the National Security Agency, a veteran codebreaker who headed its Cuba desk. One of nine children of a North Carolina railroad worker turned farmer, she grew up in a rented home without electricity or running water. A trainee teacher when World War II came, she soon found herself working as a cryptanalyst at the US Army's Arlington Hall. In 1945 she was dissuaded from returning to college, instead lingering to become a 1952 founding member of America's cryptographic centre, what became thereafter the National Security Agency. She excelled at exploiting new technologies, above all computers, for codebreaking. She was soon directing a large staff whom she occasionally called to order by whacking a hockey stick on her desk. She operated in an atmosphere of male prejudice, exemplified by one NSA boss who referred to an office in which some young women worked as 'the paint and body shop'. Off duty, she was married to an airline executive with whom she shared a mountain cabin in the Shenandoah Valley where she listened to jazz and hunted deer with a Ruger carbine.

Soon after Moody took over the Cuba department in 1961, she and colleagues noticed a step improvement in the island's communications security, obviously under Russian tutelage. Cuban wireless traffic, which had previously been easily read, became much less so: Castro's forces had begun to use a microwave system. The US Navy deployed offshore three surveillance ships – *Oxford*, *Belmont* and *Liberty* – the last later bombed by the Israeli air force in 1967. These could not, however, solve the mysteries of Soviet vessels docking at Cuban ports with cargo manifests that were shamelessly blank, declared shipments that did not match reported weights, and clandestine offloads in darkness. Moody recalled afterwards that things 'were getting hotter and hotter'. By early 1962 she was 'really getting scared'. In February, unprecedentedly, the latest top-secret NSA assessment of the Soviet build-up in Cuba was released for circulation to the wider US intelligence community, because it highlighted the Agency's alarm.

In the first week of August, construction works began on Soviet SAM anti-aircraft missile-launcher sites at Matanzas, Havana, Mariel, Bahia Honda, Santa Lucia, San Julian and La Coloma. As soon as ONE – the Office of National Estimates that was the CIA's strategic thinking cell – identified those weapons, the Soviets' cover story, that they were shipping only agricultural equipment to Cuba, was blown. The photographic evidence was bolstered by a steady stream of humint, from refugee and exile sources. The CIA's deputy director recalled his boss John McCone saying, as they discussed the growing network of anti-aircraft sites: 'They're preventing [aerial] intrusion to protect something. Now what the hell is it?' Such missiles were, in those days, an expensive and relatively scarce resource, used to protect high-value assets. The Cubans possessed few, if any, installations worthy of such cosseting.

Between 10 and 23 August, McCone gave four separate warnings to President Kennedy, highlighting his personal belief – supported by only a few others in his Agency – that the Soviets intended to deploy strategic missiles in Cuba. He said as much at a National Security Council meeting on the 17th, attended by JFK. Dean Rusk and Robert McNamara disagreed, expressing their own view that the communist build-up was designed only to reinforce the island's conventional defences.

McCone proved a key figure in the first phase of the Missile Crisis. Like most heavy-hitters in all US governments, he was a political appointee rather than a career spook. A sixty-year-old ultra-conservative California Republican, he had moved to the CIA to the consternation of the administration's liberals. Behind his benign, white-haired façade, McCone's reputation was that of a pirate. A scion of a rich San Francisco family, in World War II he moved from big steel to big shipbuilding, and became one of the businessmen who prospered mightily from the global struggle. A congressional watchdog testified after the war that McCone and his associates had made forty-four million dollars from an investment of $100,000. A General Accounting Office representative testified at the post-war investigation into such profits, in probably conscious parody of Winston Churchill: 'At no time in the history of American business have so few men made so much money with so little risk, and all at the expense of the taxpayer.'

McCone displayed a historic and questionable enthusiasm for nuclear weapons: in 1956, scientists at the California Institute of Technology came out in support of Adlai Stevenson's campaign for a test ban. As a trustee of the institute, McCone went public to assert that these 'boffins' had been deceived by Russian propaganda, and were trying to 'create fear in the minds of the uninformed that radioactive fallout from H-bomb tests endangers life'. It was widely believed, though denied by the tycoon, that he sought to get the scientists sacked.

A Catholic convert, he viewed communism not as mistaken, but rather as evil. He espoused the strategic doctrine of massive nuclear retaliation. In 1958 he was made chairman of the US Atomic Energy Commission. His appointment to the CIA was promoted by Robert Kennedy, who saw him as a man who would get things done – and who might win conservative friends for the administration, part of its 'strategy of reassurance', to use Arthur Schlesinger's phrase, in the wake of Allen Dulles's enforced resignation after the Bay of Pigs. In office, McCone proved more measured and fair-minded than the New Frontiersmen had feared, though CIA relations with the Defense Department were strained: the shadow of Operation Zapata's failure hung heavy over the Agency's reputation and over its new $65 million headquarters at Langley, Va. The incoming director, wrote a CIA staffer with grudging respect, went over every line of a report or brief 'as if it were a corporate mortgage'. He inspired fear through a fierce temper, and resentment by a taste for baubles of office that included a customized Cadillac.

On 22 August, McCone submitted a memorandum to Kennedy, speculating on the likelihood of MRBMs – medium-range ballistic missiles – being deployed in Cuba. Next day, at a meeting with the president, Rusk, McNamara, Taylor, Bundy and others, McCone again argued that the only credible rationale for the SAM deployments was to protect MRBMs. He acknowledged that he was making a judgement call, thus far unsupported by evidence, but it was to prove a good one. He said in a 1988 interview: 'We didn't see the offensive missiles. There were the ships, and we had no agents on the ships ... but some things you can deduce.'

Later that day, McCone left Washington for a month. He travelled first to Seattle, where he married thirty-nine-year-old widow Theiline McGee. The couple then departed for an extended honeymoon in France, incongruously accompanied by a CIA communications team. There is no doubt that McCone was justified in asserting later that he had been the first to sound alarm bells about what was happening in Cuba. But it seems reasonable to surmise that, if he had anticipated an imminent high noon with the Soviet Union, he would not have disappeared abroad for so long, however seductive the charms of his new wife. Moreover, at the late August meetings he did nothing to enhance his credibility, and much to alienate more responsible members of the administration, by proposing a faked Castroist assault on the US Guantánamo Bay base, as a pretext to justify the forcible overthrow of the Havana regime.

In Washington, the CIA's analysts continued to work overtime. On 29 August, they saw U-2 photographs of a new Soviet SAM site at Banes on the east coast of the island. On 1 September, the USSR announced an agreement to supply arms and military technicians to Castro. When Kennedy was asked at a press conference to comment on this, he said that the US would employ 'whatever means may be necessary' to prevent aggression, but that 'the evidence of Cuba's military buildup showed no significant offensive capability'.

Why was the administration reluctant to heed the circumstantial evidence of Soviet nuclear intentions? Many American conservatives, some of them within the intelligence and military communities, later paraded their anger towards the Kennedy brothers, for supposed naïveté. Yet an honourable case can be made for their defence. First, though McCone and the hawks proved right in the fears they expressed in August, the intelligence establishment was often wrong, frequently alarmist. CIA chiefs had been architects of the supreme folly of the Bay of Pigs. Cuban exile and dissident informants, such as offered indications of Soviet missiles, were constantly seeking to goad or frighten the US into launching an invasion. John F. Kennedy, for admirable reasons, wished to pursue détente with the Soviet Union: he was not looking for trouble. Walter Lippmann, shown a draft of Kennedy's January 1961 inaugural speech, urged replacing the word 'enemy' with 'adversary' to characterize the Russians, and Kennedy used the word not only that day, but for the rest of his life. The nuclear deployment in Cuba represented an extraordinary break with the Soviets' accustomed strategic caution, even if they shrouded the latter beneath public bombast. When the missiles were later revealed, some of the shrewdest strategic thinkers in the West avowed astonishment at Moscow's recklessness.

Moreover, against the background not only of the Bay of Pigs, but also of the ongoing CIA Operation Mongoose, nobody knew better than the Kennedys that the Castro regime and its Soviet mentors had every reason to fear American designs. In the fall of 1962 America's armed forces, and especially the USAF, were consumed with impatience to grapple the enemy, to assault Cuba and give the Soviets a bloody nose. Without higher sanction, air force chief of staff Gen. Curtis LeMay mandated the establishment of a 'Cuba attack command center' at Homestead air base in Florida. SAC's 55th Strategic Reconnaissance Wing had been conducting nine- and ten-hour sorties around Cuba since 12 September, operations with such codenames as Common Cause and Blue Ink. Maj. Gen. Richard Ellis, LeMay's executive officer, later described how fuel and munitions were discreetly positioned at air bases the length of the south-eastern United States, on the air force chief's unilateral say-so, in anticipation of operations against Castro.

Lt. Gen. Jack Merrell, a forty-seven-year-old West Pointer from Pennsylvania, described the extraordinary pre-Crisis USAF concentration in Florida: 'We had to do a hell of a lot of building up and buy a lot of additional equipment, some of it almost covertly because we didn't want too much general information of how much we might be planning to do to Cuba, and so I had to go to Congress quite a few times sort of, you might say, behind the scenes, and explain to several of the chairmen of the different committees – like the Armed Services and Appropriation Committee of both House and Senate – of what we had to do, why we had to do it, and I would normally get from them permission to reprogram funds.' From 14 September, SAC electronic surveillance aircraft, ELINT RB-47s of the 55th Strategic Reconnaissance Wing, were monitoring Soviet activity with special reference to 'Fruitset' fire control radars.

Meanwhile Marine BLTs – brigade landing teams – practised amphibious assaults on Vieques Island off Puerto Rico, to oust its fictional dictator 'Ortsac'. The carrier *Essex*, fresh out of a refit at Brooklyn Navy Yard, sailed from New York on 25 September; it reached Guantánamo on 19 October for six weeks of refresher training for a crew that included many new hands. The carrier *Independence* sailed from Norfolk, Virginia on 11 October with destroyer escorts, followed by the *Enterprise* on the 19th. These latter two giants, together with their escorts and some supporting shore-based air squadrons, were designated Task Force 135. On the 13th two Marine air groups deployed to Key West and Puerto Rico. Navy aircraft roamed the ocean not merely from carriers, but also from fields that included Argentia, Newfoundland; Lajes in the

Portuguese Azores; Bermuda; Roosevelt Roads, Puerto Rico; Guantánamo, Cuba; and stations in the east continental US.

In the face of so much visible military and naval activity in close proximity to Cuba, weeks before the missile deployment was revealed, the administration could not legitimately object to a Soviet build-up, designed to protect Castro. The one respect in which the president was unquestionably naïve was that he made a classic error in international relations – expecting his adversary to think and act like himself. He assumed that the Kremlin would be deterred from shipping offensive weapons by the strength of his own public and private warnings of the seriousness with which he would view such action, and by its own consciousness of the USSR's nuclear weakness.

Because it was obvious to the White House that a missile deployment must trigger a drastic and perhaps violent response, the president supposed that this reality would be equally apparent to the Kremlin. Yet Khrushchev's reality was not Kennedy's reality. John Hughes, special assistant to Defense Intelligence Agency director Lt. Gen. Joseph Carroll during the Crisis, wrote later that the greatest barrier to developing strategic warning is 'the tendency of the human mind to assume that the status quo will continue … Nations do not credit their potential opponents with the will to make unexpected acts.'

Late in August, Anatoly Dobrynin met privately with Ted Sorensen, the president's principal political adviser, who urged that the Soviet Union should restrain its rhetoric in the approach to the mid-term elections, since noisy threats must aid the Republicans. Some days afterwards, the ambassador reported back to the White House that Moscow understood the president's concerns; would undertake nothing ahead of the election that would raise tension, especially over Berlin. Dobrynin had no inkling of the Kremlin's Cuban nuclear plan, 'so Khrushchev's promises not to complicate the international situation', he wrote later, '… were deliberately misleading'. Kennedy nonetheless swallowed the false assurances.

The White House began unwillingly to focus its attention on the spectre of a Soviet ballistic missile deployment, in response to insistent public claims by Republican senator Kenneth Keating of New York. Keating's sources have never been identified. These were possibly in the defence or intelligence community, but also plausibly Cuban refugees or the former West German ambassador to Cuba, Karl von Spreti. The latter had been briefed by his own country's intelligence service that the Soviets were undertaking a new missile installation. In Washington in September, he approached the CIA with a narrative about nuclear weapons on Castro's island – and was rebuffed as a fantasist. Only thereafter did the German allegedly turn to Keating, on the Hill. The senator made a succession of statements, accusing the administration of negligence in its response, or lack of it, to a Soviet build-up. A successful lawyer who adopted a tough anti-communist stance, Keating was nonetheless no way-out extremist: in 1964, he would display courage by declining to endorse Barry Goldwater's Republican candidacy for the presidency.

In September 1962, Kennedy knew that Keating was talking to informed people, because photos from a 29 August U-2 flight over Cuba showed eight new SAM sites. The president ordered Gen. Marshall 'Pat' Carter, who was minding the CIA store in his boss John McCone's absence, to put the U-2 images 'in the box and nail it shut' – to maintain tight secrecy. He knew that silence would not long suffice, however, and asked Dean Rusk to draft a statement on the US government's response to the Soviet SAM deployments.

First at lunchtime and then later in the afternoon of 4 September, a group chaired by the president met twice in the White House to decide what to say about the Keating charges. In the light of what followed, these were important gatherings, at which important things were said. Dean Rusk asserted that 'any placing by the Soviets of a significant offensive capability in the hands of this self-announced aggressive regime in Cuba would be a direct and major challenge to this hemisphere and would warrant immediate and appropriate action'. McGeorge Bundy cautioned that 'we don't want to get into the position of being frightened by [the Keating] group'. But Robert McNamara supported Rusk, saying that Soviet deliveries of MiG-21 fighters provided further causes for concern.

Bundy agreed that the deployment of SAMs looked like a turning point.

McNamara spoke with considerable wisdom and foresight. He warned against making too explicit a public statement until it was plain exactly what sort of weapons the Soviets were installing on Cuba: he mentioned the possibility that these might be nuclear, though not that they might be strategic MRBMs and IRBMs. He also urged the importance of formulating a clear response ahead of such threatened developments. Bundy suggested that there need be no direct US reaction to the deployment of SAMs or surface-to-surface tactical missiles. Rusk disagreed: he feared that such weapons could turn the scale in defeating a possible US invasion, if that proved necessary. McNamara responded – again, presciently – that if the administration was to consider a future blockade to halt Soviet arms shipments, 'Why wouldn't we do it today?' The president interjected: 'Because we figure they may try to blockade Berlin.' Rusk said: 'The configuration in Cuba is still defensive.' Both he and McNamara raised the possibility of asking Congress for authority to call up reserve forces, though they were unsure whether to seek to make such a move high or low profile, headline-grabbing or otherwise. Either way, the Soviets should get the message.

Kennedy concluded by proposing to call in reporters for an off-the-record briefing, before making a public statement that evening. Bundy was wary of this notion: 'I would suggest that we be very careful, Mr. President ... because the issues involved are very grave.' Kennedy overruled him: 'That's right, but ... we can't permit somebody to break this story before we do.' He went on to say that the Cuban problem would not go away any time soon: it was sensible to assume that the Soviet build-up would continue. He himself thought that the presence of surface-to-surface missiles posed such a grave threat to a future US landing that it was unacceptable: 'The Monroe doctrine doesn't apply as it did in the past; but we still have our responsibilities ... There's certain things that would violate our national security. And we would then have to take appropriate action and such things would be the establishment of surface-to-surface missiles or the putting of, of, a nuclear weapons base.'

Dean Rusk said that when the president spoke publicly, it seemed wise for him to point out that the US had global responsibilities; that Cuba could not be viewed or addressed in isolation, as perhaps it might have been before World War II. 'We've got a million men overseas in confrontation with the Soviet bloc and this is part of that confrontation. This is the thing that makes it so agonizingly difficult.' Bobby Kennedy responded: 'Yeah, I understand that. So, therefore, I think that you really have to reach a determination of whether putting surface-to-surface missiles in Cuba would be where we'd really have to face up to it, and figure that you are going to have to take your chance on something like that. Everything you do, whether you do it in Southeast Asia, or Berlin or Cuba or wherever, is going to have some effect on the Soviet Union elsewhere.' The group then returned to drafting the press statement. Rusk opposed specifying nuclear weapons as a breakpoint: 'We would create a kind of panic that the facts themselves don't now justify.' He proposed a general warning to Moscow, rather than making specific public demands that would trap the Kremlin in a position from which it could not retreat without suffering humiliation.

The president then left the meeting to continue drafting, under Bobby Kennedy's chairmanship. However, the attorney-general soon also broke away, to meet envoy Anatoly Dobrynin at the Soviet embassy. The mission was located in an old four-storey mansion on 16th Street, three blocks north of the White House, purchased by Russia's Tsarist government in 1913 from the family of George Pullman, he who made the railroad cars. In 1962 it housed a hundred diplomats and staff, working in extremely crowded discomfort, behind windows bricked up to block American eavesdroppers. Dobrynin described his own second-floor office as 'a windowless cell'. The ambassador, knowing America well, lived a remarkably informal life, driving himself and his family at weekends; only reluctantly accepting a bodyguard as anti-Soviet demonstrations became more aggressive. He shared with the Bulgarian ambassador the unwelcome honour of claiming to be the lowest-paid envoys in Washington.

Dobrynin was one of very few Soviet diplomats who had the confidence to meet alone with Americans, up to and including the president. When he presented his credentials six months earlier, John F. Kennedy personally led the Russian in turn to the offices of Mac Bundy, Ted Sorensen and Pierre Salinger, introducing him to each 'with a wisecrack at their expense'. He also joked that he envied Dobrynin's Kremlin bosses, who had no press to worry about: 'Whatever I do, 80 per cent of the American media comes out against me.' At a later White House reception, the president introduced his brother Bobby as 'an expert in confidential contacts with the Soviet Union', whom the ambassador ought to get to know better.

This was a jibe at the attorney-general's back-channel dialogue with the Russians. RFK had become accustomed to serve as the administration's point man in deniable talks, either through Dobrynin or Georgy Bolshakov. The latter was nominally chief of the TASS news agency, but as a fluent English-speaking GRU colonel his real function was to sustain contact with Robert Kennedy and White House press secretary Pierre Salinger: between May 1961 and December 1962, he met RFK fifty-one times. US intelligence officers and FBI chiefs warned the attorney-general that the Russian peddled disinformation, but Kennedy wished to believe that he enjoyed a genuinely privileged and trusting relationship. On the other side Gromyko, Soviet foreign minister, also resented Bolshakov's role; he thought the spy a clumsy intermediary who often misinterpreted American positions. He deplored the fact that Bolshakov reported to the Soviet defence ministry, rather than to his own department. But the TASS man had powerful friends in Moscow, notably Anastas Mikoyan and Khrushchev's son-in-law Aleksei Adzhubei. In November 1961 RFK told his brother of Bolshakov's claim that Khrushchev was 'Kennedyizing USSR government, bringing in young people with new vitality, new ideas'. The president laughed and said, 'We should be Khrushchevizing the American government.'

Meanwhile the hapless Dobrynin never knew exactly what RFK and Salinger said to Bolshakov, or what the Russian told the

Americans. On the afternoon of 4 September, the attorney-general expressed the administration's acute concern about the deployment of missiles in Cuba. The ambassador responded that the island had a right to defend itself. The Soviet Union favoured a nuclear non-proliferation treaty. Dobrynin neither confirmed nor denied the missile reports 'since I had no information about them whatsoever ... At that point I never even imagined the idea of stationing our *nuclear* missiles in Cuba.' After the meeting, and Kennedy having made plain the gravity of Washington's alarm, Dobrynin sought urgent instructions from Moscow. He received the response from the foreign ministry: 'You should confirm that there are only *defensive* Soviet weapons in Cuba.' Identical instructions were given to Bolshakov, who was authorized in conversations with the Americans to attach Khrushchev's name personally to such assurances. The ambassador deplored his own government's 'mania for secrecy', of which the rickety twin-track links between Washington and Moscow were a manifestation.

RFK later claimed that he returned from the 4 September encounter with Dobrynin convinced that it was only a matter of time before the Russians installed nuclear weapons on Cuba. If that is true, it becomes even more astonishing that the administration moved so sluggishly thereafter. When the White House group reconvened at 4 p.m. that same day, it was joined by the armed forces chiefs of staff. The president cautioned the meeting against feeding a Cuba obsession: 'The fact of the matter is the major danger is the Soviet Union with missiles and nuclear warheads, not Cuba. We don't want to get everybody so fixed on Cuba ...' He wanted to remind Americans that Castro's island was just one among many scary places in the world. He then, however, invited air force chief Gen. Curtis LeMay to report on the feasibility of destroying the SAM sites from the air. He asked: 'Would that be a difficult operation?' The airman responded succinctly, characteristically and idiotically: 'No, sir.'

One of the most misbegotten military phrases of the twentieth century was 'surgical air strike'. This implied a capability for precision destruction that was seldom accomplished by any air force, in

(Above) 'Too liberal to fight': JFK was infuriated when, in September 1962, Robert Frost returned from meeting Khrushchev with Stewart Udall (pictured behind him at Idlewild airport) to report the Soviet leader's alleged mocking comment. (Below) A Soviet FKR-1 Cruise missile, one of eighteen on the island equipped with tactical nuclear warheads, ready to be deployed against prospective American invaders.

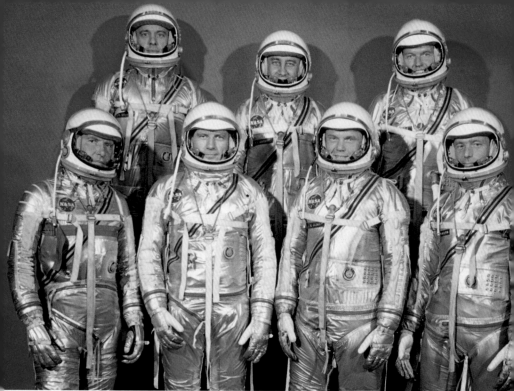

PRIDE AND SHAME across the Iron Curtain. (Top) The first generation of America's trainee astronauts. (Above and right) White rioters at the University of Mississippi protest against the admission of black student James Meredith, escorted by federal officers and troops.

(Above) At the 1962 May Day parade in Moscow, the Soviet Union shows off some of the weapons with which it seeks to terrorize the West. (Below) The only known photo of June 1962 protesters in Novocherkassk, of whom at least twenty-six were killed by Soviet troops.

SPOOKS. America's finest, or not as the case might be (clockwise from top right): Sherman Kent, Richard Bissell, Ed Lansdale, John McCone, Juanita Moody.

Some of the Russians (clockwise from top left): Georgy Bolshakov, Oleg Penkovsky, Aleksandr Alekseev, Oleg Troyanovsky, Anatoly Dobrynin, Aleksandr Feklisov.

MISSILE TRANSPORTERS

12 PROB GUIDELINE MISSILES

HEAVY EQUIPMENT

5 MISSILE DOLLIES

20' LONG CYLINDRICAL TANKS

MISSILE TRANSPORTERS

OPEN STORAGE

(Above) The aerial photograph that threatened the safety of the world: the 14 October 1962 image of a Soviet missile site in Cuba, here labelled by the CIA, which traumatized the Kennedy administration. (Below) An ironically benign study of the US president meeting at the White House with Soviet foreign minister Andrei Gromyko and on his right ambassador Dobrynin on 18 October. The Russian lied fluently for two hours, while Kennedy concealed his knowledge of the deceits.

INFLUENTIAL AMERICANS. (Above) Walter Lippmann, Kennedy's favourite columnist, also read by Khrushchev. (Inset) Georgia's Senator Richard Russell, who demanded war, a view shared by the US chiefs of staff (below, left to right) General Earle G. Wheeler, Army Chief; General Curtis E. LeMay, Air Force; General Maxwell D. Taylor, Chairman; Admiral George W. Anderson Jr., Naval Operations; and General David Shoup, Marine Corps.

Russians in Cuba, attired in comic-opera disguises. (Above) Men of a Soviet motorized rifle regiment parade in their civilian clothes. (Below) Colonel Georgi Voronkov (left) meeting with the officers who shot down Rudy Anderson's U-2.

any conflict. The USAF's 1962 advocates of swift and extreme force, some of whom after the Crisis sustained their enthusiasm for bombing, invading and occupying Cuba, were granted opportunities in Indochina a few years later, exhaustively to test their claims. US air power seldom, if ever, attained the swift, conclusive outcomes which LeMay professed that he could contrive in the Caribbean.

At 5 p.m., after the group broke up, Kennedy hosted a meeting with congressional leaders, at which 'Pat' Carter briefed them on the Soviet SAMs. In response to questioning, even LeMay conceded that such weapons were defensive, not offensive. When Sen. Alexander Wiley of Wisconsin demanded to be told whether the administration proposed 'just to sit still and let Cuba carry on?' the president responded that, so long as the weapons were seen to be intended to be protective, he thought that US armed intervention would be 'a mistake … We have to keep some proportion – we're talking about sixty MiGs [fighters supplied to Castro], we're talking about some ground-to-air missiles which from the island, do not threaten the United States. We are not talking about nuclear warheads. We've got a very difficult situation in Berlin. We've got a difficult situation in Southeast Asia and a lot of other places.'

Wiley then asked about the option of imposing a blockade. Kennedy replied: 'Well, a blockade is a major military operation, too. It's an act of war … There's no evidence that that would bring down Castro for many many months … You'd have people starving and all the rest … Berlin would obviously be blockaded too.' The president concluded that he believed the ongoing Berlin Crisis would reach 'some kind of a climax this fall', and meanwhile he was unwilling to impale the US on the Caribbean issue: 'I know a lot of people want to invade Cuba. I would be opposed to it today.'

In response to further spiky questions from his visitors, including Senators Mike Mansfield and William Fulbright, he recalled the precedent of the Anglo-French-Israeli invasion of Egypt in 1956, when the Russians exploited the worldwide focus on that debacle, brutally to crush the uprising in Hungary. Senator Richard Russell warned Kennedy that American public opinion was intensely sensitive about Cuba: 'It's in the nature of an offence to the national pride [chuckling] and there's something personal about it too. It's so close ... A man wouldn't get ruffled about something that happened in Berlin, much less Hungary or some other part of the world, but he would get upset about Cuba.'

During a meeting shortly afterwards at which the president briefed Senate majority leader Everett Dirksen on his intention to ask congressional authority for a call-up of 150,000 reserve personnel from civilian life, Dirksen echoed Russell in stressing that the president must make it plain that this action was being taken in response to the Cuban situation. Russell said that he himself had recently visited a big industrial plant, at which he found 'the only thing they wanted to talk about ... [was] Cuba. So this is very much in the average person's mind, and you'll have to lay it right on the line in any statement you make, otherwise there'll be hell-a-poppin', because of the unpopularity and disruption generated by the call-up.'

That evening Pierre Salinger, the president's chunky, flamboyant press secretary, as addicted to cigars as was Fidel Castro and also a concert-class piano-player, read a White House statement to reporters, which began: 'All Americans, as well as all of our friends in this hemisphere, have been concerned over the recent moves of the Soviet Union to bolster the military power of the Castro regime in Cuba.' The document then detailed the Soviet build-up of weapons and personnel, offering an inventory led by MiGs and SAMs that fell far short of the reality. The statement said explicitly that there was no evidence of offensive weapons being deployed which threatened the US. It concluded: 'The Cuban question must be considered as a part of the worldwide challenge posed by Communist threats to the peace ... It continues to be the policy of the United States that the Castro regime will not be allowed to export its aggressive purposes by force or the threat of force. It will be prevented by whatever means may be necessary from taking action against any part of the Western hemisphere. The United States, in conjunction with other hemisphere countries, will make sure that while increased Cuban armaments will be a heavy burden to the unhappy people of Cuba themselves, they will be nothing more.' At 7.35 p.m., Kennedy wound up the official presidential day, and went for his accustomed swim in the pool beneath the White House.

These events and conversations on 4 September are important at many levels. First, they established the parameters of US policy, as this would be sustained through the Crisis that finally broke six weeks later. The Kennedy administration would not take military action in the face of Soviet shipments of defensive arms to Cuba. It would do so, however, should Moscow seek to install offensive weapons that threatened the continent. US mid-term congressional polling day loomed in November. Beyond that would come Kennedy's 1964 presidential re-election campaign. These towering domestic factors sustained pressure on the White House to be seen to be strong, on Cuba as on Berlin and Indochina. No American president, least of all the relatively young man so narrowly elected in November 1960, could afford to tell the American people that Cuba, Castro and his nuclear-armed Russian friends did not matter. Kennedy led a nation forever schizophrenic about whether it should bask in the sunshine of a national economic triumph and a strategic might such as the world had never seen, or instead dig ever-deeper bunkers to protect itself from evil, represented by jealous enemies capable of destroying all that it held dear.

All this was well-recognized by the men around the White House table on 4 September and thereafter. A pervasive theme of Kennedy's presidency was the tension between his private optimism, good sense, rationality, highly-educated proportionality; and the political imperative demanding gestures – and, indeed, substantive policies – to assuage the considerably different impulses of middle America. Kenneth Galbraith recalled Kennedy saying later in the context of Vietnam: 'There are just so many concessions one can make to the Communists in one year and survive politically.' This consideration was equally vivid in his thoughts, when addressing Cuba in the fall of 1962. Yet on 5 September Arthur Schlesinger, after reading intelligence reports that described draft plans for a US invasion, penned a memorandum for the president urging extreme caution: 'Cuba would become our Algeria [where the French had just lost a murderous struggle against local nationalists].' It was partly as a consequence of the historian's consistent wariness about everything to do with Cuba that Schlesinger found himself marginalized during the big debate that was now imminent.

That day analysis of new U-2 images of the Cuban air force base at Santa Clara showed MiG-21s – aircraft capable of flying to 60,000 feet at speeds up to 1,000 mph – armed with infra-red air-to-air missiles as well as rockets and cannon. Next day John McCone briefly interrupted his French honeymoon activities to invite Mac Bundy, who was passing through Paris, to take a walk with him. The CIA chief warned the presidential adviser of his conviction that the Soviets would deploy offensive missiles, a message he repeated in telegrams to his subordinates at Langley. Indeed, so prolific did the so-called 'honeymoon cable traffic' become that a CIA staffer expressed doubts 'that the old man knows what to do on a honeymoon'.

Before leaving for France, McCone had ordered daily U-2 surveillance of Cuba. That instruction was countermanded by Rusk and McNamara, who feared yet another communist shootdown – a Chinese Nationalist U-2 was destroyed by a Soviet missile over the communist Chinese mainland on 8 September. Moreover, they informed Langley that McCone lacked the authority to order such flights on his own initiative, though he continued to urge them, as did Robert Kennedy. During a 10 September Washington meeting, at which the secretary of state again expressed unease about the provocative character of U-2 sorties, RFK stared almost contemptuously at Rusk and demanded: 'What's the matter, Dean, you chicken?' The Crisis did nothing to increase the Kennedys' respect for the secretary of state: they liked to quote Ken Galbraith's observation in a letter to JFK from the Delhi embassy, that trying to communicate through Rusk was 'like trying to fornicate through a mattress'.

*   *   *

There were seven million absentees from every discussion that took place in the United States: Castro's people. American decision-makers, as much as the American electorate, thought and acted upon the assumption that the Cubans had become hapless prisoners of their communist dictator, puppets of the Soviet Union. Their real thoughts and possible wishes were never discussed, during those days and months when many thousands of them faced possible extinction as a consequence of decisions being made in Washington. No consideration was given to the possibility that, after decades of servitude to the United States, Cubans might choose to endure the sacrifices imposed by an alternative bondage to Fidel, and by partnership with the Russians. Ciro Bianchi was the teenage son of a Havana construction worker: 'People had a strong conviction and great fervour, and I don't think that was because we thought the Soviet Union was going to help us, but that we trusted the leader of the Revolution Fidel Castro. Cuba as a sovereign power had the right to have those nuclear weapons.'

Nobody in America's upper reaches entertained for a moment the possibility – such as occurred to many Europeans – that, as Ciro Bianchi asserted, the Cuban government might be entitled to sanction the Soviet Union to install missiles, just as the British, Italians and Turks invited the United States to do likewise on their own territories. Even John F. Kennedy himself accepted as a given that it was for the United States to employ its enormous hemispheric power to enforce what might, or might not, be permissible on the soil of neighbouring nations.

Meanwhile Washington expended billions of dollars on defence and intelligence, yet in early September its knowledge of the decision-making of the Kremlin and the Castro regime, and of developments on Cuba, was somewhere between poor and non-existent. In the case of Havana, they relied chiefly upon cables forwarded by the UK, Brazilian, Chilean and Dutch missions. At every turn of the looming Crisis, Kennedy and his advisers were attempting to read tea leaves to discern what their enemies might be thinking. Nor was this a difficulty unique to the Caribbean: later in Vietnam, and into the twenty-first century in Iran, Iraq,

Afghanistan and the Ukraine crisis, accurate and serviceable intelligence about the mindset of adversaries remained meagre. Again and again, governments have made world-shaking decisions based upon misinformation. The fallibility of giant state information-gathering machines bewilders historians, and all nations have regularly suffered from its consequences. Every sensible national leader listens to their intelligence chiefs, but none make critical judgements solely on the basis of their claims.

Finally, even after acknowledging the failures above, we should be impressed by the quality of the discussions within the White House, both then and later. These showed men of the highest abilities, reflecting mostly prudently upon their choices. This was certainly not true of them all, especially the military. David Halberstam ironically titled his great book on the origins of the Vietnam nightmare *The Best and the Brightest*, because those same clever folks later made misjudgements about Indochina which cost hundreds of thousands of lives. But the world has reason to recall with respect the leaders around the tables in the White House during the Crisis about to unfold – even the ones who called it wrong. Those who doubt this assertion should ask: did debates of remotely comparable openness take place within the Kremlin, at any time in the history of the Soviet Union, or of today's Russian Federation?

Even those sceptical of some US Cold War claims and gambits, especially in regard to Cuba, should acknowledge the irresponsibility of the game Khrushchev chose to play; of his pigeon-chested posturing, as his Cuban operation was unfolding. The Soviet leader persuaded himself that he was conducting a clever, marvellously subtle manoeuvre. While Khrushchev was meeting Stewart Udall and Robert Frost on the Black Sea, in Moscow Marshal Malinovsky drafted a recommendation to reinforce the Cuba expeditionary force with IL-28 nuclear-capable bombers, together with the *Luna* missiles designed for tactical use in the event of a US invasion and FKR-1 cruise missiles, both equipped with nuclear as well as conventional warheads. Khrushchev's 7 September approval of the dispatch of these units represented a defiant response to President

Kennedy's public warning three days earlier: the Soviet Union, in the face of US threats of action against Cuba, was deploying war-fighting nuclear weapons that increased the risk of catastrophic consequences from a clash in the Caribbean.

Marshal Malinovsky further raised the stakes by sending new orders to Gen. Pliev, explicitly avowing the prospect of using such arms to repel American attacks. Soviet forces should be prepared, he said, 'upon signal from Moscow, to deal a nuclear missile strike to the most important targets in the [US]'. On 8 September, a message from the General Staff to Pliev raised the contingency of contact being lost between Moscow and Havana in the event of an American amphibious landing: 'You are permitted to make your own decision and to use the nuclear means of the *Luna*, IL-28 or FKR-1 [cruise missiles] as instruments of local warfare for the destruction of the enemy on land and along the coast … and to defend the Republic of Cuba.' How could the dispatch and receipt of orders couched in such language not arouse in Pliev and his officers expectations of imminent collision with the forces of the United States? How could they fail to believe that they should expect at any moment to have to fight for their lives?

On 17 September a U-2 mission over the offshore Isle of Pines was authorized by the president, but 'solid undercast' forced the pilot to abort – for all the wonders of the high-flying aircraft, its camera lenses could capture only that which was visible beneath the fuselage. Next day Sherman Kent, chief of the CIA's crystal-gazing cell ONE, presided over a meeting at which he invited his entire staff to comment upon, and to give personal opinions about, McCone's judgement that the Soviets were placing offensive missiles in Cuba. The latest SNIE – strategic national intelligence estimate – questioned this, suggesting that it was more plausible that the Soviets were building a submarine base. One of those present, Ken Absher, recalls that no one there backed McCone's view.

Kent was an Ivy Leaguer, a veteran of the wartime OSS, who chewed tobacco and favoured loud ties worn loose with an open-neck shirt. He was once described by a colleague as 'perhaps the foremost practitioner of the craft of analysis in American intelligence history'. Now he told the meeting: 'We can't just tell the President that we think the Soviets will put missiles in Cuba because Khrushchev is a son-of-a-bitch. The President knows he is a son-of-a-bitch.' He added that the evidence to support McCone's hunch simply wasn't there. Later, Kent wrote an essay in which he described the lack of humint available from Cuba on 18 September, though several relevant reports came in later.

A more important point is made by Kent's then subordinate Kenneth Absher: the ONE group issued its 18 September assessment on the assumption that regular U-2 flights were taking place which continued to reveal no strategic missile sites. This was not the case: no *successful* U-2 missions had been carried out. Kennedy and his courtiers later asserted that there was nothing the administration could have done any sooner, had the missile deployment been discovered earlier. Yet an earlier U-2 flight over western Cuba would have exposed the missiles before they came close to becoming operational.

During the weeks that followed, Kennedy sustained his declared policy of matching big-picture firmness of purpose with tactical caution. On 15 September, he told journalists there was no justification for unilateral US military action against Cuba. He did not respond to a 20 September 86-1 Senate resolution authorizing the use of force against Cuba if foreign-installed weapons there threatened US security. The CIA's ONE group delivered its new SNIE report, following up on the meeting chaired by Sherman Kent, which concluded that for the USSR to deploy nuclear ballistic missiles in Cuba 'would be incompatible with Soviet practice to date and with Soviet policy as we presently estimate it. It would indicate a far greater willingness to increase the level of risk in US-Soviet relations than the USSR has displayed thus far.'

A 28 September letter from Khrushchev to Kennedy made new threats about forcing the Berlin issue: 'The abnormal situation ... should be done away with.' This was a deliberate deception, to distract attention from Cuba, though it also complained of American threats against the island, which 'give ground to draw a conclusion that the US is evidently ready to assume responsibility for unleashing nuclear war'. The letter emphasizes the reckless-ness of the mood in the Kremlin. The more spectacularly and cynically the Americans were now deceived by Soviet behaviour, the greater must be their rage when this was laid bare. On the 28th also, McNamara returned from a visit to Berlin to report that tensions there were as bad as those in Korea during its war a decade earlier.

The president had summoned to the White House 'Chip' Bohlen and Llewellyn Thompson, two of America's most respected recent envoys to the Soviet Union. Anatoly Dobrynin described Thompson as 'the best American ambassador in Moscow during the entire Cold War'. Kennedy recalled Robert Frost's reported words from Khrushchev that the US was 'too liberal to fight', a line that still rankled. The president demanded: 'Why would [the Soviet leader] say that?' Khrushchev, responded Bohlen, probably 'thinks that the local military situation in Berlin is entirely in his favour', and that fear of nuclear war could cause the US 'to back away'; that if he moved against Berlin 'there'll be a great whooping and yelling around but that nothing will happen'.

As for Cuba, Bohlen thought Castro was feeling nervous about a US move against him, after the Russians rejected his request to join the Warsaw Pact. The president interjected: 'Why [did the Kremlin say no]?' Bohlen said: 'Because this is too much for the Russians because they're not sure what the United States might do … and they don't want to be committed to go to war over Cuba … [Yet] the Russian mind does not have the foggiest comprehension of the American political process. They really believe that you are sort of the dictator of the United States and can do any damn thing you want.' Bohlen also guessed, shrewdly, that the Soviet leader was feeling the heat of ideological pressure from Mao: 'The Chinese have been constantly attacking Khrushchev from the left, which is the first time in Bolshevik history that this has ever happened.'

Kennedy expressed his fears that, if a showdown came and the US moved against Cuba, the Russians would retaliate by seizing West Berlin. 'Well, they might have, Mr. President, and this might have led to general war. But I think the situation is getting to the

point where there are so many places ... where, if we take certain
kind of forcible actions, the Russians can retaliate ... We tend to let
the Berlin situation dominate our whole action. But this is what the
Russians are clearly trying to do.'

He suggested that, at every point, Khrushchev's aim was to test
US resolve – but without risking general war, a view Llewellyn
Thompson shared. Kennedy concluded the meeting by saying, 'I
suppose it just comes back to ... a question of how do we convince
him that the risk [of general war] is there.' Herein, of course, lay the
agonizing debate at the heart of the October Crisis.

Three significant and relevant humint reports from Cuba
reached the CIA in late September and early October. The first
came from a source who described a 9 September encounter with
Castro's personal pilot, who said that 'we have 40-mile-range
guided missiles, both surface-to-surface and surface-to-air ... There
are also many mobile ramps for intermediate range rockets. [The
Americans] don't know what is awaiting them.' This report was
circulated on 20 September, following transmission delays: it
convinced Kenneth Absher, at least, that McCone's hunches were
right. A second fragment came from the debriefing of a refugee
who claimed to have seen twenty trucks with long trailers, driven
by Russians, in the Mariano district of Havana on the night of 12
September. He drew sketches of missile-shaped artefacts aboard the
trailers. When shown a picture of an SS-4, he claimed a match. This
report was disseminated only on 27 September. Another humint
snippet was distributed on 1 October, stating that on 7 September
a large area in Pinar del Río province had been declared a restricted
military zone, where 'very secret and important work is in progress,
believed to be concerned with missiles'. This was sent in a letter
containing secret writing, mailed to a cover address in 'a foreign
city'.

As early as 1 October, more than two weeks before the Soviet
missiles were discovered in Cuba, McNamara warned the US Navy,
in the person of Atlantic Fleet commander Admiral Robert
Dennison, 'to be prepared to institute a blockade of Cuba'. That
same evening Dennison ordered his commanders to 'take all feasi-

ble measures necessary to assure maximum readiness to execute [air strike plans] by October 20'. On 3 October McCone, back from honeymoon, convened a meeting of the Cuba Special Group, attended by Rusk, Bundy and McNamara. At this he expressed fierce anger and dismay that no successful U-2 overflights had taken place. He said he would be informing the president that it was impossible to maintain that there was no evidence of offensive missiles, when no US aircraft had been able to photograph the critical western areas of Cuba. Rusk nonetheless still stubbornly resisted overflights: like many members of the US foreign policy establishment, he remained haunted by memories of the humiliation inflicted by the 1960 U-2 shootdown over Russia. Bundy argued for peripheral photography – relatively low-altitude surveillance of Cuba by aircraft flying offshore. McCone insisted, rightly, that this could not do the job.

On 6 October Robert Kennedy met Georgy Bolshakov, who said that during a recent Black Sea vacation he had met Khrushchev and Mikoyan. The first secretary had authorized him to assure the US president that 'no missile capable of reaching the United States will be placed in Cuba'; only SAMs were being installed. Why did Khrushchev choose to squander so much diplomatic capital in his relationship with the US, by telling direct lies through RFK? All nations sometimes tell untruths to each other, publicly as well as privately: JFK and his intimates had told many, following the Bay of Pigs. The answer, in the context of September–October 1962, must be that the Soviet leader believed that the prospective strategic prize – a crushing defeat inflicted upon America's young president – was worth the bankrupting of trust between Washington and Moscow. The consequence, as Ted Sorensen later wrote, was that having come to rely on the Bolshakov channel 'for direct private information from Khrushchev, he [RFK] felt personally deceived. He was personally deceived.'

In Washington the evidence of Soviet activity in Cuba, and consequent sensitivity as the mid-terms approached, mounted daily. A London *Times* report was headlined: 'Cuba Dominating American Elections. Caution Unpopular as Pressure on Mr.

Kennedy Mounts'. The paper's senior US correspondent mused: 'The testimony of Under-Secretary of State Mr. George Ball, that Cuba does not pose a military threat to the United States, is ignored because of a queer kind of national myopia that prevents a clear and dispassionate view of Cuba. This is a disease that has bothered the republic almost since its birth; even Thomas Jefferson ... always thought that Cuba should have belonged to the United States.' The *Times* writer pointed out that it was the US, and not Russia, that maintained a large military base in Cuba.

This view was characteristic of British, and indeed wider European, scepticism about America's Cuba fixation, as foreigners saw it. In Washington, however, patience had expired. On Capitol Hill, a growing number of legislators were agitating about the perceived threat. For instance, on 6 October freshman congress-man Bob Dole of Kansas wrote a note into the *Congressional Record*: 'Today, just 90 miles from the United States, anti-aircraft missiles are being installed by Soviet technicians ... it is becoming increasingly apparent that the Soviet Union is establishing a base in the Western Hemisphere from which an attack might one day be mounted against the United States. Who can say that the next step will not be the installation of short- and intermediate-range ballis-tic missiles?'

The pressures on the White House for action had become irre-sistible. The CIA, still against the wishes of Rusk and McNamara, had launched U-2 flights on 17, 26 and 29 September, none of which had been successful. Two peripheral flights on 5 and 7 October did not cover the critical regions of western Cuba, and the second was aborted with a fuel malfunction. It had become clear to all the principals that the time was past for pussyfooting about aerial reconnaissance. At a further meeting of the Cuba policy group on 9 October, the newly-installed CIA 'Special Activities' director Col. Jack Ledford gave a briefing about the risks to a 'U-bird' over Cuba from Soviet SAMs. The Agency reckoned there was a one-in-six chance that such a plane would be shot down – the real odds were much shorter, if the Russians made the decision to destroy an intruder. Yet no other US aircraft or drone was capable of doing the business. It was agreed that there should be four brief north-south U-2 overflights, one immediately addressing the western portion of the island, together with another area pinpointed by a humint report of missile activity.

There was a petulant dispute between the CIA and USAF, about whose personnel should fly the sorties, which caused Mac Bundy to observe irritably to the CIA's 'Pat' Carter, 'Looks to me like two quarrelling children.' It was eventually agreed that air force pilots would execute future Cuban missions, because if a plane was lost, it was deemed unacceptable for the CIA's civilians to be found aboard. Two senior reconnaissance pilots had U-2 experience, Majors Rudy Anderson and Steve Heyser. Anderson, however, was recovering from a shoulder injury, and thus it was Heyser who was flown on 10 October to Edwards Air Force Base in California, where the CIA's 'U-birds' were based.

Next day, the 11th, John McCone showed the president photographs of crates, presumably carrying IL-28 bombers, being loaded onto the deck of a Soviet vessel which had since arrived in Havana. Kennedy requested that the CIA director should sit on this intelligence until after the mid-terms, now less than a month away, to avoid raising the nation's blood pressure. When told that this was impossible, because the photos had already been disseminated to several military and intelligence headquarters, he asked McCone not to make too much of it.

The focus of action now shifted to a desolate runway in California where stood parked one of America's supreme aeronautical achievements, the flying wing with an engine and cockpit capable of operating far higher than any other manned aircraft in the world. Thirty-five-year-old Steve Heyser spent two days refamiliarizing himself with the technology, while waiting for the weather to clear over Cuba. Considerable logistical confusion prevailed at Edwards, about who was in charge – the USAF had sent down its own launch crew for the mission, dispossessing the CIA's technicians. Heyser himself was immensely experienced. A Korean combat veteran, he was now committed to the first of what became a historic series of photographic sorties over Cuba. His mount was a U-2F, with higher-thrust engines that delivered an extra 5,000 feet of altitude. It was CIA property, hastily repainted with new identification symbols as 'USAF 66675'. On the night of 13 October, two hours before take-off, Heyser began donning his pressure suit and painstakingly assembling his equipment. He finally climbed the ladder into his cockpit at Edwards half an hour ahead of midnight. After lifting into the night sky for the 'Brassknob' mission designated #3101, he maintained radio silence throughout the long run to Cuba, breathing 100 per cent oxygen. 'He met the sun over the Gulf of Mexico, and flew over the Yucatán Channel before turning north to penetrate denied territory,' wrote U-2 historian Chris Pocock. 'The weather was roughly as forecast: 25 per cent cloud cover. He was flying the maximum altitude profile, and by this time the U-2F had reached 72,500 feet. There was no contrail. Heyser had been briefed to scan the driftsight for Cuban fighters or, worse still, a SA-2 heading his way. If so, he was briefed to turn sharply towards it, and then away from it, in an S-pattern that would hopefully break the missile radar's lock.'

Heyser turned to coast in across the island. His huge 'B' camera, with a focal length of thirty-six inches, had been pre-programmed on the ground, so that the pilot had discretion only to alter lens angles – vertical, low or high oblique. It carried two canisters, each loaded with five thousand feet of film that exposed nine-inch by nine-inch frames. Each roll snapped pictures from seven different positions, producing a stereo image eighteen inches square. In the cockpit the pilot heard successive thumps as the camera automatically switched angle to cover a great swathe of terrain below. The resolution attained by the images was astounding: in fair weather, objects less than three feet square were distinguishable on the ground.

Heyser had been six years in the U-2 programme, and said of the Cuban sortie: 'It's the type of work we'd been preparing for all that time. It felt like … it was another day's activities, except you could hardly get away from the idea that it was considerably more important.' The aircraft made a single pass over Cuba, lasting just seven minutes, on 'an exceptionally good day weatherwise'. To the pilot's unbounded relief, he completed the overflight without interference from the ground defences, to which he was vulnerable for twelve minutes. He then turned north to land at McCoy AFB, Orlando, Florida, at 9.20 a.m., seven hours after take-off.

Heyser had exposed 928 frames. The eight cans carrying his main camera's images were hand-carried to Washington by SAC intelligence chief Brigadier Robert Smith, in a KC-135 aircraft. On landing, there was another absurd little turf squabble: it was found that the officers sent to take the film for processing at Navpic, a US Navy facility at Suitland, Maryland, were not named on Smith's list of authorized recipients. They all sat there for thirty minutes, while this issue was sorted out. Processing was a painstaking task, carried out during Sunday night, because duplicate prints had to be produced on clear acetate that could be laid out on light tables for assessment.

Only at mid-morning on Monday did the pictures reach the National Photographic Intelligence Center in the Steuart Building, a nondescript Washington government facility at 5th and K Streets, on four floors above an auto showroom. Meanwhile Maj. Gen. Robert Breitweiser, the USAF's assistant chief of staff for intelligence, was woken early. He went down to the Pentagon and waited outside the offices of Robert McNamara and Max Taylor, to brief them on their arrival. Even though the photos had not yet been subjected to analysis, 'it was evident that this was going to shake the bushes, and it did'.

Low-resolution images from the U-2's navigation tracker camera had been hijacked to SAC's Offutt base in Nebraska, and within hours were being studied independently by Gen. Power's analysts. The bomber chiefs later sought credit for having been first to spot the missiles on Cuba following Heyser's flight. Today's U-2 historical experts reject as implausible this version of the story, which merely emphasizes the bitter rivalries within the US defence establishment.

In Washington McNamara, Taylor and Breitweiser, recognizing that something big was coming, set off for meetings with the CIA in their private cars 'to avoid the outward appearance of a lot of furious activity, although it was indeed furious'. The airman was among many service officers still embittered by the Kennedys' refusal to authorize US air support for the Bay of Pigs. When the first of what became a plague of hijackings of civilian airliners to Cuba by Castro supporters took place on 1 May 1961, the president had allegedly suggested to the USAF that its fighters might fire across the planes' bows to persuade them to descend, a remark that provoked the air chiefs' scorn. Eighteen months on, they remained sceptical that the White House's principal occupant had acquired balls.

The U-2 images were scrutinized at the NPIC by three two-man joint service teams, led by the CIA's Vince Direnzo, a thirty-three-year-old Pennsylvanian. On that morning of 15 October the tension in the Steuart Building was electric, as interpreters pored over their light tables with growing excitement and alarm. It appears to have been Direnzo himself who focused upon the extraordinary length of the big tubes visible in some frames showing Soviet sites in Cuba. Nothing like them had been seen following any earlier reconnaissance mission: they were much larger than SAM ground-to-air weapons. In the archive, missile expert Jay Quantrill found pictures of Soviet SS-4 MRBMs being towed through the streets of Moscow in May Day parades. The tubes Major Heyser had snapped the previous day looked astonishingly like a match for the SS-4s, missiles capable of delivering nuclear warheads to targets across the entire south-eastern United States, as far afield as Cincinnati, Houston and Washington DC.

For confirmation, the Americans turned to the remarkable dossiers of technical intelligence supplied to them by Col. Oleg Penkovsky, Soviet GRU officer turned double agent. In 1961–62 Washington's entire understanding of Soviet nuclear capability was transformed by Penkovsky, the most significant source acquired by Western intelligence thus far during the Cold War. The CIA ran the forty-two-year-old rocket specialist jointly with Britain's SIS – his principal courier was Welsh businessman Greville Wynne. The GRU man had passed to the Westerners 111 rolls of film containing ten thousand pages of documents including operating manuals for the SS-4 and SS-5 missiles before he was betrayed by an American double agent in the summer of 1962, thereafter working under close surveillance from Soviet counter-intelligence.

The importance of Penkovsky was that his information established, with a wealth of detail, that the Soviet Union's nuclear arsenal was far less potent than Khrushchev had always pretended. A senior British intelligence officer said: 'Penkovsky really did change the way we saw things. He solved many mysteries. We were quite wrong in our existing perceptions.' U-2s had overflown the Soviet Union between July 1956 and May 1960. In August of the latter year, the first Discoverer satellite began to orbit the earth, providing unprecedentedly detailed coverage of installations across the Soviet homeland. The Americans were initially baffled to identify no ICBMs – inter-continental ballistic missiles. Only slowly did they come to understand that this was because, contrary to Khrushchev's repeated boasts, these did not then exist. Only very slowly was a modest ICBM inventory deployed: by September 1961 the CIA was making 'a sharp downward revision in our estimate of Soviet strength'. Penkovsky's data empowered NSA's photo-interpreters to assess the weapons they saw revealed by Major Heyser's images, soon reinforced by others taken during the days that followed. At 5.30 p.m. on the 15th Direnzo informed the NPIC's chief Arthur Lundahl: 'We've got MRBM's in Cuba.' Lundahl passed the news to CIA headquarters at Langley, and to deputy defense secretary Roswell Gilpatric.

It is hard to overstate the trauma that on 15/16 October struck the tightly-restricted Washington political and intelligence circle which became privy to the photo sensation. The CIA's ONE group responded with 'shock and anger', according to staffer Kenneth Absher. They had been wrongfooted. American leaders had made the cardinal error, in the eyes especially of Republicans, by trusting the assurances of a Soviet leader. GMAIC and JAEIC – respectively the US intelligence community's Guided Missile and Astronautics Intelligence Committee and its Joint Atomic Energy Intelligence Committee – began to meet daily. The Soviet Union, in the view of these Americans, and later in that of their entire nation, was

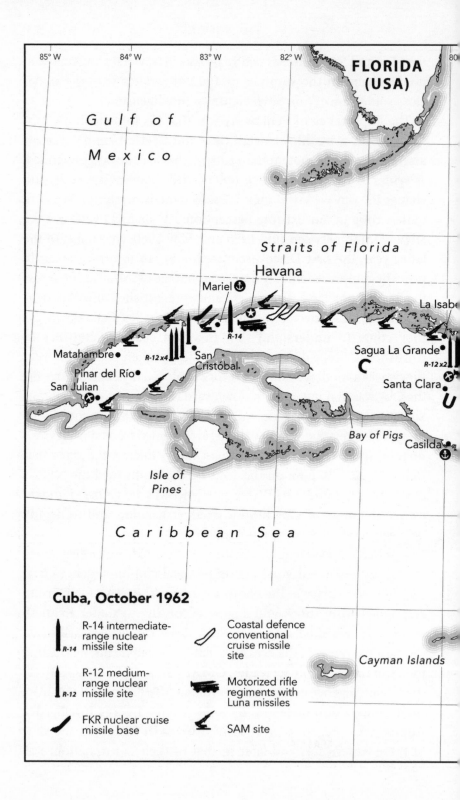

FLORIDA (USA)

Gulf of

Mexico

Straits of Florida

Havana

Mariel

La Isabe

R-14

Matahambre

R-12 x4

San Julian

San Cristóbal

Pinar del Río

Sagua La Grande

R-12 x2

Santa Clara

Bay of Pigs

Casilda

Isle of Pines

Caribbean Sea

Cayman Islands

Cuba, October 1962

R-14 intermediate-range nuclear missile site

R-12 medium-range nuclear missile site

FKR nuclear cruise missile base

Coastal defence conventional cruise missile site

Motorized rifle regiments with Luna missiles

SAM site

challenging the United States in its own backyard with the deadliest weapons in the history of mankind. Nikita Khrushchev was seeking to make a simpleton of John F. Kennedy.

Coincidentally, even as the analysts were peering through their illuminated magnifiers in the Steuart Building, Robert Kennedy presided at a meeting to review the Mongoose programme against Castro, a year after its inception. During the nineteen months that had elapsed since the Bay of Pigs, the CIA had continued to plan for a second invasion, while awaiting White House authorization for its execution. Langley sponsored repeated attempts to kill Castro by bomb, poison or bullet. Some six hundred CIA personnel were engaged in related activities, together with a much larger number of contract people.

Mongoose's principal instrument was the USAF officer Col. Edward Lansdale, among the wildest cards in America's pack, a former advertising man who had secured in the Philippines a largely undeserved reputation for skills in counter-insurgency and 'psyops'. One of Lansdale's characteristic stunts had been to plant corpses drained of blood, to convince superstitious local people that they were victims of vampires. The Cuba operation, centred upon a 1,500-acre base outside Miami, was directly overseen by an Agency veteran named Bill Harvey, whose effectiveness was impaired by advanced alcoholism. He routinely referred to the Kennedys as 'faggots' and 'those fuckers'. The Kennedys liked Lansdale, who to his credit had opposed the Bay of Pigs, but the colonel – in the words of a historian of the CIA – 'found it difficult to control the Miami station, whose over-funded and over-zealous staff launched absolutely pointless sabotage operations that only increased Castro's popularity'. There was no absurdity which the planners had not embraced, including earlier efforts to recruit mafia mobsters to kill Castro: Harvey personally supplied Italian-born John 'Handsome Johnny' Roselli with poison pills for this purpose. Lansdale's cavortings caused him to be dubbed by his staff 'F-M', meaning 'the Field-Marshal'. The Kennedys christened him, with ironic respect, 'The Ugly American', following the 1958 novel of that title, about Cold War chess games in South-East Asia.

The CIA's Miami base was home to hundreds of staff handling several thousand real or fictional agents, scores of vehicles, two planes, boats for infiltrating personnel, copious supplies of arms and explosives, all costing the American taxpayer $50 million a year. Its operations boss was thirty-five-year-old Ted Shackley, highly regarded by the Agency, and now convinced, like his Cuban exile trainees, that this time around the Kennedy administration was serious about getting rid of Castro. The moral odium which attached to the Agency's activities was less damaging to US interests than their egregious failure. The attorney-general expressed the president's dissatisfaction that so little had been achieved. At a November 1961 meeting in the White House Cabinet Room, shortly before Richard Bissell and Allen Dulles were obliged to resign from the CIA, Robert Kennedy 'chewed out Bissell' for 'sitting on his ass and not doing anything about getting rid of Castro and the Castro regime'. This prompted the veteran spook to return to Langley and revive tired old assassination plans. America's 1959–62 activities against Cuba exposed the CIA as risibly incompetent counter-revolutionaries.

Meanwhile at the Pentagon, SAC's C-in-C Gen. Thomas Power, who had worked closely under Curtis LeMay in the wartime Pacific, was newly returned from a visit to Europe. Power, like LeMay, was an expert in wholesale destruction: on 9 March 1945, he had acted as airborne director of the great B-29 firebombing attack that destroyed most of Tokyo. On 15 October, at a Cuban meeting chaired by Maxwell Taylor, even before news of the missiles had been confirmed, Power, whose hobby was personally and privately to study photo mosaics of the Soviet Union in search of missile sites, echoed his boss in recommending 'that we should destroy their air order of battle and invade'.

JFK had certainly not renounced the option of a full-scale US strike against Cuba. Robert McNamara told the joint chiefs on 15 October that the president wanted 'no military action within three months', but added that 'he can't be sure, because he does not control events' – possibly meaning that the US must be ready to take a hand, if Castro was deposed or killed. Already, during the spring and summer, high-profile US Navy exercises had taken place in the Caribbean. It seems entirely plausible that Kennedy would have taken military action against Cuba, in pursuit of his own domestic political advantage, had he been confident that this would be successful. Everything about his presidency showed a determination to be seen by the American people and the world to be tough on communism. Media credentials later issued by the Americans in South Vietnam characterized their own and allied armies deployed there in support of the Saigon regime as 'Free World Forces'. American perceptions of their Caribbean posture were no different. Robert McNamara said years later to Russian historical conference attendees: 'If I were on your side … I can very easily imagine estimating that an invasion was imminent.' And that was before the thunderburst descended upon the White House next day, which rendered such an event frighteningly plausible.

6

Drumbeat

1 THE PRESIDENT IS TOLD

That Monday evening of 15 October, secretary of state Dean Rusk was hosting a formal dinner for the German foreign minister in the State Department's eighth-floor dining room, when he was slipped a note by a waiter. He went to the phone, heard the news, returned to resume a discussion of NATO. Then, at the first break, he signalled Paul Nitze, assistant secretary of defense, to join him for a private conversation. Out on the terrace overlooking the Lincoln Memorial, he told Nitze about the photos. Meantime Robert McNamara returned home from an evening with the Bobby Kennedys at Hickory Hill to meet analysts waiting with the Cuban images.

McGeorge Bundy finished shooing out guests attending his farewell dinner for 'Chip' Bohlen, who was quitting Washington to become US ambassador in Paris, then deemed a posting of matching importance to Moscow or London and more congenial than either. The national security adviser was called to the phone to talk to Ray Cline, a deputy director of the CIA. 'Those things we've been worrying about,' said Cline cryptically. 'It looks as though we've really got something.' Bundy knew instantly what his caller meant. The forty-two-year-old egghead was hawk-visaged, bespectacled, quizzical, ungenerous with meaningful smiles; so smooth and smart that you could have played pool on him. 'Mac' was a Boston Brahmin, a star at Groton, America's gilded prep school, then at Yale before shifting to Harvard. There he had become a precociously youthful dean, when invited to serve at the White House, heedless of his Republican background. In 1962 he was offered the presidency of Yale, and might have taken it had not Kennedy insisted that he was indispensable where he was.

It would be mistaken to call Bundy impatient of fools. He merely took it as a given that nobody else was as clever as he was. This explains why he was widely respected, not much loved, least of all on Capitol Hill, which he despised. Walter Lippmann, honorary high priest to the Kennedy White House, thought that Mac should have been secretary of state. It scarcely mattered what his title was, however. The important reality was that Bundy had the ear of the president. Moreover, whatever ruderies may be applied to him now as then, he was a big thinker about how the United States should best exercise the leadership of the Western world; mastery of what he, like many humbler Americans, was confident was the greatest force for good in the history of the planet. Back when he took his college entrance board exam aged sixteen in 1936, he refused to write essays on the two appointed subjects 'How I spent my summer vacation' and 'My favourite pet'. Instead, he wrote a piece lambasting the examiners for nominating such frivolous subjects, when twentieth-century America faced vast challenges that a new generation should learn to embrace.

The downside of Bundy, like others in the White House inner circle, was that for all the high intelligence, their understanding of other cultures was meagre. None among the group, indeed, had travelled abroad as widely as had their president, nor seen much of other peoples. Most knew little about swathes of their own compatriots – the Americans who inhabited the millions of square miles that lay between Harvard and Berkeley. Yet Bundy was a natural high functionary, a supreme 'can do' man, at a time when his country had a huge amount to get done. For the national security adviser, action represented virtue; passivity doubled as vice. That night of 15 October, he faced an immediate decision: should he call the president, who was exhausted? Kennedy had been up in New York state, campaigning for the mid-terms. Bundy exercised sense in favour of a reprieve. He decided that a few hours would make no difference; Kennedy needed his rest, before confronting the crisis that undoubtedly now lay ahead.

Next morning, Tuesday 16 October, Bundy entered the president's bedroom in the White House private quarters – the Mansion – where the tenant was still in his pyjamas and the children were watching TV. He had already flicked through morning papers heavily focused on Cuba. The *Washington Post* carried a front-page article attributing to 'Communist sources' a story that the West might make concessions in Berlin in return for a slowing of the Soviet build-up in Cuba. Former president Eisenhower had made a widely-reported speech in Boston, attacking the Kennedy administration's foreign policy record. On his own watch, said the old general grumpily, 'no Walls were built. No threatening foreign bases were established.'

Bundy reported to Kennedy his sensational news: there was 'hard photographic evidence that the Russians have offensive missiles in Cuba'. The president had always made it plain that he would not tolerate such a move. The Soviets had given assurances that they would not make it. Kennedy's first reaction was to say to Bundy: 'We're probably going to have to bomb them.' He felt personally betrayed by Khrushchev, saying: 'He can't do this to me.' Then he summoned his brother, who observed with statesmanlike restraint: 'Oh shit! Shit! Shit! Those sons-of-bitches Russians.' More sober Washington analysts were equally stunned: the Soviet initiative seemed disproportionate to any plausible strategic scenario in the hemisphere. 'The dominant feeling,' wrote RFK long afterwards, 'was shocked incredulity. We had been deceived by Khrushchev, but we had also fooled ourselves.' This was true enough, but the attorney-general followed it with an untruth: 'No official within the government had ever suggested to President Kennedy that the Russian buildup in Cuba would include missiles.' It was true that the CIA's Office of National Estimates had rejected the notion that the Soviets might deploy missiles. But John McCone had several times urged on the White House that this was Khrushchev's intention.

The president now dictated to Bundy a list of fourteen people whom he wished to attend a meeting that morning to discuss the Crisis. Almost all would become daily participants in the agonized, relentlessly tense debate that would continue through the days ahead. There was the national security adviser himself; under-secretary of state George Ball; Marshall 'Pat' Carter (for that day only, deputizing for the CIA director in John McCone's absence); treasury secretary Douglas Dillon; deputy secretary of defense Roswell Gilpatric; deputy under-secretary of state for political affairs Alexis Johnson; RFK; assistant secretary of state for inter-American affairs Edwin Martin; defense secretary Robert McNamara; assistant secretary of defense for international security affairs Paul Nitze; Dean Rusk; special counsel to the president Theodore Sorensen, the man who wrote most of JFK's words of state; chairman of the joint chiefs Gen. Maxwell Taylor; vice-president Lyndon Johnson.

Kennedy wished also to summon Republican lawyer John McCloy, who though not a member of the administration was a veteran of government, direct and sharp. It transpired that McCloy was about to leave on a business trip to Germany. Kennedy did not ask him to cancel, just said: stay in touch. The rest of the group, the big players, would become known to historians as Excom, short for Executive Committee of the National Security Council, though nobody afterwards remembered that name being used at the time. Mac Bundy later wrote: 'I know no member of [Excom] for whom this was not the most intense official experience of his life.'

Ahead of the meeting, Kennedy greeted an astronaut and his family; walked into Kenny O'Donnell's office just before 10 a.m. and taunted his aide: 'You still think the fuss about Cuba is unimportant?' O'Donnell, not yet apprised of developments, responded stoutly: 'Absolutely. The voters won't give a damn about Cuba.' Then the president gave him the secret headlines. 'I don't believe it,' said the aide. 'You'd better believe it,' said Kennedy. 'Ken Keating will probably be the next president of the United States.' Thereafter, O'Donnell's role in the Crisis became much less significant than Kevin Costner made it seem, acting the aide's part in the 2000 movie *Thirteen Days*. Nor, of course, did anybody know on that first morning that the Crisis would last Thirteen Days or Thirteen Weeks; nor whether its principals would find themselves translated into ashes at some moment in between.

The president then spent a scheduled half-hour with 'Chip' Bohlen, in the latter's guise as Paris ambassador-designate. He took the opportunity to show the diplomat the Cuban photos. Bohlen's immediate response was to urge caution: if America bombed and killed Soviet citizens, the Kremlin must feel obliged to respond, and to escalate. In Excom's subsequent discussions, the diplomatic as distinct from the military path through the Crisis came to be known for a while as 'the Bohlen plan'; air strikes were dubbed the 'fast track' option.

At 11.50 a.m., Kennedy was being kept company in the Cabinet Room by his five-year-old daughter Caroline when his advisers filed in, accompanied by Arthur Lundahl and other experts from the NPIC. After the child left, the intelligence men set up labelled photo displays on easels. John McCone was again out of Washington, attending a family funeral. Thus Marshall Carter led the briefing. He described missile sites identified at the southern edge of the Sierra del Rosario in west-central Cuba. The photos of one big new camp showed at least fourteen canvas-covered missile trailers, each of which the NPIC's revolutionary new computer told them was sixty-seven feet long. Lundahl pointed out launchers and launcher-erectors; a missile trailer backing up to a launch point. His missile expert, Sid Graybeal, explained that two types had been identified: an SS-3, which had a range of 630 miles; and an SS-4, capable of delivering a nuclear charge up to 1,100 miles. Nose cones – warheads – were not visible in the photos, and probably not fitted. Robert McNamara flagged a significant point: there was no sign of fencing which, he suggested, must surely be erected before nuclear weapons were stockpiled on the sites.

The meeting promptly agreed that more data and photos were needed. On McNamara's recommendation, the president immediately authorized further U-2 flights. He then invited the secretary of state to speak. Rusk opened by saying that this was, of course, a very serious development: 'One that we, all of us, had not really believed the Soviets could carry this far.' Something must be done, but surely not unilaterally: the interests of forty-two allies needed to be considered, any or all of whom could find themselves dragged in. The choices lay between an immediate, unannounced air strike against the sites, or a protracted diplomatic engagement. Rusk favoured involving the Organization of American States, and also dispatching a warning to Castro by a back-channel – perhaps the Canadian ambassador in Havana. They even considered communicating through the Brazilians, who had previously offered themselves as interlocutors on the general Cuban impasse, though in the event nothing would be done until 27 October.

Kennedy had formed a low opinion of the State Department, which he considered limp-wristed. He once complained: 'Dammit, Bundy and I get more done in one day in the White House than they do in six months.' Arthur Schlesinger complained that in paperwork, State's staffers still used the moth-eaten phrase 'Sino-Soviet bloc', when it was becoming ever more obvious that China and Russia were nothing of the sort – instead, deadly rivals. Rusk himself seemed opaque, even at moments of crisis. Averell Harriman remarked that Kennedy was more his own secretary of state than Roosevelt had been, and he'd worked for both.

But Rusk was no fool. His conduct in the days to come reflected a steadiness and good sense some other White House advisers would have done well to match. He urged briefing former president Eisenhower, to pre-empt the old general making hostile or inflammatory public comments. He also suggested consideration of a direct approach to Khrushchev, to signal the fact that 'there is an utterly serious crisis in the making here, and that [the Soviet leader] may not himself really understand that or believe that at this point. I think then we'll be facing a situation that could well lead to general war. Now, with that we have an obligation to do what has to be done, but to do it in a way that gives everybody a chance to pull away from it before it gets too hard.'

Robert McNamara began by proposing that if the US was to unleash an air strike against the sites, this must take place before the missiles became operational. Otherwise, he thought it plausible that they could be launched against the United States before bombs disabled them. Moreover, if there were to be air strikes, these must take in a range of targets that included airfields, fighters and potential warhead storage sites. Cubans, probably several thousand of them, would be killed – the defense secretary did not then mention inevitable Russian deaths.

McNamara referred the meeting to Gen. Maxwell Taylor, chairman of the joint chiefs. Taylor, during the days that followed, would show himself a hawk, albeit not as raptorish as the USAF's Curtis LeMay and the US Navy's Admiral George Anderson. A notably handsome man who made his reputation as a World War II Airborne corps commander in North-West Europe, the general became the most trusted military member of the Kennedy administration, and later served as an ambassador to Saigon under Lyndon Johnson. Throughout the early 1960s, no military man exercised greater influence on US governments. Taylor was certainly smart, poised. He exuded experience and fluency. Some of his fellow-soldiers, however, considered him a more gifted palace intriguer than commander or strategist. His judgement on delicate politico-military issues was imperfect, to put the matter politely. When the president asked sardonically at the Cabinet table, 'Who ever believed in the Missile Gap?', Taylor's was the only hand that went up. That morning, the general recorded later, the president 'gave no evidence of shock or trepidation resulting from the threat to the nation implicit in the discovery of the missile sites, but rather a deep and controlled anger at the duplicity of the Soviet officials who had tried to deceive him'.

The general told the White House meeting that the air force was keen to strike hard and quick, before the Soviet missiles could be camouflaged, protected or made operational: 'We must do a good job the first time we go in there, pushing a hundred per cent just as far, as closely, as we can with our strike.' He also proposed a naval blockade, to halt Soviet reinforcements of men and missiles, and reinforcement of the US base at Guantánamo Bay.

In his enthusiasm for air strikes, Taylor failed to raise several key points, which he left others to headline. First, it would be impossi-

ble for the target-finders to identify all the missile sites, equipment
and SAM defensive launchers ahead of the initial sorties. Second, as
argued above, aerial bombardment remained an inexact science.
There was no possibility that even a sustained air campaign would
remove all Soviet offensive capability in Cuba, whatever claims to
the contrary were made by Curtis LeMay. Finally, Taylor failed to
mention the inevitability of heavy Soviet casualties, together with
the likelihood of retaliation elsewhere. The civilians present grasped
all these issues during the minutes, hours and days that followed. It
seems to Taylor's discredit that he himself did not flag them at the
outset, given that for weeks already the chiefs had been debating
strike options against Cuba. America's most senior professional
military man claimed to be offering the president a solution to this
boundlessly complex problem. In reality, however, he and his
uniformed colleagues were proposing only an immensely chancy
expedient.

McNamara said that he himself would take a quite different view
about air strikes if it became known that the Soviets had nuclear
warheads on the missile sites. At the same time, however, 'we don't
know what kind of communications the Soviets have with those
sites. We don't know what kind of control they have over those
warheads.' Moreover, 'I think it's really rather unrealistic to think
we could carry out an air attack of the kind we're talking about ...
because we don't know where these [Soviet] airplanes are ... We
are fearful of these MiG-21s. We don't know what they're capable
of. If there are nuclear warheads associated with the launchers, you
must assume there will be nuclear warheads associated with aircraft
... We have a serious defense problem. We're not prepared to
report to you exactly what the Cuban air force is capable of, but we
must assume that [it] is definitely capable of penetrating, in small
numbers, our coastal air defense.'

On and on the discussion ranged, often touching the foremost
enigma – Soviet motive. The Americans were rendered more troubled by the cloak of secrecy and deceit beneath which this immense
Kremlin operation had been undertaken. Moscow's commitment
decision was obviously made many months earlier; shipments had

been in progress since July. And all that time, the Russians had been serving up to the American government and to the world both public and private assurances that they were dispatching only defensive armaments to Cuba. By also making threatening noises about Berlin, they flourished matadors' cloaks to divert American attention – and had succeeded. Throughout the coming days, in Washington anxiety would continue to be matched by fears of an imminent Soviet second thrust elsewhere. America's leaders were gnawed by a belief that if Khrushchev and his advisers had planned this grandstand play so cunningly, they must be nursing a next move – pursuing some purpose way beyond the deployment in Cuba.

So obsessed about the enclave city of West Berlin had Western leaders become since 1945 that it seemed plausible, seventeen years after Hitler's death in the bunker there, that the Cuban missiles represented a Machiavellian Soviet deception; that Moscow's big event was still to come, in Europe. As well as angered, the Americans were baffled. Rusk demanded: if Khrushchev was so smart, how could he so gravely misread the significance of Cuba to the US? Why had the Soviets made no attempt to camouflage the missile sites? Why, after installing SAMs, had they not shot down the American U-2s which photographed them? The answer to all these questions, of course, was that Khrushchev had launched Anadyr without the smallest attempt to think through its prospective consequences. The irresponsibility was breathtaking, and at this stage the Americans found this impossible to credit on its own terms.

At the 16 October meeting, McNamara said that before much else could be decided, especially about military options, it seemed critical to locate the nuclear warheads, though in the ensuing days the CIA was unable to achieve this. Bundy anticipated difficulties with NATO partners, when the story broke, if the administration decided upon drastic action – 'the amount of noise we would get from our allies saying that if they can live with Soviet MRBMs, why can't we'. Deputy under-secretary Alexis Johnson said that once the US committed to a rolling programme of air strikes, such as would be essential, there seemed nothing to lose by going the whole way and invading Cuba – 'You might as well think about whether we can eradicate the whole problem ... with just as little chance of reaction.' Max Taylor concurred: 'We should be in a position to invade at any time, if we so decide ... We should be thinking that it's all bonus, if we are indeed taking out [the Soviet] weapons.'

There was discussion about how long the missile revelations could be kept secret: no one doubted the sensational impact on the world, and above all on the American people, when news of the photos broke. Taylor said that the military planning chain could be restricted to around sixty people, while the CIA was confident of sustaining its own security. McNamara guessed – a good guess – that it would be impossible to sit on the story for more than a week. Bundy pointed out that Senator Keating had said on the floor of the Senate: 'Construction has begun on at least half-a-dozen launching sites for intermediate-range tactical missiles.' It was plainly a huge embarrassment for the White House that Keating now proved to have spoken so accurately, at a time when not only was the administration denying his claims, but its senior members believed their own denials.

Vice-president Lyndon Johnson, the big and inescapably Texan former Senate majority leader, was treated by the Kennedy inner circle with a cultural condescension even greater than that which was customarily afforded by US presidents to their Veeps, and he played only a marginal role in the Excom debates of October. Yet it is striking to note that Kennedy included him in the meetings, in contrast to the lofty disdain that Franklin Roosevelt displayed towards his own vice-president Harry Truman, who was not even briefed about the atomic bomb project until after FDR's death in April 1945, when he was suddenly informed of the spectre looming over Japan.

Johnson knew little about foreigners, but more than anyone else in the room about the politics of his own nation. He said that both the choices – talk or strike – were 'very distressing', but he favoured the latter, so long as the military agreed. He was doubtful about getting much alliance support from, for instance, the Organization of American States. He agreed with Bundy that the Europeans, confronted with the Cuban missile evidence, were liable to say: so what? The American people, however, would take an intemperate view: 'The country's blood pressure is up, and they are fearful, and they're insecure.' He reminded the others of the administration's repeated pledges that if the Soviet build-up on Cuba became a threat, America would act.

The president echoed Johnson's scepticism about the fortitude of America's allies: 'I don't know how much use consulting with the British ... I expect they'll just object. Just have to decide to do it. Probably ought to tell them, though, the night before.' During the days that followed Kennedy would change his mind about much, as would almost everybody around the table. But it is striking that his first instinct favoured unilateral US action, probably military. He said later: 'If we had to act in the first twenty-four hours, I don't think probably we would have chosen as prudently as we finally did.' RFK, likewise, was among several participants who afterwards emphasized the critical importance that the president and Excom were able to work secretly and relatively slowly towards a policy. 'If our deliberations had been publicized, if we had had to make a decision in twenty-four hours, I believe the course we ultimately would have taken would have been quite different and filled with far greater risks. The fact that we were able to talk, debate, argue, disagree, and then debate some more was essential in choosing our ultimate course.'

On that morning of 16 October, the attorney-general suggested that 'dropping bombs all over Cuba' promised to be a bloody, messy business, bound to kill a lot of people. If the US was going that route, why not just invade the island? When the president surmised that such an operation might take a month or two to plan and prepare, McNamara said no – they could launch in around ten days, following a preliminary air campaign. Taylor said they could then land ninety thousand men, by air and sea. The president asked: would that be enough? Taylor replied – unwisely and almost frivolously, in language such as Khrushchev liked to use – 'At least it's enough to start the thing going.'

Both then and later, all the men around the table spoke in ignorance of the fact that there were already more than forty thousand
Soviet personnel on Cuba. Moreover, at no time did they discuss
any sort of plan for the country's post-Castro governance, other
than subsequently to float a facetious proposal to make Robert
Kennedy mayor of Havana. Presumably they planned to dress up a
new regime from among the Cuban exiles in Florida. This insouciance was, as future events in many parts of the world would show,
a chronic flaw in Western interventions abroad: governments
treated them as tactical military problems, whereas in truth the
towering and intractable issues were political. When politics was
mentioned, naïveté and ignorance predominated: at that first meeting, McNamara raised the prospect that US air strikes against Cuba
might precipitate a nationwide uprising against Castro.

The president summed up the meeting: its members, and especially the military, must prepare for some mix of three possible
options: to talk, to bomb, to invade. He was in no doubt of the
unswerving objective of the administration: 'We're going to take
out these missiles.' It was merely a question of how. For the time
being at least, nothing would be said to either the OAS or NATO.
McNamara urged that there should be some approach to the
Russians, probably direct to Khrushchev, before a strike. As the
meeting wound up, the attorney-general asked Taylor how long it
would take for US troops to occupy Cuba. The general replied: 'I
would say that in five or six days the main resistance ought to be
overcome. We might then be in there for months thereafter, clean-
ing that up.'

It was a reflection of the desperate secrecy surrounding the Crisis
that day and indeed all week, to buy time for the policy-makers,
that the president was next obliged to attend a formal lunch for the
crown prince of Libya. He had to smile graciously through a ritual
of state while his mind raced upon what was plainly the gravest
crisis of his presidency – thus, indeed, of his life. Among the guests
was UN ambassador Adlai Stevenson. Afterwards, in the White
House family quarters, Kennedy showed Stevenson the U-2 photos,
and told him the options. The loquacious, instinctively dovish

Democratic veteran said: 'Let's not go into an air strike until we have explored the possibilities of a peaceful solution.'

Later in the afternoon, Kennedy attended meetings held at the State Department with 'Chip' Bohlen and Llewellyn Thompson, at which they wrestled with the intractable, supremely important question: what was the Soviet game? The lean, gaunt, measured Llewellyn 'Tommy' Thompson was an unusual American, not least because he commanded the liking and respect of Khrushchev, of whom he had seen more than had any of his fellow-countrymen. Born in 1904, he grew up on a ranch in Colorado, joined the Foreign Service, and in 1941 was posted to the wartime Soviet Union. He never spoke Russian as fluently as did – for instance – George Kennan, partly because he also served in other countries. But he performed with distinction as ambassador in Moscow between 1957 and July 1962, and for several years thereafter was retained by the State Department as its resident Kremlinologist. Thompson, married to artist Jane Monroe Goelet, was heard with respect at every Crisis meeting. He knew the principal adversary of the United States more intimately than did anybody else around the table.

Meanwhile at Justice – an ironic venue for such a discussion – Bobby Kennedy presided over a meeting on the progress of Operation Mongoose, the CIA's campaign to undo Castro. The attorney-general mused aloud how much support the dictator would get, if the US invaded Cuba. The group briefly considered the possibility of sending émigrés to assault the Soviet missile sites, a notion mercifully dismissed.

At the Pentagon, the chiefs of staff enthused about air strikes, whether or not the Soviet missiles were operational. They believed that Moscow had not started this thing with the intention of precip-itating a nuclear war. They were confident, as only men could be confident who were unburdened by ultimate responsibility for the fate of the world, that the Soviets would endure a rain of American bombs on Cuba without launching a general nuclear exchange which they must lose. RFK later wrote about his brother's attitude to the military: 'He was distressed that the representatives with whom he met, with the notable exception of General Taylor, seemed to give so little consideration to the implications of steps they suggested. They seemed always to assume that the Russians and the Cubans would not respond or, if they did, that a war was in our national interest.'

2 THE WARMAKERS

Throughout the Crisis, opinions about alternative courses of action ebbed and flowed. In those first days, much influenced by the confidence of the nation's foremost military men, the mood shifted in favour of responding to Khrushchev's outrageous insult – for so the Cuban deployment was perceived by every American decision-maker – with devastating force. In the White House at 6.30 p.m. on 16 October, the president led a second session of Excom, which began with a new intelligence briefing. At this, Bundy urged on Marshall Carter the importance of being sure of the CIA's facts, because of the gravity of the judgements that must be made. The meeting quickly agreed that the artefacts in the photos could not be other than MRBMs. Rusk said he and his department had decided that before any drastic action was taken it was essential to talk to US allies, both in Latin America and Europe, because of the likelihood that it would precipitate a Soviet response that must impact on others. Failing such dialogue, 'we could find ourselves isolated, and the alliance crumbling'.

McNamara said that to execute an air campaign starting the following week, the chiefs needed a 'Go' order by the weekend, or in any event twenty-four hours before the first bombs could be dropped. They were convinced that a limited strike would not complete the job; that a rolling campaign of perhaps seven hundred sorties a day would be needed, requiring both USAF and Navy aircraft. Taylor described the intention as 'to take it out with one hard crack', or rather five days of bombing.

McNamara then made one of his most important interventions of the Crisis. Instead of immediately bombing Cuba, he raised the possibility of first imposing a blockade on the island, to prevent the further import of offensive weapons. The defense secretary anticipated the enormous hazards attaching to immediate violent US action, any form of which seemed almost certain to 'lead to a Soviet military response of some type, some place in the world. It may well be worth the price. Perhaps we should pay that. But I think we should recognize that possibility.' Meanwhile Kennedy still nagged at the problem of when to tell the American people and the world, and whether first to communicate privately with Khrushchev: 'He must know that we're going to find out ... But he's initiated the danger, really, hasn't he? He's the one that's playing God, not us.'

The overwhelming, finally decisive objection to communicating privately with the Soviet leader was that such a move would pass the initiative back to Moscow: Khrushchev would be empowered to rush forward his own narrative to the world, before Kennedy broadcast the American one. Ted Sorensen said later: 'I tried to write a letter that would precede our taking any action. But we never could find a formula that didn't appear to be an ultimatum or that didn't allow Khrushchev to delay responding while the missiles became operational or while he took some other kind of action. It proved impossible to do, and so we gave it up.'

Rusk and Bundy voiced agreement that the Russians were unlikely to risk nuclear war. But there remained around the table a lingering and troubled consciousness that Khrushchev, by deploying the missiles, had already acted in a way the US supposed unthinkable. What further unthinkable step might he undertake? Bundy and the president recalled that John McCone was the one member of the inner circle who had predicted the current developments. Now the national security adviser posed a general question, beyond the meeting's agreed determination to remove the missiles: what was the impact on the United States of the Cuban deployment? Did it change the strategic balance?

McNamara said that, although the chiefs of staff thought that it did, 'my personal view is: not at all'. The defense secretary embraced a supremely rationalist position, such as he sought to identify on all issues. The threat to the United States was little increased by the installation of Soviet nuclear weapons on Cuba, he argued. The US owned five thousand nuclear warheads, while the Soviets had only an estimated three hundred. An extra forty in Cuba changed nothing. As submarine-launched missiles formed an increasingly important element of both superpowers' armouries, such invisible mobile launch platforms would soon be roaming the oceans surrounding the North American continent at will, as well as those bordering the Soviet Union. What mattered most to the strategic equation of 1962 was the absolute number of missiles each side possessed, a balance that was still steeply tilted in America's favour.

Max Taylor asserted his disagreement with the defense secretary. He said that the missiles 'can become a very, rather important, adjunct and reinforcement to the strike capability of the Soviet Union. We have no idea how far they will go.' He added that to the American people it would seem enormously important that they now faced enemy nuclear missiles sited next door, rather than back in Russia. The president, in an impulsive but telling moment, said: 'That's why it shows the Bay of Pigs was really right. If we had done it right. That was [a choice between] better and better, and worse and worse.' Taylor welcomed the admission, saying: 'I'm impressed with this, Mr. President. We have a war plan over there for you. [It] calls for a quarter of a million American soldiers, marines and airmen to take an island we launched 1,800 against a year and a half ago. We've changed our evaluations about it.'

The US military and Taylor himself had been nurturing a proposal to double up on, or rather multiply many times, the Bay of Pigs. They doggedly addressed Castro's Cuba as a kinetic problem, to be resolved by soldiers, sailors and airmen. The case in their defence is that military men advising governments have a duty to offer military options, plans and scenarios. It is then for the nation's political leaders to make the choices between peace or war. Denis Healey, Britain's ablest defence minister of the post-war era, once observed tartly that he considered such decisions entirely political: he rejected any attempt by the uniformed military to influence them, as distinct from executing them. John F. Kennedy and his advisers were of the same mind, happily for humankind.

The president now articulated some of his own heart-searching. The Soviets, he said, appeared to have seized upon his public declaration that the US had no intention of invading Cuba, as giving them licence to act in the way they now had. He and the other civilians, at this early stage, certainly did not rule out war, but proposed to explore a range of options. Kennedy closed this first day of White House meetings by instructing that plans should be prepared for limited air strikes certainly against the identified missile sites – which he defined as proportional 'punishment fits the crime' – and possibly also against Cuban airfields.

Yet Robert McNamara, whose career would later come to be defined by his association with Vietnam, and whose reputation would indeed be destroyed by that conflict, was a key figure in promoting more cautious policies. He asserted that the president and his advisers, in their discussions thus far, had not talked enough about the consequences of starting a war. 'I don't quite know what kind of a world we live in after we have struck Cuba, and we've started it … Now after we've launched fifty to a hundred sorties, what kind of a world do we live in? How do we stop at that point? I don't know the answer to this. I think tonight State and we ought to work on the consequences of any one of these courses of action which I don't believe are entirely clear to any of us.' George Ball interjected: 'At any place in the world.'

Max Taylor returned to the charge, expressing the chiefs' vehement opposition to limiting a strike programme. In their view, he said, either the US launched a full air campaign, to destroy the entire Soviet offensive capability on the island, or better not start. The chiefs were also keen to ensure that, if their forces were to attack, they should enjoy the advantage of complete surprise. JFK responded: 'Don't let the Chiefs knock us out on this one, General, because I think that what we've got to be thinking about is: If you go into Cuba in the way we're talking about … then you really haven't got much of an argument against invading it.' Taylor reasserted that he opposed invasion, but supported a major air campaign.

Robert Kennedy raised a new issue: how to stop the Russians sending in more missiles, even if the USAF destroyed those now in place? McNamara said that a blockade would be essential. RFK:

'Then we're going to have to sink Russian ships. Then we're going to have to sink Russian submarines.' Taylor: 'Right. Right.' The attorney-general suggested the possibility 'if we're going to get into it at all, whether we should just get into it, and get it over with, and take our losses. And if he [Khrushchev] wants to get into a war over this ... Hell, if it's war that's gonna come on this thing, he sticks those kinds of missiles in after the warning [given by the president in September], then he's gonna get into a war over six months from now, or a year from now on something.' RFK's first ideas about many things were often terrible: Adlai Stevenson, for instance, thus dismissed him as 'a bull in a china shop'. This seems unjust. Robert Kennedy vacillated no more and no less than did most others at Excom, and his ultimate endorsement of caution was wiser than the contrary counsel of some older men.

George Ball had an inspired moment. The under-secretary, a fifty-two-year-old Iowan, was a protégé of Stevenson who had worked on the wartime Strategic Bombing Survey in London for two years; later played a leading role in guiding Europe's end of the Marshall Plan. A smart man who nonetheless often lost arguments inside the administration, Ball now raised the possibility that Khrushchev believed the missiles would not be discovered; that he had planned to appear the next month at the United Nations, to spring a devastating surprise on the United States and the world. Nobody picked up on this, but of course his hunch represented the reality of Khrushchev's thinking.

Mac Bundy said he drew modest comfort from his own conviction that the Soviets would not allow Castro discretionary control of nuclear warheads. Ball agreed: 'I think Khrushchev himself would never, would never risk a major war on a fellow as obviously as erratic and foolish as Castro.' He then raised the prospect that the missiles in Cuba were intended as a trading ploy – maybe for concessions in Berlin.

There followed one of the most famous, or notorious, exchanges of the Crisis. Kennedy mused aloud: 'It's just as if we suddenly began to put a major number of MRBMs in Turkey. Now that'd be goddam dangerous, I would think.'

BUNDY: 'Well, we did, Mr. President.'

U. ALEXIS JOHNSON: 'We did it. We [also] did it in England.'

KENNEDY: 'Yeah, but that was five years ago.'

JOHNSON: 'That's when we were short. We put them in England too when we were short of [long-range] ICBMs.'

KENNEDY: 'But that was during a different period then.'

JOHNSON: 'But doesn't he realise he has a deficiency of ICBMs vis-à-vis our capacity, perhaps? In view of that he's got a lot of MRBMs and this is a way to balance it out a bit.'

Here, of course, the White House group stumbled upon a key factor in Khrushchev's thinking, and also the major weakness in America's moral and political position. Kennedy's remarks emphasized the unwillingness of the Excom folk to consider for more than a few moments the mismatch between what had been deemed appropriate strategic conduct by the US and its allies – the British and Turkish deployment – and their outraged rejection of similar action, now undertaken by the USSR and its Caribbean client. Bundy wrote later: 'In ways which Americans did not bother to explain to themselves, the prospect of Soviet thermonuclear warheads on a next-door island was simply insupportable.' The Americans also believed, with better reason, that there was an important distinction between their own missiles, openly sited under the terms of declared treaties with host allies, and the Soviet weapons, installed in deepest secrecy and amid a barrage of Kremlin falsehoods.

JFK concluded: 'Well, it's a goddam mystery to me. I don't know enough about the Soviet Union, but if anybody can tell me any other time since the Berlin blockade where the Russians have given us so clear a provocation, I don't know when it's been.' Kennedy soon afterwards left the Cabinet Room, while the others talked on. McNamara returned to his earlier remark, that went to the heart of the matter. He refused to regard this as a military issue, he said, because he did not see that the presence of the missiles in Cuba changed the nuclear balance, which was still drastically in America's favour. It was, instead, 'a domestic political problem'.

The defense secretary meant, of course, that the challenge for the president was how to manage the inevitable fierce reaction of the American people, when they were presented with news of missiles installed on the nation's porch. Kennedy had explicitly stated that if such weapons were deployed in Cuba, he would act. And so he now must. McNamara nonetheless favoured a blockade, accompanied by overt around-the-clock surveillance of Cuba, so that the Kremlin would quickly realize that the White House knew what the Soviet Union had done. The president should issue a statement before the world that if the Russians showed any sign of using the missiles placed in Cuba, the US would respond with a full nuclear strike against the Soviet Union. The defense secretary added a gallows humour line, such as would be heard more than once during the fearsome days ahead: 'Now, this alternative doesn't seem to be a very acceptable one. But wait until you work on the others.' He got his laugh.

When the session broke up, although there were more evening meetings at the State Department and the Pentagon – where McNamara slept that night – it was deemed essential for the key players to resume agreed schedules, to avoid alerting watchful journalists. At a final farewell dinner for Charles Bohlen at Joe Alsop's house, which the president attended, JFK pulled the guest of honour out onto the porch to discuss the Crisis, and also to vent his impatience with the perceived shortcomings of the State Department: 'Chip, what's wrong with that goddamned Department of yours? I can never get a quick answer.' Bohlen responded that foreign policy did not lend itself to fast fixes. The president whispered to the ambassador's wife Avis: 'I wouldn't be too sure you are leaving. I think I may ask you to stay.'

Bohlen urged upon Dean Rusk that such a change of plan would rouse suspicion; give the Soviets a clue to American knowledge. Rusk agreed. When Kenny O'Donnell rang Bohlen at the airport next morning to say that he was urgently needed at the White House, the envoy said that he was due to make a speech in New York, for which his plane was leaving in fifteen minutes: he must go. JFK, himself called to the phone, reluctantly assented: 'Go on. I guess we'll have to do without you.' Bohlen left behind a handwritten memo, urging the dispatch of a private letter to the Kremlin, to allow Khrushchev space to back off. An air strike, said the veteran, 'will inevitably lead to war'.

Several of the White House inner circle later rejected Bohlen's explanation for his decision to proceed with his scheduled sea voyage to France, among them Robert Kennedy: '"Chip" ran out on us, which always shocked me. That wasn't necessary. He could always have postponed it. But he decided to leave the country in a crisis.' Bohlen, nursing his haunting secret knowledge, did not enjoy the subsequent five days at sea – indeed, he was visibly in a high state of nerves. He always afterwards asserted that he had felt able to sail because he trusted 'Tommy' Thompson, his successor at the Moscow embassy, to give the president the same counsel of caution that he himself would have offered. In truth, Bobby Kennedy could have been right, that Bohlen departed because he felt that he had participated in enough world dramas; was content now to take up residence in Paris for a dignified, glamorous, yet relatively undemanding posting in which he remained for the ensuing six years.

On Wednesday morning, 17 October, at the State Department there was another meeting of some of the principals. George Ball reasserted his opposition to military action. He was convinced that Khrushchev simply did not understand the enormity of what he had done. Llewellyn Thompson, however, disagreed: he believed the Soviet leader was working up to a showdown on Berlin. Maxwell Taylor and the CIA's McCone, now back in Washington, supported Thompson. McCone then drove north to Gettysburg, to brief ex-President Eisenhower. The old general described the situation as 'intolerable', and promised his support for US military action.

JFK meanwhile carried out a scheduled campaign trip in Connecticut. That day he received a memorandum from Adlai Stevenson, urging the dispatch of emissaries to both Khrushchev and Castro, rather than a resort to armed conflict: 'To start or risk starting a nuclear war is bound to be divisive at best,' the UN ambassador wrote, 'and the judgements of history seldom coincide with the tempers of the moment.' He understood Kennedy's difficulty, he said, but then urged, in a heavily underscored passage: 'the means adopted have such *incalculable consequences* that I feel you should have made it clear that the existence of nuclear missile bases anywhere is negotiable before we start anything'.

The Kennedy team regarded the Democratic veteran as a weak man; a windbag; a loser, albeit a decent and intelligent one. In the same way the other notable dove, George Ball, often displayed wisdom, and would later do so again, by arguing passionately against escalation in Vietnam. Just as Ball failed to carry his point in 1965, however, he also made little impact on the deliberations of October 1962. Both he and Stevenson appeared to promote policies of words, not deeds, which must be perceived by most of the American people as inaction. Among many uncertainties in those first days of the Crisis, the one sure thing in the minds of John F. Kennedy and his advisers was that they had to be seen to do something. Forget any McNamarish niceties about what the missiles did, or did not do, to the global nuclear balance: the Kennedy presidency faced crippling and lasting damage to its authority, if American voters believed that the incumbent displayed weakness in this supreme test of his fitness to lead them through a showdown with the Soviet Union.

There were two significant outcomes of the meetings and planning sessions held on Wednesday 17 October. First, the joint chiefs produced a menu of five alternative air campaigns, listed by Roman numerals from I to V. Attacks on missile and nuclear storage sites would allegedly require only 52 sorties; the same, with the addition of IL-28 and MiG-21 nuclear-capable aircraft, 104 sorties. If other aircraft, SAM sites, cruise missiles and missile boats were included, 194 sorties; all military targets save tanks would require 474 sorties; and a full programme of military targets as a prelude to invasion, 2,002 sorties. Senior civilians who debated the military options and possible Soviet responses reported overwhelmingly in favour of giving a diplomatic warning before such action was undertaken. McNamara and Taylor, however, feared that any such prior alert would diminish the effectiveness of the air campaign.

Another outsider was that day admitted to the secret of the Crisis, and thus joined the select group of White House confidants – Dean Acheson. A long-time hawk, Acheson was the secretary of state who had persuaded Harry Truman to dispatch a US army to Korea in June 1950, and since urged successive presidents to make a demonstration in force over Berlin. He dismissed John J. McCloy, who favoured engagement with the Russians, as a Paul Revere forever warning of dire consequences – 'one if by land and two if by sea'. He himself favoured treating Moscow with 'intelligent neglect'. Now, when shown the missile photos by Rusk, he urged immediate bombing. The weapons, he said, 'are pointing at our hearts and ready to shoot'. It was folly to allow the Crisis to become protracted – the US must go for a showdown straightaway. It was a reflection of Kennedy's anxiety to engage the widest possible range of advisers that he consulted Acheson, whom he disliked: '[Dean] thinks that nothing has been done right since he left office,' he once confided to the journalist Teddy White.

After the first sessions, Acheson attended Excom meetings through the ensuing four days. When McNamara argued that the missiles presented no more of a threat than if they were sited in Russia, the veteran statesman snorted in disgust. 'Nonsense,' he said. 'Something should be done quickly.' Nonetheless, he was no admirer of the chiefs of staff – the Korean experience had soured him on the military: 'When you get soldiers talking about policy, they want to go further and further in a military way ... until their proposals are apt to be as dangerous as the original danger.' Acheson opposed invasion; instead he favoured those misnamed 'surgical air strikes'.

Some members of Excom, including the president and Dean Rusk, came and went during its deliberations, which exasperated the veteran: he thought such behaviour frivolous, during meetings of such gravity. He felt that Bobby Kennedy had started to fill Rusk's rightful role – when JFK was temporarily absent from meetings, his brother instead assumed control. This presumptuous thirty-six-year-old responded to the sixty-nine-year-old Acheson's call for surprise air strikes: 'My brother is not going to be the

[Japanese Gen. Hideki] Tojo of the 1960s.' The old man was exasperated by Kennedy's brashness, 'moved by emotional or intuitive
responses more than by trained lawyers' analysis'. Moreover, he
was scornful of RFK's Pearl Harbor analogy, saying that for 139
years the US had been warning other nations to keep their hands
off the Western hemisphere. 'Was it necessary to employ the early
nineteenth-century method, of having a man with a red flag walk
before a steam engine to warn people and cattle to stay out of the
way?' Bobby later wrote of Acheson: 'I would never wish to be on
the other side of an argument with him.' Yet there and then, that
was almost exactly where the attorney-general was.

The same Wednesday evening RFK and Ted Sorensen drove out
to the airport to meet the president, returning from his campaign
swing. They reported on the day's meetings, and gave him a list of
some twenty unresolved issues. JFK said that he would not re-enter
the discussions until next morning; then he went home, leaving the
others to rejoin the meetings in town. Several individuals drafted
statements of their personal opinions, including treasury secretary
Douglas Dillon, who favoured an immediate, unannounced air
strike. He wrote that the Soviet Union had 'initiated a test of our
intentions that can determine the future course of world events for
many years to come'.

George Ball contrarily restated his conviction that the missile
deployments changed nothing strategically, a view that commanded
little support among men as convinced of Cuba's specialness as
were many ordinary Americans. Ball, however, declared a proposition also articulated by Robert Kennedy, that would gain increasing
traction during the coming days. He opposed any military action
without warning: 'We tried Japanese as war criminals because of
the sneak attack on Pearl Harbor.' Unannounced bombing, 'far
from establishing our moral strength ... would, in fact, alienate a
great part of the civilized world by behaving in a manner wholly
contrary to our traditions, by pursuing a course of action that
would cut directly athwart everything we have stood for during our
national history, and condemn us as hypocrites in the opinion of
the world.'

Yet while Ball was not alone in emphasizing the objections to launching a new 'Day of Infamy', he slid out on a limb when he argued that the Cuban missiles changed nothing. Even McNamara had retreated from that proposition. The top tier of the Kennedy administration was united on a central point that would remain constant through the days that followed, with Ball the only dissenter: for domestic political if not strategic reasons, the missiles must leave Cuba. On Thursday morning, 18 October, the consensus among those who reassembled in the Cabinet Room at the White House was that direct military action – bombing, perhaps followed by invasion – would likely prove necessary. McNamara had sown a seed with his proposal for blockade, which would constitute a response without necessarily precipitating a shooting war. At 11.35 a.m. that day, however, when the meeting began, this course appeared the least likely to be adopted, because it was judged the weakest of the options available to the president. Most of the other big players favoured the chiefs' choice: to launch air attacks against the Soviet nuclear weapon installations on Cuba. To go to war.

7
'They Think We're Slightly Demented on This Subject'

1 BEHIND CLOSED DOORS

This was the phase of the Crisis during which posterity can see that the White House was a command centre seething with activity. It was then invisible, however, to all save a handful of Americans, and to everyone beyond the continental shores. Elsewhere the other players – Russians and Cubans – were passive, prey to gratifying delusions of their own cleverness and subtlety. Khrushchev was briefed daily about the progress of the build-up on Castro's island. Within the Kremlin's walls members of the Presidium watched Washington intently, seeking the first hint that its gambit had been unmasked, and detecting none. Those grey-suited men presented to the world their accustomed bland faces. Khrushchev received visitors, attended events, presided at policy discussions, issued threats. The pervasive theme of Soviet conduct was business as usual.

In Cuba likewise, Russian personnel went about their duties as they had done for weeks, labouring on the missile sites in incongruous check shirts and slacks or shorts with occasional breaks for sea swimming and tourism. Local people witnessed all the sweat-stained activity, but few grasped its significance. Margarita Ríos Alducín, a nineteen-year-old mother of a small baby who lived with her mother in Havana, gazed in bewilderment at troops and anti-aircraft guns deployed around the city, but 'I never realized how serious it all was.'

In capitals across the world, governments and their peoples noted increased tension in the Caribbean, but even such close allies as the British were oblivious that the US was pondering peace or war. On the morning of 16 October, the *Glasgow Herald* headlined a speech the previous night in Edinburgh by chief of defence staff Admiral Earl Mountbatten, in which amid nuclear stalemate he called for movement towards disarmament: 'It will be no use for the West to have enough nuclear weapons to destroy Russia several times over, if Russia has enough to destroy the West once,' said the naval veteran. The London *Times* headline on the 18th reflected the stubborn European obsession with matters German: 'MR KHRUSHCHEV ASKS FOR BERLIN TALKS: POSSIBLE VISIT TO U.S. NEXT MONTH'. That week British intelligence officers including Gen. Sir Kenneth Strong, director of the Joint Intelligence Committee, chanced to be conferring in Washington at top-secret bilateral meetings with their American counterparts. The CIA's Ray Cline afterwards recorded with almost pitying condescension: 'These British friends took several occasions ... to argue with me that the Russians would never put missiles in Cuba because of the risk to their interests in Europe.'

NSA director Gordon Blake placed Juanita Moody in charge of a round-the-clock operation, to produce twice-daily sigint updates on the readiness status of the Soviet and Cuban armed forces and defences, which were teletyped to US operational headquarters as so-called 'electrograms'. Moody said later: 'I felt ... that somehow I had spent all of my career getting ready for that Crisis.' Eavesdroppers monitored the movements and trans-missions of Soviet maritime traffic. Yet, valuable as was this information, huge gaps in American knowledge persisted. Washington still believed that there were five to ten thousand Soviet personnel in Cuba, instead of the real 43,000. Beyond its ignorance of the presence of nuclear-tipped *Luna* short-range weapons and FKR-1 cruise missiles, it had no idea of the orders given to local commanders about their use, which at this date included discretion to launch in the event of an American inva-sion. Soviet cargo vessels at sea were often mislaid for hours by US Navy plotters, between pinpoints secured by reconnaissance aircraft.

The first meeting at the White House on Thursday 18th began at 11.10 a.m., with an intelligence briefing that unveiled a new sensation: U-2 photographic cover of Cuba revealed hitherto undetected missile sites which indicated the presence of IRBMs – intermediate-range ballistic missiles – twenty-one miles south-west of Havana. This information transformed several of the earlier advocates of caution into hawks. Whereas earlier debates made much of the likely scepticism or outright hostility of US allies in the face of drastic US action, Dean Rusk now said that failure to respond to a threat of such magnitude 'would undermine our alliances all over the world'. The secretary of state still favoured an approach to Khrushchev ahead of military operations, because he 'might realize he's got to back down on this'. But if such an approach failed, 'a declaration of war on Cuba' might become necessary.

Robert McNamara said that, in the light of the new information, he had become even more opposed to limited air strikes, which he believed could not eliminate the threat. If there was to be an American assault on Cuba, he favoured a full invasion, though such advocacy presumed that the ballistic missiles were not yet operational. If they were – if these weapons now posed an immediate menace to the United States – then all plans would need to be reviewed. The defense secretary said that he wanted to reassert his earlier conviction, not shared by the chiefs of staff, that the nuclear deployment in Cuba did not change the strategic balance. The US administration did not face a heightened military threat: 'It's a political problem. It's a problem of holding the alliance together. It's a problem of properly conditioning Khrushchev for our future moves [and a] problem of dealing with our domestic public.'

The president then asked: 'Which is going to strain the alliance more: this attack by us on Cuba, which most allies regard as a fixation of the United States and not a serious military threat? ... An awful lot of conditioning would have to go on before they would support our action against Cuba, because they think we're slightly demented on this subject ... A lot of people would regard this as a mad act by the United States.' This was a most significant statement by Kennedy, reflecting a recognition of allied opinion of which some others around the table, and many more legislators on Capitol Hill, were oblivious or indifferent to. 'The trouble with American cabinet ministers,' Harold Macmillan once wrote fastidiously and characteristically condescendingly, 'is they are generally drawn from either the boardroom or the common room. But neither tycoons nor academics are skilled or sensitive in politics, especially the politics of other countries.'

The rest of the world was likely to share the view expressed earlier by McNamara that the deployment did not alter the East-West strategic fundamentals. Kennedy showed a sensitivity to the perceptions of other nations, different cultures, such as few other US presidents have matched. Only a man who knew the world, who had lived as he had lived and seen what he had seen, especially in Europe before World War II, could speak in such a fashion. During the days ahead most of America's allies, when the Crisis became known to them, expressed public support for US policy as a matter of alliance solidarity. In private, however, they – and especially the British – were unsympathetic towards what JFK characterized as America's Cuba 'fixation'.

Maxwell Taylor now spoke, to urge haste – to attack before the missiles became operational: he called for an invasion, and for the order for such action to be given soon. He no longer believed that air bombardment alone would suffice. The president returned to possible Soviet responses. For the first time, importantly, he mentioned the possibility of offering the Russians a swap: if they removed their missiles from Cuba, 'we'll take ours out of Turkey'.

Llewellyn Thompson voiced his fears about air attacks which must kill a lot of Khrushchev's people, thus almost obliging Moscow to respond: 'My preference is this blockade plan ... I think it's very highly doubtful that the Russians would resist a blockade against military weapons, particularly offensive ones, if that's the way we pitched it before the world.' The US would also demand the dismantling of the missiles already on Cuba: 'We should be under no illusions, this would probably in the end lead to the same thing. But we do it in an entirely different posture and background and much less danger of getting up into the big war. The Russians have a curious faculty of wanting a legal basis despite all of the outrageous things they've done ... I think the whole purpose of this exercise is to build up to talks with you, in which we try to negotiate out the bases.'

Robert Kennedy, in one of his hawkish moments, objected that a blockade could only work slowly: 'It's a very slow death ... and during that period of time you've got all these people yelling and screaming about it, you've got the examination of Russian ships and the shooting down the Russian planes that try to land there. You have to do all those things.' Thompson predicted: 'I think Khrushchev will deny that these are Soviet bases ... He'll say: What are you getting so excited about? The Cubans asked us for some missiles to deal with these émigré bases that are threatening, have attacked and are threatening attack ... These are not missiles other than defensive. They're much less offensive than your weapons in Turkey.'

Thompson later in the meeting urged a secret communication to the Kremlin, such as Khrushchev would be obliged to share with Presidium colleagues, such as might prevent him from flying a reckless solo course. The diplomat cited the precedent of the 1960 U-2 shootdown, 'where the [Soviet] military, who normally never talked to me, came over and tried to calm me down ... showing that they were concerned that Khrushchev was being impetuous and running risks'. Thompson's astute contributions both that day and later emphasized not only his personal quality, but the virtue in all foreign policy-making of informed diplomats, with long experience of a given region. Though George Kennan remains more famous, notably through his authorship of the 1946 Long Telegram from Moscow, creating the template for containment of the Soviet Union, Thompson exercised greater influence on the Cold War crises.

He was the only foreign ambassador ever to have been invited to Khrushchev's private dacha – as distinct from the official, government one. In his Moscow days, he proved himself a notably successful poker player. His close friend 'Chip' Bohlen said that 'Tommy's outstanding characteristic was decency', a manifestation of which was a willingness to treat the Soviet Union with a respect such as many Americans declined to confer on its often boorish representatives. Now, Thompson urged the White House gathering that, whichever option they adopted, 'make it as easy as possible for him [Khrushchev] to back down'. He favoured blockade. He also emphasized some straws in the wind: 'There are a lot of little signs – but I was always curious as to why he said he would defer [a renewed confrontation over Berlin] until after the [congressional] elections. It seems to me it is all related to this.' Here Thompson meant that Khrushchev would not have displayed such sensitivity to US politics, if he was about to start a nuclear war. Unlike George Ball, however, Thompson failed to guess that the Soviet leader had scheduled the big strategic surprise for his November UN speech.

The Americans chewed over and over their puzzlement about the clumsiness with which the Soviets had launched this play, moving massive missiles across barefoot, dirt-track Cuba with scant benefit of camouflage. Surely, mused the CIA's McCone, Moscow could not suppose that nobody in Washington would notice? Both JFK and Bundy returned to the possibility of offering Khrushchev a swap for the American missiles in Turkey. The notion was canvassed, of reassuring the Turks by promising to deploy Polaris nuclear missile-armed submarines in the nearby seas. McNamara focused attention on the certainty that if the US mounted air strikes, several hundred Russians must be killed. George Ball reprised his old song: 'Mr. President, I think that it's easy sitting here to, to underestimate the kind of sense of affront that you would have in the allied countries ... if we act without giving Khrushchev some way out ... A course of action where we strike without warning is like Pearl Harbor: it's the kind of conduct that one might expect of the Soviet Union. It is not conduct that one expects of the United States.'

In the rambling discussion that followed, several speakers raised the likelihood of the Russians seizing West Berlin in response to a US assault on Cuba. American troops there would fight, before inevitably being overrun. Robert Kennedy asked: 'Then what do we do?' Maxwell Taylor said: 'Go to general war, if it's in the interests of ours.' The president asked: 'You mean nuclear exchange?' Taylor assented, almost insouciantly: 'Guess you have to.' It is difficult, after noting this remark, to regard America's top soldier as any less terrifying a counsellor than were his fellow chiefs of staff. Kennedy plainly thought so, saying seconds later: 'Now the question really is to what action we take which lessens the chances of a nuclear exchange, which obviously is the final failure.' The '*final failure*' ... the '*final failure*': it is hard to overstate the importance of the use of such language by the president of the United States at such a moment, reflecting a consciousness of its stupendous gravity for humankind which some others around the table audibly lacked. Kennedy thereafter revived discussion of blockade – whether such an action would require a formal declaration of war.

The debate that morning roamed around the houses. Arguably, this was no bad thing, because the members of Excom were still brainstorming – identifying issues, reviewing possible courses and consequences. RFK afterwards noted the oddity that the meetings had no chairman, nor did the respective ranks of the participants seem to matter: 'we all spoke as equals', and the tape transcripts show that this was so. He himself was among those who professed disgust at the armed forces chiefs' willingness to go the full distance, even to nuclear weapons: 'I thought, as I listened, of the many times that I had heard the military take positions which, if wrong, had the advantage that no one would be around at the end to know.' There was hypocrisy here, from the man who chaired the wholly disreputable Operation Mongoose, and had accused Rusk of cowardice for urging caution about U-2 overflights. But Kennedy wrote his October reminiscence in later days, when he was pitching a personal claim to statesmanship.

That Thursday morning meeting made plain that the president was far from fixing upon a path. It still seemed probable that the US would bomb the Soviet missile sites; that, indeed, such action would already have been ordered had he not been fearful of triggering a Berlin showdown as an overture for general war. JFK now spoke of announcing the news to the world next day, the 19th, and of bombing Cuba on the 20th. Max Taylor said, 'That's a little too fast for us': the air force could make Sunday, however – they could launch air strikes that day. The president revisited the Pearl Harbor analogy: 'Sunday has historic disadvantages.' This secured another uneasy laugh, following which Robert Kennedy said, 'I think George Ball has a hell of a good point', when he observed that the decisions America made during this Crisis would profoundly influence history's view of the United States. Rusk agreed: 'This business of carrying the mark of Cain on your brow for the rest of your life is something.'

RFK continued: if the US bombed Cuba without warning, after fifteen years of expressing dark fears about a treacherous Soviet surprise nuclear First Strike, it would be acting in such a fashion as the world assumed that Americans would never do. 'Now ... we do that to a small country. I think it's a hell of a burden.' Robert Kennedy later observed that during the first five days of the Crisis, Excom spent more time debating the morality as well as efficacy of a surprise air assault than any other single issue. He himself scribbled a note to his brother, yet again recalling the 'Day of Infamy': 'I now know how Tojo felt when he was planning Pearl Harbor.'

Meanwhile the president voiced a concern not hitherto mentioned by McNamara or Taylor: never mind the Russians and Cubans who would die if the US invaded Cuba – so would thousands of Americans, in the face of formidable defences: 'and I think you're in much more of a mess than you are if you take out these [presumably the Soviet missiles, from the air]'. Taylor interjected that an invasion would take a week to be ready to launch – good news from JFK's viewpoint, because it granted him more time. Thompson also thought it an entirely positive prospect that the Russians would be able to see the US embarking upon the huge extended preparations necessary for an amphibious assault, because these must cause them to reflect.

Everybody welcomed the imminence of the president's scheduled meeting that afternoon with Soviet foreign minister Andrei Gromyko, who had just arrived in the US to attend the United Nations. The men around the table agreed that his hosts should not show their hand, not reveal their secret knowledge. Instead they would merely test Gromyko; discover how much lying he was prepared to do. As for Anatoly Dobrynin, who would be accompanying the Moscow visitor, it seemed likely he knew nothing about the missiles, as indeed proved the case, and no serious historian has since disputed the Soviet ambassador's ignorance.

Maxwell Taylor suggested that it was important to secure further intelligence before making a decisive move. For that reason, he favoured holding off breaking the story until Monday, 22 October, to provide more time for aerial reconnaissance and interpretation. McNamara said that never mind intelligence, he thought the administration still lacked a coherent plan. He urged that two separate groups should convene, to plan for the only serious alternative courses being discussed: a fast move to military action or a slow build-up to it, preceded by a public statement. The defense secretary himself remained unsure which way to go, though 'I think the price of any one of these actions is going to be very high.' At the very least, he thought, for the Kremlin to agree to take its missiles out of Cuba, the US Jupiters would have to be removed from Turkey and Italy. Several men, including Bundy and Taylor, said that in addition to getting rid of the Soviet missiles, they wanted to get rid of Castro. McNamara was wisely sceptical about adding this to the administration's shopping list.

Much more was said at that meeting, but the above exchanges constituted the essentials. JFK, after lunching at the Mansion, again met Dean Acheson, who once more pressed for air strikes without warning. The old man spent more than an hour with the president, who remained patient and courteous in the face of Acheson's spasms of cantankerousness. Towards the end of their talk, Kennedy rose from his rocking chair and stared through the french doors into the Rose Garden: 'I guess I better earn my salary this week.' Acheson said: 'I'm afraid you have to. I wish I could help more.'

Beyond the Oval Office seventy-one-year-old Averell Harriman, the administration's ambassador-at-large with special responsibility for the Far East, was an old dog denied the opportunity to bark. This veteran polo-player felt bitterly frustrated that though he was made privy to the Cuban secret, his advice was not sought. During World War II, he had been Roosevelt's favourite grandee diplomat, who conducted an affair in London with Winston Churchill's daughter-in-law Pamela Digby, later dubbed 'a world expert on rich men's ceilings', which the prime minister found it expedient to ignore. Harriman, impeccably elegant and extremely shrewd, knew the Soviet Union intimately, and had twenty years' experience of its capacity for insults, sacrifices, bluffs and violence. He had parleyed with Stalin. Whatever the rival claims of Bohlen and Llewellyn, Harriman considered himself the foremost US expert on handling the Russians.

For him, however, the crisis became an exasperating and even humiliating experience. While he was kept apprised of developments, his phone seldom rang from the White House. Kennedy had a grudging respect for his record, but personally disliked him. Harriman was even used as a decoy, being instructed to be seen to drive up to the West Wing, as if the Far East and not the Caribbean headed the president's agenda. Shown into the private anteroom, he was then left to fume. 'How long do I have to sit here?' he demanded angrily. The answer proved to be: too long.

Later on that Thursday, Rusk and McNamara called several times, to report progress and brief the president for his meeting with Andrei Gromyko. This began at 5 p.m., and continued for more than two hours. When originally scheduled, it had seemed a routine diplomatic courtesy encounter. Now, instead, the meeting assumed an extraordinary significance, albeit unavowed by either side. The Russian sought clues to whether the US government had gained any cognizance of the missile deployment. The president and his advisers, including Rusk and Thompson, cradled their devastating secret knowledge; waited to discover whether the Soviet foreign minister would expose any portion of the Kremlin's actions and intentions. As the subsequent conversation unfolded, the Americans found themselves fascinated by their guest's equable mask of deceit. Gromyko emphasized the urgency of settling the future of Berlin. If there was no deal, he said, 'the Soviet government would be compelled' – and the foreign minister wished to emphasize the word *compelled* – to take unilateral action. He described the Western military presence in the city as 'a rotten tooth which must be pulled out'.

This was diplomatic bluff of a high order, and also of an ugly one. Privately, Khrushchev had not the slightest intention of moving in Berlin. Rather, he sought only to sustain pressure on the Americans, to deflect their attention from the Caribbean. Gromyko nonetheless also complained about US threats against Cuba, where he said that the Soviet Union was merely training Castro's forces in the use of defensive weapons. Ten days later Khrushchev boasted of Gromyko's cleverness: 'We and the Americans talked about Berlin – both sides with the same aim, namely to draw attention away from Cuba, the Americans in order to attack it, we in order to make the USA uneasy and postpone attacking.'

At the White House the president told the Soviet foreign minister that he had no thought of invading the island – indeed, if requested he would give a formal assurance to that effect. Yet Soviet shipments of arms continued, and had created 'the most dangerous situation since the end of [World War II]'. Here was the clearest possible hint of American knowledge, but it appears to have passed unnoticed by the visitors. Gromyko recalled the Bay of Pigs, prompting Kennedy to offer renewed pledges that there would be no further US or Cuban exile military action. Then Kennedy read aloud to his visitor from his own 4 and 13 September public statements, about the grievous consequences that must follow the deployment of aggressive weapons in Cuba.

Gromyko did not blink. He reported later to Khrushchev: 'Kennedy formulated his thoughts slowly and with great care, obviously weighing every word. During our conversation Rusk sat silent and was as red as a lobster.' There was perfunctory discussion of the ongoing negotiations about restricting nuclear testing. Kennedy agreed to meet Khrushchev when he attended the November UN meeting in New York. When the visitors left at 7.15 p.m. following this extraordinary encounter, Thompson and Rusk stayed on with the president to marvel at Gromyko's carnival of falsehoods. In the course of the Cold War both sides told plenty of untruths to each other, but Gromyko's mendacity, on a matter of such gravity, provoked real anger in the Oval Office.

The Soviet foreign minister admitted in his memoirs that this conversation was the most difficult he ever held with any of nine presidents. The Americans had played their hand superbly. Seldom if ever had a US leader sat at a poker table with a Soviet master of the game, and deceived him so successfully. Gromyko emerged confident that his host knew nothing about the missiles, and reported to Khrushchev with his accustomed obsequiousness. 'The Administration and the overall American ruling circles,' he told the first secretary, 'are amazed by the Soviet Union's courage in assisting Cuba.'

He claimed to have left his hosts apprised of the unwelcome realities of the Caribbean situation – namely, that 'the Soviet government recognizes the great importance which the Americans place on Cuba and its situation, and how painful is that issue to the USA. But the fact that the USSR, even knowing all that, still provides such aid to Cuba, means that it is fully committed to repulsing any American intervention in Cuba. There is no single opinion as to how and where that rebuff will be given, but that it will be given they do not doubt ... In these conditions a USA military initiative against Cuba is almost impossible to imagine ... Everything we know about the US position on Cuba permits the conclusion that the situation is in general wholly satisfactory.' Though all this emphasized how completely Gromyko had allowed himself to be misled, even when the foreign minister's naïveté and duplicity had been laid bare Khrushchev applauded his conduct of the meeting, telling Czech leader Antonín Novotný, 'He was lying. And how! And that was the right thing to do; he had orders from the Party.'

Kennedy's next visitor was former defense secretary Robert Lovett, who found the president still fuming about Gromyko's shamelessness. On policy and tactics, Lovett proved to share McNamara's view that the Cuban deployment did not change the strategic balance. He also endorsed Stevenson's opposition to military action, which both men believed would be highly damaging to

America's alliances. He thought the Soviets would indeed take West Berlin, for which the Europeans would blame American over-reaction in the Caribbean. Mac Bundy had separately reached the same conclusion – for now.

The president also retreated, temporarily anyway, from his earlier expressed leaning towards bombing. Dictating for the record, alone in the Oval Office that Thursday evening, JFK said: 'The consensus was that we should go ahead with the blockade beginning on Sunday night ... I was most anxious that we should not have to announce a state of war existing.' It was deemed impor-tant that next morning, the 19th, Kennedy should resume his campaign swing to support Democratic mid-term candidates in Ohio and Illinois. This was a matter of such political significance that failure to hit the hustings would lay bare to the world the exist-ence of a crisis.

Although most historians date the most dangerous days as coming later, what did *not* happen between that first Tuesday to Friday seems also critical. Bobby Kennedy noted how widely some men's opinions veered through the discussions 'from one extreme to another – supporting an air attack at the beginning of the meet-ing and, by the time we left the White House, supporting no action at all'. JFK's military advisers, influenced by their ignorance of Cuba's formidable defensive arsenal, and still with scant reflection about consequences, continued to urge on the president an imme-diate air campaign. The venerable Dean Acheson agreed, as would have done many ordinary Americans, had they been made privy to the NPIC's furnace-hot Cuban photograph album.

It should never be taken for granted that the US government would reject such counsel. And once shooting started, heedless of the personal inclinations of Khrushchev and Kennedy, forces and counter-forces would have been in play such as would have been extraordinarily difficult to contain. A first, potentially lethal phase of the Crisis passed on Thursday night, when the administration decided against immediate military action. Media eyes watched the White House day and night. In a droll vignette, most of Excom left the White House in RFK's car, hidden from public gaze by tinted windows – McCone, Taylor, the attorney-general and the driver crammed into the front seat, with six others in the back – to avoid generating excitement through the spectacle of a column of limos heading out. It remains astonishing that this huge secret was kept, in the leakiest capital on earth.

2 'IRON ASS'

On Friday morning, 19 October, before the president left Washington for his campaign trip across Ohio, he held a White House meeting with the joint chiefs. The latest intelligence estimates, which were hardening all the time, identified a third Soviet MRBM regiment with eight SS-4 launchers, east of Havana. These missiles were expected to become operational within a week. Elsewhere two sites near Guanajay were almost certainly being prepared for larger IRBMs, which required concrete launch pads. At 9 a.m., before the four chiefs saw the president, Maxwell Taylor met them to report a shift of mood at the White House, against air strikes and towards imposing a blockade. The dismayed commanders agreed to deliver to the president a renewed recommendation for surprise attack. Major Bill Smith, one of Taylor's personal aides, said: 'I was surprised by the unanimity of the Chiefs in wanting to use force because I had thought [the chairman] was a little less inclined.' They favoured following bombing with all-out invasion, a proposal from which only Taylor now dissented.

John F. Kennedy could never be characterized as anti-militarist but, surely influenced by his wartime experience as a junior naval officer, he was sensibly sceptical of brass. A few weeks earlier, he had been irked by the Army's foot-dragging when he sought to deploy federal troops in Mississippi during the disorders at the state university over the admission of black student James Meredith. The president said then about the generals: 'They always give you their bullshit about their instant reaction and their split-second timing, but it never works out. No wonder it's so hard to win a war.'

The chiefs entered the Cabinet Room at 9.45 a.m., accompanied by McNamara. Taylor, opening the meeting, was gracious enough to concede the two powerful objections to unannounced air strikes: the unlikelihood of complete success in destroying all Soviet nuclear capability in Cuba, and the damage to America's alliances abroad. The nation's top warriors nonetheless continued to urge bombs. Kennedy, in response, delivered a protracted homily, in which he stressed the need to consider why the Russians had acted as they did: 'It was a rather dangerous but rather useful play of theirs. If we do nothing, they have a missile base there, with all the pressure that brings to bear on the United States and damage to our prestige. If we attack Cuba … it gives them a clear line to take Berlin, as they were able to do in Hungary [during] the Anglo-French [1956] war in Egypt … They don't give a damn about Cuba. And they do care about Berlin and about their own society.'

In supposing that Khrushchev was indifferent to Cuba, Kennedy was mistaken. But yet again, and not for the last time, the president showed how a prospective threat to West Berlin could be exploited – perhaps in some measure cynically – as a drogue on the hawks, to the advantage of the world's prospects of survival. A Soviet seizure of the old German capital, Kennedy asserted to the chiefs extravagantly, albeit in a good cause, 'leaves me only one alternative, which is to fire nuclear weapons – which is a hell of an alternative – and begin a nuclear exchange'.

Curtis LeMay contemptuously rejected this defeatist talk. He said: 'I'd emphasize, a little strongly perhaps, that we won't have any choice except direct military action.' If the US attempted a mere blockade of Cuba, 'the first thing that's going to happen is your missiles are going to disappear into the woods, particularly your mobile ones. This blockade and political action, I see leading into war … This is almost as bad as the [1938] appeasement at Munich … Because if this blockade comes along, their MiGs are going to fly. The IL-28s are going to fly against us. And we're just going to gradually drift into a war under conditions that are at great disadvantage to us, with missiles staring us in the face, that can knock out our airfields in the south-eastern portion of [the US] … I just don't see any other solution except military intervention *right now*.'

LeMay was a remarkable person. Born into a modest family in Columbus, Ohio, he displayed precocious technical skills, manifested later when, as a hobby activity, he built a colour TV with his own hands. He joined the air force in 1928, and showed himself a skilled and courageous wartime bomber pilot, first in Europe, then as commander of the USAAF Twentieth Air Force, flying against Japan. He was always respected rather than loved: rueful subordinates dubbed him 'iron ass'. He was seldom seen without a trademark pipe – later, a cigar – clamped between his lips. Legend held that a sergeant once remonstrated with the general when, pipe and all, he climbed into the fuselage of a bomber being refuelled, saying, 'Sir, it could ignite gas fumes.' LeMay responded: 'Son, it wouldn't dare.' His chilly demeanour was not softened by the paralysis of one side of his face, the consequence of Bell's palsy.

He had applied all his ruthless energy to the direction of the fire-bombing of Japan, stage-managing one of the most devastating air attacks of the war, by B-29s against Tokyo in March 1945. That operation killed a hundred thousand people – more than the Dresden raid of the previous month, or indeed than the atomic bombings in August – and rendered 650,000 homeless. The postwar US official history of LeMay's command claimed credit for killing 310,000 Japanese, injuring 412,000, and rendering almost ten million homeless. 'Never in the history of war,' wrote the authors proudly, 'had such colossal devastation been visited on an enemy at so slight a cost to the conqueror ... The 1945 application of American Air Power, so destructive and concentrated as to cremate sixty-five Japanese cities in five months, forced an enemy's surrender without land invasion for the first time in military history.' LeMay had opposed the dropping of the atomic bombs on Hiroshima and Nagasaki because he feared, with some justification, that these would deflect attention from his own command's earlier triumphs.

This acclaimed hero of the USAF, in 1962 still only fifty-five years old, was the man who later advocated bombing the North Vietnamese communists 'back into the Stone Age'. He was a master of the one-liner: 'Successful offense brings victory. Successful defense can now only lessen defeat' ... 'To err is human, to forgive is not SAC policy'. A USAF briefing on America's nuclear strike plan concluded, with unembarrassed satisfaction, that within two hours of its initiation, 'virtually all of Russia' would be reduced to 'a smoking, radiating ruin'. In wars of national survival, such forceful leaders as LeMay can, and in his case did, make important contributions to their nations' causes: few successful battlefield commanders have been sympathetic human beings. Both sides in the Cold War owned such unyielding armourers. Their admirers advanced a case, which should not be lightly dismissed, that without their existence nuclear deterrence could never have been effective, because credible. They were mortally dangerous counsellors, however, in such a crisis as this. The airman prided himself on fearing defeat much more than war. The president was striving to avoid both.

George Anderson of the US Navy endorsed LeMay's opening remarks. The heavily-built admiral, fifty-two years old, was a former naval aviator and World War II carrier captain. His relations with Robert McNamara were already poisonous and worsening, mostly because Anderson shared the air force chief of staff's absence of trepidation about going head to head with the Russians. Now, at the White House Cabinet table, this hard-boiled sailor argued that the best deterrent against Soviet aggression in Berlin was devastating action against Cuba. For the army Gen. Earle Wheeler agreed, saying: 'In my judgement, from a military point of view, the lowest-risk course of action if we're thinking of protecting the people of the United States ... is to go ahead with a surprise air strike, the blockade, and an invasion because these series of actions progressively will give us increasing assurance that we really have got the offensive capability of the Cubans-Soviets cornered.' Gen. David Shoup, the notoriously inarticulate US Marine chief, clumsily endorsed LeMay on air strikes, though he was against invasion. Shoup's badge of honour was that he, alone among the chiefs of staff, had opposed the Bay of Pigs. He would later become a strident opponent of the Vietnam commitment.

LeMay then returned to the charge, using language that was certainly grossly impertinent, also malicious. The president, said the airman, had in the past assured the American people that Soviet weapons in Cuba were only defensive, and promised them action against offensive weapons: 'I think that a blockade and political talk would be considered by a lot of our friends and neutrals as being a pretty weak response to this. And I'm sure a lot of our own citizens would feel that way, too. In other words, you're in a pretty bad fix at the present time.'

The president, audibly astounded by LeMay's barrage of insults, demanded: 'What did you say?' The general doubled down: 'You're in a pretty bad fix.' Kennedy, with his accustomed disarming humour, batted back at LeMay, in another memorable phrase of the Crisis: 'You're in there with me.' He had said after the Bay of Pigs that he would never again allow himself to be overawed by military advice, and he did not do so now. There was a flicker of uneasy laughter, before JFK added an emphasis to his riposte: 'Personally.' It is unsurprising that Kennedy did not fire his air chief then and there, because the nation's affairs were at too grave a pass. It seems remarkable, however, that LeMay kept his job to Kennedy's death and beyond, indeed until 1965. This is only explicable by his prestige among conservative Americans: in 1968, he would become vice-presidential candidate in George Wallace's Third-Party racist run at the presidency.

At the Friday morning White House meeting Maxwell Taylor now broke the tension, saying that the chiefs were studying the blockade option, though this presented difficulties, especially of surveillance. But LeMay was not finished, interrupting Taylor: 'I think we have got to do more than take out the missiles, because if you don't take out their air at the same time you're vulnerable ... You've got to take out their air along with it, and their radar, and their communications, the whole works. It just doesn't make any sense to do anything but that ... We can be ready for attack at dawn on the 21st [Sunday] ... the optimum date would be Tuesday morning.' The discussion then continued until the president quit the meeting to set forth for Ohio, leaving the chiefs alone in the room together, unknowingly accompanied by the tape-recorder. Shoup said: 'Well what do you guys ... You, you pulled the rug right out from under him.' LeMay responded: 'Jesus Christ. What the hell do you mean?' The Marine then made some confused, barely comprehensible remarks, which ended with the angry, enigmatic words 'That was my conclusion. Don't frig around and go take a missile out.'

Anatoly Dobrynin later wrote that Robert Kennedy, in talking to the Russians, 'occasionally seemed to over-dramatise the pressure from the military, and the President's resistance to it'. In October 1962, nobody could rightfully accuse the administration's civilians of hyperbole, for emphasizing the war-hunger of America's commanders. JFK told his aide Dave Powers: 'These brasshats have one great advantage in their favour. If we listen to them and do what they want us to do, none of us will be alive later to tell them that they were wrong.' It is hard to discern a meaningful distinction between the attitude and indeed language deployed by Curtis LeMay in October 1962 and those of the maniacal General Buck Turgidson in Stanley Kubrick's satirical masterpiece *Dr. Strangelove*, filmed in 1963, about a misbegotten descent into nuclear catastrophe. '[Kennedy] just would be frantic at the end of a session with LeMay,' Roswell Gilpatric recalled afterwards, 'because, you know, LeMay couldn't listen or wouldn't take in, and he would make what Kennedy considered ... outrageous proposals ... And the President never saw him unless at some ceremonial affair, or where he felt he had to make a record of having listened to LeMay, as he did on the whole question of an air strike against Cuba. And he had to sit there. I saw the President right afterwards. He was just choleric.'

If the chiefs left the meeting dissatisfied men, the president was no happier. That Friday morning, he found that overnight his national security adviser had changed his mind: now aligning himself with the chiefs, Bundy backed surprise air strikes. He subsequently claimed to friends that he kept his proposal aloft merely to ensure that the president considered seriously all possible options before reaching a decision. It is much more plausible, however, that the national security adviser kept changing his mind. Whatever the truth, just before Kennedy's helicopter took off from the White House South Lawn for the airport, he told Bundy to keep the bombing option open until his return. He could scarcely fail to have been impressed by the strength of the chiefs' expressed sentiments. He could anticipate the political consequences for his administration, when it became known – as some time it must be – that he had rejected the professional advice, now apparently supported by his national security adviser, and instead opted for a softer option. The damage to Kennedy's prestige and authority could be very great.

In justice to the US military, it seems important to remark the bias of the historiography of the Crisis, that we have transcripts of such Washington meetings as these; yet nothing comparable from the other side. The reputations of LeMay and his comrades are tarnished, even blackened, by the evidence of their words. If a similar record existed, detailing the conversations of the Soviet Union's military leaders, it is not unlikely that they spoke with a matching absence of fear about the human consequences of their actions. No man in that era attained the summits of Moscow's armed forces while admitting to hesitation about killing people, a reality which persists in 2022. It merely seems dismaying to admirers of the United States, and adherents of the Western cause in the Cold War, that its own commanders displayed a matching brutishness.

3 THE DECISION

Even as Kennedy left Washington to go on the stump that Friday, further intense meetings took place at the State Department. Acheson, Dillon and McCone, now apparently joined by Bundy, shared the chiefs' view, represented at Foggy Bottom by Taylor. Here was a formidable quorum, supporting bombing. Ball said, sincerely or otherwise, that he was wavering. McNamara continued to promote blockade. Robert Kennedy told the others that in his own conversations with the president, they had agreed that a surprise attack was 'not in our traditions'. He favoured an option that gave the Soviets a chance to pull back, before they were bombed and – presumably – humiliated before the world. In an important expression of opinion, Justice and State Department lawyers agreed that a blockade would not require a Declaration of War.

McNamara was convinced that to have a chance of a successful negotiation with Moscow, the US missiles in Turkey and Italy must go. Despite RFK's avowed desire to do nothing that might be likened to the Japanese strike on Pearl Harbor, he was then making hawkish noises. He thought it time for some sort of showdown with the Russians: '[In] looking into the future it would be better for our children and grandchildren if we decided to face the Soviet threat, stand up to it, and eliminate it, now. The circumstances for doing so at some future time were bound to be more unfavourable, the risks would be greater; the chances of success less good.' He and others were convinced that the Russians, by attempting a covert nuclear deployment four thousand miles from home, had wrong-footed themselves as never before.

Kennedy was impressed, however, when McNamara said that imposing a blockade could, if necessary, be followed by air strikes; that starting out with the blockade option did not preclude subsequent bombing. Llewellyn Thompson was an influential supporter of this course – graduated escalation. Taylor was doubtful about its efficacy, but RFK said it was becoming obvious which way the president's decision was going to go: for a blockade preceded by a nationwide presidential broadcast, which Ted Sorensen had begun to draft. Rusk also favoured blockade, but wished to keep all options open thereafter.

It was now urgent to set in motion measures, several of which made the president's physical presence indispensable. On Saturday morning, Bobby called his brother in Chicago, saying that he should return to Washington. Feigning a cold, Jack Kennedy flew east once more. He reached the White House at 1.40 p.m., and immediately went for a swim while his brother sat by the poolside and talked down to him. Then he read Sorensen's draft of his proposed public words. Standing on the Truman balcony, the president said to the two men: 'We are very, very close to war.' Yet his sense of dark comedy broke through again: 'And there is not room in the White House shelter for all of us.' Bundy wrote later of 'the excessively gloomy view that Kennedy shared with most of the rest of us in that first week. We did not fully understand the strength of our own hand.' Here the national security adviser indicated the regional military and naval might of the US; its overwhelming strategic nuclear superiority; and the political case which Soviet duplicity would enable the White House to lay before its own people and the world.

Even as Kennedy talked on the Truman balcony, his other advisers were slipping into the Executive Mansion through back passages, assembling in its Oval Room – not the Oval Office – for a new session of Excom. This venue reflected persisting ploys to conceal signs of crisis. Kennedy opened the meeting at 2.30 p.m., making another bleak jest: 'Gentlemen, today we're going to earn our pay. You should all hope that your plan isn't the one that will be accepted.' As at earlier gatherings, there followed an updated intelligence assessment, confirming two fixed IRBM sites, showing four launcher pads apiece, under construction near Havana, with four and possibly five MRBM sites 'in a state of at least limited operational readiness'. The evidence, said the CIA's Ray Cline, indicated a probability that eight MRBMs were at readiness to be fired from Cuba immediately.

Robert McNamara then expressed his support for a blockade, while acknowledging that his uniformed advisers still wanted bombing. The president was handed a draft of Sorensen's 'blockade route' address to the American people. The defense secretary asserted the likelihood of needing to trade removal of US missiles from Turkey and Italy for disarmament of Cuba, as well as possibly setting a time limit for the US to relinquish the base at Guantánamo. He opposed an explicit ultimatum, and affirmed the planners' conviction that the USSR would flunk forcibly challenging a blockade, not least because they lacked warships to escort their cargo vessels, save a handful of submarines. 'Chip' Bohlen, before leaving New York for Paris, had expressed the opinion that the Russians would appeal to the United Nations rather than initiate a military or naval response on the worst possible tactical terms.

The defense secretary, itemizing the pros and cons, admitted that blockade might appear to the American people a weak response, and would take time to work. The big positive, however, was that it was unlikely to precipitate general war. Maxwell Taylor restated the chiefs' advocacy of air strikes, starting on Tuesday. He himself did not share McNamara's fear that nuclear weapons might be used against the US. He believed the risk of attacking the missile sites was less than that of leaving them be. America's last opportunity to destroy them by bombing was likely to come before the president went public: once the Russians knew that the Americans knew, the weapons would be hidden. Robert Kennedy now seemed to favour air strikes. A draft schedule for a bombing campaign was handed to the president; it had become known as 'the Bundy plan', and was also supported by the CIA's McCone and Dillon of the Treasury.

McNamara highlighted an important objection: even the chiefs of staff did not claim that they could achieve total success through air strikes. Subsequent evidence from Vietnam suggests that the USAF and US Navy would have struggled to knock out many if not most of the sites, and would certainly have suffered heavy losses to SAMs. The Soviets by now deployed at twenty-four sites across Cuba 144 S-75 launchers, which had proved their efficacy elsewhere by shooting down two U-2s, one American and one Nationalist Chinese.

There was a grim pause, as the meeting acknowledged the chasm between the views of the hawks and those of the McNamara camp. Deputy defense secretary Roswell Gilpatric spoke up in support of his boss, saying that the choice lay between the use of limited or unlimited force. He would not quarrel with air strikes later, but opposed them first out. McNamara emphasized that the proposed launching of eight hundred sorties would kill several thousand Russians, promote chaos in Cuba and perhaps an uprising to topple Castro. The US would almost certainly then have to invade, which he believed would prompt the Soviets to 'a very major response'. The US would lose control of the situation, which could escalate to general war. Dean Rusk supported this view. Adlai Stevenson restated his opposition to a surprise air strike. Llewellyn Thompson also supported blockade.

The blockaders prevailed. The president, on that Saturday afternoon, reached a decision which had been urged and was now supported by McNamara, Rusk, Thompson, Sorensen, Ball, Gilpatric, Lovett and Bohlen *in absentia*. He agreed to authorize all necessary preparations to launch air strikes, together with an invasion of Cuba if this proved necessary. The huge all-arms deployment that would unfold in the south-eastern United States would, of course, send a strong signal to the Kremlin. Rusk urged holding back the start of the blockade two days, until Monday, to brief allies. Kennedy acknowledged that 'the domestic political heat following his television appearance would be terrific'. Conservative America would assuredly ask, and accuse: how could he have been so wrong, in asserting a month earlier that the Soviets had only defensive weapons in Cuba?

Preparations were authorized for air strikes against the missile sites, and only the sites, ready to launch any time from Tuesday. George Ball suggested including POL – petrol, oil and lubricants – in the goods prohibited from crossing the blockade line. Dean Rusk said, surely rightly, that the US must stick with the issue of the missiles. He also pushed, and won his case, for the Navy's interdiction to be publicly characterized as a 'quarantine', not a 'blockade', for legal reasons. He made a further important point, which should have occurred to others: that the US, in focusing upon the missiles, must abandon the secondary objective, favoured by hawks, of seizing an opportunity to rid the Caribbean of Fidel Castro. Adlai Stevenson urged that, from the first moment of breaking the news to the world, America should declare its willingness to remove nuclear weapons from Italy and Turkey, in return for Soviet withdrawal from Cuba. Nobody else liked this idea at all – of offering to yield so much, before a negotiation even started.

The meeting broke up after two hours forty minutes of tense, sometimes fierce discussion. The president unleashed no harsh words, not even upon those such as Maxwell Taylor, who had pressed for bombing. He told the general: 'I know you and your colleagues are unhappy with the decision, but I trust that you will support me.' Back at the Pentagon, the chairman told the frustrated chiefs: 'This was not one of our better days.' Earle Wheeler said: 'I never thought I'd live to see the day when I would want to go to war.' Lt. Gen. David Burchinal, LeMay's deputy, later spoke with contempt about the defense secretary's role in the Pentagon debates: 'McNamara did not like the idea or the thought of nuclear weapons or nuclear forces; they were a fact of life, but he didn't like them, no question about that ... That was when the group across the [Potomac] river [at the White House] separated into hawks and doves.' McNamara allegedly said: 'I don't want to kill any of those [Soviet] technicians, but I would like to wound a couple.' LeMay responded: 'You must have lost your mind.'

The decision made on this critical day – albeit only one of a succession of critical days – represented a wise, era-defining compromise. The president rejected the proposal of McNamara and Stevenson, immediately to open a negotiation with the Soviet Union about the missiles, such as might drag on for months. He also withheld an explicit time limit for removal of the missiles – an ultimatum. Instead, he agreed to reveal the news to the world, and to insist that the weapons must be removed, while also announcing the imposition of a naval blockade to halt the introduction of further Soviet ordnance to Cuba. The men who advocated and drove through this option – McNamara, Rusk, Llewellyn Thompson, subsequently joined by McCone and Robert Kennedy, seem to deserve applause. Of them all, McNamara fought hardest, most consistently and probably with most influence, though his critics note that he, too, intermittently wavered.

As for those who argued for air strikes – to start shooting – headed by McGeorge Bundy and the chiefs of staff, the world will never know what might have happened, had they got their way. There is a plausible case that since Khrushchev did not want general war, he would have backed off, even amid carnage among Soviet personnel and massive destruction of their weapons systems. On 19 October, an SNIE – intelligence estimate – was submitted to the

White House, predicting that even if the US took direct military action against Cuba, 'the Soviet Union would not attack the U.S. ... Since [it] would not dare to resort to general war and could not hope to prevail locally, the Soviets would almost certainly consider retaliatory actions outside Cuba.' But it seems foolish now, as it was then, to have urged gambling the planet upon such a relatively benign outcome.

Bundy afterwards asserted that only the fact of the preoccupation of the White House media with the mid-term election campaign enabled the secret of the Crisis to be kept as long as it was. 'By Saturday night [the 20th]', wrote Arthur Schlesinger, 'the town was alive with speculation and anticipation. A good deal of the Government found itself late that evening at a dance given by [Washington hosts] the James Rowes. There, the gap between the witting and unwitting could almost be detected by facial expressions – on the one hand, anxiety tinged with self-satisfaction; on the other, irritation and frustration.' A succession of officials quizzed Henry Brandon, correspondent of the London *Sunday Times* and the last British journalist in Washington to command access to its innermost corridors of power, about the trip to Cuba from which he had just returned. How was the mood? they demanded. Defiant, said Brandon. So, too, was that of many Americans, irked by the perceived pusillanimity of Europeans about Cuba. New Yorker Edwin Tetlow wrote in the *Economist* correspondence column that day: 'Too much nervousness is being shown in and out of the United States about the effects on Latin-American opinion of any American action about Cuba ... The United States will be much more respected there in the long run if she disposes of Mr. Khrushchev in Cuba than if she lets him go on defying and goading her there.'

The president had hoped to address the American people next day, 21 October. The demands of the planners and requirements of the military made it necessary to push back this timetable by twenty-four hours, though by now America's precarious silence about the missiles was close to breaking point. Sunday morning brought the White House a stroke of good fortune, albeit a sorry one for peace in the sub-continent: the world's front pages were captured and dominated by a major armed clash on India's border with China, initiated by the Chinese but provoked by Indian aggression, in which Mao Zedong's troops drove forward on two fronts. Informed reporters and editors on the East Coast, however, recognized that something was also up closer to home. The *Washington Post* main headline read: 'MARINES MOVES IN SOUTH LINKED TO CUBA' – here was a first earnest of the beginnings of the US invasion deployment. Both Walter Lippmann and Joe Alsop, the nation's best-informed political columnists, knew that trouble was a-coming, involving Soviet nuclear weapons and Cuba. White House press secretary Pierre Salinger called both the *Post* and *New York Times*, to request that the titles held off the story through Monday. In those patriotic days, they did so; Salinger's call was the first the *Times* knew about it.

That Sunday had been scheduled as a liberty day ashore for much of the crew of the carrier *Essex*, anchored offshore in Guantánamo Bay. At 0330, however, the broadcast order 'Reveille, Reveille, all hands!' echoed through its vast cavernous spaces atop and below. Once under way, *Essex* remained at sea on continuous operations directed towards the Crisis until 26 November, flying off patrol and anti-submarine aircraft.

Meanwhile ashore the US Cuban base activated Operation Quicklift, as flights were informally known, to evacuate dependants ahead of the president's broadcast. 'This is not a drill,' began the officers who briefed wives and other family members. Frances Glasspoole, teenage daughter of a US naval officer, said of life in the enclave: 'We did not have a sense of what was going on in the world. Our news was filtered. The base newspaper was a little type-written newsletter. The television station didn't come on until 7 p.m., and it was just old re-runs of *The Ed Sullivan Show* and *I Love Lucy*.' JFK had been president for almost two years, yet Glasspoole had never heard his voice on the air waves. After families quit the base, the doors of their quarters were marked with a crude daubed 'V', for 'vacated'. Sailors were detailed to care for abandoned pets.

Some frightened women left clothes still in their washing machines, food on stoves. Successive groups flew out on planes that brought in arms and ammunition, while most travelled on four ships of the US Navy, bound for Hampton Roads. In all, 2,700 civilians were whisked out of harm's way, soon to be replaced by an additional three battalions of Marines.

On Sunday morning also, the president met at the White House Gen. Walter Sweeney, C-in-C of Tactical Air Command, who brought with him Col. Wilbur Creech, a thirty-four-year-old Korean veteran fighter pilot. The two airmen were invited into the Mansion with Taylor and McNamara, to brief Kennedy on the air strike plan and – in Creech's case – to answer technical questions about potential difficulties 'at the sharp end': 'I was the guy who knew all about the tactics, and I had worked with Ops Analysis on all the probabilities.' Robert Kennedy met the four men, who had ridden over together in McNamara's car, once again seeking to avoid exciting attention in a column of limousines. They were introduced to Mrs Kennedy and the children before sitting down with the president.

Creech, perhaps because he was younger and more susceptible, did not share his bosses' disdain for JFK. He said later: 'I was very impressed with the way [he] handled himself ... He listened carefully and asked a lot of good questions ... Sweeney, by the way, felt we ought to invade and get rid of Castro once and for all. In fact, he had me get a quote from *The Gathering Storm* by Winston Churchill about the circle closes, and if you wait, the time comes that it is too late. I drafted a letter for him on that theme, and he mailed it to all his flag officer acquaintances in all the services. He wanted to invade, no doubt about it. But he also was a man of great professional integrity. President Kennedy said, "General Sweeney, if I turn you loose with your forces on those Cuban missiles that Castro has, what assurance can you give me that you will get them all?" Sweeney said, "We've done the analysis and have the forces necessary. I can assure you, Mr. President, that on the first strike we will get 98 percent kill of all the missiles. Now that is not an assurance that we will get 98 out of 100. It is an assurance that for each and every missile there is a 98 percent chance that we will kill and destroy completely that missile. The second wave will come in ten minutes later and then it goes up to above 99 percent. That's followed by other waves so the odds that we won't get them all are very remote."

The President was listening intently. There was a measurable pause before Sweeney said, "That is, all that we know about."' Creech recorded: 'A look came over the President's face, and he said, "Aye, that's the rub".' Even this gung-ho air chief acknowledged that, in the wake of a US air assault, the Soviets on Cuba were likely to retain the capability to launch some nuclear missiles against the United States, should they choose to do so.

The colonel said: 'At that moment I knew we weren't going to do the air strike plan, and so did Sweeney. As we were coming down in the elevator from the White House living quarters, [the general] had this long, despondent look on his face. He said, "Well, Bill [Creech] I guess I really screwed that up, didn't I?"' His staff officer responded, 'No, Sir, you told the President what you had to say. We may not know where they all are.' Sweeney replied: 'Well, thanks for trying to make me feel better, but I'm not sure I did the right thing.' A fellow-officer described later how Sweeney explained that, if the president wanted to minimize American casualties, it would be necessary to suppress the Soviet air defences before attacking the missile sites: 'Sweeney made a very favourable impression [on Kennedy] by recognizing both the capabilities and limitations of the use of force.' The airmen and their bosses returned to the Pentagon. Creech said: 'It was an interesting moment in history because there were a lot of people agitating to invade.'

The first foreigner with whom the president discussed the Crisis was an old friend, David Ormsby-Gore, the British ambassador now summoned to the White House. He had been appointed to Washington in the previous year explicitly because of a youthful friendship with Jack, formed when the two gilded young men partied together in London before World War II, when Joseph

Kennedy was US ambassador. Ormsby-Gore, heir to Lord Harlech, was only a few months younger than the president; he had attended Eton and Oxford before serving in the wartime British Army. He then became a Conservative MP and junior Foreign Office minister, before arriving in Washington in May 1961. This intelligent, witty, cultured, slightly louche figure became a frequent guest at the White House, close to both Kennedys – following the president's death, he proposed marriage to Jackie, but proved not to be rich enough for her.

It has occasionally been suggested by fantasists about a 'special relationship' that Ormsby-Gore and prime minister Harold Macmillan hereafter became honorary members of the White House inner circle through the Crisis. This is a wild overstatement. It is probably true, however, that John Kennedy was more comfortable in the society of grand, sophisticated British people than any US president had been before, or would be again, and more so than with his own fellow-countrymen out in the boonies. The ambassador's views were more serviceable and palatable to Kennedy than were those of the prime minister, an inveterate hand-wringer on nuclear issues. RFK described Ormsby-Gore as a friend whom his brother 'trusted implicitly'. Arthur Schlesinger penned a remarkable tribute to the envoy's intimacy with the president: 'Only two men of notable character could have so delicately mingled personal and official relations, for each remained at all times the firm and candid advocate of the policies of his own nation. Their long, relaxed, confidential talks, whether at Hyannis Port or Palm Beach or on quiet evenings in the White House, gave Kennedy probably his best opportunity to clarify his own purposes in world affairs.'

Ormsby-Gore, now briefed on the situation and the options, immediately endorsed the president's judgement in favour of blockade, presenting the very arguments that the commander-in-chief had himself given to the brass. Kennedy expressed admiration for the cleverness of the Soviet play, which he interpreted far more subtly than Khrushchev could rightfully claim credit for. The president saw the Cuban deployment as a matador's cloak – though this was not his figure of speech – to provoke an American response that would justify Soviet action against West Berlin. He mused aloud to the ambassador that he himself would never be offered a better excuse to invade Cuba, even if he was not minded to go that route. He said that the Jupiter missiles in Turkey and elsewhere had negligible strategic value, and indicated that, in a deal, they would probably have to go.

Robert Lovett had joined the advisory cast at the White House earlier in the week, after the president had called him in New York saying 'come down at once', which the sixty-seven-year-old banker and former defense secretary promptly did. The lean, elegant, dome-pated Lovett, who had worked with both Henry Stimson and George Marshall, was briefed on his arrival by Mac Bundy. On the national security adviser's desk was a picture of Stimson. Lovett said, sincerely if sententiously: 'Mac, I think the best service we can perform for the President is to try to approach this as Colonel Stimson would.' Bundy agreed. On Sunday morning, Kennedy asked Lovett to help draft the 'quarantine' announcement. After lunch at Hickory Hill with RFK, the two men went to the Oval Room, where Excom was assembling for a new session.

Midway through, JFK called the new arrival, who had declined on health grounds to serve in his Cabinet, out onto the balcony overlooking the South Lawn. He asked if Lovett believed that Adlai Stevenson was up to handling a negotiation with the Soviets, if such a thing took place at the United Nations. Kennedy's question was prompted by fears about both Stevenson's sagacity and strength of purpose. The previous day, the UN ambassador had proposed immediately putting on the table America's missiles in Turkey and the US base at Guantánamo, an offer to the Kremlin which seemed to Excom gratuitously conciliatory. Lovett urged that John McCloy, not Stevenson, should do any negotiating, a nomination which RFK had already proposed. He called McCloy's secretary at home, to help track down the banker, who was then in Frankfurt, about to go partridge-shooting in Portugal. McCloy, finally contacted, proved willing to come home. The daily commercial flights to New York had already taken off, but a USAF plane was sent to convey him back across the Atlantic.

At 2.20 that Sunday afternoon, the National Security Council reconvened, again in the Executive Mansion. Its agenda was a detailed discussion of the wording of the president's national broadcast next day. Kennedy rejected Stevenson's urging to include a proposal for a summit meeting with Khrushchev. He also deleted from the draft some bleak and frightening words about the horrors of war. Admiral Anderson, chief of naval operations, reported on the forty warships already deploying to enforce the blockade. The initial rules of engagement called for any vessel that declined to stop for search to be disabled by gunfire. A Soviet warship or aircraft that fired on the Americans was to be destroyed. If a Soviet submarine sought to run the blockade, the Navy would seek permission from Washington to sink it. Kennedy asked Paul Nitze, an assistant secretary of defense, to study the implications of removing the Jupiter missiles from Turkey and Italy. He explained that his initial position would be a demand for unconditional removal of the Soviet missiles from Cuba. A negotiation was likely to follow, but there would be no upfront offer of concessions, which might suggest American panic.

At the same time an elaborate programme was prepared, of letters for foreign leaders and briefings for US embassies just ahead of the approaching, inevitable diplomatic firestorm. Key allies would receive personal visits from senior US representatives, armed with copies of the CIA photos of the missile sites. They would not, however, be invited to influence the impending White House course of action. John Foster Dulles said, in a rare 1956 moment of wisdom: 'The process of consultation should never enmesh us in a procedural web so that we fall victim to the ability of despotisms to act suddenly and with all their might.' Congressional leaders around the country were intercepted by military officers who escorted them to aircraft that flew them back to Washington, in readiness to meet the president next day, Monday 22 October. The establishment of this machinery was impressive, and it went to work efficiently, intelligently and in deadly earnest. After six days that had seemed interminable to those in the secret, America's covers were now to come off the Crisis.

8

The President Speaks

1 KENNEDY CONFRONTS HIS PEOPLE

At 10.40 a.m. on Monday 22 October, Kennedy called ex-President Eisenhower. The general had already been briefed twice by the CIA's McCone, but it seemed important to ensure that he would support the policy his successor was about to unfold. Like Dean Acheson, Eisenhower favoured an unannounced bombing campaign; but he accepted the political and diplomatic logic of blockade – he was too much a patriot to go up against his successor at such a moment. The president told him of the planned intensive air surveillance of the missile sites, and said he assumed the Soviets might well shoot down a US plane, in which case: 'I think that we probably [launch air attacks].' When Kennedy had outlined the sequence of coming moves, he was relieved when Eisenhower said: 'I thank you for telling me. And ... I personally think you're really making the only move you can.'

The old soldier added a shrewd guess: he did not think there was a linkage, in Kremlin thinking, between Cuba and West Berlin – this, though former ambassador Llewellyn Thompson had just reasserted to Kennedy his conviction that West Berlin was the place which really mattered to Khrushchev; that Cuba was a mere diversionary ploy. 'Mr. President,' said Thompson, 'he made it quite clear in my last talk with him that he was squirming ... that he couldn't back down from the position he had taken [about an ultimatum for Western troop withdrawals from Berlin]. He's come so far ... He gave an indication that time was running out.'

Still on the phone to Eisenhower, Kennedy asked: 'General, what about if the Soviet Union – Khrushchev – announces tomorrow, which I think he will, that if we attack Cuba that it's going to be nuclear war. And what's your judgement as to the chances they'll fire these things off if we invade Cuba?' Eisenhower responded: 'Oh, I don't believe that they will ... Something may make these people [the Soviets] shoot them [nuclear missiles]. I just don't believe this will.' His caller, the man now bearing the giant burden that only Ike and two other living Americans had experienced and knew the full weight of, said with a resigned and uncertain chuckle: 'Yeah, right.'

Almost as soon as Kennedy got off the phone, at 11 a.m. on what was to prove one of the toughest days of the Crisis, a small group met in the Oval Office to agree arrangements for briefing America's allies and U Thant, secretary-general of the United Nations – a much more important place then than now. JFK checked the draft of a speech which Arthur Schlesinger had prepared for Adlai Stevenson to deliver. At 11.47 a.m. another small team, the so-called Berlin group, assembled to consider contingency plans in the event the Soviets launched a surprise takeover of the city. Meanwhile Kennedy was insistent – and switched on the tape-recorder so that posterity should hear his words – that orders must be sent to the US Jupiter missile sites in Turkey, emphasizing that whatever provocation the Soviets offered, no nuclear weapon was to be unleashed without his personal authorization. 'What we've got to do,' he told under-secretary Paul Nitze, 'is make sure these fellows [the American commanders and crews] do know, so that they don't fire them off and think the United States is under attack. I don't think we ought to accept the Chiefs' word on that one, Paul.'

As events would soon demonstrate, he had reason to doubt the punctilious obedience of his armed forces commanders. Gilpatric reported that the joint chiefs objected to the dispatch of a special instruction removing the default authority for the Jupiter crews in Turkey to launch, in the event of a Soviet strike. Nitze explained that the brass considered such a presidential intervention 'compromises their standing instructions'. Only after Kennedy reiterated his absolute determination that such a constraining order should be dispatched to Turkey – 'they [in Turkey] don't know ... what we know' – was this sent.

At noon in New York, where Anatoly Dobrynin had been seeing off Andrei Gromyko, who was returning to Moscow, the ambassador was accosted by a member of the American delegation to the UN, who presented a request from Dean Rusk to call on him that evening at 6 p.m. The Soviet diplomat had business in the city, and begged a postponement until next day. No, said the messenger firmly. He must be at the State Department at six. The Russian returned immediately to Washington.

Kennedy lunched with his wife in the Executive Mansion, then worked with aides and his brother Robert before signing a memorandum belatedly to formalize the status of Excom, chaired by himself, as a committee of the National Security Council to manage the Crisis, to meet every day at 10 a.m. in the Cabinet Room. Its standing membership would consist of Lyndon Johnson, Rusk, Bundy, McNamara, Sorensen, Dillon, the attorney-general, McCone, Ball, Gilpatric, Taylor, Thompson, with others invited to attend as and when.

At 3 p.m. the full NSC convened, together with the chiefs of staff, aide Kenneth O'Donnell, and a handful of other officials. Its purpose was to ensure that all the key players knew precisely what the US government had decided to do, and why. The president began by restating the rationale for action, and for the blockade, saying: 'It may end up with our having to invade Cuba.' Thus, military preparations for such an operation would go ahead. They anticipated the lines of questioning they must face. Why had the US not launched an immediate direct assault on Cuban missile sites? Because the shock to the Western alliance 'might have been nearly fatal [and it would have] excused very drastic action by Khrushchev'.

Kennedy proposed to say that, before 16 October, there had been no evidence to support action against Cuba. Here, the CIA's McCone intervened, to caution him: 'I wouldn't be too categoric that we had no information because ... there were some fifteen, I think, various refugee reports ... that were indicative that something was going on. But we had no surveillance, I think, from August 29th till the 14th of October, that gave us positive information' – this had been the consequence of both low visibility over Cuba and also political constraints which would later become a focus of public controversy – 'Therefore we were dealing during that period with conjecture and assumptions.' Kennedy felt able to defend himself against the charge that the administration had been caught by surprise, since the Soviets were never known to have positioned nuclear missiles outside their own borders – the brief 1959 East German deployment had gone unnoticed in Washington.

Bundy warned the president against saying too much about the difficulty of hitting the sites from the air, when 'we may be doing this in a few days'. The meeting also recognized that a major difficulty in discussion with America's allies was likely to be the question of why the president was taking such action in response to Soviet missiles in Cuba, when Europe had for years lived under a comparable threat. He proposed to emphasize the Soviets' cloak of secrecy, their barrage of deceits, which promised to become an important propaganda plus for the US.

Thompson observed that it was now plain why Khrushchev had undertaken not to reactivate the Berlin crisis until after the mid-terms: the timing was decided not by diplomatic courtesy, nor anxiety to assist the Democrats, but instead by completion of his grandstand play, the missile deployment. Kennedy proposed saying nothing about the US having considered and rejected the bombing option, because it remained likely that this would have to be adopted. Instead, spokesmen could state that a surprise attack had been ruled out, because of the danger of unwelcome moral comparisons with Pearl Harbor: 'We do not do like the Japanese.'

It was a reflection of Kennedy's extraordinary discipline that, following that meeting, he spent forty-five minutes with the visiting Ugandan prime minister Milton Obote. They discussed the problems of Africa as if the host had nothing else on his mind. When Obote later watched the president's earth-shaking broadcast, he felt a sense of respect, indeed awe, which never afterwards faded.

At 5.30 p.m. in the Cabinet Room, Kennedy met twenty congressional leaders, led by Dirksen, Fulbright, Russell, Humphrey and Mansfield. After summarizing US knowledge about the ballistic missiles, John McCone responded to a question from Senator Russell about Soviet readiness on Cuba, where for several days radar had been tracking U-2s: 'While they have not fired at us, we think they will within a short time.' Russell responded: 'My God.' Llewellyn Thompson expressed to the legislators his personal view that the Cuban build-up was part of the Soviet preparation for a showdown on West Berlin. Dean Rusk said he believed there had been an ongoing power struggle in the Kremlin about strategy towards the West: 'The peaceful co-existence theme was not getting them very far ... it seems clear now that the hardline boys have moved into the ascendancy.'

In this Rusk was mistaken. Whatever private reservations some Soviet insiders later claimed, there had been no overt dissension within the Kremlin. It was certainly true that Khrushchev was being taunted as a weakling by the Chinese, and by some of the Soviet military. He nonetheless faced no direct threat to his leadership. The missile deployment was a personal initiative, undertaken after negligible real debate even by the usual standards of the Presidium, in which to invite dissenters to express their views on any policy was for the *Vozhd* to expose vulnerability. Because the bluff was so immense, so reckless, when the USSR could not conceivably hope to profit from a nuclear showdown, the Americans looked for complex causes and byzantine logic to explain it. Yet these did not exist.

Kennedy and his advisers made plain to the congressional leadership that the blockade was merely a first step, providing – in Rusk's words – 'a brief pause for the people on the other side to have another thought before we get into an utterly crashing crisis, because the prospects that are ahead of us at this moment are very serious. Now, if the Soviets have underestimated what the United States is likely to do here, then we've got to consider whether they revise their judgement quick and fast.'

Richard Russell leaped in with both feet: 'Mr. President, I could not stay silent under these circumstances and live with myself. I

think that our responsibilities to our people demand stronger steps
… It seems to me that we're at the cross-roads. We're either a first-
class power or we're not … The time is going to come, Mr. President,
when we're going to have to take this gamble in Berlin, in Korea,
and in Washington DC, and Winder, Georgia [his own town] for
the nuclear war. I don't know whether Khrushchev will launch a
nuclear war over Cuba or not. I don't believe he will. But I think that
the more we temporize, the more sure he is to convince himself that
we are afraid to make any real movement and to really fight.'

Russell, sixty-four, was a Democratic veteran from an era when
endorsement of racial segregation was written into his constituency
title deeds to public office. A lawyer, he had served in his state's
House of Representatives through the 1920s, before becoming
governor at the age of thirty-three. One of Georgia's US senators
then died in office, and Russell won the special election to succeed
him. By 1962, this lifelong bachelor had served almost three
decades, latterly as chairman of the powerful Senate Armed Services
Committee.

While back in the 1930s he had been a Roosevelt-supporting
New Dealer, in Washington he became a leader of the so-called
Southern conservative coalition. Though he was in many respects
an archetype of the old Dixie white supremacist, it would be
mistaken to suppose him a fool: on the contrary, he was much
respected on Capitol Hill. This made the posture he adopted at the
White House in October all the more disturbing for the president.
As a committed Cold Warrior, Russell spoke for powerful interests
not merely in Georgia, but across the nation.

Russell's rhetoric became wilder by the minute, as he demanded
a showdown with the Soviets in language that Curtis LeMay would
have applauded. The president finally interrupted him to say that it
was militarily impossible immediately to assault the missile sites:
'We are assembling that force, but it is not in a position to invade
Cuba in the next twenty-four or forty-eight hours.' He added,
emolliently: 'Now, I think it may very well come to that before the
end of the week.' Russell persisted, saying that every day of delay
before invasion would make it harder to act. Kennedy now

famously warned the senator: 'If we go into Cuba, we have to all realize that we are taking a chance that these missiles, which are ready to fire, won't be fired ... Is that really a gamble we should take?' McNamara catalogued the military preparations which had already begun, to execute an amphibious operation requiring ninety thousand US troops, at least two thousand preparatory bombing sorties, the assembly of over a hundred cargo vessels.

Now that Russell had seized the baton, none of his fellow-legislators wished to let it drop. Kennedy said later to Arthur Schlesinger: 'The trouble is, that when you get a group of senators together, they are always dominated by the man who takes the boldest line ... After Russell spoke, no one wanted to take issue with him. When you can talk to them individually, they are reasonable.' Everett Dirksen asked if the National Security Council had given unanimous approval to all the military planning, and was assured that it had. This was, of course, disingenuous: nothing was mentioned about the strident enthusiasm for war among the chiefs of staff. And still Russell hammered on with making that case: 'We've got to take a chance somewhere, sometime, if we're going to retain our position as a great world power.' This remark recalled an interview RFK had given almost a year earlier to the *New York Post*'s James Wechsler, in which he said that he was 'disturbed by the frustrated fury of many of his countrymen who believe our national manhood can be affirmed only by some act of bloody bluster', explicitly towards Cuba, though the attorney-general himself was no slouch at supporting rash Caribbean adventures.

Senator William Fulbright's posthumous reputation is principally ornamented by his opposition to the Vietnam War and sponsorship of international scholarships, rather than by his hostility to black American civil rights – and bellicosity on Cuba. Now, he said that he thought a US assault on the island posed fewer legal complications than the proposed blockade – 'the *worst* alternative. I'm in favour of an invasion, and an all-out one, and as quickly as possible.'

When it was all over, and the world was still there, such exchanges as this became easy to gloss over, to fast-forward; instead to cut to the chase, or rather to the relatively happy ending. Yet it is important to acknowledge, and indeed to highlight, the fact that in October 1962 some prominent and powerful Americans wished to launch military action against Soviet forces, which were present by invitation in a foreign country, and to accept the risk that this would provoke nuclear war. Such men as Richard Russell were big figures, influential politicians. They were less interested in the specifics of the situation in Cuba than in the opportunity or pretext this offered for demonstrating the superior might of the United States; for showing the Soviet Union where it got off. Their irresponsibility was breathtaking, reflected in the flippancy of Russell's next remark: 'the nettle is going to sting anyway'. Nonetheless the president had no political choice save to treat these men with courtesy and respect.

Russell kept going: 'I think we can die by attrition here. I'm through. Excuse me. I wouldn't have been honest with myself if I hadn't. So I hope you forgive me, but you asked for opinions.' The president said: 'Yeah, I forgive you. As I said, it's a very difficult problem that we're faced with.' Russell, yet again: 'Oh, my God, I know that. Our authority, and the world's destiny, will hinge on this decision.' Kennedy: 'That's right.' Russell: 'But it's coming some day, Mr. President. Will it ever be under more auspicious circumstances?' Kennedy responded by reading aloud a long letter from prime minister Harold Macmillan, who had been let into the secret during the previous evening. This emphasized the Britisher's desperate anxiety that the US should move cautiously.

Macmillan concluded: 'While you know how deeply I sympathize with all of your difficulties and how much we will try to help in every way, it would only be right to tell you there are two aspects which give me concern. Many of us in Europe have lived so long in close proximity to the enemy's nuclear weapons of the most devastating kind that we have got accustomed to it ... More worrying is that ... [Khrushchev] will try to trade his Cuba position against ambitions in Berlin and elsewhere. This we must avoid at all costs, as it will endanger the unity of the Alliance.' When the legislators left, the president confessed that he had found the meeting immensely stressful. To his brother, however, he excused the vehemence of the congressional leaders' reaction by saying that it was about the same as the mood in the White House, on first hearing of the missile deployment an eternity ago, the previous Tuesday.

Now, on this subsequent Monday afternoon, all US forces around the world were summoned to Defence Condition 3. DEFCON 5 represented normal peacetime routine. DEFCON 1 was war. DEFCON 3, and later higher, was to be sustained through the next thirty days of continuous USAF operations – 2,088 sorties and 48,532 flying hours, in which SAC's nuclear-armed bombers flew twenty million miles. Meanwhile tens of thousands of personnel, hundreds of aircraft and scores of ships began to move towards Florida and Georgia, in readiness for military action. US railroads were commissioned to marshal 3,600 flatcars, 180 gondola cars, forty boxcars and two hundred passenger coaches to move the 1st Armored Division from Fort Hood, Texas. Some US ordnance factories moved to three-shift, seven-day-week production, to meet the anticipated demand for ammunition and bombs, especially from the USAF.

Marines chanted as they exercised by companies on the flight deck of the helicopter-carrier *Okinawa*: '*Where are we gonna go?/ Gonna go to Cuba/ Whatta we gonna do?/ Gonna castrate Castro*'. Their officers studied Plan 316, a blueprint for the invasion of the island, Operation Scabbards, which called for the 1st Armored Division to land through the port of Mariel to the west, while the Marines hit Tarará beach, east of Havana. The 82nd and 101st Airborne divisions would meanwhile drop behind the beaches, as their fathers had done in Normandy eighteen years earlier. The entire invasion force would make for the identified missile sites, skirting Havana. Among these elite American formations morale, or rather self-belief, was supremely high. If their senior officers nursed a cache of secret unease about what they might meet on the island, the men knew they were The Best; they expected to walk over the Cuban army, and any Ruskies who got in the way. The prospective invaders were issued with face masks and chemical detection kits. In the event of a nuclear explosion in their vicinity,

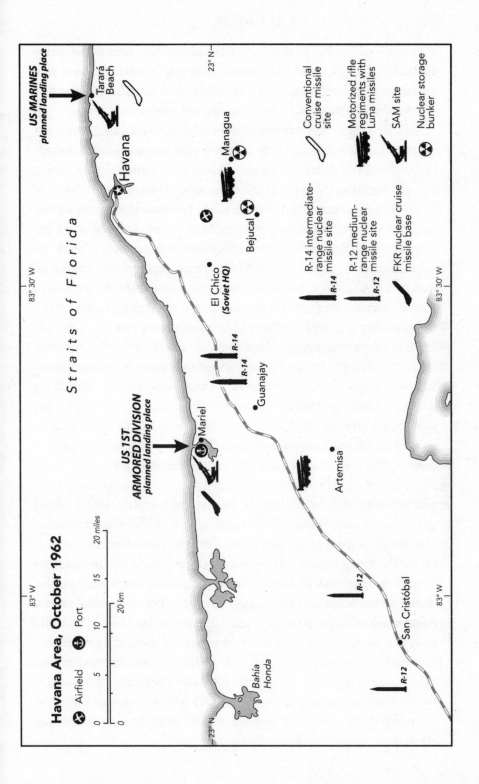

Havana Area, October 1962

⊗ Airfield   ⊕ Port

0   5   10   15   20 km

0   5   10   15   20 miles

Straits of Florida

US MARINES
planned landing place

Tarará Beach

Havana

Managua

Bejucal

El Chico
(Soviet HQ)

Guanajay

US 1ST ARMORED DIVISION
planned landing place

Mariel

Artemisa

San Cristóbal

Bahía Honda

R-14

R-14

R-12

R-12

R-12

83° W

83° 30' W

23° N

23° N

83° 30' W

83° W

⌒ Conventional cruise missile site

Motorized rifle regiments with Luna missiles

SAM site

☢ Nuclear storage bunker

R-14 intermediate-range nuclear missile site

R-12 medium-range nuclear missile site

FKR nuclear cruise missile base

they were instructed to mark contaminated areas, and report burst and yield data for 'every delivered nuclear fire'. The invasion plan anticipated a possible eighteen thousand US casualties in the first ten days of fighting, including four thousand dead.

Shortly before Kennedy met the congressional leaders, already night in London, Harold Macmillan hosted a dinner at his temporary official residence Admiralty House – 10 Downing Street was being refurbished – to mark the retirement of Gen. Lauris Norstad as NATO supreme allied commander, Europe. This was a fortuitous encounter, but the prime minister – in keeping with his extraordinary sense of alarm and anxiety for caution – took the opportunity to emphasize to Norstad that Britain would have no part of a NATO alert, such as Washington had that day urged 'in a rather panicky way'. If Britain acceded, a royal proclamation and mobilization of reservists would be required: 'I told him that we will *not* repeat *not* agree at this stage.' Norstad said he anticipated that other NATO nations would adopt the same view. Macmillan, who was thinking as much about 1914 as was Kennedy, and in his own case with personal memories, observed that mobilizations had sometimes precipitated wars. In this case, such a step would be absurd, since the forces that would be summoned to arms had no conceivable operational relevance to the immediate Crisis.

Khrushchev was at his dacha in the Lenin Hills overlooking Moscow, an impressive official residence, when he was telephoned late in the evening, to receive news of Kennedy's impending broadcast. 'They've probably discovered our missiles,' he told his son Sergei. He summoned an immediate meeting of the Presidium and drove to the Kremlin. He paused briefly at his own office on the third floor of the old Senate Building then, around 10 p.m. – still only 3 p.m. in Washington – moved on to the lofty yet harshly austere Presidium meeting room, two doors along. He understood that his Cuban missile gambit threatened to become a disaster – a very personal disaster, because he himself was its sole begetter. Even before the president spoke in Washington, he must have been conscious of his throne trembling.

The meeting began with an update from the secretary of the Defence Council on the status of Soviet forces and missile sites in Cuba. The Presidium members then addressed alternative responses to Kennedy's broadcast, all of which assumed that the nuclear deployment had been discovered. Although accounts of the meeting are fragmentary, the evidence suggests that Khrushchev was visibly alarmed, impulsive. He suggested that the US president might announce an instant invasion of Cuba.

Marshal Malinovsky calmed him by pointing out that preparations for such an operation must be conspicuous, and take many days: there were no intelligence indications of such activity. The defence minister said he thought it unlikely that Kennedy would announce an immediate assault: 'I do not think that the USA right now could embark on blitzkrieg operations. It is not such a country.' The last enigmatic sentence may be interpreted as flattering American sobriety or, more plausibly, as indicating that an open society could not readily prepare to launch a huge amphibious operation from its home ports and airfields without attracting attention. Malinovsky suggested, optimistically, that Kennedy's speech might represent some sort of 'pre-election stunt'. He added that it seemed unnecessary to raise the alert status of the Soviet Union's missile forces, a move that must increase American fears, when it was wildly unlikely that Kennedy was about to launch a nuclear First Strike.

Khrushchev agreed: 'The point is that we do not want to unleash a war. We want to frighten and restrain the USA in the matter of Cuba.' For the first time, the leader saw the trap he had set for himself by installing the missiles covertly, instead of announcing a defence treaty with Castro. Indeed, he suddenly experienced an onrush of understanding of many perils that should have been apparent in the Kremlin from the first moment of Operation Anadyr's conception: 'The tragic thing is that they can attack, and we will respond. This could escalate into a large-scale war.' The meeting scrabbled to review a wild range of options. Could they immediately arrange by radio a defence treaty with Castro? Might they place all the missiles in the island under Cuban control, asserting that the Soviet Union had nothing to do with them? It was left to Mikoyan to point out that the United States, far from being intimidated by a declaration that the USSR had transferred nuclear weapons to the unstable Castro, was likely to consider such an action the ultimate provocation.

It was agreed that Gen. Issa Pliev in Cuba should be warned to place his forces on full alert. Malinovsky proposed to dispatch an order: 'All means at "Pavlov"'s disposal [Pliev's codename] should be in a state of readiness.' Khrushchev belatedly grasped the chasm this would open. 'If [Soviet forces on the island] were to use all means without exception,' he told Malinovsky, 'that would include the missiles ... Doesn't that mean the start of a thermonuclear war? How can we imagine such a thing?' He and most of his colleagues, in those dark hours inside the Kremlin, were frightened men – probably as frightened as they had ever been, in lives richly endowed with terror.

Mikoyan's account nonetheless shows that the Presidium's 22 October meeting proposed to grant discretion to Pliev to launch the tactical and medium-range missiles, if conventional forces failed to stem an American invasion. A new draft message to Soviet head-quarters in Cuba read: 'Make all effort initially not to use atomic [weaponry]. If there is an assault landing – the tactical atomic weaponry but the strategic [not] until orders are given [from Moscow].'

In the narrowest military sense, such an order would have been rational: the Soviet Expeditionary Force in Cuba had little prospect of repelling an American invasion without resort to its tactical nuclear warheads. Yet it was finally decided to await Kennedy's broadcast before sending Pliev new orders of any kind. Fursenko and Naftali call that Presidium meeting of 22 October 'arguably the most tense of Khrushchev's career', and it is hard to dissent. The members concluded by agreeing to receive news of the Washington broadcast as a body, assembled around the table in the early hours of the morning of 23 October, so that they could discuss the USSR's response without delay.

At 6 p.m. in Washington, Anatoly Dobrynin was ushered into Rusk's office. Following a chilly exchange of courtesies, the secretary of state handed to him Kennedy's personal letter for Khrushchev, informing him of American discovery of the Cuban missiles, and declaring a US naval blockade of Cuban waters. Back in his office at the embassy, for fifteen minutes the stunned Dobrynin sat alone, attempting to puzzle out this extraordinary new situation: 'I was severely confused, since I had no instructions or advance warning of any kind from my government ... Had [Khrushchev] asked the embassy beforehand, we could have predicted the violent American reaction to his adventure.' In Cuba Fidel Castro, anticipating what was coming, mobilized his armed forces twenty minutes before Kennedy spoke. He, like Khrushchev, expected an American invasion. Dividing his island into three defence zones, he dispatched Che Guevara to command in the west, Raúl Castro to the east, while army chief of staff Juan Almeida became responsible for the centre. He himself remained in Havana.

One other significant event took place in Moscow in those hours: the jaws of the Soviet trap, poised for two months around the key Western informant Col. Oleg Penkovsky, snapped shut. His doom had been sealed since July, when the KGB Second Directorate eavesdropped on conversations between him and British business-man Greville Wynne, his courier, in a Moscow hotel room. It was surely a moment of madness that Penkovsky's Western handlers allowed such a meeting to take place, at a rendezvous that was bound to be monitored. The KGB delayed his arrest in order to accumulate further evidence, but from the date he was pinpointed as a traitor, he received no further access to sensitive sources and intelligence – which could have been invaluable to his Western beneficiaries during the looming confrontation. Penkovsky had made his last document handover on 29 August, in the bathroom of the Moscow apartment of an American agricultural attaché, receiving in return a Soviet internal passport in a false name, in case he was obliged to cut and run.

On 6 September, the KGB officer attended a film showing at the British cultural attaché's offices, which proved the final sighting of him before his arrest. On 22 October, the Soviet watchers who had continued to gather evidence, in hopes of netting collaborators of the traitor, were finally ordered to pounce. Penkovsky was confronted at his apartment and taken to the Lubyanka, the vast neo-baroque secret headquarters building that hosted so much cruelty and murder, where he immediately volunteered to confess all that he knew, 'in the interests of the Motherland'. KGB chief Vladimir Semichastny commenced a grim personal interrogation with the words: 'Tell me what harm you have inflicted on our country.' Penkovsky disclosed everything, knowing that this could not save his life, but might at least spare him from the Lubyanka's most barbarous variations upon death.

At 7 p.m. EDT, normal US TV programming was cancelled to make way for the president's statement from the Oval Office of the White House. John F. Kennedy began with words that would echo around the world: 'Good evening, my fellow citizens. This Government, as promised, has maintained the closest surveillance of the Soviet military build-up on the island of Cuba. Within the past week unmistakable evidence has established the fact that a series of offensive missile sites is now in preparation on that imprisoned island. The purposes of these bases can be none other than to provide a nuclear strike capability against the Western Hemisphere.'

The president said that confirmation of this development was now forthcoming: he detailed the known missile deployments. 'This urgent transformation of Cuba into an important strategic base ... constitutes an explicit threat to the peace and security of all the Americas, in flagrant and deliberate defiance of the Rio Pact of 1947, the traditions of this nation and hemisphere, the Joint Resolution of the 87th Congress, the Charter of the United Nations and my own public warnings to the Soviets on September 4 and 13. This action also contradicts the repeated assurances of Soviet spokesmen, both publicly and privately delivered, that the arms build-up in Cuba would retain its original defensive character.'

He then detailed statements by the Russians that were now shown to be false. '... This secret, swift and extraordinary building of Communist missiles – in an area well known to have a special and historical relationship to the United States and the nations of the Western Hemisphere – cannot be tolerated by this country if our courage and our commitments are ever to be trusted again by either friend or foe.' Kennedy made reference to the disastrous appeasement of the 1930s European dictators, before announcing his 'quarantine', or blockade, adding that this would apply only to weapons and not – as the Soviets did to Berlin in 1948–49 – halt the flow of necessities of life for the Cuban people. He stated that the US would regard any nuclear weapon launched from Cuba as representing an attack 'requiring a full retaliatory response upon the Soviet Union'.

The US, he said, had convened a gathering of the members of the Organization of American States to consider the threat, and was requesting an emergency meeting of the UN Security Council: 'Finally, I call upon Chairman Khrushchev to halt and eliminate this clandestine, reckless and provocative threat to world peace. My fellow citizens, let no one doubt that this is a difficult and dangerous effort on which we have set out. No one can foresee precisely what course it will take or what costs or casualties will be incurred. Many months of sacrifice and self-discipline lie ahead ... But the greatest danger of all would be to do nothing ... Our goal is not the victory of might but the vindication of right – not peace at the expense of freedom but both peace and freedom, here in this Hemisphere and, we hope, around the world. God willing, that goal will be achieved.' Kennedy finally addressed 'the captive people of Cuba ... Now your leaders are no longer Cuban leaders inspired by Cuban ideals. They are puppets and agents of an international conspiracy which has turned Cuba ... into the first Latin American country to become a target for nuclear war.'

Kennedy's broadcast on that Monday night, accompanied by release of the missile photos, was among the most dramatic public pronouncements of the Cold War. A droll side-effect was to make the 'spyplane', hitherto known to the public only as a source of national embarrassment, represented by the Gary Powers shootdown, into a critical weapon in the armoury of freedom. 'The once-villainous U-2 had been transformed, virtually overnight, into a heroic instrument', in the words of David Barrett and Max Holland, historians of the photo operation.

Headlines shrieked around the world next day: The entire front page of Britain's tabloid *Daily Sketch* was occupied by the story that began 'BLOCKADE! Ultimatum to Khrushchev ... Sensational Move by Kennedy'. The *New York Times* reported: 'CUBA ACTION GETS PUBLIC'S BACKING But Check of U.S. Indicates Many Fear Result'. The president's remarks about 'imprisoned' Cuba raised eyebrows among allies sensitive to America's historic record on the island. Whatever the shortcomings of Fidel Castro, which indeed were great, the conduct of his regime derived from what had gone before. But Kennedy's depiction of Castro's people seemed a necessary concession to his domestic constituency, which included many of the people who had damned President Harry Truman a decade earlier for the alleged 'loss' of China.

Years later, Mac Bundy looked back on the 22 October speech, written by Ted Sorensen, as 'a little overstated and overemotional'. Early in the relationship with Sorensen, Kennedy had urged his aide to study the rhetoric of both Lincoln and Churchill, and it showed. Sorensen himself said: 'The reason the speech was overe-motional was that the President ... was worried that the world would say, "What's the difference between Soviet missiles ninety miles away from Florida and American missiles right next door to the Soviet Union in Turkey?" It was precisely for that reason that there was so much emphasis on the *sudden* and *deceptive* deploy-ment ... We relied very heavily on words such as those to make sure the world didn't focus on the question of symmetry.'

Indeed, the president's most effective language addressed Soviet obfuscations and deceits. If Khrushchev's deployment of missiles in Cuba was legitimate, to promote the defence of an ally, why had he concealed it beneath a barrage of lies? At that period, Kennedy enjoyed critical advantages in making his case for the United States. Most of the world, despite its distaste for American arrogance, its jealousy of American wealth and fear of American excess, still acknowledged the US as standard-bearer for the free world, and as its principal protector. It recognized the Soviet Union as a citadel of terror and oppression. John F. Kennedy and his nation could expect from most fair-minded people some benefit of the doubt, such as would no longer be available a decade later, in the wake of Vietnam and Watergate. As for the American people, they took it for granted that they were right; that the Russians and Cubans were wrong; and that Kennedy was now telling them the truth. Bundy wrote: 'The President's speech was more effective than we had dared to hope beforehand. An overwhelming majority of Americans accepted the danger and supported the President's course.'

There is a further general point, about the meaning of words. All politicians sometimes posture. In the context of the Cold War, however, most Western leaders saw the issues at stake as too grave for rhetorical excess. Tensions were repeatedly intensified by Soviet, and explicitly Khrushchevian, threats and warnings that subsequently proved to have been empty, especially about Berlin. Kennedy as president, by contrast, chose his language with utmost care; he generally meant what he said, and never more so than on the evening of 22 October 1962. From the moment of the president's TV appearance the Crisis became the most public of the Cold War, played out through the six days that followed before a global audience of hundreds of millions.

The CIA's ONE staff felt a huge relief that they need no longer clutch to their bosoms the huge and deadly secret; could thereafter discuss it among the wider US intelligence community. In the streets there was a surge of panic-buying, as many American housewives shopped for a siege. The manager of a Los Angeles supermarket gazed bewildered at a woman who staggered out laden with twelve jumbo cartons of detergent, demanding: 'What's she going to do – wash up after the Bomb?' Charter planes owned by Saturn Airways flying ammunition into Guantánamo suddenly found their insurances cancelled. They were informed, not unreasonably, that they now needed to pay sky-high war-risk premiums, which Pentagon bureaucrats most unreasonably declined to cover. Sergei Khrushchev later compared the American public reaction to the president's speech to that following Pearl Harbor: 'The stance of the Joint Chiefs of Staff received powerful support. Americans, it seemed, were all prepared to perish, just as long as they could evict these uninvited guests from their neighbour's territory. No one mentioned that they were talking about another, sovereign state.'

In Cuba, following the president's broadcast and revelations of the missile deployment of which they had previously been told nothing, there was amazement. The French ambassador in Havana reported to Paris that 'the lower cadres of the revolution seem preoccupied and alarmed ... The propaganda specialists have been relying on their accustomed bluster, and have plainly not yet received instructions on how to address this new situation.' It was obvious, however, that there was almost absolute public unity behind Castro, in the face of American threats. Some Russians were astonished by the professed insouciance of Cubans about a showdown with the US. Vasil Lanovsky heard locals say: 'We can do it any time, just give us the nuclear weapons and we will show them! We will make them sit on their potty [shit themselves]!' There seemed no limit to the capacity for fantasy among the people of the island nation.

Kennedy now responded to the overnight letter he had received from Britain's Macmillan. He sought to assuage some of the old statesman's fears: 'I recognize the hazard of a riposte in Berlin, but in the wider sense I believe that inaction would be still more dangerous ... I assure you most solemnly that this is not simply a matter of aroused public opinion or of private passion against Cuba ... I have repeatedly resisted pressure for unreasonable or excessive action, and I am not interested in a squabble with Castro ... But ... our best basic course is firmness.' In a telephone conversation with the prime minister a little later that evening, during which the British leader suggested that his own fears focused upon the prospect of an extended crisis, a protracted auction of worldwide menaces, Kennedy said: 'Our action is obviously moderated by the realization that we could move very quickly into a world war over this, or to a nuclear war, or to lose Berlin, and that's why we've taken the course we've taken. Even though, as I say, it doesn't represent any final answer.' The harsh truth was that Macmillan, left to choose his own option, would have favoured an initial resort to diplomacy, which in American eyes amounted to doing nothing. For Kennedy, such a choice was unthinkable: his domestic constituency would not countenance it; and unsupported by a threat of American force, talking was likely to go nowhere.

2 KHRUSHCHEV CONFRONTS DISASTER

The Soviet Presidium had remained in session through the US presidential TV broadcast, to receive soon afterwards a transcript of Kennedy's seventeen-minute address, delivered alongside the text of his personal letter to Khrushchev, of which Dobrynin had been handed a copy in Washington. In this, the president said that during his past exchanges with the Soviet leader, 'the one thing that has most concerned me has been the possibility that your Government would not correctly understand the will and determination of the United States in any given situation'. He now asserted an absolute and unqualified commitment to securing the removal of the Soviet missiles from Cuba.

For Khrushchev, the president's public announcement signalled the failure of his gamble – that he could complete the deployment of strategic missiles in Cuba unnoticed by the Americans and the world; spring an earth-shaking surprise in November, such as might shift the balance of the Cold War. Although not a word of this was admitted at the Kremlin conference table in the early morning darkness of 23 October – the broadcast began at 2 a.m. Moscow time – there was scarcely a Russian privy to the Cuban secret who did not recognize an unfolding disaster when he saw one.

Khrushchev's professed reaction was relief that the American leader had not announced an immediate invasion. 'We've saved Cuba!' he said, snatching for a fantasy triumph that fooled none of his colleagues. He continued his commentary on Kennedy's speech: 'This is not a war against Cuba, but some kind of ultimatum.' He then took a series of rapid decisions. Sixteen ships carrying military hardware to the island, notably *Kimovsk* and *Poltava*, loaded with R-14 missiles, and *Gagarin*, carrying R-12 equipment, were to be ordered to turn back. Soviet forces worldwide were placed on a heightened alert. When all the Presidium members had read the Kennedy transcript, Khrushchev dictated a proposed response, which was then passed to others for discussion and possible amendment before dispatch. He denounced the blockade as 'an act of piracy', and accused Kennedy of pushing the world to the edge of thermonuclear war. Kremlin officials worked for the rest of the night to refine texts of these drafts.

Signals were dispatched to Maj. Gen. Igor Statsenko, commanding the missile forces in Cuba, and Col. Nikolai Beloborodov, in charge of the nuclear warheads, ordering them to alert their forces to face possible US military action. Malinovsky's earlier draft cable, presented to the Presidium for approval, would have authorized Gen. 'Pavlov' – Pliev – to use all means at his disposal to meet a US assault. That proposed message was now amended, to become an order that no nuclear warhead, tactical or strategic, should be fired without explicit orders from Moscow.

This new directive confronted the Soviet officers in Cuba with a massive challenge. Without recourse to the atomic warheads, their forces were capable only of mauling and checking a US amphibious invasion force: there was scant prospect that they could defeat it. Thus, they were obliged to wrestle with a dilemma to which an assured answer can never be forthcoming: if American forces had indeed attacked, with emotions running high and carnage among their own troops, would they have respected Moscow's belated prohibition on the release of nuclear weapons? It is impossible to be certain, especially because some senior officers in Cuba would later escalate the Crisis on their own initiative. In the Kremlin, meanwhile, the Presidium adjourned for a few hours' break. Khrushchev lay down fully clothed on a sofa in the anteroom of his office, and lapsed into a sleep that is unlikely to have been untroubled.

The Soviet Union's leaders reconvened at 10 a.m., when *Pravda* was already on the streets bearing the headline 'THE RULING CIRCLES OF THE USA ARE PLAYING WITH FIRE'. After further discussion the meeting approved a final version of

Khrushchev's defiant statement. In response to the US blockade, it was also confirmed that Soviet vessels en route to Cuba carrying weapons should be ordered to turn back, while those with innocent cargoes held their courses. There was one exception: the *Aleksandrovsk*, already close to the island with a second shipment of nuclear warheads, was ordered to complete its passage to the port of La Isabela before the US blockade was implemented – the ship docked unmolested, late that night.

One bone of contention was the disposition of the four Foxtrot submarines en route to Cuba. Mikoyan argued that they should remain outside the declared 'quarantine' zone – still close enough to Cuba to intervene if and when necessary, but without risking a clash with the US Navy. Khrushchev agreed with this proposal, but Malinovsky and three other Presidium members dissented. Here was an instance when the leader and his supporters were obliged to yield to Kremlin hardliners. The submarines sailed on.

When the gathering broke for lunch, Mikoyan again urged Khrushchev to revisit the submarine issue, which he thought serious and dangerous. Yet when they reassembled and Khrushchev once more mooted the submarines heaving to – holding their existing positions three days out from Cuba – the same members demurred, and again prevailed. Malinovsky emphasized his confidence that the Foxtrots could close the island undetected by the Americans. The marshal thus once more exposed his lack of judgement and knowledge about both submarines and the capabilities of US surveillance technology.

That evening, when the Presidium assembled for the third time since the presidential broadcast, the meeting was also attended by Admiral Sergei Gorshkov, Soviet naval chief, who briefed its members with the aid of maps. To the relief of Mikoyan and the other doves, the sailor acknowledged a high probability that the Americans would spot the submarines in shallow Caribbean waters, thickly strewn with detection devices. The submerged submarines therefore kept some distance from Cuba, though already under close American surveillance, and still holding courses that would take two of them inside the quarantine zone.

For the Russians, the most urgent imperative was to decide how to respond to Kennedy's imposition of a blockade, when a dozen Soviet vessels were still in transit towards Cuba. Despite Anatoly Dobrynin's depiction of himself in his memoirs as a career-long dove, he could not have kept his plum post for so long, had he not conformed to broad Kremlin policy and posturing. Now, in a telegram from Washington to Moscow, he assessed Kennedy's speech as an attempt to reverse the slide in US power worldwide, and to fears about Berlin. He urged taking some of the heat off Cuba by threatening a ground blockade of West Berlin, excluding air routes 'so as not to give grounds for a quick confrontation'. Yet he cautioned against haste, 'since an extreme aggravation of the situation, it goes without saying, would not be in our interests'.

Meanwhile the Soviet submarines remained at sea, though now relieved of their earlier responsibility to shadow and escort cargo vessels carrying sensitive loads, including nuclear warheads. Their sole function in the western Atlantic became that of presenting a threat-in-being to US warships. However, the decision to leave them in the theatre of operations reflected yet more confused thinking by Moscow. There was no possibility of the USSR winning a local clash at sea with the US Navy in the western Atlantic or Caribbean: thus, any actions that its warships undertook to defy the blockade must represent either bluffs or doomed gestures. It was extraordinarily self-indulgent to attempt either, in the climate of October 1962.

In the twenty-first century, many mysteries remain unresolved about the contradictions in Soviet behaviour. Even as weapon-carrying vessels stopped and turned around short of the American blockade line, in Cuba work on the ballistic missile sites continued to advance at an almost frenzied pace, as did belated camouflage activity. The most plausible explanation is a dysfunction between the alarm and caution which had now overtaken the Kremlin and a much more combative mood within the Soviet military, especially its representatives in Cuba, who had been dispatched from Mother Russia bearing such resonantly aggressive orders. If not impatient for a showdown with the US, Gen. Pliev's officers were certainly viscerally resistant to accepting a defeat or humiliation at American hands.

On 23 October in the Kremlin, whatever Nikita Khrushchev's private recognition of reality, he was still days away from acknowledging the logic of his untenable predicament in Cuba and the surrounding Caribbean, which demanded hasty retreat. He was shaken; desperate to avoid a nuclear showdown with the US.

The subsequent history of the Missile Crisis is that of the Soviet Union writhing and twisting, to find means to extricate itself without overt humiliation from a shambles of its own making. The difficulties inherent in achieving this could well have proved so great that nuclear disaster nonetheless came about through accident or miscalculation, especially on the part of subordinate commanders. But Khrushchev's adviser Oleg Troyanovsky said: 'In spite of the Soviet leader's penchant for taking risks, a war with the United States did not enter into his plans under any circumstances. He understood better than anyone else that in the modern world a military clash of the two superpowers would have evolved into a nuclear conflict with disastrous consequences for all humankind.' When Sergei Khrushchev returned to the family house from his job in a design office, he often went out walking with his father, and always asked what was happening. Sometimes Nikita Khrushchev answered him at length, but when things got really bad he said instead: 'I'm tired. Let's walk silently.' That happened more than once during the ensuing week.

Yet despite all this, Khrushchev remained determined to play out his hand to the last, to escape a defeat so explicit that it must imperil his leadership of the Soviet Union, as well as shrink his stature on the world stage. Thus, that Tuesday morning in Moscow, he determined to press the Americans to their limits, even if the cost of discovering where these lay included the risk of nuclear showdown.

9

Blockade

1 HIGH, CONFUSED SEA*

In October 1962 President Kennedy attached an importance to the opinions of allies greater than any president has since reprised, or in future is likely to, when perceived US vital national interests are at stake. He was thoroughly aware that, in private, most friendly nations were deeply sceptical about going to war for anything at stake in Cuba. Fortunately, however, amid crisis allies were prepared to go far, publicly to sustain the solidarity of the West. During the weekend of 20/21 October, high-level emissaries were dispatched from Washington to brief the leaders of the most important NATO nations, including Canada's John Diefenbaker and West Germany's Konrad Adenauer. That Saturday, Dean Acheson had retired to his farm at Sandy Spring, Maryland, disgusted at the perceived pusillanimity of Kennedy's decision merely to initiate a blockade. In the evening, Rusk called the farm: his country needed the former secretary of state. JFK would broadcast on Monday. It was important to enlist the support of the French, which meant their president, Charles de Gaulle. Ambassador-designate 'Chip' Bohlen was still in mid-Atlantic. Would Acheson go? Yes, he would. Then it was discovered that his passport had expired: the office in Washington opened specially on Sunday morning to renew it. Then Acheson found that he had no cash. In those pre-hole-in-the-wall days, State Department officials

* Nautical term.

staged a whip-round, which raised $60 to provide pocket money for the emissary of the world's richest nation.

Acheson's plane refuelled in Britain, at the USAF's Greenham Common base in Berkshire, where London ambassador David Bruce was waiting to confer. In heavy rain, the visitors disembarked and entered an airfield hut where they talked while armed Marines and Secret Service men stood guard. The plane had been alcoholically dry, but Bruce thoughtfully brought a whisky flask, to offer the distinguished emissary before he flew on to Paris.

It was already Monday night, a few hours ahead of the presidential broadcast, when Acheson finally arrived at the Élysée Palace on the Rue du Faubourg Saint-Honoré, accompanied by Cecil Lyon, who was acting as embassy chargé d'affaires, and Sherman Kent of the CIA's ONE cell. As the three men entered by basement corridors – to avoid alerting the media – Acheson the old warhorse thrilled to the drama. He recalled to his companions Dumas' *Three Musketeers*: 'Porthos, is your rapier loose in its scabbard?' They had cause to be apprehensive. The French leader, who two months earlier had survived a right-wing assassination attempt which left his car riddled with bullet-holes, possessed a notorious capacity for contrariness, rudeness, independence of thought and action, symbolized by his commitment to a French national nuclear striking force.

Yet that evening de Gaulle, master of discourtesy, astonished the Americans by his unhesitatingly supportive demeanour and language. He initially declined to scan the U-2 photos, of which they had brought copies, saying: 'I accept what you tell me as fact, without any proof of any sort needed.' He asked: what if the Soviets challenged the blockade? Acheson was unsure of the answer, but bluffed hawkishly. Only after promising France's support did the towering old general ask to see the photos, which he scanned with a magnifier: '*Incroyable*,' he remarked – not because the images revealed Soviet missiles, but instead when he was told that they had been exposed from 75,000 feet. Before the Americans left, the president said courteously to Acheson, 'It would be a pleasure to me if these things were all done through you … If there is a war, I will be with you' – note the personalization of the French nation – 'but there will be no war.' Following Kennedy's broadcast, next day there were plentiful French voices of dissent from the left, demonstrations in the streets and vociferous comment in the press. The communist paper *L'Humanité* headed its story 'MENACE CONTRE LE PAIX MONDIALE'. *Libération* told its readers 'MESURES DE GUERRE U.S. CONTRE CUBA. *Le Figaro* proclaimed 'EMBARGO SUR LES ARMES A DESTINATION DE CUBA'. Acheson later said cynically about de Gaulle's reception of him: 'This was Louis XIV saying a kind word to an ambassador from the Sultan of Turkey.' What mattered, however, was the Élysée's good word, and the Americans had got it.

By far the most important allies were the British, possessed of their own nuclear capability, bombs carried by the RAF's so-called V-Force of Vulcan bombers. It proved a striking feature of the Crisis that even among Conservatives support for the US proved equivocal; confidence in its leadership less than full-throated; fear of war greater than in either Washington or Moscow. Peter Hudson, a senior Ministry of Defence official, confessed long afterwards: 'I had the heebie-jeebies all right. The Berlin crisis was familiar pieces being played on the board. Cuba wasn't. It was an entirely different game. I'm sure it was the closest we came.'

At 10 p.m. on Sunday the 21st, Macmillan was reading in his study at Admiralty House when a duty clerk brought him an 'Eyes Only' message from the president, setting out the essentials of the Crisis. Next morning he was briefed by David Bruce, a respected grandee diplomatist, who arrived accompanied by the CIA's Chester Cooper. In response, the prime minister offered a weary view of Soviet behaviour that was widely shared by Europeans, though almost incomprehensible to Americans: British people, he said, who had been living in the shadow of annihilation for many years past, contrived to live more or less normal lives. He felt that the Americans, now confronted with a similar situation would, after the initial shock, make a similar adjustment: 'Life goes on somehow.' The prime minister was dismayed and even affronted, as later were many of his people, by the manner in which Washington's decisions were announced. He was privily briefed about what was about to happen. He was certainly not, however, consulted about its advisability.

Macmillan immediately sat down with foreign secretary Lord Home to draft the response to Kennedy, dispatched in his own name, which a few hours later the president quoted to congressional leaders, as recorded above. On Monday evening the prime minister wrote in his diary: 'First Day of the World Crisis!' At that moment, however, the European peoples, hours ahead of Washington, still had no inkling of the sensation that was about to break. British politics in the preceding weeks had been dominated by stumbling negotiations with Brussels about possible entry into the European Common Market; the trial of yet another defence worker unmasked as a Soviet agent; Uganda's independence; low-key discussion of how far Britain should, or should not, support the American trade boycott of shipping to Cuba, which had been in force for many months. The main headline in the London *Times* on 22 October, ahead of Kennedy's broadcast, addressed the Indo-Chinese border clashes: 'INDIA CALLS UP MORE RESERVES'. There was, however, a lead piece on the first foreign news page: 'BUILDUP OF US FORCES IN CARIBBEAN; TENSION OVER CUBA; PRESIDENT CUTS SHORT VISIT'. The paper's Washington correspondent wrote: 'There can be little doubt that something is going on', while confessing that he had no idea what: 'officials have been unusually evasive'.

Shortly after Kennedy addressed the American people, he telephoned Macmillan from the White House on the scrambled 'Hot Line' telephone, a primitive system which required each party in turn to flick a switch on the handset between 'speak' and 'receive'. Macmillan could never operate this without assistance from his staff: doubts persist about exactly how much of Kennedy's call he properly heard – Lord Home, for one, later expressed some scepticism. Kennedy was quintessentially a man of the twentieth century, whereas Macmillan sustained the affectations of a grandee of the nineteenth: he disliked the telephone and even more the television; referred to radio as 'the wireless'; did not possess a driving licence since his only recorded foray at the wheel precipitated himself and the car into the wall of a garage.

In their conversation, soon after midnight British time on the 22/23 October, Kennedy described the missile deployment to the prime minister as 'so deep a breach in the conventions of the international stalemate that if unchallenged it would deeply shake confidence in the United States'. Macmillan afterwards quoted this assertion to his Cabinet. Kennedy described the decision to initiate a blockade as fulfilment of 'an escalation in a way that lessens the chance of a seizure of Berlin, or World War III ... Now, we may not be able to prevent either, but at least we have served notice on him that we cannot accept the procedure and the actions which he carried out.'

The days that followed Kennedy's 22 October broadcast showed the British people far from united either in enthusiasm for the US cause or in sharing the American conviction that the Soviet Union and Cuba represented forces of unalloyed wickedness. More than a few Europeans viewed Castro's behaviour since he assumed power as representing a mere act of secession from the American empire.

Macmillan himself was committed to the US alliance and implacably hostile to communism. But he was also desperately fearful of a nuclear conflict, and of a risk that White House overreach – the mood reflected in repeated public statements by US military top brass – might precipitate one. He said in July 1961: '[Any] real war must escalate into nuclear war.' Peter Hennessy has written: 'In all his dealings with both Khrushchev and Kennedy, he never lost sight of two things: the unspeakable catastrophe of a war between East and West, which he believed would go nuclear very quickly; and the danger that world war would come through a combination of inadvertence and miscalculation as he was convinced it had in 1914.'

Macmillan's magisterially condescending 1943 words to Richard Crossman, newly arrived in North Africa where the former was serving as the British government's ministerial representative, reflected a lifelong private view of the US, characteristic of his generation: 'We, my dear Crossman, are Greeks in the American empire. You will find the Americans much as the Greeks found the Romans – great, big, vulgar, bustling people, more vigorous than we are and also more idle, with more unspoiled virtues but also more corrupt. We must run [Allied headquarters in Algiers] as the Greek slaves ran the operations of the Emperor Claudius.'

The prime minister had not much changed this view almost twenty years later, following a speech made by Robert McNamara in June 1962. In this, the defense secretary expressed his hostility to small nuclear arsenals – he specified those in the hands of the UK and France – as 'dangerous, expensive, prone to obsolescence and lacking in credibility as a deterrent'. McNamara was making a case no less valid in 2022 than it was sixty years earlier, but Macmillan vented fury to his diary about 'what terrible damage the Americans are doing in every field in Europe ... It is rather sad because the Americans (who are naïve and inexperienced) are up against centuries of diplomatic skill and finesse.' It is astonishing that he could have written these words in earnest, less than six years after serving as a prominent and complicit member of the British government that launched the grotesque Suez adventure.

Kennedy, meanwhile, had respect and even affection for the prime minister. Macmillan once told Arthur Schlesinger, with characteristic sentimentality, 'It was the gay things' – in the old sense of the adjective – 'that brought us together, and made it possible for us to talk about the terrible things.' But the old man's continued urgings upon the White House of a new summit conference, following the failures of those in Paris in 1960 and Vienna in 1961, irritated the American.

Even as Cuba forced itself upon Macmillan's attention, he retained a fixation with Berlin. Back in June 1959, he had dispatched a telegram to President Eisenhower, in which he acknowledged the imperative for the West to maintain a solid front against a threatened Soviet use of force, but added: 'It would not be easy to persuade the British people that it was their duty to go to war in defence of West Berlin. After all, in my lifetime we have been dealt two nearly mortal blows by the Germans. People in this country will think it paradoxical, to use a mild term, to have to prepare for an even more horrible war in order to defend the liberties of people who have tried to destroy us ... Nevertheless, there is a double strain of idealism and realism in these islands to which I believe I could successfully appeal, if we had first demonstrated that we have made every endeavour to put forward practical solutions and that the Russians were unwilling to accept any fair proposition.'

Macmillan's diaries show a continuing preoccupation with the former German capital. He wrote in the expectation that his words would eventually be published, and thus was establishing a record of himself for posterity. There is no doubt both of the gravity of his fears and of the strength of his instinct for caution. At Camp David in March 1959, he became tearful when pleading with Eisenhower to avoid nuclear war over Berlin, evoking the dreadful cost Britain had paid for World War I. He wrote on 13 September 1961: '... all thinking people ... know that we must have a negotiation and (with the cards we have) we cannot play the game too high'. Yet, in his anguish, he acknowledged two months later: 'What worries me all the time is the possible parallel with Munich [in 1938]. Are we "appeasing" Soviet Russia? Ought we to risk war? Is Khrushchev another Hitler?'

While opinion polls showed the steady support of two-thirds of British people for their nation's own nuclear deterrent, an equally steady and passionate one-third opposed it, believing that the Bomb should be banished from their shores. The ancient philosopher and mathematician Bertrand Russell – he was then aged eighty-nine – proclaimed at a CND youth rally in April 1961: 'We used to call Hitler wicked for killing off the Jews, but Kennedy and Macmillan are much more wicked than Hitler ... We cannot obey the murderers ... They are the wickedest people in the story of man and it is our duty to do what we can against them.' At Easter 1962, 150,000 people joined the last stage of the Campaign for Nuclear Disarmament's march from Aldermaston to Trafalgar Square. Some Labour MPs, on hearing the sensational news of the Cuban blockade, asserted that the clever Russians had baited a trap for the United States, in which Kennedy's nation would be caught if it was crazy enough to sink Soviet ships. The pacifist Labour MP Sydney Silverman denounced the American action as 'a plain, naked, brutal act of war'. The London *Evening Standard*'s front page on the 23rd emphasized its expectation of the worst: 'KENNEDY: "SINK THE GUN RUNNERS" First Clash May Come in Hours'. More than a few observers noted the curiosity that while the US embassy in Grosvenor Square became daily picketed by demonstrators demanding 'Hands off Cuba', there was no comparable protest at the Chinese embassy, against its alleged – most historians consider the Indians more blameworthy – assault on India.

Even leaving the left out of it, the British have never trusted the Americans, any more than is the case the other way around. Whatever public protestations of goodwill and admissions of dependence passed from London to Washington between 1940 and 1962, at heart many British people, together with their political leaders, lacked confidence in US fitness to arbitrate much of the world as admirably as they supposed their own forefathers to have done. Some presidents have inspired more confidence and respect than others. John F. Kennedy's glamour enthused the British public as much as the rest of the world. But the memory of the Bay of Pigs, along with a residual grievance about Eisenhower's foreclosure of the 1956 Suez adventure, and fears of American excesses in Indochina and the Middle East, were as prevalent across the British Isles as at the Cabinet table.

Not for a moment did any prime minister forget his country's dependence upon US leadership for the defence of the democracies. The West Europeans had been at one, after 1945, in inviting the US to construct an empire and to include themselves in it, to preserve their peoples from Soviet aggression. The American presence, for all its vociferous opponents represented by the likes of Russell and CND, retained a firm basis of popular support, such as the Russians never achieved for the imposition of their own troops in Eastern Europe. Some people were unkind enough to recall that the erratic, albeit brilliant Russell had made a speech in 1948, arguing that the West would be wise to fight the Soviets before they acquired their own atomic bombs, rather than afterwards. He had since changed his mind, of course, once the USSR had its own weapons, becoming an impassioned disarmer.

The prime minister's instinctive desire now, as always, was to defer escalation or even strong action; instead to seek dialogue with the Soviets. In his telephone conversation with the president, Macmillan said: 'Very few people outside the United States would consider the provocation offered by the Cubans serious enough to merit an American air attack.' He added that he could not believe 'those missiles so far landed constituted a significant military threat to the United States'. Kennedy responded – interestingly, because he was far more opaque and apparently open-minded in discussions with his advisers in the hours and days that followed – that he himself had reached the same conclusion.

Neither then, nor later in the Crisis, did Macmillan offer the Royal Navy's surface warship support in enforcing the Cuban blockade, though two British submarines under Canadian control – *Astute* and *Alderney* – joined a patrol line of ten US Navy boats, watching six hundred miles of ocean between Newfoundland and the area north-west of the Azores. Had the prime minister sought to make some conspicuous gesture of military support for the US, it is unlikely that he could have carried the British people with him. The Lord Chancellor, Lord Dilhorne, privately told the Cabinet that he believed the US blockade of Cuba was illegal, although Macmillan dismissed this consideration when he later asserted in the House of Commons: 'This is not the moment to go into niceties of international law.'

In the days after Kennedy's broadcast, in London as in many other capitals, left-wing demonstrations against the United States mustered thousands of noisy people outside American embassies. The *Guardian*, house journal of Britain's intellectual left, editorialized: 'If Khrushchev has really brought in nuclear missiles, he has done so to demonstrate to the US and the world the meaning of American bases close to the Soviet frontier.' The paper's use of a conditional was significant: millions around the world, not all of them friends of Moscow, were initially wary of accepting the word of a US president about the Cuban missiles. His country's reputation was dogged by memories of its lies about the U-2 shootdown and the Bay of Pigs.

Two days later the same newspaper added: 'In the end the United States may find that it has done its cause, its friends and its own true interests little good.' The paper urged that Britain should vote against the US at the United Nations. Sixty British academics, including A.J. Ayer, A.J.P. Taylor and Richard Titmuss, signed a letter to Macmillan attacking the blockade and urging British neutrality. This rollcall of egghead dissidents eventually swelled to six hundred. An American observer wrote unhappily: 'There was a tendency among writers in England to equate America and Russia as if their actions and responsibilities were the same.' Richard Crossman, the same to whom Macmillan had written in 1943, now transformed into a Labour front-bench MP, said that both Russian and American actions were 'insane' and that Britain 'should stop it in the future'. The left-wing weekly *Tribune* wrote: 'It may be that Kennedy is risking blowing the world to hell to keep a few Democrats in office.'

"Of course, one does see why President Kennedy's just a little nervous—after all, Washington's not *all* that much further from Cuba than London is from Russia."

"Well, dear, the principal difference as far as I can see is this—a DEfensive weapon is one with my finger on the trigger, an OFfensive weapon is one with yours."

Front-page cartoons by Osbert Lancaster that appeared in the British *Daily Express* on 24 and 26 October 1962.

After Macmillan updated his own Cabinet on 25 October, he wrote about its members' attitude to Britain's position that 'they seem quite happy to leave [this] to me and [foreign secretary] Alec Home'. That remark was tendentious: ministers were profoundly uncomfortable amid allegations being hurled by domestic critics, that the British government was serving as an American lapdog, while the country faced a threat of extinction. Since they could scarcely dispute publicly about this, however, they saw no choice save to defer to the prime minister.

The principal British beneficiaries of the Crisis were the makers of the first James Bond film, *Dr. No*, which had opened in London two weeks earlier to poor reviews and poorer box office expectations. Ian Fleming's fantastic tale of a Chinese millionaire rocket-fancier in the Caribbean, on the payroll of Moscow, suddenly seemed topical. The film became fashionable and hugely profitable – by far the most financially successful of the entire Bond franchise, measured by gross takings against production costs.

Bertrand Russell, however, was a fan neither of Bond nor of the Americans. He cabled Khrushchev, employing some of the most slavish verbiage of the Cold War: 'MAY I HUMBLY APPEAL FOR YOUR FURTHER HELP IN LOWERING THE TEMPERATURE DESPITE THE WORSENING SITUATION. YOUR CONTINUED FORBEARANCE IS OUR GREAT HOPE. WITH MY HIGH REGARDS AND SINCERE THANKS'. Khrushchev responded: 'The Soviet Union will take no rash actions, will not let itself be provoked by the unjustified actions of the United States. We will do everything which depends on us to prevent the launching of war.' Next Russell messaged Kennedy: 'YOUR ACTION DESPERATE. THREAT TO HUMAN SURVIVAL. NO CONCEIVABLE JUSTIFICATION. CIVILISED MAN CONDEMNS IT. WE WILL NOT HAVE MASS MURDER. ULTIMATUM MEANS WAR. I DO NOT SPEAK FOR POWER BUT PLEAD FOR CIVILISED MAN. END THIS MADNESS.' The president sent Russell a response notable for its good nature as well as dignity: 'I think your attention might well be directed towards the burglar rather than to those who caught the burglar.' It is sometimes alleged that both Russell's cables were dispatched by Ralph Schoenman, his American secretary, while the old sage was in bed, asleep and oblivious. Nonetheless the peer never disowned those words, and thus they must be deemed to have been his own. He also penned a pamphlet in those days entitled 'YOU ARE TO DIE', publication of which was funded by the Cuban embassy in Britain.

Dean Rusk observed ruefully to Excom: 'The mobs that we stimulated turned up in London instead of Havana ... Bertrand Russell's people stormed the embassy there. We haven't had reports of any disorder happening in Cuba.' On the eastern side of the Atlantic, however, some more temperate folk than Russell also showed themselves wary of American judgement. Only a fortnight earlier, before the Crisis broke, the *Economist*, no communist mouthpiece, had published an editorial headed 'Obsessed by Cuba'. This attacked a *Time* magazine polemic of 21 September calling for a US military assault on the island. The British magazine warned of the likelihood of 'a whole series of further Russian actions calculated to provoke new outbursts of indignation in the US, without actually breaking the rules of the Cold War game'. It urged against supposing the Monroe Doctrine of 1823 – asserting a US determination to resist any foreign intervention in the governance of Latin American nations, and implicitly a considerable measure of Washington hegemony – could still plausibly be cited to justify drastic American actions.

The London *Times* was then, as it remains today, a broadly conservative organ. Yet its comment columns throughout the crisis reflected doubts about the Kennedy administration's competence to avert catastrophe, together with limited faith in the justice of the American cause. 24 October was the first day on which the paper belatedly gave its full attention to the Crisis, under the headline '24 RUSSIAN SHIPS HEADING FOR CUBA'. Its editorial began by suggesting that, given the extravagance of past American behaviour towards Cuba, the British people were entitled to be 'extremely wary' on first hearing Washington's account of the Soviet missile deployment. It went on to admit, grudgingly: 'All that being said, the evidence appears to be hard ... By all accepted standards ... the missiles are offensive.' The leader concluded: 'It is of the utmost importance that [American objectives] remain limited. They are not to topple Castro or defeat communism.' On the following day, another editorial asserted: 'The main problem now is to find a way by which both sides can extricate themselves with some honour saved.' Yet another *Times* editorial acknowledged that it was mistaken to make a direct comparison between the US missiles in Turkey and the Soviet weapons in Cuba, but suggested that there was anyway a strong case for the former to be removed.

None of this could be described as an unreserved vote of support for Washington's stance. The paper's correspondence column was soon likewise dominated by sceptics, including a lead letter from Labour MP Philip Noel-Baker, urging that the crisis showed disarmament to be the only sane way forward for the human race. Another writer declared that Kennedy's speech 'must fill sane men with horrified foreboding. To interfere with the shipping of a nation in time of peace is piracy.' Still another recalled the Bay of Pigs and demanded: 'Are the Cubans to be denied the right of self-determination and self-defence?' A facetious correspondent said that Kennedy's speech had 'brought a refreshing breeze of simplicity into international politics. If the US has missile-launching bases at home or abroad, that is good. If another nation does it, that is bad.'

Contrary views were nonetheless given space in *The Times*. The influential Alastair Buchan, director of the Institute for Strategic Studies, opined, 'One does not have to find the US blameless in all its policy moves in recent years, or in all its reactions to the Cuban situation, to feel deeply depressed by what the incident reveals about Soviet policy; how little grasp they have of the requirements of stability in the nuclear age; or of the "balance of prudence" that is required to preserve peace.' A Canadian academic wrote describing it as 'a sad and melancholy fact that so many British people look upon President Kennedy's partial blockade of Cuba with hostility and suspicion'. He identified a widespread inclination in Britain to adopt a 'plague on both your houses', semi-neutralist posture. He suggested that such an attitude was unworthy.

The foremost point in all this is that many British people were as much afraid of what John F. Kennedy might do next, as of the behaviour of Nikita Khrushchev. If the Crisis ended in war with the Soviet Union, Britain would perforce be a belligerent – and a target – beside the US: the nuclear-armed RAF bombers now on standby for take-off were earnests of that. But for all Macmillan's public declarations of support for the president's position, there was absolutely no belief at Westminster that anything taking place in Cuba represented an appropriate *casus belli* for the Third World War. The business pages of *The Times* headlined 'HEAVY GOLD TURNOVER IN CRISIS MARKETS'.

Around Britain a lively minority of schoolchildren, including sixth-formers at Midhurst Grammar School and sixty girls at Glanmor Grammar School in Swansea, staged 'strikes' to protest the threat to their own survival, and to vent opposition to the American blockade. A group calling itself Mothers Against War sent a telegram to the Pope, urging him to halt the Catholic president Kennedy's 'dangerous' activities. Prominent nuclear disarmers Pat Arrowsmith and Wendy Butlin took refuge in the West of Ireland, telling reporters that since there seemed nothing that ordinary people could do, they had decided to take up residence in 'a place where they might survive a nuclear war'.

The pages of this narrative are dominated by what was said and done within the walls of the Kremlin, in Cuba, and in the conference rooms of the White House. However, such views as those expressed above were shared by millions around the world. Mac Bundy wrote: 'It was somewhat easier at this time to be a part of the immediate governmental process than it was being an ordinary citizen ... I do not think that the danger ever seemed instant or imminent in the mind of the United States government. I don't recall any night where it seemed too dangerous to go to sleep, while I'm sure a lot of other people did have very wakeful nights. We never did lose diplomatic contact with the Soviet government. So for us, while it was very tense, it was not unendurable.'

There spoke the ice-cold voice of Boston Brahmin reason, unconvincingly, and after the Crisis was over. Bundy's sangfroid was certainly not shared among hundreds of millions of people who were excluded from the debates in which he was a key participant. Many nations, and indeed many Americans, lived through the week that followed in a fever of uncertainty and apprehension. John Guerrasio, a child living in Brooklyn, had grown accustomed to regular Friday practice air-raid alerts, when every child crawled under their desk. Now, sitting with his family and listening to Kennedy's broadcast: 'I remember thinking the world was going to end any time now.' Major Bill Smith, Max Taylor's air force staff assistant, said: 'I was scared to death – the only time I really thought nuclear war was likely.' In New York's Greenwich Village, 'people sat around wondering if it was the end, and so did I,' said Robert Zimmerman, a little-known songster who had changed his name just two months earlier to Robert Dylan. He said later that he stayed up most of one night playing with words for 'A Hard Rain's a-Gonna Fall', to capture 'the feeling of nothingness'. He felt unsure whether he would live to write another song.

TV anchorman Walter Cronkite found himself pondering, absurdly, what he might do if he found himself in the CBS studio when missiles began to rain down on American and Russian cities: 'We have a utility room where the furnaces are, and we wondered whether we could make that into a bomb shelter of some form. We were learning, for the first time, the time that we would have after the explosion, before the fumes [and the] heat would reach us.' Cuban architecture student José Ferrara said: 'We were all in suspense about what might happen – would the button be pressed?' Mikhail Lyubimov, a KGB officer stationed in Britain, said: 'We were feeling doomed, completely powerless in an atmosphere that smelt of war, fearful that we might be destroyed by a bombardment from our own people. I had a new-born son there in London.'

Across Latin America, in addition to anti-American demonstrations there were a few ineffectual sabotage attacks on US installations by Castro sympathizers or Havana's active agents – notably explosives hurled from a motor boat at an electric power plant off Venezuela, supplying an oilfield owned by Standard Oil. The principal casualty of this attempt was the boat, blown up by its own dynamite, which killed the skipper and badly wounded his two crewmen.

On the afternoon of 23 October, Harold Macmillan briefed opposition leader Hugh Gaitskell, his deputy George Brown, together with future prime minister Harold Wilson: 'They hadn't much to say. Brown was more robust than G[aitskell]. Wilson looked very shifty. Fortunately, they all distrust each other profoundly.' The prime minister also informed the Queen, recording bathetically that she was 'naturally much interested in Cuba'. Exhausted, he then spent the evening with his confidante Ava Waverley, the raffish widow first of diplomat Ralph Wigram, more recently of wartime Cabinet minister Sir John Anderson. Macmillan's private secretary Philip de Zulueta reached his own home very late. His wife said afterwards: 'His face was a study. [He said]: "I really am most desperately sorry, but we may be at war in the morning".' Labour MP John Morris described 'a general feeling of helplessness, indeed of hopelessness'. A twelve-year-old schoolboy, nephew of the foreign secretary, wrote long after: 'I thought we were all going to die as President Kennedy called Khrushchev's bluff.' Not everyone in Britain understood the gravity of the situation, however. A BBC radio reporter canvassing opinion among passers-by on the streets of the capital was told by one woman: 'I don't know, really, I'm only in London for the day.'

In Cuba, Juan Melo drove with a fellow-worker to a hospital in Matanzas where the man had a newborn son, whom he was allowed briefly to glimpse through a ward window. As the two journeyed back to Havana, the father sighed wretchedly and said: 'To think that I may never see my son again!' Melo said: 'That was the mood of those days.' Sixteen-year-old Marta Nuñez found their predicament especially bleak, because she had grown up half American: 'For me, the crisis meant the imminent prospect of war with the United States – just four months after leaving my bubble, the American school. We really expected them to invade.' She had worked in a hospital during and after Playa Giron: 'I had already seen the dead, the amputees, the blood. I knew what war looked like.'

Many Cubans, however, were roused by the Crisis to a new intensity of emotion, hailing each other with Castro's rallying cry 'Patria o Muerte! Venceremos!' – 'The Motherland or Death! We

Shall Overcome!'; '*Viva Cuba! Viva La Unión Sovietica!*' The poet
Yevgeny Yevtushenko, then serving as Castro's bard and herald to
the Russian people, penned lines that became an editorial in
Pravda, of which the last verse ran: 'America, it will be difficult to
regain the grandeur/ That you have lost through your blind games/
While a little island, standing firm/ Becomes a great country!'

Although Russians were told less than any other nation about
the unfolding drama, many understood its gravity. Moscow diarist
Ivan Seleznev wrote in his diary, deploring the 'mad arms race'. He
was bewildered by the revelation of Soviet missiles in Cuba, which
'the Soviet government and its representatives in the UN ... had
categorically denied ... The third world war, this time involving
nuclear weapons, could break out any time.' Moscow schoolteacher
Leonid Lipkin wrote on the same day: 'There is an alarming report
in *Izvestia*. President Kennedy gave orders to the American Navy to
blockade Cuba, to stop and check vessels of any country that are
headed for Cuba. They are to stop freighters that are carrying offensive weapons. Those vessels that don't obey will be sunk. The
statement in response from TASS was quite intelligent. The armies
of the Warsaw Pact have been brought to full battle readiness. The
USA is going to set up 12 missile sites in Israel.' He nonetheless
concluded that entry on an unexpected note of optimism: 'War still
hasn't broken out over Cuba, and I don't think it will. Someone will
give in ...'

Aspiring poet Nikolai Kozakov spent hours every day attempting to manipulate his Vostok wireless to overcome the Soviet
jammers and catch foreign stations: 'The ether was filled with all
manner of fascinating information, completely devoid of any bias.
If only one could listen to all of it ... But the Red pigs that shout
about the summits of democracy and freedom, keep cutting short
every citizen's attempt to reach out to bourgeois culture and politics.' Tamara Kosykh, then fifteen, said staunchly: 'How could
Russians be really, really scared, when so many had already experienced the civil war and the Great Patriotic War? We felt that our
leaders could never allow Hiroshima and Nagasaki to be repeated.'
Valery Galenkov, eighteen, said: 'I thought Khrushchev was right.

Cuba was our ally. If we hadn't stuck our necks out, confronted the aggressors, who knows what would have happened to Cuba, and to us?'

Sixty-four-year-old Boris Vronsky wrote in Moscow on 23 October: 'The past twenty-four hours have brought us closer than ever before to the brink of terrifying war. An irreparable catastrophe can befall us at any moment, and the whole of humankind is threatened. One doesn't want to believe the worst can happen, but we did not want to believe it [in 1941], though all the warning signs of imminent war were there.' Leonid Lipkin recorded in his diary that day: 'The English dinosaur, 90-year-old Bertrand Russell, sent anxious telegrams to the heads of the USA, Russia and England. The reply from our leader was reasonable, yet sharp. It is quite hard to understand who is to blame for the conflict. Even if our leaders did set up their military base under the USA's nose in Cuba, the Yankees have also set up lots of bases around our borders. It is hard to understand these events clearly when you are in the midst of them. We, the simple folks, are only told the facts a decade afterwards, and they are often falsified, too.' He added sarcastically, even bitterly: 'We cannot be trusted with secrets. All that we can be trusted to do is to die for the benefit of the owners of dachas and limousines.'

After a lunch of borsch and millet porridge on 23 October Nikolai Kozakov wrote in his diary that although he found the Cuban imbroglio bewildering, he felt a sympathy for the US when he learned from Voice of America about the secret missile deployment: 'Who is going to like such a thing, and just [ninety miles] from their own territory? Castro most likely counted on the Shark's support and got out of hand.' When Kozakov heard Radio Moscow's account of Soviet military preparations, he felt no wiser save to be confident that someone had blundered: 'In short, a major scandal is unfolding.' He then devoted himself to trawling the air waves, searching for 'voices of freedom', foreign radio broadcasts that were not jammed: 'I stumbled by chance at 25.2m on the French RTF Russian service. The programme was already coming to an end and all that I heard was that border incidents still have not stopped between China and India, Chinese tanks have intruded into Indian territory and taken four border posts and some towns. What is going to happen if these slanted-eye pigs get out of hand? This isn't a life. This is a torture, accompanied by a never-ending fear of war. What's for sure is that thanks to Cuba, we look like becoming history.'

US domestic protests against the administration's Cuban policy were strikingly few and feeble. Little knots of demonstrators appeared, bearing banners that demanded: 'End the Arms Race, Not the Human Race'. At Indiana University a handful of anti-government placard-carriers were forced to take refuge in a library, after being heckled and harassed by a crowd of two thousand. At Cornell, two professors arguing against the US posture were forced off a platform by a shower of hurled stones and clumps of dirt. Eggs and oranges likewise assailed anti-administration professors at the University of Minnesota. At Ann Arbor, Michigan, four hundred demonstrators, mostly supporters of Women for Peace, distributed a leaflet calling for an end of the 'game of chicken, with Mankind on the bumpers'. While they attacked Khrushchev for placing missiles in Cuba, they also demanded that the US government keep its hands off the island. Yet these protesters found themselves confronted and outnumbered by six hundred jeering students who threw eggs and stoned them. In Atlanta, a woman named Alice Lynd, who was among just thirty demonstrators protesting against the government, was fired from her childcare job in consequence.

Many radicals struggled to devise a coherent position, when they deplored in equal measure Soviet totalitarianism and oppression, US imperialism and racism. At a Boston open-air rally, Marxist Barrington Moore won over scarcely any of a small audience which heard him argue that saving the world demanded 'simultaneous revolutions in the US and Soviet Union'. As the decade advanced, many young Americans would decide that they hated their own country's shortcomings – there in full view before them, especially in Vietnam – more than the invisible ones of the other side. In October 1962, however, the American left was still confused, divided and vastly outnumbered.

Elsewhere in the world, many people sincerely believed that they themselves would not survive; that their children would not live to maturity; that unborn generations were doomed. The fact that such terrors went unfulfilled should not for a moment be allowed to diminish their reality, in the minds of men, women and children of many nations who lived through October.

2 'SHOOT THE RUDDERS OFF!'

When George Ball awoke in Washington that morning of the 23rd, after an uncomfortable night on a cot in his office at the State Department, he found Dean Rusk standing over him. 'We have won a considerable victory,' said the secretary of state drily. 'You and I are still alive.' Excom met again at 10 a.m., and McNamara asked for a decision about when America's blockade of Cuba should become effective. He himself proposed that a deadline be set as soon as possible after the representatives of the OAS – Organization of American States – met in Washington later that day: the administration cherished hopes that the body would pass a supportive resolution for enforcement, which would grant American action a topdressing of legality, there being no possibility of securing UN endorsement, in the face of an inevitable Moscow veto. He also urged that the president decide forthwith what response the US would make, if a Soviet SAM in Cuba shot down a U-2. He joined with the chiefs of staff in recommending that such action should be met within two hours by the dispatch of eight strike aircraft to take out the responsible launcher. Maxwell Taylor raised a practical difficulty: it would be difficult to identify the guilty site. Nonetheless, such a response was in principle agreed.

The president asked for an update on the redeployment of US forces for military action: was everything necessary under way? Yes, he was told. The 82nd and 101st Airborne divisions, 5th Marine Division and 1st Armored were on their way to the East Coast, where some soldiers wound up bivouacked on the Gulf Stream Park racecourse at Hallandale, Florida, lining the rails to

watch thoroughbreds' early morning work-outs. There was a significant concern about air defence of local bases, strips and airports,
now crammed with combat aircraft of all types, within easy reach
of Soviet and Cuban intruders: 'This is one of these rather humor-
ous examples of the over-sophistication of our weapons,' said Max
Taylor. 'We have everything, except to deal with a simple aircraft
coming in low … Unfortunately, a lot of congestion is necessary.'
That included the West Palm Beach strip, customarily used only by
the private aircraft of super-rich vacationers. The president, of
course, knew it well: 'That's a hell of a military airport.'

They discussed a contingency deemed highly likely: that when
the Americans began to search ships inbound for Cuba, the Soviets
would intensify checks on US Army trucks heading down the highway corridor towards West Berlin. In such an eventuality, Kennedy
said, it seemed necessary to acquiesce. He and his advisers were
baffled that the latest aerial reconnaissance images of Cuba showed
aircraft lined up wingtip to wingtip on the island's airfields, with no
attempt at dispersal or camouflage. This indicated that they did not
expect to be attacked – to go to war.

Then Dean Rusk arrived, exultant. Contrary to earlier misgivings, the OAS meeting had displayed overwhelming support for the
US action. They would have the vote by 3 p.m. 'Oh, gee, wonderful!'
said a chorus of voices. 'Oh, terrific! Terrific!' It was a measure of
the enormous fears and uncertainties gripping these men that the
secretary of state now repeated his earlier expression of gratitude to
George Ball, for something bigger: 'I think it was very significant
that we were here this morning.' Although the possibility was
remote, it had hung heavy on some consciousnesses, including
Rusk's, that the Soviets, in the mood of madness which seemed to
have gripped the Kremlin, might have responded to the president's
broadcast by unleashing their missiles. 'We've passed the one
contingency: an immediate, sudden, irrational strike.' Since Vienna,
the secretary of state had harboured honest doubts about
Khrushchev's sanity.

The meeting was next told that the Russians were delaying that
afternoon's UN Security Council meeting, obviously because their

delegation was in disarray. Under-secretary Alexis Johnson said: 'That's great. That's terrific ... We really caught them with their contingencies down.' So indeed the Americans had: Soviet representative Valerian Zorin – the same man reduced to despair by Khrushchev's conduct at the Paris summit two years earlier – had been told no more than had Anatoly Dobrynin about the Cuban deployment. Robert Kennedy later wrote that the mood that morning was emphatically brighter than on previous days: 'There was a certain spirit of lightness – not gaiety, certainly, but a feeling of relaxation, perhaps. We had taken the first step, it wasn't so bad, and we were alive.' There would be many more downs before the week was out, but this was an up.

The president expressed determination to ensure that no error at the sharp end – by subordinates in charge of weapons on land, at sea or in the air – be allowed to precipitate a violent US initiative or response unless mandated by a decision taken in the White House. He reiterated this anxiety in the Oval Office later, with RFK, Sorensen and O'Donnell: 'The great danger and risk in all of this is a miscalculation – a mistake in judgement.' The president recognized the peril posed by the bellicosity, nudging intransigence, of his armed forces chiefs.

Three hours after that meeting began, there was an important development: new words from the Kremlin, the response of Nikita Khrushchev to Kennedy's letter and broadcast statement. The Soviet leader's tone was splenetic: 'I should say frankly that measures outlined in your statement represent a serious threat to peace and security of peoples. United States has openly taken the path of violation of the Charter of United Nations ... of international norms of freedom of navigation on high seas ... of aggressive actions both against Cuba and against the Soviet Union ... We cannot recognize the right of the United States to establish control over armaments essential to the Republic of Cuba for strengthening of its defensive capacity. We confirm that armaments now on Cuba, regardless of classification to which they belong, are destined exclusively for defensive purposes, in order to secure the Cuban Republic from attack of aggressor.'

The *New York Times* front page on 23 October 1962.

THE WEATHER
Mostly cloudy and cool
Tuesday with a high near 50.
See Page 62.

CHICAGO
SUN-TIMES
© 1962 by Field Enterprises, Inc.

★ ★ ★
FINAL
HOME EDITION

Vol. 15, No. 226   Phone 321-3000   TUESDAY, OCTOBER 23, 1962   •   72 Pages—7 Cents

President Orders Cuba Blockade To Halt Red Buildup

By Merriman Smith

WASHINGTON (UPI)—President Kennedy Monday night clamped a naval blockade on Cuba because Soviet intermediate-range missiles and other arms had turned the island into an armed camp capable of hurling destruction into the heart of America.

The build-up, the President said in a nationwide radio-television report to the people, now includes ballistic missiles capable of firing nuclear warheads for more than 1,000 miles.

To halt the build-up, the President ordered a seven-step program, including a strict quarantine on all shipments of offensive military equipment to Cuba.

This will involve a strict naval blockade but the blockade will not, he said, deny the Cubans the necessities of life.

In addition to the quarantine, Mr. Kennedy also announced that he had taken these "initial" steps:

1 Continued, increased surveillance of Cuba and its military build-up with orders to the armed forces "to prepare for any eventualities."

2 A declaration of American policy stating that the nation will regard any nuclear missile launched from Cuba against any nation in the Western Hemisphere "as an attack by the Soviet Union on the United States, requiring a full retaliatory response upon the Soviet Union.

3 Reinforcement of the U.S. naval base at Guantanamo Bay and the start Monday of evacuation of armed forces de-

pendents stationed there. In this connection, Mr. Kennedy ordered additional military units, apparently in this country, to stand by on an alert basis.

4 He called for an immediate meeting of the "organ of consultation" under the Organ-

President and Johnson cancel political campaigning because of Cuban crisis, Page 5.

Cuba puts military forces on alert, Page 4.

Situation in Cuba "perfectly normal," the Italian and French ambassadors in Havana tell Sun-Times city desk by telephone, Page 7.

Walter Lippmann discusses the national crisis, Page 22.

President Kennedy tells the nation the United States has thrown a naval blockade around Cuba. (UPI)

BULLETIN

WASHINGTON (UPI) —The Defense Department announced Monday night it will search, and sink if necessary, the ships of any nation that may be carrying offensive weapons to Cuba.

Turn to Page 4

"Drop it!"

Text Of Address Is On Page 6

No less had been expected by the White House. The good news – and it seemed important – was that Khrushchev made no explicit threat of resorting to force. His bombastic letter nonetheless left the president and his advisers in doubt about how the Russians proposed to respond to the US Navy's blockade. Kennedy still faced the dilemma of whether to order American warships to fire upon, and if necessary to sink, Soviet vessels that sought to defy the American edict. This issue would come to a head within hours, as the first cargo vessels, now being tracked by US aircraft, approached the ordained 'quarantine line'. At least, however, nothing in Khrushchev's communication represented an escalation, nor even a threat of it. Thus far, the letter cheered Excom.

The afternoon brought confirmation of the diplomatic good tidings: the OAS had voted solidly in support of a resolution proposed by the United States, authorizing members to use force individually or collectively, to impose a quarantine on Cuba. A cynic might note that many OAS members were US client regimes, some of them deplorable. This outcome was nonetheless useful, and positive.

At the next Excom meeting that evening, details were agreed of the Navy's Rules of Engagement for enforcing the blockade. Prominent among these was that if a Soviet ship was challenged and then turned around, it was not to be fired upon, at least not on the first day. McNamara also secured agreement that Soviet vessels would be intercepted only if they approached Cuba, not on the distant ocean. The president himself anticipated that the biggest problems for both sides would occur in the early hours after the blockade came into force, and was probably tested by the Soviets. That afternoon, a further letter was dispatched to Khrushchev via the US Moscow embassy, of which the final sentence read: 'I hope that you will issue immediately the necessary instructions to your ships to observe the terms of the quarantine, the basis of which was established by the vote of the Organization of American States this afternoon, and which will go into effect at 1400 hours Greenwich time October 24' – four hours earlier in the Caribbean.

Kennedy said to Excom: 'OK, now what do we do tomorrow morning when these eight [Soviet] vessels [identified inbound for

(Above) The president speaks to the American people and (below) the American people hear his grave words.

Members of EXCOM at one of the meetings that rank among the most momentous ever held at the White House. Clockwise from the president: JFK, Robert McNamara, Roswell Gilpatric, General Maxwell Taylor, Paul Nitze, Donald Wilson, Ted Sorensen, McGeorge Bundy (hidden), Douglas Dillon, Vice President Lyndon Baines Johnson (hidden), Robert F. Kennedy, Llewellyn Thompson, William C. Foster, John McCone (hidden), George Ball, Dean Rusk.

One of the four Soviet Foxtrot submarines trailed by the US Navy in the western Atlantic, each armed with a nuclear-tipped torpedo of which the Americans were unaware.

SAC chief Gen. Thomas Power at microphone in his headquarters, with staff officers.

Some of the US president's advisers and confidants through the Crisis. (Clockwise from top left) McGeorge Bundy, Dean Rusk, George Ball, David Ormsby-Gore, Theodore Sorensen, Curtis LeMay, Robert F. Kennedy, Llewellyn Thompson, Robert McNamara.

A critical moment in the Crisis, when US ambassador at the UN Adlai Stevenson (inset) challenged the Soviets with devastating effect to deny the reality of their missiles in Cuba. (Below) The British prime minister during a benign encounter with Khrushchev in Moscow. Harold Macmillan offered the US public backing through the Crisis, but privately feared an American overreaction.

The president at the White House with the only adviser to whom he accorded absolute confidence: his brother.

British protesters on the streets of London who shared their prime minister's fears about American judgement.

Cuba] continue to sail on? We're all clear about how we handle it?'
Maxwell Taylor said: 'Shoot the rudders off of them, don't you?'
McNamara said patiently: 'Max, this is the problem. We want to be
very careful.' In fixing upon a test case for stop-and-search, the
Pentagon must strive to identify a ship that was almost certainly
carrying offensive weapons.

The US Navy had deployed six FSU-1P Crusaders of its specialist
'Fightin' Photo' Light Photographic Squadron to Key West, from
whence they soon began to fly missions over Cuba, the first of these
on the 23rd. In three two-plane 'Loose Deuce' formations, they
approached missile sites at a speed of 350 knots and an altitude of
four hundred feet. They filmed for thirty seconds, then turned for
home. On landing at Cecil Field and surrendering their film,
Commander Bill Ecker, a World War II combat veteran, was
ordered at once to take off again and fly north to Washington, to
report direct to the chiefs of staff on his experience over Cuba. Still
in his flight suit, three hours later he reached the Pentagon and was
ushered into 'the tank' conference room. He nervously apologised
for being sweaty and smelly, causing Curtis LeMay to respond,
'Goddamn it, you've been flying an airplane, now, haven't you?
You ought to sweat and smell! Sit down.' The Navy flier told the
chiefs that his formation had attracted no ground fire; pilots had
seen a mass of equipment below, some of it newly camouflaged.
When Ecker returned to base at Key West, ground crew painted on
his fuselage the chicken symbol they used to mark each photographic sortie, beneath an image of Castro. The pilots began to dub
such flights 'chalking up another chicken'.

To understand the hubris of the US military in 1962, it is important to recall that all the services were led by men who had
participated in the supreme triumph of their nation's armed forces,
victory over Germany and Japan less than two decades earlier.
During the intervening years, American legions had been deployed
across the world to confront the communist threat, though
committed to fight significantly only in Korea. That 1950–53
conflict began badly for American arms, but ended well, with a

formidable US and allied army upholding the integrity of South Korea in the face of a Chinese host. The leading formations now being deployed for a possible invasion of Cuba – the 82nd and 101st, 5th Marine Division, 1st Armored – were successors to the heroes of D-Day and Arnhem, Iwo Jima and Bastogne, legends of which the reputations resonated across the free world, symbols of a might which their own commanders deemed invincible. In those days, never for a moment did those men who wore so many stars on their shoulders doubt that they could bury any Cuban or indeed Russian rabble that might dare to challenge them on a palm-treed Caribbean island.

On the other side Khrushchev's generals were, in their own eyes, every inch as much victors, heroes of the wartime Red Army, as were Kennedy's men among the Western allies. Pliev and his soldiers were as willing, even eager, to kill Americans as were Taylor and his subordinates to 'shoot the rudders off' Russians, figuratively or literally. The only soldier in whom President Kennedy displayed full confidence that week was Lauris Norstad, whose tenure as NATO supreme commander was due to end, but whom he temporarily retained in post, because he was impressed by the general's cool judgement in holding down NATO's alert status in Europe, to avoid increasing tension. Norstad concurred with British leader Harold Macmillan's decision to forswear all conspicuous war precautions.

The Excom meeting that Tuesday evening addressed bleak scenarios in which Russian ships refused to stop; were shot up by the US Navy; then proved to be carrying food, medical supplies and personnel. Bundy exclaimed: 'We shoot three nurses!' Kennedy concurred: 'That's what could happen. They're going to keep going. And we're going to try to shoot the rudder off, or the boiler. And then we're going to try to board it. And they're going to fire a gun, then machine-gun … So I would think that the taking of those ships are going to be a major operation. You may have to sink it rather than just take it.'

After a further messy, inconclusive discussion of complex possibilities, all grim, he said ironically, 'I'll tell you, for those who considered the blockade course to be the easy way: I told them not to do it!' An explosion of nervous laughter broke the tension. Then they resumed discussion of scenarios, in which satire kept breaking through. McNamara reported that Admiral Anderson feared a Soviet submarine might try to sink a US aircraft-carrier. The president chuckled when he said: 'Do we want to keep the *Enterprise* there? ... We don't want to lose a carrier right away.'

The mood darkened again when a Pentagon official briefed the meeting on America's preparedness to face missile attack, which addressed horrific realities: 'If nuclear weapons are used, we can draw an arc and try to address the civil defense capabilities at [a possible strike radius from Cuba of] around 1,100 nautical miles, and make a little allowance for fallout on the outer fringe. That takes in 92 million people, 58 cities of over 100,000 population.' Miami, Atlanta, Houston, Dallas, New Orleans, St Louis, Cincinnati – and Washington DC – would only be the foremost of the urban areas obliterated or merely devastated. 'A light, relatively light nuclear attack of this type, would lower the protection factors we'd use in deciding whether existing buildings would serve as adequate protection.' After a barrage of statistics, the president asked about the feasibility of evacuating all the people within that 1,100-mile radius, if a decision was made to invade Cuba: 'They may fire these weapons ... What is it we could do ... [to] take care of them, to the extent that is possible, against radiation. And then you've got the problem of blast ... I don't know how many megatons.' Not a lot of contingency stuff could be done, responded the briefer, beyond erecting shelter directional signs and prepositioning food stocks.

The meeting broke up just after 7 p.m. Robert Kennedy lingered alone, with his brother, who put down the phone from the Mansion audibly annoyed. Jackie had invited guests for dinner, led by the Maharajah of Jaipur: the last thing he needed was casual company, however gilded. Bobby picked up on the blockade prospect, asking: 'How does it look?' The president said: 'Ah, looks like hell – looks real mean, doesn't it? But on the other hand, there is no other choice. If they [the Russians] get this mean on this one, it's just a question of where they go about it next.' RFK said that, if the president had failed to act, he could have been impeached. 'That's what I think,' said JFK.

Bobby reminded Jack that it had been a good day for diplomacy, with the terrific OAS vote. The British ambassador, their friend Ormsby-Gore, was displaying more steel than his national leader – flatly asserting that the US had no choice. RFK added that Georgy Bolshakov, the GRU officer at the Soviet embassy whom the attorney-general used as a back-channel, claimed that Russian ships would defy the blockade. Bobby added, however, that Anatoly Dobrynin was always urging him to take no notice of Bolshakov, whom the ambassador considered a charlatan. The brothers yet again admitted shared bewilderment about what game the Russians were playing. RFK said he had asked Charlie Bartlett, a journalist who was a close friend, to pump Bolshakov. He sought to cheer the president by reminding him how much worse the whole thing could be: if the missile revelations had leaked before the Americans were ready to break the story on their own terms; if the OAS vote had gone differently.

That night Robert Kennedy arranged to call secretly at the Soviet embassy. Dobrynin recognized that this visitor must be treated with respect, as the mouthpiece of the president of the United States. But he had never liked or trusted Bobby, whom he found stiff and humourless, sometimes thuggish and ugly: he 'was certainly close to his brother, but he was a difficult person to deal with. He would come with a message of complaint in the name of the President, and that was that … [He was] a complex and contradictory person who often lost his temper; at such moments he behaved rudely … Having met with a rebuff, however, he usually took hold of himself but could easily wind himself up again. That is why a conversation with him tended to be uneven and broken.'

The Russian much preferred to deal with Llewellyn Thompson or Robert McNamara, cooler hands, or even Rusk, with whom he occasionally drank bourbon without getting any nearer to a démarche on Berlin. Dobrynin found the secretary of state as boringly persistent in advocating his conservative ideas as was his own boss, Gromyko, on the other side and 'not very imaginative …

'Gone Far Enough': Eddie Germano in the *Brockton Enterprise Times*,
23 October 1962.

Yet he [Rusk] never resorted to cheap propaganda or deceptive
tricks. His words could be trusted ... He was a real gentleman.' The
ambassador obviously meant: unlike the attorney-general.

That evening Robert Kennedy arrived at the embassy in what the
Russian afterwards described as 'a state of agitation'. The diplomat
met him at the entrance and led him to a private sitting-room on
the third floor, where Irina Dobrynin served coffee and then left
them. The ambassador's position was even less enviable than that of
his guest: his own government had deceived him as much as it had
deceived the Americans, yet now he was obliged to defend its stance
in the face of a tirade from Kennedy: 'What he said was markedly
repetitious,' wrote Dobrynin. '... The conversation was tense and
rather embarrassing to me.' Kennedy repeatedly denounced Soviet
deceits. Dobrynin was duty-bound to respond that he knew only
what his government had told him, which included nothing about

the missiles. The American asked what instructions had been given to Soviet ships' captains. The ambassador replied that they had been told to reject any unlawful demand to stop and be searched. This caused Kennedy to muse aloud before he departed: 'I don't know how this will end, but we are determined to stop those ships.' Dobrynin said: 'But that would be an act of war.'

The ambassador submitted to Moscow a verbatim account of this meeting, to emphasize the agitation within the US president's inner circle. He subsequently lamented 'how primitive were our embassy's communications with Moscow ... when every hour, not just every day, counted for so much'. The cable about the conversation with Robert Kennedy was manually coded into columns of numbers: 'Then we called Western Union, [who] would send a messenger ... usually the same young black man, who came to the embassy on a bicycle. After he pedalled away with my urgent cable, we could only pray that he would take it to the Western Union office without delay and not stop to chat to some girl!'

When Dobrynin's message eventually reached Moscow, foreign minister Gromyko apparently told his staff not to circulate it to other members of the Presidium, saying that instead he himself would convey its tidings to Khrushchev. No copy of such a communication survives in the foreign ministry archives, however, and thus it is doubtful Gromyko passed it on. Dobrynin was left in limbo: he received no instructions from Moscow, nor any response to the message RFK had told him to convey, about American determination to enforce the blockade.

But how, exactly, on the day and in whatever place on the ocean, was this to be done? One of the most famous, or notorious, moments of the Crisis took place when Robert McNamara visited the Navy's Flag Plot in the Pentagon, at 9.20 p.m. that Tuesday. He found himself going head to head with the service top brass, who bitterly resented the intrusion of a civilian boss whom they disliked, upon what they perceived as 'their' conflict, their right to decide, and if appropriate to fight. The big room, entered through a door guarded by armed Marines, was dominated by a wall map of the Atlantic showing the position of both American and Soviet ships.

McNamara began shooting questions at the duty flag officer: how were Soviet ships to be challenged? Did American ships have Russian interpreters on board? What orders did US warships have about how to act if a Soviet ship declined to respond to challenges? What would happen if the Soviets opened fire? The hapless sailor proved either unable or unwilling to answer most of McNamara's questions. The secretary left the Plot, marched into the office of Anderson, the chief of naval operations, nicknamed in his service 'Gorgeous George'.

Neither man had much time for the other. The admiral resented a recent auto industry executive venturing to tell the Navy its job. He had issued orders to his officers about how to enforce the blockade – which he considered a pitiful response to the Soviet missiles, 'locking the barn door after the horse has been stolen' – and he was content to leave them to get on with it. Now, the secretary asked how a Soviet ship would be challenged.

'We'll hail it.'

'In what language – English or Russian?'

'How the hell do I know?'

'What will you do if they don't understand?'

'I suppose we'll use flags.'

'Well, what if they don't stop?'

'We'll send a shot across the bow.'

'What if that doesn't work?'

'Then we'll fire into the rudder.'

'You'll not fire a single shot at anything without my express permission. Is that clear?'

Anderson then waved in the secretary's face the 1955 *Law of Naval Warfare*, setting out procedures for boarding and searching enemy warships: 'It's all there, Mr. Secretary.' The manual authorized the 'destruction' of warships 'actively resisting search or capture'. Roswell Gilpatric, McNamara's deputy and the eyewitness who later recorded this episode, recalled Anderson then exploding: 'This is none of your goddam business. We know how to do this. We've been doing it since the days of John Paul Jones. And if you'll just go back to your quarters, Mr. Secretary, we'll take care of this.'

McNamara, who was quite as angry as the naval chief, concluded: 'You heard me, admiral, there will be no shooting without my permission', before stalking out of the CNO's room.

Anderson later claimed that he did not lose his temper with McNamara, merely good-humouredly assured him that the Navy knew what it was doing. Whichever version is authentic, Anderson was an undisputed hawk, who believed that the only rightful US response to the Cuban missiles was to go in shooting; and who bitterly resented the dictatorial management of McNamara. A critical aspect of the Crisis was that it caused the political leadership of the United States to assert its absolute right to decide the issue of peace or war, in the face of strident objections from most of the armed forces brass. Even if the detail of the McNamara-Anderson exchange remains disputed, it captures a fundamental truth, and a frightening one, about the limitations of the imagination of the admiral and most of his colleagues. This was not the eighteenth century of Captain John Paul Jones. It was, instead, a late twentieth-century moment when a careless or feckless misjudgement by a naval officer at sea could ignite a powder train that led to nuclear war.

Meanwhile the president, after attending the dinner arranged by his wife, held a long conversation with David Ormsby-Gore. He told the Englishman that he could not help admiring Soviet strategy: 'They offered this deliberate and provocative challenge to the United States in the knowledge that if the Americans reacted violently to it, the Russians would be given an ideal opportunity to move against West Berlin. If, on the other hand, he did nothing, the Latin Americans and the United States' other allies would feel that the Americans had no real will to resist the encroachments of Communism and would hedge their bets accordingly.'

RFK joined the two men around 10.15 p.m., to report on his unprofitable exchange with Dobrynin. The Americans asked the lean, beaky British aristocrat what he thought the outcome would be, and received a banal response: either a negotiated settlement or war, and everybody in his right mind would prefer the former. The Englishman added that it seemed important that before there should be any question of Kennedy meeting Khrushchev, the Russian needed to harbour no delusions that the US would make unilateral concessions. In other words, the ambassador did not share his prime minister's enthusiasm for an East-West summit. Ormsby-Gore made one suggestion that had a practical impact. He urged setting the quarantine line five hundred miles out from Cuba, rather than the proposed eight hundred. This was indeed done. The president overruled McNamara's objection that the US Navy wanted interceptions to be made beyond the range of hostile aircraft taking off from Cuba. The change bought all parties some useful extra hours, before Soviet vessels approached the invisible barrier declared by Washington. Graham Allison and Philip Zelikow have plausibly argued that the effect of Ormsby-Gore's intervention was importantly benign. Had the first ship been stopped at dawn on the 24th, several hours before word was received of the Soviet turn-around, the US Navy could have challenged the *Kimovsk*, carrying a cargo of IRBMs, with incalculable consequences. This proved the only game-influencing British contribution to the Crisis.

Through the days ahead, a critical divide opened up between two of the players in this earth-shaking drama. The leaders of the United States and the Soviet Union, whatever the contents of their public statements, were alike guided by a desperate anxiety to avert war. Fidel Castro, by contrast, appeared to welcome confrontation and even conflict. Crisis suited his temperament, and the posture he had chosen to strike before the world, as a career warrior, almost invariably armed, and clad in combat fatigues and boots. Fidel was once chatting to the poet Yevgeny Yevtushenko in Havana. To illustrate a point, the Cuban casually pulled his pistol from its holster and rapped it on the table. The poet dismissed the gesture later, saying: 'He was not pointing it at me – it was just instinctive.' But the enduring portrayal of Cuba as a threatened nation, required to exist in a permanent state of military emergency, served the interests of the Castro regime incomparably better than those of the Cuban people.

The island, in those days, attained an importance in the eyes of the world far beyond any that its inherent resources, power and achievements merited. Its leader thus stood where he always demanded to be, at centre stage. The threat from the United States served both to unify his people and to justify the harsh autocracy under which he obliged them to exist. Castro was among the small and swiftly diminishing number of people on the planet who, in late October 1962, seemed unafraid of consequences. He retained a confidence in Soviet will and might, likewise in the coherence of Kremlin policy, to sustain his revolution against the worst that the *yanquis* might do to him. Cuba counted for little alongside the two nuclear superpowers, but Castro's cavortings ensured that the passions of American conservatives continued to run hot. Such people yearned not merely to humble the Russians who dared to threaten them, but also to settle accounts with the Latin revolutionary who scorned the terms the United States sought to set, for a neighbourly relationship with the island he had made his own.

On the evening of 23 October, Fidel delivered his own televised address, responding to that of President Kennedy. His tirade, as usual deploying his whole body as an instrument to accompany his high, thin voice, seized upon Kennedy's depiction of Cubans as 'captive people' and proclaimed: 'He is talking about a nation that has hundreds of thousands of men under arms. He should have said the *armed* captive people of Cuba!' The president's statement, said Castro, was not that of a statesman, 'but of a pirate'. He spoke for ninety minutes, brief by his usual standard of verbosity. For once, however, he did not exaggerate when he asserted in his peroration: 'All of us, men and women, young and old, are united in this hour of danger. All of us, revolutionaries and patriots, will share the same fate. Victory will belong to us all.' When his broadcast ended, crowds flocked onto the streets bearing torches and candles, to sing the national anthem. Although Castro had made his country a dictatorship controlled by rigid repression, in those days there was no doubt of the Cuban people's sincere determination to rally behind their leader, to resist 'liberation' by the forces of the United States.

Fidel himself spent the rest of the night at his underground command post, newly dug into a hillside across the Almendares river from Havana zoo. Sleeping conditions were oppressively hot and airless, but the facility offered protection from the expected rain of American bombs. Castro was accompanied there not only by his own staff, but also by a senior Soviet liaison officer. The leader was fuming about repeated US reconnaissance overflights, which he was determined should be met by Cuban ground fire: 'Dejalos fritos' – 'Fry them.' Whereas both John F. Kennedy and Nikita Khrushchev were now alike profoundly apprehensive about the Crisis, Castro was exalted by it. Addicted to drama, he saw himself as his people's Man of Destiny, poised to confront whatever fate now appointed for him.

10

'The Other Fellow Just Blinked'

1 HAIR TRIGGERS

On the continent close across the sea, far mightier people than Castro likewise hankered for their own moment of glory. General Thomas Power, C-in-C of Strategic Air Command, shared Curtis LeMay's philosophy of conflict. He dismissed any thought of sparing Soviet lives in the event of a nuclear showdown: 'The whole idea is to kill the bastards,' he told a RAND Corporation strategist. 'At the end of the war if there are two Americans and one Russian left, we win.' Power now occupied his command post, three floors underground at SAC headquarters in Omaha, Nebraska, where he sat with a gold telephone linking him to America's commander-in-chief, and a red one communicating with his subordinate wing and base commanders. At 10 a.m. on Wednesday 24 October, for the first time in the sixteen-year history of SAC, he was authorized to raise its readiness status to DEFCON 2, bringing 1,436 nuclear-armed bombers and 134 ICBMs to constant alert, just a heartbeat short of war.

Moreover on his own initiative, and with the deliberate intent of instilling fear in the other side, rather than issue a coded order Power made an unprecedented indicative plain-language phone call to his bases, knowing that the Russians monitored all such voice traffic. He told wing commanders: 'We are in a very dangerous situation. I know that we are all ready to do the job that we do, and I want you to know I am counting on you to do the best you can because we are ready to go and you are ready to go. We will carry out our mission. I have great confidence in you. I do have that.'

SAC's aircraft and crews were primed for war, in a fashion terrifyingly close to the *Strangelove* movie, and emphasizing the risk that Armageddon might be brought about by accident or subordinate recklessness, of the kind feared by both Kennedy and prime minister Macmillan. The number of permanently airborne USAF bombers increased fivefold, and some of these were carrying bombs for which the arming procedures had not been certified as safe. SAC regional commanders possessed authority to launch their nuclear weapons without orders from Washington, if they had 'unambiguous' evidence that war had started. It was extraordinary to have mandated such unstable figures as LeMay and Power in any circumstances to precipitate Armageddon without a direct authorization from the nation's commander-in-chief. John Lewis Gaddis writes: 'It is not too difficult … to see how the United States could have convinced itself that a nuclear attack was taking place, even if one was not.'

As the president had earlier insisted, the Pentagon issued orders that no Jupiter missiles were to be fired from Turkey without express authority from Washington. It failed, however, to extend that constraint to sixteen nuclear-armed US F-100s on fifteen-minute alert at Incirlik air base, less than an hour's flight time from the Soviet Union. Lt. Col. Robert Melgard, commander of one of those fighter-bomber squadrons, then at fifteen-minute Victor Quick Reaction Alert status, later testified that nuclear safety was 'so loose that it jars your imagination … [during the Crisis] we loaded up everything [including nuclear weapons], [slept] on a blanket on the pad for two weeks, planes were breaking down, crews were exhausted'. The ordnance on those aircraft was not then fitted with encoded locks, so that pilots were empowered to launch at their own discretion. At the time, the squadron commander implicitly trusted his men not to act irresponsibly nor, indeed, insanely, but 'in retrospect, there were some guys you wouldn't trust with a .22 rifle, much less a thermonuclear bomb'. McNamara said afterwards: 'Our commanders in the field could have started a nuclear war if they wanted to, because we didn't have PALs [Permissive Action Links].'

Back in the US some Minuteman missile crews, working with new technology, hotwired their weapons to simplify firing procedures, increasing the scope for an unauthorized launch. Even as ICBMs at Vandenberg air base were prepared for live-firing, nobody halted additional missile testing in deference to the new circumstances created by the Crisis. Thus, an Atlas which blasted off its pad in the Marshall Islands was almost certainly observed by Soviet ships that lingered offshore to monitor such activity.

Both then and later, the USAF's senior officers applauded the hair-trigger readiness moves. Thomas Power ever afterwards believed that Soviet monitoring of his phone call to bomber wings, and thus awareness that his bombers had moved to DEFCON 2, together with his personal warning to be ready to attack the Soviet Union, was in the general's own words 'a major influence' on Khrushchev's eventual retreat. The NSA's Kenneth Absher was among those who endorsed the airmen's conduct, writing that Curtis LeMay was 'perhaps the American leader most feared by the Soviets ... This Soviet fear, coupled with their ability to listen to SAC communications ... may well have been an important factor in Khrushchev's ultimate decision to back down.' Those in command at the Pentagon and in the White House had less control over America's stupendous nuclear armoury than they supposed – probably less even than LeMay and his fellow-chiefs imagined themselves to possess.

Meanwhile at sea, Khrushchev had issued instructions shortly after Kennedy's broadcast that no Soviet cargo vessel carrying weapons should challenge the US Navy. Yet some thirty hours elapsed thereafter, before the White House became aware of this critical retreat. The missile-carrying *Gagarin* had received orders from Moscow to turn around at 8.30 a.m. EDT on the 23rd. She had been steaming east, away from the quarantine line, for more than nine hours when, at 6 p.m., a US Navy Neptune with its searchlight switched on first repeatedly overflew the ship, then detonated two explosive flares ahead of her bow. An hour later another US plane made six passes, again with its searchlight beam racing across the sea, and at 7.40 p.m. a third aircraft almost clipped the Soviet vessel's masthead. Two more planes did likewise later in the night. It is remarkable that so much time elapsed after the Neptunes buzzed the *Gagarin*, before news of her course change reached the White House.

Elsewhere the US Navy's commanders chose to focus their aggression upon the Soviet submarines cruising the western Atlantic. Such harassment was justifiable only by America's sense of outrage in the face of Soviet provocation. Admiral Anderson, like the USAF's LeMay and Power, put his forces on a hair-trigger. That evening of 24 October the Navy chief reportedly told Roswell Gilpatric, 'From now on, I don't intend to interfere with Dennison or either of the admirals on the scene.' Later, when McNamara again visited the Navy Flag Plot or operations centre, he asked sharply why two US destroyers were steaming hundreds of miles outside the blockade line. Anderson explained that they were 'holding down' a Soviet Foxtrot boat. The defense secretary demanded: who authorized such action? The admiral said it was part of standard naval operating procedure to trail unidentified submarines. McNamara asked how sure was the admiral that the boat was Soviet. 'Trust me,' said Anderson. 'Isn't this dangerous?' asked the defense secretary. The admiral replied: 'If he chooses to make it so. Otherwise he can do as he has in the past few days, come up for air and charge his batteries.' McNamara considered Anderson's view recklessly casual.

The admiral warned USN commanders at sea of the risk of 'surprise attacks by Soviet submarines', though it is hard to imagine any realistic scenario in which such a move might have become a first Russian act of war. Instead of cautioning officers against provocative gestures, he advised: 'Use all available intelligence, deceptive tactics. And evasion.' This message was signed off 'Good luck, George'. The US Navy's eagerness to assert itself against the Russians would soon precipitate a potentially deadly clash. From the moment of Kennedy's broadcast to the American people, Khrushchev was a rattled man. Frightened leaders can act and react in many ways.

2 'SHOULD I TAKE OUT CUBA?'

At the Bolshoi Theatre in Moscow the previous evening, the 23rd, the big attraction was American bass Jerome Hines, in the title role of Modest Mussorgsky's masterpiece *Boris Godunov*. Hines was an interesting study. Forty-one years old, six foot six inches tall, he was an obsessive mathematician, a born-again Christian and member of the Salvation Army. That night at the Bolshoi, the Russian audience loved him. He received a standing ovation and took repeated curtain calls. Hines became not only the star on stage, but also a bit player in the Crisis. Nikita Khrushchev impulsively determined to take his entourage and visiting Romanian communist leader Gheorghe Gheorghiu-Dej to hear the opera. This was a gesture explicitly designed to suggest to the US, and to the world, that if Washington was panicking, Moscow was not.

Yet a tale of a doomed sixteenth-century Russian leader was an incongruous entertainment for an embattled twentieth-century successor more powerful than any tsar. Khrushchev never recorded whether he heeded Boris Godunov's tortured howl of anguish from the stage: '*Mine is the highest power!/ Year after year my reign was calm and peaceful and yet my heart has never known peace ... Life, fame, the heady wine of power, the people's cheers, have lost their lure/ I am betrayed, the nobles hate me, Lithuania revolts/ hungry crowds and plague and devastation prowl like angry beasts ... Russia moans for all the sorrows that Heaven sent us, to punish the sins we committed.*' At the final curtain the Soviet leader, heir to Boris Godunov, summoned Hines and other stars to what was once the theatre's royal box, to offer congratulations.

Some Bolshoi patrons may have been fooled by this charade, but before the performance Gheorghiu-Dej had witnessed Khrushchev in a towering rage, and afterwards watched him replay this. Andrei Gromyko confessed later that he had no idea what opera he was supposed to have been watching, and added: 'Probably none of the Politburo members in attendance were interested in what was happening on stage. Opera, ballet or play – it was all the same to them. Everyone was thinking of what was going on in the Western hemisphere.'

Within the Kremlin walls, Khrushchev fumed at the Americans, the blockade and above all John F. Kennedy. He knew he was in deep trouble, and was thinking furiously about how best to extricate himself. Next day, the 24th, he was still blustering when another American entered his office. William Knox, president of Westinghouse, was visiting Moscow for business conversations when abruptly summoned to meet Khrushchev and receive a message, or rather face a tirade. Although the Soviet leader had flinched from a confrontation at sea with US Navy warships enforcing the blockade, he was still minded to insist upon keeping the missiles in Cuba, and said as much to Knox: 'I'm not interested in the destruction of the world,' he told the bemused and no doubt considerably alarmed businessman, 'but if you want us all to meet you in Hell, it's up to you!' Russians disliked having NATO on its doorstep, Khrushchev continued, but had learned to live with it. Now Americans must get used to the missiles in Cuba.

In Washington Excom reassembled at 10 a.m. on Wednesday the 24th, just as the blockade came into effect. John McCone's morning briefing reported intense activity at the Soviet sites in Cuba, though partial cloud cover hampered U-2 surveillance. At that point – though of course exact numbers were unknown to the White House – forty-two nuclear missiles had been delivered to Cuba, together with forty-two nuclear-capable IL-28 bombers. The latest maritime reconnaissance reports showed sixteen Soviet dry-cargo ships and six tankers at sea, and assumed to be still on passage towards the island. Three of the former were of a type that made them suitable for carrying missiles. Overnight the Odessa station which normally controlled movements had transferred direction of the vessels to Moscow. At 11.15 p.m. EDT on 22 October, less than four hours after Kennedy spoke to the American people, the National Security Agency had intercepted signals to the cargo ships at sea, alerting them to expect a 'special instruction'. This had been duly transmitted at 12.05 a.m. on the 23rd, in a cipher the Americans could not read. Meanwhile three Soviet submarines were known to be in the western Atlantic – in reality, there were four. Dean Rusk reported a radio intercept from Havana, instructing Cuban armed forces to fire on overflying foreign aircraft only in self-defence.

Taylor highlighted the risk to US aircraft, tightly packed on Florida airstrips, if the Russians and Cubans responded to an American bombing of a SAM site with a low-level sneak attack. McNamara said that the first Soviet ships would approach the declared blockade line around noon. The two leading vessels, *Gagarin* and *Kimovsk*, were each apparently being trailed by a submerged Soviet submarine, cruising at eight knots: 'And hence it's a very dangerous situation. The Navy recognizes this, is fully prepared to meet it.' Alexis Johnson of the State Department said a message had been sent to Moscow the previous evening, establishing procedures for identifying submarines, and dropping practice depth-charges – small explosive charges – as a signal to surface. The Soviets had not responded. All the above information was many hours behind events in the Atlantic, but was assumed by Excom's members to represent a 'real time' bulletin.

Kennedy recoiled from the prospect of a clash between a Soviet submarine and US warships becoming the first armed encounter of the Crisis. McNamara nonetheless insisted that the boats must be forced to surface before a Soviet merchant vessel was stopped. This was one of the defense secretary's less impressive interventions: he was proposing a flagrant breach of international law, not covered by the declaration of blockade, and justifiable only by the Americans' conviction of their own rectitude.

In RFK's view, after the more cheerful mood that had lifted Excom the previous day, its members were now right back down. The Wednesday morning meeting would vie with that of the ensuing Saturday as 'the most trying, the most difficult and the most filled with tension'. News was constantly coming in – way behind the reality at sea – about the progress of Soviet ships approaching the blockade line – and of possible shoot-outs with US warships. When the president acceded to the Pentagon's urgings by ordering the carrier *Essex* to force a Soviet submarine to the surface by dropping practice depth-charges, RFK wrote: 'I think these few minutes were the time of gravest concern for the President. Was the world on the brink of a holocaust? Was it our error? A mistake? Was there something further that should have been done? Or not done? His hands went up to his face and covered his mouth. He opened and closed his fist. His face seemed drawn, his eyes pained, almost gray. We stared at each other across the table. For a few fleeting seconds it was almost as though no else was there and he was no longer the President.'

That passage seems both eloquent and sincere. It emphasizes that, if the conduct of Robert Kennedy was sometimes immature, often ruthless, spasmodically ugly, he was also capable of sensitivity. Then, at 10.25 a.m., a message was passed to John McCone, who made a momentous announcement: 'Mr. President, we have a preliminary report which seems to indicate that some of the Russian ships have stopped dead in the water.' Seven minutes later, a second confirmatory message reached McCone. He left the room, to seek more information.

Discussion continued in his absence, about next steps in the potentially hazardous confrontation at sea. The president said he did not want to start implementation of the blockade by sinking a Soviet submarine. McNamara continued to argue that it could be perilous for the shadowing warships not to do so. Kennedy overruled him, with a clarity of thought which was then eluding his defense secretary. Dean Rusk said: 'Mr. President, I do think it is important in our present procedures – of course, these may change later – but for us to make it, to be quite clear what the object of this present exercise is. And that is to stop these weapons from going to Cuba.'

McCone returned. 'What have you got for us, John?' asked Kennedy. The CIA chief reported that the stopped ships were all on the ocean; had been inbound for Cuba. Other Soviet vessels, much closer to the island, were still under way. Kennedy gave an order – an emphatic order – that these should be left alone. About now, Dean Rusk whispered to Mac Bundy: 'We are eyeball to eyeball, and I think the other fellow just blinked.' He was right. The order had gone out from the Kremlin many hours earlier that all Soviet weapon-carrying vessels bound for Cuba should turn back. Only those of which the cargoes were innocent should hold their courses. Far behind events at sea, the Americans now received the information that enabled them to surmise that this represented a relatively cautious Kremlin response to the blockade, entirely at odds with Khrushchev's defiant message to the White House: the other fellow just blinked. They still, however, could not be confident of this interpretation.

Max Taylor was talking on the phone to Admiral Anderson, the unwavering hawk. He returned to report: 'These ships are definitely turning back. One is the *Poltava*, we are most interested in ... Certain others are showing indications that they may be turning back.' The Americans had every reason to be 'interested in' the *Poltava*, because though its cargo manifest declared it to be bound for Algiers, in reality it was carrying twenty nuclear warheads towards Cuba. Meanwhile the troop transport *Kasimov* was in the English Channel when its passengers were bewildered to find the ship suddenly reversing its course, without explanation from the bridge. At first, men thought they were merely heading for Cuba by a more northerly route around Britain, but no. To their astonishment, the Russian soldiers found themselves making for home, as did crews of several other Cuba-bound vessels still in the Mediterranean.

The popular legend of the Crisis holds that a great drama unfolded as Soviet vessels approached the declared quarantine line on the morning of 24 October, and the White House held its breath while waiting to see whether they would stay their courses. In reality, no merchant ship carrying weapons or military personnel approached anywhere near the invisible barrier. Both the *Gagarin* and *Kimovsk* had reversed course the previous day, and by the 24th were five hundred miles from the line, heading north-east. Only submarine B-130, which had previously been trailing the *Gagarin*, was closer.

The principal cause of the confusion and tension at the White House was the inadequacy – the frightening inadequacy – of US

Navy communications. However impressive was signals technology, a limited pool of staff ashore, and even more so at sea, was available to decrypt and process messages. Thus, in those days, signals marked 'EMERGENCY' were subject to a four-hour delay, while lower-priority 'OPERATIONAL IMMEDIATE' signals were being read five to seven hours after dispatch. Moreover, beyond the 'big picture' intelligence failure running through much of the story told in this book, tactical surveillance of the Soviet ships in the Atlantic was patchy, with long pauses between sighting reports from reconnaissance aircraft.

The armed forces communications of the most powerful nation on earth, operating within a few hundred miles of its own shores, proved dangerously inadequate in the midst of a world-shaking crisis. Most blame lay with Khrushchev, for rejecting any admission to the Americans that he had instructed his ships carrying 'hot' cargoes to turn around. But the consequence was that the members of Excom, seated around the White House table on the morning of 24 October, believed that they were eavesdropping upon a showdown at sea which was unfolding even as they talked, while in reality the Russians had long since determined to duck such a confrontation.

That morning meeting was nonetheless important, because it shifted the terms of the entire debate inside the White House. Hitherto, the prevailing mood had been characterized by a commitment to take whatever military or naval action proved necessary, to get Khrushchev to back down. At 10 a.m. on Wednesday, there was no doubt of the willingness of most of the decision-makers to open fire. Now, however, and with dramatic suddenness, the tide – and explicitly the temper of the president – turned. News from the ships at sea offered a clear indication that the Soviets could be backing off; that they would not attempt to send arms through the blockade. Thereafter, though many more bad moments lay ahead, including a climactic one, Kennedy's default posture would be an unwillingness to escalate; an instinct towards sidestepping a shoot-out.

He stressed the urgency of instructing the Navy's warships to act with caution: 'You don't want to have word going out from

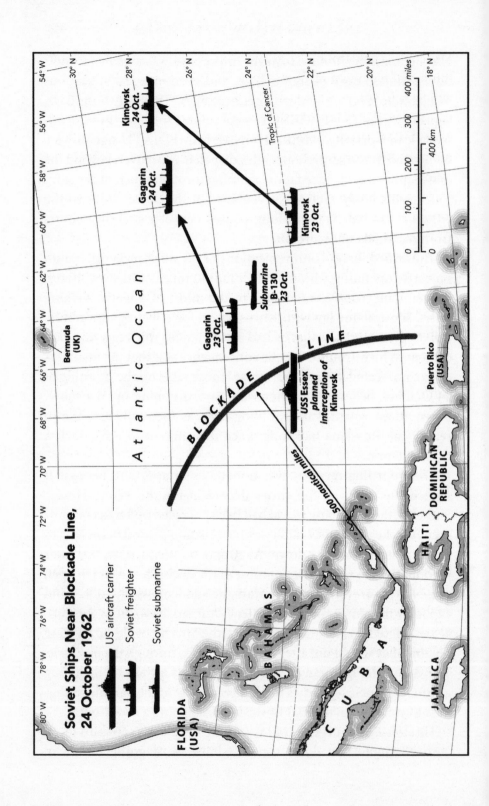

Soviet Ships Near Blockade Line, 24 October 1962

US aircraft carrier
Soviet freighter
Soviet submarine

Atlantic Ocean

FLORIDA (USA)

BAHAMAS

CUBA

JAMAICA

HAITI

DOMINICAN REPUBLIC

Puerto Rico (USA)

Bermuda (UK)

Tropic of Cancer

BLOCKADE LINE

500 nautical miles

USS Essex planned interception of Kimovsk

Gagarin 23 Oct.

Submarine B-130 23 Oct.

Kimovsk 23 Oct.

Gagarin 24 Oct.

Kimovsk 24 Oct.

0   100   200   300   400 miles

0   100   200   300   400 km

Moscow: "Turn around" and suddenly we sink a ship. So I would think that we ought to be in touch with the [carrier] *Essex*, [from which helicopters were shadowing a Soviet vessel] and just tell them to wait an hour and see whether that ship continues on its course.' RFK wrote: 'Everyone looked like a different person. For a moment the world had stood still and now it was going round again.'

Yet some Soviet ships were still approaching the blockade line, foremost among them the tanker *Bucharest*, steaming hard for Havana. At the White House, the president ordered that, once the ship identified herself, she should be allowed to proceed. Here was an advantage to the 'quarantine', later identified by Mac Bundy: 'It was far more responsive to command and control than an air attack would have been. No ship was stopped or boarded without direct authorization from the President.' Kennedy was determined to give Khrushchev extra time; not to confront him with an assault on a Soviet vessel which might cause him to feel obliged to respond with gunfire. Moreover, common sense argued that a tanker was unlikely to be carrying weapons. Whatever response was made by the captain of the *Bucharest* to a stop-and-search order, the United States must look foolish if she was stopped by force, then her cargo was found to be innocent: fuel was excluded from the US blockade prohibition list.

Strangely to posterity but significantly for an understanding of the Crisis, many hours of White House meeting time now addressed contingency planning for a new Soviet blockade of West Berlin, in response to US action in the Caribbean. More than a week since the Cuban photographs arrived, the president's fear persisted that the Soviets might open a second front in Europe; escalate on another continent. If the perils of the situation at sea seemed temporarily abated, nobody around the table in the White House was tempted to relax.

Nor did others around the world, who were denied knowledge of the surges and eddies in the decision-making of the mighty. In Gorky, diarist Nikolai Kozakov showed himself a frightened man, bereft of confidence in his nation's leaders: 'Mom lit up the stove

around 7 and started to stew the remains of a hare and some potatoes ... On the radio, they have been "branding with shame the
imperialists who are mindlessly playing with fire". They are shouting about Cuba at the top of their voices. In his turn, the bearded
usurper [Castro] is also shouting at the top of his voice: *Patria o
muerte* and *Venceremos* – or whatever it is spelt like – "We are
going to win". I don't know who is right there and who isn't but I
know one thing, that I don't need a war because of Castro. I went to
the office after dinner, to listen to the free radio [foreign stations],
but [jamming] was crackling on all the channels. I found something at 31 meters but it was pro-Soviet.'

In the White House at 5 p.m. that day of the 24th, Kennedy met
again with congressional leaders, who were first briefed by McCone
and Rusk. The latter was optimistic. He was encouraged that,
although Russian rhetoric at the UN was 'bitter and as violent as
ever', it was in some respects cautious. 'So far as we know, the
Soviets have not told their own people that they have missiles in
Cuba, which indicates ... that they think their own people may be
very disturbed ... Our best judgement is that they are scratching
their brains very hard at the present time and deciding just exactly
how they want to play this.' This was, of course, correct.

Illinois Republican Sen. Everett Dirksen mentioned Khrushchev's
message to British disarmament campaigner Bertrand Russell, in
which he proposed a summit conference to resolve the Cuban issue.
Kennedy won approval from the legislators when he said he
thought that agreement to such an encounter would be useless: it
was plain that the Soviets would only start a negotiation in anticipation of US concessions, and the president was in no mood to
make them. He also said that, with some Russian ships pressing on
while others turned back, it seemed necessary to wait for the situation to clarify, before making decisions about further American
actions.

When the meeting broke up, leaving behind some Excom
members and Robert Lovett, they discussed the mood on the Hill.
Senator Fulbright appeared to have become a supporter of the
blockade, but Richard Russell was still hawking. Lovett said the best

aspect of the blockade was that it enabled the US to probe 'the *intentions*' of the Russians. He himself was a sceptic about the efficacy of air strikes. Time was needed, 'and I don't think a decision can be made now'. Kennedy said: 'Well, I think they've got their neck [out in Cuba] just like we've got it [out in Berlin].' He meant that, missiles or no missiles, the Soviets' fundamental strategic position in the Caribbean, a few minutes' flight time from the US, was as exposed as that of the Western garrisons in the Berlin enclave.

Then a message arrived from UN secretary-general U Thant, which Kennedy read aloud. The Burmese diplomat called for calm; for a voluntary suspension of all arms shipments to Cuba, and also of the US quarantine measures. The president promptly ordered a response, via Adlai Stevenson: the US insisted that all work on the Cuban missile sites should cease, and be subjected to UN verification, before consideration could be given to lifting the quarantine.

That evening, Kennedy spoke again with Harold Macmillan. This time around, recorded the prime minister, the president asked him 'straight out the 64 thousand dollar question "Should he take out Cuba?" I said I would like to think about this and send an answer (it's just like a revue called "*Beyond the Fringe*" which takes off the leading politicians) ... Meanwhile the "guilty" ships seem to be turning away.' The prime minister said news of this retreat was 'a great triumph' for the president.

But what about the missiles still on Cuba? This remained, indeed, the critical question. Kennedy said that once the quarantine was firmly in place, 'We're going to make the judgement as to whether we're going to invade Cuba, taking our chances, or whether we hold off and use Cuba as a sort of hostage in the matter of Berlin.' Macmillan said that obviously there would have to be a negotiation, but hopefully not one where Khrushchev 'has all these cards in his hands'. Kennedy replied: 'He has Cuba in his hands, but he doesn't have Berlin. If he takes Berlin, then we will take Cuba. If we take Cuba now, we have the problem of course of these missiles being fired, or a general missile firing, and we certainly will have the problem of Berlin being seized.' It is doubtful that Kennedy saw this match as might twenty-first-century observers: the Cuban people no more desired an American 'liberation' than did the citizens of West Berlin seek a Soviet one.

Macmillan said he thought Khrushchev was 'a bit wondering what to do'. But so was Kennedy. Even assuming the quarantine worked, the only resolution of the Crisis acceptable to the US was removal of the missiles already in place. 'Do we then tell them that if they don't get the missiles out, that we're going to invade Cuba? He [Khrushchev] will then say that if we invade Cuba that there's going to be a general nuclear assault, and he will in any case grab Berlin. Or do we just let the nuclear work go on, figuring he won't dare fire them, and when he tries to grab Berlin, we then go into Cuba? That's what I'd like to have you to think about.' Macmillan asserted courteously that the issue was 'very well put, if I may say so'. He added that he thought U Thant's UN proposal 'rather tiresome ... because it looks sensible and yet it's very bad'. The prime minister then gave voice to his perennial enthusiasm for a summit. Once more the president brushed aside this ill-judged notion.

Labour MP John Strachey wrote later: 'Mr. Macmillan's public pronouncements and what one heard about his private reactions sounded to me rather like those of a fussy old retired nanny, forever calling out: "Oh, oh, Master Jack, do be careful or the bad men will get you!" The role of Britain in this confrontation of the two nuclear powers could only be a modest one. When there was little that we could say which made any difference, might it not have been more dignified to assert our solidarity with our ally, and, for the rest, keep silence?'

Walter Cronkite, America's favourite uncle, told viewers of *CBS Evening News*: 'It was beginning to look this day as though it might be one of armed conflict between Soviet vessels and American warships on the sea-lanes leading to Cuba. But there has been no confrontation as far as we know ...' Cronkite nonetheless concluded: 'There is not a great deal of optimism tonight.' The Kennedys' journalist friend Charles Bartlett, dining with them in the Mansion, suggested a toast to celebrate the turn-around of some Soviet ships, but the president said: 'You don't want to celebrate in this game this early.'

Soon afterwards the State Department received another angry, bombastic message from Khrushchev, which Kennedy read at 9.30 p.m. This began: 'Imagine, Mr. President, that we had posed to you those ultimative conditions which you have posed to us by your action. How would you have reacted to this? I think that you would have been indignant at such a step on our part ... You, Mr. President, are not declaring quarantines, but advancing an ultimatum and threatening that unless we subordinate ourselves to your demands, you will use force.' The Soviet leader declined to accept the US demands. He said that he refused to stop the ships heading for Cuba: 'Our instructions to Soviet mariners are strictly to observe the generally recognized norms of navigation in international waters and not to retreat from them by even one step. And if the American side violates these rules, it must realize what sort of responsibility will rest on it in that case. Of course, we shall not be simply observers of piratical actions of American ships on the high seas. We will then be forced for our part to take the measures which we deem necessary and adequate in order to protect our rights. For this we have all that is necessary. Respectfully yours, N. Khrushchev'.

Kennedy and his advisers pored over the fine print of this letter. It appeared to make plain a determination to test the blockade, albeit – as Soviet behaviour of the previous day indicated – without breaching the US list of prohibited cargoes. After reading it, Kennedy called Bartlett, his earlier dinner guest, and told him laconically: '[Khrushchev] said those ships are coming through.' The State Department's George Ball saw no option but to let events take their course; to see what happened in the morning. Doubts persisted about whether to search the *Bucharest*, now inside the quarantine zone. Meanwhile Adlai Stevenson, as ever desperate for compromise, was wringing his hands about the US rejection of U Thant's proposed solution. Kennedy dismissed the ambassador's groaning. At 2 a.m., a stern message was sent to the UN, while another was dispatched to Moscow. To Khrushchev, in many fewer words than the Russian leader had employed, Kennedy reaffirmed American resolve: the missiles in Cuba had to go.

Khrushchev received this early on the 25th. 'I ask you to recognize clearly, Mr. Chairman,' wrote Kennedy, 'that it was not I who issued the first challenge in this case and that in the light of this record these activities in Cuba required the responses I have announced.' The blockade would be enforced. That same day the Russians intercepted, as they were intended to do, SAC's communications about the move to DEFCON 2 and Gen. Power's call to his officers. The American's words and actions achieved precisely the purpose for which they were designed – to convince the Russians that they were serious – but at high risk to peace. Khrushchev was now sincerely fearful that the US, if further provoked, would not only invade Cuba, but also launch a nuclear strike against the Soviet Union. His rage, in the hours and days that followed, was prompted by a conviction that he must retreat or face war, together with a determination, almost impossible to reconcile with this knowledge, that he should continue to present a masquerade of defiance not merely to frighten the West, but also to preserve his authority over his comrades and rivals within the Kremlin and across the communist world.

11

Khrushchev Looks for an Out

1 'EVERYTHING TO PREVENT WAR'

Early on Thursday 25 October, a message reached the White House from Harold Macmillan. Kennedy had asked for his opinion, and now he got it. The British leader was drawing back from his earlier acquiescence in American courses, expressed on the telephone the previous night. Now shifting ground, he was assuredly influenced by a rising tide of domestic dismay, most of it directed towards perceived American brinkmanship. This extended beyond thousands of anti-war demonstrators on the streets, into the editorial columns of newspapers. There was a belief that Kennedy was being pushed towards war by his own hysterical electorate. When Europe had lived for a decade under the shadow of Soviet nuclear attack capability, why should not Americans do the same? What legitimate case had the US to determine which side Cuba chose in the Cold War?

The *Economist* feared that Washington was driving Moscow into a corner. It spoke of 'the ominous possibility ... that the blockade does not mark the end of American plans for action against Dr. Castro's land'. It also emphasized Europeans' continuing fears about Berlin. An angry American reader, Roger Coe of Flushing, NY, wrote in the magazine's correspondence column, deploring its condescension to a supposed American 'obsession' with Cuba: 'Yes, we are "obsessed", obsessed with the burning desire to return freedom to our Caribbean neighbours. This is the same freedom for which our soldiers are dying in Laos and for which so many of your countrymen died in preventing the world conquest of Hitler.' The expression of such views intensified British alarm that Americans wished to promote an agenda with which they had scant sympathy, for Cuban regime change.

The prime minister was mocked by some of his own people, for alleged passivity in the face of US bellicosity. The great cartoonist Vicky drew an image for the *Evening Standard* of Eisenhower pulling back the coat-tails of prime minister Eden from a brink labelled 'Suez', while Macmillan stood supine behind Kennedy on a brink marked 'Cuba'. Now, in his message to Washington, the old statesman urged Kennedy to call off his blockade if the Russians would accept UN inspection of the Cuban missile sites, and open a negotiation. He effectively endorsed U Thant's proposal. He added weakly: 'You must no doubt continue with your military build-up for any emergency.' Though the president's reaction is unrecorded, he cannot have been impressed by the message, which reflected a caution for which conservative Americans – especially uniformed ones – despised the 'Brits'. They considered that the attitudes of many of Macmillan's people reflected an unworthy indulgence and indeed fear of the communists, symbolized by the disarmers' slogan 'Better Red than dead'.

It was this belief that encouraged some Americans to see in the Missile Crisis an opportunity to show the world that the Soviet Union was a paper tiger – if only their president would summon the steel to act decisively. US military superiority, above all in air power and nuclear weapons, was undisputed even inside the Kremlin. Now was the moment to exploit this, argued such people as Senator Russell and the joint chiefs. Major Bill Smith, Max Taylor's USAF aide, said: 'The Kennedy Administration up to that point had not done anything very successfully.' This thirty-seven-year-old from Arkansas, veteran of scores of combat sorties in Korea, added contemptuously, 'They wanted to use force preferably without killing anyone ... Once they decided to do something, they tried to shave it so thin that it just didn't work ... They didn't want to use any more force than was absolutely necessary. The trouble is, you don't know what that is.'

* * *

In Moscow on the morning of 25 October, Khrushchev chaired a new Presidium meeting at which he is alleged to have crowed: 'the Americans have chickened out', because there was no sign of an invasion fleet setting sail for Cuba. In language designed to suggest triumphalism but which did not fool his comrades, the first secretary made a statement that later proved to have shown his path to retreat: 'Kennedy is telling us to take our missiles out of Cuba. And we reply: Give us firm guarantees, a promise, that the Americans won't attack Cuba. That's not bad.' In return for such a guarantee, the Soviets would remove their R-12s. 'We will strengthen Cuba, and save it for two or three years. In a few years' time, it will be even harder [for the US] to deal with it.'

It was among the precepts of the Soviet Union's governance that unpalatable truths were seldom, if ever, explicitly voiced even within the Presidium. Its membership, however, was expert in reading the runes – interpreting oblique signals from the top. Khrushchev's colleagues thoroughly understood that their leader declined to face a war with the US over Cuba, and was establishing the terms for Soviet retirement. On Friday 26 October, *Pravda*'s drum-banging bellicosity of previous days was replaced by a headline: 'EVERYTHING TO PREVENT WAR Reason Must Prevail'.

The Kremlin's deliberations were confused by consistently poor reporting from its US intelligence apparatus, which identified McNamara as leader of a hawkish faction within the administration, and Douglas Dillon as a dove. Gossip from Washington's National Press Club, where the Lithuanian-born barman was a KGB informant, suggested that a US invasion of Cuba was imminent, and that reporters were being briefed to 'embed' with the troops. Soviet knowledge of US policy-making compared unfavourably with that which was available to the Kremlin twenty years earlier. During World War II communist sympathizers, some of them holding important positions in the US government, were briefing Russian agents, who enjoyed remarkable licence. Senator McCarthy was not wrong about everything: an astonishing volume of authoritative intelligence reached Stalin.* In 1962, by contrast, Kremlin understanding was threadbare, partly because the Soviet Union – especially since the brutal 1956 suppression of the Hungarian Uprising – had lost much of its allure for Western leftists. The spurious credibility accorded by the KGB, and then by the Kremlin, to the National Press Club scuttlebutt ranks in grotesquery alongside the intelligence reports conveyed to Moscow a generation later, during the Reagan presidency, claiming that the US was close to launching a nuclear First Strike against the Soviet Union.

The language of Soviet official narratives and documents was relentlessly mechanical. Yet the Kremlin minute of the meeting chaired by Khrushchev on 25 October deserves to be quoted at length, as an example both of such gatherings and of the manner in which they were recorded:

> Point 1. On the response of the Chairman of the USSR Council of Ministers Comrade N. S. Khrushchev to the letter of US President Kennedy.
>
> Comrade N. S. Khrushchev says he decided to convene a session of the Presidium in connection with the further events in Cuba.
>
> The further course of events is proceeding in the following way. The Americans say that the missile installations in Cuba must be dismantled. Perhaps this will need to be done. This is not capitulation on our part. Because if we fire, they will also fire. There is no doubt that the Americans became frightened, this is clear. Kennedy was sleeping with a wooden knife. (To Cde. A. I. Mikoyan's question (in jest), "Why with a wooden one?" N. S. says, jokingly, that when a man goes bear-hunting for the first time, he takes with him a wooden knife so that it will be easier to clean his trousers.)
>
> Cde. N. S. Khrushchev goes on to say that we have now made Cuba a country that is the focus of the world's attention. The two systems have clashed. Kennedy says to us, take your missiles out

* See the author's *The Secret War* (William Collins 2015), for some detail.

of Cuba. We respond: "Give firm guarantees and pledges that the Americans will not attack Cuba." That is not a bad [trade]. We could pull out the R-12 [SS-4] missiles and leave the other missiles there. This is not cowardice. This is a fallback position, it is possible we will have to meet with them at the UN. We have to give the opponent a sense of calm and, in return, receive assurances concerning Cuba. Beyond that, it is not worth forcing the situation to the boiling point. We can strike the USA from the territory of the USSR. Now Cuba will not be what it was previously. They, the Americans, are threatening an economic blockade, but the USA will not attack Cuba.

We should not inflame the situation and should conduct a reasonable policy. In this way we will strengthen Cuba and will save it for 2–3 more years. Within several years it will be harder [for the Americans] to deal with [Cuba]. We have to play, but we should not get out and lose our heads. The initiative is in our hands, there is no need to be afraid. We began and got cold feet. It is not to our benefit to fight. The future depends not on Cuba but on our country. That is correct.

All the members of the Presidium and the Secretaries endorse and support Cde. N. S. Khrushchev. Cde. N. S. Khrushchev proposes to think about information [to give to] F. Castro. We must draft a document in which we say where we are heading. Some things worked out well, others did not. What we have right now is a positive moment. What is the positive side of this? The fact that the entire world is focused on Cuba. The missiles played their positive role. Time will pass, and if need be, the missiles can appear there again. Perhaps Cdes. Gromyko, Ponomarev, and Ilichev will think a bit about this document. Notes taken by A. K. Serov on 25 [October] 1962.

None of the above Soviet deliberations, and preparations for retreat, were known or even guessed at in the White House. Early that Thursday morning at sea, a drama unfolded in real time, as US warships intercepted the Soviet tanker *Bucharest* when it approached the quarantine line, an encounter reported on live network TV. Millions of people held their breath. Inside the Soviet embassy, where diplomats knew no more about Kremlin processes than did the US administration, Anatoly Dobrynin described this day as 'the most memorable in the entire period of my long service as ambassador'. In his memoir he dates the episode to Wednesday 24th, but in reality it took place on the 25th. Russian staffers crowded around TV sets as the tanker approached the line, while the presenter counted down the miles, with US destroyers and aircraft riding herd. Anti-climax followed. Around 7 a.m. the US Navy challenged the tanker to identify herself. She did so, declaring her cargo to be petroleum products from the Black Sea, destined for Cuba. The Americans, as decreed by the White House, allowed her to proceed. The world breathed again.

Excom's next meeting took place soon after Khrushchev made his remarks to the Presidium – it is striking to contrast the latter's stiff formality with the freewheeling style of the Washington discussions. It began, as usual, with John McCone's report: work on the Cuban missile sites continued unabated, said the CIA chief. Meanwhile, of twenty-two Soviet cargo ships known to be on passage to Cuba, fourteen had turned back. Five of the remaining eight were tankers, unlikely to be carrying weapons or personnel. The alert status of Soviet forces in Europe appeared high, but unchanged. Warsaw Pact media were playing up Khrushchev's call for a summit, and also the efforts by the UN to establish machinery for easing tension.

McNamara opened a discussion about procedures for implementing the blockade. Following the decision to allow the *Bucharest* to proceed, Excom agreed that morning to start enforcing stop-and-search procedures against non-Soviet bloc vessels, to establish a routine. At the same time US aircraft would maintain low-altitude surveillance on all inbound shipping. Good news was that the Soviet Navy's KOMAR missile boats remained moored in Cuban harbours, their weapons covered; no take-offs were reported from Castro's military airfields. The SAM sites were now under camouflage netting. Kennedy mused that 'some day' he would like somebody to explain to him what had been the Soviet game plan.

Why had they not camouflaged the missiles at the outset? And if not then, why now? These were fair questions, to which rational answers were never forthcoming, because they did not exist.

The defense secretary proposed establishing regular low-level surveillance of Cuban installations by flights of US aircraft, consistent with attack behaviour. This would create a deception template, if the time came to launch bombing sorties. The Cubans should also be warned diplomatically of the intended overflights. That morning, in the minds of those around the table the prospect of a US air campaign remained very real. There was speculation about why the ground defences remained silent in the face of American aerial activity: had the Soviets made a top-level decision to allow the US to fire the first shots, and obliged the Cubans to conform?

The meeting havered about whether the *Bucharest*, still some hours out from Cuba, should be permitted to dock at Havana unsearched. McNamara favoured renewed interception and scrutiny. Granted, it was carrying fuel not covered by the American embargo. But might the Soviets trumpet its free passage as evidence that American will was weakening? It was indeed true that inside the Kremlin some functionaries drew exactly this conclusion. Ted Sorensen suggested that the *Bucharest* was the best sort of ship to search, because obviously innocent: 'They'll never let you board a ship that really has something serious on it' – such as nuclear warheads. The *Bucharest* was not, in the end, stopped.

Attention shifted from conduct of the blockade to the intractable issue of the missiles already sited in Cuba. The president said: 'I just don't want a sense of euphoria to get around. That message of Khrushchev is much tougher than that.' There was still profound uncertainty about whether an attempt to force a quick showdown – a high noon at sea – would serve the US better than allowing matters to drag on for weeks, through diplomatic exchanges. McNamara played party-pooper to the optimists by saying: 'I don't see any way to get those weapons out of Cuba. I never have thought we'd get them out ... without the application of substantial force.' Though the defense secretary had been an early advocate of blockade as a means of graduated escalation, he had certainly not

abandoned a belief that an invasion of Cuba might yet prove necessary.

At 2 p.m., the Americans dispatched Kennedy's formal reply to U
Thant, responding to the UN secretary-general's proposals. The key
sentence of the letter read: 'The existing threat was created by the
secret introduction of offensive weapons into Cuba, and the answer
lies in the removal of such weapons.' Adlai Stevenson, the president
told the Burmese diplomat, would be happy to discuss a role for the
United Nations in bringing about such an outcome. It bears restating that in those days the UN was a vastly more important forum,
its principal official a bigger personality, than they are today.

Bundy read aloud to Excom Kennedy's letter to Khrushchev,
dispatched the previous night, in which the president described
how, back in August and September, he had urged restraint on
America's hawks, because he had accepted the Soviet chairman's
assurances that only defensive weapons were being installed in
Cuba: 'and then I learned beyond doubt what you have not denied
– namely, that all these public assurances were false'. Here again, as
through all the exchanges of the Crisis, the Americans were able to
make hay with charges of Kremlin duplicity, because the world
could readily understand them. The prominence of this issue did
much to deflect unwelcome discussion from others, such as the
right of Cubans to deploy missiles on their own soil. Khrushchev's
lies created a solid foundation for the American diplomatic offensive, which the Russian leader was extraordinarily foolish to have
provided.

That morning at the White House, McNamara said that it was
time to look ahead – to the possibility that say, next day, work on
the Soviet missile sites continued and the UN Security Council
provided no support, and 'we have to escalate'. His critics have
focused upon such remarks to emphasize that the defense secretary
was not an unwavering dove; that he, like the others, changed his
mind. Excom first considered, then rejected, a proposal to discuss
alternative courses later that day. It seemed essential first to allow
the UN to have its moment. The president said: 'This is not the
appropriate time to blow up a ship.'

When the NSA's top Cuba analyst Juanita Moody saw the latest intelligence about Soviet vessels changing course, she knew that Adlai Stevenson was due to address the UN Security Council meeting earlier postponed at the USSR's request. Deciding that it was urgent that he should be kept abreast of the latest developments, she rang him in New York City. When State Department staffers declined to connect her, she tracked him to his hotel room, saying later: 'I did what I felt was right, and I really didn't care about the politics.'

The Security Council commenced its meeting at 4 p.m. The White House group clustered around a TV to watch the session with little enthusiasm, because they lacked confidence in the resolve of their own standard-bearer. The lanky sixty-two-year-old Californian, a former governor of Illinois and twice Democratic nominee for the presidency, in 1952 and 1956, was one of the most profoundly decent people in American public life, as well as an electrifying orator. But both Kennedys despised this admirable citizen as 'rather prissy and ineffective', in the words of Robert Dallek. The bald egghead – almost literally so – was too clever for many Americans to understand him. Bobby, especially, mocked Stevenson's crusade to lift Illinois's public institutions from their accustomed mire of corruption. Stevenson, in his turn, privately dismissed the Kennedys as 'cold and ruthless'. The administration had grudgingly appointed him to the UN job, only because his stature in the Democratic Party required that he should be given something.

Yet this proved to be Adlai Stevenson's finest hour. His adversary, Soviet representative Valerian Zorin, faced a hopeless task and a galvanized US spokesman. Anatoly Dobrynin, who worked for Zorin for five years, characterized him as 'an intelligent and kind person', though a Western diplomat found him 'a ghastly old Stalinist hack'. Whichever depiction is just, that afternoon Zorin, blindsided by both the Kremlin and the Americans, was obliged to stonewall, in the face of repeated questions about whether the USSR had installed ballistic missiles in Cuba. Again and again, Stevenson demanded an answer: 'Yes or no – don't wait for the translation – yes or no?' Zorin floundered like an ox in a morass, saying that Stevenson would have to wait for an answer: 'I am not in an American courtroom, and therefore I do not wish to answer a question that is put to me in the fashion in which a prosecutor puts questions.'

Stevenson said: 'You are in the courtroom of world opinion right now, and you can answer yes or no.' Zorin again prevaricated pitifully: 'You will have your answer in due course.' The American returned to the charge, saying staunchly, 'I am prepared to wait for my answer until hell freezes over.' Jack Kennedy, standing before the White House TV, said with unworthy condescension: 'Terrific. I never knew Adlai had it in him.' John McCloy, back from Europe at the president's behest, had arrived at the UN building to stiffen Stevenson's spine. He found the ambassador no longer in need of such support – instead, transformed into a 'hopping mad hawk' by Zorin's evasions and deceits, though in truth these were little worse than those that Stevenson himself had perpetrated in the same forum the previous year, about the Bay of Pigs. Now, however, the Americans were unequivocal victors in a gladiatorial moment carried live on TV, and seen by hundreds of millions around the world.

2 THE KREMLIN DECISION

That afternoon of the 25th in Moscow, though Khrushchev could not yet bring himself to inform either Kennedy or Castro of his intention, he ordered Malinovsky to dispatch a message to Pliev, announcing in unequivocal terms the Soviet Union's commitment to withdrawal: 'In connection with the fact that US Navy is blockading approaches to Cuba, we made a decision not to send 665 and 668 RP [missile regiments] to you. You should not unload warheads for R-14s from transport ship *Aleksandrovsk*, if they are already unloaded organize secret loading back onto *Aleksandrovsk* ... [which] with the warheads for R-14s should be prepared for transportation back to the Soviet Union.' In case of an emergency – probably envisaged as a US invasion of Cuba – the ship's captain was ordered to scuttle *Aleksandrovsk*, sink the warheads.

Britain's Joint Intelligence Committee guessed that the Kremlin was now seeking 'to safeguard what they have already established in Cuba and to reduce to a minimum the possible loss of face which might be caused by a failure to do so or to respond firmly'. This was so, but Khrushchev's stubborn pride required the world to remain in its condition of extreme terror through three days still to come, while a host of fingers hovered over both Soviet and American firing buttons. Sergei Khrushchev described how, that evening, for the first time his father told him the missiles in Cuba would probably have to be removed, to which the young man responded with disbelief: 'I was shocked and could hardly restrain my anger. To my mind retreat was associated with national humiliation ... I couldn't understand how Father had decided to trust the word of a U.S. president [that he would not invade Cuba]. I sensed that he had no alternative. Until then Father had held the opinion that the imperialists, especially Americans, could not be trusted ... Now he had softened ... He did not convince me.'

Another development that day of the 25th generated new confusion between Washington and Moscow: a nationally-syndicated column was published in the *New York Herald Tribune*, written by Walter Lippmann, an intimate friend of the administration. Khrushchev had met Lippmann, always an advocate of détente: back in 1946 the columnist deplored Winston Churchill's famous Iron Curtain speech at Fulton, Missouri. The Soviet leader cherished a longstanding respect for the liberal sage's work, though he appears not to have made much of the concluding line of an earlier piece which we know that he also read: 'This being the nuclear age,' Lippmann wrote in September 1961, 'it is the paramount rule of international politics that a great nuclear power should not put another great nuclear power in a position where it must choose between suicide and surrender.'

Now, Lippmann suggested that the Missile Crisis should be resolved by exchanging the removal of Soviet weapons in Cuba for that of American ones in Turkey. Although the comparability issue had been much bruited abroad, this was the first mention of such a proposal in an authoritative American organ. When the column was drawn to Khrushchev's attention, late on the 25th by Moscow's clocks, the first secretary seized upon it. He took it for granted that what Lippmann wrote reflected thinking within the White House, and he was by no means wrong. For the first time the Russian leader saw the attraction of such a trade. He set about belatedly incorporating the idea in the Soviet diplomatic agenda, with a clumsiness that would shortly baffle the Americans.

In Washington, that afternoon's Excom began with an update on ships still in transit to Cuba, including the tanker *Grozny*, still a thousand miles out, which carried suspect deck cargo. There was also an East German passenger vessel, bearing 1,500 industrial workers. Robert Kennedy suggested that it might be better to go ahead with air attacks on the missile sites, rather than to confront the Soviets at sea. It was decided that, while events waited upon both the UN's and Khrushchev's next moves, the US Navy should hold off action. Walt Rostow, the president's economic adviser who later became one of the most prominent Vietnam hawks, urged extending the list of transit goods prohibited by the blockade to include fuel. Such a move could quickly strangle the Cuban economy, he said, citing the effectiveness of US attacks on German fuel supplies in World War II. Rostow won no supporters for his proposal, which was ill-considered: the president had already forsworn an assault on Castro and his people, in favour of a prudent focus upon the Soviet missiles, and only the missiles.

Kennedy then left the meeting, to speak again on the telephone to Harold Macmillan. In this latest conversation, he made no mention of the prime minister's urgings, in the written message received at the White House that morning, that the US should avoid an armed collision. Instead, the two leaders discussed the diplomacy, and American uncertainty about which ships to board where and when. Macmillan suggested that the key issue remained that of 'immobilizing the weapons in Cuba, which is your major point, isn't it?' Yes, said the president. But it was less urgent than decisions about tactics at sea.

*   *   *

By Friday morning, 26 October, it was deemed to have become essential to demonstrate to the world that the US Navy was in earnest about enforcing the blockade, rather than merely satisfying itself with having frightened Khrushchev into turning around his arms-carrying ships. The president personally selected the Lebanese vessel *Marucla*, on charter to the Soviets, as an appropriate test case, because it was unlikely either to be carrying weapons or to resist boarders. The US destroyers *Pierce* and *Joseph P. Kennedy*, the latter named for the president's elder brother killed in World War II, were tasked to intercept. Around 6 a.m., their crews were called to General Quarters without the accustomed broadcast reassurance 'this is a drill, this is a drill'. The warships closed on the vessel with orders to avoid provocations: 'Take no menacing actions. Do not train ships' guns in direction merchantmen.'

The boarding party that crossed to the *Marucla* was unarmed, and dressed in naval whites. At 7.50 a.m., the Americans reached the ship's deck via a rope ladder obligingly let down for them, and were promptly offered coffee by its mostly Greek crew. The boarders examined deck cargo of trucks and farm machinery, with more vehicles, sulphur and auto parts below – some said also toilet paper. After two hours, the visitors returned to their respective warships. The US Navy had fulfilled its purpose – to be seen to execute a first search in implementation of the blockade, without risking a showdown with the Russians. The *Marucla* was permitted to steam on towards Cuba.

This was the day, according to Robert Kennedy, when the president began reluctantly to accept that American moves thus far had failed to induce the Russians to conform to his central demand – for removal of their nuclear missiles already deployed in Cuba. A renewed gloom settled upon Excom, prompted by fears that the Soviets still intended to defy the United States. Its members were convinced that Kennedy's presidency was doomed, unless the Russian nuclear missiles were removed. His personal authority would have been set at naught, and it still seemed Khrushchev's intention to seek to achieve this. Kennedy ordered a sharp increase in air surveillance missions over Cuba, and told the State

Department to embark upon a crash programme to plan an interim civil government, if the US felt obliged to invade and occupy the island. That morning Adlai Stevenson flew down from New York to attend the meeting, accompanied by John McCloy. It was plain that the UN Security Council could play no further role that might serve American purposes, given the oft-exercised Soviet power of veto over its votes. But the American representatives would meet U Thant that afternoon, and needed fresh instructions.

While all this was happening the largest concentration of US armed forces since Korea was massing behind the south-eastern seaboard, preparing to execute at twelve hours' notice Operation Scabbards. This was a seven-day rolling programme of air strikes, likely to be followed by an invasion. Speculation about such an assault dominated that morning's newspapers. Castro had spoken the previous evening, denouncing US actions. The Cuban leader also proclaimed, without consulting the Kremlin, that US over-flights would no longer be tolerated. McNamara reported that while the US armed forces' chiefs still advocated invasion, heavy American casualties were likely to follow. The Soviet missiles on Cuba either had achieved, or would soon achieve, operational read-iness.

John McCone updated the meeting on Operation Mongoose. At Robert Kennedy's urging, early in the Crisis the CIA had acceler-ated work on this programme against Castro, including landing parties of exiles by submarine to collect intelligence, commit sabo-tage and possibly even attack the missile sites – these last representing projected follies of a high order. It was decided to hold a separate Mongoose meeting that afternoon, which also needed to discuss the role of the Cuban exiles during and after a prospective US invasion. Mac Bundy offered a memorable understatement: 'Post-Castro's Cuba is the most complex landscape.'

McCone asserted that the Mongoose group, run by the clownish Col. Edward Lansdale, was now well-organized. This claim went unchallenged, but was absurd. Following the Bay of Pigs fiasco, it is extraordinary that the White House still placed such faith in the capability of the exiles to play any significant role in discomfiting

Castro. Arguably the least impressive, most discreditable aspect of all the discussions that took place during the Missile Crisis were those that concerned Cuba's political future. In a fashion that echoed Washington policy-making across Latin America, and foreshadowed its conduct in Vietnam, Kennedy and his advisers made unembarrassed assumptions about their own right to ordain the political future of Cuba, and to puppeteer its management from Washington. To be sure the Soviets did the same, in managing their East European empire: but America aspired to be better.

When discussion turned to the blockade, strong views were expressed, that it had become urgent to shift the focus of global attention from Soviet ships to the weapons already deployed in Cuba. Dean Rusk said that he wanted to pursue diplomatic efforts – for instance, to promote United Nations inspections of the missile sites – before a military commitment was made. He suggested asking for UN members to volunteer to take over the quarantine at sea with their own warships. It was obvious that Moscow would reject such a plan, but it would strengthen America's hand to be able to brand the Russians with obduracy. The president said the Crisis had a long way to run: 'Obviously we can't expect them to remove [the missiles] … without a long negotiation.'

But then Kennedy used words that would prove critical to the outcome. 'I thought the proposal was they would remove these weapons if we guaranteed the territorial integrity of Cuba … Obviously we're going to have to pay a price in order to get those missiles out without fighting to get them out.' Suddenly, a core issue was on the table. Nikita Khrushchev asserted that the reason he had installed missiles on Cuba was to defend the island against American aggression. Even if this claim was disingenuous, it formed the professed justification for his action. And even if the Kennedy administration had – before the Crisis – no immediate intention to launch an invasion, it was the oft-expressed desire of the president and almost every member of his government to eliminate Fidel Castro.

Here was a glimpse of a window for fulfilling the commitment of the United States to secure removal of the Soviet missiles, while allowing Khrushchev to achieve his own expressed objective. Robert McNamara was doubtful whether a non-aggression declaration from Washington would mean much. The president, however, reasserted: 'If that's one of the prices that has to be paid to get these [missiles] out of there, then we commit ourselves not to invade Cuba.' It deserves emphasis that he had already indicated a willingness to do this to Gromyko on 18 October, four days before the missile deployment was even publicly avowed.

Yet the CIA's ever-hawkish McCone was dismayed by the proposal: 'That would sort of insulate Castro from further actions. Long before these missiles were there, his link with the Soviet Union and the use of Cuba as a base of operations to communize all of Latin America was a matter of great concern to us. Now what this [would do] is more or less leave him in that position.' Bundy, however, backed the president: 'The very simple, basic structural purpose of this whole enterprise ... is to get these missiles out ... If we can bring Castro down in the process, dandy ... But if we can get the missiles out ...' The president reaffirmed: 'If we can get the missiles out, we can take care of Castro.' Adlai Stevenson said he thought a guarantee of the territorial integrity of Cuba could prove critically important to securing an outcome. Llewellyn Thompson returned to the issue of possible UN inspections of the missiles, saying that he thought the Russians would find it far less painful just to take them out than to have UN personnel crawling over their launch sites.

That morning's discussions became rambling and fractious. Stevenson wished to promote a scenario in which the status quo on Cuba was sustained while a negotiation took place, which he acknowledged would take weeks. Others, audibly unhappy, insisted that the missiles must be stood down – rendered inoperable – ahead of any talks. McCone remained wary of any concession to the Soviets while the US was under threat. Stevenson left the room for several minutes to speak from the president's office to his own deputy in New York, Charles Yost, who was due to meet U Thant and needed instructions. The ambassador told Yost, 'There's a lot of flap down here', explaining that the deputy should consent to no

UN-supervised 'standstill' and lifting of the blockade while the Soviet missiles were still operational.

The Excom meeting meanwhile continued, with all the participants on short fuses. They felt that the US was making little progress towards achieving its principal goal. They had no confidence in Stevenson – nor, indeed, in the UN – and were suspicious that even with McCloy at his elbow, he would yield too much. Max Taylor believed the US government was not sounding angry enough: 'During any negotiation, Mr. President, shouldn't we be raising the noise level of our indignation over this?' For starters, he proposed increasing combat air activity over Cuba. Kennedy conceded: 'In some ways [the air strike option] is more advantageous than it was even a week ago.'

After the meeting broke up, the president spoke by telephone to David Ormsby-Gore, who asked how long the US could wait for U Thant to achieve a verified standstill in Cuba. Kennedy responded: not long. At noon he met intelligence officials, who reported increased operational readiness at the Cuban missile sites, together with identification of possible tactical nuclear weapons – FROGs. McCone emphasized his conviction that there should be no negotiation with the Soviets unless or until the missiles were stood down – weapons separated from launchers. Kennedy said: 'There are only two ways to do this, as I said this morning. One is the diplomatic way. Which I doubt – I don't think it will be successful. The other way is, I would think, a combination of an air strike and probably invasion.'

He discussed with McCone and Arthur Lundahl the possibility of landing Cuban exiles to attack the missile sites. The CIA director raised the newly-flagged threat that the Soviets had also deployed tactical nuclear weapons. The president still toyed with sabotage. Might a fuel trailer be blown up with a single bullet? Doubtful, said Lundahl, it would spew forth fuming red nitric acid. And FROGs were solid-fuelled. The CIA chief struck a sudden, unexpected note of caution, saying: 'Invading is going to be a much more serious undertaking than most people realise ... It's very evil stuff they've got there. Rocket-launchers and self-propelled gun carriers, half-tracks ... They'll give an invading force a pretty bad time. It would be no cinch by any manner of means.' Kennedy said: surely air power could 'chew them up'? Yes indeed, responded McCone, 'but you know how it is. It's damn hard to knock out these field-pieces. That was the experience we had in World War II and then Korea.'

It is striking to perceive the influence of mutual deterrence on the entire Washington debate, not to mention the Moscow one. The Americans would already have taken military action – certainly air strikes and probably also invasion and the removal of Castro – but for fear first, that the Kremlin would respond by seizing West Berlin; second, that bombing would be ineffective in destroying all the missile sites, and might conceivably provoke the Russians to launch nuclear weapons; and now, also, that an invasion would become a bloody business for attackers as well as defenders. McCone made his assessment on the basis of a drastic underestimate of Soviet strength on Cuba. Even if the Russians defending the island did not launch tac nukes, they had the firepower grievously to maul, just conceivably to repulse, an American invasion.

Kennedy, haunted by memories of the Bay of Pigs fiasco, knew that such a new outcome would be a catastrophe. A defeat on that scale would almost certainly have destroyed his presidency as assuredly as would the 1980 collapse of the Iranian hostage rescue mission later wreck that of Jimmy Carter. The American people will forgive almost anything but failure. There could be nothing more humiliating than to precipitate a bloodbath, never mind an outright defeat, on America's doorstep. It was not fear of taking military action, nor doubts about the morality or legitimacy of bombing or invading Cuba, that held back John F. Kennedy. It was apprehension that such a course would prove unsuccessful or, more likely, an inconclusive mess. This caused him to persevere with the diplomatic route even as his uniformed brass, and some of his civilian advisers, bayed for bombing. As McNamara shrewdly and even brilliantly articulated at the outset of the crisis: the fundamental issue was always political, not strategic.

* * *

From 23 October onwards, while the world's attention fixed upon the movements of Soviet cargo vessels in the Atlantic, a considerably different reality existed at sea, imperfectly understood at the White House, and influenced by the swashbuckling mood of the US Navy's commanders. Within hours of Kennedy's broadcast, Khrushchev had turned around all those Soviet vessels bound for Cuba which carried missiles, conventional weapons or military personnel. Only those carrying fuel, food and suchlike were holding their courses. This left essentially purposeless the Soviet submarine flotilla that had been trailing the merchant ships, constrained by their maximum underwater speed of nine knots.

US Navy secretary Fred Korth subsequently described the quarantine operation as 'the most demanding test of the Navy's Anti-Submarine Warfare (ASW) capabilities since World War II'. American warships actively pursued twenty-nine suspected submerged submarine contacts, of which six proved to be authentic. British and Canadian submarines reported other contacts in the wider Atlantic. 'So far as can be determined, no Russian submarines committed to the Cuban operation escaped detection and tracking,' Korth claimed – mistakenly, because B-4 was never pinpointed. 'By tracking these submarines – and by being capable of destroying them if necessary – the Navy denied their effective use to the USSR.' The Navy secretary failed to add, however, that if shooting started the Soviet Foxtrots were capable of exacting a devastating price for their own destruction.

The senior US naval commander in the Atlantic, Admiral Robert Dennison, chose to regard the presence of the submarine flotilla in 'his' ocean as a threat comparable with that posed by the missile deployment in Cuba, 'because it demonstrates a clear Soviet intent to position a major offensive threat off our shores … the first time Soviet submarines have ever been positively identified off our East Coast'. At 11.04 a.m. EDT on the 24th, a P5 Marlin floatplane out of Bermuda spotted a snorkel mast five hundred miles south of the island. This report prompted the dispatch of a task group centred upon the *Essex*, to shadow the presumed – and indeed actual – Soviet submarine B-130 commanded by Captain Nikolai Shumkov.

The skipper had plenty of problems of his own, even before the US warships approached his position. Before sailing he had requested new batteries for his boat, and been refused. Now, his old ones would not long hold a charge, limiting his best underwater speed to six to eight knots. Thus, he had no choice but to surface at regular intervals, to recharge the cells. Moreover, as he approached the Sargasso Sea only one of his diesel motors, which powered the boat on the surface, was functioning. His noisy, rattletrap craft was appallingly vulnerable, as Soviet commanders should have recognized before it sailed.

Yet Shumkov had one asset unknown to the Americans: a 10-kiloton nuclear torpedo, boasting more than half the power of the bomb that destroyed Hiroshima. The captain was in no doubt that this piece of equipment, at least, was fully serviceable. A year earlier, on 23 October 1961, he had himself fired the first live-tested T-5 weapon in the Arctic, then observed through his periscope the stupendous flash as it exploded five miles away, sending shockwaves pulsing through his craft. This vessel and this weapon, together with three more like it, were now loose in the Atlantic, where senior US Navy officers were determined to treat them as immediate threats, though knowing nothing of their nuclear torpedoes. Two of the Foxtrots – one of them Shumkov's B-130 – had been ordered by Moscow to move well back from the US blockade line. The third, B-36, was ordered to set a course through the Silver Bank passage, between Grand Turk and Hispaniola, while B-4 positioned itself two hundred miles to the north-west.

Here again, the Kremlin's desperate and dangerous confusion of purpose was apparent. Khrushchev had already made his decision to pull back from confrontation, to avoid war with the United States. But he still could not bring himself to retreat on all fronts, to accept the logic of his own mindset. Thus, at 8.19 a.m. on Friday 26 October, the gleaming black hull of B-36 was pinpointed by a US Navy spotter plane, on the surface eighty miles east of Grand Turk – four hundred miles south-west of B-130 and inside the quarantine zone. Yet again, the Americans found themselves alarmed and baffled. What was the submarine's business? What new mischief or threat might its presence signify? The Russians aboard B-36 were equally distressed, when air-dropped practice depth-charges and sonobuoys began to explode in the boat's vicinity after it dived, as the US Navy strove to sustain its positional fix.

It was a characteristic of Soviet tanks, aircraft and warships that their designers took little heed of human comfort. This was notably true of the Foxtrots now plying the western Atlantic. After four weeks at sea, the crews of the submarines, and especially B-36, were suffering from extreme heat that had brought out ugly rashes in many, who also endured water rationing and extreme tension. Anatoly Andreev, assistant to the captain of B-36, wrote in a letter to his wife: 'For the past four days we have been unable even to come up to periscope depth. My head is bursting from the foul air … Today again three men fainted from heat exhaustion … Those off-duty sit motionless, staring at some fixed spot.' Andreev complained bitterly about the state of his commander's nerves, 'shot to hell. He's yelling at everyone and torturing himself … He is becoming paranoid, scared of his own shadow … The heat's driving us crazy … It's getting harder and harder to breathe.' The stench of rotting meat compounded that of human bodies, as refrigeration machinery ceased to function.

The boats' captains later testified that they expected every hour to receive word from Moscow that war with the United States had begun. Captain Dubivko in B-36 said afterwards: 'The success of being the first to use our [nuclear] weapons depended on timely reception of the signal to start combat operations.' Yet to receive any communication from their base, they needed to rise to periscope depth, then float a wireless antenna. This they were often unable to do, while under intensive surveillance from the Americans. Confused though their orders were before departure, one point every Soviet submarine officer understood: he must strive to the limits of his own ability and the powers of his boat and his crew to avoid the humiliation of being forced to the surface by the warships of the US Navy. And in the absence of news or fresh orders from home, save knowledge that a deadly crisis was in progress, in Dubivko's words: 'We were expecting a [war] signal from one hour to the next.' American warships, chivvying the submerged Russians and as a result denying them communication with their bases, made the Atlantic Ocean as dangerous a place as was Cuba already, because so much thus turned upon the discretion of individual boat commanders.

3 'A TRIAL OF WILL'

That morning of the 26th, two Soviet submarines were obliged to surface to charge their batteries, in the threatening presence of US warships. Meanwhile a Swedish cargo ship, the *Coolangatta*, under charter to the Soviet Union and carrying potatoes from Leningrad, had somehow escaped American notice until fifty miles out from Havana. Now, the US destroyer *Perry* raced to close upon the vessel and signal: 'Will you stop for inspection?' The Swedish captain ignored the request; steamed on. When this news was passed to McNamara, he ordered the Navy to leave the ship be. Such forbearance further excited the Pentagon's already angry and impatient brass, who demanded: was the administration serious about blockade enforcement, or was it not? The defense secretary insisted that, at a time when the diplomacy was intensifying, it would be mistaken to precipitate a possible showdown at sea.

When Charles Yost met U Thant at the United Nations, the secretary-general gave him important news: the Soviets were indicating that they might accept a deal whereby they withdrew their missiles from Cuba, in return for a formal US pledge not to invade. Dean Rusk phoned the president to report this, together with similar indications from Canadian diplomats. Rusk said: 'So it's just possible that this may move faster than we had expected.' Kennedy, still audibly ruminating on this idea, said: 'I think we'd have to do that, because we weren't going to invade them anyway.' Rusk: 'That's right.' Kennedy: 'Right.'

That afternoon, events continued to develop – or rather, there were further signs that such a deal as U Thant trailed was indeed in Khrushchev's mind. ABC News journalist John Scali was approached by the veteran Soviet KGB station chief, forty-eight-year-old Aleksandr Fomin, real name Aleksandr Feklisov, who operated in Washington under journalistic cover. Col. Feklisov, who had achieved notoriety as handler of the executed atom traitor Julius Rosenberg, floated the prospect of the missiles being removed, in a trade for a US pledge to leave Castro alone. Scali immediately reported this conversation to Rusk, who urged him to keep talking, and to tell the KGB man that the Americans were indeed interested. The news caused Kennedy to rework the evening White House statement, which was confined to a flatly factual report, about the continuing progress of work on the missile sites, revealed by air reconnaissance.

The president reported to Macmillan in London on the apparent Soviet trial balloon – 'a couple of hints, not enough to go on yet'. The Britisher once again urged Kennedy to hold back on military action: 'At this stage any movement by you may produce a result in Berlin which would be very bad for us all.' The president, however, refused to offer the reassurance the prime minister sought: 'If at the end of forty-eight hours we are getting no place, and the missile sites continue to be constructed, then we are going to be faced with some hard decisions.' He thus implied that he would certainly bomb, probably also invade. All that he yielded to the prime minister was a promise that there would be no new US action without forewarning to London.

Macmillan, in his turn, offered Kennedy the modest aid of allowing the introduction of UN supervisors to US Thor nuclear missile sites in Britain, in return for UN monitoring of the Soviet missiles in Cuba. Kennedy responded warily: 'Sure, Prime Minister, let me send that over to the [State] Department. I think we don't want to have too many dismantlings. But it is possible that that proposal might help. They [the Soviets] might also insist on Greece, on Turkey, and Italy [where Jupiter missiles were stationed].' Kennedy briefed only his brother in detail about these exchanges, almost certainly because he knew that few Excom members would be impressed by them.

Meanwhile in Washington Averell Harriman was at least as dovish as Macmillan, because he knew how often displays of

Kremlin aggressiveness were driven by morbid private consciousness of Soviet weakness. Harriman called Schlesinger, urging that
Khrushchev was not behaving like a man who wanted war. He
feared that Kennedy was driving the Soviet leader into a corner, in
which he might feel obliged to do the unthinkable: 'If we do nothing but get tougher and tougher, we will force them into
counter-measures. We must give Khrushchev an out ... He has an
opportunity now, to move the world back from the abyss of
destruction.' But Schlesinger, who agreed, was likewise shut out of
the Excom loop.

Kennedy, nursing the candle flame of hope of a trade with the
Soviets, angrily rebuked a US government spokesman for asserting
at the State Department's daily press briefing that the administration was ready to embark on 'further action', if a peaceful solution
was not soon forthcoming: 'Christ, we're meeting every morning
on this to control this, the escalation ... You have to be goddamn
careful.' The spokesman, Lincoln White, apologized profusely.

A few minutes later, at 7.40 p.m., as the president walked across
to the White House Mansion, a cable began to arrive from the US
Moscow embassy, forwarding in sections a 2,748-word message
from Khrushchev, delivered in the Soviet capital at 4.43 p.m. local
time. This was translated, encrypted and decrypted with the agonizing sluggishness of so many communications in the Crisis. Its
complete text had taken almost ten hours to travel between
Khrushchev and Kennedy – hours which were properly too
precious to have been thus wasted.

The Soviet leader's letter opened in his accustomed haughty,
condescending fashion: 'I see, Mr. President, that you are not
devoid of a sense of anxiety for the fate of the world, of understanding, and of what war entails. What would war give you? You are
threatening us with war. But you well know that the very least
which you would receive in reply [to any nuclear attack] would be
that you would experience the same consequences as those which
you send us ... I have participated in two wars and I know that war
ends when it has rolled through cities and villages, everywhere
sowing death and destruction.'

Khrushchev then blustered: 'In the name of the Soviet Government and the Soviet people, I assure you that your conclusions regarding offensive weapons in Cuba are groundless ... The same forms of weapons can have different interpretations ... We want ... to compete with your country on a peaceful basis. We quarrel with you, we have differences on ideological questions. But our view of the world consists in this, that ideological questions ... should be solved on the basis of peaceful competition.

'You have now proclaimed piratical measures, which were employed in the Middle Ages, when ships proceeding in international waters were attacked ... I assure you that on those ships which are bound for Cuba, there are no weapons at all. The weapons that were necessary for the defense of Cuba are already there ... If assurances were given by the President and the government of the United States that the USA itself would not participate in an attack on Cuba and would restrain others from actions of this sort, if you would recall your fleet, this would immediately change everything ... Then the necessity for the presence of our military specialists in Cuba would disappear.'

There were another two thousand words of baroque Soviet rhetoric, but here was the core of the communication: an apparent confirmation of that morning's message relayed by U Thant and later echoed by others. Kennedy and his close advisers retired to bed on that Friday night more hopeful than they had been for days.

Others, however, were less so. Dean Rusk summoned Dean Acheson, returned from his visit to de Gaulle in Paris. The past and present secretaries of state drank Scotch in Rusk's seventh-floor office at Foggy Bottom while awaiting completion of the translation of the Soviet missive. Acheson still stubbornly advocated 'firm' US action – which meant the military kind. The Soviet missiles remained on Cuba, and time was running out. Only an air strike could eliminate them. He agreed with the State Department guess that Khrushchev had personally composed the latest letter; he imitated the pudgy first secretary pacing the Kremlin, waving a stubby finger and dictating. That same evening Rusk briefed the British, French and West German ambassadors about the likely US timetable for destroying the missile sites, unless work on them was halted. Ormsby-Gore reported to London that he expected this to happen on Tuesday 30 October.

On the afternoon of Friday 26th, Fidel Castro summoned Aleksandr Alekseev to his command post. News reaching him from New York indicated a US commitment imminently to invade Cuba. He, Castro, was convinced that the Americans were coming. He had been dismayed by Khrushchev's decision to halt the inbound Russian warhead-carrying vessels, which suggested an unworthy lack of resolve. Yet it still did not occur to the Cuban leader that the mighty Soviet Union might be so infirm of purpose as also to bow to US demands for removal of the stupendous weapons already deployed in Cuba, which had made the island so gratifyingly important.

Thus, he assumed that Soviet staunchness would be met by American aggression, and thus he prepared his forces to fight to repel this. An overwrought President Osvaldo Dorticós, Castro's puppet president, told the Yugoslav ambassador on that Friday that a US assault was 'inevitable'. All this Alekseev reported to Moscow, where it intensified the fears of Khrushchev, incomparably less eager than Fidel for a showdown with the forces of capitalism.

Castro meanwhile dispatched a communication to the secretary-general of the UN: 'Cuba does not accept the vandalistic and piratical privilege of any warplane to violate our airspace, as this threatens Cuba's security and prepares the way for an attack on its territory. Such a legitimate right of self-defence cannot be renounced. Therefore any warplane that invades Cuban airspace does so at the risk of meeting our defensive fire.' He also visited the Soviet command post at El Chico south-west of Havana, where he was told that all Russian troops and most of the missile units were at full readiness. He urged Gen. Pliev first, to order his men to throw away their absurd civilian dress and don uniforms; then to switch on their radars, hitherto determinedly dormant. Pliev did not comply with the first proposal; he did, however, assent to the second. American eavesdroppers reported to Washington that the

ether had suddenly come alive – scores of Soviet electronic installations, including fire control systems, had been activated. Pliev
messaged Malinovsky in Moscow: 'In the opinion of the Cuban
comrades, we must expect a US air strike on our sites in Cuba
during the night of Oct. 26–27, or at dawn on Oct. 27. Fidel Castro
has decided to shoot down American warplanes with his anti-aircraft artillery in the event of an attack on Cuba. I have taken
measures to disperse *tekhnika*' – warheads – 'within the operating
zone and to improve our camouflage. In the event of American air
attacks on our sites, I have decided to use all air defence means
available to me.'

Most of the Soviet warheads were stored in an underground
bunker, undetected by the CIA, near the small town of Bejucal.
Once they had been conveyed to the missile sites, thirty minutes'
labour was required to strip the canvas cover off each R-12 and fit
its nuclear charge. A further two hours were needed thereafter to
mount the assembled missiles on launchers, couple electrical
cabling and set the weapons at designated angles, in conformity
with target cards. Pliev made the decision on his own authority to
move the warheads nearer to the missiles, in contravention of the
latest order from Moscow. The Presidium endorsed his action
when he reported it, but he was again cautioned that no nuclear
weapon must be fired without Kremlin authority. Further to
confuse the situation, a succession of signals warned Pliev: 'Stop all
work on deployment of R-12 and R-14 – you are aggravating the
United Nations … Camouflage everything carefully, work only at
night.'

In the absence of technical safeguards, compliance remained
dependent upon the will of the general and his subordinates, who
retained authority to fire SAMs. Pliev, a sick man, was by now also
an exasperated one. He was obliged to grapple with an emotional
local dictator convinced that his hour of destiny was at hand; troops
who had slaved in almost intolerable tropical conditions to prepare
a nuclear arsenal for action, but who were now told to disarm their
most potent weapons; an imminent American invasion threat
which both the Russians and Cubans were committed to resist, but

which Pliev and his subordinates were instructed to defeat without using extreme force; and a government in Moscow bent upon beating a retreat, but desperate not to be seen to be doing so. It is unsurprising that, amid such confusion, Soviet officers responsible for Cuba's air defences were eager to use their weapons to frustrate America's arrogant overflights, and interpreted their muddled and almost contradictory orders as giving them discretion to do so. Sergei Mikoyan said later: 'Under conditions where Moscow and Washington are anxious not to do anything, and when commanders don't know what to do, *anything* can happen.'

Concurrently Khrushchev still saw sufficient evidence of US vacillation in its enforcement of the blockade – the passage of some ships unchallenged – to discern scope for hustling Kennedy; for salvaging something from the looming wreck of the supremely ambitious and epically clumsy Operation Anadyr. The last sentence of Harold Macmillan's diary for 26 October read: 'The situation is very obscure and dangerous. It's a trial of will.'

12

Black Saturday

1 CASTRO FRIGHTENS KHRUSHCHEV

On the morning of 27 October outside Gorky – today's Nizhny Novgorod, a large city on the Volga – young Nikolai Kozakov was still obsessed with the Crisis, but little wiser: 'I got up at 9.30 and took time making myself presentable since it's a Saturday. I shaved, washed, worked on my appearance. After breakfast, I took a pencil and started thinking about a hot-button poem on Cuba. I took the winged phrase *Venceremos* [Spanish for 'We shall overcome'] as the title and the theme. Of course, I could not express my own thoughts as they don't agree with the communist views. I had to pretend to be an ardent Bolshevik and follower of Khrushchev. The poem started coming together; by lunchtime I had three verses. I ate some thin soup and carried on working ... I completed five verses today, I just needed the last one ... But before that I had to glue my boots as they had holes in them.'

At about the time Kozakov got out of bed, in deep darkness half a world away Fidel Castro arrived at the Soviet embassy in Havana, a two-storey mansion in the leafy, elegant Vedado area, once owned by a sugar magnate's family who quit Cuba after the Revolution. It was 2 a.m. on the 27th. The *maximo lider* repeated to Aleksandr Alekseev what he had been saying to the Soviet generals: an American invasion was 'inevitable'. Once again, he embraced the language of melodrama, urging that when war began, it must become thermonuclear war; that he was happy to die along with his people '*con suprema dignidad*'. The ambassador, struggling to distinguish rhetoric from reality in Castro's torrent of words, messaged Moscow at once to report the visitor's presence at the embassy, together with the prediction of imminent bloodshed. Alekseev also alerted Khrushchev that he would shortly be receiving a personal letter from his devoted Cuban ally. Through several hours of night that followed, sitting in the bunker beneath the embassy in case of a sneak American attack, the Russian sought to assist his guest in drafting a message to the leader of the Soviet Union, couched in language Castro considered appropriately grandiose, to match the drama of the hour.

At one point in the two men's discussion the exasperated, exhausted envoy demanded of the Cuban: 'Do you want to say that we should deliver a nuclear First Strike?' No, said Castro, unwilling to be so explicit. Nonetheless, he finally settled upon a form of words that was quite alarming enough: 'If … the imperialists attack Cuba with the purpose of occupying it, the danger facing all mankind … would be so great that the Soviet Union must in no circumstances permit the creation of conditions that would allow the imperialists to carry out a first atomic strike against the USSR … If they carry out an attack on Cuba, a barbaric, illegal and immoral act, then that would be the time to think about liquidating such a danger forever through a legal right of self-defence. However harsh and terrible such a decision would be, there is no other way out, in my opinion … With fraternal greetings, Fidel Castro.'

Alekseev was later at pains to urge upon historians that his visitor did not, by these phrases, seek to demand that the Soviet Union should launch a pre-emptive strike against the US. Such an accusation, asserted the former KGB man, became merely Khrushchev's figleaf, to justify betraying the island's people. In this, the ambassador may have been very narrowly correct. But the evidence is overwhelming, from many sources, that Fidel Castro was so obsessed with the maintenance of his own power and glory – the opportunity to emblazon for the admiration of posterity his courage in defying the might of the United States – that he displayed an absence of fear of nuclear war unworthy of any human being, never mind the leader of seven million Cubans. When the visitor finally took his leave of the Soviet embassy at 5 a.m., after Alekseev had passed the letter to his staff for encryption, Fidel suggested that the ambassador might wish to accompany him to his own underground bunker, in a cave outside Havana. The Russian instead remained at the mission, while the Cuban departed to prepare for what he believed would prove the climactic hours of his life.

Castro's letter to Khrushchev, clearly proposing to embrace the prospect of a nuclear exchange in response to a US invasion, deserves to define his reputation in the eyes of posterity. Khrushchev's response, when it arrived many hours later, began in bathos: 'Dear Comrade Fidel Castro, I consider this proposal of yours incorrect, although I understand your motivation.' The Soviet leader then bluntly clarified Castro's suggestion: that a US invasion of Cuba should provide a sufficient justification to initiate a global conflict, 'that we should be the first to launch a nuclear strike against the territory of the enemy'.

Narcissism had been a prominent characteristic of Castro throughout his life, and especially since he secured power over his little country. But a unique brand of egoism was required to promote the first, and almost certainly last, thermonuclear war, in order to protect his own polity. Khrushchev's testimony, as well as that of others, shows that Castro's message belatedly persuaded the Soviet premier that, though he did not cease to like, even to love Castro as a revolutionary, this was not a man who should be permitted any part in the pilotage of a mortally dangerous crisis. Khrushchev wrote afterwards: 'We understood that he failed to think through the obvious consequences of a proposal that placed the planet on the brink of extinction.'

Castro's message did not reach Khrushchev until Sunday morning the 28th in Moscow, by which time both the White House and the Kremlin had experienced many other traumatic shocks. It thus did not directly influence the course of events on 'Black Saturday', as participants would later come to call the 27th. The letter nonetheless reflected the almost hysterical, yet fatalistic mindset then prevailing in Cuba, which afflicted Soviet commanders more dangerously than Castro's own forces, because they controlled incomparably more alarming weapons systems.

While Castro was closeted with Alekseev in the embassy many Soviet troops, warned that 'a landing is expected tonight', were digging trenches around the missile-launchers and their own positions. Near the seashore, rock proved impenetrable even with jackhammers, but they did their best. In the darkness an alarm sounded and thousands of men leaped down from their tiered bunks and stood to arms until daylight. On the shoreline in the small hours twenty-year-old naval signaller Vitaly Semenozhenkov was among those who took up positions with AK-47s, four magazines apiece and a box of F-1 grenades: 'All our units were on the highest alert, our nerves were extremely strained as we expected a landing at any time. The silence was oppressive. It was completely dark, and all we could see was the glimmer of enemy ships' lights, far too close' – though in reality most unlikely to have been those of US warships. 'Senior sailor Voznyuk had brought down his accordion, and we were ready to don our striped shirts and sailors' caps, to fight in uniform with orchestral accompaniment.'

Missile engineer Rafael Zakirov said: 'We slept with our weapons beside us; we struggled to pick up bulletins from Radio Moscow; remained on full battle alert.' When at last he could write home – though still without being permitted to specify where he was stationed – he told his family: 'It is very hard to live here, and the situation is pretty tense as you are probably aware from the newspapers. But I think that everything will be alright. Don't worry about me ... This is a very unusual and dangerous period of my service, but I take pride in it ... I am very homesick, Hugs and kisses to you all.'

As for the Cuban forces, not all the weapons with which the Soviets had supplied them were state-of-the-art. Juan Melo, employed degreasing Mauser rifles for issue to the militia, noticed their swastika symbols. He realized that these must be war booty, captured by the Red Army from Hitler's legions. Conchita Alfonso, like millions of Cuban wives and mothers, had a backpack ready for each child, containing a can of milk, a little rice, clothes and essentials, 'because if the invasion comes, they will bomb Havana'. She was then teaching at the university, where the entire faculty was summoned, to swear a new oath of loyalty to the Revolution. Like the rest of the Cuban people, Alfonso had heard nothing official about the missiles on their soil until the Americans revealed them.

Nineteen-year-old María Regueiro had hitherto concealed her militia uniform from disapproving bourgeois parents. Now she showed up at home proudly wearing green trousers, blue shirt, with a Czech sub-machine gun as a fashion accessory. Her father demanded indignantly: 'What are you doing, dressed up as a man?' She responded: 'I am not a man, I am a militiawoman, and I came to tell you, because I don't know if I shall be coming back.' If those were melodramatic words, it was a melodramatic time. María continued: 'From that day, my father understood that I was not going to change.' She spent the rest of the Crisis guarding her workplace, a depot where the authorities stored cars confiscated from fugitives who quit the country. She always looked back on those days as a time when there was 'a lot of determination, a lot of courage'. She was moved that her father, who hated communism and almost everything that had happened since the Revolution, in October nonetheless rallied to Fidel and the flag, training as a paramedic. When she asked him why he did so he responded: 'Make no mistake, if the United States attacks Cuba, I shall be first in the line of our people defending it.'

In Washington early that Saturday morning J. Edgar Hoover, unworthy director of the FBI through six presidencies, did nothing to assist the attorney-general's peace of mind by reporting to him that Soviet personnel in New York had been ordered to prepare to destroy confidential documents, in anticipation of a US invasion of Cuba that would precipitate war. Like much information disseminated by Hoover, this was untrue, but was widely believed, as were rumours of similar incendiary activity at Dobrynin's Washington embassy.

Nonetheless, a Soviet attaché at the United Nations told journalist Murray Kempton that he felt unable to attend a performance that afternoon by visiting violinist the great David Oistrakh: 'We must meet to consider whether we are to evacuate,' said the diplomat sombrely. 'I do not want to be here when the Russian bomb falls.' This remark caused Kempton to sally with the blackest humour: 'There are Red dawns which even the best of Bolsheviks do not wish to see.' Elsewhere around the world German chancellor Konrad Adenauer, addressing the German people on TV, described the Crisis as 'the gravest threat to peace since 1945'. In Buenos Aires American conservatives' favourite evangelist Billy Graham preached to ten thousand people on 'The End of the World'.

Alongside the hemispheric mobilization and deployments, accidents provoked by haste and harsh operating conditions were killing people on both sides. A US Navy transport carrying ammunition to Guantánamo exploded on landing, taking out its eight-man crew, as ordnance in the wreckage continued to detonate for hours. Only a few miles away, two Russian soldiers and a Cuban bystander died when their truck overturned on a rough jungle road, while shifting heavy weapons towards the US base. A US Navy RB-47 reconnaissance plane crashed on take-off from Bermuda, killing its four-man crew, as a result of human error by ground technicians.

John Guerrasio, a child in Brooklyn, had been summoned into the kitchen the previous morning with his five siblings, to be addressed by their mother: 'We may not see each other again,' she told them emotionally. 'The world may end this afternoon.' Then they recited a prayer together: 'She had found some poem which described New York City in a nuclear attack with the skyscrapers forming canyons that filled with water like in one of those disaster movies. And she read us that poem and kissed us and we all walked off to school thinking that was the end of it. And I was pretty amazed when three o'clock came, and I got to go home and watch *The Three Stooges* again.' Likewise in Galina Artemieva's Moscow home: 'The family had serious discussions about what to do if a bomb fell on us.'

* * *

At 9.09 a.m. on the 27th, the USAF's Major Rudolf Anderson took off from McCoy Air Force Base outside Orlando, on yet another U-2 photographic surveillance flight. This would be Anderson's sixth Cuban sortie since the Crisis began, checking out Soviet deployments in the eastern part of the island, with special reference to Guantánamo. After leaving US airspace he would sustain radio silence, crossing the coastline on a south-easterly heading to Camagüey, then flying onward to Manzanillo on the southern coast of Cuba before heading directly east towards Guantánamo. He was briefed thereafter to make a final turn – away north-west towards Florida, crossing the coast homebound at Banes. He would pass over several batteries of Soviet SAM missiles, in the course of almost three hundred miles overflying Castro's country, but he and a succession of his fellow recon pilots had done likewise during the previous week, without provoking a ground response.

Anderson, an eager-beaver U-2 man who loved his work at the extremity of manned flight, had volunteered for this mission, which was being reinforced elsewhere by US Navy Crusaders' low-altitude photographic passes. His minimum-weight plane carried no active defensive equipment to counter ground-to-air missiles, of the kind fitted to bombers. If fired upon, he must rely solely upon evasion. The dispatching officer slapped him on the shoulder before the hood closed, saying, 'Okay Rudy, here we go, have a good trip. See you when you get back.' Anderson gave him a thumbs-up, then turned to taxi for take-off, leaving behind Jane, his pregnant wife, and two young children. The pilot's USAF chiefs failed him significantly: he was not informed at briefing that the previous day the Russians on Cuba had activated their air defence radars, previously either switched off or operating on low power. The only rational conclusion to be drawn from this step was that Soviet installations were now operating at heightened readiness, and expected to fire upon aerial intruders.

On that Saturday morning at the White House, Kennedy met a delegation of state governors alarmed about inadequate civil defence precautions. One of them, 'Pat' Brown, sometimes hailed as the founder of modern California, demanded spikily: 'Mr. President, many people wonder why you changed your mind about the Bay of Pigs and aborted the attack. Will you change your mind again?' Here was a reminder of the many Americans who perceived toughness towards the communist enemy as the highest good. Kennedy responded unapologetically: 'I chose the quarantine because I wondered if our people are ready for the Bomb.'

Meanwhile the nuclear routines of both Soviet armed forces and SAC were sustained, making no concessions to the heightened tension created by the Crisis. Late on the previous night, though early on Saturday in Russia, a Soviet Tu-95 Bear bomber had released and detonated in the atmosphere above Novaya Zemlya in the Arctic Circle a small bomb with twenty times the explosive power of Hiroshima's Little Boy. Now the Americans played catch-up. In darkness a B-52 Stratofortress armed with an 800-kiloton nuclear weapon took off from Hawaii bound for Johnson Island, a federal bird sanctuary turned nuclear test site in the midst of the Pacific. The previous day, a missile had been successfully test-flown from Johnson. Today an explosion was scheduled to follow as part of a thirty-bomb programme, planned in response to the Soviets' resumption of atmospheric testing.

At 11.46 a.m. EDT, on the plane's fourth pass over the designated target area, SAC's most proficient bombardier Major John Neuhan released his four-ton canister on three parachutes, designed to slow its descent to enable the aircraft to clear the proximate airspace before the detonation of its barometric fuse. Just 87.3 seconds later, while the crew sheltered behind thermal curtains in their cockpit, they blinked amid a flash of white light in the wake of their flight path, followed minutes later by a series of shock-waves. The mushroom cloud from the bomb rose above sixty thousand feet. At Excom in Washington nobody troubled to mention this event, so frequent were the occurrences of such explosions in the diary of the Cold War, though so rightly shocking to posterity. Since the beginning of October the Soviet Union had exploded nine nuclear weapons in the atmosphere, the US five. It seems inadequate to describe these stupendous roars of thermonuclear menace as sabre-rattling, but they represented nothing less.

At a meeting in the Pentagon 'tank' on the morning of the 27th, Curtis LeMay renewed his demands that the chiefs of staff should submit a paper calling for a full US invasion of Cuba. The initial air strike programme, OPLAN 312-62, would commit fifty-two aircraft to a first wave of bombings of anti-aircraft, transport and communications hubs, increasing after six hours to 384, and after twelve hours to 470. An amphibious assault – OPLAN 316-61 – would follow, in turn succeeded by airborne landings. McNamara joined the meeting at 1.30 p.m., to be informed of the chiefs' recommendation. This was still being discussed when an officer interrupted with news of a U-2 missing on a flight over the North Pole. Here was yet another potentially disastrous mission-of-choice, which had been allowed to proceed even as the world held its breath.

The Americans received their first intimation of this dramatic friction-flight in the face of the Soviet Union's defences at 12.30 p.m. Gen. Thomas Power, C-in-C of SAC, was on the Offutt base golf course near his headquarters outside Omaha when he was told of an intercept by Soviet air defences: the Russians had scrambled fighters to engage a U-2 aircraft high above their north-eastern airspace, indeed three hundred miles inside Russia. An officer telephoned the 4080th Strategic Wing, to demand 'What the hell you are doing with a U-2 over Russia?' Col. John des Portes answered that he knew nothing about this aircraft, but was instead alarmed about the failure of Major Anderson to return as scheduled from a Cuban mission. Further calls revealed that this second plane could only be that of Major Charles 'Chuck' Maultsby, who had taken off the same morning in pitch darkness from a USAF base in Alaska, bound upon a routine air-sampling mission, seeking data on fallout from the Soviet nuclear tests.

Just over an hour later, the president was telephoned by McNamara with this news, together with a report that USAF fighters had been scrambled to protect the U-2 whenever they could reach it. Kennedy responded calmly but not unreasonably sorely:

'There's always some sonofabitch who doesn't get the word.' He knew, they all knew, that the Soviets might assess this aircraft as flying an intelligence mission ahead of an impending bomber attack. Yet the USAF had wilfully withheld from the administration, for a potentially lethal interval, the information that its plane was missing, and thrusting ever deeper into Russia.

It was, of course, an act of carelessness trending towards madness to have permitted a US aircraft to fly anywhere near the Soviet Union in the midst of a crisis of such magnitude, but there it – and the hapless Maultsby – was. The Americans' initial responses were hampered by an unwillingness to allow the other side any hint of a supreme secret: that they possessed the capability to monitor Soviet air defence communications. Less than two months earlier another U-2 had strayed into Russian airspace near Sakhalin island, prompting a formal US apology to Moscow. That incident, however, took place before Cuba erupted.

Meanwhile Maultsby was lost, frightened and supremely lonely, voicing plain-language 'MAYDAY, MAYDAY, MAYDAY' emergency calls across the air waves while hearing Russian folk music in his headphones and watching his fuel gauge sink. He began to receive instructions from an unfamiliar voice – which he rightly assumed to be Russian – to turn sharply right, a course that would take him still deeper into the Soviet Union. He was also receiving US transmissions from Alaska, but these were growing weaker. He had become sure that he was overflying Russia, and was terrified of finding himself 'another Gary Powers'. Maultsby had special reason: a decade earlier, he had spent almost two years as a communist prisoner, after his F-80 Shooting Star fighter was shot down over North Korea. It seems remarkable that he was still willing to accept such flight assignments as this one, after what he had endured as a PoW. The only explanation is that a flier is a flier is a flier. Many pilots throughout history have taken to the air in the face of all odds, logic and prospects of self-preservation, because challenging the sky is the only thing they know how to do, or wish to do.

He understood that he was far off track. Gyro compasses were useless in those extreme northern latitudes. He depended instead upon celestial navigation, which failed him when he experienced unexpectedly high Aurora Borealis activity: the flashing lights in the northern sky made it impossible for him to use his sextant to establish a position. Now he turned steeply until the position of the overhead stars suggested that he might be flying east once more. Fortunately for his already extravagant pulse rate, he was unaware that two successive pairs of MiG-17Ps were pursuing him, and continued to do so for three hundred miles. The Soviet planes, however, reached their 60,000-foot ceiling while still far below the wandering flier. In the operations centre at SAC, all these movements were being tracked. Fearful that the MiGs would catch the U-2, the Americans had scrambled two F-102 fighters from Western Alaska. These were armed with Falcon air-to-air missiles. Which were nuclear-tipped, capable of destroying everything within a half-mile of their detonation point. Nobody at SAC seems to have reflected that it would have been better to risk the loss of the unarmed U-2 than to precipitate a shoot-out between Soviet fighters and American planes equipped with such weapons.

LeMay's deputy Lt. Gen. David Burchinal later testified that when word reached the chiefs in 'the tank' about the lost U-2, McNamara panicked: 'He turned absolutely white and yelled hysterically "This means war with the Soviet Union. The President must get on the hot line to Moscow!" And he ran out of that meeting in a frenzy.' This story more vividly illustrates the contempt of the USAF's brass for the defense secretary than any plausible version of his behaviour, but there is no doubt that Maultsby's unwanted adventure represented yet another very bad moment of the Crisis.

Over the Kola Peninsula, shortly before 2 p.m. EDT on Saturday the U-2 pilot shut down his engine, cockpit pressurization, heating and electrics. Already airborne for nine and a half hours, he sought to preserve a meagre reserve for a further emergency, and to exploit his aircraft's extraordinary glide capability, derived from an eighty-foot wingspan, twice its fuselage length from nose to tail. His emergency oxygen supply kicked in, preventing his blood from exploding in the thin air thirteen miles up. He began his ever-so-slow, silent descent until, after an eternity of suspense, he saw ahead a faint glow of dawn that told him he was assuredly heading east. A few minutes later – morning in Alaska – he met the pair of F-102s that had been searching for him, above the snow-covered wasteland which he now glimpsed from twenty-five thousand feet. 'Welcome home!' said one of the American pilots on the emergency frequency. They guided him down towards a primitive ice strip at Kotzebue Sound, where a US radar station was based.

At a thousand feet, one of the fighter pilots became convinced that the U-2 would crash and yelled, 'Bail out! Bail out!' Maultsby ignored him, triggered his braking parachute, belly-flopped onto the runway and skidded into a patch of deep snow. A huge American in a parka knocked on his cockpit hood, grinned 'welcome to Kotzebue', then lifted the numbed pilot out of his seat, out of the plane, 'and placed me on the snow as if I'd been a rag doll'. Other Americans and half a dozen Inuit people gathered around, while overhead the two F-102s buzzed the strip and waggled their wings before turning for their own home runway. Maultsby had to be assisted to remove his helmet, exposing him to a blast of icy-cold air. He staggered away a few feet, to empty a bursting bladder. He had been airborne for ten hours and twenty-five minutes, the longest-ever recorded flight of a U-2.

It was 2.25 p.m. in Washington. One of the dozen pocket crises within the Crisis was over. Yet again there proved a wanton absence of communication between the two sides. Nobody troubled to tell the Soviets what the U-2 had, or had not, been doing, three hundred miles into their airspace. Khrushchev appeared relieved when Marshal Malinovsky reported to him that the MiGs had been unable to catch the American intruder. 'The plane was probably lost,' said the first secretary. 'There was nothing for him to do over Chukotka', easternmost region of the USSR. The *Vozhd* admitted the possibility, however, that the overflight could have been a deliberately provocative act by the USAF's chiefs, and claimed as much in his next missive to the White House.

2 THE SOVIETS SHOOT

And even as the Maultsby drama unfolded over north-eastern Russia, another U-2 had become the focus of an even graver confrontation: above Cuba. Although the Americans now knew much about Soviet deployments, there were still important gaps in their intelligence. They were unaware, for instance, that *Luna* missiles had been moved into launch positions around Guantánamo Bay. The US Marine garrison of the base had been reinforced to a strength of more than five thousand men, dug in to resist an assault by the Cuban army. Such measures would avail them nothing, however, if the Soviets unleashed the nuclear-tipped *Lunas*, which could incinerate them in seconds. Thirty-six 2-kiloton warheads were held at a bunker dug into a hill a few miles above the town of Managua, while twelve 1-megaton R-12 missile warheads were cached at Bejucal. Neither site had been identified by the CIA, despite immense efforts being made to do so. The photo-interpreters spotted activity at Bejucal, but rejected it as a possible warhead location because it was only carelessly fenced, and approached through an open gate. The analysts assumed that extreme security would surround any nuclear site, which the Soviets must surely regard as the most sensitive of all their secrets in Cuba. The analysts were too rational, and thus wrong.

Many of Gen. Pliev's men on the island had become exasperated by their commanders' passivity, as US reconnaissance aircraft repeatedly streaked through the sky above them. Some Russians were taunted by Cubans, demanding 'Why have you come, then?', if not to shoot down *yanqui* intruders. Castro himself had been visiting the San Antonio de Los Baños command post on 25 October when it was overflown by two US F-101s, prompting from the dictator expressions of indignant anger at their impunity.

Tens of thousands of Cubans manning the defences were keyed to the highest pitch of excitement and expectation. At 3.41 p.m. on Saturday six more US Navy Crusaders took off on Cuban recon-naissance missions. Having crossed the sea low enough to meet bursts of spray, they climbed above their photo targets – and met

Cuban AA fire. Scores of the defenders began firing at them with every weapon to hand, and nearby Russians joined in. 'I pulled out my pistol,' recorded Lt. Dmitry Senko later, 'and started shooting. Of course my bullets could never reach, but one of the planes started bleeding smoke and lost height.' This was almost certainly an illusion, but no matter. Elsewhere Vasil Voloshchenko's tank unit had been on full alert since the previous day. Asked afterwards the Russians' feeling towards the Americans in those hours, he said: 'What feeling could you have, when we were living on top of a barrel of gunpowder? We saw their planes skimming the palm tree tops, tracked by our AA guns. We weren't scared – we just thought of the Americans trying to tell everybody everywhere what to do.'

Within the hour word was passed to the White House that an American plane had been hit by a 37mm shell. This was untrue, but caused Excom – not wrongly – to perceive a Cuban escalation. Nonetheless, the president and McNamara, still deeply alarmed by news of the U-2 intrusion deep into Soviet airspace, decided that this was no moment further to excite their own country's media. It was agreed that nothing should be said about the Crusaders coming under fire. At that stage, both the White House and the Kremlin were still oblivious of the much more serious episode, which had taken place hours earlier.

Soviet air defence headquarters for eastern Cuba was based in a former church at the centre of the old colonial town of Camagüey, its interior now dominated by a massive screen showing aerial movements in the region. Since the system was belatedly activated on Friday night, Russian monitors – still incongruously clad in civilian check shirts and slacks – had been watching take-offs from Guantánamo, together with US Navy activity offshore. The local commander Col. Georgi Voronkov had passed the night on duty, in constant expectation of a US amphibious assault.

During the hours of darkness nuclear warheads continued to be trucked across country to several Soviet IRBM missile-launch sites, despite repeated obstacles and hazards, and at least twenty-four hours after Moscow had sent orders to Pliev to prepare for the return of these weapons to the Soviet Union. The explanation must lie partly in the chaos attending many Soviet military operations throughout history, and into 2022; the general's poor state of health; and, above all, the shared expectations of Soviet and Cuban forces on the island that an American assault was imminent. Russian personnel were exhausted by heavy labour and hours of apprehension. American communications to and from 'the sharp end', about developments both in the air and at sea, were often badly delayed. It is thus unsurprising that the same was true on the Soviet side. Gen. Pliev's order, that his forces should fire only if they came under direct attack, was issued at 8 a.m. on the 27th following the new instructions received from Moscow. But there appears to have been no discussion with his subordinates about the exact interpretation of the words 'under direct attack' – whether US reconnaissance aircraft should be considered attackers – before the general left his command post at El Chico to catch up on some sleep. He was ailing, driven to exasperation by successive changes of directive. His grip on his forces and subordinates was weak.

Major Anderson's U-2 was tracked by Camagüey from the moment it approached the Cuban coast, passing over the town at 9.22 a.m. local time without responding to an electronic challenge. In the operations centre, this pulsating dot on the screen was designated Target 33. Its presence was also noted at El Chico, by the overall air defence commander Lt. Gen. Stepan Grechko and his deputy Maj. Gen. Leonid Garbuz. Both men, like all Soviet officers in Cuba, were keyed to the highest pitch of tension. They tried to alert Gen. Pliev to the intruder, but were unable to raise him by telephone.

By that point Anderson's plane had passed over Guantánamo; was heading north again, his camera laden with exposed images of Soviet installations. He would soon be out of Cuban airspace. While Grechko and Garbuz were still deciding their course of action, the U-2 passed through the zone of the Soviet 701st AA Regiment. Only when Anderson had already been over Cuba for more than an hour did Soviet Central Command in Havana – Pliev's two senior subordinates – message 27th AA Division at Camagüey: 'Destroy

Target No. 33'. This formation's commanding officer, Col. Voronkov, promptly ordered the 507th Regiment, commanded by Col. Yuri Guseinov, to launch a salvo of missiles. The U-2 was then flying at an altitude of more than thirteen miles over Banes, formerly a United Fruit Company town, where Fidel Castro celebrated his first wedding on 11 October 1948 ... in its American club.

The US aircraft had been tracked for several minutes by the 507th's No. 4 missile battery, commanded by a Major Gerchenov. US eavesdroppers offshore reported that a 'Big Cigar' or Soviet 'Fruitset' fire control radar was locked onto an aircraft above the island. Target officer Lt. Aleksei Ryapenko and three corporals had only recently relieved the night watch in the radar cabin of the battery when their commander gave an order such as none of the Russians had ever before received in earnest: 'Locate target azimuth 130, range 110, altitude 23 [km].' When the range closed to 60 kilometres – 36 miles – Ryapenko ordered his crew to engage electronically: 'The tracking was stable, equipment was working fine. I felt absolutely confident we would hit the target, and ordered the crew to switch to automatic tracking.'

As the American plane entered the SAM launch zone, it lost some height. The regimental chief of staff was repeatedly demanding from headquarters confirmation of the shootdown order, and hearing nothing. The heat in the control cabin was intense, and in Ryapenko's words, 'so was the situation. Still no instructions.' Major Gerchenov demanded down the telephone: 'What do we do? Fire?' Sweat trickling down their faces, the missile crew watched the U-2 enter their firing zone, monitored by the Automatic Launch Apparatus. Suddenly Gerchenov called out 'Destroy target with a salvo of three [missiles]!' Ryapenko electronically armed his SAMs, and pressed the firing button. As the first missile soared skywards and the tracking beam locked on, he reported 'target engaged'. Ten seconds later, the second SAM fired, then the third. A torrential rainstorm descended as crews at the launch pad raced to manhandle missiles onto the ramps, to replace those streaking towards the intruder.

In the stifling cabin, the Russians could neither see nor hear what was happening in the sky. Then, on their radar screens, they were mesmerized by the sight of a cloud replacing the previously sharp image, as the plane disintegrated. After the second missile exploded, the broken fragments lost altitude rapidly, and Ryapenko reported laconically, 'Target destroyed.' 'There were no more targets in our zone,' he recorded later. 'Major Gerchenov reported to the command post of the regiment that target No. 33 was no more. He gave everybody the news over our loudspeaker system, then applauded me for performing confidently and calmly.' The crew, stunned and also thrilled, emerged from the control cabin. 'The rain had stopped. All the officers and operators assembled on the launch pad, chattering excitedly. Our CO said: "Well done everyone!" Then they picked me up and started tossing me into the air, which wasn't hard as I weighed just fifty-six kilos. My crew had also done a great job.' Both Gerchenov and Ryapenko were awarded combat decorations for their achievement – but not until 1 October 1964, more than two years after the event. The U-2's tail fell into Banes Bay, while the pilot's corpse and other wreckage smashed into a cane field at Veguitas, six miles south-east of the SAM launch site.

Lt. Gen. Stepan Grechko had made the spontaneous decision to authorize the launch of SAM missiles in the knowledge that the Cubans were already firing promiscuously at US aircraft. He said later that he chose thus to assume that war had broken out; that all constraints were lifted, despite the absence of an order to that effect from the summit of the Soviet military command chain. Gen. Gribkov later excused his subordinates: 'These officers did not so much disobey orders as react, in a reasoned military manner, as they understood the situation required.' It is more plausible that, in the atmosphere of extreme stress prevailing among Soviet and Cuban forces, he found it irresistible to prick the balloon of American arrogance that he, like so many of his compatriots, perceived in the overflights. As Cubans demanded of a host of local Russians: if they were not to shoot at intruding Americans, why had they come? This was precisely why Kennedy, especially, and

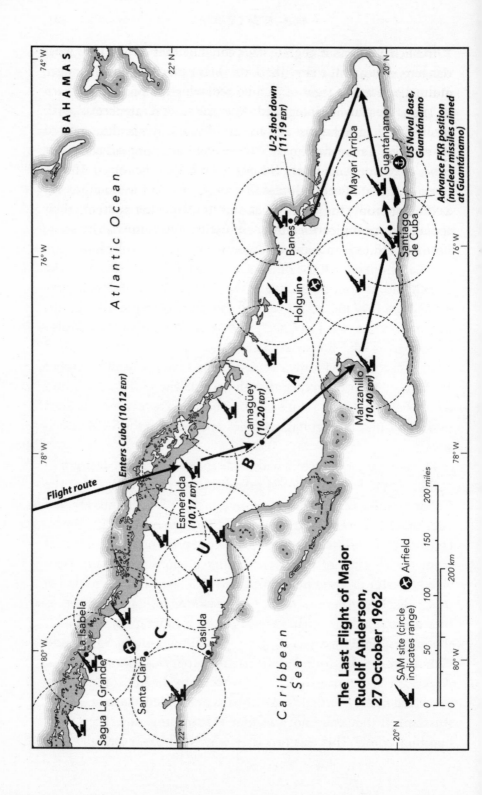

The Last Flight of Major Rudolf Anderson, 27 October 1962

BAHAMAS

Atlantic Ocean

Caribbean Sea

Flight route

Enters Cuba (10.12 EDT)

Esmeralda (10.17 EDT)

Camagüey (10.20 EDT)

Manzanillo (10.40 EDT)

U-2 shot down (11.19 EDT)

Banes

Holguín

Mayarí Arriba

Santiago de Cuba

Guantánamo

US Naval Base, Guantánamo

Advance FKR position (nuclear missiles aimed at Guantánamo)

Sagua La Grande

La Isabela

Santa Clara

Casilda

SAM site (circle indicates range)

Airfield

0   50   100   150   200 km

0   50   100   150   200 miles

80° W   78° W   76° W   74° W

22° N

20° N

Khrushchev in lesser degree, feared losing control of vastly more dangerous weapons than the SAMs, which could also be launched at the discretion of their respective generals in Cuba.

The shootdown dramatically raised tension, at precisely the moment Khrushchev in the Kremlin had become desperate to de-escalate. As for the Americans, several hours elapsed before the news of Major Anderson's extinction reached the White House. Even in the late twentieth century, when oblivion was supposedly at the fingertip command of national leaders, long and perilously tenuous communications threads stitched from the battlefield to both the White House and the Kremlin.

13

The Brink

The Saturday morning intelligence briefing to Excom, as usual given by McCone, confirmed no change in the status of the ballistic missiles in Cuba: they appeared ready for firing. Three Foxtrot-class submarines had been pinpointed, one of these inside the quarantine line. As for sentiment around the world, there had been anti-American demonstrations in Buenos Aires, Caracas and La Paz, but opinion in Europe, increasingly conscious of Soviet recklessness, appeared to be rallying to the United States. The *Economist* wrote that day: 'Mr. Khrushchev's motives for placing in Cuba the missiles which he appears to have withheld from other satellite countries remain alarmingly obscure.'

The British *Spectator* was strongly supportive of the US stance, asserting that President Kennedy 'had no real choice in the face of a direct and obvious Soviet testing of American will. The legal niceties of the American [blockade] are not the crux ... The defence of our liberties, and of peace, depends on our strength. The core of that strength is the power of the United States. A direct threat to that power, if not firmly rebuffed, would mean the crumbling of the sole real guarantee of freedom and law throughout the world.' This sentiment – essentially, 'our side in the Cold War, right or wrong' – commanded significant and still growing European popular support.

As some Soviet cargo vessels continued to steer towards the blockade zone, an American message was dispatched to Moscow, routed via U Thant, to ensure that the Russians knew where this was drawn. At Excom McNamara spotlighted the *Grozny*, a tanker then six hundred miles out. He recommended that it should be boarded and searched –'Use force if necessary' – in a measured toughening of US tactics. At Barksdale, Louisiana, USAF 2nd Air Force staff charged with surveillance of the inbound Russians suffered technical headaches. C-in-C Gen. John Ryan suddenly realized that his pilots might not be able to read the name *Grozny* in Russian lettering. An officer was hastily dispatched to the nearby liberal arts Centenary College, who found there a Russian-speaker and got him to write out *Grozny* in Cyrillic script. Then – before the existence of fax machines – the airman painstakingly explained over the telephone to the planes' home base at Lake Charles, how the name would look on the ship's side, 'like you might do with kids', in the words of 2nd Air Force's Col. Bill Garland.

Aircraft took off to maintain rotational surveillance of the *Grozny*, which appeared to the Americans likely to be carrying missiles, though in reality innocent. After the tanker failed to respond to a challenge, Admiral Dennison ordered nearby US warships to load their guns with live ammunition, then clear them by firing in the opposite direction to the tanker. When darkness fell, the warships also lit up the night sky with occasional starshell illuminants. 'The US Military behaved more and more aggressively,' wrote Sergei Khrushchev. 'I would even say insolently.'

At noon in Moscow, early morning in Washington, Khrushchev displayed to the Presidium some of his former ebullience, saying: 'They're not going to invade now.' The fact that Kennedy had responded to U Thant's proposal indicated that the US would not embark upon military action while still pursuing diplomacy. The Soviet leader had acknowledged, within the Kremlin walls at least, that the missiles in Cuba would have to be withdrawn: he remained nonetheless committed to salvaging redemptive terms for doing so. 'We won't be able to liquidate the conflict unless we satisfy the Americans and tell them that our R-12 rockets are indeed there. If we can get them to liquidate their bases in Turkey and Pakistan in exchange, then we will have won.'

This was the moment at which Khrushchev embraced the 'Lippmann proposition'. He drafted yet another letter to Kennedy, proposing an explicit deal: 'You are worried about Cuba. You say it worries you because it is only ninety miles across the sea from the shores of the United States. However, Turkey is next to us. Our sentinels are pacing up and down and watching each other. Do you believe you have the right to demand security for your country and the removal of weapons that you considered to be offensive, while not recognizing the same right for us? That is why I make this proposal. We agree to remove these weapons from Cuba that you categorise as offensive. We agree to state this commitment to the United Nations. Your representatives will make a statement to the effect that the United States, bearing in mind the anxiety and concern of the Soviet state, will evacuate its analogous weapons from Turkey.'

In the interests of both speed and tactical advantage, this message was broadcast by Radio Moscow at 5 p.m. that Saturday, 10 a.m. in Washington. Meanwhile Khrushchev caused his defence minister

"INTOLERABLE HAVING YOUR ROCKETS ON _MY_ DOORSTEP!"

Vicky's cartoon in the London *Evening Standard*, 24 October 1962.

to message Gen. Pliev in Havana: 'It is categorically confirmed that it is forbidden to use nuclear warheads for the missiles, FKRs, and *Lunas* without approval from Moscow. Confirm receipt.' If the White House was frustrated by the difficulties of keeping pace with Khrushchev's lurches of position, so was the Soviet media bureaucracy. *Izvestia*'s front page that day carried the story that the Kremlin had confirmed the presence of Soviet missiles in Cuba, previously denied, and also reported the offer to withdraw them in exchange for the removal of US missiles from Turkey. Unfortunately a page two commentary lagged behind this development, heaping scorn on American claims of the missile deployment, and dismissing talk of a swap as the work of the fevered 'Pentagon propaganda machine'.

Khrushchev's latest open letter to Kennedy, an exercise in megaphone diplomacy, made headlines around the world. At the White House the president read aloud from a news agency report, handed to him by Ted Sorensen, the announcement that Khrushchev was offering the US a trade of its Jupiters in Turkey for the Soviet missiles in Cuba. Bundy said: 'Hmm. He didn't.' The president and his advisers were once more confused, indeed angered. Moscow was proposing different terms from those set out in the previous day's private letter to the president. Excom searched for coherence in this sequence of Soviet communications, but in reality they reflected wild vacillation, as Khrushchev groped for an exit door handle.

No American response was possible until more was known. The group in the Cabinet Room agreed that pending clarification, it was vital to keep the heat on the Russians, not least through intensified air surveillance of the missile sites: they as yet knew nothing of the fate of Major Anderson. Far from Excom members understanding that Khrushchev was preparing to beat a historic retreat, most still believed that only American air attack and invasion would remove the nuclear missiles from Cuba.

They discussed the possibility that the Soviet offer on Turkey was genuine. Even if it was, most opinion around the table opposed such a deal. Not only would the Turks be infuriated, but it would signal to other allies a willingness to throw them to the wolves, for the sake of a short-term US advantage. Paul Nitze said: 'I think everybody else [in other nations] is worried that they'll be included in this great big trade if it goes beyond Cuba.' Yet in the eyes of the world, such an offer might seem a fair proposition. The president said: '[Khrushchev's] got us in a pretty good spot here. Because most people would regard this as not an unreasonable proposal … I think we have to assume that this is their new and latest position, and it's a public one.' RFK wrote later of Excom's dismay, after studying the latest open communication from Moscow: 'The proposal the Russians made … did not amount to a loss to the United States or to our NATO allies.' The White House group agreed that, while the perceived incompatibility of the two Kremlin messages, one private and one public, argued confusion in the Soviet camp, in the attorney-general's words: 'There was confusion among us, as well.' It merits emphasis that whatever opposition was expressed around the table to the Turkish trade, privately – at this stage – the president himself was minded to accede to it.

They puzzled over whether the real Soviet position was that of the previous day's private letter, or of that day's public statement. They had become increasingly attracted to a deal based on a pledge that the US would leave Cuba alone; they were ever more dismayed by contemplation of one that appeared to sacrifice Turkey, even if – as the Pentagon emphasized – the Jupiter missiles there had no strategic value. Kennedy, who had now been handed a transcript of Khrushchev's public statement, said: 'He's put this out in a way to cause maximum tension and embarrassment … The Turks are bound to say that they won't agree to this.'

In Gorky, aspiring poet Nikolai Kozakov listened with his accustomed cynicism to the broadcast of his national leader's letter to Kennedy: 'Levitan [the Radio Moscow announcer] started ranting at 5 p.m.: "Attention! Attention!" What is going on? It turned out that they were broadcasting a message from Shark [Khrushchev] to Kennedy. That he welcomed their decision on the immunity of our ships in the Caribbean, and let's send over UN representatives with comprehensive instructions. He kept making jabs at Kennedy, that they had bases in Turkey, then why couldn't we make ourselves comfortable in Cuba? So, the pig admitted that we had rockets there, that is, that Cuba had our rockets, and our officers were looking after them. And so, don't you be afraid, nothing unforeseen can possibly happen.

'But what an imprudent step that was, to give the Cubans the missiles! They are descendants of the conquistadors, after all, hot and impulsive people. Now [Shark] just needs to give nuclear weapons to China, as well. And the bastard says: we are only giving Cuba defensive weapons. What is he talking about? Rockets and long-range aircraft, for defence?! Not they, but we, are playing with fire, poised on the brink of a war. Perhaps my thinking is very primitive, but this is my firm view. I have nothing against Cuba, but I feel ready to grind the "wise man" Khrushchev into powder ...'

McNamara said in exasperation: 'How can we negotiate with somebody who changes his deal before we even get a chance to reply, and announces publicly the deal before we receive it?' That group of clever, puzzled Americans felt driven to a conclusion – a false conclusion – that Khrushchev was struggling against foes inside the Kremlin; that the latest proposal superseded the earlier one, because the Soviet leader had been obliged by Presidium comrades to make it. They could not grasp the reality, that Khrushchev was floundering in a morass of his own creation, rewriting his script between takes – to mix metaphors – most recently after reading Walter Lippmann's column.

RFK threw out a proposal: might it be possible to provide the Turks with some means of reassurance that would enable the US to progress a deal such as Moscow offered in its latest broadcast letter? Most of the group, worn down by Russian equivocations and sincerely confused about the authentic Kremlin position, were against yielding ground; showing anything that might be construed as weakness. But the president urged buying Turkish time – persuading Ankara not to announce any irrevocable hardline position until the situation clarified. 'There isn't any doubt. Let's not kid ourselves. They've [the Soviets] got a very good proposal, which is the reason they've made it public – with an announcement ... Emotionally, people will think this is a rather even trade ... Therefore it makes it much more difficult for us to move [militarily against Cuba] with world support.'

The White House that morning sought to create some space, by responding to Khrushchev's public offer with a complaint – an entirely legitimate complaint – that 'several inconsistent and conflicting proposals' had come out of Moscow in the previous twenty-four hours. There could be no negotiation while work continued on the Cuban missile sites. It was a reflection of the chasm between America's armed forces leaders and political reality that even while Max Taylor was attending Excom, the other chiefs occupied themselves in drafting yet another memorandum to the president, urging him to authorize a massive air strike against Cuba either next day, 28 October, or on the 29th, and thereafter to invade the island.

Throughout the crisis, European attitudes, and especially that of British prime minister Harold Macmillan, were strongly influenced by their own circumstances: 'To us who face nearly 500 of these missiles in Russia trained on Europe,' wrote the prime minister, 'there is something slightly ironical about these 20–30 in Cuba ... As I told the President, when one lives on Vesuvius, one takes little account of the risk of eruptions.' Nonetheless on 'Black Saturday' Macmillan summoned to Admiralty House Britain's chief of air staff, Sir Thomas Pike, to discuss the alert status of the RAF's V-Bomber force. Air Chief Marshal Pike later reported to his fellow armed forces bosses that the prime minister remained anxious to hold off any measure such as mobilization, that might be interpreted as a step preparatory to war.

If the situation deteriorated further, Macmillan intended to call a Cabinet meeting on the following afternoon, which he would invite the chiefs of staff to attend. For the time being, however, he did not want the chief of the defence staff, Admiral Lord Mountbatten, recalled to London – or rather, to be seen by the media to be recalled – from his country home in Hampshire. The prime minister proposed only that the V-bomber force should be placed on a slightly higher state of alert, which was done at 1 p.m. on Saturday – 8 a.m. in Washington. The logbook of RAF Bomber Command's No.1 Group recorded: 'All key personnel were required to remain on station and operations staff to be available at short notice. Although no generation of aircraft was ordered, some preparations were made to ensure rapid generation if necessary. All measures were unobtrusive.'

The following day the strength of the standing alert flight of three huge nuclear-armed bombers was increased to six. This was the spearhead of a total force of 166 nuclear-capable aircraft, of which 120 were then operationally available. Meanwhile the sixty Thor nuclear missiles deployed at RAF bases in Britain had been called to readiness. Some officers, like their American counterparts, interpreted Macmillan's instruction more enthusiastically than he would have wished. The prime minister supposed that he had authorized only Readiness State One-Five – aircraft armed and ready, with crews at fifteen minutes' warning. In reality, Bomber Command's alerted aircraft were at Readiness State Zero Five, just five minutes from take-off. The CO of 100 Squadron at RAF Wittering, W/Cdr. Mike Robinson, spent the afternoon of Black Saturday sitting with his crew in their Victor, ready to go: 'The aircraft was loaded with its Yellow Sun Mk. 2 [hydrogen bomb] and we had the Go-Bag with all the necessary target and route instructions.' A young navigator, a member of the crew of a Vulcan bomber, said afterwards: '[If] the signal … had been received … we would have done it unhesitatingly. I really mean unhesitatingly.'

Mike Robinson and his fellow-professionals were overwhelmingly preoccupied not with the possibility of looming oblivion, but instead with their professional duty to ensure that the aircraft should start up immediately, in the event of a 'Readiness State Zero Two' or Scramble order. They had tested every system. They were acutely conscious that, in the event of a Soviet attack, Britain's defences could expect only the briefest window of opportunity to act. The Ballistic Missile Warning System being constructed at RAF Fylingdales, high on the Yorkshire Moors, promising Bomber

Command four minutes before its incineration, would not be operational until the following year. In the meantime Britain was dependent on existing systems in Alaska and Greenland, together with Manchester University's Jodrell Bank radio-astronomy installation in Cheshire.

Projections about the nation's fate in the event of war – and no one supposed for a moment that the UK might be spared, if the Soviet Union attacked the US – were then based on 1955 estimates that ten 10-megaton H-bombs would kill twelve million of the country's forty-six million people, and incapacitate many more. A later 1964 estimate would have been more realistic: A Soviet attack, this stated, 'would cause the United Kingdom to cease to exist as a corporate political entity'.

The slightest delay in issuing the war order could be fatal to the V-Force's prospect of take-off, which is why rotating elements of SAC's B-52 strength were kept permanently airborne. Once aloft, British crews were required to listen out for a coded signal to proceed to their targets inside Russia – or to return to base. Despite the prime minister's anxiety to sustain the lowest possible temperature in Britain's corner of the Crisis, any observer on the public road outside RAF Wittering could have watched the activity inside the perimeter that Saturday afternoon, and even heard orders being passed to crews over the station's public address system. Transmission of a message prefixed with the words 'Mickey Finn' indicated that Britain was at war. After spending four torrid hours in cockpits, they were permitted to descend, play bridge or *Risk!* in the cramped ready-rooms at Wittering and nearby Waddington, where 44 Squadron was based. One evening at Wittering, a posse of aircrew wives marched into the officers' mess and demanded to be told what plans had been made for their evacuation. In the words of S/Ldr Kevin Dalley, 'Answer came there none.' Some mothers thus made their own futile preparations to head northwards with their children, for the remote Pennines or Western Isles of Scotland, if they learned that their husbands had taken off.

Britain's chiefs of staff anticipated that the likeliest Soviet response to an American assault on Cuba, such as seemed imminent, would be an assault and seizure of West Berlin with its US, British and French garrisons. The city was indefensible, but inevitably the three governments intended to respond militarily to such Russian aggression. To that end, the British chiefs of staff proposed to press the politicians to raise Bomber Command's readiness to Alert Condition 2. Even if Britain did not mobilize, as the chiefs wished, such a step would demonstrate solidarity with the US. British defence minister Peter Thorneycroft later recalled seeing Whitehall deserted and silent that weekend: 'Rather a lovely morning, and just walking in there to the Ministry and thinking "My God, I wonder whether this really is it".'

In Cuba, Fidel Castro indulged himself in a rising tempo of rage and indignation. The superpowers were talking only to each other, to the exclusion of himself. The Americans were preparing to invade his country; the Russians perhaps to precipitate its destruction, without the meanest pretence at consultation with its leader. Though he was obliged to acknowledge his absolute dependence on the Soviet Union, he never thereafter loved Khrushchev as he had loved him before October, because events forced him to confront the reality that he strutted amid a small, weak polity, important only because the two superpowers had been rash enough to make it the stage for a confrontation between each other.

On that Saturday afternoon, a massive crowd on the Mariel waterfront greeted the arriving Soviet vessel *Vinnitsa*, whose captain gave a colourful account of braving an American offshore armada to defy the blockade. The crowd shouted '*Fidel, Jruschov, estamo' con los dos!*' – 'Fidel, Khrushchev, we are with you!' Against the urgings of the US Navy, McNamara had ordered that the ship should be allowed to pass unchallenged: while diplomacy offered some hope, it seemed frivolous to precipitate a clash at sea. If there had to be an escalation, this seemed likely to be a historic one, ashore.

The contradiction about the mood inside the White House that afternoon was that the Americans were now in possession of Kremlin proposals that would provide the world's escape route from the brink of the abyss. Yet because of their anger about perceived Soviet duplicity, increased by the reported U-2 shoot-down and mingled with a determination to force an outcome, on that Saturday they seemed to approach closer to launching US military action than at any previous moment. When the president returned to the Cabinet Room after an absence, he was handed a new draft of a proposed American letter to Khrushchev, composed by members of Excom. Bundy said by way of explanation: 'The justification for this message is that we expect it to be turned down, and expect to be acting [against Cuba] tomorrow or the next day. That's what it's for, and it's not good unless that's what happens.' Rusk followed: 'I think we've got to make a judgement here as to whether ... the Soviet Union, in putting this further demand [for an exchange of foreign-based missiles] is putting it forward as a real sticking point up to the point of shooting, or whether it is an attempt at the last minute to try to get something more. After they had indicated last night that they would settle for something less.' This was about right.

McNamara said that it now seemed necessary to prepare for US military action: 'I am not prepared at this moment to recommend air attacks on Cuba. I'm just saying that I think we must now begin to look at it more realistically than we have before.' That day the C-in-C of North American Air Defense Command, Gen. John Gerhart, sought advance clearance from the chiefs of staff to use nuclear weapons against prospective incoming enemy bombers. In response, he was told that such authorization would not be forthcoming if only Cuban aircraft attacked US forces, but would be given if it became plain that they faced a general 'Cuban and Sino-Soviet attack'.

Meanwhile Admiral Robert Dennison, increasingly alarmed about what Soviet *Lunas* might do to a US invasion armada, proposed arming his forces with 'an atomic delivery capability'. Rear-Admiral Edward O'Connell, commanding at Guantánamo, also sought authority to treat any movement of *Lunas* into a launch position within range of the base as 'an offensive act unacceptable to the United States'. He was unaware that overnight such Soviet missiles had indeed been advanced to sites from which they could annihilate his five-thousand-man garrison. Curtis LeMay had in the interim secured authorization to arm his F-100 Super Sabres in Europe with tactical nuclear weapons, in readiness for strikes against thirty-seven priority Warsaw Pact targets – airfields and command centres. At that date, no electronic locking devices were fitted to these weapons, which could thus be launched and detonated by pilots. Moreover, senior air force officers with a sense of responsibility worried about the security of the 136 Minuteman missiles on full alert, in silos at remote launch sites across the northern United States. Some were technologically capable of being dispatched by their two-man crews without higher authorization.

At Excom, the defense secretary raised the possibility of replacing the Jupiters deployed in Turkey with Polaris missiles, aboard a submarine to be deployed in the Mediterranean, to reassure the Ankara government. This proposal was generally approved. The president and his advisory group also endorsed the summoning of a NATO Council committee next day, to discuss such a scenario and its implications for the alliance, 'so that they all have a piece of it'. The council would meet knowing that the US had formally responded to U Thant, accepting the Soviet proposal to exchange removal of the missiles for a pledge not to invade Cuba. It would be told that, if the Soviets refused to accept this, there could be a trade of the Jupiters in Turkey and Italy for the Cuban weapons.

The allies would be dismayed by such action, but would then be confronted by a more brutal reality, described by the president: 'They don't have any notion that we're about to do something [bomb and invade Cuba]. And that's going to be on them. You see that hasn't been explained to NATO, and I'd like to have them get into *that* before they reject [the Cuba-Turkey trade].' Whatever the allies' unhappiness about the US pulling missiles out of Europe in the face of Soviet threats, it would be less than their fears about the consequences of a US invasion of Cuba. More than one party now faced American threats, in this fantastically confused situation. Kennedy observed drily: 'We all know how quickly everybody's courage goes when the blood starts to flow, and that's what is going to happen to NATO.'

McNamara emphasized the gravity of the state of affairs, which he thought it important that all parties recognized: 'Mr. President … If we act in Cuba, the only way we can now is with a full attack. I don't think we can take any of these limited attacks when they are shooting at our reconnaissance aircraft … The moment we take out the SAM sites and the MiG airfields we're up to the 500-sortie program. If we send 500 sorties in against Cuba we must be prepared to follow up with an invasion in about seven days … It seems to me that the Soviets are very likely to feel forced to reply with military action someplace.'

Which might include air strikes against the Jupiter launchers behind the Black Sea. The Americans were now talking much more about the perils of a Soviet attack on Turkey in reprisal for bombing of Cuba than about Berlin, focus of their earlier apprehension. Opinion shifted against calling a NATO Council for next day. All that mattered was that such a gathering should take place before air strikes, which now seemed likely to be delayed at least until Monday, to give time for the Soviets to respond to the president's latest message to U Thant. There was much discussion of whether to publish Khrushchev's earlier, supposedly private letter to Kennedy, making a proposal which the Americans were ready to accept, before the Russians pre-empted it with their new, public demands. It seemed overwhelmingly likely that revealing the letter would strengthen international support for the American position.

Kennedy sought to focus attention on one central matter: the unshakeable US demand for all activity at the Cuban missile sites to halt, and to be subjected to UN verification, pending discussion of wider issues – '*that* we're all in agreement on'. Llewellyn Thompson thought that there was still a realistic prospect of Moscow backing down, accepting the non-invasion pledge demanded in the private letter, forgetting the Turkish trade. John McCone said: 'The important thing for Khrushchev, it seems to me, is to be able to say: "I saved Cuba. I stopped an invasion."' Bobby Kennedy said: 'He must be a little shaken up, or he wouldn't have sent the message to you in the first place.' Max Taylor reported the chiefs of staff's renewed formal recommendation, for air strikes followed by invasion. There was another flash of scaffold laughter when the attorney-general quipped, 'Well, I'm surprised.' He and most of his Excom colleagues had given up on LeMay and company as counsellors.

The exchanges recorded here represent only a small fraction of the discussions that afternoon and evening, by men under enormous stress, conscious at every moment of clocks ticking; of the *Grozny* approaching the quarantine line; of the need for a decision on whether to sustain air surveillance of Cuba amid almost certain ground fire; of what to say and when to say it to the Turks, to NATO, to the world. Only a few blocks from the White House, at the Statler Hilton hotel early that evening, a second meeting took place between ABC's John Scali and KGB station chief Aleksandr Feklisov. In a studied display of histrionics the journalist accused the KGB officer of 'a stinking double cross' – stalling for time – by proposing the 'hands-off Cuba deal' when Moscow was about to demand the Cuba-Turkey missile swap. The American asserted that US forces were on the brink of launching an assault on the island. The Russian insisted that he had transmitted a legitimate offer.

There is still no conclusive evidence about whether Khrushchev authorized Feklisov to act as a back-channel to Kennedy through Scali. The colonel's original message was certainly the first hint to reach the White House of a complete change of course in Moscow. Anatoly Dobrynin later downplayed the role of Feklisov, but this may have been partly to inflate his own: the ambassador was a man of considerable virtues, but modesty was not among them. In a much later letter to Khrushchev, President Kennedy warned him against ever using as an intermediary a journalist such as Scali, because neither side could be sure of what might eventually appear in print. The ambassador believed that Feklisov's approach to Scali, if such it was, represented merely one of many attempts by both sides' intelligence services to acquire insider information, of which the CIA and KGB were alike starved. This is plausible. It is unlikely that the Scali-Feklisov exchanges had any significance, save at the outset to offer a hint to the Americans that Khrushchev was preparing to back off.

At the White House, already steeped in sensation that day, confirmation came that the U-2 missing over Cuba had been shot down by a Soviet missile. The president said sombrely: 'Well now, this is much of an escalation by them, isn't it?' The defense secretary responded: 'Yes, exactly. And this – relates to the timing. I think we can defer an air attack on Cuba until Wednesday or Thursday but only if we continue our surveillance, and fire against anything that fires against a surveillance aircraft, and only if we maintain a tight blockade in this interim period.' Kennedy then mused: 'How do we explain the effect of this Khrushchev message of last night? And their decision [to shoot down the U-2], in view of their previous orders [to fire only if attacked], the change of orders?' McNamara responded: 'I don't know how to interpret it.' They were all astonished by this sudden act of violence, against the background of Khrushchev's several peace offers. Nobody professed to be able to answer Kennedy's questions. Nitze shrugged: 'They've fired the first shot', a remark that seemed to presume there would be a second. Once again, Excom assumed a coherence and intent behind this latest dramatic Soviet act, which was in reality absent.

The Americans took the U-2 shootdown incomparably more seriously than the fire directed at the Navy's Crusaders, because the former was done by missiles obviously acting under authority – assumed to be that of the Kremlin – rather than by mere trigger-happy Cubans. They puzzled over the difficulty of renewing reconnaissance sorties next day, without shooting: pilots lacking gunfire cover could not be asked to face SAMs. They debated whether to admit the loss of the plane, already announced by Radio Havana. Roswell Gilpatric pointed out to the president that he had earlier publicly promised that any such act by the Russians would meet an American response. McNamara proposed a declaration that surveillance would resume next morning, protected by fighter aircraft.

Kennedy left the room briefly, returning to report that Castro had just announced that any intruder in Cuban airspace would be fired upon. The discussion which followed became more confused, uncertain, rambling than any previous conference of the Crisis. Much of it focused upon how to reconcile US NATO allies to a trade of the Turkish missiles for the Cuban ones, with war as the alternative.

A difficulty for historians posed by the recorded Excom meetings is that these chronicle what people said, but not what they thought. It was entirely reasonable, indeed admirable, that they changed their minds, in some cases repeatedly. First, their predicament was unprecedented. It created perils not merely for the US, but for humankind. Next, the situation kept changing. Then again, despite the vast information-gathering resources of the White House through open and covert sources including newspapers, diplomatic channels, codebreaking, wireless interception and other forms of intelligence, a miasma of uncertainties persisted. Nobody in Excom, least of all the president of the United States, wished posterity to observe him as having sounded weak, pusillanimous. Yet the only people in the close circle of American decision-makers whose posture remained unchanged throughout – rocklike in its certainty – were the chiefs of staff.

That early evening, McNamara talked at length about likely scenarios, all grim. Once air attacks started, he said, the US would lose aircraft every day, and the only way to halt such attrition would be through invasion – overrunning the air defence sites in Cuba. In that event, the Soviets would probably attack the Turkish missiles, in which case 'we *must* respond'. One possible riposte would be to use conventional weapons to attack Soviet bases and warships in the Black Sea: 'that to me is the absolute minimum'. He thought the only way to remove the risk of a Soviet assault on Turkey was through removal of the US nuclear weapons there – which might indeed avert war. Walt Rostow said: 'We've been going around at the State Department and day and night we've talked about this. And we said we'd be *delighted* to trade those missiles in Turkey for the thing in Cuba.' Most of Excom chimed in to say that, after days in which they had been fearful of Soviet demands focused on Berlin – where there could be no conceivable concessions – there should be relief that Moscow was instead talking about Turkey.

At the news of the U-2 shootdown, in RFK's words 'there was the feeling that the noose was tightening on all of us, on Americans, on

mankind, and that the bridges to escape were crumbling'. JFK said:
'We are now in an entirely new ballgame.' At first, there was almost
unanimous Excom agreement that next day – Sunday – the SAM
sites in Cuba must be attacked and destroyed. Only as the minutes
and then hours passed, did arguments for continued restraint come
to seem more persuasive, above all to the president. These were
perhaps his finest hours of the Crisis: when he had every possible
justification for military action, in retaliation for the shootdown;
yet stayed his hand.

Graham Allison and Philip Zelikow have written: 'President
Kennedy becomes the driver of the debate. We see a president as
analyst-in-chief. On each issue, he presses his colleagues to probe
deeper implications of each option; to explore ways of circumvent-
ing seemingly insurmountable obstacles; to face squarely
unpalatable trade-offs; and to stretch their imagination.' These
words, far from being breathlessly reverential, seem just. Bundy
perceived Kennedy at every stage examining Khrushchev's latest
move as if playing out a chess game with him, and thus determinedly approaching one decision at a time, rather than pursuing
some illusory grand strategy, save the overarching purpose of
securing removal of the missiles from Cuba. The maturity of the
president's conduct stands in stark contrast to the impulsiveness of
some of those around him. Indeed, there is a good argument that
Kennedy displayed quite as much courage in resisting the Excom
voices demanding early violent action – especially that of Bundy –
as in facing down Khrushchev.

'Those hours in the Cabinet Room,' wrote RFK, 'could never be
erased from the minds of any of us. We saw as never before the
meaning and responsibility involved of the power of the United
States, the power of the President, the responsibility he had to
people around the world who had never heard of our country or
the men sitting in that room determining their fate, making a decision which would influence whether they would live or die.' The
president said: 'We won't attack tomorrow. We shall try again.'
That line would have been no contemptible epitaph.

2 THE HOUNDING OF B-59

At the Excom meeting during the early evening of 27 October, Vice-President Lyndon Johnson made one of his few contributions to the debate, scarcely remarked by his colleagues at the table. The afternoon session had been one of the most alarming of the week, during which the group was made aware both of Captain Maultsby's intrusion over Russia and the shootdown of Major Anderson. Now its members were discussing procedures for stopping the tanker *Grozny*, and a need to warn the Russians of the noisy, spectacular firework displays inseparable from night surveillance of their vessels. Neither the president nor his brother were then present in the room, so Johnson's remarks had no impact on events. These were nonetheless significant, in the context of what was then taking place almost a thousand miles out in the western Atlantic.

'I've been afraid of those damn flares ever since they [the Navy] mentioned them,' said the vice-president. In the absence of a clear warning, if a plane suddenly approached a Soviet vessel at low level, it could provoke shooting: 'Imagine some crazy Russian captain doing it. The damn thing [flare] goes "blooey" and lights up the sky. He might just pull a trigger. Looks like we're playing Fourth of July over there or something. I'm scared of that.' Johnson said he could not see what advantage the Navy gained from flashlight photography, when it knew perfectly well what Soviet vessels were out there. 'Psychologically, you scare [the Soviets]. Well, hell, it's always like the fellow telling me in Congress, "Go on and put the monkey on his back." Every time I tried to put a monkey on somebody else's back, I got one. If you're going to try to psychologically scare them with a flare, you're liable to get your bottom shot off.'

Almost at the moment the vice-president spoke, the US Navy was playing a game with Soviet submarine B-59 of exactly the kind Johnson conceived, and at risk of provoking a far more deadly outcome than the mere shootdown of a reconnaissance aircraft. Harassment or hazing of each other's aircraft and warships, sometimes also ground forces, had been a routine part of both sides' games since the Cold War began. They played it eagerly, roughly, sometimes clumsily and dangerously, as with the US-Soviet tank face-offs in Berlin. Common sense might suggest that, in such days as these, US and Soviet military and naval chiefs would alike have issued orders to their forces to exercise caution.

Instead, earlier that day Khrushchev's men had defied prudence, to shoot down Major Anderson in the air. Now it was the turn of Kennedy's officers at sea to play childish games in a nuclear scenario. McGeorge Bundy later described Kennedy as 'startled' by the revelation on 24 October that US warships were forcing Soviet submarines to the surface by dropping small charges around them. His alarm had not, however, caused him to instruct Admiral Anderson to abandon this practice. It may be that the president did not understand the risks the US Navy was taking because he himself, like the rest of Excom, had never been on the receiving, clanging, echoing end of underwater explosions in a submarine.

Of the Soviet boats originally dispatched to support Operation Anadyr in September one, the Zulu-class B-75, was recalled from the eastern Atlantic as soon as the US quarantine was announced, and reached Murmansk on 10 November. A second Zulu boat, B-88, was stationed off Pearl Harbor in the Pacific, with orders to attack the US naval base in the event of war. It remained in that area until recalled in late November.

Meanwhile the four Foxtrot-class boats of the 69th Brigade had been lingering in the western Atlantic, two of them in the Sargasso Sea well outside the quarantine line, since this was announced. The brigade's commander, Vitaly Agafonov, was aboard B-4, while his chief of staff Vasily Arkhipov was in B-59. All were armed with twenty-one conventional torpedoes and a single nuclear-tipped weapon, which on detonation was capable of destroying an entire cluster of shipping on the surface above. An officer explicitly responsible for the nuclear warhead was carried aboard each boat.

The Foxtrots, like many Soviet aircraft and ships, were primitive in all respects save their capacity to inflict destruction. Crews suffered discomfort, which sometimes became severe. Ventilation was poor; engine noise-levels rendered the boats highly vulnerable to detection by enemy warships. In vessels bereft of tropicalization equipment, crew conditions became oppressive, especially in machinery areas. Temperatures in the electrical-technical compartments at times rose above sixty-five degrees. Drinking water was harshly restricted; the norm was 250ml per person per twenty-four hours. This caused many sailors to develop a sweating fever, and some repeatedly to collapse at their posts – according to Captain Dubivko, his crew's average weight fell by one-third.

The peril they faced was worsened by the shallow waters in which the two westerly boats, especially, were operating. Anastas Mikoyan and the Soviet Navy's C-in-C Admiral Sergei Gorshkov had opposed the deployment in the Caribbean; then, when American wrath was unleashed on 22 October, had argued for their withdrawal. Yet no recall order was transmitted, though the vessels were instructed to hold back from Cuban waters. B-4, around four hundred miles from the island, was not pinpointed by the Americans, though sonobuoys were dropped in its vicinity. It escaped close harassment by the US Navy, such as the others endured for days. On the afternoon of the 24th US Navy aircraft had spotted another Soviet submarine, B-36, on the surface four hundred miles north of Puerto Rico and inside the quarantine line, which they labelled Contact C-18.

On that fearsome Saturday the Americans began to drop noisy, though non-lethal, grenades around the boats, designed to force them to surface. The most dramatic experience befell Captain Valentin Savitsky of B-59, who determined to resist, to reject harassment which he – like the Soviet air defence officers in Cuba – judged to be illegal and insulting to their country. B-59 was first spotted off Bermuda on the evening of 25 October, and designated C-19 by Navy plotters. It was sighted again further south twenty-four hours later. An urgent effort began to concentrate warships at its reported position and force it to surface.

Through two nights and days that followed, the Soviet boat remained submerged some six hundred miles north-east of Cuba. The heat inside the vessel grew ever more oppressive, the air harder to breathe. Savitsky used every evasion technique of changing course and depth to throw off his pursuers, at the cost of using up battery life. At 4.59 p.m. on the 27th, the destroyer *Beale* began

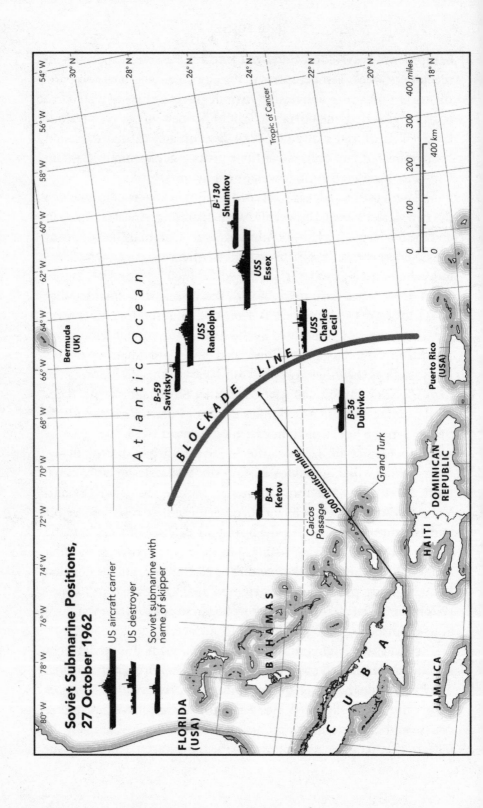

Soviet Submarine Positions, 27 October 1962

US aircraft carrier
US destroyer
Soviet submarine with name of skipper

FLORIDA (USA)

BAHAMAS

CUBA

JAMAICA

HAITI

DOMINICAN REPUBLIC

Puerto Rico (USA)

Bermuda (UK)

Atlantic Ocean

Tropic of Cancer

BLOCKADE LINE

Caicos Passage

Grand Turk

500 nautical miles

B-4 Ketov

B-36 Dubivko

B-59 Savitsky

B-130 Shumkov

USS Randolph

USS Essex

USS Charles Cecil

0   100   200   300   400 km
0   100   200   300   400 miles

80° W   78° W   76° W   74° W   72° W   70° W   68° W   66° W   64° W   62° W   60° W   58° W   56° W   54° W

30° N   28° N   26° N   24° N   22° N   20° N   18° N

(Above) American opera star Jerome Hines, who entertained Khrushchev in Moscow in the midst of the Crisis, playing the doomed tsar Boris Godunov. (Below) Emotional propaganda ruled the streets of Havana.

(Above) US Navy reconnaissance aircraft overflies a Soviet merchant vessel in the western Atlantic. (Left) Cuban anti-aircraft guns await the expected US invasion. (Inset) Defence minister Raúl Castro, with – right of picture – Soviet commander Gen. Issa Pliev, still incongruously dressed in 'civvies'. (Below) Khrushchev meets with his closest advisers, including here Malinovsky and Mikoyan (centre).

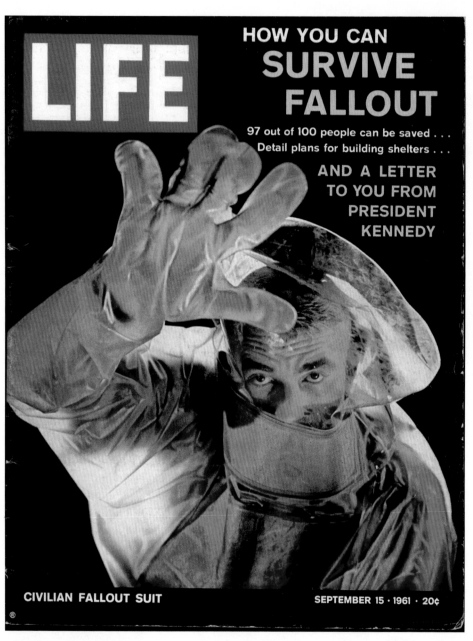

Although *Life* magazine's cover pre-dated the Crisis, it captures the mood that overtook much of the world during the Thirteen Days.

AMERICAN AIRMEN.
(Top) U-2 pilots Major
Chuck Maultsby and
Major Rudy Anderson.
(Centre) A view from the
cockpit of the highest-
flying aircraft in the world.
(Below) US Navy Crusader
photo-recon pilots 'chalk
up another chicken',
congratulating each other
as they mark a fuselage
after a sortie over Cuba.

Motor pool   Former dormitories   To Havana →

Mission number   Date of mission

N-62 2623 26 OCT62 SECRET

(Above) A US Navy reconnaissance photo of Soviet military headquarters in Cuba, at El Chico. (Below) A U-2 in flight.

(Above) A disconsolate Castro with Pliev, who also had suffered humiliation in Cuba. (Below) Mikoyan, with ambassador Alekseev behind him, during the visit to Cuba on which he was charged to reconcile Castro to Khrushchev's deal with Kennedy.

(Above) Flotsam of the war that never was, mercifully for the world: a Soviet SA-2 missile, of the type that shot down Anderson. (Below) After it was all over, JFK visited SAC headquarters. Here, Gen. Power addresses Lyndon Johnson. The bitterly disappointed Curtis LeMay stands left, in spectacles, with behind him Mac Bundy.

dropping practice depth-charges, and thirty minutes later its consort USS *Cory* detonated five grenades.

The White House had been at pains to communicate to Moscow this maritime 'advance and be recognized' challenge procedure, and the Soviet vessel's officers had been informed of it. Yet it was a matter of pride that they should reject such attempts to make them abase themselves. They were being asked to acknowledge that, while the western Atlantic was an international waterway, it lay within the United States's legitimate sphere of influence, the US Navy's rightful domain of dominance. They later said that the resounding blows on their hull caused them to believe themselves under attack. Lt. Vadim Orlov, who led the submarine's hydrophone team, said afterwards: 'They exploded next to the deck. It was as if you were sitting in an iron barrel that was being beaten with a sledgehammer.' His reaction, and that of his captain, were understandable. It remains an extremely moot point, whether the US Navy was justified in adopting such provocative tactics far outside the declared blockade zone, when tensions were already running high.

As the air worsened in the submarine hull, only emergency lighting remained operational. Both the temperature and carbon dioxide level were almost unbearable, and caused several men to collapse. After four hours, Orlov noted a much louder explosion: 'The Americans slammed us with something stronger than a grenade – obviously it was practically a depth charge … We thought: this is it, it's all over!' Savitsky, Orlov claimed, had now had enough. Exhausted after hours of manoeuvring under extreme stress, the boat's skipper summoned the officer in charge of the nuclear torpedo, and ordered it made ready for firing: 'Perhaps war has already started up above, and we're going nuts here … Now we'll hit them with everything we've got! We'll die and drown everyone, but we won't disgrace the fleet.'

This was exactly the fashion in which John F. Kennedy, Harold Macmillan, Anastas Mikoyan and others with vivid imaginations imagined the world ending: not following the deliberate decisions of national leaders, but instead through the impulsive action of one

or more half-crazed individuals, undergoing supreme stress and
unable to contain themselves in the face of responsibilities such as
no human beings, least of all relatively junior operational
commanders, should have been entrusted with. Mercifully for the
world, brigade chief of staff Vasily Arkhipov and deputy political
officer Ivan Maslennikov succeeded in calming the agitated
Savitsky; they persuaded him to give the order to surface.

In darkness at 8.50 p.m. on that Saturday, the Soviet submarine
broke the surface of the Sargasso Sea, to find its glistening black
hull bathed in the glare of searchlights from the destroyer USS
Cory, one of the Navy task group led by the carrier *Randolph*.
Russian crewmen emerged blinking from below, tearing off their
clothing as they breathed in the steamy yet blissful night air.
Signallers on the *Cory* flashed a request for the sub to identify itself,
to receive the bland response 'Soviet ship X'. The Americans
demanded: 'DO YOU REQUIRE ANY ASSISTANCE?', and were
promptly told '*NYET*'. The submarine began the long, slow process
of recharging its almost exhausted batteries. This operation was
abruptly interrupted by the roar overhead of a low-flying Neptune
aircraft which dropped a string of explosive incendiary devices,
prompting the Russians on the submarine bridge to disappear
below, the boat to change course. *Cory*'s captain ordered his signallers to flash an apology for the aircraft's apparently aggressive
behaviour – which appeared to be accepted. A second version of
events aboard B-59 holds that Savitsky's loss of temper and reason
took place following the Neptune's violent pyrotechnic display,
rather than while the boat was still submerged; that it was then that
he ordered the nuclear torpedo to be readied.

Orlov's vivid and colourful narrative has formed the basis for
many accounts of this dramatic moment in the Crisis. Vasily
Arkhipov, the officer who allegedly calmed Savitsky and countermanded his order to arm the nuclear torpedo, has been hailed as
the man who saved the world from war, such as would assuredly
have followed the detonation of such a weapon in the darkness,
with annihilatory consequences for the surface warships of the US
Navy's hunter-killer group.

No definitive account of what took place aboard B-59 during those hours is possible, unless or until further Russian documentation becomes available. Some Soviet submarine veterans of those days have cast serious doubts on Orlov's account; they question whether his boat or its captain ever came anywhere near to precipitating a nuclear explosion. Three keys were required to arm the weapon on board, and the evidence seems overwhelming that this process was never completed – probably not even commenced. Svetlana Savranskaya makes the significant point that it is unsurprising captains resorted to extravagant rhetoric, partly to sustain the concentration and morale of their crews in exceptionally testing circumstances. However, there is no doubt of the extraordinary tension of the encounter between the submarine and the US Navy's warships, which pushed to the limits their questionable justification for harassing the Foxtrot. Khrushchev and his admirals had taken a huge risk, by committing the flotilla to the western Atlantic in such circumstances, armed with such weapons. If the officers aboard B-59 had chosen to interpret their orders as freely as did Soviet air defence commanders in Cuba that day, they had the power to do something very terrible. It is relatively unimportant whether the details of Orlov's account of events that afternoon and evening are sensationalized. The potential for catastrophe in the Sargasso Sea is impossible to dispute.

3 THE OFFER

At the White House where Excom was still in session, around 6.30 p.m. Bundy raised an absurdly banal question: 'Do people want dinner downstairs, do they want trays, or do they want to wait?' McNamara said dismissively, perhaps testily: 'Well let's wait … eating is the least of my worries.' He addressed the more urgent issue of the next day's plan for air surveillance of Cuba: 'We're just going to get shot up sure as hell. There's just no question about it. Then we're just going to have to go in and shoot.' What a SAM had done to Major Anderson that morning, it could and probably would do to other American pilots next day. Not by a hint from the

Kremlin had the Soviets indicated to the Americans that the shoot-down contravened Khrushchev's wishes.

McCone proposed a direct appeal to the Soviet leader, to stop firing upon unarmed reconnaissance planes. McNamara, tacking somewhat after his hawkish remarks earlier in the afternoon, said that he continued to be nagged by a belief that, though they should be ready to take violent action, they should defer pressing the trigger. There was an edgy exchange between Robert Kennedy and Lyndon Johnson about whether the blockade was working – the former thought it was, the latter believed not. The vice-president then led a drearily repetitive review of the day's exchanges, or lack of them. Johnson warned that American public opinion, of which few men had a better understanding than himself, was shortly going to lose patience, demanding: '"The President made a fine speech, what else have you done?" ... They want to know what we're doing.' They then read each other drafts of proposed messages to Khrushchev, to U Thant, to NATO and the Turks.

Around 7.20 p.m. the president returned to the Cabinet Room. He approved the draft of a new letter to Khrushchev. The United States was now offering the terms that the Soviet leader had days earlier privately determined to accept. 'You would agree to remove these weapons systems from Cuba under appropriate United Nations observation and supervision,' wrote the US president, 'and undertake, with suitable safeguards, to halt the further introduction of such weapons into Cuba.' In return, the government of the United States would agree '(a) to remove promptly the quarantine measures now in effect, and (b) to give assurances against an invasion of Cuba'.

Kennedy also agreed with his advisers that his brother should seek a further secret meeting with the Soviet ambassador, Dobrynin, in his office at the Justice Department, at which he would deliver a copy of this missive. Excom had now been in session for three and a half hours. Some of its members were no longer young, and they were tired. Kennedy was sheering off an imminent assault. He said: 'We can't very well invade Cuba, with all this toil and blood it's going to be, when we could have gotten [the Soviet missiles] out by making a deal on the same missiles in Turkey. If that's part of the record, then I don't see how we'll have a very good war.' Once again, deterrence was casting its spell: the president, McNamara, McCone and others had become hesitant about bombing and invading Cuba, not because they thought such a course morally, strategically or politically wrong, but instead because they believed – even while still ignorant of the Soviet tactical nuclear weapons – that the defenders could exact a brutal price from US forces, whether or not general war followed.

Then this longest of all Excom meetings broke up. Ahead of RFK's meeting with Dobrynin, the president summoned into the Oval Office his most trusted advisers – excluding Lyndon Johnson and McCone, notable hawks – to discuss what verbal message the attorney-general should deliver. McNamara, Rusk and Bundy joined the Kennedy brothers. It was Rusk's idea to promise Khrushchev withdrawal of the Turkish missiles as a voluntary act by the US, independent of a publicly-acknowledged Cuban settlement. Only the Americans present in the Oval Office were to be privy to such an arrangement, which would become instantly void if the Russians disclosed it. Twenty minutes later, around 8 p.m., Kennedy's personal message to Khrushchev was finally transmitted, while his brother carried away to his own office the copy that he was to hand to Ambassador Dobrynin.

The president's letter, worked and reworked by Excom and Ted Sorensen through the course of the day, began by emphasizing the urgency of halting all activity at the Cuban missile bases. If this was done, Kennedy said that he had instructed the US delegation at the UN to prepare to work out a permanent solution to the Crisis with U Thant and the Soviet ambassador, 'along the lines suggested in your letter of October 26'. This meant that all offensive weapons systems would be removed from Cuba under UN observation and supervision. The US would immediately lift its blockade – 'the quarantine measures' – and 'give assurances against an invasion of Cuba'. If this could be agreed, Kennedy saw no reason why arrangements should not be completed and announced within two days. If such a settlement came about, the president would welcome wider disarmament talks: 'The United States is very much interested in reducing tensions and halting the arms race.'

The meeting between the attorney-general and the Soviet ambassador was stiff and tense. Robert Kennedy emphasized the escalation represented by the U-2 shootdown. Dobrynin demanded that the Americans should abandon their reconnaissance overflights of Cuba. Kennedy rejected this notion at once, saying that they were indispensable to US security. He told the Russian that many Americans – not only the military – were 'itching for a fight'. He said that time was running out. Decisions would be taken within the next twelve to twenty-four hours. If ground defenders shot at US planes, the Americans would shoot back. When Castro's people complained about violations of their airspace, 'if we had not been violating Cuban air space then we would still be believing what he – Dobrynin – and Khrushchev had said: that there were no long-range missiles in Cuba'.

The ambassador was hamstrung by a continuing absence of instructions from Moscow. It was, thus, on his own initiative that he abruptly asked the American about the Turkish missiles – the possibility of a trade. Kennedy had expected the question, and was ready with his answer: if these represented the only obstacle to a settlement, the president saw no insurmountable difficulties. Nothing could be publicly announced, because of the damage to the NATO alliance. The offer must be kept strictly confidential, or it would be off the table. RFK stressed the urgency of making the deal. 'Throughout the whole meeting,' wrote Dobrynin, 'he was very nervous ... the first time I saw him in such a state ... He just kept repeating that time was pressing, and we should not waste it.'

Robert Kennedy later recalled his own words: 'We had to have a commitment by at least tomorrow that those bases would be removed. This was not an ultimatum, I said, but just a statement of fact ... If they did not remove those bases, then we would remove them.' He urged haste in contacting Khrushchev, because unless there was a good word from him by next day, 'there would be drastic consequences'. The exchange lasted a mere fifteen minutes. Some doubts persist, about whether Kennedy went further in this conversation than his brother the president had authorized, in warning the ambassador of the likely imminence of US military action. In any event, Dobrynin's subsequent report of the conversation to Moscow was, if not apocalyptic, profoundly alarming for its recipients. Before the Russian left the building, Kennedy gave him a telephone number, to make direct contact with the White House.

By 8.40 p.m. the attorney-general was back with his brother. The president had had a brief swim, and was eating with his aide Dave Powers. Bobby gave a bleak account of his meeting with Dobrynin, while Powers gobbled. 'God, Dave,' said the president, 'the way you're eating up all that chicken and drinking up all my wine, anybody would think it was your last meal.' Powers, unabashed, rejoined: 'The way Bobby's been talking, I thought it was.' All the news seemed bad. Zorin, the Soviet UN ambassador, had refused to receive the document setting out the exact limits of the Atlantic quarantine zone, because the USSR declined to recognize its legitimacy. Castro had delivered another bellicose speech to the Cuban people. The Defense Department was struggling to draft a statement for a clamorous press, on the American response to the U-2 shootdown.

At 9 p.m., Excom reconvened. Dean Rusk reported that the administration was still no wiser about the Kremlin's intentions. It had been agreed that next day the Navy would intercept, stop and search the tanker *Grozny*; the air force would shoot up any Cuban or Soviet ground AA battery or SAM missile-launcher that sought to impede surveillance. It might well be decided to add POL – petrol, oil and lubricants – to the index of cargoes denied access to Cuba. McNamara urged against further sorties by U-2s, because of their proven vulnerability to SAMs. The president said that he wanted no firing on ground defences until Monday. It had just been announced that Castro had invited the UN secretary-general to make an immediate visit to his island, and the proposal had been accepted. The Americans would concede time for its outcome to emerge. Kennedy meanwhile approved McNamara's request to mobilize twenty-four Air Reserve squadrons to operate three

hundred troop transport aircraft that would be needed for an invasion of Cuba. Reserve shipping, he agreed, should start to be
brought out of mothballs.

As the meeting broke up, the tape recorded an exchange between
the attorney-general and defense secretary:

'How are you doing, Bob?'

'Well. How about yourself?'

'All right.'

'You got any doubts?'

'No,' said Robert Kennedy. 'I think that we're doing the only
thing we can do, and on. You know.'

McNamara urged: 'I think the one thing, Bobby ... We ought to
seriously do before we attack them [the Soviets], you've got to be
damned sure they understand it's coming ... You need to really
escalate this ... And then we need to have two things ready: a
government for Cuba, because we're going to need one, after we go
in with bomber aircraft. And secondly, plans for how to respond to
the Soviet Union in Europe because sure as hell they're going do
something there.' Bobby Kennedy said, only half-facetiously: 'I'd
like to take Cuba back. That would be nice.' An unidentified voice
echoed him: 'Yeah, and let's take Cuba away from Castro ... Get all
of the Mongoose [CIA operatives].' This earned a round of laughter.

Yet the prevailing mood that night, according to Sorensen, was
'rancorous', amid general exhaustion around the table, and a deep
divide between the exponents of bombing and the continuing
believers in diplomacy. Sorensen observed that 'the President was
under tremendous pressure at that point for military action'.
McNamara admitted he 'wasn't sure I would ever see another
Saturday night'.

Two further American actions on the 27th deserve notice, not
because they led to significant consequences, which they did not,
but instead because they emphasize how desperate was still the
mood within the White House; how far Excom was from cherish-
ing hopes that a peaceful resolution of the confrontation was
imminent. A message approved by JFK and Excom was dispatched

to the Brazilian government via the US ambassador in Rio. The Brazilians had earlier offered to act as intermediaries between Washington and Havana. Now they were authorized to promise Castro that, if he caused the Soviets to remove their missiles from his country, Cuba would be welcomed back into the hemispheric fraternity of nations. This message was not read in Havana until after it had ceased to be relevant. But its dispatch reflects the fact that the president was still urgently anxious to explore any exit route from the Crisis – and remained unconvinced that Moscow would provide this.

The second late-night action was a further twist in the 'Turkish trade' issue. Robert Kennedy, in his conversation with Dobrynin, had been instructed to insist upon its confidentiality. However, the administration also dug a reserve position, only disclosed by Dean Rusk a quarter-century later, in a letter to the Hawk's Bay historical conference. At the president's behest, the secretary of state telephoned Andrew Cordier, a former senior UN official by then translated to become dean of the School of International Affairs at Columbia University in New York. Rusk dictated a statement, to be passed to U Thant, if Cordier was so directed. The message informed the UN secretary-general that, if he proposed an open exchange of the Soviet missiles in Cuba for the American ones in Turkey, this deal would be accepted by the United States. In other words, for domestic political reasons Kennedy was most anxious that it should *not* be known that he had made an apparent substantial concession to the Soviets, to purchase Khrushchev's retreat. But if this became essential, to preserve global peace, then the deal might be avowed. The Cordier conversation led to nothing, because it was overtaken by events. The fact that it took place, however, underlined the extremes of anxiety persisting in the White House at close of play on 27 October.

Excom broke up for the night, though officials laboured on through the darkness, preparing diplomatic messages for NATO and US ambassadors in allied capitals. A brief, sententious message came in from Harold Macmillan: 'The trial of wills is now approaching a climax. Khrushchev's first message, unhappily not published to the world, seemed to go a long way to meet you. His second message, widely broadcast and artfully contrived, adding the Turkey proposal, was a recovery on his part. It has made a considerable impact. We must now wait to see what Khrushchev does.'

This was an unoriginal summary of realities recognized all day in the White House, and contributed nothing to easing the president's dilemmas. The prime minister thereafter spent Saturday night and Sunday morning toying with proposals which much dismayed his British Cabinet colleagues, because absurdly unrealistic: for extending invitations for the rival national leaders to attend a summit in London at which Macmillan saw himself acting as arbitrator. Dissuaded from this by colleagues, at noon on Sunday he dispatched a vapid plea to Khrushchev, calling upon him to accept Kennedy's demands. This was to prove Britain's final contribution to the Crisis, and was of a piece with the general debility of Macmillan's conduct, deriving from his knowledge of the British people's lack of enthusiasm for becoming victims of a war over Cuba.

That Saturday evening in the Oval Office, the two Kennedy brothers talked alone. The president mused about his conviction that the Soviets no more wanted war than the US did; but that events threatened to enforce an outcome, which would engulf and destroy mankind. He himself was determined to do everything within his power to avert such a calamity, which meant offering the Russians every opportunity to back off. He knew that, if the decision-makers in Washington and Moscow got it wrong, new generations would be snuffed out, without the opportunity to live lives, make their own choices and decide their own fates. It seems mistaken to dismiss Robert Kennedy's account of this conversation as extravagantly theatrical. Rather, it seems right to be impressed by the fact that the United States then had a leader capable of articulating such feelings and beliefs.

In Florida the 5th Marine Expeditionary Brigade began boarding the ships that would carry it to war. Even as its men did so, thousands of fearful local people took to their automobiles, making the futile gesture of driving north, to put as much distance as possible between themselves and Khrushchev's missiles. The city of St.

A cartoon by Illingworth in Britain's *Daily Mail*, 27 October 1962.

Petersburg found itself almost bare of tourists – but densely crowded with warriors. The USAF's Lt. Gen. Jack Merrell testified afterwards: 'We went down to Homestead Airport, and I thought the whole southern tip of Florida was about ready to sink. It had so many troops down here getting ready ... We went around to some of the different tactical crews and got their briefing, heard them describe their targets to us, what they were going to do. In fact, at that time – it looked like it might be tomorrow, literally at that time, the next day, and they each had their targets picked out. They'd brief us how they were going to identify their targets – when they went in low level, make a bomb run on the targets.'

At Homestead and other bases, aircraft were repeatedly bombed-up, de-bombed and rearmed, as their loads were switched between high explosive and napalm when targeting plans were refined or changed. The air force was embarrassed to find that, on a demonstration run, some of the ordnance merely popped, rather than flamed, the tanks of incendiary napalm jelly having been held too long in storage. Most of the fourteen thousand air force reservists summoned to active duty prepared to join their squadrons, though some wilfully absented themselves. Scores of anti-aircraft batteries were deployed, to protect against possible Soviet or Cuban air strikes on the Florida airfields. Almost a hundred warships of the US Navy rode on the Atlantic and Caribbean swells, their crews braced for a shoot-out or an invasion.

The president, in no haste to sleep, sat down with Dave Powers to watch a screening of *Roman Holiday* with Gregory Peck and Audrey Hepburn. Earlier that evening, Powers had taken advantage of Jackie Kennedy's overnight absence to smuggle into the Mansion Mimi Beardsley, a Wheaton College student and intern in the White House press office. Her inability to type was no handicap to her real role, as one of the president's teenage lovers. Although Beardsley allegedly chatted to Kennedy that evening, she found him understandably grave and preoccupied, and no sexual encounter took place. Even the relentlessly priapic president had too much else on his mind. The nineteen-year-old, according to her own account, slept in the next room while the two men watched their movie. That night, amid continuing silence from Moscow, many of the American decision-makers thought it likely that next day, their forces would have to fire upon the Russians at sea, and attack both Cuban and Soviet anti-aircraft defences on land, with untold consequences.

Khrushchev was at his villa in the Lenin Hills, where Sunday was already started. He had summoned a morning meeting of the Presidium at a nearby government guesthouse, and suggested to his wife and son that they should drive to the family dacha in the country, where he would join them once the conference was done with. At 1 a.m., however, he was telephoned from the Kremlin with news of Castro's histrionic message, together with his warning of a US invasion that was expected within hours. The letter was read over the telephone to the Soviet leader who several times interrupted, to ask for key passages to be repeated. It was this conversation that persuaded him – or at least caused him hereafter to profess – that his Cuban ally was demanding a Soviet pre-emptive nuclear strike. Even before Khrushchev heard of the U-2 shootdown, announced that night by the Pentagon, he became acutely alarmed. In the small hours of Sunday morning, he began to think and act with a sense of urgency that had been absent from his deliberations and words even a few hours earlier.

Both Robert Kennedy and ambassador Dobrynin afterwards asserted that their meeting the previous evening – when the Turkish offer was made – became the turning point of the crisis. Khrushchev endorsed this version in his memoirs, because it supported his own claims to have extracted the concession of removal of the US missiles in Turkey, before he yielded in Cuba. In truth, however, the evidence from other sources is plain: even before the ambassador's Washington cable reached Moscow later on Sunday, the Soviet leader had made his choice – the only sane choice – between peace and war.

14

Endgame

1 TIME RUNS OUT

Sunday morning, 28 October, began in the United States with an electrifying alarm. Just before 9 a.m. 'Falling Leaves' early warning radar at Moorestown NJ detected a ballistic missile launch from Cuba. The operator instantly telephoned NORAD air defence command in Colorado Springs to predict an impact at 9.02, eighteen miles west of Tampa, Florida. SAC was alerted. The duty personnel endured heart-stopping minutes until it was reported that no impact had taken place, or at least no nuclear warhead had exploded. Then Moorestown came back to NORAD with an update: the alert had been triggered when its operators ran a test tape, simulating an attack, just as another radar site pinpointed a satellite.

Meanwhile in Moscow, Marshal Malinovsky reported to Khrushchev 'eight American violations of Cuban airspace' on the previous day, during one of which Major Anderson's U-2 was shot down 'with the aim of not permitting the photographs to fall into US hands'. Even by the Kremlin's accustomed standards, this was a less than convincing justification. As the Russians knew to their cost, the Americans already had an abundance of images of Soviet installations on Cuba: those of the 27th could have changed nothing. Moreover, here again was a critical delay between an event on the 'battlefield' and cognizance at the top: the USSR's leader was apprised of the momentous shootdown only some sixteen hours after it took place. A formal reprimand was dispatched to Pliev for exceeding his orders – or rather, for being passively complicit in his subordinates doing so.

Khrushchev guessed correctly that the Soviet SAM network commanders had allowed themselves to become infected by Cuban anticipation of imminent war. 'It seems likely,' wrote Mac Bundy in 1988, 'that the shoot-down of Anderson ... a severe shock ... was a powerful influence in persuading Khrushchev to step back from danger. To recognize and honor Anderson's role in this result is a better repayment to his memory than any act of vengeance could have been.' The national security adviser was almost certainly right, in suggesting that the downed U-2 caused the Soviet leader to approach the forthcoming meeting of the Presidium profoundly alarmed; even more urgently anxious to secure an escape from the brink.

At noon, while in Washington those capable of sleep were hours short of regaining consciousness, the USSR's leaders assembled in the government guesthouse at Novo-Ogaryovo, an imposing building with a neo-classical pillared façade in the western suburbs of Moscow that was once the dacha of the disgraced Georgy Malenkov, and indeed had been constructed in 1954 to the design of his architect daughter. The meeting took place in its big dining room, around a table covered with a white cloth and strewn with intelligence and defence folders of many colours – red, pink, green, grey-blue. Before each Presidium member's place was a stack of messages and reports, newly delivered by couriers from the Kremlin. Also present were Malinovsky and a handful of functionaries, eighteen men in all.

Khrushchev, who arrived after a ten-minute drive from his own suburban dacha, initially spoke for an hour. He informed the gathering about the latest exchange with Washington. The atmosphere in the room was 'electric', according to Oleg Troyanovsky. '[The first secretary] was keenly aware, as were all of us, that in the situation that had arisen, when nerves' – on both sides – 'were strained to breaking point, a single spark might cause an explosion.' On the previous evening, the leader had advertised to these same men his intention to do a trade with Kennedy for the Turkish missiles. Now he asked them to approve a deal without fulfilment of this condition. He likened their predicament to that of Lenin towards the close of World War I: 'There was a time when we advanced, as in October 1917. But in March 1918 we had to retreat, having signed the Treaty of Brest-Litovsk with Germany. That decision was dictated by our interests: we had to save Soviet rule. Now we find ourselves face to face with the threat of war and nuclear catastrophe, as a result of which human civilization may perish. To save humanity, we should retreat. I have called you all together to take counsel and consider whether you agree with such a decision.' The meeting recognized the urgency, in the light of reports from the KGB residency in Havana, echoing Castro, that an American assault on Cuba was imminent. Khrushchev still had not abandoned his parade of toughness: he reasserted a commitment to devastating Soviet retaliation, if the island was indeed invaded.

For the preservation of his own power and dignity, he emphasized that once the deal was struck Castro would be safe, because the US would formally undertake to pursue no further military operations against Cuba. Nobody around the table was much impressed by representing this as a great Soviet victory, however, since he also explicitly avowed that Operation Anadyr was aborted; the USSR's ballistic missiles were to be brought home. Troyanovsky recalled that when the chairman concluded his remarks only Mikoyan and Gromyko spoke: 'The others preferred to remain silent, as if giving to understand that "it was you who got us into this mess, now get yourself out of it".'

Although some of those around the table privately seethed with rage towards Khrushchev, for the perceived humiliation he was about to inflict upon the USSR, all bowed to the inevitability of the outcome. The Presidium had already rubber-stamped the decision to withdraw the missiles from Cuba, when Troyanovsky was called to the telephone. He was informed of a telegram from Dobrynin about his latest exchange with Robert Kennedy, which the ambassador characterized to Moscow as an ultimatum. Time was running out: the US chiefs of staff were clamouring for war. But the president's brother also promised removal of the Turkish missiles.

Soon after Troyanovsky returned to report this development to the Presidium, reading aloud from scrawled notes, the Defence Council secretary Gen. Ivanov was likewise called away. He returned to say that the military had secured intelligence from Washington that President Kennedy would deliver a new broadcast address to the American people at 5 p.m., EST. All those around the table assumed this must mean Kennedy would announce either an invasion of Cuba or, at the very least, a US air assault on the missile sites.

This information was false – yet another clumsy error by the Soviet intelligence apparatus: no presidential address was scheduled, only a repeat of Kennedy's 22 October broadcast, for viewers who had missed Monday's transmission. The report nonetheless further galvanized Khrushchev and his colleagues, who supposed themselves to be working against the clock. It was now the Soviet leader who carried a wooden knife to his bear hunt, the crude figure of speech he had employed in such jocular fashion earlier that week. 'Comrade Gromyko,' Khrushchev told the foreign minister, 'we don't have the right to take risks. Once the president announces there will be an invasion, he won't be able to reverse himself. We have to let [JF] Kennedy know that we want to help him.' The foreign ministry was ordered to dispatch an immediate telegram, instructing Dobrynin to inform RFK that his deal would be accepted.

It was only that Sunday morning, according to Khrushchev, even as his staff were working on the draft of his formal letter to Kennedy, which in the interests of haste would be broadcast by Radio Moscow, that he was informed of Castro's missive to himself, appearing to demand a nuclear First Strike on the US in the event of an invasion of Cuba. 'When this was read to us,' he wrote in his memoirs, 'we, sitting in silence, looked at each other for a long time.' Aleksandr Alekseev was later reprimanded for having been party to the composition of Castro's letter. Whether or not the Cuban leader ever intended to suggest that Khrushchev should unleash nuclear weapons to defend his polity, there is no doubt that Castro saw glory in a showdown with the United States, a vision which few other inhabitants of the planet could share, none of them seated around the table at Novo-Ogaryovo.

Khrushchev suddenly found himself eyeball to eyeball not only with the Americans, but also with the wild Latin American revolutionary whom he had chosen to embrace. Two days later, he told Czech communist leader Antonín Novotný: 'We were completely aghast. Castro clearly has no idea about what thermonuclear war is. After all if a war started it would first be Cuba that would vanish from the face of the Earth. At the same time it is clear that with a First Strike one cannot today know the opponent is out of the fight … Only a person who has no idea what nuclear war means, or who has been so blinded, like Castro, by revolutionary passion, can talk like that.'

Khrushchev thus recognized an intractable new challenge – to break news to Havana which Castro must perceive as a betrayal, while averting the further huge embarrassment for the USSR, of being denounced by the Cubans as a traitor to their Revolution. The Soviet leader chose to address this by announcing the withdrawal decision to the world before he informed the missiles' Caribbean host. Alekseev said later: 'I still cannot understand why Khrushchev had not informed Castro that he might decide to withdraw the missiles. However [he] possibly took the view because he knew how unyielding Fidel was; that he would not agree with this decision, and thus time might be lost [while the Cuban argued with Moscow].'

A critical feature of the Crisis was the snail-like pace of communication between Washington and Moscow, impeded by bureaucracy, imperfect technology and the requirements of ciphering and deciphering, followed by physical delivery of messages to intended recipients in the Kremlin, Soviet embassy, US State Department and White House. By now Khrushchev was thoroughly aware of all this. Troyanovsky wrote: 'There was a great deal of commotion and nervous tension in Moscow on that last day, with alarming reports in from Washington and Havana. Time seemed to be running out.' Khrushchev himself said, in his conversation with Novotný: 'We had to act very quickly. That is also why we even used radio to contact the President, because the other means might have been too slow. This time we really were on the verge of war.'

Radio Moscow was alerted that an important bulletin was coming. Yuri Levitan was summoned from home to the studio, to read the text over the air. Yet, when speed might be a matter of humankind's life and death, the black government Chaika limousine carrying Khrushchev's message to the radio building first lost its way, then became delayed by traffic. It is not difficult to envisage the intemperate scenes inside the vehicle between the driver and the Presidium's chosen messenger Leonid Ilichev, Central Committee secretary responsible for ideology. When this *apparatchik* finally dashed into the building, he found that one of its six elderly lifts was being held in readiness, for his exclusive passage to the studio floor. Even as he ascended, however, this conveyance abruptly halted, stranded between floors. This being a Sunday, no engineer was on duty. The hapless Ilichev tried to push the document through the jammed lift doors to station staff, but thick wax seals made this impossible: the envelope tore. Then, suddenly and inexplicably, the lift once more juddered into life, delivering Ilichev to the studio. Levitan, whose deep voice had made him Stalin's favourite mouthpiece, made his historic broadcast.

The critical passage of Khrushchev's missive to Kennedy, now read to the world, stated: 'I have received your message of October 27, 1962. I express my satisfaction and gratitude for the sense of proportion and understanding of the responsibility borne by you at present for the preservation of peace throughout the world which you have shown. I very well understand your anxiety and the anxiety of the United States' people in connection with the fact that the weapons which you describe as "offensive" are, in fact, grim weapons ... In order to complete with greater speed the liquidation of the conflict dangerous to the cause of peace, to give confidence to all people longing for peace, and to calm the American people, who, I am certain, want peace as much as do the people of the Soviet Union, the Soviet government, in addition to previously-issued instructions on the cessation of further work at building sites for the weapons, has issued a new order on the dismantling of the weapons which you describe as "offensive" and their crating and return to the Soviet Union.'

Two signals to Pliev in Cuba were dispatched that Sunday by Malinovsky, undoubtedly prompted by Khrushchev and perhaps dictated by him: 'We believe that you were too hasty in shooting down the US U-2 reconnaissance plane, at the time an agreement was emerging to avert, by peaceful means, an attack on Cuba ... We have made the decision to dismantle the R-12s and remove them. Begin to implement the measure. Confirm receipt ... In addition to the order not to use [SAM] S-75s, to avoid clashes with US reconnaissance planes you are ordered not to "scramble" fighters.' Moreover, the general was instructed that when U Thant and his UN delegation arrived in Cuba on their imminently scheduled peace mission, they were to be permitted to visit the Soviet missile sites, to confirm the dismantling.

It is not difficult to comprehend the anger and resentment of the senior Soviet officers in Cuba who read these signals. None had sought to be posted to the Caribbean, the sick Pliev least of all. They had striven in an extraordinarily hostile environment, amid fractious and excited local people, to execute orders which required them, essentially, to prepare to confront the Americans in arms. Now they were told that all their labour and hardships had been wasted. They were to retire with no glory and little honour. Thoughtful men among them may have appreciated the value of Kennedy's new guarantee of Cuban inviolability. Mac Bundy wrote in 1988 that Khrushchev 'had saved much from the shipwreck of his bold venture'. Some Russians may also have felt gratitude for their own deliverance from the looming threat of incineration. There were few such on the island, however, in those last days of October.

Yet another signal was dispatched by Soviet naval authorities to vessels at sea, which caused US warships in the western Atlantic to report before dawn on the status of the tanker *Grozny*, inbound towards the blockade line with its cargo of ammonia: 'Contact dead in the water since 0430'. Soon after 9 a.m. in Washington, afternoon in Europe, the contents of the broadcast from Radio Moscow began clattering off the world's news agency wire machines. The president read the words that promised to avert war as he prepared to leave the White House Mansion to attend mass. 'I feel like a new man now,' he told Dave Powers. Bundy said: 'It was a very beautiful morning and it had suddenly become many times more beautiful.'

At the Pentagon, the US chiefs of staff refused to believe a word of it. They messaged the president: 'The JCS interpret the Khrushchev statement, in conjunction with the [Soviet] buildup, to be efforts to delay direct action by the United States while preparing the ground for diplomatic blackmail.' The chiefs asked Kennedy to order a full air strike against Cuba for next day, to be followed by invasion. Maxwell Taylor duly forwarded this recommendation, while telling McNamara that he himself dissented. Curtis LeMay did not trouble to hide his rage that the USAF's beautiful programme of air strikes, designed to devastate Cuba, at a stroke appeared redundant. While McNamara, who had slept at the Pentagon since the Crisis began, strove to calm the service brass, all save Taylor persisted with their insistence that the Kremlin message was a ruse, designed to buy time to hide the missiles. Robert Kennedy observed with some disdain: 'Admiral Anderson's reaction to the news was "we have been had". This caused the President to say wearily "The military are mad. It's lucky for us that we have McNamara over there."'

The attorney-general had started that morning by fulfilling a longstanding promise to take his daughters to a horse show at the Washington Armory. It was there that he received a call from Dean Rusk, reporting the news. The attorney-general drove immediately through the deserted Sunday morning streets of the capital to the White House, where he received a request to meet Anatoly Dobrynin, and thus left again for his own office. There, the Soviet ambassador told him that he had been requested by Khrushchev to convey best wishes to both Kennedy brothers.

RFK returned to the White House, to share with the president an overwhelming surge of relief. As he then left the Oval Office, JFK offered another characteristic witticism, almost unbearably painful to posterity in the light of what came thirteen months later. Recalling Lincoln, he said: 'This is the night I should go to the theater.' His brother said: 'If you go, I want to go with you.' Then the president sat down to write to Jane Anderson, widow of the downed U-2 pilot.

At 11.10 a.m. the Excom group reassembled in a mood of euphoria. Dean Rusk said that eight days earlier the president had remarked ironically that whatever course they adopted, those who advocated it would wind up being sorry. Now, however, 'I think there is some gratification for everyone's line of action, except [for those who wanted] to do nothing.' Bundy said that, after days when some had been hawks and others doves, this was a day of the doves. The president urged his advisers to display caution in their public statements. The Cuban quarantine would remain in place until all other arrangements were made: 'No interview should be given, no statement made, which would claim any kind of victory ... [I]f it was a triumph, it was a triumph for the next generation and not for any particular government or people.'

When the meeting broke up soon after noon, following a session lasting less than an hour, Kennedy telephoned in succession America's three living ex-presidents to pass on the news, with RFK listening in. Eisenhower asked warily: 'Did [Khrushchev] put any conditions in whatsoever, in there?' Kennedy said, far from truthfully: 'No, except that we're not going to invade Cuba ... [Although] my guess is that, by the end of next month, we're going to be toe to toe on Berlin.' Harry Truman said generously: 'I'm just pleased to death the way these things came out.' Herbert Hoover said: 'It seems to me these recent events are rather incredible ... That represents a good triumph for you.' Then Kennedy left Washington to join his wife and children at Glen Ora, their rented weekend house at Middleburg, Virginia.

At Novo-Ogaryovo, once the letter had been dispatched to Radio Moscow, Khrushchev's hitherto grim demeanour brightened. He threw open the meeting-room doors to call on the flunkeys outside to produce lunch. The senior guard excused the staff for some delay, saying that they had been unable to lay the table. The

Presidium members left their chairs and began chatting inconse-
quentially while the meal was set out. Sergei Khrushchev wrote:
'The entire atmosphere changed, as if the sun had come out after a
thunderstorm.' The family had been awaiting Nikita Sergeyevich at
their dacha, ten minutes' drive away from the guesthouse where the
Presidium was meeting. They ate lunch without him; first heard the
news of what he had been doing on the 5 p.m. bulletin.

Once the Presidium members had listened to Radio Moscow's
broadcast, Khrushchev said abruptly, in an uncanny echo of
Kennedy's words to his brother: 'Why don't we go to the theatre?
We'll show the whole world there's nothing to fear.' As always, no
one dissented. What was playing downtown? They were told there
was a final performance that night by a visiting Bulgarian ensemble.
'That's good,' said the first secretary. 'Let's go and see the
Bulgarians.' It was almost six o'clock, and he merely paused briefly
at his own dacha to change a shirt before the show.

Harold Macmillan, writing his diary on Sunday night, the 28th,
was a man bewildered as well as exhausted: 'Impossible to describe
what has been happening in this hour-by-hour battle ... The Turkey
offer to Khrushchev was very dangerous ... The press today ... were
awful. It was like Munich [1938] ... All through Saturday night, the
strain continued ... As we were finishing luncheon together, the
news came (by radio) that the Russians had given in! First they
admit to the ballistic missiles (hitherto denied by Communists and
doubted by all good fellow-travellers in every country).' Here,
Macmillan referred to the throngs of demonstrators who not
merely blamed the US for its response to the Crisis, but had also
swallowed Moscow's denials of the reality of the threat. The prime
minister initially found it hard to credit the outcome: 'A complete
climb-down (*if* they keep their word).' His scepticism was at least
partially merited. President Kennedy did not inform the British –
nor, indeed, any other ally – of his private pledge on removal of the
Turkish missiles.

A curious sense of let-down, of anti-climax however welcome,
overtook Macmillan's room at Admiralty House. He said to the
little cluster of intimates who remained, after his ministers and

senior advisers had gone home: 'It's like a wedding when there is nothing left to do but drink the champagne and go to sleep.' In New York veteran CBS News correspondent Charles Collingwood told millions of American viewers: 'This is the day we have every reason to believe the world came out from under the most terrible threat of nuclear holocaust since World War II.' Khrushchev's letter to the US president, he said, represented a 'humiliating defeat for Soviet policy'.

While both the White House and the Kremlin felt tolerably confident that the Crisis was within sight of ending, the threat of Armageddon lifted, many ordinary people remained fearful. A notably wary leader in the London *Times* of 29 October acknowledged that the worst might be past, but declined to take the good news for granted. Elsewhere the distinguished columnist Murray Kempton wrote from New York: 'There were many indications, and still are, that the President is under great pressure to invade Cuba and get it over. Europe must remember that there is no peace party in the United States [resembling the anti-nuclear movements in Europe]. There is seldom a peace party in any nation in a crisis like last week's.' Kempton feared that some forces in the US might derive the lesson from the events of October that the only way to treat the Soviets was to adopt a hard line 'whenever a direct confrontation can be made'.

David Ormsby-Gore wrote in a personal letter to the president: 'I am lost in admiration for the superb manner in which you have handled the tremendous events of the critical week we have just lived through. Well done.' Walter Lippmann applauded the way in which Kennedy had 'so narrowed his objectives to what he had the power to achieve', then exercised that power to secure them. Iverach McDonald, foreign editor of *The Times*, together with Lippmann, lunched in London the following week with foreign secretary Lord Home. The British minister, in a spirit echoing that of the US president, warned against any parade of Western triumphalism. Home added: 'The chief frightening thing about it all is that Khrushchev could have miscalculated so badly. It could mean that he could blunder into war another time.' The *Spectator* agreed:

'One of the most striking lessons of the whole affair has been the view it has given us of the quality of the Soviet leadership.' The editorial characterized the Kremlin's conduct as 'shallow, irresponsible adventurism ... the peasant Machiavellianism, the cheap conman's and gambler's quality of mind, which came as a surprise even to those of us who have not credited the Russians with any great sense in the past.'

France's *Le Monde* headed its comment 'An unexpected turn of events', then expressed astonishment that only twenty-four hours after Moscow had proposed a swap, 'Mr. Khrushchev simply bowed to Mr. Kennedy's terms and conditions ... One is left with the feeling that he had no choice. However, serious difficulties persist. Mr. Fidel Castro's tone stood in stark contrast to that of Mr. Khrushchev.' The *Economist*'s editorial of 3 November expressed both astonishment at the completeness of the Soviet climbdown and effusive praise for the fashion in which Kennedy had played his hand. Such enthusiasm contrasted with the mistrust of American judgement often voiced in the magazine's pages. It also offered 'unstinted credit' to the president for his promise not to undertake further military action against Cuba. This seemed to most British people to represent wisdom, quite independent of the need to offer the Soviets a deal. They had been appalled by the possibility of a global war over Castro's island.

Most of Kennedy's own countrymen, even those unimpressed by other things he had done or not done since January 1961, applauded his handling of the Crisis. His personal approval rating, measured by Gallup, rose to a stellar 74 per cent, up from 63 per cent two months earlier. In the congressional elections held on 6 November, against the historic tide of most mid-term contests the Democrats strengthened their dominance of the Senate, winning an additional four seats, and increased their margin of the popular vote in the House polls, despite losing one seat.

A few of those in the American military loop likewise commended the administration's handling of the Crisis. USAF intelligence officer Maj. Gen. Robert Breitweiser said: 'I thought it was brought off rather skillfully. The eyeball-to-eyeball bit in which the Soviet supply vessels turned around at the last minute was a pretty good piece of standing firm without overdoing it.' This was a minority armed forces view, however. Most of Breitweiser's comrades deplored the outcome; continued loudly to lament Kennedy's failure to exploit a perceived opportunity to rub in the dirt the noses of both the Soviets and Cubans. Curtis LeMay said: 'We would have gotten not only the missiles out of Cuba, we could have gotten the Communists out of Cuba ... In my mind there wasn't a chance that we would have gone to war with Russia because we had overwhelming strategic capability, and the Russians knew it.'

Another USAF general, World War II fighter pilot Bruce Holloway, said: 'I think if we had cleaned out that rats' nest, it would have cut back a lot of the Communist growth in South America for a long, long time.' Holloway thought air strikes alone would have done it: 'I was surprised we didn't actually go in there. I thought we were going.' The USAF's Lt. Gen. David Burchinal, LeMay's forty-seven-year-old deputy, said: 'There were two big arguments going on. One was the nuclear confrontation that we had already solved. That we won hands down. The second one was do you invade Cuba or don't you? And of course the military and the hawks wanted to go in and clean it out – take out Castro, get rid of the problem decisively for all time, and the other side [in the White House] didn't want to invade, just talk. "We will do a little of this, a little of that." We just fiddled around ... We had the capability to do the job but in the final analysis it was the indecision ... at the top. Nobody would bite the bullet.'

When, a few months later, the order came down to remove the Jupiter missiles from Turkey, USAF deputy chief of staff Major-General Gabriel Disosway, who had negotiated the original deployments, was disgusted: 'They had the Russians on the run and they figured they had to give them a way out so they negotiated ... We never got to make any inspection of whether the missiles were gone. They could still be in Cuba as far as we know ... As we said around the Pentagon, we snatched defeat out of the jaws of victory.' Such views, from the US Air Force's most senior officers, emphasize the strength of military passions in those days, to which the secretary of defense was the striking hold-out. The USAF's deputy director of plans Col. Jerry Page described McNamara as 'the greatest menace to the safety of the United States that's ever been in Washington'.

Dean Acheson, unusual among the civilians in that he had been an unwavering hawk, even now privately declined to acknowledge that he might have been wrong. He described White House management as 'a gamble to the point of recklessness', its success 'home to plain dumb luck'. Acheson nonetheless wrote graciously to the president: 'May I congratulate you on your leadership, firmness and judgement over the past tough week. We have not had these qualities at the helm in this country at all times. It is good to have them again. Only a few people know better than me how hard these decisions are to make, and how broad the gap between the advisers and the decider.'

Dean Rusk said: 'Those who experienced the Missile Crisis came out of it a little different people from what they were before they went into it.' He intended to suggest, of course, that they had explored the furthest reaches of global peril, diplomacy and statesmanship. Yet it is hard to accept that, beyond the president himself, those tested in the fire of Excom membership thus achieved a great accession of wisdom, since those same men would march the United States into Vietnam, and keep it there for the best part of a decade.

As for reaction within the Soviet Union, the *Economist* noted sardonically that the aged and oft-disgraced Marshal Kliment Voroshilov 'had to be picked from the dustbin of history to proclaim in *Pravda* mankind's gratitude to Mr. Khrushchev for his performance'. Nikolai Kozakov wrote on 28 October: 'Shark [Khrushchev] has sent Kennedy another letter. Of course, it is very long and not free of threats, but what matters is that he has ordered a halt to construction work on the missile sites in Cuba, the return of the weapons to the USSR. In short, he has put his naked arse into the stinging nettles. Kennedy, in turn, has guaranteed that they will not attack Cuba. Of course, a lot of diplomatic manoeuvring will follow, but the crisis has been resolved, in the USA's favour. I finished my poem [about the Crisis] and read it to my mum. She approved, but she also thinks that it is too late now' – and so thought Kozakov's editors.

Muscovite Ivan Seleznev wrote in his diary that it seemed humiliating for such a nation as the Soviet Union, 'that deeds proved to be so different from words. Second, everything was done in a childishly secret fashion ... They [now] say that common sense dictated the decision to remove [the missiles]. But clearly this was absent when they took them [to Cuba].' He wrote sarcastically about the decisions of the Kremlin: 'How can we possibly live with these wise and brilliant folks?'

Russians love animal figures of speech. Ukraine Communist Party secretary Petr Shelest likened the conduct of Kennedy and Khrushchev to that of two goats which met on a narrow cliff path, and refused to give way to each other. The goats, he observed, both fell into the abyss. In the Crisis, by contrast, the winner was 'good sense'. Amid all the conflicting claims made by national leaders, wrote Shelest, 'one thing is clear: we found ourselves on the brink of war because we precipitated the so-called Caribbean crisis by deploying rockets and bombers in Cuba. We created fantastic military tension, and now claim that by somehow extricating ourselves from it we have created an "achievement", almost a "victory".'

Some Russians, however, were happy to accept a benign view of their own leadership. Twenty-eight-year-old Romen Nazirov wrote in his diary for 6 November: 'Khrushchev has saved the world from the threat of a nuclear war. American newspapers announced his decision to withdraw the bases with headlines like: "Reds are Retreating from Cuba", etc. They are even mocking us. But Khrushchev's moral victory is obvious. He is right in one thing: about war and peace. As for the prestige ... well, let them laugh! *Rira bien, qui rira dernier!*' Gen. Gennady Obaturov, then commanding 6th Guards Tank Army in Ukraine, wrote in his diary later: 'We came out winners in the Cuba region ... [but] God save us from such victories if they take the world to the brink of nuclear war.'

In Cuba twenty-year-old José Ferrara described a slow dawning of realization of the gravity of the issues: 'People had become more and more conscious of what was at stake. They heaved a sigh of relief when the issue was resolved, the rockets removed.' One Cuban, however, celebrated nothing. Fidel Castro was beyond rage. He perceived the outcome as a humiliation for himself and his nation, as much as for Khrushchev. Having provided the Soviet Union, at mortal risk, with a stage on which to play out the drama of the missiles' deployment, the Russians had not even troubled to warn him about the impending Radio Moscow announcement of their withdrawal. The first that he knew of it was on hearing the broadcast news, which prompted him to smash a mirror. At the height of his fury towards Khrushchev, he abused him as a 'faggot' – '*mericon*' – the most savage epithet this savagely *macho* Latin American could deploy.

Inside the Kremlin Gen. Obaturov described Khrushchev addressing a Central Committee meeting in the wake of the Crisis: 'As always he spoke without notes, haltingly, nervously, stammering. Afterwards we went upstairs to the reception hall, where tables were set up. Toasts were offered:

- Khrushchev, to the People, Party and Army
- Malinovsky, to Party, Central Committee and Khrushchev
- Eremenko, to Khrushchev
- Khrushchev finally raised his glass to the Army and all those present. He said that any fool could start a war. But it was harder to find one clever enough to end one well, in this era of nuclear weapons.'

On 30 October Kennedy wrote to Mrs Paul Mellon, who had recently supervised a replanting of the White House Rose Garden: 'I need not tell you that your garden has been our brightest spot in the somber surroundings of the last few days.' That day also, the Kennedy administration formally, albeit secretly, stood down the CIA's Operation Mongoose. The 'Special Group' directing it was abolished, though the Kennedys' rage against Castro remained unabated.

2 THE CUBANS CUT UP ROUGH

Sunday 28 October has been defined by posterity as the last of the thirteen days of the Crisis during which the world stood in peril. On the 29th the *Kansas City Times* bore the front-page headline 'REDS BACK DOWN ON CUBA'. The *New York Herald Tribune* led with 'Khrushchev Offers to Scrap Cuba Missiles'. The *New York Times* stated: 'US and Soviets Reach Accord on Cuba: Kennedy Accepts Khrushchev Pledge to Remove Missiles Under UN Watch'. The dismantling of the missiles was quickly completed, and the long, deadly, drab-green cylinders began to be moved to the ports in broad daylight. Two days later, all the designated weapons had been loaded by crews working day and night. The first vessels carrying warheads, *Aleksandrovsk* and *Divnogorsk*, sailed from Mariel with their nuclear cargoes on 6 November, and remained under US air surveillance until they entered respectively the Baltic and Black Sea. That evening, the destroyer USS *Blandy* closed on the *Divnogorsk* and demanded to send a boarding party to search it. The ship's captain refused, and after exchanges of lamp signal and tense discussions aboard both the Soviet vessel and the destroyer, the Americans contented themselves with watching from their own bridge as canvas covers were stripped off, to expose the missiles lashed on deck. By 9 November forty-two nuclear missiles, 1,056 pieces of equipment and 3,289 officers and men had left Cuba.

Yet acute tensions persisted between Moscow and Washington through a further two weeks, while some nuclear warheads remained in Cuba, and one man battled against their removal. This was not Nikita Khrushchev, but Fidel Castro. Moscow had failed to warn its Havana ambassador, Aleksandr Alekseev, about the imminent 28 October broadcast letter to Kennedy. Thus, when Cuba's outraged President Dorticós demanded to be told what was happening, the envoy in good faith dismissed the US broadcast claims; urged him not to believe stuff he heard on American radio. Hours later, when Alekseev received a copy of the Kremlin letter, intended for delivery to Castro, the disgusted Cuban leader refused to meet him. That day Fidel delivered a bellicose and defiant '5

Points' public statement, asserting that, as far as he and Cuba were concerned, the Missile Crisis was not at an end. When he relented next day, the 29th, and met Alekseev, the ambassador handed him both Khrushchev's message and another from the entire Presidium, urging him publicly to endorse the US-Soviet missile deal. Castro, angry and depressed, said sulkily that he would consider the proposal. He rejected out of hand the notion of allowing UN inspectors to visit the missile sites – a 'humiliating procedure'.

The Czech ambassador in Havana enjoyed privileged access to his Soviet counterpart, Alekseev, as the representative of a Warsaw Pact state. He reported to Prague: 'The Cubans have unfortunately not at all understood the historic steps by Khrushchev and indeed believe that the USSR has backed down from the USA, and that Cuban defences are thus weakened.' Within the Cuban government 'there is apparently a total confusion of opinions. They do not view the situation from a global perspective, only from a Cuban one, and their only objective remains the fulfilment of Fidel's demands. There are even suggestions about a new Munich.'

In Khrushchev's 30 October letter to Castro, he again reproached the Cuban for the insouciance with which he had seemed willing to countenance headlong conflict between the superpowers: 'Of course the United States would have suffered enormous losses, but the Soviet Union and the whole socialist bloc would also have suffered greatly. It is even difficult to say how things would have ended for the Cuban people ... We struggle against imperialism not in order to die but to draw on all our potential, to lose as little as possible, and later to win more, so as to be a victor and make communism triumph.'

Castro responded with his accustomed truculence, writing as if he was addressing an equal: 'I do not see how you can state that we were consulted in the decision you took ... The imperialists are talking again of invading our country, which is proof of how ephemeral and untrustworthy their promises are.' When U Thant arrived in Havana on 30 October, in fulfilment of the invitation from Castro issued three days earlier, the Cuban remained immovable in his refusal to allow UN inspectors to view the missile sites:

'We have not violated any law ... To the contrary, we have been the victims, in the first place of a blockade, which is an illegal act. And secondly we have been victims of another country's claim to determine what we have the right to do or not to do within our own borders. It is our understanding that Cuba is a sovereign state, no more and no less so than any other member state of the United Nations ... As I see it, all this talk about inspection is one more attempt to humiliate our country. We do not accept it.' Moreover, when Alekseev asked Gen. Pliev to meet the UN's Gen. Indar Jit Rikhye, U Thant's military adviser, the Russian refused to do so, having already swallowed humiliations enough. Pliev merely permitted his deputy to talk to the visitor. In reluctant compliance with Moscow's orders, that officer provided to the UN a full account of the schedule for dismantling the nuclear missiles.

Kennedy's initial agreement with Khrushchev addressed only the ballistic missiles in Cuba. He had said nothing about the IL-28 bombers and their nuclear weapons, together with the *Luna* and FKR-1 nuclear-tipped cruise missiles. These the Soviet leader at first aspired to retain on the island, to appease Castro. Their status became the focus of ill-tempered dispute. Neither superpower seriously supposed itself to be still on the brink of war. But the US chiefs of staff clung to hopes that residual Soviet and Cuban obduracy might yet secure them authorization for an invasion of Cuba, which their forces in the south-eastern United States remained poised to undertake.

At sea, of the four Soviet Foxtrot submarines which had been hunted by the Americans one, B-4, north-east of the Bahamas inside the quarantine zone, escaped surveillance and retired towards its home waters, submerged in the daylight hours. B-130 played an ignominious role, because three of its four diesel engines ceased to function. On 25 October it was obliged to rise to periscope depth, and thereafter to face repeated harassment – grenade and practice depth-charge explosions – which caused its captain to believe himself under real attack, especially when one charge exploded against his hull, starting a leak. US warships sustained their threatening activities until, on 30 October, with its battery power entirely exhausted, B-130 surfaced before the USS *Blandy*. When efforts to repair its diesels failed, the Soviets dispatched a tug to drag the boat to Murmansk, where it eventually arrived. This episode took place more than two hundred miles east of the quarantine line, on the open Atlantic.

Dubivko's B-36, inside the blockade zone, was likewise hunted by the USS *Charles Cecil*, which during the hours of darkness hove to, showing no lights, thoroughly alarming the Russians when they surfaced to recharge batteries and found the destroyer's silent, shadowy bulk almost alongside. Dubivko promptly ordered a crash-dive, and later reported that the Americans had fired a torpedo, which missed. This is most unlikely, but reflects the Soviet sailors' state of mind in those days and nights, hearing the screws of the US Navy's anti-submarine vessels thrashing the water overhead, accompanied at regular intervals by the detonations and resonant clanging of charges. The captain eventually surfaced in the presence of the Americans on 31 October. Nonetheless, and almost contradictorily: 'We have to be fair to the enemy – the destroyer did not bother us, but adopted a parallel course at a distance of 50 to 150 meters.' A week later, homeward bound, two of his three diesel motors broke down. As the boat wallowed, heroic engineers were obliged to cannibalize both, to build a single replacement motor that enabled them to complete their passage to Russia.

US warships continued to surround the surfaced B-59, more than a hundred miles outside the quarantine line, until the hounds were called off – the Americans were ordered to withdraw. All four Foxtrot captains, on their return to the USSR, were treated by their commanders as having disgraced themselves – contributed to the general Soviet humiliation by permitting themselves to become playthings of the enemy. Dubivko said: 'Marshal [Andrei, army C-in-C of Warsaw Pact forces] Grechko refused to listen to my report on our problems and difficulties. He was unable to understand why a submarine had to charge its batteries every night in stationary mode. The only thing he understood was that we violated the secrecy requirements, were discovered by the Americans, and for some time stayed in close contact with them ... The head of the Operations Department of the Navy General Staff ... said "I would rather have been sunk than surfaced."' In truth, of course, blame for the Foxtrots' misfortunes lay entirely with the Soviet high command. Dubivko said that Navy C-in-C Admiral Gorshkov was the only senior officer who gave credit and praise to the submariners for what they had endured.

Meanwhile the Kremlin remained embarrassed by Castro's fierce resistance to removal of the Soviet IL-28 bombers. Khrushchev had battled to salvage some pride and dignity from the debacle by securing the American guarantee, safeguarding Cuba from further aggression. However, its dictator, far from displaying gratitude, continued to assail the Soviet premier with public claims of betrayal, which weakened Khrushchev's grip upon power at home, and on the respect of fellow-Socialists abroad. The *Detroit Free Press* headline reflected a widespread international take on the situation: '*CUBANS* WONT GIVE UP *RUSSIAN* JET BOMBERS'. Then, and indeed for two years that followed, Khrushchev found himself in the grotesque position of being obliged first to appease, then to solace, and latterly to cherish the leader of the threadbare Caribbean republic to which he had so rashly shackled himself. 'Father felt deeply hurt,' wrote Sergei Khrushchev. 'He had given his heart to the bearded leader and now regarded him almost as a son.'

When Moscow received a cable from its Havana ambassador, warning of Castro's bitterness, Khrushchev told Mikoyan: 'Look, they don't understand. Haven't we saved them from invasion? We've saved them, but he [Castro] doesn't understand our policy.' The Soviet leader declared vaingloriously in a later version of his memoirs: 'The aim of the American aggressors was to destroy Cuba. Our aim was to preserve Cuba. Today Cuba exists. So who won? It cost us nothing more than the round-trip expenses for transporting the rockets to Cuba and back.'

Yet amid Castro's furious rejection of such assertions, Khrushchev said to Mikoyan: 'We can't explain it in writing, but we need to do so, or they won't get the message. Somebody needs to go there and do it properly. You need to go.' Mikoyan said nothing. Ashkhen, his wife of forty-one years, was dying. Khrushchev interpreted his silence as reluctance, and pressed his point: 'They know you there. You just need to present the case.' Mikoyan finally agreed, and at the close of the meeting ordered Aeroflot to prepare a plane. The foreign ministry was told to arrange visas; refuelling in Scotland; a stop in New York to meet Stevenson and McCloy – this last was suggested by Khrushchev. After some difficulties about the American landing permissions, a call to Dobrynin in Washington secured consent from the State Department.

Mikoyan arrived in New York on 1 November, en route to Cuba. He met with U Thant, then dined with Adlai Stevenson and John McCloy. The Soviet representative briefly attempted to adopt a tough line with the US representatives, demanding an immediate end to the blockade. He retreated from this, however, when it became apparent that the Americans were now confident of holding the cards, and thus of dictating the agenda. The blockade would end, they said, only when withdrawal of the missiles from Cuba had taken place, and been verified. They summarily rejected a new demand, for US evacuation of its Guantánamo Bay base, as a sop to Castro. Since the Cuban leader refused to accept on-site verification of the nuclear warheads' removal, he was deemed to have no claim upon any goodwill gesture from Washington.

The Kremlin's emissary landed next day in Havana. Thereafter, it would require three weeks of his dogged, patient diplomacy to secure Castro's grudging acquiescence in the Moscow-Washington agreement, 'which he was quite capable of sabotaging', in Mikoyan's words. The deputy premier had brought with him an instructional aid – a copy of Sergei Eisenstein's great film *Ivan the Terrible*. When the talks bogged down, Mikoyan urged taking a break to watch the movie, 'so that you understand what power is'. Later the Kremlin envoy claimed, somewhat implausibly, that the screening impressed the Cuban leader. After both Castro and Che Guevara bitterly rebuked Mikoyan, he responded in like spirit: 'We see your readiness to die beautifully, but we believe that it isn't worth dying beautifully.' On 3 November Mikoyan learned of his wife's death, but felt unable to quit the tense negotiations to return home for her funeral on the 5th. Khrushchev broke a promise to attend, excusing himself to his emissary's son, Sergei Mikoyan, by saying tersely: 'I don't like funerals. After all, it's not like going to a wedding, right?'

Most of the forty thousand Russians in Cuba were disgusted by the outcome of the Crisis, and aggrieved by its souring of their relationships with Castro's people. Gennady Chudik, running a missile regiment's workshop on the island, wrote: 'The Cubans simply could not understand the USSR's strategy. Here was the country that conquered fascist Germany in 1945, while Cuba in 1961 had defeated the Americans' mercenaries at Playa Giron. One salvo of Soviet missiles at North America, they thought, and victory would be ours. Relations with local people deteriorated pretty badly.'

Nurse Elvira Dubinskaya, a passionate communist working at the Soviet military hospital in Havana, felt ashamed that her country let down the Cubans: 'Our commanders did the wrong thing when they withdrew and told no one, and the Cubans were left on their own. But they did not have a choice.' The 428th Missile Regiment quit the island on 6 November, its armament conspicuously lashed to the ship's sides for the benefit of the American planes and warships that shadowed its early passage. Through the years that followed, the crews would be forbidden on pain of the harshest sanctions to discuss their experience of Cuba. But Rafael Zakirov, an officer of a support unit responsible for nuclear warheads, was one of many who shared Dubinskaya's bitterness about the manner of their departure: 'It was traumatic for our soldiers – embarkation at night from deserted piers, with no traditional farewells from our Cuban comrades. We left in a fashion that suggested we were guilty of some crime, though in reality we had fulfilled with devotion and self-sacrifice our duties as soldiers, and our orders from the Motherland.' During the voyage home, they consoled themselves with rotting oranges.

On 12 November Mikoyan informed Castro of Moscow's determination to take home its bombers. The Cuban absolutely rejected this decision. His own response was to issue a new order, effective from 6 a.m. on 18 November, for the air defences to shoot down any American reconnaissance aircraft that entered Cuban airspace. Relations between the Soviets and the regime became glacial. During a dinner in their own embassy Castro taunted them, saying that if Stalin had still been in charge, no such shameful surrender would have taken place. When this remark was repeated to the Kremlin, Khrushchev's fury intensified. He told Mikoyan, still in Havana, to warn Castro that unless he withdrew his shootdown order, all Soviet forces in Cuba would be withdrawn. Malinovsky informed the Presidium that Pliev had been instructed that on no account were Soviet weapons to fire upon US aircraft, even if Castro ordered them to do so.

On the evening of 19 November, the Cuban bowed to the inevitable. He belatedly informed Mikoyan that, if the American blockade was lifted, he would agree to cancel his shootdown order, and acquiesce in removal of the IL-28s. His surrender came not a moment too soon: that day at the White House, a renewed Excom meeting discussed the apparently gloomy prospects for an acceptable settlement with Moscow. The chiefs of staff reprised their agitation for an invasion of Cuba, which they asserted that US forces were now 'in an optimum posture to execute'. The administration warned the Kremlin repeatedly through Robert Kennedy's back-channel, of the pressures on the president to attack, unless a settlement was finalized, its terms swiftly fulfilled. 'Bobby's notion is there's only one peace-lover in the government,' said Mac Bundy, describing the characterization of the president which the attorney-general sought to transmit to Moscow via Georgy Bolshakov, 'and he's entirely surrounded by militarists and it's not a bad image.'

On 20 November, Marshal Malinovsky instructed Pliev in Cuba to dispatch back to the Soviet Union his holding of eighty nuclear warheads for the FKR-1 cruise missiles, together with twelve such warheads for the *Lunas* and six nuclear bombs for the IL-28s. The missiles themselves, with conventional warheads, remained on the island. So also, through the years ahead, did a Soviet motorized infantry brigade and supporting elements, as earnests of Moscow's continuing defence commitment. That same day, which chanced to be the US attorney-general's thirty-seventh birthday, Anatoly Dobrynin walked into RFK's office to declare with a beaming smile: 'I have a birthday present for you' – news of Russia's agreement to withdraw all the IL-28 bombers. That evening the president addressed a press conference in the State Department auditorium, at which he announced Khrushchev's surrender, and said that in response the American naval quarantine would be lifted.

The Crisis that had come so terrifyingly close to war thus ended, without a bang but with many whimpers: from disgruntled Soviet Presidium members and commanders; from Cubans; from US uniformed brass. The prospective invasion forces in the south-eastern United States were at last stood down. Anatoly Dobrynin wrote: 'Khrushchev's failure to insist on a public pledge [on the US missiles in Turkey] by Kennedy cost him dearly. Kennedy was proclaimed the big winner in the crisis ... Khrushchev had been humiliated into withdrawing our missiles from Cuba with no obvious gain.' He added that the outcome intensified the sense of inferiority that so often drove the Kremlin to excesses: 'The Soviet leadership could not forget a blow to its prestige bordering on humiliation when it was forced to admit its weakness before the whole world ... Our military establishment used this experience to secure for itself a new large-scale program of nuclear arms development ... a new stage in the arms race.'

Khrushchev designated deputy foreign minister Vasily Kuznetsov, a fluent English-speaker who had studied at the Carnegie Institute of Technology, to finalize details of the peace deal with the Americans. John McCloy, Kennedy's nominee, talked ruthlessly toughly, even resisting confirmation of the US pledge not to invade Cuba, until explicitly ordered to concede this by the White House. Nonetheless, Kennedy escaped formalizing this undertaking, because Castro still refused to allow UN on-site monitoring of the removal of the Soviet missiles. One of the final sessions of the negotiations took place at McCloy's house in Stamford, Connecticut, in the last days of November. Talking in the garden because of Kuznetsov's fears of eavesdropping devices, the two men seated themselves on a wooden fence rail. The Russian said, 'Well, Mr. McCloy, we will honour this agreement. But never will we be caught like this again!'

15

'This Strange and Still Scarcely Explicable Affair'

Unlike the United States, Britain retained a diplomatic mission in Cuba. Ambassador Herbert 'Bill' Marchant, a fifty-six-year-old wartime Bletchley Park codebreaker, sent a personal message to the foreign secretary in the first days of November, in which he wrote: 'Any record [of the Crisis] must necessarily read more like a wildly improbable sequel to [Graham Greene's novel] *Our Man in Havana* than a Foreign Office despatch.' Prime minister Harold Macmillan characterized the events of October as 'this strange and still scarcely explicable affair'. He meant that, once the initial surge of relief passed, it was replaced by bewilderment about what on earth had been the Kremlin's game, to deploy nuclear missiles in Cuba, then hastily to remove them in the face of American rage that was inevitable. Even in the eyes of Soviet sympathizers, Khrushchev was left appearing foolish, because he had perpetrated so many falsehoods that were bound to be exposed; and weak, because he was obliged to yield. The Chinese Communist Party, which had become the Kremlin's deadly foe, denounced the Soviet leader for both 'adventurism' in deploying the missiles and 'capitulationism' in removing them.

Oleg Troyanovsky said: 'Andrei Gromyko and a number of others in Moscow later claimed that ... there was no threat of nuclear war, that Khrushchev had evaluated all the positive and negative factors beforehand ... This argument is difficult to accept. Even if we concede that neither government wanted a nuclear war, they still could have been drawn into one against their will, due to some unexpected circumstance or even an accident ... Khrushchev could not foresee all possible developments. He certainly misjudged the main factor, the scale of the American reaction.'

Britain's Joint Intelligence Committee argued that even if Kennedy had committed US forces against Cuba, Khrushchev would not have permitted the struggle to become nuclear because of Moscow's understanding that the USSR would be the big loser – if such words can be employed in such a context – from an exchange. The JIC had predicted back in February, before the missile deployment was conceived, 'we ... believe that the Soviet leaders, provided they remain rational, will not plan to initiate general nuclear war as a deliberate act of policy'. The committee now anticipated that the Russians would respond to every American move with a proportionate response, designed to avoid escalation to all-out superpower conflict. They did not expect a drastic move against West Berlin: '[The Soviets'] overriding concern therefore is likely to be to limit their reply to the least dangerous possible place.' In such an event, they would flag to Washington 'that this went as far as they intended to go at present stage'. That forecast proved correct, but was nonetheless remarkably optimistic, following the revelation of the missiles.

In the eyes of all save Americans, a piece is missing from both the fevered October 1962 discussions in Washington and most histories published since. US leaders took it for granted that their country could not be expected to endure the presence of Soviet missiles in Cuba. It was undoubtedly the case that domestic opinion regarded the deployment as representing as much a mortal insult as a deadly peril. But, echoing Harold Macmillan's courteous observation to JFK, there was no more logical or legal cause why the Cubans should not choose to host nuclear weapons on their soil than that the Turks, Italians or British should be denied such a right. European NATO members had lived for years with a proximate Soviet atomic threat. The American debate was conducted by men wearing historical blinkers – sharing the assumption that the United States had privileges in determining what was, and was not, acceptable in Cuba such as were a commonplace to President Theodore Roosevelt, but represented an anachronism in 1962. This is why Robert McNamara was absolutely correct, albeit electorally insensitive, to tell Excom at the outset of the Crisis that the missiles posed a political rather than a strategic challenge to the United States.

The absence of freedom, denial of an unfettered public opinion, in communist and totalitarian states is customarily measured against Western liberties, to the latter's advantage. Yet democratic forces by no means always exercise their influence benignly. In the winter of 1950, Dean Acheson persuaded Harry Truman to permit Gen. Douglas MacArthur to lead his disastrous march to North Korea's Yalu river border with China, chiefly to appease American conservatives who threatened, and eventually destroyed, Truman's presidency. In South-East Asia the overreaches of the Kennedy administration and its successors were prompted scarcely at all by consideration of the interests of the indigenous peoples; instead by the perceived expectations of voters at home, in the wider context of the Cold War.

Our gratitude for Kennedy's handling of the Missile Crisis, and respect for his memory, must be increased by recognizing that less than half his successors as America's commander-in-chief could have been relied upon to make the same calls. He adopted a strategy that emphasized his own and his nation's resolve, while rejecting courses that might have precipitated Armageddon. His remarkable gifts as a listener were seen to utmost advantage in the meetings of Excom at the White House, which concluded with clear, rational executive decisions. Against the instincts not only of the military but of much domestic opinion, almost from the outset he determined to strike a bargain with the Soviets. He expected to pay a price in order to secure peacefully his unwavering objective – removal of the missiles from Cuba.

The most important achievement of the 'quarantine' was that – as Kennedy, McNamara and others hoped – it bought time for the Soviets to reflect and draw back before the US started shooting. White House promises to Moscow were critical, in offering the Soviets a path for retreat while salvaging some fragments of pride. Nonetheless it deserves an emphasis which would delight the

shades of the US chiefs of staff, that the principal driver in persuading Khrushchev to yield was fear of the imminent bombing and
invasion of Cuba. There was never a credible, wholly diplomatic
escape route: the threat of American force was indispensable.
Walter Lippmann and later his biographer Ronald Steel argued that
Kennedy should have quietly told Khrushchev to remove the
missiles from Cuba, before announcing the blockade. McGeorge
Bundy commented acidly and convincingly: 'Neither Steel nor
anyone else has told us why Khrushchev should have agreed to
such a "quiet" request.'

Bundy also asserted in 1988 that in October 'the objective risk of
escalation to the nuclear level may have been as large as 1 in 100'.
This seems far too low, because it discounts human misjudgement.
Perhaps the former national security adviser recognized as much
when he conceded: 'In this apocalyptic matter the risk can be very
small indeed and still much too large for comfort.' The president
himself was less sanguine, putting the odds against war 'somewhere
between one out of three and even'.

The menace to the planet was not that the Russians would
purposefully launch a First Strike against the US, but instead that the
Americans, provoked at their most sensitive point, would consider
that the missile deployment justified devastating military action
against Cuba. It seems mistaken to take for granted that President
Kennedy would resist the urgings of his military chiefs to go to war,
or that a conflict could thereafter have been confined to conventional weapons, since the choice would have been partially dependent
upon the discretion and restraint of Soviet officers under American
bombardment on Cuban battlefields. Robert McNamara saw this
spectre, saying: 'If the United States attacked conventionally, the
Politburo probably would not have authorized a nuclear response.
So that's not the danger. But what about the second lieutenant?'

It remains a huge enigma how events might have unfolded had
Khrushchev not yielded on 28 October. McGeorge Bundy went to
his grave convinced that Kennedy would have held off from launching an air campaign; would probably instead merely have tightened
the blockade. McNamara and Sorensen endorsed this view. Three

of the foremost modern American scholars of the period, Jim Hershberg, Fred Logevall and Sheldon Stern, are alike convinced that the president never came close to yielding to Excom's hawks, or to the chiefs of staff. This is a counter-factual. If indeed JFK was not intending to bomb Cuba in the days ahead then his brother's remarks to Dobrynin represented a massive bluff, which seems a large historical assumption. Domestic pressure on the White House was rising fast, in the wake of the U-2 shootdown. Kennedy's personal coolness was astonishing, in the face of the sometimes reckless proposals advanced by others around the Excom table. He stood head and shoulders above them, not merely through the power of his great office, but by his exercise of it. Yet it is hard to believe that the diplomatic path was indefinitely sustainable: events might at any moment have been tilted by – for instance – an unintended clash between a Soviet submarine and US warships at sea. It is fortunate that Kennedy's patience and restraint were not tested to destruction.

If the above are tactical factors which influenced the outcome, we must also acknowledge the strategic ones: neither Khrushchev nor his generals doubted the overwhelming nuclear superiority of the US, and thus their own inability to win a general war. On the American side, the same knowledge persuaded the joint chiefs of staff to urge its exploitation, to secure an outright victory over both the Soviet Union and Castro. The quality of Kennedy's judgement was emphasized by his refusal to attempt to do this.

When the president talked afterwards about the performance of Excom's membership, he said that he was especially proud of his brother's showing. He also highlighted McNamara as having been 'superb', Llewellyn Thompson 'wise'. These three, he thought, had been the committee's stars. Meanwhile Mac Bundy flipflopped repeatedly, changing his mind more even than other Excom members. The president retained an enduring respect for the national security adviser's intellect and academic prowess, but it is remarkable that Bundy kept his job through the years ahead, after his erratic showing in October. He went on to play an even less admirable role in Vietnam escalation.

Kennedy was unimpressed by the State Department's contribution, rebuking Dean Rusk for being wrongfooted when Khrushchev's broadcast missile swap proposal arrived on Saturday 27th. He asserted that Foggy Bottom staff were caught unawares: 'We were not really prepared to know what we were going to say,' said Kennedy. Somebody, he told the secretary of state sharply, should have addressed contingencies ahead of time, to meet a range of scenarios. Robert Kennedy declared contemptuously that Rusk 'had a virtually complete breakdown mentally and physically'. That remark says more about the shortcomings of the attorney-general than about those of the secretary of state. Sheldon Stern describes the comment as 'outrageous', and this seems just. The Kennedys never learned to think much of either Rusk or his department, but he served his country admirably through the Crisis. RFK, especially, was diminished by his refusal to recognize this.

Among the host of historians who have examined the record of the White House October meetings, few have questioned Thompson's contribution. We now know that he misjudged the Kremlin's appetite for opening a second front elsewhere: when on 23 October Soviet deputy foreign minister Vasily Kuznetsov proposed a Berlin blockade to counter the American Cuban one, Khrushchev blew up: 'We're just beginning to get ourselves out of one adventure, and you're suggesting we climb into another!' Thompson was nonetheless importantly right in urging that Khrushchev did not want war; that thus the US should not launch precipitate military action.

Robert Kennedy, though far less steady, seems to deserve credit for counselling against an unheralded air assault. His later assassination conferred upon him a martyr's status, not far behind that of his elder brother. RFK was always, however, a charismatic politician, rather than a plausible statesman. Meanwhile Robert McNamara was the principal advocate of blockade; of graduated escalation. Most of what he is recorded as saying at Excom's meetings represented both reason and prudence.

That was more than could be said for the contributions of the US chiefs of staff. Maxwell Taylor's posthumous reputation has fared better than his record merits: during the Thirteen Days, he showed himself little wiser than were his colleagues, 'a twofold hawk from start to finish', to use his own crassly confident words. Military men are, by the nature of their calling, required to show themselves strong; to be undaunted by the human cost of war, because the generation of disciplined violence is their business. The Kaiser's Gen. Paul von Hindenburg observed gruffly in 1912: 'I never read poetry. It might soften me', and many warriors through the ages have shared such self-conscious pride about the iron in their souls. Moreover, the commanders of 1962 were practised in mass death. Soviet officers had experienced it in the Great Patriotic War; LeMay, Power and their comrades inflicted it upon Japan, and were rewarded for their achievement by becoming national heroes.

These were men of their time and place, few as yet attuned to a new world, in which traditional warrior virtues – above all, an appetite for mortal combat – posed a threat to the planet. Military chiefs must always be ready to obey a political order to fight, but should never be permitted to arbitrate the big decisions, when humankind's extinction is at stake. Nonetheless, it seems necessary reluctantly also to recognize that Pentagon bellicosity, well-known in the Kremlin, constituted a significant weapon in the president's Crisis armoury. His disgust at the chiefs' irresponsibility was unfeigned. It well served his diplomacy, however, that few informed Russians doubted the eagerness to attack among America's foremost warriors, spurred by confidence in their capability to prevail.

Some modern analysts question McNamara's claims to have played a pivotal and constructive role – Sheldon Stern, influenced by the defense secretary's many retirement untruths and evasions, sustains a deeply sceptical view. Critics also emphasize intemperate remarks made and attitudes struck by both Kennedys, when tape-recorders were absent. Yet it seems just to assess personalities by outcomes, not by verbal lunges. RFK acknowledged that 'none was consistent in his opinion from the very beginning to the very end'. This reflected an intelligent flexibility, not – as the chiefs of staff chose to believe – a flaccid infirmity of purpose. Within the White House senior Republican former office-holders and advisers worked to assist in shaping policy alongside the Democratic incumbents, without a hint of partisanship. Though this had previously been the case throughout American history, especially in national emergencies, such conduct becomes remarkable in the context of the twenty-first-century chasm in the US polity.

RFK wrote: 'The final lesson ... is the importance of placing ourselves in the other country's shoes ... President Kennedy spent more time trying to determine the effects of a particular course of action on Khrushchev or the Russians than on any other phase of what he was doing. What guided all his deliberations was an effort not to disgrace Khrushchev, not to humiliate the Soviet Union, not to have them feel they would have to escalate their response because their national security or national interests so committed them.' Respect is central to international relations, even between adversaries. Where it is denied by one party or both, whether in 1962 or in our own times, the public weal is the loser.

America's allies afterwards applauded the president. British prime minister Harold Macmillan contrasted Kennedy's handling of the Missile Crisis with that of the Suez debacle six years earlier by his own predecessor in office Anthony Eden, much to the American's advantage: '[Kennedy] played a firm *military* game throughout – acting quickly and being ready to act *as soon as* mobilized. This was Eden's fatal mistake – in which we all shared the responsibility.' Here, he alluded to President Nasser of Egypt's nationalization of the Suez Canal on 26 July 1956, following which Anglo-French forces did not invade Egypt until 5 November. Moreover, 'President K did not bluster – but everyone knew that (if no other solution was found) there w[oul]d be an invasion. He played the *United Nations* admirably.'

Much later, Macmillan eulogized JFK as 'always ready to listen to advice, generous in giving weight to opinions, however diverse ... he had the supreme quality, shared by only very great men, of refusing to evade or cushion his final responsibility'. Though all that was true, the transcripts of British exchanges with the White House, read together with Macmillan's diary, make plain his unease that the Americans might overreach themselves. The mood music in Europe was much influenced by exasperation – muted on the part of governments, vocal on the part of demonstrators – that Cuba had dragged the world to the brink of extinction, when few non-Americans sympathized with the US obsession with the island, as they viewed it.

Nonetheless in January 1963 British communist journalist and nuclear disarmer Philip Toynbee published a frank *mea culpa* about the naïveté of himself and his kind. At the outset of the Crisis, he said, 'I believed the blockade was a monstrous and cold-blooded [American] election stunt; that there were no Russian missiles on Cuba and that the physical invasion of Cuba was the next step in this wicked US plot.' Later he recognized that JFK had told 'the literal truth' and 'I was forced to make an immediate volte-face'. This seems an important and enduring point. In the wake of the Missile Crisis, support for Britain's Campaign for Nuclear Disarmament declined steeply. After years in which more than a few Europeans, especially those on the left, perceived a moral equivalence between the superpowers, there was thereafter a growing understanding that the Soviet Union bore a lion's share of rightful blame, for having dragged the world to the brink. The United States was guilty of its own share of Cold War deceits, and its global credibility would again suffer grievously in the Vietnam era. In October 1962, however, John F. Kennedy was able to wield truth as a potent weapon in his own and his country's cause, while the revelation of Nikita Khrushchev's lies contributed critically to his defeat.

The Soviet leader's silences proved equally dangerous. Following Kennedy's 22 October broadcast, Khrushchev almost immediately elected not to risk war, yet was too proud and stubborn to adopt the only responsible course – that of signalling this decision to the US administration privately, if not at once publicly. Instead, he allowed uncertainty to persist in the White House through five days that followed, with consequences that could have been disastrous.

Harold Macmillan wrote in his diary on 4 November: 'This *has* been a battle, in which everything was at stake.' He identified a tension in his own mind between 'the frightful desire to *do* something' and '… the knowledge that *not* to do anything (except talk to the President and keep Europe and the Commonwealth calm and firm) was probably the right answer.' Here Macmillan touched upon a significant point about both the October Crisis and foreign policy-making generally. While his own country lacked the power to undertake any initiative that could influence the main event, Excom in Washington suffered spasms of impatience for the US to embark upon violent action. The president's foremost manifestation of wisdom was that he did not succumb to this impulse, while adopting conspicuous measures to alert his adversary to America's military preparedness to fight.

Operation Anadyr failed in the attempt to reconfigure the Soviet Union's nuclear posture – to reinforce the strategic threat which it might present to the United States. Khrushchev and, almost equally culpably, his defence minister Rodion Malinovsky, utterly failed to think through the consequences and implications of launching a forward deployment of Soviet forces and nuclear weapons in a region where the US possessed unchallengeable dominance. Anadyr was successful, however, in the secondary purpose of securing the Cuban Revolution. This caused British Labour's Harold Wilson to claim that the outcome of the Crisis was 'just what Khrushchev had intended it to be'. The Soviet leader said on 30 October, speaking to Czech communist chief Antonín Novotný as he strove to restore his battered authority amid the anger of much of the Presidium: 'Who won? I am of the opinion that we won. One must start from the final aims we set ourselves. What aim did the Americans have? To attack Cuba and get rid of the Cuban Republic, to establish a reactionary regime. Things did not work out as they planned ... We wrenched the promise out of the Americans that they would not attack Cuba and that other countries on the American continent would also refrain from attacking Cuba. That would not have happened without our missiles in Cuba. The USA would have attacked ... The whole world now sees us as the ones who saved peace. I now appear ... as a lamb. That is not bad either. The pacifist [Bertrand] Russell writes me thank-you letters. I, of course, have nothing in common with him, except that we both want peace.'

Khrushchev wrote in his memoirs: 'A number of years have passed and we can be grateful that the revolutionary government of Fidel Castro still lives and grows. So far the United States has abided by its promise not to interfere in Cuba.' It is an anomaly of history that the Cuban leader, incomparably the smallest and least admirable of the three men who dominated the missile saga, prospered for decades the longest, having become its big winner. The Cuban people proved thus its big losers, because they remained victims of Fidel's disastrous economic and brutal repressive policies. To this day they enjoy the freedom from American suzerainty for which they yearned, but at the figurative as well as sometimes actual cost of empty larders and crumbling townscapes. Castro also exploited his inviolability to become one of the foremost exporters of socialist revolution, albeit with little success.* Meanwhile the non-invasion pledge saved America from itself, by ensuring that subsequent Washington administrations, though exasperated by Cuban intransigence, remained debarred from undertaking a military intervention, which could never have wrought happy consequences for either Castro's people or John F. Kennedy's.

SAC's Gen. Power said sourly as the Crisis wound down: 'Now, I don't think that this means [Khrushchev] has decided to become a peaceful citizen of this world and abandon his plans for world domination.' The Cold War did not end in November 1962. However, despite Power's enduring paranoia, East-West relations somewhat improved. 'After the crisis,' said Troyanovsky, 'Khrushchev's attitude towards East-West relations underwent a marked change. His pugnacious behaviour during the Berlin crisis and the U-2 incident faded into the background ... Gone was his condescending attitude towards the American president. He no

---

* In 1976 the author, reporting on the civil war in Angola for BBC TV's *Panorama*, interviewed four Cuban prisoners held by the UNITA guerrilla movement at a prison in Silvaporto. Castro's unhappy conscript 'freedom-fighters', among the 36,000-strong contingent he committed to aid the communist regime, seemed to have scant notion of why they were in Africa. Ever since we left them, I have harboured doubts that they enjoyed long and happy lives thereafter.

longer had doubts about Kennedy's statesmanlike qualities or his ability to take the right decisions. Gone too was the suspicion that the President could be or was manipulated by the so-called forces of reaction.' On 29 November 1962 Anastas Mikoyan stopped in Washington en route home from Havana, and spent three and a half hours in talks at the White House with Kennedy, almost exclusively about Cuba. If the discussions were tense, the outcome was conciliatory. Following the events of October, in the course of the Cold War neither side again initiated a direct challenge to the other, in their respective acknowledged spheres of influence.

As all the participants knew would happen, Soviet nuclear missile-armed submarines, of which primitive examples had been operational since 1955, were soon routinely stationed within range of the continental United States, posing a threat far greater than any weapons deployed in Cuba, and no more vulnerable to Washington protests than were the US Navy's Polaris-equipped counterparts to the anger of the Kremlin about their presence within range of Russian shores. This emphasized the symbolic, rather than genuine strategic nature of the East-West confrontation about the Cuban missiles. Likewise, mutual American and Russian space satellite surveillance soon rendered redundant such camera platforms as the U-2 aircraft.

Harold Macmillan, like other European leaders, continued to be haunted by the vulnerability of Berlin: '[The US] can take Cuba. The enemy can only reply by all-out nuclear war. But this applies to Berlin. The Russians can take Berlin by conventional means. The Allies *cannot defend* or *re-capture* it by any conventional means (the conclusion to be drawn is rather sinister).' He meant, of course, that any armed clash about an objective deemed vital by one side or the other was almost bound to go nuclear. It remained the case until the end of the Cold War that NATO forces would have been obliged to resort to the use of tactical nuclear weapons to enjoy any realistic prospect of repelling a Warsaw Pact offensive in Europe.

In the House of Commons the Tory government's critics, headed by Labour's Gaitskell and Wilson, portrayed the Crisis as having unfolded not merely without Washington consulting London, but in a manner which indicated that the British were treated with contempt. Charges were hurled about the collapse of the vaunted, albeit always largely illusory, 'special relationship'. Macmillan privately lamented that the taped conversations between himself and Kennedy could not be made public to silence such critics. He wrote: 'Our secrets were almost too well kept ... We are doing something to let the truth be known through judicious leaks [prompting published news stories, asserting that the president had consulted daily (sic) with the prime minister] ... The British people must not feel themselves slighted.' Yet Lawrence Freedman in his history of nuclear strategy characterizes as 'minimal ... the consultation Britain enjoyed' during the Crisis. The essential point is that Kennedy confided in Macmillan more than in any other US ally about what he intended – but only after his big decisions were made. The prime minister exercised scant influence upon American courses of action. The most he could justly claim was that he banked goodwill with the US president through his public expressions of support.

He cashed this at the bilateral Anglo-American summit on Nassau in December 1962. Against the better judgement of Kennedy and the absolute opposition of Robert McNamara, the prime minister pulled off the diplomatic coup of his life by persuading the Americans to sell to Britain Polaris submarine-launched nuclear missiles, following cancellation of the US Skybolt air-launched weapon which had been intended to become the British deterrent. The old 'actor-manager', as half-cynical, half-admiring colleagues characterized Macmillan, staged a display of histrionics, addressing Kennedy 'about the great losses and the great struggles for freedom', in the words of his private secretary Philip de Zulueta, and showcasing Britain as 'a resolute and determined ally, who was going to stand firm, and that it was very unreasonable for the United States not to assist her to do so ... And there wasn't a dry eye in the house.' The French considered that the Polaris deal committed Britain to such close linkage with, and shameless dependence upon, the US that they perceived Macmillan as having forfeited his country's freedom of action, and thus its claims to join the European Common Market. The Nassau outcome made a major contribution to de Gaulle's decision to inflict upon Macmillan the humiliation of vetoing Britain's application for membership, belatedly accepted only in 1972.

After the Crisis the CIA received a surge of refugee reports, headlined in some American newspapers, alleging that the Soviets had secreted nuclear missiles in Cuban caves. On 5 February 1963, the Kennedy administration felt obliged to order John McCone to reassure the American people by issuing a statement, declaring that the US National Intelligence Board was 'convinced beyond reasonable doubt' that all offensive weapons had been removed from Cuba.

Less than two years later, Khrushchev was ousted from the leadership of the Soviet Union in an October 1964 Kremlin coup. His comrades of the Presidium, notably including Marshal Malinovsky, vented the spleen, frustration and resentment they had nursed since Anadyr, about the humiliation which they saw the first secretary as having inflicted upon their country. Deputy premier Dmitry Poliansky, one of the silent men when the Cuban commitments were approved, now spoke for them all, denouncing Khrushchev: 'He insisted that our missiles be sent to Cuba. That produced a tremendous crisis, bringing the world to the verge of nuclear war, and terribly frightening himself, the organizer of so dangerous a venture. Having no other recourse, we were forced to accept all the demands and conditions of the USA, including the shameful inspection of our ships by the Americans.' Malinovsky, forgetful of his own complicity in Anadyr – possibly even enthusiasm for it – said likewise: 'Neither the Russian nor the Soviet army had ever suffered such humiliation.'

Nikita Khrushchev became more popular and respected among his own people after his ousting, as Russians saw him succeeded by ever less impressive national leaders. He died in 1971, having been permitted to spend his retirement in relative comfort, though intense bitterness of spirit.

Despite the shutdown of Operation Mongoose, America's siege of Cuba has persisted into the twenty-first century, promoted by the implacable exile community in Florida and its Republican supporters. The stand-off provided a justification for Fidel Castro to posture for the rest of his days as a warrior, often clad in military fatigues. An old revolutionary intelligence officer said later – ruefully matter-of-factly, as if stating a truth that was self-evident – 'Fidel was a megalomaniac. A lot of people don't understand that.' Both sides in the Cold War suffered from association with intractable allies. During the Vietnam conflict Moscow found its dealings with Hanoi's North Vietnamese communists almost as thankless as did Washington the relationship with its own Saigon clients. As late as the 1980s the US sought to justify its support for murderous Latin American tyrannies. But Nikita Khrushchev paid an especially and deservedly high price, for having risked so much alongside Castro.

Revolutionaries were the rock stars of 1960s radical politics. Mao Zedong in China, Ho Chi Minh in Vietnam, Fidel Castro and Che Guevara in Cuba, were foremost among those who rose to power by delivering nations from colonial servitude, an achievement that caused them to become imbued with romance. They exercised global influence, especially upon the young, by offering utopian visions, which only slowly did it become apparent that they were incapable of fulfilling, and which imposed dreadful human sacrifices. Castro was a remarkable personality, who may claim to have endowed the Cuban people with a self-respect in which defiance of the United States constituted an important element. Yet whatever the successes of revolutionaries as propagandists and liberators, the record shows that few have thereafter proved themselves capable of governing competently, or willing to do so humanely. Carlos Prío Socarrás, Batista's predecessor who ruled Cuba between 1948 and 1952, remarked in old age: 'They say I was a terrible president. That may be true. But I was the best president Cuba ever had.' His claim was possibly valid.

Russian support for Castro persisted, though the Cuban never entirely forgave Khrushchev for his perceived betrayal. Aleksandr Alekseev remained ambassador in Havana until 1968. The USSR paid up to eleven times the world price for Cuban sugar, as a means of sustaining its showcase of Caribbean communism; trade with the Soviet Union accounted for 80 per cent of Cuba's entire overseas earnings. The island, having been a prize snatched from the jaws of American hegemony, hailed as a jewel in the new Soviet empire, became an expensive embarrassment to Moscow.

More than two decades elapsed before the end of the Cold War precipitated a dramatic change of the Russian mood towards the Caribbean. Many of the same comrades who once embraced Castro tired of the island's cost. They reset the old song of the Revolution with fresh words: *'Cuba, give us back our bread!/ Cuba, take back your sugar!/ We've had enough of your hairy Fidel/ So, fuck off Cuba.'* In 1989 Castro declared void his country's treaty with the Soviet Union. Two years later Moscow withdrew its remaining troops and economic support. Russian oil deliveries to the island fell from thirteen million tons in 1989 to three million tons in 1991. Cubans entered an era of desperate economic hardship, though Castro was able to sustain his Marxist polity by the ruthless repression of dissent. His regime became numbered among the fiercest critics of Mikhail Gorbachev's new Russian Federation.

Vladimir Putin's ascent to power brought about a restoration of cordial relations between the two countries, but there has been no renewal of Soviet largesse. Early in the twenty-first century left-wing journalist and KGB informant Richard Gott wrote in a history of Cuba: 'By the bleak standards of Latin America the island has an educated and healthy population, but many Cubans are fed up with pulling themselves up by their bootstraps. Like the gaudy papier-mache fish selling at the market stalls that litter the heritage zones of Old Havana, they have their mouths wide open, gulping thirstily in anticipation of the great draughts of capital that will surely inundate the country as soon as the ancient *maximo lider* – "supreme leader" – dies. This is not an outcome that would have been expected by the revolutionary enthusiasts of yesteryear.' Yet the dominance of Cuba by descendants of the *barbudos* has persisted beyond Castro's death in November 2016, after he outlived John F. Kennedy by more than half a century and Nikita Khrushchev by little less. Fidel's eldest legitimate son Fidelito, a nuclear physicist, killed himself eighteen months later, aged sixty-eight. Raúl Castro succeeded his brother, wielding power until his retirement in 2021. The Cuban people still await their opportunity to join the twenty-first century.

When the dust of October began to settle in Washington, the Kennedys paid some scores. Robert Frost sent a congratulatory message to the president via Interior Secretary Udall: 'Great Going', but received no reply. JFK, so gracious when he wished, was unforgiving of such brutal jibes as the poet had delivered less than two months earlier, after visiting Khrushchev. The president held no further communication with Frost before the old man's death in January 1963, though he then delivered a majestic eulogy. Another victim of fallout was Georgy Bolshakov, whom the Americans had tired of. The Soviet embassy discovered that Joe Alsop and Charlie Bartlett, the Kennedys' favourite journalists, were about to publish an article which spotlighted the GRU officer's role as a back-channel to Moscow. Bolshakov rushed to the attorney-general to protest; begged him to intervene, to suppress the piece. Kennedy rebuffed the Russian: 'We believe that in the Cuban crisis we have been deceived by everybody, including you.' The Alsop/Bartlett piece duly appeared in the *Saturday Evening Post* on 8 December 1962, blowing Bolshakov's cover: he was recalled to Moscow. The same article stated that during the Missile Crisis Adlai Stevenson had 'wanted a Munich' – appeasement of the Soviets through a withdrawal of the Jupiters in Turkey. This was, of course, a travesty on several counts, driven by the Kennedy camp's unworthy malice towards their own UN ambassador.

Although the Crisis ended in November, US domestic reverberations persisted for a further six months. Many Republicans were galled that the White House had secured such spectacular political gains from its outcome. During the post-mortems, inquisitive journalists and political opponents honed in upon two issues: first, had the US made secret concessions to secure the Soviet retreat, specifically over the Jupiter missiles in Turkey? Again and again, the most senior members of the administration denied this, some because they did not know the truth, most because they were privy to the Turkish trade, but determined to deny the Republicans the formidable political weapon its exposure would offer them. Robert Kennedy, in particular, was haunted by fears that his own political career would be damaged by exposure of his secret trafficking with Dobrynin.

The second contentious issue was what became known as 'the photo gap'. How had it been possible, during the autumn of 1962, for the Soviets to deploy their ballistic missiles in Cuba, for weeks undetected by the US? As early as 31 October Hanson Baldwin, influential military correspondent of the *New York Times*, raised questions in a piece headed 'An Intelligence Gap'. David Lawrence wrote in the *Washington Star* on 6 November: 'A case of sheer negligence, if not incompetence, can be made out.' A series of congressional inquiries explored this vexed question, which the administration met with a procession of deceits. Maxwell Taylor, Robert McNamara and John McCone – in McCone's case, through gritted teeth – publicly denied that U-2 surveillance had been inhibited by political restrictions imposed by the White House and State Department. They emphasized that missions had been carried out in August and September, without acknowledging that during the latter month the most sensitive areas of western Cuba had been explicitly excluded from photo-targeting, for reasons that many non-Americans still find worthy of respect, but Republicans would assuredly not.

The CIA's internal report conducted by Jack Earman, the Agency's inspector-general, recorded: 'It took nearly a month [in reality from 10 September to 14 October] to get the coverage CIA had sought to get in a single [U-2] mission.' Clark Clifford, who would have become Kennedy's CIA director in preference to McCone had he not declined the post, wrote in his 1991 memoir *Counsel to the President* that when later investigating the 'photo gap' as a member of the President's Intelligence Board, 'we were faced with a dilemma. We did not wish to criticize the president, who had handled the crisis brilliantly once the Soviet missiles had been positively identified by American intelligence, but we felt the length of time it had taken to discover the missiles was dangerously and inexcusably long.' The board's final report laid blame for this on the professionals, rather than where it mostly belonged – with the politicians. It accused the CIA and other agencies of lacking 'a focused sense of urgency or alarm that might well have stimulated a greater effort'. It was encouraged in this finding by its members' personal dislike of McCone, now shared by the White House.

Through the winter of 1962 and spring of 1963 sceptical journalists and politicians recognized that they were onto something, but remained uncertain exactly what. Senator Kenneth Keating, who had sounded a fire alarm about Cuban missiles back in September, returned to the charge that winter. Republican congressman Gerald Ford told his Michigan constituents that while he applauded the Kennedy administration's handling of the Missile Crisis once it broke, 'from the middle of September to the middle of October the administration had solid evidence which should have, but did not, prompt them to step up surveillance of the island'.

Richard Rovere wrote in the *New Yorker* in the early spring of 1963: 'It would have been almost impossible to believe in early November of last year that the respect and admiration the President had won ... could have almost completely disappeared by February. Yet this seems to be the case – or close to it.' Rovere considerably overstated Kennedy's fall from grace. Nonetheless, it was indisputably true that many informed Americans by then recognized that the picture of seamlessly assured White House crisis-management, which back in November dominated perceptions both in Washington and the country, had overlooked important fumbles, even if these did not deserve to alter the overall positive view of the administration's performance.

Events following the Crisis did little to diminish the Kennedys' distrust of the CIA. Bill Harvey, the Agency's drunken Miami station chief, claimed at a White House meeting that the Kennedys had been to blame for the Cuban missile deployment, causing JFK to storm out of the Cabinet Room. John McCone told an aide: 'Harvey has destroyed himself today. His usefulness has ended.' The president was further infuriated to be told that exile advance parties, landed in Cuba in expectation of a US invasion, could not be extracted. When Agency veteran Desmond Fitzgerald was appointed to succeed Harvey as head of the 'Special Affairs' staff in January 1963, he told a colleague, 'All I know is that I have to hate Castro.' He wrote soon after to his daughter: 'My first job was to convince the Administration that anyone from my firm dealing with the Cuban situation is not necessarily a Yahoo bent on disaster.' The CIA persisted with its clumsy covert attempts to secure Castro's death. On 19 June 1963 the president approved a new sabotage programme in Cuba 'to nourish a spirit of resistance and disaffection'. Assassination attempts against the island's dictator were not discontinued until 1965, and Robert McNamara's dogged, persistent denials of the reality of these did no more service to his memory than did those of Arthur Schlesinger to his own.

The president became weary of John McCone privately telling everyone who would listen that he, and only he, had called the Crisis correctly. McGeorge Bundy, write Holland and Barrett in their study of the 'photo gap', 'had long since concluded that [McCone] was selling himself on Capitol Hill as the lone figure in the Kennedy Administration who had had the courage and insight to insist in August and September that the Soviets were placing strategic missiles into Cuba'. On 4 March 1963 the Kennedy brothers discussed their difficulties with the CIA director in a phone conversation during which the president said: 'Yeah, he's a real bastard that John McCone ... Of course everybody [within the administration] is onto him now ... Everybody's saying he's a horse's ass.' The attorney-general said: 'Well, he was useful at one time', to which JFK responded, 'Yeah, but boy, it's really evaporated.' Though Kennedy kept the CIA director in his job, thereafter he had little time for him. 'You were right all along,' Kennedy told this career hawk sourly. 'For the wrong reasons.'

In justice to McCone, although his arrogance was indisputable, and a conspicuous gap opened between Robert McNamara's narrative of the administration's pre-14 October actions and that of the CIA chief, the latter preserved sufficient discretion to save the White House from an outright security scandal. Although the 'photo gap' issue rumbled on through the spring of 1963, both in Congress and the media, it never exploded in such a fashion as seriously to threaten the president's credibility.

A young reporter named Jules Witcover, writing for the Advance News Service, came closer than any other journalist to pinpointing the truth in a story published by the *Los Angeles Times* on 10 March 1963: 'Fear of another U-2 incident now appears to have been the major impediment to earlier discovery of the Soviet missile buildup in Cuba.' Witcover was entirely correct, but was then too obscure a journalist for anyone to trouble to follow his story. In May the Preparedness Investigating Sub-Committee of the Senate, last significant political inquiry into the events of the previous autumn, published its interim report, which found no evidence of an important and culpable 'photo gap', nor of post-facto deceits by the administration. It was wrong on both counts – according to the conservative belief in an absolute US right to photograph sovereign nations from their own airspace – but the sub-committee's verdict caused the story to peter out. Not until 1989 did Anatoly Dobrynin reveal, and US official sources confirm, the secret Turkish deal struck in 1962, and omitted from *Thirteen Days*, Robert Kennedy's posthumously published account of the Crisis. Ted Sorensen, who edited the book following RFK's assassination, explained that he had sought thus to protect his fallen hero's reputation.

On 16 May 1963 the Russians tied up a loose end of their own, when their executioners dispatched Col. Oleg Penkovsky – according to some reports, with extreme cruelty. Before his capture, the GRU officer had made a critical contribution to Western policy-making, by providing the US and Britain with the evidence – the ammunition – to address the October Crisis confident of absolute American nuclear superiority, and of the Soviets' understanding of their own vulnerability.

On 10 June 1963, Kennedy gave a commencement address at American University under the heading 'A Strategy for Peace', which Khrushchev privately called 'the best president's speech since Roosevelt'. Kennedy announced a moratorium on US nuclear testing, and later an outright ban on atmospheric testing, though China and France persisted with such activity. There had been an informal US-Soviet moratorium on testing since 1961, albeit interrupted in the following year, but in July 1963, Kennedy invited John McCloy to become his chief negotiator at a resumption of formal nuclear test ban talks. When McCloy begged off, Averell Harriman accepted the role. On 5 August a partial test ban treaty was signed by Britain, the Soviet Union and the US, and has been applauded ever since as a significant step towards East-West détente.

Both sides recognized that during the Crisis poor communications between Moscow and Washington had threatened the planet. Never again would such a factor be permitted to impede emergency dialogue in the fashion they did in 1962. A Pentagon-Kremlin teletype hotline was installed, which became operational early in the following year. Today replaced by a secure email link, it is constantly tested and occasionally used by national leaders. A policy decision was made to eschew a phone connection, because speech is vulnerable to misinterpretation.

Nonetheless, a further communication obstacle persisted which mere technology could not remove. Kennedy, granted the falsehoods of the Bay of Pigs, strove to speak frankly to the Kremlin, both in public and private. Khrushchev, by contrast, remained the prisoner of a lifetime of mendacity in the service of Bolshevism. He could never comfortably avow what he did, or did not, intend. The threat of nuclear annihilation had been his rhetorical weapon of choice against the West since the day he secured power. He felt unable to relinquish this, even when he understood that his conduct had driven the Americans to the brink of courses from which there might have been no turning back.

Khrushchev invites the respect due to any man who rose so high from such unpromising origins. He led a nation that suffered unimaginable loss and hardship. His conduct was far less cruel than that of Stalin, his mentor and predecessor. He made sincere, albeit ineffectual efforts towards domestic reform. But he had secured leadership of his country through a system in which authority derived from the generation of fear together with the imposition of oppression, and his style of governance reflected this. The languishing of many of his programmes at home, and consequent threat to his own authority within the Kremlin – albeit at that stage only implicit – contributed much to his adventurism abroad. His 1959 visit to the US made a lasting impact, because thereafter he was obliged to co-exist with the pain of consciousness of the relative material failure of socialism, alongside the plenty created by capitalism.

His boorishness, poverty of manners and wealth of vanity did no favours to the cause of his country abroad. Kennedy once observed, a little ruefully, that the world's expectations of Khrushchev the thug and bully were so low that it was irksome to behold the gratitude showered upon the Soviet leader whenever his conduct rose above the brutish. The United States must accept blame for some of the blunders that landmarked the Cold War. The Soviet Union and its leaders did worse things, however, and more of them.

John F. Kennedy was a profoundly different human being from Khrushchev, endowed with a grace such as the Russian premier had seldom encountered – and for which he might somewhere, perhaps, have nursed a worm of envy. Yet Kennedy's claims upon the mantle of King Arthur remain doubtful. He was a man apparently at ease as only the very rich can be at ease, because they are spared from the material concerns that dog the lives of lesser mortals. He inherited from his father a ruthlessness that was no less ugly because the world seldom saw it laid bare, together with a view of women as mere playthings, to be exploited and discarded, which is not rendered less repugnant by the fact that more than a few loved him.

While Kennedy's rhetoric emphasized the plight of less fortunate humanity, his conduct in office showed limited concern for it, until the last months. He was far more interested in becoming the foremost statesman of his time than in succouring the afflicted, either at home or abroad. His enduring, murderous grudge against Castro and Cuba diminished him, and fulfilment of domestic aspirations was crippled by his indifferent political skills. His successor Lyndon Johnson, a brilliant politician, got much more done before destroying his administration in Vietnam.

Kennedy nonetheless proved outstandingly suited to lead his country through the Missile Crisis, his finest and most courageous achievement. Among the unwisest of popular proverbs is that which holds 'Cometh the Hour, Cometh the Man'. History shows that momentous events are often managed by inadequate national leaders – think of Europe in 1914, or the world in 2022. By contrast, Kennedy's conduct of policy during the Thirteen Days makes an almost unanswerable claim for his greatness, because a lesser president might have consigned the planet to perdition. Hundreds of millions of people, both at home and abroad, understood this. In March 1963 a Pew poll showed that, whatever reservations Washington cherished about JFK, reflected in Richard Rovere's column quoted above, 74 per cent of Americans expected their president to secure re-election the following year.

When Kennedy was assassinated on 22 November, Khrushchev personally visited the US embassy in Moscow, bearing a wreath. He wrote in his memoirs that the fallen head of state was 'someone we could trust'. Perhaps so or perhaps not, but the Soviet leader certainly feared that the stunned American people might find cause to attribute to the Kremlin responsibility for his death. Something of the same apprehension seized Fidel Castro, when he beheld his own people celebrating the killing. Soviet nurse Elvira Dubinskaya, serving in Havana, saw exultant locals hurling water, eggs and bottles at the movie screen on which film reports of the Dallas horror story appeared: 'A Cuban was sitting there, and I explained to him – "This is bad! Kennedy's death is bad for you!"' Her neighbour seemed unmoved.

Castro said grimly: 'They're going to say it was us. They're going to say we did it.' Lee Harvey Oswald was an active member of the 'Fair Play for Cuba' group. Yet it remains implausible that even the *maximo lider* at his most erratic, vengeful, violent, would have dared to precipitate or to sponsor the killing of the US president. His supreme purpose was the preservation of his own power. Had the United States been able to attribute the Kennedy assassination to the man in Havana, it is overwhelmingly likely that direct action would have followed, which must have undone Castro and his

Revolution. There is no credible evidence to support the conspiracy theories that either Cuba or the USSR had any share of responsibility for the president's killing.

The November 1989 fall of the Berlin Wall was widely perceived as representing the triumph of capitalism and freedom over the forces of oppression and discredited doctrine of communism. The Soviet Union collapsed two years later with its vast armed forces and nuclear arsenal intact. John Lewis Gaddis wrote in 1997: 'It may be that the West prevailed during the Cold War ... because that conflict just happened to take place at the moment in history when the conditions that had for thousands of years favoured authoritarianism suddenly ceased to do so.'

A quarter of a century on, and especially following Vladimir Putin's murderous assault upon Ukraine, it is impossible to sustain that judgement. Lawrence Freedman wrote recently that the optimistic mood of the first post-Cold War decade appears naïve: 'A return to great power competition is now described as a defining feature of the 2020s.' Autocracies are widely ascendant, above all President Xi's China. Economic failure was the fundamental cause of the collapse of the Soviet empire. Yet one of the most remarkable and dismaying achievements, not only of the USSR but also of the Russian Federation that succeeded it, has been to exercise a baleful influence upon world affairs, from a strategic position of ever-worsening weakness. In the twenty-first century, Russia's only significant exports are oil, gas and extreme violence. Nonetheless, these have enabled President Putin to wield astonishing clout, for unflaggingly malign purposes. He exerts less trammelled personal authority than did Khrushchev in the era of the Soviet Presidium. All the while the institutions of the United States find themselves under siege from within, by forces some of which must be characterized as neo-fascist, in a fashion that America's leaders of 1962 would find incomprehensible and terrifying. The liberal order is imperilled as much by its domestic enemies as by its foreign foes.

Although this narrative has included strictures upon US policy, especially towards Cuba, no citizen of the modern West should lose sight of a fundamental reality: in the Cold War America led forces that aspired to advance human freedoms, such as the Soviet Union ideologically opposed. In politics and international affairs good and evil are always relative. All of us who inhabit democracies have cause to be grateful that the United States prevented the communist superpowers from securing victory, even if the outcome – viewed from the distance of decades – has proved to represent something less than the comprehensive triumph for freedom which visionaries hailed in 1991.

The most important fact of the struggle is that the world survived it without a nuclear catastrophe. This reflected a collective wisdom on both sides that transcended the misjudgements of both the Kremlin and the White House: the sum of their statesmanship was greater than its parts. It has been observed that both Khrushchev and Kennedy were bad at crisis avoidance, effective at crisis management. Among some of today's Western leaders and military commanders, a nostalgia is discernible, such as would have seemed unimaginable back in 1991, for that era's adversarial certainties. International order and stability are banished, perhaps forever. It does not seem merely nostalgic to suggest that Khrushchev was a more rational and measured Russian leader than is Putin.

What is happening today is not, for many reasons, a replay of the old Cold War, though it may well represent the start of a new one. Territorial dominance and influence, rather than ideology, are at stake. As Rodric Braithwaite wrote recently: 'The Soviet Union's role as the second superpower is no longer available [to Russia] ... being taken by China.' This change does not, of course, make the world a safer place. There are trigger points, led by Taiwan and the entire Russian periphery, that threaten consequences as grievous for humankind as those which beckoned sixty years ago, and are highlighted by the invasion of Ukraine. In one respect, this latest crisis is a mirror reflection of the 1962 Cuba: just as the USSR found itself hopelessly strategically wrongfooted on an island ninety miles off the North American coast, so the West faces severe difficulties in securing the future of a vulnerable state that is Russia's immediate neighbour. Understanding between the leaderships of China, Russia and the US is as remote as ever it was, and mutual sympathy seems unattainable. The scope for a catastrophic miscalculation is as great now as it was in 1914 Europe or in the 1962 Caribbean.

During the Missile Crisis, even the Kremlin's hawks recognized that in a nuclear showdown there could be only one winner – if such a word can be used even pejoratively – which would not be the USSR. This knowledge had a decisive impact on their decisions. Today, by contrast, many strategy gurus believe that China, exploiting the superiority of its hypersonic weapons, might well prevail in an air and naval collision with US forces off its own coast. Whereas in 1962 Khrushchev's nation merely masqueraded as an equal of the US, sixty years on China is close to justifying a claim upon peer status, with a GDP eight times the size of Russia's, which makes it correspondingly more dangerous.

Meanwhile Vladimir Putin's obsessive resentment, his craving for respect and willingness to take huge risks and to initiate hideous atrocities around Russia's borders in pursuit of a pan-Slav fantasy, is increased by his consciousness of China's giant progress, of America's continuing innovative technological mastery, alongside Russia's relative stagnation. Putin's view of history is skewed by a mingling of ignorance, amorality and nationalism, blended with his country's long-cherished narrative of grievance and victimhood. We should be in no doubt that the Russian invasion of Ukraine is an act of a far graver moral order than was Khrushchev's deployment in Cuba. The Soviet Union in 1962 had some sort of case for its actions. Putin in 2022 has none.

Yet we should also acknowledge a widely-held Russian belief and grievance, that for decades the Americans exploited their nuclear and conventional dominance, most conspicuously in the Missile Crisis, to frustrate Moscow's aspirations and to sustain dominance of the vast US sphere of influence. Georgy Shakhnazarov, who served Mikhail Gorbachev in the Kremlin, addressed American Excom veterans attending a 1987 historical conference: 'All of you believed yourselves in both a military and a moral position of superiority. You speak of deception, and so on. But, according to international law, we had no reason to inform you beforehand [of the Cuban deployment]. You did not inform us of your intention to put missiles in Turkey ... The conflict was political, and the moral case was unclear.' Putin is not the only modern Russian who sees hypocrisy in the West's attempts to frustrate – for instance – the Kremlin's hegemony over Ukraine. Shakhnazarov continued: 'The United States did not want to recognize others' right to equal security. It desired to keep its superiority ... According to international law both sides have equal rights to make arrangements with third parties to protect their security.'

The passage above does not represent an assertion of the smallest enthusiasm for the modern Kremlin regime – a desire to become what Germans now contemptuously call a *Putinversteher* or Putin apologist. Instead, it merely seeks to explain something of how differently the world appears, as viewed from Moscow, than from Washington or London. As we age, we learn that there is no single universal truth or logic: every culture cherishes its own narrative. In the twenty-first century, as when Shakhnazarov spoke, Americans and Russians retain contrasting perspectives on the Missile Crisis, and much else.

Walter Lippmann wrote wisely that the word appeasement has often been abused since 1938, to denounce those seeking necessary international compromises: 'You can't decide these questions of life and death for the world by epithets like appeasement. I don't agree with the people who think we have to go out and shed a little blood to prove we're virile men.' Professor Sir Michael Howard said in old age: 'Appeasement is often a very sensible policy, when you are dealing with a leader less satanic than Adolf Hitler.'

Yet it is difficult, if not impossible, to make any principled case for appeasement of Vladimir Putin, as distinct from acknowledging the practical and strategic difficulties of frustrating his ambitions. It may be impossible politically for Western troops directly to engage the Russian aggressors in Ukraine, but it is assuredly necessary to deploy NATO forces prepared to do so in the Baltic states and Poland. The dangers of a general war with Russia are real – but so also are those of passivity in the face of a grave threat to European order and security.

It has been a theme of this book that those who today dismiss the risks inherent in the Missile Crisis, because neither Kennedy nor Khrushchev wanted nuclear war, are mistaken. In 1962, the world got lucky. Our hopes for averting future catastrophe must rely upon twenty-first-century national leaders never for a moment losing sight of the magnitude of the perils posed by the weapons at their command. The risk of nuclear conflict, which at the height of the Cold War often dominated front pages, has been for decades since scarcely discussed among ordinary citizens, far more preoccupied with the threats posed by climate change, pandemics, conventional clashes and terrorism. If any fragment of good has emerged from the terrible evil of the 2022 invasion of Ukraine, it has been to awaken oversleeping Westerners to the vital importance of security, which must include powerful elements of both military capability and political will. The US administration could not have achieved a tolerable outcome of the Missile Crisis without being known in Moscow to possess the weapons to unleash overwhelming force in support of its diplomacy.

In 2022 the means still exist for humankind to destroy itself. Power to initiate a nightmare is shared among a growing number of nuclear-armed nations. In the nature of technology, checks upon the use of terrible weapons by careless or deranged subordinates are imperfect. A rightful motto for every national leader is: Be Afraid. Neither John F. Kennedy nor Nikita Sergeyevich Khrushchev was deficient in personal courage, but what distinguished them from Fidel Castro and from some military commanders on both sides of the Iron Curtain is that the two men were prudently haunted by consequences. Winston Churchill said, in his last major speech to Britain's House of Commons on 1 March 1955: 'It may well be that by a process of sublime irony we have reached a state in this world where safety is the sturdy child of terror and survival the twin brother of annihilation.'

Such is the optimistic view. Yet even so dauntless a statesman as Churchill could not fail to be troubled by the rise of authoritarian adventurers whose most conspicuous characteristic is an appetite for both oppression and aggression. This is shared by President Xi,

President Putin and North Korea's Kim Jong-Un. All consider themselves shielded from consequences of their most extravagant actions by a stage-set façade of electoral legitimacy, together with possession of nuclear weapons. Yet, beyond constructively confronting climate change, our planet's best hope of surviving the twenty-first century relies upon an imperative: that no national leader shows themself deficient in the fear which must lie at the heart of wisdom, and which was indispensable to a peaceful resolution of the Cuban Missile Crisis.

Acknowledgements

This book was the brainchild of my formidable agent Andrew Wylie, to whom I am happy to pay my first debt of gratitude, followed by thanks due now – as for so many years – to the wonderful HarperCollins team in London, foremost among them Charlie Redmayne, Arabella Pike and Helen Ellis, together with Jonathan Jao at HarperCollins in New York. Iain Hunt has proved an exemplary copy editor, who has meticulously corrected my text, not least by addressing my besetting weakness for tautology.

The Covid pandemic created unprecedented and persisting difficulties for scholars and researchers all over the world, with the closure of many archives, together with the difficulty and indeed, for long periods, impossibility of international travel. Britain's National Archives have been almost inaccessible for most of the past two years, and I was obliged to cancel my planned programme of travel in both the US and Cuba. Thus I have been more dependent than for any previous book which I have researched upon earlier published works and online sources. In America George Cully made an invaluable contribution, by scouring to great effect the USAF Historical Archive at Montgomery, AL. Margaret MacMillan flagged for me a host of links to material in the Wilson Center's Cold War International History Project, and I have also profited immensely from sources available online through US National Security Archive, the CIA historical website, and the Miller Center, Virginia.

I have quoted several messages and documents held in the US Navy's Historical Archive that I hoped to revisit myself, but this time around have instead been obliged to copy from Michael Dobbs's excellent *One Minute to Midnight*. Michael has given me further invaluable assistance with maps and images, and by putting me in touch with Svetlana Savranskaya of George Washington University, who knows probably more than anyone about the activities of Soviet submarines in the Crisis, and kindly checked my account of their stories.

For British material I should express special appreciation to Peter Hennessy's book *Winds of Change: Britain in the Early Sixties*, published in 2019. Meanwhile aviation specialist Chris Pocock is a mine of information about the U-2 programme: he has kindly corrected and criticized the passages of my book addressing the plane's extraordinary role in the Crisis. Ian Ballantyne gave advice about submarines, derived from research for his own important books. Sir Rodric Braithwaite, a distinguished historian of the Cold War as well as a former British ambassador in Moscow, has read and commented upon my text.

Several other kind friends, notably Margaret MacMillan and George Walden, have done likewise. I am especially grateful to Fred Logevall, in the midst of his magisterial JFK biography of which the first volume has been universally acclaimed, for finding time to offer some important criticisms and corrections of my passages on the president, which I am only relieved to have been able to address before this book was published, and not afterwards. At least as important is the contribution of Jim Hershberg, Professor of History and International Affairs at George Washington University, who has been studying and writing on the Missile Crisis for decades. His detailed comments and corrections have been invaluable. Sheldon Stern, for twenty-two years resident historian at the John F. Kennedy Library, likewise scanned my narrative and made suggestions almost all of which I have acted upon. My debt to the generosity and wisdom of these distinguished scholars is immense, but of course they bear no responsibility for either my persistent errors or my judgements.

The London Library has made its usual wonderful contribution to my work, and before the 2019 death of my dear friend Professor

Sir Michael Howard, OM, CH, MC, I was able to borrow importantly from his shelves and files. My secretary Rachel Lawrence remains indispensable to my work, as she has been for most of the past thirty-five years. Her role is surpassed only by that of my wife Penny, who likes to say that it is fortunate that I can write and talk a bit, because my other talents are – how shall we say? – finite.

Notes and References

In the narrative above, in accordance with my usual practice I have not given explicit attributions for quotations from major players that have been long in the public domain. All quotes of words spoken inside the White House, unless otherwise sourced, derive from the 2001 edition of the May-Zelikow transcripts published as *The Kennedy Tapes*, though I have checked wording against Sheldon Stern's profusely detailed catalogue of errors. UKNA below signifies material from the National Archives in Britain. Interviews in Cuba for this book were carried out by Alexander Correa Iglesias, and with former Soviet armed forces personnel in Ukraine, by Oleksii Ivashyn, to whom I want to express a special debt of gratitude in these days when he is fighting for his country. Russian material has been translated for me by Dr Lyuba Vinogradova, unless otherwise attributed; she also conducted the quoted interviews inside Russia.

Introduction

xviii 'That was horrifying' Tamayo, Juan 'Secret Nukes: The Untold Story of the Cuban Missile Crisis' *Miami Herald* 13.10.2012 and Don Oberdorfer 'Cuban Missile Crisis More Volatile Than Thought' *Washington Post* 14.1.1992

xix 'Ken, you will never know' Galbraith, J.K. *Name-Dropping: From FDR On* Houghton Mifflin 1999, p.105

xx 'Nuclear weapons … had a remarkably *theatrical*' Gaddis, John Lewis *We Now Know: Rethinking Cold War History* Oxford 1997 p.258

xxii 'The historian Peter Hennessy' Hennessy, Peter *Winds of Change: Britain in the Early Sixties* Penguin 2019 p.318

xxii 'You know, if there's one of these four-minute warnings' anecdote from W/Cdr Graham Perry, RAF retd.

xxiv 'Meanwhile others felt' Information from Sheldon Stern 10.3.22 who wrote
      to the author: 'It is supremely ironic that when the announcement was
      made in 1973, after the Butterfield testimony at the Watergate hearings,
      that the Kennedy Library did have secret tapes, Rusk called the director of
      the Library to express his outrage at being taped without his knowledge. By
      sheer chance I was chatting with the director when Rusk called and he put
      his hand over the receiver and whispered, "It's Rusk and he's bullshit
      [furious] about the tapes." Too bad he did not live to see that the tapes
      were his *deus ex machina*.'

Prologue: Operation Zapata 17–19 April 1961

   4 'OK, Artime, you are our friend' Johnson, Haynes *The Bay of Pigs*
      Hutchinson 1965 p.27
   4 'They said there was going to be an invasion' ibid. p.50
   5 'We must attempt to strengthen' ibid. p.49
   6 'My philosophy … was that the ends justified the means' Thomas, Evan
      The Very Best Men: The Daring Early Years of the CIA Simon & Schuster
      1995 p.340
   7 'Arthur, standard-bearer for the memory' Schlesinger, Arthur *Robert F.
      Kennedy and His Times* Andre Deutsch 1978 pp.490–3
   7 'We all felt that the Castro regime' Joseph, Peter *Good Times: An Oral
      History of America in the Nineteen Sixties* Morrow 1974 p.12
   7 'There can be no long-term living' Schlesinger *RFK* p.473
   8 'The elimination of Castro' Schlesinger, Arthur *A Thousand Days* Andre
      Deutsch 1965 p.160
   8 'we all listened transfixed' ibid. p.218
   8 'The people of Cuba' ibid. p.222
   8 'The historian discussed with the president' ibid. p.223
   9 'an enormous confidence in his own luck' ibid. p.234
  11 'Most of the Cubans were there' Johnson p.76
  11 'It was a great spectacle' ibid. p.77
  12 'The operation didn't go deep' Taylor Committee *Operation Zapata*
      University Publications of America 1981 p.339
  12 'blew up the detail' ibid. p.96
  13 'only served to make Castro angry' ibid. p.119
  14 'We were in the middle of a class' Ferrara interview 21.9.20
  15 'wasted their ammunition in excessive firing' *Operation Zapata* p.37
  15 'The effectiveness of the Castro military forces' ibid. p.41
  15 'When the going got tough' ibid. p.123
  16 'There is evidence that the president' Hershberg, James *Saving the Bay of
      Pigs Prisoners* National Security Archive Electronic Briefing Book #759,
      29.4.21
  17 'I don't understand Kennedy' Khrushchev, Sergei *Nikita Khrushchev and
      the Creation of a Superpower* Pennsylvania State University Press 2000
      p.436
  18 'None of you will come back' Johnson p.230
  18 'Harvard's dissidents took the Kennedy administration' Gitlin, Todd *The
      Sixties: Years of Hope, Days of Rage* Bantam 1993 p.90

18 'I underestimated the cost of failure' Joseph p.12
19 'shoestring operation run by amateurs' Barrett, David 'The Bay of Pigs Fiasco and the Kennedy Administration's Off-the-Record Briefings for Journalists' *Journal of Cold War Studies* Spring 2019 pp.3–26, p.14
20 'probably some countries can't be saved' ibid. p.20
20 'seized the lead in Cuban policy' Schlesinger *RFK* p.505
20 'The time has come for a showdown' RFK memorandum to JFK 19.4.61, *Foreign Relations of the United States* 1961–63 10:304
20 'Che Guevara met in Uruguay' Bird, Kai *The Color of Truth: McGeorge Bundy and William Bundy: Brothers in Arms* Touchstone 1998 p.201
21 'The president sometimes expressed regret' Schlesinger *RFK* p.452
21 'but Britain and France' Schlesinger *A Thousand Days* p.260
21 'He better not publish that memorandum' ibid. p.262

1: *Cuba Libre*

1 THE AMERICAN COLONY

23 'I felt as if I had sailed with Captain Silver' Churchill, Winston *My Early Life* 1930 p.91
24 'as the advance guard of civilization' Kagan, Robert *Dangerous Nation* Knopf 2006 p.416
25 'The host who had sold Elvis to middle America' Perrotet, Tony *Cubra Libre!* Blue Rider Press 2019 pp.3–4
27 'We are responsible for keeping order' Hansen, Jonathan *Young Castro: The Making of a Revolutionary* Simon & Schuster 2019 p.348
28 'When you finished at Ruston' Yepe interview 4.8.20
28 'it was where all the rancid bourgeoisie' Nuñez interview 24.10.20
29 '*Te la voy a pelar, Americano!*' Hansen p.129
32 'It was not that a majority of Cubans' Ferrer, Ada *Cuba: An American History* Simon & Schuster 2021 p.280
32 'Naty, what a formidable school this prison is!' Hansen p.215
34 'but we must be with it' Johnson p.71
34 'Cuba's previous president, Carlos Prío Socarrás' Ferrer p.310

2 *GRANMA*

36 'a continent with imperfect self-control' Fleming, Peter *Brazilian Adventure* World Books 1940 p.53
39 'I hate Soviet imperialism' Hansen p.345

3 THE LIBERATOR

46 'We began to be afraid of what to do' *Cuba Libre* TV documentary series 2020, Rodríguez Menier
46 'the revolution became heavy-handed' Ferrara interview 21.9.20
46 'Americans of every kind' Yepe interview 19.8.20
47 'Most of us did not know what socialism was' *Cuba Libre* documentary series 2020
48 'I don't know if I'm interested in the Revolution' Perrotet p.333
48 'They saw in him, I think, the hipster' Schlesinger *A Thousand Days* p.199

48 'either incredibly naïve about Communism' Ambrose, Stephen *Nixon: Vol. 1: The Education of a Politician 1913–62* Simon & Schuster 1987 p.516
49 'Don't talk about Tomasito' Gomez interview Sept. 2020
49 'My father was a gourmet' Nuñez interview 5.10.20
50 'María Regueiro's impeccably middle-class father' Mallo interview 19.10.20
50 *'Después del triunfo'* DePalma, Anthony *The Cubans* Bodley Head 2020 p.6
50 'He gave Cuba a sense of worth' Valido interview 17.6.20
50 'Without the Revolution that would have been impossible' Gomez interview Sept. 2020
50 'I don't know what communism is' Melo interview 22.4.20
51 'Damn you, Fidel, you're a real tight-wad!' ibid.
51 'a great politician, a great statesman' Ferrara interview 21.9.20
51 'I have a lot to thank the Revolution for' Valido interview 17.6.20
52 'We relied for the country's defence' Lara interview 21.8.20
52 'Cuba's economic weakness' Fursenko interview Alekseev 1994 & Alekseev cable to Center 7.2.60 File 78825 pp.108–12 SVR
52 'Because he has the power to lead' Ambrose p.516
52 'thorough consideration' Church Committee Interim Report 94 Congress, I Sess 1975, 92
55 'sewed for the street' Margarita Ríos Alducín interview 23.6.20
56 'It was hard. When we returned' Gomez interview Sept. 2020
56 'There was mistrust if you were a revolutionary' Alfonso interview
56 'many Cubans who might otherwise' Macmillan, 25 July 1960, in *Foreign Relations of the United States* 1958–1960 6:1033
57 'The troubles of the poor are always the same' Alducín interview 23.6.20
57 'Avoiding Adventures' *Spectator* 19.10.62

2: Mother Russia

1 TRIUMPH IN SPACE, HUNGER ON EARTH

59 'find us reduced to Fortress America' Kissinger, Henry *The Necessity for Choice* Harper & Row 1960 p.1
59 'It lays bare the rickety, rackety' Walker, Stephen *Beyond: The Astonishing Story of the First Human to Leave Our Planet* William Collins 2021
59 'The general in charge of the arsenal' Braithwaite, Rodric *Armageddon and Paranoia: The Nuclear Confrontation* Profile 2017 p.238
60 'We do not answer political questions' information from George Walden
60 'Khrushchev is right to say' https://prozhito.org/person/1646.Shelest 2.11.62
60 'My neighbours fought so much' Chirakhov interview 24.8.20
60 'She was fascinated to learn' Mikhlova interview Feb. 2021
62 'A goat now equals a cow!' https://prozhito.org/person/1646 Saveliev 7.7.62
62 'While there is more or less enough black bread' ibid. 9.10.62
63 'Illiterate *muzhiks* ploughing fields' https://prozhito.org/person/1646 Seleznev diary 1962
64 'going through a period' Dobrynin, Anatoly *In Confidence* Times Books 1995 p.25

64 'The fifties were a time of hope' Artemieva, Galina *Memuary schastlivoi zhenshchiny* (*Memoirs of a Happy Woman*) p.186

65 'Life seemed good' Valery Galenkov interview March 2021

66 'We could not compare our country' ibid.

66 'We knew absolutely nothing' Kosykh interview March 2021

66 'Although the cause of the tragedy has never been acknowledged' Kasatkin, Vasiliy (17 April 2008). 'Dangerous Sky (in Russian: Опасное небо)'. Krasnoyarskiy Rabochiy (in Russian: Красноярский рабочий)

67 'Some paid with their lives' Alexeyeva, L. & Chalidze, V. *Mass Unrest in the USSR* US Department of Defense 1985

67 'Life is better now' https://prozhito.org/person/1646 Vronsky diary 16.6.61

67 'Galina Artemieva's aunt Anya' Artemieva p.202

67 'Comrades! How much longer' Hornsby, Robert *Protest, Reform and Repression in Khrushchev's Soviet Union* Cambridge 2013 p.156

67 'A few months earlier Nina Barbachuk' ibid. p.167

67 'approving of life in the U.S.' ibid. p.49

68 'Bread was brought to the village' *Menya okruzhayut stoletia* (*Centuries Surround Me*) Moscow 2017 p.263

69 'I realized that the workers' demands' Mikoyan, Anastas *Tak bylo* (*That's How It Was*) Vagrius 1999 p.658

69 'which he received from Khrushchev' ibid. p.659

69 'they did not tear down portraits' Baron, S. *Bloody Saturday* Stanford University Press 2001 p.37

69 'The disillusionment and dissatisfaction' in Taubman, William & Khrushchev, Sergei & Gleason, Abbott eds *Nikita Khrushchev* Yale 2000 p.6

69 'was racked by guilt' Sergei Khrushchev p.501

70 'The workers kicked up a row' ibid. p.495

70 'ready for war tomorrow' https://prozhito.org/person/1646 Nazirov diary 6.11.62

2 'THE SHARK'

71 'The victors are above judgement!' Nekrasov quoted Zubok, Vladislav *A Failed Empire: The Soviet Union in the Cold War* University of North Carolina 2007 p.4

71 'One of the most popular held that' see Nancy Condee in Taubman & others p.179

71 'Why was all this published?' ibid. p.185

72 'The country was ruled for so long' ibid. p.199

72 'We were hushed by the solemnity' Artemieva p.210

72 'There is no limit to Khrushchev's adventurism' see Nancy Condee in Taubman & others p.205

74 'Khrushchev assisted in the arrest' Taubman, William *Khrushchev: The Man and His Era* Free Press 2003 p.98

74 'because they had put everybody else' Mikoyan p.659

74 'Those who survived' Hayter, William *Russia and the World* Secker & Warburg 1970 p.28

74 'He was transported and bewitched' in Taubman & others p.87
77 'The paradox or, conversely, the logic' ibid. p.65
77 'Stalin is nowadays branded almost a criminal' https://prozhito.org/person/1646 Seleznev diary 11.11.61
77 'He went through battles together with our people' Taubman & others p.37
77 'It's not a face he's got ...' Artemieva p.198
78 'He's either all the way up' Taubman p.xxx
78 'What do you think Mexico is?' ibid. p.243
78 'Neither man had any common language' Dobrynin p.34
78 'He was a real rough diamond' Mikoyan p.645
80 'blended pragmatism and communist idealism' Sergei Khrushchev in Taubman & others p.242
82 'It was trying to fly' Sakharov, Andrei *Memoirs* Knopf 1990 p.175
82 'In spite of all the talk about disarmament' https://prozhito.org/person/1646 Seleznev 19.12.60

3 KHRUSHCHEV ABROAD

84 'Nikita Khrushchev was the driving force' Troyanovsky in his contribution to Taubman & others p.210
84 'In the 21st century, it is easy to forget' private conversation with the author 2013
85 'main street Americans' Zubok p.131
85 'There are insistent rumours' https://prozhito.org/person/1646 Kamanin diary 9.2.62
86 'We lived all the time' Kendall, Bridget *The Cold War: A New Oral History* BBC 2017 pp.236–7
86 'determined not only to seem fearless' Taubman p.332
86 'Father was extraordinarily proud' Sergei Khrushchev p.211
87 'a man who is insecure' Taubman p.408
88 '*I* see US missiles in Turkey' Gaddis *We Now Know* p.264
88 'atomic blackmail against the USSR' Khariton quoted Zubok p.27
89 'Joke with him, urged the veteran' Isaacson, Walter & Thomas, Evan *The Wise Men* Faber 1986 p.608
90 'Khrushchev launched a diatribe' UKNA FO371/160546
90 'Nobody in Moscow dared to tell him' Sergei Khrushchev p.329
91 'What sort of camp is it?' ibid. p.327
91 'One sometimes felt embarrassed' Lyubimov interview 25.i.21
91 'Newspapers are full of Khrushchev' https://prozhito.org/person/1646 Nazirov 20.9.59
92 'Michael Howard described his own first visit' Howard, Michael *Captain Professor* Continuum 2006 p.169
92 'a *military* capital' Howard, Michael *Liberation or Catastrophe*, Hambledon Continuum 2007 pp.100–1
93 'I was no longer in full control' Taubman p.447
93 'It was his [Khrushchev's] fault' Mikoyan p.654
95 'What a situation!' Troyanovsky in his contribution to Taubman & others p. 226
96 'Oh, you missed so much!' ibid. p.229

97 'probably had the world's lowest expectations' Heren, Louis *Growing Up on The Times* Hamish Hamilton 1978 p.226
97 'an instance in which our political posture' Beschloss, Michael *Mayday: Eisenhower, Khrushchev and the U-2 Affair* Faber 1986 pp.162–3
98 'Berlin threatened a war' Schlesinger *A Thousand Days* p.353
98 'The situation is tense' information from George Walden

3: *Yanquis, Amerikantsy*

1 AMERICAN PIE

99 'Capitalism works' Galbraith, J.K. *The Affluent Society* Houghton Mifflin 1958 p.103
99 'The success of capitalism has created' Joseph p.65
100 'Taking all things together' Anderson, Terry *The Sixties* Texas A & M 1999 p.9
100 'that great race for membership' Joseph p.xxvii
100 'We talk about ourselves' Chafe, William H. *America since World War II* OUP 1986 p.112
101 'I believed that Castro and Khrushchev' Kendall p.240
101 'Whatever first there was' Joseph p.75
101 'which for over forty years' Twining, Nathan E. *Neither Liberty Nor Safety: A Hard Look at US Military Policy & Strategy* Holt, Rinehart & Winston 1966 p.56
101 'anti-nuclear intellectuals' ibid. p.65
102 'Kennedy has chosen to identify himself' quoted Schlesinger *A Thousand Days* p.431
102 'I am the first American who is practising peaceful' Dobrynin p.62
103 '1950s extended: students were very concerned' Brokaw, Tom *Boom! Talking about the Sixties* Random House 2007 p.218
103 'The whole image of the Administration' Chafe p.189
104 'I thought President Dwight Eisenhower' Gitlin p.1
105 'Every time you pass civil rights legislation' Joseph p.127
105 'We will wear you down' *Washington Post* 2.1.60
106 'It is in the American tradition' Anderson p.22

2 JACK

108 'George Ball once observed' Hodgson, Godfrey *In Our Time: America from World War II to Nixon* Macmillan 1976 p.119
108 'a quiet, agreeable man' Schlesinger *A Thousand Days* p.150
108 'He brings me solutions' Thatcher said this of David Young, later Lord Young of Graffham. Most of his 'solutions', like those of most snakeoil salesmen, turned out to be illusory
109 'They [the administration] certainly were not great believers' USAF Oral History Smith K239.0512-2040
110 'it soon became evident' USAF Oral History Breitweiser K239.0512-877
110 'The president discussed with Philip Graham' Schlesinger *RFK* p.441
111 'He was a little bastard' Dobbs, Michael *One Minute to Midnight* Hutchinson 2008 p.10

111 'If Harvard produced generals' Halberstam, David *The Best and the Brightest* Random House 1972 p.40

113 'He was on fire' Joseph p.54

113 'In all men who lead multitudes' to Arthur Vandenberg in 1951 Steel, Ronald *Walter Lippmann and the American Century* Routledge 1980 p.519

114 'The face was more lined' Schlesinger *A Thousand Days* p.575

114 'He seemed very little changed' White, Theodore *The Making of the President 1960* Pocket Books 1961 p.451

115 'All at once you had something' Joseph p.3

116 'almost British in his style' Halberstam p.96

116 'It is not true that suffering' Maugham, Somerset *The Moon and Sixpence* p.64. JFK himself misquoted these lines, but their meaning was the same

116 'Yet if this struck a chord' Schlesinger *A Thousand Days* p.88

116 'Walter Lippmann was among liberal critics' Steel p.543

116 'When a wartime comrade' Logevall, Fredrik *JFK: Coming of Age in the American Century 1917–56* Viking 2020 p.231

117 'There was a spontaneity' Joseph pp.7–8

118 'Indians firing occasional arrows' Halberstam p.77

118 'it's about time somebody got the son-of-a-bitch' Brokaw p.10

3 NUKES

119 'We live in an age of nuclear giants' quoted in article by Daniel Ellsberg 5.8.2009 on www.Truthdig.com

119 'a nuclear war would not arise' Allison, G.T., Carnesale, A. & Nye, J.S. eds *Hawks, Doves and Owls: An Agenda for Avoiding Nuclear War* Norton 1985 p.210

119 'Nor, for that matter, Nikita Khrushchev' Dallek, Robert *John F. Kennedy: An Unfinished Life* Little, Brown 2003 p.505

121 'There is no evidence that the Russians' Braithwaite p.179

121 'While the Unthinkable file today' UKNA CAB120/691

121 'The principal fault of the process' Garthoff, Raymond *Assessing the Adversary* Washington 1991 p.51

122 'By all but a tiny number of experts' Howard *Captain Professor* p.167

122 'not long, they reckoned' ibid. p.172

122 'His basic assumption, common to so many' ibid. p.173

122 'whom I found to be deeply humane' ibid. p.175

123 'just as frightened of the West' ibid. p.178

123 'The Americans were politely uninterested' ibid. p.178

123 'there were madmen on both sides' Hennessy p.290

123 'urged President Eisenhower to deploy' James Hagerty diary 27.7.54 quoted Gaddis *We Now Know* p.227

123 'might well feel their policies' UKNA CAB158/29 JIC (57) 62

124 'When all these questions' Dobrynin p.45

125 'was committed to the peace' ibid. p.36

125 'Roughest thing in my life' Reston, James *Deadline: A Memoir* Random House 1991 pp.290–1

125 'The President seemed rather stunned' ibid.

127 'A month later, according to his own account' Taubman p.505
127 'This is a way out of [Khrushchev's] predicament' Dallek p.426
127 'The Americans have got very excited' unpublished Macmillan diary entry, quoted Hennessy p.237
128 'We are the masters of Berlin' https://prozhito.org/person/1646 Obaturov 8.2.63
128 'He had to hammer away' Taubman p.538
129 'could not read our intentions' quoted by James Wood Forsyth in *Strategic Studies Quarterly* New York 1995 p.307
129 'in a nuclear war there will be no winner' Wardak, G.D., Turbiville, G.H. & Garthoff, R.L. *The Voroshilov Lectures* Washington 1989 p.72
129 'American grand strategy' Braithwaite p.160
131 'I agree the following' UKNA CAB21/6081
131 'In a final touch of satire' UKNA PREM11/5223

4: The Red Gambit: Operation Anadyr

135 'Then we'll try something else' Sergei Khrushchev p.305
137 'You Americans must realize' quoted Gaddis *We Now Know* p.181
137 'Fidel was entirely correct' Hansen p.412
138 'if need be, Soviet artillerymen' quoted in Fursenko, Aleksandr & Naftali, Timothy *'One Hell of a Gamble': The Secret History of the Cuban Missile Crisis* Norton 1997 p.52
138 'Castro was waiting for us' Talbott, Strobe ed. *Khrushchev Remembers* Little, Brown 1970 pp.477–9
138 'brilliant ... he was very good' Mikoyan p.653
139 '[The Cubans] became heroes' Kendall p.236
139 'fascinated by Cuba and its revolution' Artemieva p.188
139 'For a Soviet person' Vail, Petr & Genis, Aleksandr *60-e, Mir Sovietskogo Cheloveka* (*The Sixties: The World of a Soviet Person*) Moscow 2013, Corpus 2021 ebook
139 'I haven't changed' Heikal, Mohammed *The Sphinx and the Commissar* Harper & Row 1978 p.84
140 'Why not invite Cuba?' Sergei Khrushchev p.429
141 'before we get it ready' Moskalenko in February 1962
141 'The Americans ... would learn just what it feels like' Khrushchev Vol. 1 p.494
142 'Don't ask for trouble' Dobrynin p.52
142 'Something had to be done' Khrushchev Vol. 1 p.494
143 'I later learned from [the general's] orderly' https://prozhito.org/person/1646 Kamanin diary 4.12.44
143 'Malinovsky was a man who loved women' Talbott ed. p.458
144 'After the war, the marshal' Shirokorad 'Love at the Front' *Nezavisimaya Gazeta* 14.10.16
145 'Khrushchev possessed a rich imagination' in Troyanovsky's contribution to Taubman & others p.235
145 'had become extremely conceited' Mikoyan p.654
145 'My thinking went like this' Khrushchev Vol. 1 p.494
146 'Nedelin, the first deputy thought' Mikoyan p.654

146 'more cruel but more rational' Blight, James & Welch, David *On the Brink: Americans and Soviets Reexamine the Cuban Missile Crisis* Hill & Wang 1989 p.252, at Cambridge conference

146 'During that period the Presidium' Sergei Khrushchev p.486

147 'What's up? I didn't realise' Mikoyan p.648

147 'Your appointment is linked with our decision' Dobrynin p.72

148 'nearly turned me to ice' Alekseev, A. I. 'Caribbean Crisis: The Way It Was' in Popov, N.V. ed. *Otkryvaya novye stranitsy ... Mezhdunarodnye voprosy: sobytiya i lyudi* (*Opening New Pages ... International Aspects, Events and People*) Politizdat 1989 pp.157–72

148 'Foreign minister Andrei Gromyko confided to Alekseev' www.Cubanos.ru Alekseev

149 '*Patria o Muerte!*' https://prozhito.org/person/1646 Obaturov 8.2.63

151 '*única*, what Cuban poet' DePalma p.328

151 'with the impression that Cuba's leaders' Gribkov, Anatoli & Smith, William *Operation ANADYR* Chicago 1994 p.20

152 'without knowing the facts' Dobrynin p.74

152 'He initially suggested dispatching' Sergei Khrushchev p.503

155 'They were then told' Sputnik website Belarus Alyoshin testimony

155 'as if we were nobodies' ibid.

156 'that five hundred officers' Plokhy, Serhii *Nuclear Folly: A New History of the Cuban Missile Crisis* Allen Lane 2021 p.93

156 'He and his mates' www.Cubanos.ru Chudik memoir

156 'The Turks were bribed' Sergei Khrushchev p.510

158 'The sun was merciless' Zakirov interview 2020

159 'He was national leader' Voloshchenko interview 15.5.19

159 'Every day you looked at them' ibid.

160 'On Castro's orders, the only available' Nazirov interview op. cit.

160 'a Cuban who pestered the guards' www.Cubanos.ru Vitaly Semenozhenkov

161 'There were no potatoes' Probachai interviewed Sept. 2020 by Oleksii Ivashin

161 'It was depressing' ibid.

162 'Guys, would you like to do it' ibid.

162 'Cuba was a wonderfully romantic' Lyubimov interview 25.1.21

162 'The country amazed us' Sputnik website Belarus

163 'It wasn't much, but he was so happy' Elvira Dubinskaya interview 2020

163 'with a big Russian website' Dmitriev, Anatoly Boevye Deistviya i Poteri Sovetskoi Gruppy Voisk v Respublike Kuba v Period Karibskogo Krizisa i VSO 'Anadyr' (Combat Operations and Losses of the Soviet Group of Troops during the Caribbean Crisis and the Anadyr Operation), 1961–1964

164 'There was some *machismo*' Ferrara interview 21.9.20

164 'saying that he belonged' Yepe interview 19.8.20

165 'very strange people' Lara interview 21.8.20

166 'It is ... totally beyond my comprehension' Troyanovsky in his contribution to Taubman & others p.236

167 'we did not plan any alternative' www.Cubanos.ru Alekseev

167 'From the start, the undertaking' Gribkov & Smith p.15
167 'You don't have to worry' Fursenko & Naftali *One Hell of a Gamble* p.196
168 'The mistake with the camouflage' Blight & Welch p.241
168 'We are a planned society' ibid. p.251
169 'Father got no sensible answer' Sergei Khrushchev p.562
171 'the special weapon in the following cases' Plokhy p.408
172 'He, too, had been invited to meet the leader' Udall, Stewart 'Poetry, Stalinism and the Cuban Missile Crisis' *Los Angeles Times* 30.10.88
173 'Soon all hell will break loose' Troyanovsky in his contribution to Taubman & others p.236

5: The Shock

174 'Soviet ships passing through the English Channel' Lympne Airfield Historical Society Bulletin Nov. 2021 *Lympne and the Cuban Missile Crisis*
175 'She excelled at exploiting' Wolman, David 'Cuba Confidential: On the Brink of Nuclear War America's Bold Response' *Smithsonian* magazine March 2021
176 'They're preventing [aerial] intrusion' ibid. p.69
178 'as if it were a corporate mortgage' Jeffreys-Jones, Rhodri *The CIA and American Democracy* Yale 1989 p.124
178 'We didn't see the offensive missiles' Kenneth Absher interviewed 28.8.88
178 'Moreover, at the late August' Holland & Barrett p.4
179 'Walter Lippmann, shown a draft' Steel p.525 & Schlesinger *A Thousand Days* p.147
180 'Cuba attack command center' USAF *History of the 55th Recce Wing* K-W6-55-HI
180 'later described how fuel' USAF Oral History Ellis K239.0512-1412
180 'We had to do a hell of a lot' USAF Oral History interview K239.0512.1179
181 'the Soviet Union should restrain' Dobrynin p.69
181 'so Khrushchev's promises' ibid. p.68
182 'Only thereafter did the German' Henning, Heiko *Senator Keating's Source* 21.2.17 Wilson Center blogpost
185 'Whatever I do, 80 per cent' Dobrynin p.60
185 'We should be Khrushchevizing' Schlesinger *RFK* p.499
186 'since I had no information' Dobrynin p.69
186 'mania for secrecy' ibid. p.39
190 'Cuba would become our Algeria' Bird p.243
190 'Indeed, so prolific' Holland, Max & Barrett, David *Blind Over Cuba* Texas A & M 2012 p.11
190 'like trying to fornicate' Parker, Richard *The Legacy of John Kenneth Galbraith* Farrar Straus and Giroux 2005 p.351
191 'People had a strong conviction' Kendall p.235
193 'You are permitted to make your own decision' signal of 8.9.62 published in Gribkov & Smith *Operation Anadyr* p.183
193 'perhaps the foremost practitioner' Steury, Donald ed. *Sherman Kent and the Board of National Estimates* collected essays CIA 2004 p.ix
194 'in which he described' Kent, Sherman *A Crucial Estimate Relived* Center for the Study of Intelligence 1994

195 'the best American ambassador' Dobrynin p.63
196 'we have 40-mile-range guided missiles' McAuliffe, Mary S. ed. & CIA
     History Staff *CIA Documents on the Cuban Missile Crisis* CIA October
     1992 pp.103, 105, 107–8
197 'Cuba Dominating American Elections' *The Times* 11.10.62
198 'Who can say that …' US *Congressional Record* 6.10.62, 22738
200 'The weather was roughly' Pocock, Chris *Fifty Years of the U-2* Schiffer
     Publishing 2005 pp.166–7
200 'It's the type of work' USAF Oral History Heyser interview 27.11.62
     K239.0512-749
201 'it was evident that this was going to' USAF Oral History Breitweiser
     K239.0512-877
201 'They all sat there …' *SAC Intelligence Quarterly* 1984 'Project Warrior'
     narrative of the Crisis, declassified in 1999
201 'The bomber chiefs later sought credit' see SAC's 1984 narrative 'The
     Missiles in Cuba 1962: The Role of SAC Intelligence' and Chris Pocock's
     authoritatively dismissive commentary
202 'its fighters might fire across the planes' bows' USAF Oral History Ellis
     K239.0512-1412
203 'Penkovsky really did change' Hennessy p.231
203 'shock and anger' Absher, Kenneth Michael *A Personal Account of the
     Cuban Missile Crisis* 2009: https://lccn.loc.gov/2009438710 p.56
206 'faggots' Thomas p.290
206 'found it difficult' Jeffreys-Jones p.131
206 '"F-M", meaning "the Field-Marshal"' Thomas p.289
207 'chewed out Bissell' ibid. p.271
207 'that we should destroy their air' USAF Oral History Power interview
     15.11.62 K239.0512-748
208 'If I were on your side' Blight & Welch p.250

6: Drumbeat

1 THE PRESIDENT IS TOLD

211 'Oh shit! Shit! Shit!' Brugioni, Dino *Eyeball to Eyeball* Random House 1991
     p.223
212 'I know no member' Bundy, McGeorge *Danger and Survival: Choices about
     the Bomb* Random House 1988 p.407
214 'They even considered communicating' see Hershberg, James in 'The
     United States, Brazil, and the Cuban Missile Crisis, 1962' *Journal of Cold
     War Studies* 2004, in two parts Spring & Summer
214 'Dammit, Bundy and I' Schlesinger *A Thousand Days* p.365
215 'Who ever believed in the Missile Gap?' Schlesinger *RFK* p.449
219 'If we had to act in the first twenty-four hours' Schlesinger *A Thousand
     Days* p.686
219 'If our deliberations had been publicized' Kennedy, Robert *13 Days*
     Macmillan 1969 p.108
221 'He was distressed that the representatives' ibid. p.116

2 THE WARMAKERS

223 'I tried to write a letter' Blight & Welch p.245, at 1987 Cambridge conference
227 'In ways which Americans' Bundy p.413
229 '"Chip" ran out on us' Kennedy Library Oral History interview Feb. 1965
232 'I would never wish to be' Kennedy p.41

7: 'They Think We're Slightly Demented on This Subject'

1 BEHIND CLOSED DOORS

234 'I never realized how serious' Alducín interview 23.6.20
235 'These British friends took several occasions' Deacon, Richard *C: A Biography of Sir Maurice Oldfield* Futura 1984 p.135
235 'I felt ... that somehow I had spent all of my career' Wolman p.72
237 'The trouble with American cabinet ministers' Macmillan, Harold *At the End of the Day* Macmillan 1974 p.123
240 'we all spoke as equals' Kennedy p.49
240 'I thought, as I listened' ibid. p.51
241 'Now ... we do that to a small country' ibid. p.42
244 'We and the Americans talked about Berlin' Novotný in https://digitalarchive.wilsoncenter.org/document/115219.pdf?v=5a0f522cdf60 d7d5c7cc06da1ffa6a1a (originally published in CWIHP *Bulletin* 17/18 (Fall 2012) pp.401–3)
245 'the Soviet government recognizes' Gromyko to CPSU Central Committee 19.10.62
245 'He was lying. And how!' CWIHP *Bulletin* 17/18 (Fall 2012) p.402
246 'from one extreme' Kennedy p.46

2 'IRON ASS'

247 'I was surprised by the unanimity' USAF Oral History Smith K239.0512-2040
249 'LeMay had opposed the dropping' for a full account of this saga and its accompanying controversies, see the author's *Nemesis: The Battle for Japan 1944–45* HarperCollins 2007
250 'virtually all of Russia' Rosenberg, David Alan '"A Smoking Radiating Ruin at the End of Two Hours": Documents on American Plans for Nuclear War with the Soviet Union' *International Security* 6:1 (Winter 1981/82), pp.3–38
252 'occasionally seemed to over-dramatise' Dobrynin p.76
252 '[Kennedy] just would be frantic' Dallek, Robert 'JFK's Second Term' *The Atlantic* June 2003 & Gilpatric in O'Brien interviews for JFK Oral History Program 30.6.70 and 13.8.70
252 'He subsequently claimed to friends' Bird p.234

3 THE DECISION

255 'We are very, very close' Sorensen, Theodore *Kennedy* Harper & Row 1965 pp.1–2
255 'the excessively gloomy view' Bundy p.547

255 'Gentlemen, today we're going to earn our pay' Stern p.133
258 'McNamara did not like the idea' USAF Oral History Buchinal K239.0512-
     837
259 'the town was alive with speculation' Schlesinger A Thousand Days p.692
259 'Too much nervousness' Economist 20.10.62
260 'We did not have a sense' Kendall p.233
261 'I was the guy who knew' USAF Oral History Creech K239.0512-2050
263 'trusted implicitly' Kennedy p.68
263 'Only two men of notable character' Schlesinger A Thousand Days p.379
264 'He mused aloud' UKNA PREM11/3689 24020

8: The President Speaks

1 KENNEDY CONFRONTS HIS PEOPLE

272 'The trouble is, that when you get' Schlesinger A Thousand Days p.694
272 'disturbed by the frustrated fury' New York Post 22.9.61
276 'in a rather panicky way' Macmillan, Harold The Macmillan Diaries Vol. 2
     1959–1966 ed. Peter Caterall Pan 2012 p.510
278 'Make all effort initially' Presidium Protocol No. 60 in Prezidium TsK KPSS
     1954–1964 ed. Fursenko Moscow 2003, Vol. 1
278 'arguably the most tense' Fursenko & Naftali Khrushchev's Cold War
     Norton 2006 p.221
278 'The members concluded' Anastas Mikoyan's 19.1.63 memorandum about
     his visit to Cuba, Russian archive RGASPI F.84.Op 3.D.115.L.115–20
279 'I was severely confused' Dobrynin p.79
281 'The once-villainous U-2' Holland & Barrett p.28
282 'a little overstated' Blight & Welch pp.245–6, at 1989 Cambridge
     conference
283 'The President's speech was more effective' Bundy p.404
283 'The stance of the Joint Chiefs of Staff' Sergei Khrushchev p.557
284 'the lower cadres of the revolution' Wilson Center Telegram 538.540
     French ambassador to foreign ministry 23.10.62
284 'We can do it any time' Lanovsky interview 11.12.2019

2 KHRUSHCHEV CONFRONTS DISASTER

288 'since an extreme aggravation' Dobrynin to Foreign Ministry 23.10.62 in
     CWIHP Bulletin 5 (Spring 1995) pp.70–1

9: Blockade

1 HIGH, CONFUSED SEA

292 'MENACE CONTRE LE PAIX MONDIALE' L'Humanité 23.10.62
292 'MESURES DE GUERRE U.S. CONTRE CUBA' Libération 23.10.62
292 'EMBARGO SUR LES ARMES A DESTINATION DE CUBA' Le Figaro
     23.10.62
292 'This was Louis XIV' Brinkley, Douglas Dean Acheson: The Cold War Years
     1953–71 Yale 1992 pp.264–8
292 'I had the heebie-jeebies' 2007 personal interview quoted Hennessy p.220

292 'Life goes on somehow' Kent, Sherman 'The Cuban Missile Crisis of 1962: Presenting the Photographic Evidence Abroad' *Studies in Intelligence* 10/2 (Spring 1972) pp.22–3
293 'First Day of the World Crisis!' Macmillan *Diaries* 22.10.62
293 'Lord Home, for one' private information from Alan Petty
294 'so deep a breach' UKNA CAB128/36
294 '[Any] real war must escalate' UKNA PREM11/3815
294 'In all his dealings' Hennessy p.226
294 'We, my dear Crossman' Horne, Alastair *Macmillan 1894–1956* p.160
295 'what terrible damage' Macmillan *Diaries* 19.6.62 pp.478–9
295 'It was the gay things' Schlesinger *A Thousand Days* p.341
295 'It would not be easy to persuade' UKNA PREM11/2686
296 'Macmillan's diaries show' Macmillan *Diaries passim*
296 'What worries me' ibid. 4.12.61
296 'We used to call Hitler wicked' Hennessy p.303
297 'a plain, naked, brutal act of war' Hansard 31.10.62 col.207
297 'More than a few observers ...' It deserves notice that, for instance, Neville Maxwell's authoritative *India's China War* Cape 1971 holds the Delhi government overwhelmingly blameworthy for the clash
298 'those missiles so far landed' Macmillan p.192
298 'that he himself had reached the same conclusion' ibid. pp.190–4
298 'This is not the moment' UKNA CAB129/11 Dilhorne memorandum & Hansard 25.10.62 col.1060
298 'If Khrushchev has really' *Guardian* 23.10.62
299 'There was a tendency' Deweerd, H.A. *British Attitudes in the Cuban Crisis* Rand Corporation P-2709 Feb. 1963, published 2008 p.8
299 'should stop it in the future' Hansard 31.10.62 col.218
300 'they seem quite happy' Macmillan *Diaries* 25.10.62 p.512
300 'MAY I HUMBLY APPEAL' Driver, Christopher *The Disarmers* Hodder 1964 p.146
300 'I think your attention' Hennessy p.305
302 'The main problem now' *The Times* 25.10.62
302 'brought a refreshing breeze' ibid.
302 'One does not have to find the US blameless' ibid. 26.10.62
302 'a sad and melancholy fact' ibid. 27.10.62
303 'HEAVY GOLD TURNOVER IN CRISIS MARKETS' ibid. 24.10.62
303 'It was somewhat easier' Joseph p.14
304 'I remember thinking' Kendall p.238
304 'I was scared to death' USAF Oral History Smith K239.0512-2040
304 'people sat around wondering' Heylin, Clinton *Bob Dylan: Behind the Shades Revisited* HarperCollins 2001 pp.102–3 & Dylan interview with Studs Terkel 1.5.63
304 'We have a utility room' Walter Cronkite interview in CNN *Cold War* series, episode ten
304 'We were all in suspense' Ferrara interview 21.9.20
304 'We were feeling doomed' Lyubimov interview 15.1.21
305 'They hadn't much to say' Macmillan diary unpublished entry quoted Hennessy p.255

305 'His face was a study' ibid. p.545 Hennessy 2008 conversation with Lady de
     Zulueta
305 'a general feeling of helplessness' Hansard 31.10.62 col.226
305 'I thought we were all going to die' Douglas-Home, Andrew *A River Runs
     Through Me* Elliott & Thompson 2022 p.193
305 'I don't know, really' information from George Walden
305 'That was the mood' Melo interview 22.4.20
305 'For me, the crisis meant the imminent prospect' Nuñez interview
     5.10.20
306 'mad arms race' https://prozhito.org/person/1646 Seleznev diary 1962
306 'There is an alarming report in *Izvestia*' https://prozhito.org/person/1646
     Lipkin diary 23.10.62
306 'The ether was filled' https://prozhito.org/person/1646 Kozakov diary
     6.11.62
306 'How could Russians be' Kosykh interview March 2021
306 'I thought Khrushchev was right' Galenkov interview March 2021
307 'The past twenty-four hours' https://prozhito.org/person/1646 Vronsky
     diary 23.11.62
307 'The English dinosaur' https://prozhito.org/person/1646 Lipkin diary
     23.10.62
307 'Who is going to like such a thing' https://prozhito.org/person/1646
     23.10.62

2 'SHOOT THE RUDDERS OFF!'

311 'There was a certain spirit' Kennedy p.60
311 'The great danger and risk' ibid. p.65
318 'was certainly close' Dobrynin pp.6 & 61
318 'not very imaginative' ibid. p.58
319 'a state of agitation' ibid. p.81
320 'how primitive were our embassy's' ibid. p.96
322 'You heard me, admiral' there are many accounts of this legendary episode,
     notably that of Gilpatric in the JFK Library, as given in his O'Brien
     interviews for the Oral History programme. Here I have largely followed
     Dobbs, pp.72–3, who himself made the significant contribution of dating
     the Pentagon clash to Tuesday, not Wednesday as often stated
322 'They offered this deliberate' May & Zelikow *Kennedy Tapes* p.207
323 'Graham Allison and Philip Zelikow' Allison, Graham & Zelikow, Philip
     Essence of Decision: Explaining the Cuban Missile Crisis Addison Wesley
     Longman 1999 p.384
323 'He was not pointing it' Volkov, Solomon *Dialogi s Evgeniem Evtushenko*
     (*Conversations with Yevgeny Yevtushenko*) Moscow 2018 p.63

10: 'The Other Fellow Just Blinked'

1 HAIR TRIGGERS

326 'The whole idea' *Boston Globe* 26.12.2008, obit of William Kaufmann
326 'We are in a very dangerous situation' USAF Oral History Smith
     K239.0512-2040

327 'It is not too difficult … to see how the United States' Gaddis *We Now Know* p.273

327 'in retrospect, there were some guys' Sagan, Scott *The Limits of Safety: Organizations, Accidents and Nuclear Weapons* Princeton 1993 Lt. Col. Robert Melgard to Sagan p.110

327 'Our commanders in the field' Blight & Welch p.275

328 'a major influence' USAF Oral History Power interview 15.11.62 K239.0512-748

328 'perhaps the American leader most feared' Absher p.67

329 'Isn't this dangerous?' Brugioni pp.400–1, 415–17

329 'Good luck, George' Anderson message 230003Z CNO Cuba USNHC quoted Dobbs p.90

2 'SHOULD I TAKE OUT CUBA?'

330 'probably none of the Politburo members' Gromyko, Andrei *Pamiatnoe* (*Memories*) Izdatelstvo polititcheskoi literatouri Moscow 1988 p.489

333 'I think these few minutes were the time of gravest concern' Kennedy p.71

337 'Everyone looked like a different person' ibid. p.74

337 'It was far more responsive' Bundy p.422

337 'Mom lit up the stove' https://prozhito.org/person/1646 Kozakov diary 24.10.62

339 'straight out the 64 thousand' Macmillan *Diaries* p.531

340 'Mr. Macmillan's public pronouncements' Strachey *Observer* 11.11.62

341 '[Khrushchev] said those ships' Beschloss, Michael *The Crisis Years: Kennedy & Khrushchev 1960–63* HarperCollins 1991 pp.501–2

11: Khrushchev Looks for an Out

1 'EVERYTHING TO PREVENT WAR'

343 'the ominous possibility' *Economist* 27.10.62

343 'yes, we are "obsessed"' ibid. 27.10.62

344 'The Kennedy Administration' USAF Oral History Smith K239.0512-2040

346 'Point 1. On the response of the Chairman' Protocol No.61 Wilson Archive Digital Archive F.3, Op.16, D.162 L.170–3

348 'the most memorable' Dobrynin p.83

351 'I did what I felt was right' Moody quoted in Wolman, *Smithsonian* op. cit.

351 'rather prissy' Dallek p.94

351 'an intelligent and kind person' Dobrynin p.28

351 'a ghastly old Stalinist hack' George Walden to the author

2 THE KREMLIN DECISION

352 'In connection with the fact' Wilson Center document 117324, Archive of the President Russian Federation Special Declassification 2002

353 'to safeguard what they have' UKNA CAB158/47 26.10.62 JIC962 62 97

353 'I was shocked' Sergei Khrushchev p.581

353 'Khrushchev had met Lippmann' Steel p.429

353 'This being the nuclear age' Lippmann in the *New York Herald Tribune* 4.9.61

3 'A TRIAL OF WILL'

369 'Stop all work' Wilson Archive documents no. 117326 & 117325
370 'Under conditions where Moscow' Blight & Welch p.271

12: Black Saturday

1 CASTRO FRIGHTENS KHRUSHCHEV

371 'I got up at 9.30' https://prozhito.org/person/1646 Kozakov diary 27.10.62
372 'Alekseev was later' www.Cubanos.ru Alekseev
374 'All our units were on the highest alert' Vitaly Semenozhenkov interview
      op. cit.
374 'He realized that these' Melo interview 22.4.20
376 'We must meet to consider' Spectator 2.11.62
376 'We may not see each other again' Kendall p.239
381 'He turned absolutely white' USAF Oral History Buchinal K239.0512-837
382 'The Vozhd admitted the possibility' Sergei Khrushchev p.609

2 THE SOVIETS SHOOT

384 'What feeling could you have' Voloshchenko interview op. cit.
387 'These officers did not' Gribkov & Smith p.67

13: The Brink

1 IMPASSE

390 'had no real choice' Spectator 26.10.62
391 'like you might do with kids' USAF Oral History Garland K239.0512-1707
391 'The US Military behaved' Sergei Khrushchev p.645
394 'The proposal the Russians' Kennedy p.92
394 'There was confusion' ibid. p.94
396 'To us who face nearly 500' Macmillan Diaries 4.11.62 p.515
397 'All key personnel were required to remain on station' UKNA AIR25/173
397 'The aircraft was loaded' Robinson 2007 interview with Peter Hennessy,
      quoted Hennessy p.268
397 '[If] the signal … had been received …' Robson 16.7.2001 quoted Hennessy
      p.220
398 'would cause the United Kingdom' UKNA CAB134/940 & CAB134/4291
398 'One evening at Wittering' information from S/Ldr Kevin Dalley
399 'Rather a lovely morning' JFK Presidential Library, 1966 Thorneycroft Oral
      History transcript
403 'In a much later letter' it was dispatched on 14.12.62
406 'President Kennedy becomes the driver of the debate' Allison & Zelikow
      p.337
406 'Bundy perceived Kennedy' Bundy p.427
406 'Those hours in the Cabinet Room' Kennedy p.98
406 'We won't attack' ibid. p.98

2 THE HOUNDING OF B-59

407 'Almost at the moment the vice-president spoke' this account derives chiefly from that of Svetlana Savranskaya, in the April 2005 *Journal of Strategic Studies*. There have since been other, more sensational versions, some information from which I have incorporated, but aspects of this story will remain uncertain and disputed unless or until relevant Moscow documentation is released to scholars
408 'startled' Bundy p.422
409 'Yet no recall order' Fursenko & Naftali *Khrushchev's Cold War* pp.478–80
411 'They exploded next to' Orlov in Plokhy p.409
413 'Svetlana Savranskaya makes the significant point' in a message to the author January 2022

3 THE OFFER

416 'Throughout the whole meeting' Dobrynin p.89
418 'rancorous' Bird p.240
419 'But its dispatch reflects' Hershberg in the 2004 *Journal of Cold War Studies*
422 'Earlier that evening, Powers' Alford, Mimi *Once Upon a Secret: My Affair with President John F. Kennedy and Its Aftermath* Random House 2013 pp.93–4

14: Endgame

1 TIME RUNS OUT

424 'Then Moorestown came back' Sagan pp.130–1
428 'We were completely aghast' Novotný in https://digitalarchive. wilsoncenter.org/document/115219.pdf?v=5a0f522cdf60d7d5c7 cc06da1ffa6a1a (originally published in CWIHP *Bulletin* 17/18 (Fall 2012) pp. 401–3)
428 'There was a great deal of commotion' Troyanovsky in his contribution to Taubman & others p.237
428 'We had to act very quickly' Novotný in https://digitalarchive.wilsoncenter. org/document/115219.pdf?v=5a0f522cdf60d7d5c7cc06da1ffa6a1a (originally published in CWIHP *Bulletin* 17/18 (Fall 2012) pp. 401–3)
429 'Levitan, whose deep voice' Sergei Khrushchev pp.xvi–xvii
430 'had saved much from the shipwreck' Bundy p.441
431 'It was a very beautiful morning' Bird p.240
431 'Admiral Anderson's reaction' Schlesinger *RFK* p.524
432 'This is the night I should go' Kennedy p.108
433 'The entire atmosphere changed' Sergei Khrushchev p.632
433 'Why don't we go to the theatre?' ibid. p.636
433 'Impossible to describe' Macmillan *Diaries* pp.513–14
434 'It's like a wedding' Evans, Harold *Downing Street Diary* Hodder 1981 p.224
434 'There were many indications' *Spectator* 2.11.62
434 'I am lost in admiration' JFK Library President's Office File JFKFOF127-08 30.10.62

434 'so narrowed his objectives' Steel p.537
434 'The chief frightening thing' McDonald, Iverach *A Man of The Times* p.184
435 'One of the most striking lessons' *Spectator* 2.11.62
435 'Mr. Khrushchev simply bowed' *Le Monde* 30.10.62
435 'I thought it was brought off' USAF Oral History Breitweiser K239.0512-877
436 'We would have gotten' USAF Oral History LeMay K239.0512-2115
436 'I think if we had cleaned out' Joseph p.90
436 'I was surprised' ibid. p.91
436 'They had the Russians' USAF Oral History interview K239.0512-974
437 'the greatest menace' USAF Oral History Fairweather K239.0512-1826
437 'a gamble to the point' Isaacson & Thomas p.629
437 'Those who experienced' Joseph p.58
437 'had to be picked from the dustbin' *Economist* 10.11.62
437 'Shark [Khrushchev] has sent Kennedy' https://prozhito.org/person/1646 Kozakov diary 28.10.62
438 'that deeds proved to be so different' https://prozhito.org/person/1646 Seleznev diary November 1962
438 'Khrushchev has saved the world' https://prozhito.org/person/1646 Nazirov 6.11.62
438 'We came out winners' https://prozhito.org/person/1646 Obaturov 8.2.63
439 'People had become more and more' Ferrara interview 21.9.20
439 'As always he spoke' https://prozhito.org/person/1646 Obaturov 8.2.63

2 THE CUBANS CUT UP ROUGH

441 'The Cubans have unfortunately' Wilson Center Telegram 11208 30.10.62
443 'We have to be fair to the enemy' https://nsarchive2.gwu.edu/NSAEBB/NSAEBB75/Dubivko.pdf
443 'Marshal [Andrei, army C-in-C of Warsaw Pact forces] Grechko refused to listen' Dubivko report https://nsarchive2.gwu.edu/NSAEBB/NSAEBB75/Dubivko.pdf
444 '*CUBANS* WONT GIVE UP *RUSSIAN*' *Detroit Free Press* 5.11.62
444 'Father felt deeply hurt' Sergei Khrushchev pp.642 & 658
444 'The aim of the American' Schecter, J.L. & Luchkov, V. eds *Khrushchev Remembers: The Glasnost Tapes* Little, Brown 1990 p.180
445 'which he was quite capable' Mikoyan p.655
445 'so that you understand' Volkov p.73
445 'We see your readiness' Soviet transcripts of Mikoyan conversations with Cubans on 3 & 5 November 1962
446 'The Cubans simply could not understand the USSR's strategy' Chudik memoir
446 'Our commanders did the wrong thing' Elvira Dubinskaya interview 2020
446 'It was traumatic for our soldiers' Zakirov interview 2020
447 'and he's entirely surrounded' Coleman transcript of Excom meeting 14.11.62 quoted in Fursenko & Naftali *'One Hell of a Gamble'* p.499
448 'Khrushchev's failure to insist' Dobrynin p.91
448 'The Soviet leadership could not forget' ibid. p.93

15: 'This Strange and Still Scarcely Explicable Affair'

450 'Any record [of the Crisis] must' UKNA FO371/162408 Marchant to Home 10.11.62

450 'this strange and still' Kennedy p.15

450 'Andrei Gromyko and a number of others' Troyanovsky in his contribution to Taubman & others p.237

451 'Khrushchev would not have permitted' UKNA CAB158/47 JIC(62) 10

451 '[The Soviets'] overriding concern' UKNA CAB158/47 JIC (62) 99

453 'In this apocalyptic matter' Bundy p.461

453 'somewhere between one' Sorensen p.705

453 'If the United States attacked' Blight & Welch p.275

453 'McGeorge Bundy went to his grave convinced' Bundy p.427

453 'McNamara and Sorensen' see Blight & Welch p.266

453 'Three of the foremost' in 2022 private exchanges with the author

455 'had a virtually complete breakdown' JFK Library Oral History Program interview 27.2.65 and Schlesinger *RFK* p.507

455 'Sheldon Stern describes the comment' message to the author 28.2.22

455 'We're just beginning' Troyanovsky, Oleg *Cherez gody i rasstoyanya: Istorya odnoi sem'i* Moscow 1997 p.247

456 'none was consistent' Kennedy p.35

457 'The final lesson ...' ibid. p.121

457 '[Kennedy] played a firm *military*' Macmillan p.219

457 'always ready to listen' Kennedy p.17

458 'I believed the blockade' Toynbee, Philip *Encounter* January 1963 p.95

458 'This *has* been a battle' Macmillan *Diaries* 4.11.62 p.514

459 'just what Khrushchev had intended' Hansard 31.10.62 col.218

459 'Who won?' https://digitalarchive.wilsoncenter.org/document/115219. pdf?v=5a0f522cdf60d7d5c7cc06da1ffa6a1a (originally published in CWIHP *Bulletin* 17/18 (Fall 2012) pp. 401–3)

460 'A number of years have passed' *Khrushchev Remembers* p.504

460 'Khrushchev's attitude towards East-West relations' Troyanovsky in his contribution to Taubman & others p.238

461 '[The US] can take Cuba' Macmillan *Diaries* 4.11.62 & Macmillan p.219

462 'Our secrets were almost too well kept ...' Macmillan p.220

462 'minimal ... the consultation Britain' Freedman, Lawrence *The Evolution of Nuclear Strategy* Macmillan 1982 p.310

462 'about the great losses' Hennessy p.308

463 'He insisted that our missiles' Artizov, Andrei & others *Nikita Khrushchev 1964* Moscow 2007 p.198

464 'Fidel was a megalomaniac' *Cuba Libre* documentary series 2020

464 'They say I was a terrible president' Schlesinger *A Thousand Days* p.216

465 'By the bleak standards' Gott, Richard *Cuba: A New History* Yale 2004 p.324

466 'We believe that in the Cuban crisis' Dobrynin p.92

467 'the photo gap' Holland & Barrett *passim*

467 'It took nearly a month [in reality from 10 September to 14 October] to get the coverage' ibid. p.41

467 'we were faced with a dilemma' Clifford, Clark *Counsel to the President* Random House 1991 pp.353–5

468 'a focused sense of urgency' PFIAB report 4.2.63 in McAuliffe ed. *CIA Documents* pp.363–5
468 'from the middle of September' Gerald R. Ford Library, undated Ford Speech Notes undated Box D-16
468 'It would have been almost impossible' Richard Rovere 'Letter from Washington', *New Yorker* 22.3.63
468 'Harvey has destroyed himself' Thomas p.289
469 'My first job was to convince' ibid. p.119
469 'had long since concluded' Holland & Barrett p.84
469 'Yeah, but boy' ibid. p.88
469 'You were right' Jeffreys-Jones p.136
470 'Fear of another U-2 incident' Holland & Barrett p.67
473 'someone we could trust' *Khrushchev Remembers* p.513
473 'A Cuban was sitting' Elvira Dubinskaya interview 2020
473 'They're going to say' Castro to French journalist Jean Daniel *Cuba Libre* documentary series 2020
474 'It may be that the West prevailed' Gaddis *We Now Know* p.295
474 'A return to great power competition' Freedman, Lawrence in IISS *Survival* Dec–Jan 2022 p.40
475 'It has been observed that' Blight & Welch p.312
475 'The Soviet Union's role as the second superpower' Braithwaite, Rodric IISS *Survival* Feb–March 2022 p.43
476 'All of you believed' Blight & Welch p.247, at Cambridge conference
477 'The United States did not want' ibid. p.257
477 'You can't decide these questions' Steel p.530
477 'Appeasement is often a very sensible' Howard to the author in 2017
478 'It may well be that by a process' Hansard 1.3.55 col.218

Bibliography

The literature of the Missile Crisis is vast. Rather than seek to catalogue the entire library, an absurdity, I have here adopted a more pragmatic policy, of listing only titles that I have personally consulted in the course of writing this book. The omission of many works bears no suggestion of their inadequacy or irrelevance.

Confusingly, there are three versions of Nikita Khrushchev's memoirs, edited to achieve coherence from successive fragments that made their way to the West. Many passages are factually inaccurate or questionable, but all are deemed credibly to reflect the former Soviet leader's views in old age.

Articles and online sources

Absher, Kenneth Michael *A Personal Account of the Cuban Missile Crisis* 2009: https://lccn.loc.gov/2009438710

Barrett, David 'The Bay of Pigs Fiasco and the Kennedy Administration's Off-the-Record Briefings for Journalists' *Journal of Cold War Studies* Spring 2019 pp.3–26

Borzunov, Boris *Life of Marshal Malinovsky in Photographs and Documents* SM144 7.9.202

Byrne, Malcolm *National Security Archive: CIA Assassination Plot Targeted Cuba's Raul Castro* AssH-Diplo posted 18.4.21

— *National Security Archive Did JFK Send a Secret Warning to Fidel Castro?* James Hershberg H-Diplo posted 29.4.21

Chudik, G.R. Memoir published on Sait veteranov 8 otdelnoi armii PVO – website of 8th Independent Anti-Aircraft Defence Army 22.10.16

Crandall, Russell review essay of Simon Hall's *Ten Days in Harlem, Survival* Vol. 63 no. 2 April 2021 pp.173–80

http://cuban-exile.com/doc_351-375/doc0358.html

www.Cubanos.ru This is the website of Russian experiences of Cuba in times gone by

DeWeerd, H.A. *British Attitudes in the Cuban Crisis* Rand Corporation P-2709 Feb.1963, published 2008

Dmitriev, Anatoly Boevye Deistviya i Poteri Sovetskoi Gruppy Voisk v Respublike Kuba v Period Karibskogo Krizisa i VSO 'Anadyr' (Combat Operations and Losses of the Soviet Group of Troops during the Caribbean Crisis and the Anadyr Operation), 1961–1964 Bishkek 2017

Dobrynin, Anatoly telegram to Soviet Foreign Ministry 23.10.62 in CWIHP *Bulletin* 5 (Spring 1995) pp.70–1

Ferrer, Ada *Cuba: An American History* 31.1.22 a Wilson Center webinar

Freedman, Lawrence 'The Crisis of Liberalism and the Western Alliance' in *Survival* Dec–Jan 2022 pp.37–43

Goldgeier, James; Simons, Thomas W.; Pechatnov, Vladimir; Zubok, Vladislav; Caldwell, Dan; Thompson, Jenny; Thompson, Sherry (2019-08-01) 'Cold War Adviser: Llewellyn Thompson and the Making of U.S. Policy toward the Soviet Union' *Journal of Cold War Studies* 21 (3): 222–257. doi:10.1162/jcws_c_00899. ISSN 1520-3972. S2CID 199465404

Henning, Heiko Senator Keating's Source Wilson Center blog post 21.2.2017

Hershberg, James New Russian Evidence on Soviet-Cuban Relations, 1960–61 Wilson Center February 2019

— 'The United States, Brazil, and the Cuban Missile Crisis, 1962' *Journal of Cold War Studies* 2004, in two parts Spring & Summer

Izvestia interview with Fyodor Burlatsky 22.10.2002 JFKlibrary.org

Kamanin, Nikolai diaries available online at http://militera.lib.ru/db/kamanin_np/index.html

Kent, Sherman 'The Cuban Missile Crisis of 1962: Presenting the Photographic Evidence Abroad' *Studies in Intelligence* 10/2 (Spring 1972) pp.22–3

— 'A Crucial Estimate Relived' Center for the Study of Intelligence 1994

Kommersant newspaper 15.2.2017

Lympne Airfield Historical Society Bulletin *Lympne & the Cuban Missile Crisis* November 2021

McAuliffe, Mary S. ed. & CIA History Staff *CIA Documents on the Cuban Missile Crisis* CIA October 1992

Mpofu-Walsh, Sizwe https://ora.ox.ac.uk/objects/uuid:1989894d-1e20-419e-8b39-84a02b53cf05/download_file?safe_filename=Mpofu-Walsh._Obedient_Rebellion._DPhil_Thesis._Final_Draft._2020.pdf&type_of_work=Thesis

Novotný, Antonín minutes of 30.11.62 meeting with Khrushchev https://digitalarchive.wilsoncenter.org/document/115219.pdf?v=5a0f522cdf60d7d5c7cc06da1ffa6a1a (originally published in CWIHP *Bulletin* 17/18 (Fall 2012) pp. 401–3)

https://openvault.wgbh.org/catalog/V_35708B61D5AB4E7AAD9E03CCF38764A0

Overton, J. 'Urgent: Put This in Your Purse' https://warrom.armywarcollegedu.special series/dusty-shelves/in-your-purse

Paterson, Thomas G. 'The Historian as Detective: Senator Kenneth Keating, the Missiles in Cuba and His Mysterious Sources' *Diplomatic History* Vol. 11, No. 1 1987 pp.67–70

Plokhy, Serhii book talk at the Wilson Center 21.4.21 https://www.wilsoncenter.org/event/book-talk-nuclear-folly?utm_campaign=happ&utm_

medium=email&utm_source=newsletter&emci=4ed31472-319e-eb11-85aa-0050f237abef&emdi=7b509809-bc9e-eb11-85aa-0050f237abef&ceid=153298
https://prozhito.org/person/1646 – a Russian website that contains much excellent historic diary material
Reid, Tim 'Soviet Submariner "Saved the World" in Cuban Crisis' *The Times* 14.10.2002
Savranskaya, Svetlana 'New Sources on the Role of Soviet Submarines in the Cuban Missile Crisis' *Journal of Strategic Studies* 24.1.2007 https://doi.org/10.1080/01402390500088312
Scherer, John 'Reinterpreting Soviet Behavior during the Cuban Missile Crisis' *World Affairs* Vol. 144, No. 2 (Fall 1981), pp.110–25
Shirokorad, Aleksandr 'Love at the Front' *Nezavisimaya Gazeta* 14.10.2016 Soviet submarine links flagged and translated by Svetlana Savranskaya: https://nsarchive2.gwu.edu//NSAEBB/NSAEBB399/docs/Report%20of%20the%20submarine%20mission.pdf
https://nsarchive2.gwu.edu//NSAEBB/NSAEBB399/docs/asw-II-16.pdf
https://www.youtube.com/watch?v=AII2KNH18Jc
https://nsarchive2.gwu.edu//NSAEBB/NSAEBB399/
https://nsarchive2.gwu.edu/NSAEBB/NSAEBB75/Dubivko.pdf
Sputnik website, Belarus
Stern, Sheldon 13.12.2020 'Reflections on Fredrik Logevall's *JFK: Coming of Age in the American Century, 1917–1956*' History News Network, Columbian College of Arts & Sciences
— 17.3.2004 'Errors Still Afflict the Transcripts of the Kennedy Presidential Recordings' History News Network
Steury, Donald ed. *Sherman Kent and the Board of National Estimates* collected essays CIA 2004 p.ix
Trachtenberg, Marc 'The Influence of Nuclear Weapons in the Cuban Missile Crisis' *International Security* Vol. 10, No. 1 (Summer 1985) pp.137–63
Udall, Stewart 'Poetry, Stalinism and the Cuban Missile Crisis' *Los Angeles Times* 30.10.88
The Wilson Center.org offers a wonderful and invaluable range of digital material relating to the Missile Crisis
Wolman, David 'Cuba Confidential: On the Brink of Nuclear War America's Bold Response ...' *Smithsonian* magazine March 2021
Zelikow, Philip *Response to National Security Archive Saving the Bay of Pigs Prisoners* H-Diplo posted 29.4.21

Books

Abel, Elie *The Missile Crisis* Bantam 1966
Alford, Mimi *Once Upon a Secret: My Affair with President John F. Kennedy and Its Aftermath* Random House 2013 pp.93–4
Allison, Graham & Zelikow, Philip *Essence of Decision: Explaining the Cuban Missile Crisis* Addison Wesley Longman 1999
Allison, G.T., Carnesale, A. & Nye, J.S. eds *Hawks, Doves and Owls: An Agenda for Avoiding Nuclear War* Norton 1985
Ambrose, Stephen *Nixon: Vol. 1: The Education of a Politician 1913–62* Simon & Schuster 1987

Anderson, Terry *The Sixties* Texas A & M 1999

Ballantyne, Iain *Hunter-Killers* Orion 2013

— *The Deadly Trade* Weidenfeld & Nicolson 2018

Benson, Thomas W. *Writing JFK: Presidential Rhetoric and the Press in the Bay of Pigs Crisis* Texas A & M Press 2004

Beschloss, Michael *The Crisis Years: Kennedy & Khrushchev 1960–63* HarperCollins 1991

Bird, Kai *The Color of Truth: McGeorge Bundy and William Bundy: Brothers in Arms* Touchstone 1998

Blight, James & Welch, David *On the Brink: Americans and Soviets Reexamine the Cuban Missile Crisis* Hill & Wang 1989

Boot, Max *The Road Not Taken: Edward Lansdale and the American Tragedy in Vietnam* Head of Zeus 2018

Braithwaite, Rodric *Armageddon and Paranoia: The Nuclear Confrontation* Profile 2017

Brinkley, Douglas *Dean Acheson: The Cold War Years 1953–71* Yale 1992

Brokaw, Tom *Boom! Talking about the Sixties* Random House 2007

Brugioni, Dino *Eyeball to Eyeball* Random House 1991

Bundy, McGeorge *Danger and Survival: Choices about the Bomb* Random House 1988

Burleigh, Michael *Day of the Assassins: A History of Political Murder* Picador 2021

Chafe, William H. *America since World War II* OUP 1986

Chang, Laurence & Kornbluh, Peter eds *The Cuban Missile Crisis 1962: An NSA Documents Reader* New Press 1998

Clifford, Clark *Counsel to the President* Random House 1991

Colman, Jonathan *The Cuban Missile Crisis: Origins, Course and Aftermath* Edinburgh 2016

Crump, Thomas *Brezhnev and the Decline of the Soviet Union* Routledge 2014

Dallek, Robert *John F. Kennedy: An Unfinished Life* Little, Brown 2003

DePalma, Anthony *The Cubans* Bodley Head 2020

Dobbs, Michael *One Minute to Midnight* Hutchinson 2008

Dobrynin, Anatoly *In Confidence* Times Books 1995

Ellsberg, Daniel *The Doomsday Machine: Confessions of a Nuclear Planner* Bloomsbury 2017

Evans, Harold *Downing Street Diary* Hodder 1981

Ferrer, Ada *Cuba: An American History* Simon & Schuster 2021

Freedman, Lawrence *The Evolution of Nuclear Strategy* Macmillan 1982

— *Atlas of Global Strategy* Equinox 1985

Fursenko, Aleksandr & Naftali, Timothy *'One Hell of a Gamble': The Secret History of the Cuban Missile Crisis* Norton 1997

— *Khrushchev's Cold War* Norton 2006

Gaddis, John Lewis *We Now Know: Rethinking Cold War History* Oxford University Press 1997

— *The Cold War* Allen Lane 2005

Galbraith, J.K. *The Affluent Society* Houghton Mifflin 1958

— *Name-Dropping: From FDR On* Houghton Mifflin 1999

Gitlin, Todd *The Sixties: Years of Hope, Days of Rage* Bantam 1993

Gott, Richard *Cuba: A New History* Yale University Press 2004
Gromyko, Andrei *Pamiatnoe (Memories)* Izdatelstvo polititcheskoi literatouri
     Moscow 1988
Guerra, Lillian *Visions of Power in Cuba* UNC Press 2012
Halberstam, David *The Best and the Brightest* Random House 1972
Hale-Dorrell, Aaron *Corn Crusade: Khrushchev's Farming Revolution* Oxford
     2019
Hall, Simon *Ten Days in Harlem: Fidel Castro and the Making of the 1960s* Faber
     2020
Hansen, Jonathan *Young Castro: The Making of a Revolutionary* Simon &
     Schuster 2019
Hastings, Max *Nemesis: The Battle for Japan 1944–45* Harper Press 2007
Helms, Richard *A Look Over My Shoulder* Random House 2003
Hennessy, Peter *Winds of Change: Britain in the Early Sixties* Penguin 2019
Hodgson, Godfrey *In Our Time: America from World War II to Nixon*
     Macmillan 1976
Holland, Max & Barrett, David *Blind Over Cuba* Texas A & M 2012
Hornsby, Robert *Protest, Reform and Repression in Khrushchev's Soviet Union*
     Cambridge 2013
Howard, Michael *Captain Professor* Continuum 2006
Humphrey, Nicholas & Lifton, Robert Jay *In a Dark Time* Faber 1984
Isaacson, Walter & Thomas, Evan *The Wise Men* Faber 1986
Isserman, Maurice & Kazin, Michael *America Divided: The Civil War of the
     1960s* Oxford 2000
Jeffreys-Jones, Rhodri *The CIA and American Democracy* Yale 1989
Johnson, Haynes *The Bay of Pigs* Hutchinson 1965
Joseph, Peter *Good Times: An Oral History of America in the Nineteen Sixties*
     Morrow 1974
Kagan, Robert *Dangerous Nation* Knopf 2006
Keep, John *Last of the Empires: The Soviet Union 1945–91* Oxford 1995
Kendall, Bridget *The Cold War: A New Oral History* BBC 2017
Kennedy, Robert *13 Days* Macmillan 1969
Khrushchev, Nikita ed. Thomas Whitney *Khrushchev Speaks* University of
     Michigan 1963
— ed. Strobe Talbott *Khrushchev Remembers* Vol. 1 Deutsch 1971
— ed. Strobe Talbott *Khrushchev: The Last Testament* Vol. 2 Deutsch 1974
Khrushchev, Sergei *Nikita Khrushchev and the Creation of a Superpower*
     Pennsylvania State University Press 2000
Kissinger, Henry *The Necessity for Choice* Harper & Row 1960
Kornbluh, Peter ed. *Bay of Pigs Declassified* New Press 1998
Laqueur, Walter *The Dream That Failed* Oxford 1994
Logevall, Fredrik *JFK: Coming of Age in the American Century 1917–56* Viking
     2020
Macmillan, Harold *At the End of the Day* Macmillan 1974
— *The Macmillan Diaries Vol. 2 1959–1966* ed. Peter Caterall Pan 2012
Maultsby, Charles *Towards the Unknown: Memoirs of an American Fighter Pilot*
     Bookbaby 2013
Maxwell, Neville *India's China War* Cape 1970

May, Ernest & Zelikow, Philip eds *The Kennedy Tapes: Inside the White House during the Cuban Missile Crisis* Norton 2002

Menya okruzhayut stoletia (Centuries Surround Me): a history of the twentieth century through the eyes of schoolchildren Moscow Mezhdunarodny Memorial 2017

Mikoyan, Anastas *Tak bylo (That's How It Was)* Vagrius 1999

Munton, Don & Welch, David *The Cuban Missile Crisis* Oxford 2012

O'Donnell, Kenneth & Powers, David *Johnny, We Hardly Knew Ye* Boston 1972

Parker, Richard *The Legacy of John Kenneth Galbraith* Farrar Straus and Giroux 2005

Perrotet, Tony *Cubra Libre!* Blue Rider Press 2019

Plokhy, Serhii *Nuclear Folly: A New History of the Cuban Missile Crisis* Allen Lane 2021

Pocock, Chris *Fifty Years of the U-2* Schiffer Publishing 2005

Popov, N.V. ed. *Otkryvaya novye stranitsy ... Mezhdunarodnye voprosy: sobytiya i lyudi (Opening New Pages ... International Aspects, Events and People)* Politizdat 1989

Reeves, Richard *President Kennedy: Profile of Power* Simon & Schuster 1994

Sagan, Scott *The Limits of Safety: Organizations, Accidents and Nuclear Weapons* Princeton 1993

Salinger, Pierre *With Kennedy* Doubleday 1966

Sandbrook, Dominic *Never Had It So Good* Little, Brown 2005

Sandford, Christopher *Harold & Jack* Prometheus 2014

Schlesinger, Arthur *A Thousand Days* Andre Deutsch 1965

— *Robert F. Kennedy and His Times* Andre Deutsch 1978

Scott, Len *The Cuban Missile Crisis and the Threat of Nuclear War* Continuum 2007

Shchekochikhin, Yuri *Raby GB* Moscow 2000

Steel, Ronald *Walter Lippmann and the American Century* Routledge 1980

Stern, Sheldon *The Cuban Missile Crisis in American Memory: Myths Versus Reality* Stanford 2012

— *Averting the Final Failure* Stanford University Press 2003

Talbott, Strobe ed. *Khrushchev Remembers* Little, Brown 1970

Taubman, William & Khrushchev, Sergei & Gleason, Abbott eds *Nikita Khrushchev* Yale 2000

Taubman, William *Khrushchev: The Man and His Era* Free Press 2003

Taylor, Maxwell *Swords and Plowshares* W.W. Norton 1972

Taylor Committee *Operation Zapata* University Publications of America 1981

Thomas, Evan *The Very Best Men: The Daring Early Years of the CIA* Simon & Schuster 1995

Troyanovsky, Oleg *Cherez gody i rasstoyaniya: Istorya odnoi sem'i* Moscow 1997

Twining, Nathan *Neither Liberty Nor Safety* Holt, Rinehart & Winston 1966

Vail, Petr & Genis, Aleksandr *60-e, Mir Sovetskogo Cheloveka (The Sixties: The World of a Soviet Person)* Moscow 2013

Volkov, Solomon *Dialogi s Evgeniem Evtushenko (Conversations with Yevgeny Yevtushenko)* Moscow 2018

Walker, Stephen *Beyond: The Astonishing Story of the First Human to Leave Our Planet* William Collins 2021

Westad, Odd Arne *The Cold War: A World History* Allen Lane 2017
White, Theodore *The Making of the President 1960* Pocket Books 1961
Zubok, Vladislav *A Failed Empire: The Soviet Union in the Cold War* University
  of North Carolina 2007

Index

Absher, Ken, 193, 194, 196, 203, 328
Acheson, Dean, 10, 120, 231, 242, 246,
    253, 290–2, 367, 437, 452
Adams, John Quincy, 24
Adenauer, Konrad, 85, 290, 376
Adzhubei, Aleksei, 140, 185
aerial bombardment/air strikes: active
    USAF preparations for, 274, 326–7,
    356, 401, 421–2; air strikes dubbed
    'fast track' option, 213; air strikes
    without warning option, 214, 230,
    231–2, 239, 242, 247–8, 250, 252,
    257; chiefs of staff press for, 221,
    222, 225, 233, 246, 247–8, 250, 251,
    252–3, 256, 258, 396, 402–3, 431;
    EXCOM discussions on, 214–16,
    217–18, 222, 225, 230–2, 233, 239,
    240–1, 242, 246, 256–8, 354, 359;
    impossibility of destroying all
    targets, 186–7, 215–16, 247–8, 256,
    261–2, 360; limited air strike option,
    222, 225, 236, 257; 'surgical air
    strike' term, 186–7, 216; US air
    campaign plans, 230, 240–1, 256,
    257, 261–2, 367–8, 379; US planning
    for (pre-Crisis), 196–7, 216
Aeroflot Flight 902 crash (1962), 66
Afghanistan, Soviet intervention
    (1979–89), xviii
Africa, 145, 269
Agafonov, Vitaly, 170, 408
Agüero, Andrés, 43
Alducín, Margarita, 55, 57, 234
Alekseev, Aleksandr, 135, 164–5, 442,
    464; and Anadyr, 147–8, 150, 167;

and Castro, 52, 147, 150, 368, 371–3,
    374, 427, 428, 440–1
Alfonso, Conchita, 56, 374–5
Allison, Graham, 323, 406
Almeida, Juan, 32, 39, 279
Alsop, Joseph, 113, 114, 121, 228, 260,
    466
Alyoshin, Valentin, 155, 162–3
Anadyr, Operation: and Alekseev,
    147–8, 150, 167; camouflage failure,
    168–9, 217, 239, 348–9; Castro
    agrees to, 149–51; Cuban
    communications security, 176;
    Cubans urge openness, 151–2, 167;
    expeditionary force, 152–3, 154–9;
    fantasy claims of fighting/battles,
    163; impact of heat on missiles, 160;
    Kenneth Keating's public claims,
    181–3; Khrushchev's thinking, 142,
    144–9, 165–7, 197, 217, 226–7,
    238–9, 263–4, 270, 277–8, 285; lack
    of coherent Soviet strategy, 151, 167,
    168, 169, 170–2, 217, 223, 288–9,
    318, 368–70, 384–5; map showing
    missile sites/bases, 204–5; McCone's
    warnings, 176–7, 178, 179, 190,
    193–4, 196, 199, 211, 223, 268–9;
    Pliev appointed to command
    mission, 153–4; policy on Pliev's
    authority to fire weapons, 168, 193,
    278, 286, 369, 393; RFK meets
    Dobrynin over (4 September),
    184–6; Russians' relations with
    locals, 159, 160–3, 164–5; and SAM
    anti-aircraft missiles, 155, 159, 169,

Anadyr, Operation (*cont ...*)
176, 178–9, 182–4, 186, 188, 256,
386–9, 402, 406, 417; and secrecy,
142, 145–6, 149, 152, 154–6, 163,
165, 166, 169–70, 174–5, 216–17,
277; secret treaty in Moscow (1962),
150; Soviet delegation to Cuba,
148–9; Soviet doubters, 145, 147,
148; submarine flotilla, 170–2;
transit of ballistic missiles across
Cuba, 159–60; US intelligence
failures over, 174; US surveillance
of, 171, 174–80, 182, 190, 198–206,
209, 315, 377, 383–4, 404, 467–8;
utter failure of, 459; weapons/
equipment/manpower deployed,
152–3, 155, *157*, 168, 169–70, 192–3,
235 *see also* Cuban Missile Crisis
Anderson, Admiral George, 215, 250,
265, 317, 321–2, 329, 334, 408, 431
Anderson, Jane, 432
Anderson, Major Rudolf, 199, 377,
379, 404, 405–6; shot down over
Cuba, 385–9, *388*, 393, 400, 404–8,
413–14, 416, 417, 422–3, 424–5, 430,
454
Anderson, Sir John, 305
Andreev, Anatoly, 363
Andropov, Yuri, 144
Angolan Civil War, 460*
appeasement policy of 1930s, 248, 281,
296, 477
Arbenz, Jacobo, 5
Argentina, 7–8
Arkhipov, Captain Vasily, 170, 408,
412
Arnaz, Desi, 48
Arrowsmith, Pat, 303
Artemieva, Galina, 58, 64–5, 67, 72,
77, 139, 376
Artime, Manuel, 3–4, 16
Atomic Energy Commission, US, 177
Ayer, A.J., 299

Baldwin, Hanson, 467
Ball, George, 108, 198, 212, 225, 253,
257, 268, 309; correct hunch on
Khrushchev's thinking, 226, 239;

opposition to military action, 226,
229, 230, 232–3, 239, 241
Baltic states, 83, 478
Barbachuk, Nina, 67
Barquín, Colonel Ramón, 43
Barrett, David, 282, 469
Barsukov, Nikolai, 69, 77
Bartlett, Charlie, 318, 340, 341, 466
Batista, Fulgencio, 24–5, 26–33, 36–43,
44, 47, 50, 51, 54–5
Bay of Pigs invasion (Operation
Zapata, April 1961), xviii, 1–6, 7–22,
54, 108, 125, 139, 202, 224
BBC, 66, 460*
Beardsley, Mimi, 116, 422
Beloborodov, Col. Nikolai, 286
Beria, Lavrenti, 75, 153
Berle, Adolf, 27
Berlin: autobahn access to West
Berlin, 96–7, 120, 127, 310; Berlin
Wall built (August 1961), 127–8;
Blockade (1948–49), xvii, 88, 96;
brief Soviet nuclear deployment
near (1959), 154, 269; 'Checkpoint
Charlie,' 128; fear of retaliatory
blockade, 183, 187, 337; flight of
refugees through, 96–7, 126–7; JFK's
'*Ich bin ein Berliner*' speech, xxi; and
Kennedy administration, 124–7,
187, 194–6, 229, 248, 250, 263–4,
266–7, 269, 284, 288, 294, 339–40,
360; Khrushchev threatens to cut off
access to, 92, 98, 120; Khrushchev's
'ultimatums'/threats, 79, 91, 97–8,
120–1, 124–5, 126, 135, 142, 169,
194–6, 243–4, 283; and Macmillan,
125–6, 127–8, 273, 284, 295–6, 365,
461; as obsession of West, 96–7,
124–8, 217, 235, 248, 263–4, 266–7,
295–6, 322, 343, 365, 461; potential
for Great Power showdown in, 57,
97–8, 124–8, 140, 194–6, 239, 240,
245–6, 248, 339–40; Llewellyn
Thompson on, 266, 269, 270, 455;
Western garrisons of, 96, 153, 266,
339, 398–9
Berlin, Isaiah, 76
Bevan, Aneurin, 87

Bianchi, Ciro, 191
Biryuzov, Marshal Sergei, 146, 149, 151, 166
Bissell, Richard, 6, 8, 52, 207
Blake, Gordon, 235
Bohlen, Charles 'Chip,' 75, 195–6, 209, 213, 221, 228–9, 238–9, 255–6, 290
Bolshakov, Georgy, 185, 186, 197, 318, 447, 466
Boris Godunov (Mussorgsky opera), 330–1
Borzunov, Sergei, 143
Bowles, Chester, 118
Bradley, Gen. Omar, 119
Braithwaite, Rodric, 121, 129, 475
Brandon, Henry, 259
Braun, Wernher von, 101
Brazil, 10, 214, 418–19
Breitweiser, Maj. Gen. Robert, 110, 201–2, 435–6
Brezhnev, Leonid, xxxvi
Britt, May, 117–18
Brokaw, Tom, 118
Brown, Governor Edmund Gerald 'Pat,' 377–8
Brown, George, 305
Brown, Harold, 129
Bruce, David, 291, 292
Buchan, Alastair, 302
Buckley, William F., 101–2, 112
Bulganin, Nikolai, 75
Bundy, McGeorge, 108, 112, 190, 197, 199, 209–10, 246, 255, 337, 431, 447, 469; at 4 September 1962 meeting, 182–3; account of Crisis (1988), 425, 430, 453; and Bay of Pigs, 7, 8, 9, 18, 21; 'Bundy plan' (bombing schedule), 256; erratic performance during Crisis, 252–3, 454; at EXCOM meetings, 217–18, 222–3, 226–7, 239, 242, 269, 316, 350, 356, 358, 393, 400, 413, 432; on JFK's 22 October speech, 282, 283; pressures JFK to yield to hawks, xix, 252–3, 258–9, 406; on public's fears during Crisis, 303–4; role in Kennedy White House, 210–12; and Colonel Stimson, 264

Burchinal, Lt. Gen. David, 258, 381, 436
Burlatsky, Fyodor, 146, 168
BURLINGTON (leadership bunker in Wiltshire), 132
Butlin, Wendy, 303

California Institute of Technology, 177
Campaign for Nuclear Disarmament (CND), 296, 297, 458
Cardona, José Miró, 9–10
Carmichael, Stokely, 102
Carroll, Lt. Gen. Joseph, 181
Carson, Rachel, *Silent Spring* (1962), 103
Carter, Gen. Marshall 'Pat,' 182, 187, 199, 212, 213, 222
Carter, Jimmy, 360
Casals, Pablo, 115
Castro, Fidel: accepts Soviet weapons, 52, 56–7, 135–6, 140–1; appears on *The Ed Sullivan Show*, 25–6; and assassination of JFK, 473–4; background of, 29–30, 31; baiting of USA, 3, 4–5; and Bay of Pigs, 3, 5, 14, 15, 16, 18; becomes leader of Cuba, 43–4; behaviour at end of Crisis, 435, 439, 440–2, 444–7; bellicose speeches during crisis, 324, 356, 417; as big winner of Crisis, 460; brutal and repressive rule of, 13, 18, 45–6, 49, 324, 464; character of, 29–30, 31, 40, 45, 137; and communism, 33, 41, 54–5, 136–7, 145; and Cuban economy, 52; death of (2016), 465; embraced by Khrushchev in New York, 6, 138; exaggerated reverence for a peasant ideal, 30; executions in first year of regime, 44, 46, 53; exile in Mexico (1955–56), 33–5; first wife Mirta, 30, 31, 33; as hero to young Russians, 139; imprisonment of (1953), 32–3; as incompetent ruler, 45, 47–8, 51, 54, 56–7, 136, 149, 282, 460, 464; interviews with visiting journalist (1957–58), 38, 39, 40; leads 'the Movement,' 31–2, 33–44; letter to

Castro, Fidel (*cont ...*)
  Khrushchev (27 October), 372–4,
    422, 427–8; mobilizes armed forces
    (22 October), 279; and Moncada
    assault (1953), 31–2, 33; narcissism/
    megalomania of, 45, 57, 137, 372–4,
    427–8, 464; Nixon on, 48, 52;
    oration at show trial of, 32; Pliev's
    relations with, 154; recklessness of,
    29, 137, 149–51, 323–5, 371–4,
    427–8; refuses UN on-site-
    monitoring, 441–2, 445, 448;
    relationship with Cuban people,
    50–2, 284, 305–6, 324, 375, 399; as a
    sensationalist, 55, 57, 132, 323,
    371–4, 427–8; in Sierra Maestra
    mountains (1956–58), 37–42; Soviet
    alliance, 137–41, 147–52, 178–9,
    277–8, 324–5, 368–9, 371–4, 399;
    superstar celebrity of, xxi, 3, 25–6,
    45, 48, 104, 138, 464; threatens US
    planes (25–27 October), 356, 368,
    369, 404; and U Thant, 368, 417,
    430, 441–2; US plans for killing/
    overthrow of, 7, 20, 21, 26, 52–3,
    134, 140, 165–6, 175, 179–80, 206–8,
    357, 469; visits to USA, 34, 48, 52–3,
    55, 138; visits Voloshchenko's unit,
    159; young Westerners enthused by,
    48, 104, 149, 464
Castro, Fidelito, 44, 465–6
Castro, Raúl, 7, 31–3, 37–9, 41, 46, 49,
    150, 279, 466
Central America, 137–8
Chafe, William, 103
Checker, Chubby, 100
chess, 143
Chiang Kai-shek, 166
China, xvii–xviii, 4, 55, 88, 110, 123,
    471; armed clash with India
    (October 1962), 260, 297, 307–8; as
    ascendant today, 474, 475, 476;
    challenge to Soviets, 95–6, 145, 195,
    450; Nationalists in Formosa, 166,
    190; Truman's 'loss of,' 101, 118,
    165–6, 282
Chirakhov, Aziz, 60
Chudik, Gennady, 156, 158, 446

Chukhrai, Grigory, 70
Churchill, Winston, xxiii, xxiv, 6–7,
    23, 114, 121, 243, 261, 282, 478–9;
    Iron Curtain speech at Fulton, 353
Cienfuegos, Camilo, 39, 42, 43, 44,
    45–6
Civil War, Russian, 73
Clifford, Clark, 467–8
Cline, Ray, 209, 255
Coffin, William Sloane, 105
Cold War, xvii–xviii, 56–9, 89, 92,
    100–4, 121–3, 460–1; end of, 465,
    474; and human freedom, 474–5;
    JFK's desire to win, 113; nostalgia
    for as discernible today, 475; nuclear
    weapons as central to, xx, 120–31,
    461; 'owls,' 119–20, 127–8
Collingwood, Charles, 434
Columbus, Christopher, 23
communications: Cuban security, 176;
    frightening inadequacy of US Navy,
    334–5; machinery in Britain for
    nuclear warning, 131; Pentagon-
    Kremlin teletype hotline, 471;
    snail-like pace of during Crisis, 320,
    366, 385, 389, 393, 428–9, 471;
    US-UK scrambled 'Hot Line'
    telephone, 293
communism, xxvi; in 1950s Cuba, 27,
    28; absence of freedom in
    totalitarian states, 452; and Castro,
    33, 41, 54–5, 136–7, 145; conditions
    leading to in Latin America, 7–8; fall
    of the Berlin Wall (1989), 474; of
    Guevara and Raúl Castro, 41, 46;
    JFK's need for anti-communist
    credentials, 5, 208; Khrushchev's
    absolute faith in, 79–80; McCarthy
    witch-hunts, 30, 64, 101, 110, 116;
    Soviet-China competition for
    leadership, 95–6, 145, 195, 450; US
    fear of, 100, 101–2, 121–3, 177; US
    view on popularity of, 7, 8–9
Congolese Republic, 7
contraceptive pill, 103
Cooper, Chester, 292
Cordier, Andrew, 419
Cornell University, 308

Costner, Kevin, 212
Covid-19 pandemic, xxv
Creech, Col. Wilbur, 261, 262
Cronkite, Walter, 304, 340
Crossman, Richard, 87, 294–5, 299
CUBA
    'Después del triunfo,' 50–2; '26th July
    Revolutionary Movement' (M-26-7),
    31–42, 43–4; at centre stage due to
    missiles, 151, 324, 368; dismantling
    and shipping of missiles, 440; exile
    community in US, 2–6, 8, 9–13,
    14–17, 55, 356–7, 359, 463–4;
    hijackings of civilian airliners to,
    202; history of (pre-1959), 23–5,
    26–34, 35–43, 47, 50, 53, 54–5;
    immaturity/irresponsibility of
    Castro regime, 47, 49, 137, 149–50,
    371–4, 427–8; and machismo, 164;
    military forces, 2, 9, 12, 374, 383–4;
    misgovernment of Castro regime,
    45, 47–8, 51, 54, 56–7, 136, 149, 282,
    460, 464; nationalizations of
    US-owned enterprises, 26, 49, 53,
    54–5; post-Crisis history of, xxvi,
    447–8, 459–60, 464–6; public
    reaction to end of Crisis, 439;
    revolution (1959), 1, 4, 25–6, 43–4;
    right of to deploy missiles on its own
    soil, 191, 350, 451; Soviet alliance,
    137–41, 147–52, 178–9, 277–8,
    324–5, 368–9, 371–4, 399; Soviet
    delegation to (1960), 136–7; storage
    of Soviet warheads, 369; support for
    Castro during Crisis, 284, 305–6,
    324, 375, 399; survival of communist
    regime in, xxvi, 465–6; united by
    Bay of Pigs, 13–14, 18; US claims/
    assumes privileges over, 10, 26, 191,
    198, 339–40, 357, 451–2; US
    obsession with, 98, 140, 236, 237,
    269, 272, 282, 290, 301, 458; White
    Russian refugees, 158
Cuba policy group, 197, 198–9
Cuba Study Group, 7
Cuban Missile Crisis: B-59 submarine
    incident, 409–13; 'the Bohlen plan'
    (diplomatic path), 213; 'Bundy plan'
    (bombing schedule), 256;
    continuing work on missile sites
    during, 288, 339, 348, 350, 359;
    Cuban escalation (27 October),
    383–4, 404; danger of accidents/
    mistakes, xix–xx, 311, 327–8,
    379–80, 411–12, 453, 478; Day 1
    (Tuesday 16 October), 211–28; Day
    2 (Wednesday 17 October), 229–33;
    Day 3 (Thursday 18 October), 233,
    236–47; Day 4 (Friday 19 October),
    247–54; Day 5 (Saturday 20
    October), 254–9, 290; Day 6 (Sunday
    21 October), 259–65, 290–3; Day 7
    (Monday 22 October), 266–85,
    293–4; Day 8 (Tuesday 23 October),
    285–9, 305, 309–23, 324, 328, 330–1;
    Day 9 (Wednesday 24 October),
    326–8, 329, 331–42, 336; Day 10
    (Thursday 25 October), 343–54; Day
    11 (Friday 26 October), 355–60,
    364–70; Day 12 (Saturday 27
    October), 371–89, 390–406, 407,
    409–22; Day 13 (Sunday 28
    October), 424–35; diplomatic
    developments of 26 October, 364–5,
    366–7; end of (28 October 1962),
    431–40; Essex forces Soviet
    submarine to surface, 332–3, 408;
    'fast track' option (military path),
    213; final peace deal, 448–9; full-
    scale US invasion option, 207–8,
    217–18, 219, 220, 236, 237, 241, 247,
    250, 256–7, 349–50, 359–60, 402–3,
    431; full-scale US invasion plans,
    224, 272, 274–6, 309–10, 356, 379;
    Havana conference on (1992), xviii;
    historiography of, xxi, xxiii, xxiv–
    xxvi, 253, 454; influence of mutual
    deterrence on the entire debate, 360,
    414–15; instinctive disbelief in
    threat of annihilation, xxi–xxii;
    JFK-Gromyko meeting (18
    October), 241–2, 243–5; JFK's
    broadcast to nation (22 October),
    280–6; JFK's personal letter for
    Khrushchev (22 October), 278–9,
    285; Khrushchev's open letter to JFK

Cuban Missile Crisis (*cont ...*)
(27 October), 392–5, 399–400;
Khrushchev's private letter to JFK
(26 October), 366–7, 393–4, 402,
415; Khrushchev's radio missive to
JFK (28 October), 429–30, 431;
Kremlin's desperate/dangerous
confusion of purpose, 288–9, 362–4,
369–70, 384–5, 391–6, 404; letter to
Khrushchev offering terms (27
October), 414, 415–16; parameters
of US policy established, 189;
Pentagon bellicosity as significant
factor, 328, 342, 456; peril/gravity of,
xviii, xix–xx; Pliev activates radar on
Cuba, 368–9, 377, 384; as political
issue rather than strategic one, xx,
223–4, 227–8, 360, 476–7; Bertrand
Russell's cables to Khrushchev and
JFK, 300–1, 307, 338; Soviet motive
issue, 216–17, 221, 223, 226–7, 239,
248, 348–9; Soviet secrecy as
propaganda plus for the US, 269,
282–3, 350; telegram from Moscow
accepting RFK's deal (28 October),
427; threat of American force as key,
452–3, 478; US graduated escalation
idea, 254, 349–50; White House
tapes of, xxiii–xxiv, xxv–xxvi, 120,
405; worldwide fears/apprehensions
during, 303–4, 305, 309, 374–6,
383–9, 420–1 *see also* Anadyr,
Operation; blockade of Cuba, US;
Executive Committee of the
National Security Council
(EXCOM)
Cuban Missile Crisis, US blockade
during: *Bucharest* allowed to
proceed (25 October), 347–8, 349;
comes into force (24 October),
314–15, 331; continues after Crisis
ends, 445; declared (22 October),
279, 281; enforcement of, 314–17,
319, 320–3, 328–9, 331–7, 348–9,
355, 361–4, 390–1, 399, 407–13,
442–4; fear of retaliatory Berlin
blockade, 183, 187, 337; formal
declaration of war issue, 240, 254;

Lyndon Johnson's view of, 414;
lifting of, 448; Lovett on, 338–9;
McNamara requests starting date,
309; military view of, 215, 248, 250,
251, 254, 255, 256; missiles still on
Cuba as critical question, 339–40,
341–2, 349, 355–6, 357–9; most
important achievement of, 337,
452–3; as not precluding subsequent
bombing/invasion, 254, 268, 270,
349–50, 355–6, 359–60; OAS
supports, 310, 314, 318; opposed as
inadequate by right-wing opinion,
248, 251, 270–1, 272, 290, 338; plan
chosen by JFK/EXCOM, 257–8,
263–4, 266, 268; as policy option,
183, 187, 196–7, 222–3, 225–6, 228,
233, 237–40, 246, 247–8, 251, 253–6;
publicly characterized as a
'quarantine,' 257; quarantine line
distance/position, 323, 390–1; and
Soviet Navy, 265, 287, 288, 314, 317;
Soviet response to JFK broadcast,
285–7, 311–14; and Soviet
submarines, 288, 317, 329, 332–3,
361–4, 390, 408–13, *410*; Soviet
vessels ordered to turn back (22
October), 285–6, 287, 328–9, 331,
333–4, 335, 361; stop-and-search
orders/procedures, 265, 310, 314–15,
321–2, 337, 348, 355; views of US
allies on, 290–303
Cuban Revolutionary Council, New
York, 13, 15

Dallek, Robert, 351
Dalley, S/Ldr Kevin, 398
Davies, John Paton, 110
Davis Jr, Sammy, 117–18
de Gaulle, Charles, 94, 124, 290–2,
463
Dear Comrades! (Andrei
Konchalovsky film, 2020), 68
Dennison, Admiral Robert, 196–7,
361, 391, 400
DePalma, Anthony, 50, 151
Diefenbaker, John, 290
Digby, Pamela, 243

Dilhorne, Lord, 298
Dillon, Douglas, 212, 232, 253, 256, 268
Direnzo, Vince, 202
Dirksen, Everett, 188, 272, 338
Disosway, Major-General Gabriel, 436
Dobbs, Michael, *One Minute to Midnight* (2008), xxv
Dobrynin, Anatoly, 64, 98, 102, 141–2, 195, 252, 403, 431, 448; and *Bucharest* incident, 348; dislike of RFK, 318, 319–20; ignorance of Anadyr, 144, 152, 181, 242, 279, 311, 319–20; meets Rusk (22 October), 268, 278–9, 285; memoirs of, xxv, 124, 288; RFK's 4 September meeting with, 184–6; RFK's meeting with (23 October), 318–20, 322; RFK's meeting with (27 October), 414, 415, 416–17, 419, 423, 426, 454, 467; and RFK's secret Turkish offer, 416, 419, 423, 426, 427, 467, 470; on Zorin, 351
Dole, Robert, 198
Dorticós Torrado, Osvaldo, 47, 368, 440
Dr. No (Terence Young film, 1962), 300
Dr. Strangelove (Stanley Kubrick film, 1963), xxii–xxiii, 252, 327
Droller, Gerard ('Frank Bender'), 4
Dubinskaya, Elvira, 156–8, 162, 163–4, 446, 473
Dubivko, Captain, 171, 363–4, 409, 443–4
Dulles, Allen, 5, 6, 19, 52–3, 177, 189, 207
Dulles, John Foster, 265
Dylan, Bob, 304

Earman, Jack, 467
East Germany, 95, 96–7, 126, 127–8
Ecker, Commander Bill, 315
the *Economist*, 112, 259, 301, 343, 390, 435, 437
Eden, Anthony, 457
Edwards Air Force Base, California, 199–200

Eisenhower, Dwight, 5, 26, 94, 97, 101, 115, 126, 130, 211, 296; briefing of during Crisis, 214, 229, 266–7, 432; CIA anti-Castro activity under, 3, 7, 52, 54; foreclosure of Suez campaign (1956), 297, 344; and golf courses, 48, 104, 107; and Khrushchev's official visit (1959), 90, 91; support for Latin American dictators, 30, 47; and U-2 incident (May 1960), 93–4, 95; and USAF's SIOP-62 plan, 128
El Encanto department store, Havana, 13, 26–7
Elizabeth II, Queen, 305
Ellis, Gen. Richard, 180
Escalante, Anibal, 145

Fangio, Juan, 40
Federal Bureau of Investigation (FBI), xli, 375
Feklisov, Aleksandr (Aleksandr Fomin), 364–5, 403
Ferguson, Don, 115
Ferrara, José Ramón Linares, 13–14, 46, 51, 164, 304, 439
Ferrer, Ada, *Cuba: An American History* (2021), xxv, 32
film and cinema, 70, 164, 300
First World War, 143, 296, 426; causes of, xviii–xix, 119–20, 276, 294
Fitzgerald, Desmond, 469
Fleming, Ian, 115, 300
Flynn, Errol, 26
Fokin, Admiral Vitaly, 170
Forbes, Malcolm, 99
Ford, Gerald, 468
Ford Motors, 108–9
Formosa (Taiwan), 166
Fox, Frederic, 117
France, 90, 92, 228–9, 435, 462–3, 471; Algerian war, 21, 190
Franco, Francisco, 104
Freedman, Lawrence, 462, 474
Frondizi, Arturo, 7–8
Frost, Robert, 172–3, 192, 195, 466
Fulbright, Sen. William, 8, 9, 105, 187, 272, 338

Gaddis, John Lewis, xx, 327, 474
Gadea, Hilda, 34
Gagarin, Yuri, 58, 59, 83, 145
Gaither, H. Rowan, 100–1
Gaitskell, Hugh, 73, 305, 461–2
Galbraith, J.K., xix, 58–9, 99, 112, 118, 189, 190
Galenkov, Valery, 65, 66, 306–7
Garbuz, Maj. Gen. Leonid, 385
Garland, Col. Bill, 391
Garst, Roswell, 80
Garthoff, Ray, 121
Gdansk shipyard strikes (1970), xviii
Gerchenov, Major, 386, 387
Gerhart, Gen. John, 400
Germano, Eddie, 319
Gheorghiu-Dej, Gheorghe, 330
Gilpatric, Roswell, 131, 203, 212, 252, 256, 267, 268, 321
Gitlin, Todd, 18, 103–4, 106
Glanmor Grammar School, Swansea, 303
Glasspoole, Frances, 101, 260
Glenn, Col. John, 103
Goelet, Jane Monroe, 221
Goldwater, Barry, 182
Gomez, Maximo, 27, 49, 50, 55–6
González, María Antonia, 34
Goodwin, Richard, 8, 20–1
Gorbachev, Mikhail, 465, 476
Gorshkov, Admiral Sergei, 171, 287, 409
Gott, Richard, 465
Gould, Loyal, 105–6
Graham, Billy, 376
Graham, Philip, 110
Granma (cruiser), 35–6
Graybeal, Sid, 213
Grechko, Marshal Andrei, 443
Grechko, Lt. Gen. Stepan, 385, 387
Greece, 365
Greene, Graham, Our Man in Havana (1958), 25, 450
Gregory, Dick, 104–5
Gribkov, Gen. Anatoly, 148, 167, 387
Gromyko, Andrei, 148, 185, 241–2, 243–5, 268, 320, 330–1, 358, 427
Guantánamo Bay US base, 12, 17, 41, 101, 178, 180, 198, 215, 376, 384; and Anderson's U-2 flight, 377, 385; imperialist nature of, 28; Operation Quicklift, 260–1; as possible part of Crisis deal, 255, 264, 445; powerful roving searchlight, 161; Soviet missiles target, 160, 383, 400
Guardian newspaper, 298–9
Guatemala, training camp in, 4, 5, 6
Guerrasio, John, 304, 376
Guevara, Ernesto 'Che,' 20–1, 45, 46, 49, 138, 139, 149, 279, 445, 464; and '26th July Revolutionary Movement' (M-26-7), 35–6, 37, 39, 41, 42, 43, 44; first meeting with Castro (1955), 33–4; visits to Soviet Union, 56, 150, 167
Guillén, Nicolás, 23
Guseinov, Col. Yuri, 386
Guthrie, Woody, 100
Guys and Dolls (Broadway musical based on Damon Runyon stories, 1950), 24

Halberstam, David, 111, 116, 192
Hamer, Fannie Lou, 105
Hammarskjold, Dag, 78
Harriman, Averell, 89, 124, 214, 242–3, 365–6, 471
Harris, Robert, The Second Sleep, xvii
Harvey, Bill, 206, 468
Havana University, 28, 29–30, 43–4, 51
Hayter, William, 74, 75, 87
Healey, Denis, 224
Heikal, Mohammed, 139
Heller, Joseph, Catch-22, 104
Helms, Richard, 20, 21
Hemingway, Ernest, 24–5
Hennessy, Peter, xxii
Heren, Louis, 97
Hershberg, James, xxiii, 454
Heyser, Major Steve, 199–201, 202, 203
Hindenburg, Gen. Paul von, 456
Hines, Jerome, 330
Ho Chi Minh, 45, 149, 464
Hodgson, Godfrey, 108

Holland, Max, 282, 469
Holloway, Gen. Bruce, 436
Home, Lord, 293, 300, 434
Hoover, Herbert, 432
Hoover, J. Edgar, 375
Howard, Professor Sir Michael, 84, 92, 122, 123, 477
Hudson, Peter, 292
Hughes, John, 181
Humphrey, Senator Hubert, 86-7
Hungarian Uprising (1956), xviii, 17, 91, 136, 140, 187, 248, 346

Iglesias, Alexander Correa, xxvi
Ilichev, Leonid, 429
Illingworth (cartoonist), 421
Incirlik air base, 327-8, 401
India, 260, 297, 307-8, 479
Indiana University, 308
Ingenieros, José, 28
international relations: appeasement/ compromise needed today, 477-8; Cuba's potential for Great Power showdown, 57; difficulties of reading intentions of adversaries, 129, 179; and fog of ignorance, xx; Garthoff on, 121; good and evil as always relative, 475; respect as central to, 457; scope for catastrophic miscalculation today, 475-6; and unexpected/irrational acts, 181
Ireland, 54
Italy, American Jupiter missiles in, 88, 145, 151, 242, 254, 255, 257, 265, 365, 401, 451
Ivan the Terrible (Sergei Eisenstein film, 1944), 445
Ivanov, Gen., 427

Jaipur, Maharajah of, 317
Janney, Gordon, 174
Jefferson, Thomas, 198
Jodrell Bank radio-astronomy installation, 398
Johnson, Alexis, 212, 217-18, 227, 311, 332
Johnson, Lyndon, 117, 212, 218-19, 268, 407, 414; author's meeting with,

xxii; domestic policy achievements of, 472
Johnson Island, 378
Joseph, Peter, 100

Kagan, Robert, 24
Kaganovich, Lazar, 74, 76
Kalatozov, Mikhail, 70
Kamanin, Gen. Nikolai, 85, 143
Karzhavin, Fyodor, 23
Keating, Kenneth, 181-3, 212, 218, 468
Kempton, Murray, 375-6, 434
Kennan, George, 221, 238
Kennedy, Jacqueline, 114, 263, 317
Kennedy, John F.: 4 September 1962 meetings, 182-4, 186-9; and Addison's disease, 124; administration's policy to oust Castro, 20, 21, 134, 165, 166, 175, 179-80, 207-8, 257, 357; and Alliance for Progress, 53; anti-communist credentials, 5, 208; assassination of (22 November 1963), 473-4; assumes office as President, 98, 107; and Bay of Pigs, 3, 5, 8-9, 10, 13, 17, 18-20, 21-2; briefs congressional leaders (22 October), 270-4; broadcast to nation (22 October), 280-6; as Castro-hater after Bay of Pigs, 20, 22, 134, 472; cites Tuchman's August 1914, xviii-xix, 119-20; as Cold War 'owl,' 119-20; conservative attacks on, 101-2, 251, 377-8; and conservative opinion, 5, 6, 133, 177, 189, 197-9, 227-8, 233, 236, 257, 282, 285, 452, 1132-3; consults Acheson, 231-2, 242; and decision of 20 October, 257-8; declared policy in weeks before Crisis, 194; default posture changes after 24 October, 335-7; and diplomatic developments of 26 October, 364-5, 366-7; dislike of Harriman, 243; domestic policy problems, 112-13, 117-18, 247, 472; and end of Crisis, 431-2; error in assumptions over Soviet thinking,

Kennedy, John F. (*cont ...*)
181, 263–4, 270; extraordinary
discipline of, 269; '*final failure*'
comment, 240; finest hours of Crisis
for (evening, 27 October), 406, 420;
as highly disciplined dissembler,
115–16; hunger for greatness as
statesman, 113–14, 472; immediate
intimates of, 111–12; inner frailty
and pain, 116, 124; intelligence and
culture of, 114–15, 189, 237, 472;
Kamanin on, 85; and Khrushchev's
provocations, 89; Khrushchev's view
of as weak, 17, 125; large character
flaws, xxi, 116–17, 472; meets
congressional leaders (24 October),
338; message to Khrushchev (24–25
October), 341–2, 350; Ormsby-Gore
friendship, 262–4, 322–3, 359, 434;
pledge to put man on the moon,
103; and political consequences of
failure, 230, 360, 454; pre-Crisis
warnings to Moscow over Cuba,
140, 181, 186, 188–9, 192–3, 226,
280; promotes myth of 'missile gap,'
89; on prospects for blockade,
317–18; as prudently haunted by
consequences, 478, 479; rise in
approval ratings after Crisis, 435; on
risks of mistakes/miscalculations,
311; scheduled campaign trips
during Crisis, 229, 232, 246, 247,
251–2, 253, 254–5; Second World
War service, 112, 237, 247; seeks
détente with Khrushchev, 123–5,
179; sensitivity to perceptions of
other nations, 219, 233–7, 290, 322,
401; sexual behaviour, 116–17, 422,
472; speech at American University
(June 1963), 470–1; superb handling
of Crisis, 406, 452, 454, 458, 459,
473; and targeted killing of national
leaders, 6–7; told news of
photographic evidence, 211–12; on
US support for Batista, 47; usual day
at White House, 114; Vienna
summit with Khrushchev (June
1961), 124–5, 310; view of the

military, 221–2, 240, 247, 251,
267–8, 456; views expressed at 16–27
October meetings, 219, 220, 224–5,
227, 236–7, 240, 241, 357–8, 359,
414–15; views expressed to
Macmillan (24 October), 339–40,
343; views on EXCOM members'
performances, 454–5; and White
House tapes of Cuban Missile Crisis,
xxiii–xxiv, 120; *Profiles in Courage*,
117
Kennedy, Joseph, 116, 262–3
Kennedy, Robert: at 27 October
EXCOM meeting, 395, 402–3, 406,
414; on Acheson, 232; and air
strikes option, 231–2, 256, 354; and
all-out invasion option, 219; and
Anadyr intelligence, 184, 190, 211;
appoints McCone, 177–8; as
Attorney-general, 111; author's
meeting with, xxii; back-channel
dialogue with Russians, 184–6, 197,
318, 447; and Bay of Pigs, 10, 20;
and black civil rights, 117; and
blockade of Cuba option, 225–6,
238; and Bohlen's departure, 229;
and Cuba Study Group, 7; and
decision of 20 October, 258; dislike
of Stevenson, 351; and end of Crisis,
431–2; on EXCOM discussions,
219, 240, 241, 246, 333, 337, 355,
456–7; and graduated escalation,
254; on improved mood of 23
October, 311; on JFK's view of the
military, 221–2, 252; on
Khrushchev's open letter (27
October), 394, 395; meeting with
Dobrynin (27 October), 414, 415,
416–17, 419, 423, 426, 454, 467; on
national obsession with Cuba, 272;
and Operation Mongoose, 20, 21,
206, 207, 221, 356; opposes
no-warning attack, 253–4; on
Ormsby-Gore, 263; performance at
EXCOM, 454, 455; on prospects for
blockade, 317–18; secret visit to
Soviet embassy (23 October), 318,
319–20, 322; on U-2 shootdown,

405–6, 416; ultimate endorsement of caution, 226, 232; unfair view on Rusk, 455; and White House tapes of Cuban Missile Crisis, xxiii–xxiv; *Thirteen Days*, 240, 470

Kent, Sherman, 193–4, 291

Ketov, Captain Ryurik, 170–1

Khariton, Yuli, 88

Khrushchev, Nikita: absolute faith in communism, 79–80, 86, 139; acknowledges need to withdraw missiles, 391, 423, 426; announces withdrawal of missiles (28 October), 429–30; and assassination of JFK, 473–4; background of, 73–4, 91, 471; and Bay of Pigs, 17; Berlin 'ultimatums'/threats, 79, 91, 97–8, 120–1, 124–5, 126, 135, 142, 169, 194–6, 243–4, 283; biggest mistakes over Anadyr, 165, 166–7, 277–8, 350; Castro's public claims of betrayal, 444–5; change in behaviour after Crisis, 460–1; character of, 73, 74, 75, 77–80, 81, 84–91, 94–8, 124–6, 131, 138–9, 472; comparison with Putin, 475; Cuban alliance, 137–41, 147–52, 178–9, 277–8, 324–5, 368–9, 371–4, 399; dacha in the Lenin Hills, 276, 422; death of (1971), 463; dictatorial authority of, xxxvi, 146–7, 270; domestic policy of, 60, 67, 68, 73, 76, 79–81, 471; embraced by Castro in New York, 6, 138; embraces 'Lippmann proposition,' 391–6, 403, 420, 423, 425–6, 448; EXCOM suggestion of direct approach to, 214, 220, 223, 229–30, 236, 238; foreign policy objectives, 84–8, 89–96, 97–8, 121, 128, 141–2, 244; at Geneva (1955), 130; greatly damaged by Crisis outcome, 444, 448; illiberal rule of, 67, 68–70, 71, 73, 76; impact on of shootdown of Anderson, 422–3, 424–5; and intellectual world, 81–2; irresponsibility of, 192–3, 194–5, 217, 238, 283, 471; and Kennedy broadcast (22 October), 276–7;

leadership style, 73, 78–80, 471–2; lends Castro a plane, 53; letter to Castro (30 October), 441; lies during Anadyr/Crisis, 181, 186, 197, 211, 244, 245, 282, 350, 450, 458, 471; Mao Zedong's threat to, 127, 128, 195, 270; masquerade of defiance towards end of Crisis, 334, 341, 342, 345, 353, 367, 393, 426; message to State Department (24 October), 341; as not wanting general war, 196, 226, 258, 277, 289, 366, 455; and Novocherkassk massacre, 68–70, 154; nuclear threats/boasts by, 85, 86–7, 89–90, 92, 121, 151, 203, 283, 471; nuclear weapons as central to defence policy, 82, 86–7, 130, 143; official response to JFK's letter/broadcast, 311–14; official visit to US (1959), 80, 90–1, 135–6, 472; at the opera (23 October), 330–1; as opportunist/gambler, 135, 145, 167, 169, 192–3, 238, 285; orders ships to turn back (22 October), 285–6, 287, 328–9, 331, 333–4, 335, 361; ousted in Kremlin coup (1964), 463; political rise of, 74–7, 471; at Presidium meetings during Crisis, 276–8, 285–8, 345, 346–7, 391–4, 425–8, 432–3; and pretence of Soviet strength/success, 85–6, 87, 89–90, 132–3, 141, 203, 366; provocations and surprises from, 85, 86–7, 89–90, 92–3, 135, 165, 194–5, 283; as prudently haunted by consequences, 478, 479; rage towards the West, 84–90, 124–6; recognized as *Vozhd* (Leader), 76–7; reduces size of army, 82–3; releases of political prisoners by, 73; response to Castro's letter of 27 October, 373; Robert Frost's comments, 172–3, 195; romantic excitement over Cuba, 138–9, 144–5, 152, 165; Bertrand Russell's cables to, 300–1, 307, 338; sabotages Paris summit (May 1960), 94–5; 'secret speech' denouncing Stalin (1956), 71–2, 76; seeks path to

Khrushchev, Nikita (*cont ...*)
retreat, 289, 345–7, 352–4, 357–8, 361, 362, 367, 389, 393; sensitivity to perceived Western slights, 63; in small hours of 28 October, 422–3; Soviet public opinion on, 67, 69, 72, 77, 85; and Stalin, xxi, 71–2, 73, 74, 75, 77, 88; thinking behind Cuban missile deployment, 142, 144–9, 165–7, 197, 217, 226–7, 238–9, 263–4, 269, 270, 277–8, 285; tirades against JFK at Vienna, 124–5, 310; tour of Asia (1955), 75; verbal assaults on the West, 87–8, 89–91, 93–6, 124–5, 127, 154, 169; view of JFK as weak, 17, 125, 126, 172–3, 195; vulnerability to Kremlin hardliners, 94–5, 128, 142–3, 270, 287; White House efforts to give retreat space to, 229, 236, 239, 337, 366, 396, 457
Khrushchev, Sergei, 69–70, 80, 84, 86, 135, 140, 146, 289, 391, 444; on end of Crisis, 433; on JFK's 22 October speech, 283–4; on removal of missiles, 353
Kim Il-Sung, 45, 88
Kim Jong-Un, 479
King, Col. J.C., 52
King, Martin Luther, 105, 106
Kirilenko, Andrei, 147
Kirk, Admiral Alan, 112
Kissinger, Henry, 59, 122
Knox, William, 331
Korea, partition of (1945), 110
Korean War (1950–53), xvii–xviii, xx, 64, 88, 113, 118, 165–6, 231, 315–16, 380
Korolev, Sergei, 59
Korth, Fred, 361
Kosykh, Tamara, 64, 66, 306
Kozakov, Nikolai, 77, 306, 307–8, 337–8, 371, 394–5, 437–8
Kozlov, Frol, 68–9, 70
Krock, Arthur, 113–14
Ku Klux Klan, 105–6
Kuznetsov, Vice-Admiral Nikolai, 82, 448–9, 455

Lancaster, Osbert, *299*
Lanovsky, Vasil, 284
Lansdale, Col. Edward, 206, 356
Lansky, Meyer, 24, 27, 43
Lara, José Bell, 51–2, 165
Latin America: anti-American feeling during Crisis, 304, 390; anti-nuclear sentiment in, 147, 148, 150; and legend of Castro, 137–8; and US Alliance for Progress, 53; US domination of, 24, 27, 30, 137–8; US support for murderous tyrannies, 464
Lawrence, David, 467
Ledford, Col. Jack, 198
LeMay, Gen. Curtis, 129, 179–80, 186–7, 207, 215, 216, 253, 258, 315, 328; background and character of, 248–50; barrage of insults at JFK (19 October), 251, 252; calls for full US invasion of Cuba, 379, 403; desire for war with Soviet Union, 88–9; and fire-bombing of Japan, 249, 456; prestige among conservative Americans, 251; rage at peaceful outcome to Crisis, 431, 436; and tactical nuclear weapons, 327, 401
Lenin, V.I., 33, 72, 135
Leningrad, siege of, 61–2
Lesnik, Max, 137
Levitan, Yuri, 58, 429
Lincoln, Abraham, 282
Lipkin, Leonid, 306, 307
Lippmann, Walter, 100, 113–14, 116, 179, 209, 260, 353–4, 392, 395, 434, 453, 477
Liverpool, xxii
Logevall, Fred, 454
Lorenz, Marita, 45
Lovett, Robert, 245–6, 264, 338–9
Lundahl, Arthur, 203, 213, 359
Lynd, Alice, 308
Lyon, Cecil, 291
Lysenko, Trofim, 80
Lyubimov, Mikhail, 91, 304

MacArthur, Gen. Douglas, xvii–xviii, 88, 113, 118, 166, 452

Macmillan, Harold, xxiii, 56, 85, 131–2, 263, 276, 300, 305, 316, 370, 451; actions on 27 October, 396–8; on Americans, 237, 294–5; and Berlin issue, 125–6, 127–8, 273, 284, 295–6, 365, 461; as Cold War 'owl,' 119, 120, 127–8; communications with JFK during Crisis, 273, 284–5, 292–4, 298, 339–40, 343–4, 354, 365, 419–20, 462; on end of Crisis, 433–4; JFK's respect for, 295; Nassau agreement on Polaris, 462–3; at Paris summit (May 1960), 94, 95; perennial enthusiasm for a summit, 298, 340, 344, 420; view of Crisis in retrospect, 450, 457, 458–9

MacMillan, Professor Margaret, xxvi

Maddox, Lester, 105

mafia, US, 24, 27, 30, 43, 54–5

The Magnificent Seven (John Sturges film, 1960), 70

Mailer, Norman, 117

Malcolm X, 52

Malenkov, Georgy, 75, 76, 130, 425

Malinovsky, Marshal Rodion, 95, 142–4, 352, 382, 424, 430, 463; and Anadyr, 142, 144, 150, 154, 166, 167, 168, 171, 192–3, 459; at Presidium meetings during Crisis, 277, 278, 286, 287, 425, 447

Malraux, André, 115

Mansfield, Senator Mike, 7, 187

Mao Zedong, 45, 96, 101, 127, 128, 149, 166, 195, 464

Marchant, Herbert 'Bill,' 450

Marks, Herman, 44

Marshall Islands, 328

Marshall Plan, 108, 226

Martí, José, 25

Martin, Edwin, 212

Marvell, Andrew, 115

Marx, Karl, *Das Kapital*, 33

Mary I, Queen of England, 22

Maslennikov, Ivan, 412

Matos, Huber, 46

Matthews, Herbert, 38, 47–8

Maugham, Somerset, 24, 33, 116

Maultsby, Major Charles 'Chuck,' 379–82, 384, 407

McCarthy, Joseph, 30, 64, 101, 110, 111, 116

McCloy, John J., 126–7, 212, 231, 264, 352, 356, 359, 445, 448–9, 471

McCone, John, 20, 239, 253, 270, 338, 390, 402, 463; background of, 177–8; briefs Eisenhower, 229, 266; and decision of 20 October, 258; at EXCOM meetings, 331, 333, 348, 414, 415; Kennedy brothers' dislike of, 468, 469; and lack of U-2 overflights, 197; at NSC meeting (22 October), 268–9; and Operation Mongoose, 356; opposes negotiations, 358, 359; on perils of invading Cuba, 359–60, 415; and 'photo gap,' 467, 468, 469–70; during Second World War, 112; supports 'Bundy plan,' 256; warns White House about missiles, 176–7, 178, 179, 190, 193–4, 196, 199, 211, 223, 268–9

McDonald, Iverach, 434

McNamara, Robert: at 16 October EXCOM meetings, 212, 214–15, 216, 217, 218, 219, 220, 222–4, 225, 227–8; at 18–26 October EXCOM meetings, 236, 242, 255–7, 258, 309, 317, 332, 333, 348, 349–50, 356, 358; at 27 October EXCOM meetings, 400, 401, 402, 404, 405, 413–14, 415, 417–18; and Air Reserve mobilization (27 October), 417–18, 421–2; and air strikes option, 236, 239, 256; and all-out invasion option, 207–8, 219, 220, 222, 236, 256–7, 272, 356, 402, 405; and Anadyr intelligence, 176–7, 182–3, 190; author's meeting with, xxii; and Bay of Pigs, 8; on Berlin issue, 195; and blockade of Cuba option, 183, 196–7, 222–3, 225–6, 228, 233, 253, 255–7, 258; and bogus 'missile gap' claims, 124, 132; clashes with Anderson, 321–2, 329; corporate management career, 108–9; on

McNamara, Robert (*cont ...*)
danger of accidents/mistakes, 327–8,
453; and decision of 20 October,
258; at Defense, 108–10; denials over
Castro assassination plots, 469;
Dobrynin on, 318; and enforcement
of blockade, 314, 315, 320–2, 323,
329, 332, 333, 348, 364, 391, 399;
and 'flexible response' doctrine, 126,
132; and graduated escalation, 254,
349–50; and Heyser's U-2F flight
images, 201–2, 209, 213; hostility to
small nuclear arsenals, 295;
ignorance of Cuban politics, 220; on
Khrushchev's open letter (27
October), 395; on loose US nuclear
safety, 327–8; and Maultsby's plane,
379–80, 381, 384; and military
chiefs, 250, 258, 320–2, 329, 431,
437; on Missile Crisis as political
issue, 223–4, 227–8, 360, 451–2; and
nuclear warheads issue, 214–15, 216,
217; performance at EXCOM, 454,
455, 456; and plans to remove
Castro, 165, 208, 242; resists U-2
overflights, 190, 197, 198, 467; SIOP-
63 plan, 129; on strategic impact of
Cuban missiles, 223–4, 227–8, 231,
233, 236, 237, 245; and US fear of
communism, 101; and Vietnam
War, xviii, 225; as wartime
statistician, 108, 112
Melgard, Lt. Col. Robert, 327
Mellon, Mrs Paul, 439
Melo, Juan, 27, 50–1, 305, 374
Memorias del Subdesarrollo
('*Memories of Underdevelopment*,'
Tomas Gutierrez Alea film, 1968),
164
Meredith, James, 106, 247
Merrell, Lt. Gen. Jack, 180, 421
Mexico, 33–5
Meyer, Karl, 40
Miami International Airport, 2,
12–13
Michigan, University of, 308
Midhurst Grammar School, 303
Mikhlova, Svetlana, 60–1

Mikoyan, Anastas, 124, 146, 147, 168,
171, 185, 197, 370, 409, 411, 426;
bloodstains on record of, 68–9, 136;
on Khrushchev, 78–9, 93, 138, 145;
memoirs of, xxv, 69, 74; at
Presidium meetings (22–23
October), 278, 287; talks with JFK
(November 1962), 461; visits Cuba
(early November 1962), 444–7; visits
Cuba (February 1960), 136–7
Mikoyan, Sergei, 168
Miller Center, Virginia, xxv–xxvi
Minnesota, University of, 308
Miret, Pedro, 32
Mississippi, University of, xxi, 106,
247
Modi, Narendra, 479
Molotov, Vyacheslav, 76
Moltke, Helmuth von, 119
Moncada barracks, Santiago, 31–2, 33
Mongoose, Operation, 20, 21, 139–40,
179, 206–7, 221, 356, 439
Monroe, Marilyn, 102, 118
Monroe doctrine, 183, 301
Moody, Juanita, 175–6, 235, 351
Moore, Barrington, 308
Morgan, William, 41
Morris, John, 305
Mosnes, Thomas, 41
Mountbatten, Admiral Earl, 235, 396
Munich Agreement (1938), 477
Murrow, Ed, 26

NASA, 103
Nassau, 175
Nasser, Gamal Abdel, 139, 140
NATO, 140, 168, 217, 220, 331, 394,
401, 402, 414, 419, 451; alert status
in Europe, 276, 316; and Berlin, 97,
98, 120, 126; and nuclear missiles in
Europe, 87–8, 401, 405, 416; and
tactical nuclear weapons, 461; US
briefings to, 290 *see also* allies of
USA
Naumov, Vladimir, 74
Nazirov, Romen, 91, 438
Nazi-Soviet Pact (1939), 83
Nedelin, Marshal Mitrofan, 123, 146

Nekrasov, Viktor, 71
Neuhan, Major John, 378
Newhart, Bob, 107
Newman, Joseph, 8–9
Nicaragua, 11
Nitze, Paul, 8, 100–1, 209, 265, 267, 394, 404
Nixon, Richard, 48, 52, 93, 115
Noel-Baker, Philip, 302
NORAD air defence command, Colorado Springs, 424
Norstad, Gen. Lauris, 276, 316
North Korea, 123, 479
North Vietnam, 45, 47, 55, 464
Novocherkassk massacre (1962), xxi, 68–70, 154
nuclear weapons, xvii–xviii, xviii, xix; atmospheric testing of during Crisis, 378–9; atomic bombing of Japan (1945), 88, 249; bogus 'missile gap' claims in US, 89, 121–2, 124, 132; brief Soviet deployment near Berlin (1959), 154, 269; centrality to Cold War, xx, 120–31, 461; civil defence preparations for, xxi–xxii, 131–2, 377–8; and Cold War 'owls,' 119–20, 127–8; exposure to radioactivity during testing, 81–2; Falcon air-to-air missiles, 381; First Strike as only Soviet option, 141; FKR-1 cruise missile-launchers, 168, 192, 193, 235, 393, 442, 447; FROGs, 359; IRBMs, 150, 152, 169, 183, 236, 247, 255, 384–5; JFK announces test moratorium/ban, 470–1; JFK on personal authorization, 267–8, 327; Khrushchev's view of, 85, 86–8, 89–90, 92; loose safety protocols, 327–8, 383, 401; Luna missiles, 168, 192, 193, 235, 383, 393, 400–1, 442, 447; map showing sites/bases on Cuba, 204–5; and McNamara, 109, 129, 295; Minuteman missile crews, 328, 401; MRBMs, 150, 152, 178, 183, 202, 203, 222, 226–7, 247, 255; numbers delivered to Cuba by start of blockade, 331; partial test ban treaty (August 1963), 471; Pliev's discretion removed, 286, 369, 393; post-Crisis Soviet expansion programme, 448; Pugwash disarmament conferences (1960/61), 122–3; R-14 (SS-5) missiles, 168, 203, 352, 369; R-16 liquid-fuelled long-range rockets, 141; Soviet production of its own bomb, 88; Soviet rejection of subtle nuances of strategy, 129–30; Soviet Strategic Rocket Forces, 154; Soviet Tu-95 Bear bombers, 378; SS-4s (R-12s), 202, 345, 346, 348, 369, 383, 391, 430; Stevenson's campaign for test ban, 177; strategic impact of Cuban missiles, 223–4, 227–8, 231, 233, 236, 237, 245; subordinate/local officers' control of, xix–xx, 168, 169, 193, 235, 278, 286, 327; symmetry/comparability question, 191, 226–7, 238, 269, 282, 298, 302, 331, 353–4, 392, 392, 451, 476–7; T-5 weapons, 362; Thor missiles, 365, 397; US chiefs of staff advocate use of, 88–9, 400–1; US strategic superiority, 128, 131, 141, 203, 223–4, 454; USAF's SIOP-62 plan, 128–9
Nuñez, Marta, 28, 49–50, 305

Obaturov, Gen. Gennady, 128, 149, 438, 439
Obote, Milton, 269
O'Connell, Rear-Admiral Edward, 400
O'Donnell, Kenny, 111, 212, 228, 268
Oistrakh, David, 376
Oliva, Erneido, 2, 4, 6, 11
On the Beach (Stanley Kramer film, 1959), 130
'One Hell of a Gamble' (Aleksandr Fursenko and Timothy Naftali, 1997), xxiv–xxv, 278
'Operation Peter Pan,' 49
Organization of American States (OAS), 214, 218–19, 281, 309, 310, 314, 318
Orlov, Lt. Vadim, 411, 412, 413
Ormsby-Gore, David, 262–4, 322–3, 359, 368, 434

Pakistan, 391
Paris summit conference (May 1960), 92, 93, 94–5
Parrott, Thomas, 111
Pasternak, Boris, 72, 81
Pawley, William, 42
Pearson, Drew, 102
Penkovsky, Col. Oleg, 202–3, 279–80, 470
Perez, Leander, 105
Perry, Wing-Commander Graham, xxii
Petrovna, Nina, 78
Philippines, 24, 96
Pike, Sir Thomas, 396
Platt Amendment, 25
Playboy Club, 102, 104–5
Pliev, Gen. Issa, 169, 288–9, 316, 369–70, 383, 424–5, 442, 447; activates radar on Cuba, 368–9, 377, 384; appointed to command Anadyr, 153–4; and authority to fire weapons, 168, 193, 278, 286, 369, 393; brutality and ruthlessness of, 153–4; ill health of, 154, 369, 430; and Novocherkassk massacre, 69, 154; signals sent to (28 October), 430; and Soviet commitment to withdrawal, 352, 369, 384–5
Pliusch, Leonid, 80–1
Plokhy, Serhii, xxv, 156
Pocock, Chris, 200
Poland, 136, 153
Poliansky, Dmitry, 463
Porro, Ricardo, 14
Portes, Col. John des, 379
Power, Gen. Thomas, 121, 201, 207, 326–7, 328, 342, 379, 456, 460
Powers, Dave, 114, 417, 422
Powers, Gary, 93
'Prague Spring' (1968), xviii, 66
Prío Socarrás, Carlos, 34, 464
Probachai, Nikolai, 161–2
Puerto Rico, 180
Pullman, George, 184
Putin, Vladimir, xx, xxiv, 89, 465, 474, 475, 477–8, 479

Quantrill, Jay, 202
Quevedo, José, 42

race issue in USA: Freedom Riders' mixed-race bus demonstrations, 105; and Fulbright, 272; and Kennedy administration, 106–7, 112, 113, 117–18, 247; and poverty, 106; Southern racists, 104–6, 271; as towering social issue, 104–5; University of Mississippi riot (1962), xxi, 106, 247
Radford, Admiral Arthur, 88
Radio Liberty (CIA-funded station), 66
Radio Moscow, 429–30, 431
RAND think-tank, 101, 122, 326
Rashidov, Sharaf, 149
Rassokho, Admiral Anatoly, 170–1
Reagan presidency, 346
Regueiro, María, 50, 375
Reston, James 'Scotty,' 107, 125
Revuelta, Naty, 32, 33
Rhee, Syngman, 123
Rice University, USA, 103
Rikhye, Gen. Indar Jit, 442
Rio Pact (1947), 280
Rivas, Filiberto, 55
Rivero, Elena, 151
Rivero, Manuel Ray, 12
Roberts, Frank, 90
Robinson, W/Cdr. Mike, 397
Rockefeller, Nelson, 73
Rodin, Judith, 103
Rodríguez, Zoila, 39
Roosevelt, Franklin, 115–16, 218
Roosevelt, Theodore, 24, 25, 53
Roselli, John 'Handsome Johnny,' 206
Rosenberg, Julius, 365
Rostow, Walt, 21, 112, 354, 405
Rovere, Richard, 468, 473
Rusk, Dean: at 16 October meetings, 213–14, 217, 222, 223; at 23–28 October EXCOM meetings, 309, 310, 332, 333, 357, 400, 417, 432; admirable behaviour during Crisis, 214, 455; and Anadyr intelligence,

176–7, 182–3, 184, 190; anger at White House tapes, xxiv; author's meeting with, xxii; background of, 110; and Bay of Pigs, 8, 19; and Bohlen's departure, 228; and briefing of congressional leaders, 270, 338; briefs European ambassadors (26 October), 367–8; on British protests, 301; calls Acheson, 290; and Cordier conversation, 419; and decision of 20 October, 258; and diplomatic developments of 26 October, 364, 365; Dobrynin on, 318–19; favours blockade plan, 254, 257; and Heyser's U-2F flight images, 209; and IRBM evidence, 236; on JFK, 113; at JFK-Gromyko meeting (18 October), 243, 244–5; Kennedy brothers' view of, 455; and Khrushchev's escalating rhetoric, 98; and letter to Khrushchev (27 October), 415; meets Dobrynin (22 October), 268, 278–9, 285; on personal impact of Crisis, 437; questions Khrushchev's sanity, 125, 310; resists U-2 overflights, 190, 197, 198, 240

Russell, Bertrand, 296, 297–8, 300–1, 307, 338, 459

Russell, Sen. Richard, 105, 187–8, 270–2, 273, 338, 344

Russian Federation, 192, 465, 474, 476, 477

Ryan, Gen. John, 391

Ryapenko, Lt. Aleksei, 386, 387

Sackellson, James, 107

Sakharov, Andrei, 71, 81–2, 123

Salinger, Pierre, 19, 185, 188–9, 260

Samuelson, Paul, 58–9

San Romain, Jose Perez 'Pepe,' 1–2, 5, 6, 8, 11, 12, 15, 16, 18

Sánchez, Celia, 38, 40, 42

Sánchez, Universo, 35

Santiago, Cuba, 31–2, 43, 44

Sargasso Sea, 171, 362, 408–13

Sarria, Pedro Manuel, 31

Savitsky, Captain Valentin, 170, 409, 411–12

Scabbards, Operation, 274, 356

Scali, John, 364–5, 403

Scannell, Vernon, 81

Schlesinger, Arthur, xxii, 7, 8–9, 20, 98, 112, 122, 189–90, 259, 267, 469; on Castro, 48, 54; on JFK, 114, 115; on McNamara, 108; opposes Bay of Pigs, 9, 21; on Ormsby-Gore, 263; role in Kennedy White House, 112; shut out of Excom loop, 366; on State Department, 214; and 'strategy of reassurance,' 177; The Vital Center: The Politics of Freedom (1949), 111–12

Schoenman, Ralph, 300–1

scientists, Soviet, 70–1, 81–2, 123

Second World War: fire-bombing of Japan, 249, 456; Hitler's Operation Barbarossa (June 1941), 130; JFK's service in, 112, 237, 247; Katyn massacre (1941), 136; and Khrushchev, 74–5; legacy of in Soviet Union, 61–2, 63, 66, 71, 83–4, 97, 130, 316, 456; Malinovsky's service in, 143; Pliev's operations during, 153–4; Soviet intelligence in US during, 345–6; in US memory, 113, 315, 316

Seleznev, Ivan, 63, 77, 82, 306, 438

Semenozhenkov, Vitaly, 160–1, 374

Semichastny, Vladimir, 280

Senko, Lt. Dmitry, 384

Shackley, Ted, 207

Shakhnazarov, Georgy, 476–7

Shaposhnikov, Gen. Matvey Kuzmich, 69

Shelest, Petr, 60, 438

Shostakovich, Dmitri, 76

Shoup, Gen. David, 250, 252

Shumkov, Captain Nikolai, 361–2

Shute, Nevil, On the Beach (1957), 130

Sidey, Hugh, 125

Silverman, Sydney, 297

Sizykh, Lyubov Illarionovna, 78

Skelly, Jack, 29

Skyfotos, 174
Smith, Brigadier Robert, 201
Smith, Earl, 41, 42, 43
Smith, Major Bill, 109, 247, 304, 344
Smith, Sydney, 54
Solzhenitsyn, Aleksandr, 62, 63–4, 81, 139
Somoza, Luis, 11
Sorensen, Ted, 111, 181, 185, 197, 393, 415, 418, 470; drafts public broadcast of 22 October, 254–5, 282; as EXCOM member, 212, 223, 268
South Korea, 123, 315–16
South Vietnam, 7, 464
SOVIET UNION
abuse of psychiatric institutions, 83; access to foreign media, 66, 306, 307–8; Castro accepts weapons from, 52, 56–7, 135–6, 140–1; chaos of military operations through history, 385; Cold War blunders, xvii, xviii; collapse of (1991), 474; craving for respect at heart of foreign policy, 84, 85–8, 132–3; delegation to Cuba (1960), 136–7; glasnost, xxiv; imperialism of, 28, 45; intelligence services, 185, 202–3, 279–80, 304, 318, 345–6, 364–5, 403, 426, 466, 470; legacy of Great Patriotic War, 61–2, 63, 66, 71, 83–4, 97, 130, 316, 456; low productivity in, 59, 61, 63; minorities in, 83; national narrative of sacrifice, 61–2, 63, 70, 83–4; post-Stalin economy, 58–60, 61–3, 64–5, 67–8, 79–81; Presidium meetings during Crisis, 276–8, 285–8, 345, 346–7, 391–4, 425–8, 432–3; public opinion in during Crisis, 306–8, 337–8; public opinion/sentiment in Khrushchev era, 58, 60–5, 66–8, 69, 71–2, 83–4; public protests/disorder in, 66–7, 68–70, 154; public reaction to end of Crisis, 437–8; quality of life in, 60–3, 64–6, 67–8, 80–1; repression of religion, 83; scientific secret cities, 70–1; shestidesyatniki ('Sixties generation'), 70; Tu-114 airliner;

urbanization in late-1950s, 60; view of US atomic bombing of Japan (1945), 88
Armed Forces:
Air Force: 381, 382; IL-28 nuclear-capable bombers, 192, 193, 199, 247, 331, 442, 444, 446–7, 448; MiG-21 fighters, 182–3, 187, 188, 190, 216, 247, 402
Army: 153, 160–3, 316, 374, 446; AA units in Cuba, 383–4, 385–9, 388; legacy of Great Patriotic War, 316; sexual practices of, 164; S-75 missiles, 93, 157
Navy: 153, 158–9, 170, 348, 408, 430; and US Cuban blockade, 265, 287, 288, 314, 317
Submarines: B-130 boat, 334, 361–3, 442–3; B-36 boat, 171, 172, 362–4, 409, 443; B-4 boat, 361, 362, 408, 409, 442; B-59 boat, xxiii, 170–1, 407–8, 409–13, 443; B-75 boat, 408; B-88 boat, 408; Foxtrot-class, xix, 170–2, 287, 288, 329, 332–3, 361–4, 390, 408–13, 442–4; K-3 submarine at North Pole, 66; left in theatre during blockade, 265, 288, 317, 329, 332–3, 361–4, 390, 408–13, 410; not designed for human comfort, 363, 408–9; in post-Crisis era, 461; Zulu-class, 408
Intelligence Services, 144, 203, 277, 345–6, 427; GRU, 185, 202–3, 318, 466, 470; KGB, 52, 69, 91, 135, 147–8, 162, 164–5, 279–80, 304, 345–6, 364–5, 403, 426
Ships: Admiral Nakhimov, 156; Aleksandrovsk, 171, 287, 352, 440; Bucharest, 337, 341, 347–8, 349; Coolangatta (Swedish cargo ship), 364; Divnogorsk, 440; Gagarin, 285–6, 328–9, 332, 334; Grozny (tanker), 354, 391, 403, 407, 417, 430; Kimovsk, 285–6, 323, 332, 334; Maria Ulyanova, 155; Marucla (Lebanese vessel), 355; Poltava, 285–6, 334; Stavropol, 158; Vinnitsa, 399

Space Programme, 58, 59, 85, 101, 139, 145; R-16 launch pad disaster, 59, 146
Spain, imperialism of, 24, 25, 28, 53
Spanish-American War (1898), 24, 25, 53
Sparkman, John, 104
Spectator magazine, 57, 390, 434–5
Spreti, Karl von, 182
Sputnik satellite, 58
Stalin, Josef, xxi, 28, 61, 64, 74, 75, 146, 153; accepts 1944–45 deal with West, 86; Berlin Blockade (1948–49), xvii, 88, 96, 281; corpse removed from Leaders' mausoleum, 72; doctors' plot rumour, 71; Khrushchev denounces (1956), 71–2, 76; Soviet public opinion on, 71, 72, 77; and West Germany, 121, 137
Standard Oil, 304
Statsenko, Maj. Gen. Igor, 286
Steel, Ronald, 453
Steinem, Gloria, 102–3
Stern, Sheldon, xxiii, 454, 455, 456
Steve Allen Plymouth Show (NBC), 24
Stevenson, Adlai, 104, 226, 258, 265, 339, 341, 350, 445; at 26 October EXCOM meeting, 356, 358–9; and Bay of Pigs denials at UN, 13, 152, 352; campaign for nuclear test ban, 177; dislike of Kennedy brothers, 351; Kennedy team's view of, 230, 264, 351, 352, 466; opposition to military action, 220–1, 229–30, 245–6, 257; performance at UN (25 October), 351–2; speech at UN (22 October), 267
Stimson, Col. Henry, 264
Strachey, John, 340
Strong, Gen. Sir Kenneth, 235
submarines, 224, 239, 298, 401, 461, 462–3
Suez crisis (1956), xviii, 21, 86, 187, 248, 295, 297, 344, 457
Sullivan, Ed, 25–6

Swan Islands, 54
Sweeney, Gen. Walter, 261–2

Taiwan (Formosa), 166, 475
TASS news agency, 185
Taubman, William, 74, 86
Taylor, A.J.P., 299
Taylor, Gen. Max, 7, 201–2, 254, 431, 467; at 16 October meetings, 212, 215–16, 218, 219, 220, 222, 224, 225, 226; at 18–27 October EXCOM meetings, 237, 239–41, 242, 256, 257–8, 309, 310, 315, 332, 334, 359, 396, 402–3; as chairman of the joint chiefs, 111, 207, 212, 215, 239–40, 247–8, 251; as hawk during Crisis, 215–16, 218, 219, 222, 224, 225, 226, 229, 230, 237, 239–40, 256, 257–8, 456; performance at EXCOM, 455–6; posthumous reputation, 455–6; secret report into Bay of Pigs, 12, 15–16, 19
Teller, Edward, 130
Tetlow, Edwin, 259
Thatcher, Margaret, 108
Thirteen Days (Roger Donaldson film, 2000), 212
Thomas, George, 114
Thompson, Llewellyn, 93–4, 125, 195, 221, 229, 237–8, 241, 254, 258, 358, 402; on Cuba as diversion for Berlin, 266, 269, 270, 455; Dobrynin on, 318; at JFK-Gromyko meeting (18 October), 243, 244–5; knowledge and experience of Russia, 238–9; performance at EXCOM, 238, 454, 455
Thorneycroft, Peter, 399
Times newspaper, 301–2, 303
Titmuss, Richard, 299
Toynbee, Philip, 458
Treaty of Relations (1934), 25
Troyanovsky, Oleg, xxv, 84, 92, 96, 128, 145, 166, 173, 289, 450–1, 460–1; at Presidium meeting (28 October), 425, 426–7, 428
Truman, Harry, 118, 218, 231, 282, 432, 452

Tuchman, Barbara, *August 1914* (1962), xviii–xix, 119–20
Tulane University, 102
Turkey, US nuclear missiles in: idea of swap, 237, 239, 242, 254, 255, 257, 264, 265, 353–4, 391–6, 401, 403, 404–5, 414–15; Khrushchev on, 87–8, 142, 145, 148; Khrushchev embraces swap idea, 391–6, 403, 420, 423, 425–6, 448; and launch authorization, 267–8, 327; as openly deployed, 151, 227; order for removal of, 436; Polaris replacement option, 401; political constraints on withdrawal of, 132, 239, 365, 394, 395–6, 401, 404–5, 416; secret US offer on (27 August), 415, 416, 419, 423, 426, 427, 433, 466–7, 470; symmetry/comparability issue, 191, 226–7, 238, 282, 302, 353–4, 392, *392*, 451, 476–7; US fear air strikes on, 402
Turner, Admiral Stansfield, 120
Tuxpan, Mexican port, 35
Twining, Gen. Nathan, 101

U Thant, 267, 368, 390–1, 419, 445; and Castro, 368, 417, 430, 441–2; proposed solution to Crisis (24 October), 339, 340, 341, 344, 350; relays Russian peace proposal (26 October), 364, 367, 391, 401, 415; relays US response (27 October), 401, 402; US meeting with (26 October), 356, 358–9, 364
U-2 reconnaissance planes: Anderson failed by USAF chiefs, 377; Anderson's plane shot down, 385–9, *388*, 393, 400, 404–8, 413–14, 416, 417, 422–3, 424–5, 430, 454; detail of surface images, 166–7, 200; further flights authorized (16 October), 213; Heyser's flight over Cuba (13 October 1962), 199–201, 202, 203, 209; images of SAM sites, 169, 176, 178–9, 182; lack of pre-Crisis flights over Cuba, 194, 197, 269; Maultsby's plane intercepted (27 October),

379–82, 384, 407; missile photos published (22 October), 281–2; over Soviet Union (1956–60), 95, 203; overflights during Crisis, 236, 377–89; plans for 28 October flights, 404, 413–14, 417; possibility of shootdown over Cuba, 198–9, 217, 256, 270, 309, 377; replaced by space satellite surveillance, 461; resistance to overflights in EXCOM, 190, 193, 194, 240, 467–8, 470; resumption of Cuba overflights, 198–201; shootdown over Russia (May 1960), 92–4, 95, 197, 238, 256, 298–9
Udall, Stewart, 169, 172–3, 192
Ukraine, xxv; Russian invasion of (2022), xvii, xxvi, 84, 474, 475, 476, 478; in Soviet era, 60, 73–4, 75, 83
Ulbricht, Walter, 127
United Fruit Company, 5
United Kingdom: American nuclear deployment in, 151, 227, 365, 451; Anglo-Irish relations, 54; Ballistic Missile Warning System, Fylingdales, 397–8; equivocal support for US during Crisis, 292–3, 295, 298, 300, 301–3, 457–8; French veto of EEC application, 463; imperialism of, 28; intelligence services, 123, 202, 353, 451; and JFK's friendships, 262–4, 322–3, 359, 434; Khrushchev's nuclear threats against, 90, 92; left-wing opinion in, 296–7, 298–9, 300–1, 302, 305, 340, 458; as nuclear power, 292, 295, 296, 397; perspective on Cuban Missile Crisis, xxi–xxii, xxiii; public opinion on Crisis, 294, 296–7, 298–9, 302–3, 343–4, 458; RAF readiness level on 27 October, 397–9; Royal Air Force (RAF), 292, 303, 396–9; Royal Navy, 298; Suez crisis (1956), xviii, 21, 86, 187, 248, 295, 297, 344, 457; supplies planes to Batista, 40; US treatment of during Crisis, 219, 234–5, 263–4, 292–3, 295, 365, 452; view of Soviet-Cuban alliance, 140, 191 Vulcan bombers, RAF V-Force of, 292, 303,

396, 397, 398 *see also* Macmillan,
Harold
United Nations: and Bay of Pigs, 13,
152, 352; Castro addresses
(September 1960), 52–3, 55, 138;
Castro refuses on-site-monitoring
by, 441–2, 445, 448; Charter of, 280;
during Crisis, 264, 281, 310–11, 339,
340, 341, 344, 348, 350, 356, 358–9,
364, 402, 415; Khrushchev's shoe-
banging at, 96, 138; November 1962
meeting, 142, 239, 244; Security
Council meeting (25 October),
310–11, 350–2; as vastly more
important forum than it is today,
267, 350
UNITED STATES OF AMERICA
appeasing of conservative opinion
in, 5, 6, 101–2, 112–13, 133, 177,
251, 257, 452; atomic bombing of
Japan (1945), 88, 249; breaks
diplomatic relations with Cuba
(1961), 53; Castro's visits to, 34, 48,
52–3, 55, 138; claims/assumes
privileges over Cuba, 10, 26, 191,
198, 339–40, 357, 451–2; Cold War
blunders, xvii–xviii; covert hostility
to Batista, 40–1, 42–3; Cuban exile
community in, 2–6, 8, 9–13, 14–17,
55, 356–7, 359, 463–4; domestic
reverberations of Crisis (1962–3),
466–70; during first year of Castro
regime, 46–7, 48–9; forces at
DEFCON 2 (24 October), 326–7,
328, 342; forces at DEFCON 3 (22
October), 274; Guevara's proposal to
(August 1961), 20–1; imperialism of,
24, 25–9, 53, 108; Justice
Department, US, 221; Khrushchev's
official visit to (1959), 80, 90–1,
135–6; left-liberal politics in, 18,
103–4, 106, 308; major weakness in
moral/political position, 226–7;
military preparations for attack on
Cuba, 196–7, 257, 261–2, 268, 272,
274–6, 309–10, 326–8, 356, 400–1,
417–18, 420–2; native inhabitants of,
24; nuclear weapon-building

programme, 121–2; post-1959
relations with Cuba, 53–5, 56–7;
post-war prosperity/contentment,
99–100; power exuded by Kennedy
White House, 107–12; preparations
for possible invasion, 179–81; public
opinion during Crisis, 308, 344;
Southern racists, 104–6; space
programme, US, 103; support for
Batista, 24, 26, 27–9, 30–1, 32, 40–1,
47, 50, 54–5; twenty-first-century
chasm in polity, 457, 474; view of
Cuban public opinion, 3, 7, 8–9
Allies of: contingency plans in
Europe, 121, 131–2; Cuba seen as
US obsession, 98, 140, 236, 237, 269,
282, 290, 458; and Cuba's right to
defend itself, 140, 166, 294, 302;
fears of US misjudgement, xxiii, 294,
301, 302–3, 457–8; as ignorant of
Crisis in early days, 234–5; JFK's
recognition of allied opinion, 219,
233–7, 290, 322, 401; JFK's
scepticism about fortitude of, 219,
401; praise for JFK's performance,
xxiii, 457; National Intelligence
Board, xli; National Photographic
Interpretation Center (NPIC), xli,
175, 201, 202, 203, 213; National
Security Agency (NSA), xli, 175–6,
235; National Security Archive, xxv;
National Security Council, xli, 268–9
(*see also* United States, Executive
Committee of the National Security
Council (EXCOM)); public defence
treaties, 167, 227; sensitivity to US
arms reduction ideas, 132, 394, 401,
404–5; solidarity of, 97, 237, 290,
297; and symmetry/comparability
issue, 269; terrors aroused by Berlin
issue, 90, 96–8, 295–6, 461; US
briefings to US on Crisis, 265, 267,
273, 290; views of during Crisis,
xxiii, 273, 276, 284–5, 290–303, 322,
394, 401, 404–5; views/interests
considered in EXCOM, 214, 217,
218–19, 222, 236–7, 248, 257, 269,
404–5 *see also* NATO

Armed Forces
 Aerial Reconnaissance/Surveillance:
 and Anadyr/Cuban missile build-up,
 169, 174–80, 182, 190, 198–206, 209,
 467–8; Cubans fire at planes, 383–4,
 404; SAC's 55th Strategic
 Reconnaissance Wing, 180; space
 satellite surveillance, 166, 203, 461;
 technical limitations, 193; US Navy,
 315, 377, 383–4, 404 see also U-2
 reconnaissance planes
 Air Force (USAF): atmospheric
 testing of nuclear bombs, 378; and
 bitterness over Bay of Pigs, 202;
 dislike of McNamara in, 110, 381,
 437; dispute with CIA over
 overflights, 199; electronic
 surveillance aircraft, 180; fighter
 aircraft, 381, 382, 383; fighter-
 bomber squadrons, 327, 401; JFK
 briefed on air strike plan, 261–2; and
 Maultsby's plane, 379–82; pre-Crisis
 concentration in Florida, 180;
 preparations for air strikes on Cuba,
 274, 326–7, 401, 421–2; rage at
 peaceful outcome to Crisis, 431,
 436–7; RAND think-tank, 101, 122,
 326; SIOP-62 and SIOP-63 plans,
 128–9; Strategic Air Command
 (SAC), xxii–xxiii, 101, 121, 180, 201,
 207, 326–7, 328, 342, 379–82;
 surveillance of Russian ships, 391;
 and tactical nuclear weapons, 327–8,
 401; urging of war by command of,
 xix, 88–9, 121, 179–80, 186–7, 207,
 249–52 see also LeMay, Gen. Curtis
 Army: 274, 309, 315, 316
 Army Air Forces (USAAF): 108, 249
 Marines: 180, 274–6, 309, 316, 420
 Navy: Anti-Submarine Warfare
 (ASW) capabilities, 361–3; and Bay
 of Pigs, 16, 17; and blockade of
 Cuba, 314–17, 320–3, 328–9, 331–7,
 348, 355, 361–4, 391, 399, 407–13,
 442–4; and blockade of Cuba option,
 196–7, 265, 314; Flag Plot at
 Pentagon, 320–2, 329; frightening
 inadequacy of US communications,

334–5; harassment of Soviet ships/
 submarines, 328–9, 407–8, 409–13,
 442–4; Law of Naval Warfare
 (1955), 321; Light Photographic
 Squadron, 315; pre-Crisis
 concentration near Cuba, 207–8;
 preparations for possible invasion,
 180–1, 422; reconnaissance planes,
 376; surveillance ships, 176
Central Intelligence Agency (CIA):
 xli, xlii; anti-Castro sentiment/
 activity, 3, 7, 20, 52, 54, 134, 179,
 206–7, 356, 469; and Batista, 40; and
 Bay of Pigs, 1, 2, 3–5, 6, 8–9, 11, 13,
 15–16, 17, 19, 178; confirms missiles
 removed, 463; and Cuban missile
 deployment intelligence, 176–7,
 178–9, 190; dispute with USAF over
 overflights, 199; Kennedy brothers'
 distrust of, 468–9; Office of National
 Estimates (ONE), xli, 176, 193–4,
 203, 211, 283; overthrow of Arbenz
 in Guatemala, 5; and 'photo gap,'
 467, 468, 469–70; propaganda
 during Missile Crisis, 66
Defense Department: xli, xlii, 108–10,
 178
Executive Committee of the National
 Security Council (EXCOM): xxii,
 xxiii; absence of plan for post-Castro
 governance, 220, 418; and all-out
 invasion option, 217–18, 219, 220,
 224, 236, 237, 241, 256–7, 309–10,
 359–60; blockaders prevail on 20
 October, 257–8, 263–4; high quality
 of discussions, 192, 452, 456–7; and
 idea of military action without
 warning, 232–3, 239, 241, 247–8,
 253–4, 256–7; immediate military
 action rejected, 246–7; keeping
 knowledge of missiles secret, 218,
 219, 220, 223, 246–7, 255, 259–60;
 meetings of 16 October, 212–20,
 222–8; meeting of 18 October,
 236–42; meeting of 20 October,
 255–8; meetings of 21 October, 264,
 265; meetings of 23 October,
 309–11, 314–15, 316–17; meeting of

24 October, 331–7; meetings of 25 October, 348–9, 354; meeting of 26 October, 355–9; meetings of 27 October, 390, 393–6, 399–400, 401–3, 404–6, 407, 413–15, 417–19; meeting of 28 October, 432; members of, 212–13; moral issues discussed, 241; and Pearl Harbor analogy, 231–2, 239, 241, 254, 269; and removal of Castro, 242, 257, 357; RFK's 'we all spoke as equals,' 240; and timing of making news public, 223, 242; White House tapes of proceedings, xxiii–xxiv, xxv–xxvi, 120, 405

Intelligence Services: xli–xlii; archives of, xxiv; codebreaking/cryptography, 175–6, 235; fallibility of to present day, 191–2; GMAIC, 203; humint reports from Cuba, 176, 194, 196, 199, 268–9; information from during Crisis, 236, 247, 255, 258–9, 268–9, 310, 331–2, 333–5, 348, 351, 354, 359, 383; JAEIC, 203; as often wrong, 179; 'the photo gap' (autumn 1962), 467–8, 469–70; political constraints on, 174, 190, 194, 197, 240, 269, 467–8, 469–70; President's Intelligence Board report, 174, 467–8; strategic national intelligence estimate (SNIE), 193, 194, 258–9; tracking of ships during Crisis, 331–2, 333–5, 336, 348, 351, 354, 361, 391 see also aerial reconnaissance/surveillance, US; United States Central Intelligence Agency (CIA); U-2 reconnaissance planes

Joint Chiefs of Staff: advocates of use of nuclear weapons in, 88–9, 239–40, 250, 326; air strike plans, 230, 233, 240–1, 256, 257, 379, 402–3, 431; air strikes pressed for by, 221, 222, 225, 233, 246, 247–8, 250, 251, 252–3, 256, 258, 396, 402–3, 431; all-out invasion plans, 224, 356, 379, 431; all-out invasion pressed for by, 247, 250, 379, 402–3, 431;

contempt for Kennedy White House, 109–10, 202, 250, 251, 258, 321–2, 381; continued hopes for invasion after Crisis, 442, 447; desire for war, xix, 88–9, 101, 179–80, 186–7, 221–2, 225–6, 233, 239–40, 248–53, 272, 283–4, 426, 454; hubris of in early 1960s, 315–16, 456; JFK's meetings with during Crisis, 247–51, 268–9; JFK's view of, 221–2, 267, 456; as mortally dangerous counsellors during Crisis, 215–16, 250; and nuclear weapon authorizations, 267–8, 327–8, 400–1; power and influence of, 109–10; pressure on JFK from, xix, 224, 225–6, 246, 247–53, 257–8, 311, 332–3, 344, 453, 454, 455–6; and prospective deaths in nuclear exchange, 128–9, 317; and strategic impact of Cuban missiles, 223, 224, 236; support for Bay of Pigs, 6, 250; Max Taylor chairs, 111, 207, 212, 215, 239–40, 247–8, 251, 455–6; unchanged posture throughout Crisis, 405

Ships: Beale (destroyer), 409–11; Belmont (surveillance ship), 176; Blandy (destroyer), 440, 443; Charles Cecil, 443; Cory (destroyer), 412; Enterprise (carrier), 180, 317; Essex (carrier), 180, 260, 332–3, 337, 361–2, 408; Independence (carrier), 180; Liberty (surveillance ship), 176; Okinawa (helicopter-carrier), 274; Oxford (surveillance ship), 176; Perry (destroyer), 364; Pierce (destroyer), 355; Randolph (carrier), 412

State Department: 8, 9, 40, 41, 42, 110, 253–4, 309; JFK's opinion of, 214, 228, 455; Thompson as resident Kremlinologist, 221, 238–9

USSR see SOVIET UNION

Valido, Marcolfa, 50, 51
Vandenberg air base, 328

Velichko, Sergeant Pavel, 160, 162
Venezuela, 304
Vicky (cartoonist), 344, *392*
Vieques Island, 180
Vietnam War, xviii, xxii, 10, 107–8,
  192, 208, 250, 283, 452, 458, 472;
  and George Ball, 230; Fulbright's
  opposition to, 272; intractable allies
  during, 464; and Kennedy
  administration, 104, 189; and
  McNamara, xviii, 225; and members
  of EXCOM, xviii, 225, 357, 437, 454;
  and USAF's fondness for bombing,
  187, 249, 256; and young Americans,
  103, 308
Vinogradova, Dr Lyuba, xxv
Voloshchenko, Lt. Vasil, 155–6, 159,
  384
Voronkov, Col. Georgi, 384, 386
Voroshilov, Marshal Kliment, 437
Vronsky, Boris, 67, 307

Wagner, Robert, 48
Wallace, George, 251
Warsaw Pact, 120–1, 136, 140, 195;
  archives of, 121
Watergate scandal, 283
Waverley, Ava, 305
West Germany, 90, 95, 96–7, 121, 145,
  376

West Side Story (Robert Wise film,
  1961), 100
Westinghouse, 331
Wheeler, Gen. Earle, 250, 258
White, Lincoln, 366
White, Theodore H., 114
Wigram, Ralph, 305
Wiley, Sen. Alexander, 187
Wilhelm II, Kaiser, 119
Williams, Robert, 54
Wilson, Harold, 305, 459, 461–2
Wilson Center, Washington, xxv
Witcover, Jules, 470
Wohlstetter, Albert, 122
Wynne, Greville, 202, 279

Xi, President, 474, 479

Yepe, Manuel, 28, 46–7, 136, 164–5
Yevtushenko, Yevgeny, 147, 306, 323
Yost, Charles, 358–9, 364

Zakirov, Rafael, 158, 159, 160, 374,
  446
Zelikow, Philip, 323, 406
Zhukov, Marshal, 82, 153
Zorin, Valerian, 95, 152, 311, 351–2,
  417
Zulueta, Philip de, 305
Zuniga, Mario ('Juan Garcia'), 13

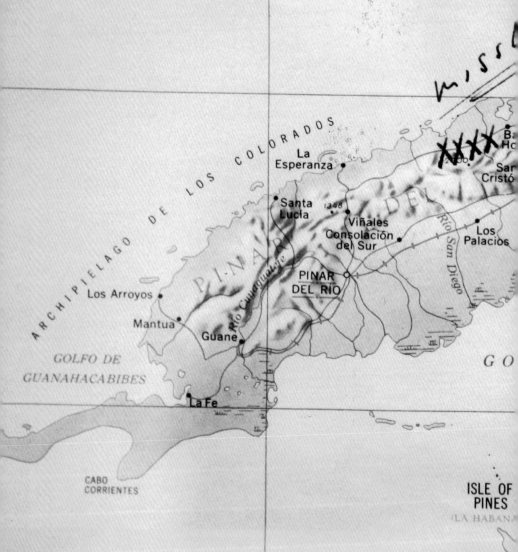

GULF OF MEXICO

missil

B
Ho

XXXX
2000

Sar
Cristó

La
Esperanza

Santa
Lucia   1348

Viñales
Consolación
del Sur

Los
Palacios

PINAR
DEL RIO

Los Arroyos

Mantua

Guane

GOLFO DE
GUANAHACABIBES

La Fe

CABO
CORRIENTES

ISLE OF
PINES

LA HABANA

CAB
PEP

The annotations on this map were made in October 1962, by President John F. Kennedy